CQ Press, an imprint of SAGE, is the leading publisher of books, periodicals, and electronic products on American government and international affairs. CQ Press consistently ranks among the top commercial publishers in terms of quality, as evidenced by the numerous awards its products have won over the years. CQ Press owes its existence to Nelson Poynter, former publisher of the *St. Petersburg Times,* and his wife Henrietta, with whom he founded Congressional Quarterly in 1945. Poynter established CQ with the mission of promoting democracy through education and in 1975 founded the Modern Media Institute, renamed The Poynter Institute for Media Studies after his death. The Poynter Institute (*www.poynter.org*) is a nonprofit organization dedicated to training journalists and media leaders.

In 2008, CQ Press was acquired by SAGE, a leading international publisher of journals, books, and electronic media for academic, educational, and professional markets. Since 1965, SAGE has helped inform and educate a global community of scholars, practitioners, researchers, and students spanning a wide range of subject areas, including business, humanities, social sciences, and science, technology, and medicine. A privately owned corporation, SAGE has offices in Los Angeles, London, New Delhi, and Singapore, in addition to the Washington DC office of CQ Press.

CONGRESSIONAL PROCEDURES AND THE POLICY PROCESS

For Janet, Mark, and Eric

NINTH EDITION

CONGRESSIONAL PROCEDURES AND THE POLICY PROCESS

WALTER J. OLESZEK

Los Angeles | London | New Delhi
Singapore | Washington DC

Los Angeles | London | New Delhi
Singapore | Washington DC

FOR INFORMATION:

CQ Press

An Imprint of SAGE Publications, Inc.

2455 Teller Road

Thousand Oaks, California 91320

E-mail: order@sagepub.com

SAGE Publications Ltd.

1 Oliver's Yard

55 City Road

London, EC1Y 1SP

United Kingdom

SAGE Publications India Pvt. Ltd.

B 1/I 1 Mohan Cooperative Industrial Area

Mathura Road, New Delhi 110 044

India

SAGE Publications Asia-Pacific Pte. Ltd.

3 Church Street

#10-04 Samsung Hub

Singapore 049483

Printed in the United States of America

A catalog record of this book is available from the Library of Congress.

978-1-4522-2603-3

This book is printed on acid-free paper.

Acquisitions Editor: Charisse Kiino

Associate Editor: Nancy Loh

Production Editor: Laureen Gleason

Copy Editor: Megan Granger

Typesetter: C&M Digitals (P) Ltd.

Proofreader: Laura Webb

Indexer: Judy Hunt

Cover Designer: Auburn Associates Inc.

Marketing Manager: Erica DeLuca

Permissions Editor: Jennifer Barron

Certified Chain of Custody
Promoting Sustainable Forestry
www.sfiprogram.org
SFI-01268

SFI label applies to text stock

13 14 15 16 17 10 9 8 7 6 5 4 3 2 1

Contents

About the Author

Walter J. Oleszek is a senior specialist in the legislative process at the Congressional Research Service. He has served as either a full-time professional staff aide or consultant to every major House and Senate congressional reorganization effort, beginning with the passage of the Legislative Reorganization Act of 1970. In 1993, he served as policy director of the Joint Committee on the Organization of Congress. A longtime adjunct faculty member at American University, Oleszek is a frequent lecturer before various academic, governmental, and business groups. He is the author or coauthor of several books, including *Congress Under Fire: Reform Politics and the Republican Majority* (with C. Lawrence Evans) and *Congress and Its Members,* 14th edition (with Roger H. Davidson, Frances E. Lee, and Eric Schickler).

Tables, Figures, and Boxes

BOXES

Preface

CONGRESS IS constantly adapting to change. New procedures, processes, and practices come about in response to developing conditions and circumstances. Some procedural innovations are incorporated formally into the rules of the House or Senate; others evolve informally. For all their variability over time, the rules of the House and Senate are constant in this sense: They establish the procedural context within which individual members and the two chambers raise issues and make—or avoid making—decisions. Members of Congress must rely on rules and procedures to expedite or delay legislation, to secure enactment of a law, or to defeat a bill.

Congressional Procedures and the Policy Process was first published in 1978, in the aftermath of major changes that affected legislative decision making and the political system. Many of these developments on Capitol Hill diffused policymaking influence widely throughout Congress. Six years later, when the second edition appeared, the House and Senate had undergone further procedural transformations. The House, for instance, began gavel-to-gavel television coverage of its floor proceedings. The third edition was published in the late 1980s. By then, the Senate also had begun gavel-to-gavel television coverage of its floor proceedings. Furthermore, Congress had revamped its budgetary practices with the enactment of Gramm-Rudman-Hollings I and II; the House Rules Committee had crafted unique new rules for regulating floor decision making; and greater use had been made of comprehensive bills, or packages, to process much of Congress's annual workload. One effect of these and other changes was to recentralize authority in fewer legislative hands.

The fourth edition was updated during another time of momentous change on Capitol Hill. After 40 years as the "permanent minority," Republicans captured control of the House in the November 1994 elections and reclaimed control of the Senate as well. The fifth edition, published in 2001, examined many of the rules and practices introduced on Capitol Hill by the Republican majority and the new fiscal environment of surpluses, not deficits. The sixth edition, published in 2004, focused on a number of significant procedural and political developments that shaped the lawmaking process, such as the return of fiscal deficits, innovative rules from the House Rules Committee, and attempts to change the Senate's cloture rule.

The seventh edition was published at a time of major change on Capitol Hill. For the first time in a dozen years, congressional Democrats took charge of both chambers as a result of the November 2006 elections.

What made the 110th Congress (2007–2009) especially significant, in addition to important procedural and agenda changes, was the election of the first woman in congressional history—Nancy Pelosi of California—to be Speaker of the House, the highest elective post ever held by a woman in American history. As a history maker, Speaker Pelosi was under intense scrutiny from her colleagues, the minority party, the president, the media, and many others as she employed the formidable procedural and political resources of her high office to address the country's pressing issues. The November 2008 elections also proved momentous. Barack Obama became the first African American to be elected president. As he said, "I don't look like all those other presidents" on our currency. Further, the 111th Congress (2009–2011) saw Democrats expand their number of seats in the House by double digits, just as they did in the prior election. Back-to-back electoral successes of this magnitude have not occurred for more than 50 years. Democrats also gained seats in the Senate. The return of unified government enabled the Democratic Congress and President Obama, despite vigorous opposition from Republicans, to enact truly consequential legislation, such as overhauling health care and revamping the financial regulatory system.

The 112th Congress, however, was another story. Democrats took heavy losses in the 2010 midterm elections. They held the Senate narrowly but lost control of the House to Republicans, many of them Tea Party supported. It was a Congress filled with bitter clashes among the chambers, branches, and parties. Much of the focus of the 112th Congress was the agenda of the 111th Congress, such as repealing the health care law and cutting federal spending. Legislative gridlock was commonplace. Some analysts called the 112th the worse Congress in recent memory. As the 113th Congress begins, with President Obama elected to a second term in November 2012 and Democrats winning eight additional seats in the House (still in GOP hands) and two in the Senate, legislators face a series of manufactured deadlines, such as raising the statutory borrowing limit, dealing with sequestration (automatic spending cuts in domestic and defense programs), and funding the government. How such matters are resolved will doubtless influence the 113th Congress's 2-year actions and activities.

This new edition highlights many of these procedural developments, including several major changes that shape the lawmaking process. These include the heightened importance of campaigning by legislating, policy and political messaging, centralizing more authority in the principal party leaders of both chambers, and policymaking by brinksmanship. Add to these happenings, among many others, the rise of acrimonious partisanship that encourages a quasi-parliamentary style (party-line voting) of decision making; the skeptical view of compromise held by many of today's lawmakers; the intense legislative focus on fiscal austerity; and the decline of the "regular order," which emphasizes the role of committees, deliberation, and openness, and the rise of an irregular lawmaking order that bypasses traditional deliberative processes, such as secret negotiating and policymaking by a handful of key actors inside and outside the Congress.

The fundamental objective of *Congressional Procedures and the Policy Process* is to discuss how Congress makes laws and how its rules and procedures shape domestic and foreign policy. The theme of the book is that the interplay of rules, procedures, precedents, and strategies is vital to understanding how Congress works. I emphasize the rules and procedures most significant to congressional lawmaking; I do not attempt to survey all the rules and procedures used by Congress.

Every chapter of the ninth edition has been revised to incorporate new developments and insights. Chapter 1 presents an overall view of the congressional process. Chapter 2 examines Congress's budget process, which shapes much legislative decision making.

Chapter 3 turns to the initial steps of the legislative process—the introduction of legislation, referral of bills to House and Senate committees, and committee action on measures. Chapter 4 explains how legislation that has emerged from committee is scheduled for floor consideration in the House. Chapter 5 then examines the main features of floor decision making in the House. Chapter 6 puts the spotlight on the Senate, with discussion of how legislation is scheduled in that chamber. Senate floor action is the subject of Chapter 7. In a significant procedural development, the 113th Senate imposed restrictions on the use of the filibuster. This incremental change, which was adopted with large support, is discussed in this chapter.

Chapter 8 describes how House–Senate differences are reconciled when each chamber passes a different version of the same bill and then discusses the president's veto power. Chapter 9 deals with how Congress monitors the implementation of the laws it has passed. Finally, Chapter 10 reexamines the legislative process, pulling together the major themes of the book.

Anyone who writes nine editions of a book is intellectually indebted to numerous scholars and colleagues, and I welcome the opportunity to acknowledge their generous advice and assistance. Let me start with the talented professionals at CQ Press. Laureen Gleason and Eric Garner served as production editors for this edition and did a careful and thorough job. Megan Granger, copy editor, used her exemplary editorial skills to improve the manuscript. Finally, my sincere appreciation goes to Brenda Carter, executive editorial director, and Charisse Kiino, publisher of political science books, both of whom encouraged and helped me with this book over the years.

Much credit for whatever understanding I have of the congressional process goes to my colleagues at the Congressional Research Service (CRS). Over the years I have learned the intricacies of the House and Senate from scores of current and former CRS associates. Their research endeavors have expanded my understanding of Congress's role and responsibilities. I especially want to acknowledge Stanley Bach, Richard Beth, Colton Campbell, Curtis Copeland, Christopher Davis, Louis Fisher, Valerie Heitshusen,

William Heniff, Frederick Kaiser, Robert Keith, Michael Koempel, Megan Lynch, Betsy Palmer, Morton Rosenberg, Paul Rundquist, Elizabeth Rybicki, James Saturno, Judy Schneider, Colleen Shogan, Stephen Stathis, Sylvia Streeter, and Jessica Tollestrup. CRS, I should note, bears no responsibility whatsoever for the views or interpretations expressed within these pages. I must also emphasize that whatever errors remain in this book are mine alone.

I am indebted also to scores of past and present House and Senate members and professional congressional aides who have shared ideas and observations and deepened my understanding of the legislative process. My deep gratitude goes to all the past and present official parliamentarians of the House and Senate for trying to improve my understanding of Congress's procedural intricacies.

In addition, I am grateful to numerous colleagues in academia who have created, with their research studies, a reservoir of knowledge about congressional activities and operations. Here I would like especially to acknowledge my collaborators in various projects—Roger H. Davidson, C. Lawrence Evans, Frances E. Lee, Eric Schickler, and James Thurber—who are always generous with their time and who provide excellent suggestions. My intellectual debt also extends to Donald R. Wolfensberger, resident congressional scholar at the Bipartisan Policy Center and former staff director of the House Rules Committee, and veteran House staffer Matt Pinkus, for their parliamentary advice over the years. I would also like to thank the reviewers of this edition: Michael Crespin (University of Georgia), Diane Schmidt (California State University–Chico), Charles Finocchiaro (University of South Carolina), Jason Casellas (University of Texas), and Craig Goodman (Texas Tech University)

Finally, I dedicate this ninth edition to family members—Janet, Mark, and Eric. They provided a loving and encouraging home environment, patience, and support throughout the preparation of every edition.

Walter J. Oleszek
Fairfax, Virginia

CHAPTER 1

Congress and Lawmaking

CONGRESSIONAL RULES and procedures are a complex mix of intricate features that can be used to expedite, slow down, or stop action on legislation. Adroit lawmakers may influence how expeditiously legislation moves through Congress, but in doing so they must navigate around procedural obstacles. This legislative reality typically means that measures move slowly through the congressional maze, or sometimes not at all. At times, members can employ parliamentary procedures to bypass lawmaking stages to accelerate even controversial measures through the usually slow-moving Congress. Crises often trigger expedited legislative action. A classic example is a Depression-era emergency banking bill sent to Congress on March 9, 1933, by President Franklin D. Roosevelt. It passed both chambers in a matter of hours and was signed into law that same day.[1] Fast-forward to today's economic times, which witnessed the collapse of banking giants, the housing market, and Wall Street brokerage firms that all contributed to an ailing economy with persistent unemployment. In one response, the 111th Congress (2009–2011) moved rapidly, over a span of 3 weeks (January 26 to February 17, 2009), to enact the president's nearly $800 billion economic stimulus package, bypassing committee consideration of the legislation (H.R. 1) in both chambers.

Too much haste in passing major legislation can sometimes have profound and unforeseen implications. Two classic examples highlight the dangers of insufficient deliberation by lawmakers and legislative speediness, especially in granting the president the equivalent of a declaration of war. In early August 1964, President Lyndon Johnson informed the country and Congress that North Vietnamese PT boats had twice attacked U.S. naval ships in the Gulf of Tonkin. (Analysts disagree on whether there was a second attack.) On August 5, 1964, the president asked Congress to pass a measure (the Gulf of Tonkin Resolution) authorizing the chief executive "to take all necessary measures" to deter further aggression in Southeast Asia. Two days later, on August 7, both chambers overwhelmingly approved the measure after limited debate: 414 to 0 in the House and 88 to 2 in the Senate. The resolution provided legal support for the administration's military expansion of the war in Indochina.

Nearly four decades later and reminiscent of the Gulf of Tonkin Resolution, Congress in October 2002 granted the president a blank check to invade Iraq on the grounds that dictator Saddam Hussein had ties to al Qaeda—the terrorist organization that organized the September 11, 2001, terrorist attack against the United States—and that he possessed weapons of mass destruction. Both allegations proved to be false. Debate in both chambers on the use-of-force resolution in Iraq was abbreviated, and each voted by large margins to pass the measure, which authorized the president to decide whether to launch preemptive military action against Iraq. On March 23, 2003, the United States attacked Iraq and toppled the Saddam Hussein–led regime within a matter of weeks.

The Vietnam and Iraq wars each divided the nation, killed and maimed thousands of U.S. military personnel and tens of thousands of local civilian residents of those nations, and cost the federal treasury hundreds of billions of dollars. Whether all this could have been avoided if Congress had spent more time evaluating the credibility of presidential claims can never be known. Wars and crises tend to strengthen the executive branch, as Congress and the country look to the White House for leadership. However, it is Congress's job not simply to defer to the president but to rigorously and vigorously debate, deliberate, challenge, and question administration plans and proposals. Such actions by Congress may prevent presidential miscalculations, as well as engage the citizenry in a national debate.

Conflicts and disputes are commonplace when Congress debates controversial issues or party priorities. These matters arouse the partisan or ideological zeal of lawmakers on each side of the issue and make compromises hard to come by. As stated by John D. Dingell, D-Mich., the longest serving House member ever, "Legislation is hard, pick-and-shovel work," and it often "takes a long time to do it."[2] Whether Congress can overcome the procedural and substantive wrangling regularly associated with many bills depends on numerous factors, such as backing from the public and presidential leadership. What remains constant, however, is Congress's ability to initiate ideas on its own, to refine and crystallize public debate, and to delay, block, or modify legislative proposals.

Congress is an independent policymaker as well as the nation's premier forum for addressing the economic, social, and political issues of the day—from agriculture to housing, environment to national security, health care to taxes. However, Congress is not impermeable to pressures from other governmental and nongovernmental forces (including the executive branch, the media, members' constituents, and lobbying groups) or from formal and informal procedural changes that affect policymaking. The lawmaking process, which can be complicated and variable, is governed by rules, procedures, precedents, and customs and is open to the use of some generally predictable strategies and tactics.

This book examines the most significant House and Senate **rules** and practices that influence the lawmaking process. Because it is unusual on Capitol Hill for any idea to avoid a range of parliamentary processes if it expects to become law, this book looks at some related questions, such as, Why does Congress have rules? How do House and Senate rules differ, and what impact do those differences have on policymaking? How are rules applied strategically to accomplish partisan goals? What procedures frame budgetary debates on Capitol Hill? Can House and Senate rules be set aside to expedite consideration of legislation?

THE CONSTITUTIONAL CONTEXT

Congress's central role in policymaking can be traced to the Constitution. James Madison, Alexander Hamilton, and the other framers developed a political system in which Congress would serve as the lawmaking body and set out its relationship with the other branches of government and with the people. As a legislative scholar noted:

> The Constitution has successfully provided two features of national political life that seem unassailable. The first is a Congress that is institutionally robust and capable of gathering information and seeking opinions independently of the president. The second is that Congress is still linked directly to the people through elections. The president is a stronger rival than he once was, but he is not the only game in town. It is that unbreakable electoral link that provides [Congress's] continuing legitimacy, ensuring real political power.[3]

Several familiar basic principles underlie the specific provisions of the Constitution: limited government, separation of powers, checks and balances, and federalism. Each principle continues to shape lawmaking today, despite the enormous changes that have transformed and enlarged the role and reach of government in American society.

Limited Government

The framers of the Constitution wanted a strong and effective national government, but at the same time they wanted to avoid concentrating too much power in the central government lest it threaten personal and property rights. The Constitution is filled with implicit and explicit "auxiliary precautions" (Madison's phrase), such as checks and balances and the Bill of Rights. The framers believed that limits on government could be achieved by dividing power among three branches of national government and between the nation and the states. The division of power ensured both policy conflicts and cooperation, because it made officials in the several branches responsive to different constituencies, responsibilities, and perceptions of the public welfare. The framers believed that the "accumulation of all powers, legislative, executive, and judiciary, in the same hands ... may justly be pronounced the very definition of tyranny."[4] As men of practical experience, they had witnessed firsthand the abuses of King George III and his royal governors. They also wanted to avoid the possible "elective despotism" of their own state legislatures.[5]

Wary of excessive authority in either an executive or a legislative body, the framers were familiar with the works of influential political theorists, particularly John Locke and Baron de Montesquieu, who stressed the separation of powers, checks and balances, and popular control of government.

Separation of Powers

The framers combined their practical experience with a theoretical outlook and established three independent branches of national government, none having a monopoly of governing power. Their objective was twofold. First, the separation of powers was designed to restrain the power of any one branch. Second, it was meant to ensure that cooperation would be necessary for effective government. As Justice Robert Jackson wrote in a 1952 Supreme Court case, *Youngstown Sheet and Tube Co. v. Sawyer*: "While the Constitution diffuses power the better to secure liberty, it also contemplates that the practice will integrate the dispersed powers into a workable government."[6] The framers held a strong bias in favor of lawmaking by representative assemblies, and so they viewed Congress as the prime national policymaker. The Constitution names Congress the first branch of government, assigns it "all legislative power," and grants it explicit and implied responsibilities through the so-called elastic clause (Section 8 of Article I). This clause empowers Congress to make "all Laws which shall be necessary and proper for carrying into Execution" its enumerated or specific powers.

In sharp contrast, Articles II and III, creating the executive and judicial branches, respectively, describe only briefly the framework and duties of these governmental units. Although separation of powers implies that Congress "enacts" the laws, the president "executes" them, and the Supreme Court "interprets" them, the framers did not intend such a rigid division of labor. The Constitution creates a system not of separate institutions performing separate functions but of separate institutions sharing functions (and even competing for predominant influence in exercising them). Indeed, the overlap of powers is fundamental to national decision making. The founders did, however, grant certain unique responsibilities to each branch and ensured their separateness by, for example, prohibiting any officer from serving in more than one branch simultaneously. They linked the branches through a system of checks and balances.

Checks and Balances

An essential corollary of separation of powers is checks and balances. The framers realized that members of each branch might seek to aggrandize power at the expense of the other branches. Inevitably, conflicts would develop. In particular, the Constitution provides Congress and the president with an open invitation to struggle for power.

To restrain each branch, the framers devised a system of checks and balances. Congress's own legislative power is effectively "checked" by its structure; it is a bicameral body that consists of a House of Representatives and Senate. The measures Congress passes may be vetoed in turn by the president. Treaties and the president's high-level executive, diplomatic, and judicial appointments require the approval of the Senate. Many decisions and actions of Congress and the president are subject to review by the federal judiciary.

Checks and balances have a dual effect: They encourage cooperation and accommodation among the branches—particularly between the popularly elected Congress and the president—and they introduce the potential for conflict. Since 1789, Congress and the president have cooperated with each other and protected their own powers. Each branch depends in various ways on the other. When conflicts occur, they are resolved most frequently by negotiation, bargaining, and compromise.

Federalism

Just as the three branches check each other, the state and federal governments also are countervailing forces. This division of power is another way to curb and control governing power. Although the term *federalism*—like *separation of powers* or *checks and balances*—is not mentioned in the Constitution, the framers understood that federalism was a plan of government acceptable to the 13 original states. The Constitution's "supremacy clause" makes national laws and treaties the "supreme Law of the Land"; however, powers not granted to the national government remain with the states and the people. The inevitable clashes that occur between levels of government are often arbitrated by the Supreme Court or worked out through practical accommodations or laws.

Federalism has infused congressional proceedings with "localism." As a representative institution, Congress and its members respond to the needs and interests of states and congressional districts. The nation's diversity is given ample expression in Congress by legislators whose tenure rests on the continued support of their constituents. Federalism is a perennial issue, as many lawmakers often advocate the return of federal functions to state and local governments. Conversely, lawmakers also advance legislation expanding the federal role in areas traditionally left to states and localities, such as education.

The Constitution outlines a complicated system. Power is divided among the branches and between levels of government, and popular opinion is reflected differently in each. Both Congress and the president, each with different constituencies, terms of office, and times of election, can claim to represent majority sentiment on national issues. Given each branch's independence, formidable powers, different perspectives on many issues, and intricate mix of formal and informal relationships, important national policies reflect the judgment of both the legislative and the executive branches and the views of many others—constituents, influential persons, special interests, and the like.

FUNCTIONS OF RULES AND PROCEDURES

Any decision-making body needs formal and informal rules, procedures, and conventions to function. The rules and conventions described in Box 1.1

BOX 1.1 Major Sources of House and Senate Rules

U.S. Constitution. Article I, Section 5, states: "Each House may determine the Rules of Its Proceedings." In addition, other procedures of Congress are addressed, such as quorums, adjournments, and roll call votes.

Standing Rules. The formal rules of the House are contained in the Constitution, *Jefferson's Manual,* and *Rules of the House of Representatives,* commonly called the House Manual. The Senate's rules are in the *Senate Manual Containing the Standing Rules, Orders, Laws, and Resolutions Affecting the Business of the United States Senate.* Each chamber prints its rulebook biennially as a separate document.

Precedents. Each chamber has many precedents, or unwritten law, based on past rulings of the chair. The modern precedents of the Senate are compiled in one volume prepared by the Senate parliamentarian. It is revised and updated periodically, printed as a Senate document, and entitled *Senate Procedure: Precedents and Practices.* House precedents are contained in several sources. Precedents from 1789 to 1936 are found in 11 volumes: *Hinds' Precedents of the House of Representatives* (from 1789 through 1907) and *Cannon's Precedents of the House of Representatives* (from 1908 through 1936). Precedents from 1936 on can be found in the 18 volumes that make up *Deschler's Precedents of the United States House of Representatives and Deschler-Brown-Johnson Precedents of the United States House of Representatives.* A summary of important precedents through 1984 is found in *Procedure in the U.S. House of Representatives.* In addition, *House Practice: A Guide to the Rules, Precedents, and Procedures of the House* (2011) by William Holmes Brown, Charles W. Johnson, and John V.

---

establish the procedural context for both collective and individual policy-making action and behavior.

The Constitution authorizes the House and Senate to formulate their own rules of procedure and also prescribes some basic procedures for both houses, such as overrides of presidential vetoes. Thomas Jefferson, who as vice president compiled the first parliamentary manual for the Senate, emphasized the importance of rules to any legislative body:

> It is much more material that there be a rule to go by, than what that rule is; that there may be a uniformity of proceeding in business not subject to the caprice of the Speaker or captiousness of the members. It is very material that order, decency, and regularity be preserved in a dignified public body.[7]

Rules and procedures in an organization serve many functions. Among other things, they provide stability, legitimize decisions, divide responsibilities, protect minority rights, reduce conflict, and distribute power.

Sullivan examines selected contemporary precedents as of the 108th Congress. Asher C. Hinds, Clarence A. Cannon, Lewis Deschler, William Holmes Brown, Charles Johnson, and John Sullivan were parliamentarians of the House.

Statutory Rules. Provisions of many public laws have the force of congressional rules. These rulemaking statutes include, for example, the Legislative Reorganization Act of 1946 (P.L. 79-601), the Legislative Reorganization Act of 1970 (P.L. 91-510), and the Congressional Budget and Impoundment Control Act of 1974 (P.L. 93-344).

Jefferson's Manual. When Thomas Jefferson was vice president (1797–1801), he prepared a manual of parliamentary procedure for the Senate. Ironically, in 1837 the House made it a formal part of its rules but the Senate did not grant it such status. The provisions of his manual, according to the House Manual, "govern the House in all cases to which they are applicable and in which they are not inconsistent with the standing rules and orders of the House."

Party Rules. Each of the two major political parties in each chamber has its own set of party rules. Some of these party regulations directly affect legislative procedure. The House Republican Conference, for example, has a provision that affects the Speaker's use of the suspension of the rules procedure.

Informal Practices and Customs. Each chamber develops its own informal traditions and customs. They can be uncovered by examining sources such as the *Congressional Record* (the substantially verbatim account of House and Senate floor debate), scholarly accounts, and other studies of Congress. Committees and party groups may also prepare manuals of legislative procedure and practice.

Stability

Rules provide stability and predictability in personal and organizational affairs. Individuals and institutions can conduct their day-to-day business without having to debate procedure. Universities, for example, have specific requirements for bachelor's, master's, and doctorate degrees. Students know that if they are to progress from one degree to the next they must comply with rules and requirements. Daily or weekly changes in those requirements would cause chaos on any campus. Similarly, legislators need not decide each day who can speak on the floor, offer **amendments**, or close debate. Such matters are governed by regularized procedures that continue from one Congress to the next and generally afford similar rights and privileges to every member.

To be sure, House and Senate rules change in response to new circumstances, needs, and demands. The history of Congress is reflected in the evolution of the House and Senate rules. Increases in the size of the House in the 19th century, for example, produced limitations on debate for individual representatives. As Democratic Senator Robert C. Byrd of West Virginia, the longest serving member ever in either the House or Senate, once said about Senate proceedings:

> The day-to-day functioning of the Senate has given rise to a set of traditions, rules, and practices with a life and history all its own. The body of principles and procedures governing many senatorial obligations and routines . . . is not so much the result of reasoned deliberations as the fruit of jousting and adjusting to circumstances in which the Senate found itself from time to time.[8]

Procedural evolution is a hallmark of Congress. The modern House and Senate differ in important ways from how each operated only a few decades ago. For example, the House today operates with more procedural and political powers centralized in the **Speaker** than it did in the past. In the contemporary Senate, the use or threat of dilatory procedures is a growth industry. Increasingly, the Senate finds it harder to reach unanimous consent agreements as a way to avoid parliamentary stalemates and to facilitate the lawmaking process. In brief, the rules of each chamber are used by lawmakers and congressional parties to enhance their policy, power, and reelection requirements.

Legitimacy

Students typically receive final course grades that are based on their classroom performance, examinations, and term papers. Students accept the professors' evaluations if they believe in their fairness and legitimacy. If professors suddenly decided to use students' political opinions as the basis for final grades, a storm of protest would arise against such an arbitrary procedure. In a similar fashion, members of Congress and citizens generally accept legislative decisions when they believe the decisions have been approved according to orderly and fair procedures.

For years Congress grappled with the issue of applying to itself many of the laws it passes for the private sector and executive branch. Issues of legitimacy abound in this area. As a House member highlighted in a story he told the House Rules Committee:

> Mr. Chairman, at one town meeting recently a constituent stood up and said, "Congressman, how are we supposed to believe the laws you guys pass are good for America, when you're telling us they're not good for Congress?" He was right. To ensure confidence in our laws we need to apply them to ourselves as well.[9]

Congress, therefore, devised a process consistent with constitutional principles to bring itself into compliance with appropriate workplace and employee protection laws (e.g., age discrimination, civil rights, and health and safety laws). The landmark bill, titled the Congressional Accountability Act of 1995, was signed into law by President Bill Clinton.

Division of Labor

Any university requires a division of labor to carry out its tasks effectively and responsibly, and rules to establish the various jurisdictions. For that reason, universities have history, chemistry, and art departments; admissions officers and bursars; and food service and physical plant managers, all with specialized assignments. For Congress, **committees** are the heart of the legislative process. They provide the division of labor and specialization that Congress needs to handle the roughly 8,000 measures introduced biennially and to review the administration of scores of federal agencies and programs. Like specialized bodies in many organizations, committees do not make final policy decisions but initiate recommendations that are forwarded to their respective chambers.

The jurisdiction, or policy mandate, of Congress's standing (permanent) committees is outlined in the House and Senate rules. Legislation generally is referred to the committee (or committees) having authority over the subject matter. As a result, the rules generally determine which committee, and thus which members and their staffs, will exercise significant influence over a particular issue such as defense, taxes, health, or education.

Rules also prescribe the standards that committees are expected to observe during their policy deliberations. These include **quorum** requirements, public notice of committee meetings and hearings, and the right to counsel for witnesses. These rules also allocate staff resources to committees and subcommittees.

Protection of Minority Rights

Colleges and universities have procedures and practices to make certain that minority ideas and beliefs are protected from suppression. Tenure for faculty members ensures that professors are free to expound unconventional views without fear of reprisal from academic administrators. Student handbooks are replete with policies and guidelines to ensure fairness and due process in the adjudication of academic grievances or violations. A fundamental purpose of the collegiate experience presumably is to encourage students to explore new areas, examine diverse ideas, and engage persons who think and believe differently than they do.

Congress provides procedural protections for individual lawmakers regardless of their party affiliation and for the minority party. However, the House and Senate differ in the extent to which they emphasize majority rule versus minority rights. The principle of majority rule is embedded in the rules, precedents, and practices of the modern House. Still, there are procedural protections for minority members and viewpoints. For example, the minority party is represented on every standing committee; any lawmaker with contrary views can claim one third of the debate time on conference reports if the Republican and Democratic floor managers both support it; and any committee member is entitled to have supplemental, additional, or minority views printed in committee reports on legislation. A House member declared: "This body, unlike the other, operates under the principle that a determined majority should be allowed to work its will while protecting the rights of the minority to be heard."[10] An insightful analysis of procedural change in the House by political scientist Sarah Binder states that the minority party may see some of their parliamentary rights reduced "when members of the majority party believe rules changes are necessary to secure favored policy outcomes; minority parties have recouped some of those rights when cross-party coalitions emerge to demand new rights from a weakened majority party."[11]

The Senate, by contrast, operates with rules and procedures that advantage minority rights. Prime examples include the right of every senator to speak at great length—the filibuster—and to offer amendments, including nongermane amendments. If the House errs on the side of majority rule, putting decision over deliberation, the Senate tilts toward minority rights, even if that thwarts the will of the majority. As political scientist Richard F. Fenno Jr. said about the awesome procedural prerogatives afforded each senator, "Every member of the Senate has an atomic bomb and can blow up the place. That leads to accommodation."[12]

Conflict Resolution

Rules reduce conflicts among members and units of organizations by distinguishing appropriate actions and behavior from the inappropriate. For example, universities have procedures by which students may drop or add classes. There are discussions with faculty advisers, completion of appropriate paperwork, and the approval of a dean. Students who informally try to drop or add classes may encounter conflicts with their professors as well as sanctions from the dean's office. Most of the conflicts can be avoided by observance of established procedures. Similarly, congressional rules reduce conflict by, for example, establishing procedures for the orderly consideration of floor amendments or to settle bicameral disputes on legislation. Rep. Clarence A. Cannon, D-Mo. (1923–1964), House parliamentarian and later chair of the Appropriations Committee, explained:

> The time of the House is too valuable, the scope of its enactments too far-reaching, and the constantly increasing pressure of its business too great to justify lengthy and perhaps acrimonious discussion of questions of procedure which have been authoritatively decided in former sessions.[13]

Distribution of Power

A major consequence of rules is that they generally distribute power in any organization. Rules, therefore, are often a source of conflict themselves. During the 1960s, college and university campuses were the scene of struggles among students, faculty, and administrators over curricula. Unhappy students charged that their courses were irrelevant. As a result, many schools changed the rules of the game for curriculum development. Students, junior faculty, and even community groups became involved in reshaping the structure and content of educational programs. Recent years have witnessed comparable concerns as groups on various campuses have persuaded university officials to adopt rules, guidelines, or codes regarding speech that is perceived as offensive to, for example, minority groups or women (the so-called political correctness movement).

Like universities, Congress distributes power according to its rules and customs. Informal party rules establish a hierarchy of leadership positions in both chambers. House and Senate rules accord prerogatives to congressional committee chairs that are unavailable to others. Majority party leaders in both chambers exercise large influence over the floor agenda and schedule.

Rules are not neutral devices. They help shore up the more powerful members and influence the attainment of member goals such as winning reelection, gaining internal influence, or winning congressional passage of legislation. Newt Gingrich, R-Ga., who served as Speaker from 1995 to 1999, once said, "The rules of the House are designed for a Speaker with a strong personality and an agenda."[14] Attempts to change the rules almost invariably are efforts to redistribute power.

RULES AND POLICYMAKING IN CONGRESS

Rules play similar roles in most complex organizations. However, Congress has its own characteristics that affect the functions of the rules. First, members owe their positions to the electorate, not to their congressional peers or to influential congressional leaders. No one in Congress has authority over the other members comparable to that of university presidents and tenured faculty over junior faculty or to that of a corporation president over lower-level executives. Members cannot be fired except by their own constituency. (Under the Constitution, either chamber may expel a member by a two-thirds vote, but the authority is rarely used. The authority was last employed on July 24, 2002, when the House voted 420–1 to expel Rep. James A. Traficant Jr., D-Ohio, for corruption.) And each member has equal voting power in committees and on the floor of the House or Senate.

The rules of Congress, unlike those of many organizations, are sensitive to the rights of minorities, including the minority party, ideological minorities, and individual members. Skillful use of the rules enables the minority to check majority action by delaying, defeating, or reshaping legislation. Intensity often counts as much as numbers—an apathetic majority may find it difficult to prevail over a well-organized minority. Except in the few instances in which extraordinary majorities are needed, such as overriding presidential vetoes (requires a two-thirds vote), Senate ratification of treaties (a two-thirds vote), and ending a filibuster in the Senate (a three-fifths vote), the rules of the House and Senate require a simple majority to decide public policies.

Congress also is different from many other organizations in its degree of responsiveness to external groups and pressures. The legislative branch is not as self-contained an institution as a university or a corporation. Congress is involved with every significant national and international issue. Its agenda compels members to respond to changing constituent interests and needs. Congress also is subject to numerous other influences—particularly the president, pressure groups, political parties, state and local officials, and major external events or developments, such as the September 11, 2001, terrorist attacks, global climate change, or persistent joblessness.

Finally, Congress is a collegial, not hierarchical, body. Power flows not from the top down, as in a corporation, but in practically every direction. While presidents can say, as did Harry S Truman, "The buck stops here," responsibility in Congress is generally circular, with everybody and nobody appearing responsible for action or inaction. "The congressional system is not set up to have the buck stop somewhere," observed Charles E. Schumer, D-N.Y. (House, 1981–1999; Senate, 1999–).[15] Congressional policies are not produced by fiat but are made commonly by shifting coalitions that vary from issue to issue. And Congress's deliberations are more accessible and transparent to the public than those of perhaps any other kind of organization. These, then, are some of the characteristics that set Congress apart from other bodies. Inevitably, these differences affect the decision-making process.

Procedure and Policy

Legislative procedures and policymaking are inextricably linked in at least four ways. First, procedures affect policy outcomes. Congress processes legislation by complex rules and procedures that permeate the institution. Some matters are only gently brushed by the rules, while others become locked in their grip. Major civil rights legislation, for example, failed for decades to win congressional approval because Southern senators used their chamber's rules and procedures to kill or modify such measures.

Congressional procedures are employed to define, restrict, or expand the policy options available to members during floor debate. They may prevent consideration of certain issues or presage policy outcomes. Such structured procedures enhance the policy influence of certain members, committees, or party leaders; facilitate expeditious treatment of issues; grant priority to some policy alternatives but not others; and determine, in general, the overall character of policy decisions.

Second, policy decisions often are expressed as procedural moves. Robert H. Michel, R-Ill., who served as House minority leader from 1981 to 1995, highlighted the procedure–substance linkage:

> Procedure hasn't simply become more important than substance—it has, through a strange alchemy, become the substance of our deliberations. Who rules House procedures rules the House—and to a great degree, rules the kind and scope of political debate in this country.[16]

Or as Representative Dingell phrased it, "If you let me write the procedure, and I let you write the substance, I'll [beat] you every time."[17] Dingell's adage can be modified, however. With ample time, sufficient votes can overcome procedural maneuvers to produce substantive wins.

Representatives and senators on various occasions prefer not to make clear-cut decisions on certain complex and far-reaching public issues. Should a major weapons system be continued or curtailed? Should the nation's energy production needs take precedence over environmental concerns? Should financial assistance for the elderly be reduced and priority given to disadvantaged children? On questions such as these, members may be cross-pressured—the president may exert influence one way, while constituent interests dictate another approach. Legislators sometimes lack adequate information or time to make informed judgments. They may be reluctant to oppose powerful interest groups, or they may feel that an issue does not lend itself to a simple "yes" or "no" vote.

As a result, legislators employ various procedural devices to handle knotty problems. A matter may be postponed on the grounds of insufficient study in committee. Congress may direct an agency to prepare a detailed report before an issue is considered. The House or Senate may establish an outside commission to study a problem. Or the House or Senate may table a measure, a procedural vote that effectively defeats a proposal without rendering a clear judgment on its substance.

Third, the nature of the policy can determine the use of certain procedures. The House and Senate generally consider noncontroversial measures under expeditious procedures; controversial proposals normally involve lengthy deliberation. The House commonly passes noncontroversial or relatively noncontroversial legislation by suspending the rules, a procedure that limits debate to forty minutes, prohibits floor amendments, and requires a two-thirds vote for passage. Legislation with overwhelming bipartisan support can be passed quickly by way of the suspension route.

Fourth, policy outcomes are more likely to be influenced by members with procedural expertise. Members who are skilled parliamentarians are better prepared to gain approval of their proposals than those who are only vaguely familiar with the rules. Just as carpenters and lawyers must learn their trade, members of Congress need to understand the rules if they expect to perform effectively. Congressional procedures are confusing to members. "To table, to refer to committee, to amend—so many things come up," declared a junior senator. "You don't know whether you are coming or going."[18] John W. McCormack, D-Mass., who served as House Speaker from 1962 to 1971, once advised House newcomers:

> Learn the rules and understand the precedents and procedures of the House. The congressman who knows how the House operates will soon be recognized for his parliamentary skills—and his prestige will rise among his colleagues, no matter what his party.[19]

Members who know the rules will always have the potential to shape legislation to their ends and become key figures in coalitions trying to pass, modify, or defeat legislation. Those who do not understand the rules reduce their proficiency and influence as legislators. Some members even become parliamentary watchdogs or use guerrilla warfare tactics to harass the opposition or stymie majority steamrollers.

Conventional Versus Unconventional Lawmaking

A fundamental strength of Congress's lawmaking process—a principal characteristic of the legislative process apparent from Congress's earliest days—is its capacity to adjust and adapt to new circumstances. The House and Senate, not surprisingly, regularly modify, either formally or informally, their procedures and practices, making the procedures associated with lawmaking something of a moving target. What is conventional or orthodox in one era or for specific types of bills may seem unconventional or unorthodox when different patterns of congressional decision making emerge.

In recent years, some commentators and scholars have noted procedural deviations from a textbook Congress, or the regular order. The "regular order" refers to what the House or Senate rulebook prescribes for the consideration of legislation. Much of the time in each chamber, many of these rules are not observed because they are too cumbersome to apply in practice. Instead, each chamber creates special procedures, such as "rules" from the Rules Committee in the House or unanimous consent agreements in the Senate. Thus, the regular order can be conceived as the default procedures in the standing rules that will be observed except when they are set aside.

Speaking of the regular order as a specifically prescribed way by which ideas become laws is somewhat misleading. Instead, this term generally refers to procedural expectations or norms for how legislation should normally be considered in the House or Senate. During the 1950s, 1960s, and early 1970s, for example, the regular order—or textbook version of lawmaking—meant introduction and referral of bills to committees; committee hearings, markups, and reports; wide amendment opportunities on the House or Senate floor; the bicameral resolution of chamber differences on legislation; and presidential consideration. This pattern, shown in Figure 1.1, still holds true for most public laws enacted by Congress, because most neither arouse much controversy nor sharply divide the two parties.

Yet the procedural expectations prevalent in certain eras have always been subject to variations and innovations, especially for priority or "must pass" legislation. During the 1990s and 2000s, deviations from the regular order have increased, because Congress is less insular, more partisan, more ideological, and more permeable to outside forces than ever before. Understandably, changes in the broader political environment—the election of activist lawmakers, the cost of congressional campaigns, the proliferation of interest groups, the rise in issue complexity, partisan polarization,

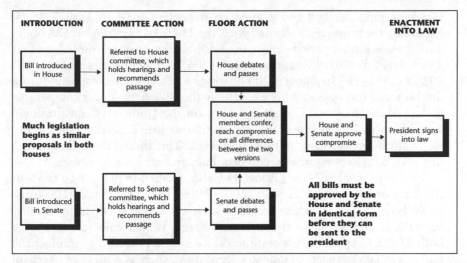

| INTRODUCTION | COMMITTEE ACTION | FLOOR ACTION | | ENACTMENT INTO LAW |

FIGURE 1.1   How a Bill Becomes Law

breakthroughs in communications technology, clashes with presidents, crises, and more—are reflected in the procedural practices and politics of the House and Senate.

Contemporary lawmaking is a more fluid and less predictable process. Party leaders and individual members simply have more procedural room for strategic maneuvers. For example, scholars and commentators talk about obstructionism or gridlock in today's Senate. Why? The past two decades have witnessed the rise of a more polarized, individualistic, and closely divided Senate (even 50–50 during the first 5 months of 2001), with the result that senators now have more incentives to push their procedural prerogatives to the limit. And omnibus bills have gained prominence since the 1980s, in part because party and committee leaders can package or bury controversial provisions in one massive bill to be voted up or down with limited debate and few (if any) amendments. In another development, party leaders tend to bypass the standing committees more often or make adjustments in legislation after it is reported out of committee. Such leadership decisions are made to prevent major bills from getting bogged down in committee and to promote favorable action on important measures.

Procedural change is a persistent feature of the House and Senate. For example, in one of Congress's most dramatic and landmark legislative sessions, the House in early 1995 reviewed, debated, and voted on virtually everything associated with the GOP's Contract with America (a 10-point program of issues, such as tax cuts, welfare reform, and a constitutional balanced budget amendment). The contract had served as a 1994 campaign document for Republicans—who promised to enact it within the first hundred days of the historic 104th Congress (1995–1997) if the electorate gave them majority control—and as a governing document around which GOP

House members rallied and focused on from January 4 to April 7, 1995. Reflecting the unusual accelerated pace, the House was in session 528 hours during the contract period—more than double the session hours of the first 13 weeks of the 103rd Congress (1993–1995) and almost triple those of the 102nd (1991–1993). About 1,200 hearings and markups were held during the hundred days—one third more than the 800 held in the comparable period of the previous Congress.[20] "I'm on the [Judiciary] constitutional subcommittee," said Democratic Representative José E. Serrano, N.Y., "and we're amending the Constitution every week. This should not be happening this way, but [Republicans] have a deadline, and we have no choice."[21]

Similarly, Speaker Nancy Pelosi, D-Calif., pushed the House to enact at the start of the 110th Congress (2007–2009) the Democratic "100 legislative hours" agenda, which included such measures as ethics and lobbying reform and a hike in the minimum wage. With Democrats in charge both of the 111th Congress and the White House ("unified government"), party lawmakers enacted landmark legislation, such as a massive overhaul of both the health care and financial regulatory systems. When Republicans reclaimed control of the 112th House (2011–2013), Speaker John Boehner, Ohio, and his GOP majority made evisceration of both laws a top priority. Their political slogan on the health law was "repeal and replace," and their principal aims were to slash spending, reduce the reach and role of government, and eliminate burdensome regulations. In June 2012, the U.S. Supreme Court upheld the constitutional thrust of the Affordable Care Act. Nonetheless, Speaker Boehner announced that in the 113th Congress (2013–2015) House Republicans would conduct aggressive oversight of the law's implementation and promotion.

Several recent House Speakers, such as Thomas P. "Tip" O'Neill Jr., D-Mass. (1977–1987), employed partisan or bipartisan task forces to facilitate passage of legislation and to draft legislation. However, Speaker Newt Gingrich, R-Ga., accelerated the creation of task forces, most composed only of GOP lawmakers. A Capitol Hill newspaper suggested that Gingrich was "implementing a new House structure that relies heavily on task forces to carry out responsibilities handled by committees."[22] This was an overstatement, but Gingrich did create a large number of these ad hoc groups, several of which exercised important policy influence. For example, the "Design Group," composed of the principal Republican lawmakers with expertise in health care issues, crafted Medicare reform legislation. "This bill, right from the start, was written in the Speaker's office," said a committee chair.[23]

Speaker J. Dennis Hastert, R-Ill. (1999–2007), who succeeded Gingrich, deemphasized the use of task forces and employed them selectively and for purposes beyond policy development. Like Hastert, Speaker Pelosi (2007–2011) had little need to create task forces since the majority Democrats use the standing committees to craft legislation. However, she did initiate the formation of a bipartisan ethics task force to strengthen ethics enforcement in the House. The task force recommended the creation of an independent

Office of Congressional Ethics, which the House established in 2008. Speaker Boehner (2011–) formed a GOP task force on cybersecurity to develop ideas for protecting the nation's critical Internet sites from domestic or foreign hackers. In the Senate, Minority Leader Mitch McConnell, R-Ky., established a High Tech Task Force to counter an initiative of Majority Leader Harry Reid, Nev., who named Senator Mark Warner, Va., to be the Democratic point person "in reaching out to corporate board rooms and executive suites from Silicon Valley to Wall Street."[24]

Ideas can become law with little or no committee or floor debate in either the House or Senate. Few statistics have been kept on the number of times this has occurred,[25] but congressional insiders suggest that it is on the increase. A convenient venue for this practice is the **conference** stage. For example, with no committee hearings or floor debate in either chamber, a one-sentence, 46-word, $50 billion tobacco industry tax break was quietly inserted into a budget conference report, and the president signed the resulting bill into law. When word leaked out about the tax break, it was repealed in another law.[26] As another example, when the Senate debated President Obama's 2009 economic stimulus package, it added restrictions on the use of federal bailout money for the millions of dollars in bonuses paid to Wall Street executives. During conference negotiations, however, the Senate's restrictive language was dropped and new language was added in its place that specifically protected the large bonuses paid to the executives. The public was outraged, as were many lawmakers. But no one came forward to say, as Rep. Steve LaTourette, R-Ohio, expressed it, "I took out the first language and I put in the [substitute] language."[27] An apt summary of what often characterizes contemporary lawmaking was voiced by Senator Bill Nelson, D-Fla.: "If you want to get anything done . . . you have to figure out how to get there. Sometimes it's not a straight line. Sometimes it's a circuitous path."[28]

Precedents and Folkways

Congress is regulated not only by formal rules but also by informal ones that influence legislative procedure and member behavior. Two types of informal rules are precedents and folkways. Precedents, the accumulated past decisions on matters of procedure, represent a blend of the formal and informal. They are the common law of Congress and govern many procedures not explicitly covered in the formal rules. As noted House parliamentarian Lewis Deschler wrote, the great majority of the "rules of all parliamentary bodies are unwritten law; they spring up by precedent and custom; these precedents and customs are this day the chief law of both Houses of Congress."[29] For example, formal rules prescribe the order of business in the House and Senate, but precedents permit variations through the unanimous consent of the members. The rulings of the Speaker of the House and presiding officer of the Senate form a large body of precedents. They are given formal status by the parliamentarians in each chamber and then become part of the accepted rules and procedures.

Folkways are unwritten norms of behavior that members are expected to observe. Like rules and precedents, folkways evolve in response to new times, demands, and lawmakers. During the 1950s, for example, scholars wrote about norms of "apprenticeship" (junior lawmakers should listen and learn from their more seasoned colleagues before actively getting involved in policymaking), "courtesy" (members should be solicitous toward their colleagues and avoid personal attacks on them), or "specialization" (a member should master a few policy areas and not try to impress colleagues by attempting to be a jack-of-all-trades). Today, these particular norms are "torn and frayed."[30] In both chambers, lawmakers enter a partisan and "entrepreneurial" environment where the incentives—both inside and outside Congress—are to get quickly involved in lawmaking, publicity seeking, and campaign fundraising.

The "to-get-along, go-along" culture of the 1950s and 1960s Congresses is mainly a thing of the past. Newcomers who sit back quietly and defer to their elders are likely to be viewed as unusual, especially in the Senate, where norms of individualism pervade the institution. On the other hand, when Senators Hillary Clinton, D-N.Y. (later a secretary of state), and Al Franken, D-Minn., entered the Senate, each famous in their own right, they deferred to their senior colleagues for much of the first year, focusing on constituency service and downplaying their celebrity status. Each wanted to earn the respect of their colleagues and constituents as legislative "work horses" and not media-oriented "show horses." Still, in today's Senate, a member

> feels minimally constrained by consensual codes of behavior. The relevant distinction in his life is not between the Senate and the rest of the political world but between himself (plus his staff) and everything else. . . . With the help of the Senate's formal rules, he knows he can bring the collective business to a halt. He can be a force to be reckoned with whenever he wants to be.[31]

Congressional decision making, then, is shaped by each chamber's formal and informal structure of rules, precedents, traditions, goals, and expectations.

CONGRESSIONAL DECISION MAKING

The congressional decision-making process is constantly evolving, but it has certain enduring features that affect consideration of all legislation. The first is the decentralized power structure of Congress, characterized by numerous specialized committees and a central party leadership that works hard to promote party and policy coherence. A second feature is the existence of multiple decision points for most pieces of legislation. The many decision points mean that at each step of a bill's progress a majority coalition must be formed to move the measure along. This leads to the third important feature of the process: the need for bargaining and compromise to form a winning coalition. Finally, each Congress has only a 2-year life cycle in which to pass legislation once it has been introduced. The pressure of time is an ever-present force underlying the process.

Decentralized Power Structure

Congress's decentralized character reflects both political and structural realities. Politically, legislators owe their reelection to voters in widely differing states and localities; structurally, the legislative branch has an elaborate division of labor to help it manage its immense workload. Responsibility for specific subject areas is dispersed among more than 200 committees and subcommittees.

Structural decentralization means that policymaking is subject to various disintegrative processes. Broad issues are divided into smaller subissues for consideration by the committees. Overlapping and fragmented committee responsibilities can impede the development of comprehensive and coordinated national policies. Many House and Senate committees consider some aspect of broad subject areas such as health care, trade, homeland security, or energy policy. For example, a major global climate change bill (called a "cap and trade" system) that passed the House was referred to nine standing committees (see Box 1.2).[32] Jurisdictional controversies occur as committees fight to protect or expand their turf. Finally, committees develop special relationships with pressure groups, executive agencies, and scores of other interested participants. These alliances, often called *subgovernments, issue networks,* or *sloppy large hexagons,* influence numerous policy areas. Committees, then, become advocates of policies and not simply impartial instruments of the House or Senate.[33]

Political parties can sometimes provide the cohesive force needed to balance the centrifugal influences of a fragmented committee system. They serve to organize their members and elect the formal leaders of Congress. Democrats and Republicans regularly meet in their committees and in informal groups to discuss substantive and political issues. Neither party, however, commands the consistent support of all its members. Too great a spread of ideological and policy convictions exists within each party. Too many countervailing pressures—constituency, region, individual conscience, career considerations, or committee loyalty—also influence the actions of representatives and senators. "I'll fight for my district even though it may be contrary to my national goals," once declared a House majority whip.[34] Many public policies are enacted because diverse elements of both parties temporarily coalesce to achieve common goals. On the other hand, today's polarized Congress functions at times like a quasi-parliamentary body. Large majorities of one party vote in lock-step against the similarly united opposition party.

Congressional party leaders, especially in the Senate, understand that attempts to dictate policy are fraught with difficulties because they often lack the means to force agreement among competing party factions or autonomous committees and subcommittees. Box 1.3 discusses the leadership structure of Congress. "What influence I have is based upon . . . respect and reasoned persuasion and some sensitivity to the political and other concerns of individual Senators," said a Senate majority leader. "I don't have a large

BOX 1.2 One Down, Eight More House Committees to Go

After winning approval by the House Energy and Commerce Committee, legislation (H.R. 2454) that would create a "cap and trade" system addressing climate change was referred to eight other House committees, each with jurisdiction over parts of the bill.

Committee	Issues Facing the Committee
Agriculture	Establishment of a program to help national forests adapt to climate change. May share jurisdiction with the Financial Services Committee for the new financial derivatives market that would be created by buying and selling carbon emissions credits.
Education and the Workforce	Creation of training programs in alternative-energy technology and university grants for studying climate issues.
Financial Services	Creation of new energy use standards for housing. May share jurisdiction with the Agriculture Committee for the new financial derivatives market that would be created for buying and selling carbon emissions credits.
Foreign Affairs	Establishment of international programs to mitigate carbon emissions and climate change. Reduction of international deforestation and establishment of an international carbon offset market. Establishment of a State Department office aimed at exporting clean-energy technology.
Natural Resources	Establishment of a federal program aimed at adaptation of wildlife, oceans and public lands to the effects of climate change.
Science, Space and Technology	Creation of programs to research new low-carbon energy technology, including carbon sequestration and electric vehicles.
Transportation and Infrastructure	Creation of carbon emissions requirements for state and regional transportation infrastructure planning. Creation of emissions requirements for vehicles including planes, trains and ships.
Ways and Means	Oversight and allocation of the billions in new revenue that the federal government would receive from selling carbon emissions credits to polluters.

SOURCE: *CQ Today* by Coral Davenport. Copyright 2009 by Congressional Quarterly Inc. Reproduced with permission of Congressional Quarterly Inc.

NOTE: The GOP-controlled 112th House (2011–2013) changed the names of the Education and Labor Committee to Education and the Workforce, and the Science and Technology Committee to Science, Space and Technology.

bag of goodies to hand out to Senators nor do I have any mechanism for disciplining Senators."[35] Because some legislators are not particularly dependent on their state or local parties for reelection, party leaders cannot count on automatic party support and so must rely heavily on their skills as bargainers and negotiators to influence legislative decisions. In addition, the power and style of any party leader depend on several factors, some outside the leader's control. Among them are personality, intellectual and political talent, the leader's view of the job, the size of the majority or minority party in the chamber, whether the White House is controlled by the opposition party, the expectations of colleagues, and the political complexion of the House or Senate during a particular historical era.

To be sure, there are eras when the leaders of the majority party exercise a large influence over committee chairs and their rank-and-file colleagues. For example, there were times during the dozen years (1995–2007) when the House was under GOP control that it operated in a parliamentary or quasi-parliamentary manner, with rank-and-file Republicans often following the lead and direction of their top party leaders, including President George W. Bush, to approve priorities on largely party-line votes. Speaker Dennis Hastert, R-Ill. (1999–2007) even articulated a governing philosophy reminiscent of parliamentary bodies. His policy, he said, is to bring legislation to the floor only when it has the support of the majority of the majority party. This view precludes floor consideration of various issues supported by a bipartisan coalition. As former GOP Rep. Mickey Edwards, Okla., explained, House members tended "to see themselves less as members of a separate and equal institution with its own oath of office and obligations, and more as either a part of the president's team or part of the opposition to the president."[36]

Speaker Pelosi's leadership style tracked the "top-down," centralized model of her two immediate predecessors (Gingrich and Hastert). She was a forceful, energetic, and hands-on leader who was not reluctant to give directions and deadlines to her standing committee chairs. When Barack Obama became president (with a larger House Democratic majority), Speaker Pelosi loosened her reins somewhat on the chairs and delegated major law-writing authority to a select number of trusted committee leaders.[37]

Speaker Boehner has a different leadership approach. After observing how Gingrich, Hastert, and Pelosi (all of whom he served with) centralized operational control of the House and made key decisions behind closed doors, Speaker Boehner—a former chair of the Education and the Workforce Committee—opted for the regular order. Let committees work their will on measures with a generally open floor amendment process to follow. As Speaker Boehner stated,

> [after] 20 years of watching leaders tighten down the process, tighten down the process, tighten down the process, trying to reconfigure all the rules in order for them to pass their agenda, the leader's agenda. That is not [how I view] my job.[38]

BOX 1.3 Leadership Structure of Congress

The party leadership in the House and Senate is crucial to the smooth functioning of the legislative process. In the House, the formal leadership consists of the Speaker, the majority and minority leaders, whips from each party, assistants to the whips, and various partisan committees. The vice president of the United States serves as **president of the Senate;** in the vice president's absence, the **president pro tempore** or, more commonly, a temporary presiding officer of the majority party presides. The Senate also has majority and minority leaders, whips, assistant whips, and party committees.

The Speaker's fundamental power is to set the agenda of the House. Speakers achieve their influence largely through personal prestige, fundraising ability, mastery of the art of persuasion, legislative expertise, and the support of members. Among the Speaker's formal powers are presiding over the House, deciding points of order, referring bills and resolutions to committee, scheduling legislation for floor action, and appointing House members to select, joint, and House–Senate conference committees. Speakers infrequently participate in debate and usually vote only to break a tie. Their institutional prerogatives are buttressed by their role as leader of the majority party. For example, Speakers may chair their party's committee assignment panel and can expedite or delay floor action on legislation.

His willingness to run the House in a more open manner, encouraging the input of his rank-and-file party colleagues, while "not the most efficient process," according to then Rep. Jeff Flake (now a senator), R-Ariz., "certainly makes for a more fair process."[39]

Multiple Decision Points

Although Congress can act quickly, normally legislation works its way slowly through multiple decision points. One congressional report identified more than a hundred specific steps that might mark a "bill's progress through the Congress from introduction to possible enactment into law."[40]

After a bill is introduced, it usually is referred to committee and then frequently to a subcommittee. The views of executive departments and agencies also are often solicited. As a head of the Justice Department's office of legislative affairs has described it, "Almost every bill that is moving in Congress is sent to my office . . . by the committees for a reaction."[41] The full committee and subcommittee hold hearings and issue reports on the bill. The bill is then voted out of the full committee and is ready to be scheduled for consideration by the majority party leadership. After floor debate and final action in one chamber, the same steps generally are repeated in the other house. At any point in this sequential process, the bill is subject to delay, defeat, or modification. "It is very easy to defeat a

The majority and minority parties of the House and Senate elect, respectively, majority and minority leaders. The House majority leader has considerable influence over the scheduling of bills and day-to-day management of the floor. He ranks just below the Speaker in importance. The minority leader heads his or her party in the House. Among other things, he or she develops policy alternatives to majority initiatives, serves as party spokesperson, and devises strategies to win back majority control of the House.

In the Senate, the majority leader is the most influential officer because neither the vice president nor the president pro tempore holds substantive powers over the chamber's proceedings. Everyday duties of the minority leader correspond to those of the majority leader, except that the minority leader has less authority over scheduling legislation. Agenda-setting is the prime prerogative of the majority leader. The minority leader speaks for his party and acts as field general for his party, promoting partisan cohesion and searching for ways to reclaim majority control of the chamber.

Each party in the House and Senate elects a whip and appoints a number of deputy, assistant, or regional whips to aid the floor leader in implementing the party's legislative program. The diversity of whips provides greater geographical, ideological, and seniority balance in the party leadership structure. At its core, the whips' job is to know where the votes are and to produce the votes on behalf of party objectives.

bill in Congress," President John F. Kennedy once noted. "It is much more difficult to pass one."[42]

At each stage of the process, measures and procedures must receive majority (and sometimes supermajority) approval. All along the procedural route, therefore, strategically located committees, groups, or individuals can delay, block, or change proposals if they can form majority coalitions. Bargaining may be necessary at each juncture to forge the support that advances the bill to the next step in the legislative process. Thus, advocates of a piece of legislation must attract not just one majority but several successive majorities at each of the critical intersections along the legislative route. And at each legislative intersection, the strategies for constructing winning coalitions can vary to accommodate diverse issues, external circumstances, and member goals.

Bargaining and Coalition Building

Three principal forms of bargaining are used to build majority coalitions: logrolling, compromise, and nonlegislative favors. "The way you get the votes to pass anything is to ask whoever would possibly vote for something, what do they want," declared a House Ways and Means chair. "It is an additive process."[43] The additive process was much in display when the House narrowly passed (219–212) a landmark bill to curb greenhouse gases linked to global warming. To win the support of wavering lawmakers, committee and party leaders made numerous compromises and provided billions of dollars in vote-getting projects to undecided members. A major opponent of the bill, GOP representative Joe Barton of Texas, sarcastically told members, "If you haven't made your deal yet [with the House Energy and Commerce chair], come on down to the floor."[44]

During Senate consideration of President Obama's landmark health care reform plan, Majority Leader Harry Reid, Nev., made various policy concessions to four centrist, on-the-fence, party colleagues to win their support on a pivotal procedural vote. Democratic Senator Mary Landrieu, La., for example, secured more Medicaid funding for her state (dubbed the "Louisiana Purchase"). Democratic Senator Ben Nelson, Neb., won similar favorable treatment for his state, called the "Cornhusker Kickback" by critics. Liberal Senators were not happy with the use of such provisions to woo the votes of party holdouts. Despite their misgivings, liberal senators had no choice but to go along with Reid's policy concessions; they needed their colleagues' votes to prevail. Senate Republicans charged that various policy concessions were added to the health legislation to "buy" the votes of wavering Democratic senators.

Logrolling is an exchange of voting support on different bills by different members of Congress. It is an effective means of coalition building because members rarely are equally concerned about all the measures before Congress. For example, representatives A, B, and C strongly support a bill that increases government aid to farmers. But A, B, and C are indifferent toward a second bill that increases the minimum wage, which is strongly supported by representatives D, E, and F. Because D, E, and F do not have strong feelings about the farm bill, a bargain is struck: A, B, and C agree to vote for the minimum-wage bill, and D, E, and F agree to vote for the farm bill. Thus, both bills are helped on their way past the key decision points at which A, B, C, D, E, and F have influence. Logrolling may be either explicit or implicit. A, B, and C may have negotiated directly with D, E, and F. Alternatively, A, B, and C may have voted for the minimum-wage bill, letting it be known through the press or in other informal ways that they anticipate similar treatment on the farm bill from D, E, and F. The expectation is that D, E, and F will honor the tacit agreement because at a later date they may again need the support of A, B, and C.

Compromise, unlike logrolling, builds coalitions through negotiation of the content of legislation. Each side agrees to modify policy goals on a given bill in a way that is generally acceptable to the other. A middle ground is often found—particularly for those bills involving money. A, B, and C, for example, support a $50 million education bill; D, E, and F want to increase the funding to $100 million. The six meet and compromise on a $75 million bill they all can support.

Note the distinction between logrolling and compromise. In the logrolling example, the participants did not modify their objectives on the bills that mattered to them; each side traded voting support on a bill that meant little in return for support on a bill in which they were keenly interested. In a compromise, both sides modify their positions. "Anyone who thinks that compromise is a dirty word," remarked a House member, "should go back and read one of the fascinating accounts of all that happened in Philadelphia in 1787" (when the Constitution was drafted).[45] As one senator put it, "In politics there are no right answers, only a continuing flow of compromises between groups resulting in a changing, cloudy, and ambiguous series of public decisions where appetite and ambition compete openly with knowledge and wisdom."[46] Compromise, in short, is an essential component of governance, but it is not easy to achieve on contentious measures. This reality is certainly the case in today's polarized and acrimonious political environment, where many lawmakers view "compromise" as a sell out of their principles or a sign of political weakness.

Nonlegislative favors are useful because policy goals are only one of the many objectives of members of Congress. Among other objectives are winning assignment to a prestigious committee, raising campaign funds, running for higher office, obtaining larger office space and more staff, or being selected to attend a conference abroad. The variety of these nonpolicy objectives creates numerous bargaining opportunities—particularly for party leaders, who can dispense many favors—from which coalitions can be built. As Senate majority leader from 1955 to 1961, Lyndon B. Johnson of Texas was especially skillful at using his powers to satisfy the personal needs of senators—all with the goal of building support for legislation he wanted.

> For Johnson, each one of these assignments contained a potential opportunity for bargaining, for creating obligations, provided that he knew his fellow senators well enough to determine which invitations would matter the most to whom. If he knew that the wife of the senator from Idaho had been dreaming of a trip to Paris for ten years, or that the advisers to another senator had warned him about his slipping popularity with Italian voters, Johnson could increase the potential usefulness of assignments to the Parliamentary Conference in Paris or to the dedication of cemeteries in Italy.[47]

In this way, Johnson made his colleagues understand that there was a debt to be repaid.

The Congressional Cycle

Every bill introduced in Congress faces the 2-year deadline of the congressional term. (The term of the 113th Congress, elected in November 2012, began at noon on January 3, 2013, and expires at noon on January 3, 2015.) Legislation introduced must be passed by both the House and the Senate in identical form within the 2-year term to become law. But because Congress normally adjourns prior to the end of the 2-year term, bills usually have less than 2 full years to germinate. Bills that have not completed the required procedural journey before final adjournment of a Congress automatically die and must be reintroduced in a new Congress to start the legislative process anew. Inaction or postponement at any stage of the process can mean the defeat of a bill.

Many measures considered by Congress come up in cycles—such as those bills required each year to finance the activities of federal agencies and programs. Generally, this kind of legislation appears regularly on the congressional agenda at about the same time each year. Other legislation comes up for renewal every few years. Emergencies demand immediate attention. Other matters become timely because public interest, international events, or the president has focused on them; health care, terrorism, joblessness, Social Security overhaul, gun control, and immigration reform are examples of such issues in the 2000s.

Complex legislation is often introduced early in the congressional term because it takes longer to process than a simple bill. A disproportionately large number of major bills are enacted during the last few weeks of a Congress. Compromises that were not possible in July can be made in December. By this time—with the 2-year term about to expire—the pressures on members of the House and Senate are intense, and lawmaking can become frantic and furious. "It is a time when legislators pass dozens of bills without debate or recorded votes, a time when a canny legislator can slip in special favors for the folks back home or for special interest lobbyists roaming Capitol corridors."[48] Members plan purposefully to take advantage of the end game through deadline lawmaking.

Finally, many ideas require years or even decades of germination before they can be enacted into law. Controversial proposals—reintroduced in successive Congresses—may need a 4-, 6-, or 8-year period before they win passage. Many of the 1960s policies of Presidents Kennedy and Johnson, for example, first were considered decades ago by earlier Congresses. Bankruptcy reform legislation required the action of four consecutive Congresses before it eventually surmounted hurdles and roadblocks to become public law in 2005. In 1994, President Bill Clinton and first lady Hillary Clinton tried unsuccessfully to win congressional approval of a comprehensive health care reform proposal. Fifteen years later, President Obama made overhaul of the health care system a top priority. In 2010, he signed the Patient Protection and Affordable Care Act into law. To be sure, health care reform will occupy center stage well into the 21st century, given America's aging society and the escalating cost of new drugs and medical technology.

THE HOUSE AND SENATE COMPARED

The "House and Senate are naturally unalike," observed Woodrow Wilson.[49] Each chamber has its own rules, precedents, and customs; different terms of office; varying constitutional responsibilities; and different constituencies. "We are constituted differently, we serve different purposes in the representative system, we operate differently, why should [the House and

Senate] not have different rules," said Senator Wayne Morse, D-Ore. (1945–1969).[50] Or as former Speaker Hastert noted, "Even though the Senate is only 30 yards away across that [Capitol] Rotunda, sometimes it's like they're 30 miles away." Table 1.1 lists some of the major differences between the chambers.

Probably the three most important structural differences are that (1) the House is more than 4 times the size of the Senate, (2) most senators represent a broader constituency than do representatives, and (3) senators serve longer terms of office. Relatedly, the most significant procedural differences between the House and Senate are (1) the germaneness requirement for amendments in the House but not the Senate; (2) unlimited debate in the Senate but not the House, which has a **motion** (the previous question; see Chapter 4)

TABLE 1.1   Several Major Differences Between the House and Senate

House	Senate
Shorter term of office (2 years)	Longer term of office (6 years)
Adheres closely to procedural rules on floor activity	Operates mostly by unanimous consent
Narrower constituency	Broader, more varied constituency
Originates all revenue bills	Sole power to ratify treaties and to advise and consent to presidential nominations
Policy specialists	Policy generalists
Less press and media coverage	More press and media coverage
Power less evenly distributed	Power more evenly distributed
Less prestigious	More prestigious
More expeditious in floor debate	Less expeditious in floor debate
Strict germaneness requirement for floor amendments	No general germaneness rule for floor amendments
Less reliance on staff	More reliance on staff
More partisan	Somewhat less partisan
Strict limits on debate	Unlimited debate on nearly every measure
Method of operation stresses majority rule	Traditions and practices emphasize minority rights

to cut debate off; (3) the Speaker has discretionary and unchallengeable **recognition** authority compared with the Senate's presiding officer, who must recognize the first person he or she sees seeking recognition (with a few exceptions, such as priority for the majority leader); and (4) a Rules Committee in the House—but not the Senate—that can determine the ground rules for debating and amending legislation on the floor. These differences affect the way the two houses operate in a number of ways.

Complexity of the Rules

Size explains much about why the two chambers differ. Because it is larger, the 435-member House—441 if the six delegates and resident commissioner representing places such as the District of Columbia or Puerto Rico are included—is a more structured body than the 100-member Senate. Indeed, the restraints imposed on representatives by rules and precedents are far more severe than those affecting senators. House rules for the 113th Congress consume more than 1,400 pages. Its precedents from 1789 to 1936 are in 11 huge volumes; those from 1936 and later are recorded in the 18 large tomes of *Deschler's Precedents of the United States House of Representatives* and *Deschler-Brown Precedents of the United States House of Representatives* (see Box 1.1). By contrast, the 113th Senate's rules, standing orders, resolutions, and laws affecting the business of the chamber are contained in over 1,400 pages and its precedents in one 1,608-page volume.

Whereas Senate rules maximize freedom of expression, House rules "show a constant subordination of the individual to the necessities of the whole House as the voice of the national will."[51] Furthermore, House and Senate rules differ fundamentally in their basic purpose. House rules are designed to permit a determined majority to work its will. Senate rules are intended to slow down, or even defer, action on legislation by granting inordinate parliamentary power (through the filibuster, for example) to individual members and determined minorities. "Senate rules are tilted toward not doing things," remarked Jim Wright, D-Tex., who served as Speaker from 1987 to 1989. "House rules, if you know how to use them, are tilted toward allowing the majority to get its will done."[52] Ironically, moving legislation is easier in the larger House than in the smaller Senate because of the differences in their rules. A simple majority is sufficient to pass major and controversial legislation in the House. In the Senate, at least 60 votes (necessary to break a filibuster) might be needed—sometimes more than once—to move legislation to final passage. The House acts on the basis of majority rule; the Senate stresses minority rule and often functions as a supermajoritarian institution in which 60 votes are crucial to the enactment of legislation or the confirmation of executive branch or judicial nominees.

The Senate, as a result, is more personal and individualistic. "The Senate is run for the convenience of one Senator, to the inconvenience of 99," said one senator.[53] It functions to a large extent by unanimous consent, in effect adjusting or disregarding its rules as it goes along. It is not uncommon for votes on a bill to be rescheduled or delayed until an interested senator can be present. Senate party leaders are careful to consult all senators who have expressed an interest in the pending legislation, because "under the rules of the Senate any one Senator can hold up the works here," said Senator Robert C. Byrd, D-W.Va., the acknowledged expert at the time on Senate procedure.[54] In the House, the majority leadership focuses on party colleagues and usually consults only key members—often committee and factional leaders—about upcoming floor action. It is then no wonder that bills often take longer to complete in the smaller Senate than in the larger House. All senators can participate actively in shaping decisions on the floor given their unique prerogatives: unlimited debate and unlimited opportunities to offer either relevant or nonrelevant floor amendments to almost any bill. House members typically get involved on the floor only on measures reported from the committees on which they serve. To be sure, far-reaching issues such as health care, energy, or defense proposals will trigger floor participation by many representatives.

Policy Incubation

Incubation entails "keeping a proposal alive, while it picks up support, or waits for a better climate, or while the problem to which it is addressed grows."[55] Both houses fulfill this role, but policy incubation is promoted in the Senate particularly because of that body's flexible rules, more varied constituent pressures on senators, and greater press and media coverage. As the chamber with greater prestige, lesser complexity, longer term of office, and smaller size, the Senate is, news outlets find, easier to cover than the House.[56] The Senate is more involved than the House in cultivating national constituencies, formulating questions for national debate, and gaining general public support for policy proposals. The policy-generating role is particularly characteristic of senators having presidential ambitions; they need to capture headlines and national constituencies.[57]

However, when the House began televising its floor sessions in 1979 over C-SPAN (Cable-Satellite Public Affairs Network)—the Senate began gavel-to-gavel coverage in mid-1986—many activist representatives recognized the technology's bully-pulpit potential. For example, when Newt Gingrich was elected to the House in 1978, he quickly saw C-SPAN as a means for mobilizing grassroots support behind the GOP's agenda and for attacking Democrats and their decades-long control of the House. He organized floor debates and speeches, even when there was hardly anyone in the chamber, to highlight Republican ideas to the C-SPAN viewing audience and to persuade them that they ought to put the House in Republican hands. He was successful.

As Speaker of the 104th and 105th Congresses (1995–1999), Gingrich was a well-known national figure who took the public role of the Speaker to new heights.[58] For example, he went on prime-time national television after the House successfully completed action on the Contract with America, emulating presidents who address the nation. By contrast, his GOP successor, Dennis Hastert, played a less visible public role, sharing the spotlight with other party members.

As the first female Speaker (the highest elective position for a woman in U.S. history), Nancy Pelosi could not avoid a public role, as press and media representatives sought her views on the major issues of the day and the management of the House and her party. House Republicans launched periodic media attack ads against Speaker Pelosi (a "San Francisco liberal") as a way to boost their members' reelection chances.[59] Speaker Boehner is the principal spokesperson for House Republicans. A seasoned party leader, Speaker Boehner meets regularly with the press to explain and defend the GOP's agenda. He shares the public messaging responsibility with other party leaders. In a 24/7 media environment, public relations strategies—message politics—are increasingly important in moving party priorities through the legislative process.

Today, many Senate Republicans and Democrats who had previously served in the House emulate their former House colleagues in certain ways by conducting organized, often early morning, speeches to a largely empty chamber. These orchestrated speeches are designed to bolster their party's image and agenda. As in the House, Senate Democrats and Republicans each have their own informal message group, which takes the floor periodically to highlight and advance party ideas and priorities to the C-SPAN viewing public. Members of each message group also challenge and critique the other party's agenda and actions. On a broader level, lawmakers recognize that, as one scholar noted, "ideas do not sell themselves." The side that prevails in legislative battles "will depend as much on which one has its messaging right as on which has its policies right."[60] In brief, the party that frames the debate is likely to frame the outcome.

Specialists Versus Generalists

Another difference between the chambers is that representatives tend to be known as subject-matter specialists while senators tend to be generalists. "If the Senate has been the nation's great forum," a representative said, then the "House has been its workshop."[61] The House's greater workforce and division of labor facilitate policy specialization. "Senators do not specialize as intensively or as exclusively in their committee work as House members do" because senators must spread their "efforts over a greater span of subjects than the average representative."[62] During the 113th Congress, for example, the average senator served on about 12 committees and subcommittees, compared with about 6 for the average representative.

One reason for the specialist–generalist distinction is that most senators represent a more heterogeneous constituency than House members. This difference compels the former to generalize as they attempt to be conversant on numerous national and international issues that affect their state. With their 6-year term, senators are less vulnerable to immediate constituency pressures. They can afford to be more cosmopolitan in their viewpoints than House members. Journalists tend to expect senators, more than representatives, to have an informed opinion on almost every important public issue. Senators, too, suffer from what Senator Byrd has called "fractured attention."[63] They are often away from the Senate raising campaign funds, appearing on television, giving speeches, or engaging in other activities that limit their ability to participate in floor deliberations.

One result of the generalist role is that senators must rely more than House members on knowledgeable personal and committee staff aides for advice in decision making. House members are more likely to be experts themselves on particular policy issues. If not, they often go to informed colleagues rather than staff aides for advice on legislation. "House members rely most heavily upon their colleagues for all information," one study concluded, while senators "will often turn to other sources, especially their own staffs, for their immediate information needs."[64] Consequently, Senate staff aides generally have more influence over the laws and programs of the nation than do their House counterparts. Many experienced senators, however, certainly can hold their own with knowledgeable House members on various policy issues.

Distribution of Power

Another difference between the two chambers is that the power to influence policy is more evenly distributed in the Senate than in the House. Unlike most representatives, senators can readily exercise initiative in legislation and oversight, get floor amendments incorporated in measures reported from committees on which they are not members, influence the scheduling of bills, and, in general, participate more widely and equally in all Senate and party activities. Moreover, every senator of the majority party typically chairs at least one committee or subcommittee.

This ability to make a difference quickly is one reason the Senate is so politically attractive to House members. "I've found the Senate to be a very liberating experience," said a former representative who was elected to the Senate. "The House is so structured by its rules, and Members are so compartmentalized by ideologies or interests. Sometimes it's hard to make an impact."[65] In the 113th Congress, 50 senators were former House members; by contrast, no representative served previously in the Senate. House procedures, in short, emphasize the mobilization of voting blocs to make policy; deference to individual prerogatives is the hallmark of senatorial decision making. Senator Pat Roberts, R-Kans., a former House member, noted that a House member must legislate by coalition, but a senator has to "work with each individual senator."[66]

Similarities

The House and Senate have many similarities. Both chambers are essentially equal in power and share similar responsibilities in lawmaking, oversight, and representation. Both have heavy workloads, decentralized committee and party structures, and somewhat parallel committee jurisdictions. The roles and responsibilities of one chamber interact with those of the other. House and Senate party leaders often cooperate to coordinate message themes and action on legislation. Cooperation in moving agenda priorities generally is made easier when the same party controls both houses.

Importantly, a whole range of institutional, partisan, and policy connections turns bicameralism into a force that shapes member behavior and policy outcomes. Along with traditional interchamber jealousies and rivalries, evident even when the same party controls both chambers, House members often hold negative views against what they perceive as Senate obstructionism. As House members sometimes say, "The other party is only the opposition, the Senate is the enemy!" When Nancy Pelosi served as Speaker, she sometimes was dismayed that the Democratic-controlled Senate could not quickly move House-passed measures through their chamber.[67] Nonetheless, Pelosi and Senate majority leader Reid consulted and coordinated regularly about policy, political, procedural, and message priorities and strategies. In the 113th Congress, Speaker Boehner and Senate GOP leader McConnell meet regularly, and their staffs consult, communicate, and coordinate on a daily basis. Boehner and McConnell have developed a close and cordial relationship. "We work hard at not surprising each other," remarked Senator McConnell.[68]

Part of the House's frustration and exasperation with the other body is the ability of any senator to block legislation through means such as filibustering, placing a "hold" on measures, or offering nonrelevant amendments. Senators have their own complaints about House procedures and policymaking. Upset that the House was trying to impose a controversial budget procedure called "reconciliation" (see Chapter 2) on the Senate, a GOP senator exclaimed: "How outrageous is that?"[69] Suffice it to say that the within-chamber procedures of each body influence the policymaking activities of the other. The two houses are interlocked with national policies fundamentally shaped by the bicameral connection.

In recent years, the two chambers have become more similar in some unexpected areas. Today's House members are more dependent on staff than were their colleagues of a few decades ago, in part because issues are more complex and because more informed constituents look to Capitol Hill for assistance and information. Senators are much more involved in constituency service than ever before. Like House members, they travel frequently to their states to meet in diverse forums with their constituents. In fact, two scholars found that small-state senators "have even more contact with their constituents than the House members in those states do."[70]

Many senators, too, emulate their House colleagues by preparing to run for reelection almost immediately after being sworn into office. This situation reflects contemporary electoral developments unforeseen by the framers—the escalating costs of election races, the professionalization of campaigns (the need to hire consultants, pollsters, and the like), and the emphasis on the new media (blogs, e-mail, YouTube, Facebook, and more) and video politics—that make senatorial races more competitive than most House contests.

House members enjoy more incumbent protection than senators because they attract fewer effective, well-known, or politically experienced challengers (in part by scaring off opponents with their money-raising ability), receive more favorable press and media attention, represent more homogeneous—and gerrymandered—areas, and court their constituents assiduously. Thus, representatives are more likely than senators to survive periodic electoral tides that oust numerous incumbents. But not always.

A year before the November 2010 congressional elections (following the "wave" elections of November 2006 and 2008 that produced large wins for Democrats and losses for Republican incumbents), Democratic strategists debated whether the party should run on local rather than national issues. Some consultants suggested that regardless of what Democrats might prefer, the midterm 2010 election would be a referendum on President Obama's job performance and voters' view of the success of his agenda. That prospect did not please Democratic lawmakers who represented GOP-leaning areas. These Democrats "need to localize, not nationalize," exclaimed a party consultant, by highlighting local issues and their qualifications.[71] Republicans, meanwhile, focused largely on national issues and themes, such as the sorry state of the economy. An angry electorate ousted many Democratic incumbents, regardless of their campaign message approach. It was a "shellacking" for Democrats, exclaimed President Obama. Eighty-seven new House Republican freshmen (many Tea Party endorsed or supported), compared with only nine freshmen Democrats, entered the lower chamber. The margin of GOP control was 242 to 193 compared with 257 to 178 for Democrats in the 111th Congress. Republicans also picked up seats in the 112th Senate (53 to 47), compared with the 60-to-40 advantage for Democrats in the previous Congress.

PRESSURES ON MEMBERS

In making their legislative decisions, members of Congress are influenced by numerous pressures—the White House, the news media, constituents, lobbyists and interest groups, and their own party leadership and colleagues on Capitol Hill. These pressures are a central feature of the congressional environment; they affect the formal procedures and rules of Congress. All these pressures are present in varying degrees at every step of the legislative process. The interests and influence of groups and individuals outside Congress have a considerable impact on the fate of legislation.

The President and the Executive Branch

The president and executive branch are among the most important sources of external pressure exerted on Congress. Many of the president's legislative functions and activities are not mentioned in the Constitution. The president is able to influence congressional action through techniques such as the manipulation of patronage, the allocation of federal funds and projects that may be vital to the reelection of certain members of Congress, and the handling of constituents' cases in which senators and representatives are interested. National or international crises, such as the global battle against terrorist groups, trigger a flow of power to the president and away from Congress. The September 11, 2001, terrorist attacks clearly strengthened President George W. Bush's assertion of executive power. President Obama reversed several of his predecessor's counterterrorism policies, such as banning illegal "enhanced interrogation," but he also supported many of them as well, such as the "state secrets" privilege (a common-law doctrine that allows the government to argue in court that certain information required in legal cases cannot be disclosed because it would threaten national security).[72]

As leaders of the Democratic or Republican Party, presidents are their party's campaigner-in-chief. By most accounts, the Republicans won a historic midterm election in 2002 in which the president's party won, rather than lost, seats in both the House and Senate, something that had not occurred since 1934 for a first-term chief executive. The gains were attributed to President George W. Bush's elevated stature as commander in chief following the September 11, 2001, terrorist attacks, and his fundraising prowess and aggressive electioneering for GOP candidates. Six years later, Barack Obama won the White House, in part because of voter dissatisfaction with the two-term Bush administration. Obama made history not only because he is the first African American president but also because he was a superb fundraiser—raising a record-setting $745 billion, which increased to $1 billion in 2012—and campaigner for the Democratic Party.[73] The 2008 election saw the return of unified government and the first back-to-back, double-digit election victory for the House majority party since the 1950 and 1952 electoral cycles. Democrats also gained seats in the Senate, eventually reaching 60 when Al Franken of Minnesota was declared the victor over his GOP opponent, Norm Coleman, after an 8-month legal battle.[74] The 2010 midterm elections, as noted, ended unified government. The 2012 elections maintained the party status quo: Barack Obama in the White House, Republicans in control of the House, and a Democratic Senate.

The president also has ready access to the news media for promoting his administration's policies and commanding headlines. This bully-pulpit role, as Theodore Roosevelt described it, enables presidents to mold public opinion and build popular backing for White House proposals. With advances in communications technology and the amplifying power of the media, the bully pulpit is arguably the president's most significant resource. "Teledemocracy"—satellite press conferences, cable TV, interactive technology, talk-show formats, YouTube, Facebook, blogs, televised town hall meetings, the Internet, and more—enables public officials to bypass traditional news outlets and communicate directly with the electorate. As a White House pollster put it, enacting the president's agenda "is not simply a matter of presenting a policy proposal, sending it to Congress and letting Congress do its work. Now you need an effort to keep the American public with you."[75]

The president's role as legislative leader derives from the Constitution. While the Constitution vests "all legislative Powers" in Congress, it also directs the president to "give to the Congress Information of the State of the Union, and recommend to their Consideration such Measures as he shall judge necessary and expedient." This function has been broadened over the years. The president presents to Congress each year, in addition to the State of the Union message, two other general statements of presidential aims: an economic report, including proposals directed at maintaining maximum employment, and a budget message outlining appropriations requests and policy proposals. During a typical session, the president transmits to Congress scores of other legislative proposals and ensures that the White House and executive agency liaison offices keep tabs on legislative activities and lobby for administration policies. The president's constitutional power to veto acts passed by Congress (a two-thirds vote in each house is needed to **override a veto**) often promotes legislative–executive accommodations.

The Media

Of all the pressures on Congress, none is such a two-way proposition as the relationship between legislators and the media. Although senators and representatives must contend with the peculiarities of the newsgathering business, such as deadlines and limited space or time to describe events, and with constant media scrutiny of their actions, they also must rely on news organizations to inform the public of their legislative interests and accomplishments. At the same time, reporters must depend to some extent on inside information from members, a condition that makes many of them reluctant to displease their sources lest the pipeline of information be shut off.

But Congress is basically an open organization. Information flows freely on Capitol Hill, and secrets rarely remain secret for long. An enterprising reporter can usually find out what is newsworthy. Moreover, Congress has taken a variety of actions during the past few decades to further open its proceedings to public observation. For one thing, it has allowed nationwide, gavel-to-gavel coverage over C-SPAN and C-SPAN II of House and Senate floor proceedings. Instead of relying on press accounts of congressional actions, many citizens now have an opportunity to watch the floor sessions (and many committee sessions) via the electronic gallery and make their own legislative judgments.

Recently, the Congress–media connection has undergone changes that significantly affect individual lawmakers, the two parties, and the legislative branch itself. On an individual basis, lawmakers are exploiting a large array of technologies to communicate with their constituents, generate favorable publicity, and promote their policy proposals. As Rep. David E. Price, D-N.C., described this aspect of his legislative experience:

> My staff and I also try to maintain effective contact with the news media in the district. Members of the media, especially television, are often attracted to campaign fireworks, but it takes considerably more effort to interest them in the day-to-day work of Congress. We send television feeds by satellite to local stations from Washington, offer radio commentary about matters of current interest, and arrange interviews on these topics when I am home. We provide a steady stream of press releases to newspaper, radio, and television outlets; most of these either offer news about my own initiatives or give some interpretation of major items of congressional business, often relating them to North Carolina. We also furnish copies of my statements and speeches and let stations know when they can pick up my floor appearances on C-SPAN.[76]

Lawmakers employ a variety of high-tech devices and techniques—smartphones, Twitter, Facebook, e-mail, teleconferencing (meeting constituents in their states or districts without ever leaving Capitol Hill), social networking, blogging, and more—in addition to their traditional means—newsletters, franked mail, telephone calls, town hall meetings, radio, and television—for contacting constituents or promoting issues. Members may field questions online from computer users as part of their effort "to be armed with favorable comment [on their legislation] from beyond the Beltway sent to them over the information superhighway."[77] As a sign of the times, more lawmakers are creating blogs, such as Rep. Jan Schakowsky, D-Ill. "My real goal here is to . . . explore this medium for getting people to take action and be more involved," she said. A GOP lawmaker from Illinois who also blogs added that members "who rapidly update [their web] sites are going to improve communication with [their] constituents, especially younger ones."[78] About a quarter of the membership of the House and Senate "tweet"—that is, send messages of up to 140 characters—on Twitter (a social-networking service). For example, former Rep. Judy Biggert, R-Ill., "bypassed the local media and used Twitter as a direct response to a robocall that criticized her on troop pay raises."[79]

From a party perspective, Democratic and Republican leaders devote considerable attention to ways of using the media and the Internet to frame the terms of public debate on substantive and political issues so that they promote the outcome they want. In recent years, congressional party leaders—in collaboration with a president of their party and partisan-oriented outside groups—have regularly employed sophisticated electronic communications strategies to highlight their goals and messages to the American public. "New technologies make it possible to keep the public informed of what we're doing and receive instant feedback," said a spokeswoman for Steny Hoyer, D-Md., minority whip in the 113th House.[80] Opinion polling, televised ads, mobilization and coordination of interest groups, town hall meetings, think tanks, airport rallies, radio and television interviews, op-ed articles, blogs, and more are employed to muster public support. Daily and weekly "theme" team meetings are also held "to plan the message of the [day or] week for the speeches at the beginning and end of each legislative day."[81]

The two parties employ electronic technology and message techniques to get their ideas and views out to the public, including giving their members "talking points," video materials, or other information for meetings with constituents. The politics of strategic message sending are also employed by both parties in the Senate as a way to project a favorable public image and to activate and energize their core electoral supporters. For example, the Senate Republican Conference provides GOP lawmakers with various communications services, such as graphic design, Internet support, and radio and television consulting. During debate on President Obama's landmark health care reform bill, Senate Minority Leader Mitch McConnell created a "rapid response team" to challenge and rebut the ideas and views publicized by Democratic senators and their "war room" operation. Senate Democrats and Republicans have their own "theme" teams and outreach programs designed to shape the national political debate. An issue for lawmakers in both chambers is that they have nothing comparable to the powerful megaphone of the Obama White House. It is simply harder for them to get their messages and ideas delivered to and heard by the general public.

From an institutional perspective, scholarly research has shown "that press coverage of Congress has declined in volume and increased sharply in negativity, while moving from coverage of what the institution does as a legislature to increased emphasis on reports, rumors, and allegations of scandal, individual and institutional."[82] The implications that flow from this finding are several, including heightened public disrespect for the legislative branch. In the judgment of Senator Frank Lautenberg, D-N.J.:

> Democracy simply cannot function in an atmosphere of distrust. After all, when citizens view everything the Congress does in the worst possible light, they are similarly skeptical about the legislation we propose. That makes it extremely difficult to build public support. And without public support, it becomes almost impossible to address major social problems in a meaningful way.[83]

Michael Gerson, a former speechwriter for President George W. Bush, worries that the ideological polarization of various media outlets means that many Americans "get their information from sources that agree with them—sources that reinforce and exaggerate their political predispositions."[84]

Constituent Pressures

Although many pressures compete for influence on Capitol Hill, the constituents—not the president or the party or the congressional leadership—still grant and take away a member's job.[85] A member who is popular back home can defy all three in a way unthinkable in a country such as Great

Britain, where the leadership of the legislature, the executive, and the party are the same.

The extent to which members of Congress seek to follow the wishes of their constituents is determined to a considerable degree by the issue at stake. Few members would actively oppose issues deemed vital by most constituents. A farm-state legislator, for example, is unlikely to push policies designed to lower the price of foods grown by those who elect him. Likewise, few members would follow locally popular policies that would endanger the nation. Between these extremes lies a wide spectrum of different blends of pressure from constituents and from conscience. And members must make most of their decisions in this gray area. It is no coincidence that the committee assignments sought by senators and representatives are often determined by the type of constituency the legislator serves.

A fundamental change from a generation ago is that lawmakers spend more time with the people they represent. Today, most members travel weekly to their states or districts to meet with constituents. Technology, too, enables members to maintain a constant presence in their state or district, even when they are not physically present. Since the advent of the cyber-Congress, lawmakers can exchange e-mails with constituents no matter where their legislative business takes them. Some lawmakers use video e-mail. "The messages feature a 30-second to 40-second video next to a list of options that constituents can click, sending them to a lawmaker's Web site or allowing them to send a reply."[86] A freshman representative uses her House website to expand her outreach to constituents "so that I can hear about people's needs" and solicit their suggestions, she said. "The dialogue will help me make my decisions [on legislation], and work with other legislators."[87]

Lawmakers are in close and constant touch with voter sentiments back home, but they may be too hypersensitive to constituency opinion. From a member's perspective, doing a good job on constituency service is understandably the road to electoral success. However, it tends to push lawmakers toward something more resembling an ombudsman role than a leadership role in which citizens are educated about major problems and solutions and about the unpopular decisions and difficult choices that their member of Congress may have to make to serve the national interest. As Walter Mondale (former senator, vice president, and ambassador to Japan) stated in testimony before a joint congressional reorganization panel:

> Good constituent service is, of course, necessary—and honorable—work for any member of Congress and his staff. Citizens must have somewhere to turn for help when they become victims of government bureaucracy. But constituent service can also be a bottomless pit. The danger is that a member of Congress will end up as little more than an ombudsman between citizens and government agencies. As important as this work is, it takes precious time away from Congress' central responsibilities as both a deliberative and a law-making body.[88]

Members, then, regularly confront the dilemma of how to maintain a rough balance between serving the often-contradictory impulses of their constituents (provide more government services without raising taxes, for example) and the larger national interest.

Washington Lobbyists

Lobbyists and lobby groups play an active part in the legislative process. The corps of Washington lobbyists has grown markedly in number and diversity since the 1930s, in line with the expansion of federal authority and its spread into new areas. Given today's economic crisis—growing joblessness, plant closings, home foreclosures, bank failures, and more—the Obama administration and Congress have taken numerous actions to help restore the economic well-being of the nation. "Not since Lyndon B. Johnson and Franklin D. Roosevelt," wrote a congressional journalist, has a president like Obama "moved to expand the role of government on so many fronts—and with such a demanding sense of urgency."[89]

The federal government has become a tremendous force in the life of the nation, and the number of fields in which changes in federal policy may spell success or failure for special interest groups has grown enormously. Thus, commercial and industrial interests; labor unions; ethnic, ideological, health care, education, environmental, and racial groups; professional organizations; state and local governments; citizen groups; and representatives of foreign interests—all from time to time and some continuously—seek by one method or another to exert pressure on Congress to attain their legislative goals.

Pressure groups, whether operating at the grassroots level to influence public opinion or through direct contact with members of Congress, perform some important and indispensable functions. These include helping inform both Congress and the public about problems and issues, stimulating public debate, opening a path to Congress for the wronged and needy, and making known to Congress the practical aspects of proposed legislation: whom it would help, whom it would hurt, who is for it, and who is against it.

Lobbyists also work closely with sympathetic party leaders, legislators, and their staffs drafting legislation, developing strategy, and preparing speeches. Party leaders in both chambers often work with lobbying organizations on matters such as the floor agenda, election goals, policy initiatives, or the enactment of priority legislation. As a House GOP whip stated, "we look at the outside groups as an extension of the Whip operation" during key legislative battles.[90] In 2006 and 2007, public and legislative concern about the actions of a small number of lobbyists who gave gifts, expensive foreign trips, and campaign funds in exchange for official acts prompted each chamber to pass new lobbying restrictions. The Honest Leadership and Open Government Act of 2007 requires lobbyists, for instance, to file quarterly (rather than semiannual) reports of their activities with the secretary of the Senate and clerk of the House; forbids lawmakers from accepting gifts or travel from lobbyists; and imposes criminal, not civil, penalties for those who "knowingly and corruptly" do not comply with the law.

Interest groups may, in pursuing their own objectives, lead the legislature into decisions that benefit a particular pressure group but do not necessarily serve other segments of the public. A group's ability to influence legislation is based on a variety of factors: the quality of its arguments; the size, cohesion, and intensity of the organization's membership; the group's ability to augment its political power by forming ad hoc coalitions with other associations; its financial and staff resources; and the shrewdness of its leadership.

These groups understand the potency of grassroots lobbying, mobilizing constituents to pressure lawmakers using phone calls, faxes, Twitter, blogs, letters, e-mails, or personal visits. Interest groups also make efforts to build global grassroots campaigns via the Internet on behalf, for example, of the inclusion of labor and environmental standards in international trade agreements. Even if grassroots activity is manufactured, members realize they cannot simply ignore these expressions of voter opinion. Thus, a crucial phase in determining whether a bill is passed, defeated, or amended on Capitol Hill is the struggle among competing interests in members' states or districts.

The proliferation of interest groups and their sophistication in using campaign funds, expert information, and technology to affect legislative decisions has, on the one hand, added to the demands on lawmakers and created difficulties in organizing winning coalitions. On the other hand, the very proliferation of these groups often enables lawmakers to play one against another. "The power of interest groups is not, of course, exercised without opposition," notes one group of scholars. "The typical issue has some interest groups on one side and some on the other, or many interest groups on many sides, not necessarily with an equal balance of power."[91] Although lawmakers must contend with more interest groups, no single one is likely to exercise dominant influence over policy formation, as sometimes occurred in the past.

NOTES

1. As House GOP leader Bertrand Snell, N.Y., exclaimed: "The House is burning down, and the President of the United States says this is the way to put out the fire." See *Congressional Record*, March 9, 1933, 67.
2. Margaret Kriz, "Still Charging," *National Journal*, December 6, 1997, 2462.
3. Charles Stewart III, "Congress and the Constitutional System," in *The Legislative Branch*, ed. Paul Quirk and Sarah Binder (New York: Oxford University Press, 2005), 30.
4. Paul L. Ford, ed., *The Federalist: A Commentary on the Constitution of the United States by Alexander Hamilton, James Madison and John Jay* (New York: Henry Holt, 1898), 319. James Madison wrote the commentary "Separation of the Departments of Power" (*Federalist* No. 47).

5. Thomas Jefferson, "Notes on Virginia," in *Free Government in the Making*, ed. Alpheus Thomas Mason (New York: Oxford University Press, 1965), 164.
6. *Youngstown Sheet and Tube Co. v. Sawyer*, 343 U.S. 579 (1952), 635.
7. *Constitution, Jefferson's Manual, and Rules of the House of Representatives*, 111th Cong., 2d sess., 2011, H. Doc. 111–157, 129.
8. *Congressional Record*, April 8, 1981, S3615.
9. Statement of Rep. Earl Pomeroy, D-N.D., on the application of laws to Congress, hearing before the House Rules Subcommittee on Rules, March 24, 1994, 1.
10. *Congressional Record*, September 16, 1982, H7097.
11. Sarah Binder, *Minority Rights, Majority Rule* (New York: Cambridge University Press, 1997), 2.
12. Adam Clymer, "In House and Senate, 2 Kinds of G.O.P.," *New York Times*, November 15, 1994, B8.
13. Clarence Cannon, *Cannon's Procedure in the House of Representatives*, 86th Cong., 1st sess., 1959, H. Doc. 86–122, iii.
14. John M. Barry, "The Man of the House," *New York Times Magazine*, November 23, 1986, 109.
15. "Lawmakers Were Warned of Abuses at HUD.," *New York Times*, July 3, 1989, 9.
16. Testimony before the GOP Task Force on Congressional Reform, House Republican Research Committee, December 16, 1987, 3.
17. *National Review*, February 27, 1987, 24.
18. *Los Angeles Times*, February 7, 1977, sec. 1, 5.
19. *Congressional Record*, March 9, 1976, 5909.
20. *CQ Daily Monitor*, April 17, 1995, 1.
21. *Washington Post*, March 7, 1995, A1, A6.
22. Deborah Kalb, "Government by Task Force: The Gingrich Model," *The Hill*, February 22, 1995, 3.
23. Eric Pianin and John Yang, "House Passes Medicare Reform Bill," *Washington Post*, October 20, 1995, A4.
24. Alan Ota, "Warner to Act as Democrats' Liaison to Business World," *CQ Today*, May 15, 2009, 1, 14.
25. See Barbara Sinclair, *Unorthodox Lawmaking*, 2d ed. (Washington, DC: CQ Press, 2000), 94.
26. Edwin Chen, "$50-Billion Tobacco Tax Break Rejected by Senate, 95–3," *Los Angeles Times*, September 11, 1997, B5.
27. *Congressional Record*, June 22, 2009, H6676.
28. David Nather, "Daschle's Soft Touch Lost in Tough Senate Arena," *CQ Weekly*, July 20, 2002, 1921.
29. Quoted in *Deschler-Brown Precedents of the United States House of Representatives*, vol. 1, 94th Cong., 2d sess., 1976, H. Doc. 94–661, iv.
30. Judd Choate, *Torn and Frayed: Congressional Norms and Party Switching in an Era of Reform* (Westport, Conn.: Praeger, 2003).
31. Richard F. Fenno Jr., "Adjusting to the Senate," in *Congress and Policy Change*, ed. Gerald C. Wright Jr., Leroy N. Rieselbach, and Lawrence C. Dodd (New York: Agathon Press, 1986), 134–136. See also Edward V. Schneier, "Norms and Folkways in Congress: How Much Has Already Changed?" *Congress and the Presidency* (Autumn 1988): 117–138; David W. Rohde, "Studying Congressional Norms: Concepts and Evidence," *Congress and the Presidency* (Autumn 1988):

139–145; and Chester W. Rogers, "New Member Socialization in the House of Representatives," *Congress and the Presidency* (Spring 1992): 47–63.

32. See John M. Broder, "House Backs Bill, 219–212, To Curb Global Warming," *New York Times*, June 27, 2009, A1. (The table is from *CQ Today*, June 2, 2009, 32.)

33. Roger H. Davidson and Walter J. Oleszek, *Congress Against Itself* (Bloomington: Indiana University Press, 1977); Roger H. Davidson, "Breaking Up Those 'Cozy Triangles': An Impossible Dream?" in *Legislative Reform and Public Policy*, ed. Susan Welch and John G. Peters (New York: Praeger, 1977), 30–53; Hugh Heclo, "Issue Networks and the Executive Establishment," in *The New American Political System*, ed. Anthony King (Washington, DC: American Enterprise Institute for Public Policy Research, 1978), 87–124; and Charles O. Jones, *The United States Congress: People, Place, and Policy* (Homewood, Ill.: Dorsey Press, 1982), 360. "Sloppy large hexagons," a phrase coined by Jones, refers to the large number of participants who shape policy issues.

34. Jeff Raimundo, "Cool Whip," *California Magazine*, April 1987, 64.

35. Richard E. Cohen, "Sen. Mitchell, a Lame Duck, Sizes Up '94," *National Journal*, March 12, 1994, 598.

36. George F. Will, "New Speaker, Old Virtues," *Newsweek*, December 4, 2006, 76.

37. See Richard E. Cohen and Brian Friel, "Chairmen Rising," *National Journal*, January 24, 2009, 22–32, and Richard E. Cohen, "Pelosi's Shift," *National Journal*, June 6, 2009, 31–34.

38. John Stanton, "Boehner's Changes Put to Test," *The Hill*, July 20, 2011, 8.

39. Jonathan Allen, "Speaker Still Searches for Keys to His House," *Politico*, November 4, 2011, 13.

40. Committee on House Administration, "The Bill Status System for the United States House of Representatives," July 1, 1975, 19.

41. *New York Times*, October 31, 1984, B6.

42. Donald Bruce Johnson and Jack L. Walker, "President John Kennedy Discusses the Presidency," in *The Dynamics of the American Presidency*, ed. Donald Bruce Johnson (New York: Wiley, 1964), 144.

43. *Congressional Record*, April 2, 2004, H2120.

44. Steven Mufson, David Fahrenthold, and Paul Kane, "In Close Vote, House Passes Climate Bill," *Washington Post*, June 27, 2009, A4. See John M. Broder, "Adding Something for Everyone, House Leaders Won Climate Bill," *New York Times*, July 1, 2009, A1, and Edward Felker, "Sweetener Helped Sway Vote on House Climate Bill," *Washington Times*, July 1, 2009, A1.

45. *Congressional Record*, March 17, 1994, H1483.

46. *Congressional Record*, May 20, 1987, S6798.

47. Doris Kearns Goodwin, *Lyndon Johnson and the American Dream* (New York: Harper and Row, 1976), 11.

48. *Los Angeles Times*, October 6, 1982, sec. 1, 1.

49. Woodrow Wilson, *Constitutional Government in the United States* (New York: Columbia University Press, 1911), 87.

50. *Congressional Record*, February 7, 1967, 2838.

51. Asher C. Hinds, *Hinds' Precedents of the House of Representatives*, vol. 1 (Washington: U.S. Government Printing Office, 1907), v.

52. Janet Hook, "Speaker Jim Wright Takes Charge in the House," *Congressional Quarterly Weekly Report*, July 11, 1987, 1486.

53. *New York Times*, November 22, 1985, B8.
54. *Congressional Record*, September 10, 1987, S11944.
55. Nelson W. Polsby, "Policy Analysis and Congress," *Public Policy* (Fall 1969): 67.
56. Michael Green, "Obstacles to Reform: Nobody Covers the House," *Washington Monthly*, June 1970, 62–70.
57. See Robert L. Peabody, Norman J. Ornstein, and David W. Rohde, "The United States Senate as a Presidential Incubator: Many Are Called but Few Are Chosen," *Political Science Quarterly* (Summer 1976): 236–258.
58. See Douglas Harris, "The Rise of the Public Speakership," *Political Science Quarterly* (Summer 1998): 193–212.
59. Reid Wilson, "GOP Sees Pelosi as Dems Achilles' Heel," *The Hill*, June 11, 2009, 14, and Charlie Cook, "A Bit of Advice, Madam Speaker," *National Journal*, May 23, 2009, 64.
60. Drew Westen, "Selling Health Care? Watch What You Say," *Washington Post*, June 28, 2009, B3.
61. Charles Clapp, *The Congressman* (Garden City, NY: Doubleday, 1963), 39.
62. Richard F. Fenno Jr., *Congressmen in Committees* (Boston: Little, Brown, 1973), 172.
63. Robert C. Byrd, *Operations of Congress: Testimony of House and Senate Leaders, Hearing Before the Joint Committee on the Organization of Congress*, 103d Cong., 1st sess., February 2, 1993, 4.
64. Norman J. Ornstein, "Legislative Behavior and Legislative Structure: A Comparative Look at House and Senate Resource Utilization," in *Legislative Staffing*, eds. James J. Heaphey and Alan B. Balutis (New York: Wiley, 1975), 175.
65. Ed Henry, "The Senate's Freshman Firestorm: Torricelli 'Liberated' by His Move to Upper Chamber," *Roll Call*, June 2, 1997, 24.
66. Lindsay Sobel, "From House Chairman to Senate Freshman, Pat Roberts Rides in Smaller Farm Pasture," *The Hill*, June 11, 1997, 20.
67. Tory Newmyer and Emily Pierce, "A Marriage of Convenience?" *Roll Call*, January 12, 2009, 1.
68. Carl Hulse, "For 2 Republican Leaders, a Bond, Not a Rivalry," *New York Times*, July 2, 2011, A11.
69. *Congressional Record*, March 31, 2009, S4025.
70. Francis Lee and Bruce Oppenheimer, *Sizing Up the Senate* (Chicago: University of Chicago Press, 1999), 56.
71. Nathan Gonzales, "Democrats Face Pros and Cons in Nationalizing 2010 Races," *Roll Call*, November 11, 2009, online edition.
72. Peter Baker, "A 'Surgical Approach' to Policy, and Its Pitfalls," *New York Times*, May 22, 2009, A1. See also Louis Fisher, *The Constitution and 9/11* (Lawrence: University Press of Kansas, 2008).
73. Kenneth P. Doyle, "Record-Shattering $1.8 Billion Cost For '08 Presidential Campaign, FEC Says," *Daily Report for Executives*, June 9, 2009, A-10.
74. Peter Bacon Jr., "Franken Wins Senate Battle," *Washington Post*, July 1, 2009, A1.
75. Thomas B. Rosenstiel, "Presidents' Pollsters: Who Follows Whom?" *Los Angeles Times*, December 28, 1993, A5.
76. David E. Price, *The Congressional Experience,* 3d ed. (Boulder, Colo.: Westview Press, 2004), 245.

77. Andrew Mollison, "Lawmakers for Balanced Budget Take Case to Computer Network," *Washington Times*, February 15, 1994, A8. See also James Thurber and Colton Campbell, eds., *Congress and the Internet* (Upper Saddle River, NJ: Prentice Hall, 2003).

78. Staci Zavattaro, "Members Seeing Advantage of Plugging Into Blogosphere," *National Journal's CongressDailyAM*, October 25, 2005, 8. See also K. Daniel Glover, "The Rise of Blogs," *National Journal*, January 21, 2006, 30–39.

79. Erika Lovley, "Twitter as a Weapon," *Politico*, May 26, 2009, 21.

80. Emily Yehle, "Members Grapple With Media Trends," *Roll Call*, November 11, 2009, 3.

81. Robin Toner, "G.O.P. Mobilizes for Contract Deadline," *New York Times*, March 30, 1995, A21.

82. Norman J. Ornstein, "If Congress Played a Better Host to Guests, Maybe It Would Improve a Crummy Image," *Roll Call*, March 31, 1994, 15.

83. *Congressional Record*, March 25, 1994, S4025.

84. Michael Gerson, "Journalism's Slow, Sad Death," *Washington Post,* November 27, 2009, A25.

85. For a valuable discussion of constituent pressures, see David Mayhew, *The Electoral Connection* (New Haven, Conn.: Yale University Press, 1974).

86. Glenn Simpson, "Now Showing on an E-Mail Screen Near You: Your Congressman, Produced by Joe Taxpayer," *Wall Street Journal*, January 7, 2000, A16.

87. Richard E. Cohen, "Kilroy Reaches Out on Health Care as GOP Hones Attacks," *National Journal's CongressDailyAM*, June 26, 2009, 3.

88. Walter F. Mondale, hearing before the Joint Committee on the Organization of Congress, 103d Cong., 1st sess., July 1, 1993, 33.

89. Janet Hook, "Obama's Budget is the End of an Era," *Los Angeles Times*, February 27, 2009, online edition.

90. Kate Ackley, "Coalitions: Lobbyists' Holy Grail," *Roll Call*, November 8, 2005, 16.

91. John P. Heinz, Edward O. Laumann, Robert L. Nelson, and Robert H. Salisbury, *The Hollow Core: Private Interests in National Policy Making* (Cambridge, Mass.: Harvard University Press, 1993), 391. See also Allan J. Cigler and Burdett A. Loomis, *Interest Group Politics*, 7th ed. (Washington, DC: CQ Press, 2006).

CHAPTER 2

The Congressional Budget Process

T HE FRAMERS of the Constitution deliberately lodged the power of the purse in Congress because it is the branch of government closest to the people. "This power of the purse," wrote James Madison in *Federalist* No. 58, "may, in fact, be regarded as the most complete and effectual weapon with which any constitution can arm the immediate representatives of the people, for obtaining a redress of every grievance, and for carrying into effect every just and salutary measure." Or as Senator Robert C. Byrd, D-W.Va., said more than 200 years after Madison: "The greatest power of the Legislative Branch is the power of the purse."[1] Under Article I of the Constitution, only Congress is empowered to collect taxes, borrow money, and authorize expenditures. And the executive branch can spend money only for the purposes and in the amounts specified by Congress. As Section 9 of Article I proclaims: "No Money shall be drawn from the Treasury, but in Consequence of Appropriations made by Law." The House has the constitutional authority to originate revenue measures, which the Senate can amend. If the House believes the Senate has trespassed on its revenue-initiating authority, it will subject the measure to a "blue-slip" rejection: a notification on blue paper to the Senate that it has contravened the constitutional prerogatives of the House. The Sixteenth Amendment to the Constitution permits Congress "to lay and collect" income taxes.

The Constitution did not prescribe a budget system for the legislative branch. Instead, it evolved over time to reflect new demands and pressures, such as the huge increase in the size and cost of government from the Great Depression through today. In the U.S. system of separate institutions sharing power, the president exercises significant fiscal authority through the constitutional veto power and a wide-ranging ability to influence the law-making process. Congress, which also recognizes the value of the president's role in budgeting, delegated to the president in the Budget and Accounting Act of 1921 statutory responsibility for preparing an annual federal budget. Using this responsibility, presidents have been able to spotlight their priorities, frame the budgetary debate, and require Congress to respond to their budgetary proposals. Congress is not bound by the president's recommendations, but it typically uses them as a starting point for the legislative budget process.

If Madison and the other constitutional framers returned today, they might wonder about the overall effectiveness of the congressional purse strings. After all, about 60% of federal expenditures are considered to be relatively uncontrollable under existing law—that is, the government is required to spend money automatically for certain purposes because of laws previously enacted by Congress. These uncontrollables include interest on the public debt ($1.4 trillion in fiscal 2012), entitlements (laws that require mandatory payments to all eligible individuals, such as Social Security, Medicare, and government pension programs), and contractual obligations that must be paid when due (such as the Defense Department's procurement arrangements with various businesses).

One consequence of uncontrollables is clear. If the 113th Congress adjourned immediately after convening on its opening day in January 2013, without passing any laws, federal government spending for 2013 would still be significantly more than $1 trillion.[2] Furthermore, spending each year thereafter would continue—and increase—because many federal programs are indexed to the cost of living. Congress can convert uncontrollables into controllables by changing the basic law that establishes governmental obligations and authorizes automatic funding without regular legislative review. (There are different degrees of controllability, however. Interest on the national debt and the interest rates to finance that debt are largely beyond Congress's control.) But members who want to amend the law and subject uncontrollables—entitlement programs primarily—to annual budgetary scrutiny can incur serious political risks. Congress chooses to place programs in the uncontrollable category for a variety of reasons. Stability, certainty, and preferred status are among the values that accrue to such programs. Retirees, for example, would have "to live under a great deal of financial uncertainty" if Congress subjected Social Security to annual review.[3]

The federal budget reflects the president's and Congress's choices among competing national priorities and identifies where the nation has been, where it is now, and where the administration and legislative branch plan to make future fiscal as well as policy commitments.[4] Thus, the nation's budget is both an economic and a political document. As a Democrat on the Senate Budget Committee once said:

> By their nature, debates on the budget tend to be more partisan than other debates. After all, setting a broad plan for allocating resources necessarily depends on judgments based on established principles we bring with us from our views and priorities influenced by our respective partisan affiliations.[5]

The bitter partisan fiscal battles over numerous fiscal issues in the 112th Congress—for instance, the threat of two government shutdowns (May and December 2011) and a default on raising the federal debt ceiling (August 2011; more on the shutdown and default threats below)—underscore the wide gap between the two parties on how to reduce the fiscal deficit and grow the economy. President Barack Obama and most congressional Democrats want to raise taxes on the well-off and enact federal policies that both reduce the deficit gradually and stimulate the economy to create more jobs. Republicans oppose revenue increases and castigate an oppressive government that hampers business productivity through burdensome regulations and unnecessary taxes. Thus, the budget is more than just numbers for both parties and the chief executive. It is "the document through which an administration announces just what sort of polity it envisions, and which fights it is willing to take on to realize that vision."[6]

In broad terms, federal budgeting is composed of four main phases:

1. Preparation and submission of the budget by the president to Congress

2. Congressional review of the president's budget and action on required budgetary matters

3. Execution of budget-related laws by federal departments and agencies

4. Audits of agency spending

The first and third steps are controlled primarily by the executive branch; the fourth is conducted largely by the Government Accountability Office (GAO), a legislative support agency of Congress. This chapter focuses on the second stage, the basic elements and features of Congress's budgetary process.

AUTHORIZATION–APPROPRIATIONS PROCESS

Fundamental to the congressional budget process is the distinction between authorizations and appropriations. As Senate Democratic leader Harry Reid, Nev., explained:

> Authorizations allow programs to be created and funded. When we pass an authorizing bill, we hope the authorized level will be looked at in [the] appropriations committee—as I did as a longtime member. But we realize there are competing priorities, and full funding doesn't come very often.[7]

House and Senate rules created this two-step, sequential process. Authorizations establish, continue, or modify agency programs or policies; appropriations fund authorized agency programs and policies. An authorization, in brief, can be viewed as a "hunting license" for an appropriation. (Congress may also "deauthorize," or eliminate, programs and agencies.) Both authorizations and appropriations bills must be approved by both houses and presented to the president for signature or veto.

Authorizations

In the first step, Congress passes an **authorization bill** that establishes or continues—a reauthorization—an agency or program and provides it with the legal authority to operate. Authorizations are commonly limited to one or more years, and such legislation typically recommends, as guidance to the appropriators, specific funding levels for programs and agencies. That is, these bills include statutory language (such as "hereby authorized to be appropriated") that permits, or authorizes, the enactment of appropriations to fund agency and program activities. The basic purposes of an authorization are highlighted in Box 2.1. Note that the example in Box 2.1 shows authorization covering fiscal year 2010; further, it recommends specific allocations for various Coast Guard expenses.

Today, it is usual for most authorizations to be multiyear—with a few exceptions, such as defense, which is authorized annually. As Senate Armed Services Chair Carl Levin, D-Mich., stated, "Every year since 1961 there has been an annual defense authorization bill enacted" into law.[8] This record of success has come close to being broken several times because of major conflicts over military policy among the House, the Senate, and the White House. Recent controversial issues such as allowing gays in the military, trying alleged terrorists in either military or civilian courts, or the deployment of military units to Libya are examples of the contentious topics that threatened but did not prevent the annual enactment of this legislation.

Another sometimes annual authorization worth noting is for the intelligence community. Bicameral and legislative–executive disagreements prevented Congress for 6 years in the 2000s from passing such legislation. That was not the case in 2010, 2011, and 2012, however. "What this means," said Diane Feinstein, D-Calif., chair of the Senate Intelligence Committee, "is that Congress, through the House and Senate Intelligence Committees, is restoring oversight over the intelligence community and fulfilling our responsibility to thoroughly examine intelligence policies and budgets."[9]

Until the 1950s, most federal programs and entities were permanently authorized. Permanent authorizations (the Library of Congress is an example) remain in effect until changed by Congress and provide continuing statutory authority for ongoing federal programs and agencies. Then, in the 1960s and 1970s, authorizing committees won enactment of laws that converted many permanent authorizations into temporary authorizations. Two major factors precipitated this change. First, the authorizing committees wanted greater control of and oversight over executive and presidential activities, especially in view of the interbranch tensions that stemmed from the Vietnam War and the Watergate scandal of the Nixon Administration. Second, short-term authorizations put pressure on the appropriating committees to fund programs at levels recommended by the authorizing panels.

Appropriations

Today, much of the federal government is funded through the annual enactment of 12 regular appropriations bills. No constitutional requirement exists

BOX 2.1 Authorization of Appropriations Language

An Excerpt from Coast Guard Authorization Act of 2010

* * * * *

TITLE I—AUTHORIZATION

SEC. 101. AUTHORIZATION OF APPROPRIATIONS.

Funds are authorized to be appropriated for fiscal year 2010 for necessary expenses of the Coast Guard as follows:

(1) For the operation and maintenance of the Coast Guard, $6,838,291,000, of which—
   (A) $24,500,000 is authorized to be derived from the Oil Spill Liability Trust Fund to carry out the purposes of section 1012(a)(5) of the Oil Pollution Act of 1990 (33 U.S.C. 2712(a)(5));
   (B) $1,110,923,000 shall be available only for paying for search and rescue programs;
   (C) $802,423,000 shall be available only for paying for marine safety programs; and
   (D) $2,274,312,000 shall be available only for paying for ports, waterways, and coastal security.

(2) For the acquisition, construction, rebuilding, and improvement of aids to navigation, shore and offshore facilities, vessels, and aircraft, including equipment related thereto, $1,597,580,000, of which—
   (A) $20,000,000 shall be derived from the Oil Spill Liability Trust Fund to carry out the purposes of section 1012(a)(5) of the Oil Pollution Act of 1990, to remain available until expended;
   (B) $1,194,780,000 is authorized for the Integrated Deepwater System Program; and
   (C) $45,000,000 is authorized for shore facilities and aids to navigation.

(3) To the Commandant of the Coast Guard for research, development, test, and evaluation of technologies, materials, and human factors directly relating to improving the performance of the Coast Guard's mission in search and rescue, aids to navigation, marine safety, marine environmental protection, enforcement of laws and treaties, ice operations, oceanographic research, and defense readiness, $29,745,000, to remain available until expended, of which $500,000 shall be derived from the Oil Spill Liability Trust Fund to carry out the purposes of section 1012(a)(5) of the Oil Pollution Act of 1990.

* * * * *

SOURCE: *Coast Guard Authorization Act of 2010*, 111th Congress, 1st Session, H.R. 3619.

for annual appropriations, but the practice since the First Congress has been to appropriate for a single year. Another long-standing precedent is that the House originates appropriations bills based on its constitutional authority to initiate revenue-raising measures.

Appropriations bills are of three main types: (1) annual—also called regular or general; (2) **supplemental appropriations bills**—to address unexpected contingencies, such as emergency funding for natural disasters; and (3) continuing—often called **continuing resolutions,** or CRs—to provide stop-gap (or temporary) funding for agencies (on a formula basis, such as the previous year's level) that did not receive an annual appropriation by the start of the fiscal year. The fiscal year runs from October 1 to September 30. Congress enacts about 15 or so appropriations bills every fiscal year: the 12 regular bills, one or more supplementals, and one or more continuing appropriations.

When Congress is unable to complete action on one or more of the dozen regular appropriations bills by the start of the fiscal year, it provides temporary funding for the affected federal agencies through a CR, also called a continuing appropriation. CRs provide Congress with additional time to resolve funding differences between the two parties and among the House, Senate, and White House. (A record high of 21 CRs was passed in the last year of the Clinton Administration.) Traditionally, CRs have been employed to keep a few government agencies in operation for short periods, ranging from several days or weeks to a few months. Congress also may pass CRs that extend beyond the November elections and even into the next congressional session. Sometimes CRs have become major policymaking instruments of massive size and scope. In 1986 and 1987, for example, Congress packaged the then 13 regular appropriations bills into CRs.

Packaging all or a number of appropriations bills together creates what are called "mega," "omnibus," or "minibus" measures. These bills authorize and appropriate money to operate the federal government and make national policy in scores of areas. These omnibus bills grant large powers to a small number of people who put these packages together—party and committee leaders and top executive officials. Omnibus measures usually arouse the ire of the rank-and-file members of Congress, because typically little time is available in the final days of a session to debate these massive measures or to know what is in them. Absent enactment of annual appropriations bills or a CR, federal agencies must shut down, furloughing their employees. Moreover, "uncertainty about final appropriations leads many [federal] managers to hoard funds; in some cases, hiring and purchasing stops."[10] (The structure of a regular appropriations **act** is depicted in Box 2.2.) CRs usually do not permit agencies to initiate new programs or activities.

At the start of the 112th Congress (2011–2013), House Republicans wanted to avoid year-end omnibus appropriations bills and return to

---

BOX 2.2   Excerpts From the Structure of a Regular Appropriations Act

An Act

[Title]

Making appropriations for Agriculture, Rural Development, Food and Drug Administration, and Related Agencies programs for the fiscal year ending September 30, 2010, and for other purposes.

[Enacting clause]

Be it enacted by the Senate and House of Representatives of the United States of America in Congress assembled, That the following sums are appropriated, out of any money in the Treasury not otherwise appropriated, for Agriculture, Rural Development, Food and Drug Administration, and Related Agencies programs for the fiscal year ending September 30, 2010, and for other purposes, namely:

AGRICULTURAL RESEARCH SERVICE
SALARIES AND EXPENSES

For necessary expenses of the Agricultural Research Service and for acquisition of lands by donation, exchange, or purchase at a nominal cost not to exceed $100, and for land exchanges where the lands exchanged shall be of equal value or shall be equalized by a payment of money to the grantor which shall not exceed 25 percent of the total value of the land or interests transferred out of Federal ownership, $1,179,639,000, of which $44,138,000 shall be for the purposes, and in the amounts, specified in the table titled "Congressionally Designated Projects" in the statement of managers to accompany this Act: Provided, That appropriations hereunder shall be available for the operation and maintenance of aircraft and the purchase of not to exceed one for replacement only:

* * * * *

SOURCE: Public Law 111–80, *Agriculture, Rural Development, Food and Drug Administration, and Related Agencies Appropriations Act, 2010* (October 21, 2009).

---

the "regular order." The regular order in this context means Congress completing action on the 12 general appropriations bills as stand-alone measures—something that previously occurred in 1996—prior to the October 1 start of the new fiscal year. GOP Speaker John Boehner, Ohio, had publicly said at various times that one of his goals was to do away with comprehensive spending bills. The reality of governing in a contentious legislative environment led to the abandonment of the Speaker's plan.[11] Two case examples from the first session (2011) of the 112th Congress provide a summary review of the partisan and bicameral clashes that compelled the packaging of appropriations bills, required several CRs to keep the government functioning, and threatened twice to produce a partial government shutdown.

The Spring Contretemps. Although Republicans controlled the 112th House, they had to deal with the appropriations bills left them by the previous Democratic Congress. In 2010, Democrats could not win enactment into law of any of the 12 annual appropriations bills because of disputes within the parties and the two chambers. The result: Democrats in December 2010, coming off a huge midterm election defeat the previous month, enacted a CR that kept the government running until March 4, 2011. House Republicans were now responsible for devising a longer term spending plan. As most GOP lawmakers said on the campaign trail, "We want to shrink the record-setting deficits by cutting federal spending and reducing the role and reach of the government." Scores of House Republicans—particularly the 87 Tea Party–endorsed or supported freshmen—clamored for fast action to restrain federal spending.

Speediness did not occur, however. The Democratic Senate and the Obama Administration vehemently disagreed with the spending cuts advocated by House Republicans, such as prohibiting the use of federal funds to implement the president's health care reform law (the Patient Protection and Affordable Care Act). Democrats recognized that many voters wanted to pare back spending but not in a way that would, in their estimation, hinder needed investments and economic growth. Republicans contended that cutting federal spending would spur economic growth and create jobs.

The two parties and chambers were at a standoff. They appeared unwilling to pass a CR by the statutory deadline of March 4 and prevent a government shutdown. Federal agencies prepared to stop non-essential activities as the two sides engaged in brinksmanship: Each party wanted the other to "cave" to its demands. In early March, both chambers passed a 2-week CR that gave the two parties additional time (until March 18) to negotiate an accord. The two parties supported the CR because they were uncertain which one would be blamed by voters for stopping government services. (Many congressional Republicans remembered the public relations disaster they faced in December 1995 and January 1996 when the government shut down twice. Speaker Newt Gingrich pushed the shutdown strategy in an unsuccessful attempt to force President Bill Clinton to agree to the GOP's fiscal agenda.)

Two additional weeks proved insufficient to achieve a compromise. House and Senate legislators agreed on only two things: "Congress should avoid a government shutdown and spending bills should include some measure of funding reduction."[12] Despite the 2-week extension, no compromise materialized. So in mid-March, both chambers passed a 3-week CR with an expiration date of April 8. Less than 2 hours before April 8 ended, congressional leaders from each chamber reached a compromise that would cut $39 billion from spending projections. "Americans of different beliefs came together," said President Obama, to agree to "the largest spending cut in our history."[13]

Because additional time was required to draft the continuing appropriations act to include the various negotiated agreements, Congress passed another CR lasting until April 15. The day before the mid-April deadline, Congress enacted legislation funding the government through September 30, 2011. As Senate GOP leader Mitch McConnell, Ky., stated: "We've taken care of the business [the 111th Congress] Democrats left unfinished last year, and we've taken a small but crucial step in getting Washington to live within its means without disrupting people's lives."[14]

The Fall–Winter Conflict. Several months later, the House and Senate witnessed a reprise of the earlier conflict. Only this time, instead of completing the work of the 111th Congress, House Republicans could put their own financial stamp on federal agencies and programs. Still, passage by October 1, 2011 (the start of fiscal year 2012), of all 12 regular appropriations bills could not be accomplished. There were simply too many sharp party disagreements over where and how to reduce spending, as well as controversy over the severity of the cutbacks. Moreover, a fierce interparty battle in August over raising the statutory debt ceiling (see the discussion below) only aggravated the already hostile partisan environment on Capitol Hill.

As part of the August debt-ceiling accord, Congress agreed to a spending cap of just over $1 trillion to fund the government for fiscal years 2012 (and beyond). But the many weeks required to resolve the debt-ceiling issue, combined with Congress's traditional August recess and other factors, left little time for the two chambers to enact the regular appropriations measures by October 1. By mid-September, plans were under way for Congress to pass a CR to fund government operations until November 18. Brinksmanship again came into play as each party wanted to use the hard deadline to try to gain political and policy leverage over the other.

At least two key factors gave rise to the threat of a government shutdown. First, in 2011, the nation had a record number (83) of natural disasters: hurricanes, floods, earthquakes, tornadoes, and wildfires. Both parties wanted to provide financial assistance to the devastated communities, but the two parties and chambers had sharply divergent spending approaches. House Republicans wanted "offsets"—cutting the budgets of other federal programs—to pay for hikes in disaster assistance. They targeted as an offset a clean energy program strongly supported by Democrats.

In response, House and Senate Democrats voiced strong opposition to the GOP's approach and argued that assisting disaster areas constituted emergency funding and required no offsets. "It has long been a tradition of Congress to approve disaster assistance without need for [an] offset," declared Senate Appropriations Chair Daniel Inouye, D-Hawaii.[15] Not so, said House Appropriations Chair Hal Rogers, R-Ky., who noted that there have been "over $60 billion in emergency offsets since 2001."[16] With neither party nor chamber budging, Congress was poised for another "game of chicken."

Second, more than 50 House Republicans opposed the statutory spending cap agreed to as part of the August debt-ceiling deal. They wanted to make deeper cuts in overall discretionary spending for fiscal year 2012. On September 21, much to the shock of GOP leaders, the House rejected (195 to 230) the short-term CR to keep the government functioning until November 18. Conservative Republicans who wanted deeper spending cuts and Democrats who opposed offsets for disaster relief combined to defeat the CR. Suddenly, the chances for a government shutdown seemed more likely. "They're threatening to shut down the government to get what they want," said Senate Majority Leader Reid.[17]

The threat never materialized. The next day, ignoring Democrats, Speaker Boehner won the support of enough wavering Republicans—he retained the offsets and cut an additional $100 million from a solar energy program lauded by President Obama—to win passage (219 to 203) of the CR. On September 23, the Senate rejected (59 to 36) the House-passed CR and went home for the weekend. When the Senate returned on Monday (September 26), with both chambers slated to be on recess for at least part of that week, it voted 79 to 12 to pass a CR (H.R. 2608) with the November 18 deadline. In addition, just in case more time for bicameral negotiations was needed before action on H.R. 2608 was completed, the Senate also sent another, shorter term CR (H.R. 2017) to keep the government open for a few days past the October 1 deadline. Both measures were returned to the House. Unexpectedly, the House–Senate conflict over offsets for disaster funds ended when the Federal Emergency Management Agency (FEMA)—the lead agency for disaster relief—discovered that it had enough money to assist the hard-hit communities.

With the House in recess for the week and both measures before it, Speaker Boehner "held a conference call with rank-and-file [Republican] members Monday night [September 26]" to get their input on a course of action.[18] The result: The House met 3 days later and, with only three lawmakers in attendance, it enacted in minutes the short-term CR (H.R. 2017) by unanimous consent, which kept the government operating until October 4.[19] When the entire House reconvened after its weeklong break, it agreed on October 4 (by a 352 to 66 vote) to the Senate's amendment of the CR (H.R. 2608) that kept the government running until mid-November. Thus, the struggle to keep the government open at least to November 18 was resolved but not the battle to pass some or all of the remaining nine annual appropriations bills.

Sentiment was growing in both chambers and parties by this time to enact the outstanding appropriations bills. "My goal is not to do CRs," remarked House Appropriations Chair Rogers.[20] Subsequently, both chambers agreed to assemble a "minibus" composed of three annual appropriations bills. The legislation was named the "Consolidated and Further Continuing Appropriations Act of 2012." Both chambers convened a conference committee (see Chapter 8) on an agriculture appropriations measure and added to it the Commerce-Justice-Science and Transportation-HUD appropriations bills. The conference report also contained, as noted by House Appropriations Chair Rogers, "a continuing resolution to keep the rest of the government operating until December 16."[21] The House enacted (298 to 121) the conference report on November 17, as did the Senate on the same day, by a 69-to-30 vote.

The remaining nine appropriations measures were then subsumed in the Military Construction–VA appropriations conference report. On December 16, the House adopted the nine-bill conference report by a 291-to-121 vote. In addition, the House enacted two CRs (one expiring December 17 and the other December 23) to provide additional time to clear the bill for presidential consideration, if it was needed. On December 17, the Senate approved (67 to 32) the conference report carrying the nine appropriations measures, as well as the two CRs passed by the House. Thus ended an intense and frustrating appropriations process that provided the government with operating funds for fiscal year 2012.

These two examples underscore what might be a trend in a polarized Congress. Just avoiding government shutdowns might be the new standard of success for the appropriations process rather than, as in times past, gaining the punctual enactment of the 12 yearly bills. As one legislative budget expert opined, "The primary reason for delayed or nonexistent [annual] appropriations" is pure politics.

> Threatening a government shutdown is [viewed] as an appropriate, even desirable, legislative strategy. Refusing to make a decision on an appropriation until the very last minute and creating agony and [heartburn] along the way is thought of as a proper negotiating tool.[22]

In sum, the deadlines in CRs (and other laws and matters) and the repeated threats of shutdowns have at least five noteworthy consequences. First, they compel Congress to address issues that otherwise might "languish due to partisan differences or legislative inertia." Second, they "give leverage to those legislators who are least concerned about going over the brink."[23] Third, they impose money and morale costs on federal agencies that must prepare to shut down. Fourth, they consume the valuable time of legislators and the legislative branch, time that might be better spent dealing with other important matters. Fifth, they undermine citizens' trust and confidence in

Congress's capacity to govern and to resolve longer term issues. Yet, as one lawmaker said about Congress and time crunches, "This place, like it or not, works better on deadlines."[24]

More on Appropriations. Most activities or functions that individuals usually associate with the federal government—the Federal Bureau of Investigation (FBI), the Coast Guard, the national park system, interstate highways, defense, space exploration, homeland security, foreign aid, medical research, and so on—are funded through the annual enactment of the 12 general appropriations bills. The fiscal reality is that the annual appropriations process controls only around 38% to 40% of all federal spending. This controllable, discretionary spending funds most domestic and defense programs. The other 60% or so of federal spending consists of automatic payments for either interest on the national debt or entitlements. Entitlements represent 50% or so of federal spending (Social Security, Medicaid, and Medicare are the largest). Money for these programs is continuously available to eligible beneficiaries under the terms of previously enacted statutes. Appropriated entitlements, such as Medicaid and several veterans' programs, are funded through, but not controlled by, the regular appropriations process. Any shortfall in spending for appropriated entitlement programs must be covered by supplemental appropriations.

Congressional analysts distinguish between *discretionary spending,* which is controlled through the annual appropriations process, and *direct spending,* which is used primarily to fund entitlement programs that are provided for in authorization laws. Direct spending is under the jurisdiction of the authorizing, not the appropriating, committees. Discretionary spending has borne the brunt of reductions over the years, because politicians have been eager to reduce the size and cost of government. However, the direct spending side of the budget has escalated, because Congress cannot easily control mandatory expenditure levels for the entitlement programs (e.g., Medicare and Social Security) established by permanent law. Congress does not set annual expenditures for these programs; instead, their financial costs reflect the eligibility criteria and benefit levels established in the statute.

Figure 2.1 highlights the ratio of discretionary expenditures to entitlement expenditures over time. Yes, Congress can modify those statutes, but doing so can be both difficult and an electorally risky venture. The elderly, who are well organized and who turn out to vote, are not reluctant to tell lawmakers, "Keep your hands off my Medicare and Social Security!"

Budget Authority and Budget Outlays

Another budgetary distinction to bear in mind is that between *budget authority* and *budget outlays.* Appropriations approved by Congress provide **budget authority,** which allows government agencies to make financial commitments, up to a specified amount, that eventually result in

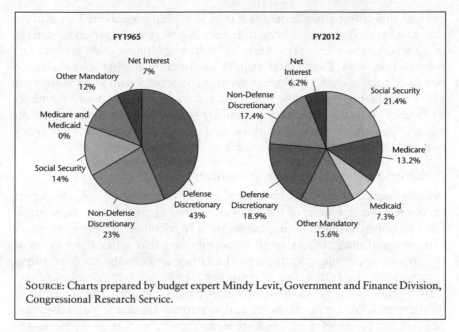

FY1965

Net Interest
7%

Other Mandatory
12%

Medicare and
Medicaid
0%

Social Security
14%

Non-Defense
Discretionary
23%

Defense
Discretionary
43%

FY2012

Net
Interest
6.2%

Non-Defense
Discretionary
17.4%

Social Security
21.4%

Medicare
13.2%

Medicaid
7.3%

Other Mandatory
15.6%

Defense
Discretionary
18.9%

SOURCE: Charts prepared by budget expert Mindy Levit, Government and Finance Division, Congressional Research Service.

FIGURE 2.1   Federal Spending by Major Category, Fiscal Years 1965 and 2012

budget outlays—that is, the spending of dollars. As one budget analyst explains it:

> Congress does not directly control the level of federal spending that will occur in a particular year. Rather, it grants the executive branch authority (referred to as budget authority) to enter into obligations, which are legally binding agreements with suppliers of goods or services or with a beneficiary. When those obligations come due, the Treasury Department issues a payment. The amount of payments, called outlays, over an accounting period called the fiscal year (running from October 1 to September 30) equals federal expenditures for that fiscal year. Federal spending (outlays) in any given year, therefore, results from the spending authority (budget authority) granted by Congress in the current and in prior fiscal years.[25]

To state it differently, budget authority is like putting money in a checking account, and obligations are like writing a check; when the check is cashed, the dollars (outlays) are dispensed to the appropriate recipient.

The conversion of budget authority to outlays depends on a variety of factors, including the character of the program or activity. Budget authority granted annually to pay federal salaries is typically converted to outlays that same year. Budget authority to build a highway is converted to outlays at a variable rate over several years as highway planning costs give way to construction costs. Lawmakers require both figures so they can assess the projected total cost of a multiyear program or project compared with what will be spent on it annually. Legislators are mindful that budget authority figures—instead of the outlay numbers—are the better predictors of an agency's growth or decline. Outlays, however, are reflected in each year's national deficit or surplus (an uncommon occurrence) levels.

Authorizing and Appropriating Committees

Whether agencies receive the budget authority they request depends in part on the recommendations of the authorizing and appropriating committees. Each chamber has authorizing committees (Agriculture, Commerce, Small Business, and many others) with responsibilities that differ from those of the two appropriating committees—the House and Senate Appropriations Committees. The authorizing committees are the policymaking centers on Capitol Hill. As the substantive legislative panels, they propose solutions to public problems, create agencies and departments, define administrative policies and priorities, and advocate what they believe to be the necessary level of appropriations for new and existing federal agencies, activities, and programs, specifying either a specific amount of money or an indefinite level of funding ("such sums as may be necessary").

Each house's appropriations committee and their 12 parallel subcommittees recommend how much federal agencies and programs will receive in relation to available fiscal resources and economic conditions. The full committee and subcommittee chairs of the House and Senate Appropriations Committees are collectively known in their respective chambers as the "College of Cardinals" because of their large influence over spending issues. For decades, these chairs often included "earmarks" in bill text or, more commonly, in their committee reports or as part of appropriations conference reports (and their accompanying joint explanatory statements) that set aside specific funds for projects or programs in lawmakers' districts or states. This type of particularistic spending is sometimes called "spending with a zip code," "member projects," "congressionally directed spending," or, more negatively, "pork." By whatever name, earmark requests often come from lawmakers' constituents who want funds for school construction, highways, sewer grants, flood control programs, and the like. Tax and authorization bills also contain earmarks, such as tax breaks or transportation projects, but those in appropriation measures usually receive more public and media attention.

Earmarks Under Fire. Earmarks have come under critical review since the early 2000s for three main reasons. First, the scandals associated with the criminal indictments of lobbyist Jack Abramoff and former Rep. Randy "Duke" Cunningham, R-Calif., prompted increased scrutiny of earmarks.

Abramoff, who referred to each chamber's appropriations panel as the "favor factory," developed ties with influential lawmakers and staff aides by, among other things, "wining and dining" them and presenting them with gifts. He then persuaded his Capitol Hill contacts to quietly insert earmarks into legislation for his clients, who, in turn, would contribute to these lawmakers' campaigns. Cunningham, who took $2.4 million in bribes, used his position on the Defense Appropriations Subcommittee to earmark millions of dollars for favored defense contractors. In Cunningham's case, the lack of transparency—there are both "white" (public) and "black" (secret) aspects to budgeting—enabled him to slip earmarks into the secret intelligence budget without anyone's knowledge. The classified part of budgeting, said Senator John McCain, R-Ariz., a longtime champion of earmark reform, "deserves extra scrutiny now because Duke Cunningham was able to perpetrate some of his egregious crimes through exactly that vehicle."[26]

Second, there was a dramatic increase in the number and dollar value of earmarks. Senator McCain, citing data compiled by the Congressional Research Service, spotlighted the explosion.

> In 1994, there were 4,126 congressional earmarks added to the annual appropriations bills. In 2005, there were 15,877 earmarks, the largest number yet, that's an increase of nearly 300 percent! The level of funding associated with those earmarks has more than doubled from $23.2 billion in fiscal year 1994 to $47.4 billion in fiscal year 2005.[27]

A December 2009 update by the Congressional Research Service found that between 2008 and 2009, the "total number of appropriations earmarks decreased 6 percent, from 12,810 to 12,099. However, the total value of earmarks increased 6 percent, from $28.9 billion to $30.7 billion."[28] (To be sure, numerous earmarks in the budgets are proposed by presidents.)

Various factors accounted for the surge of earmarks. For example, narrow partisan divisions in the House and Senate prompted party leaders to use earmarks to attract the votes needed to pass priority legislation and to help vulnerable lawmakers "bring home the bacon" to appreciative constituents who would then return the incumbent to office. In addition, members did not want to relinquish the "power of the purse" to unelected administrators. As a House Appropriations chair stated: "Members know the needs of their districts better than civil servants working in Washington, DC."[29]

Third, aggressive "watchdog" groups were not reluctant to embarrass Congress by publicizing what they viewed as wasteful spending on bad programs or projects. (Various groups, such as Taxpayers for Common Sense, have websites that permit citizen involvement in monitoring earmarks.) An oft-cited example was the so-called bridge to nowhere—a "mile long, 200-foot-high span [costing $223 million] that will connect Ketchikan, [Alaska,] a town with fewer than 8,000 people, to an island that has 50 residents and a small airport."[30] Critics also highlighted the unseemly and sometimes improper connection between earmarks granted to favorite clients who then contributed to lawmakers' campaign war chests (the so-called "pay-to-play" syndrome). Some ex-lawmakers who join or form lobbying shops have as clients those whom they won earmarks for when they served in Congress.[31]

Earmark Reforms. The proliferation of earmarks and the public controversy associated with egregious examples of wasteful spending on earmarks prompted the 110th (2007–2009) and 111th Congresses (2009–2011) to adopt a number of reforms. These reforms merit review because they are still in the House and Senate rulebooks. The 112th Congress observed a different practice, a voluntary ban on earmarks (discussed below).

The fundamental goals of the reforms are to infuse disclosure and transparency in the earmarking process, which includes limited tax and tariff benefits. House Rule XXI and Senate Rule XLIV define explicitly what constitutes an **earmark** (called a "congressionally directed spending item" by the Senate), **limited tax benefit**, and **limited tariff benefit**. Both chambers adopted somewhat comparable disclosure rules. A lawmaker who requests earmarks or limited tax and tariff provisions must provide a written statement to the committee of jurisdiction that includes these five elements: (1) the name of the requesting member; (2) the name and address of the intended recipient or, if there is no specific recipient, the location of the intended activity; (3) in the case of a limited tax or tariff benefit, the identification of the individual or entities expected to benefit, if known to the member; (4) the purpose of the earmark or limited tax or tariff benefit; and (5) a certification that the lawmaker (or spouse) has no financial interest in the earmark or limited tax or tariff benefit.

To ensure that lawmakers and the public have knowledge of the congressional sponsors of earmarks, both chambers have rules that constrain floor consideration of legislation, amendments,[32] or conference reports unless a list of the earmarks and their sponsors is publicly available in relevant committee reports, on an appropriate legislative website, or in the *Congressional Record.* Senate Rule XLIV also prohibits what are called "air-dropped" earmarks: provisions included in a conference report (see Chapter 8) that neither chamber included in its version of an appropriations bill committed to conference. This particular rule, like so many others in both chambers, is not self-enforcing (a lawmaker must raise a **point of order** against procedural violations) and can be set aside by a three-fifths vote of the Senate or by House adoption of a special rule issued by the Rules Committee.

In the 112th Congress, House and Senate leaders imposed a moratorium on all lawmaker-directed projects. Skyrocketing fiscal deficits and the election of numerous Tea Party–backed congressional Republicans who opposed earmarks triggered the prohibition. One consequence: The majority and minority leaders on the House Appropriations Committee sent a series of "Dear Colleague" letters to lawmakers warning that "earmarks, as defined by . . . the Rules of the House will not be considered."[33] In short, anything that looked like an earmark for a specific recipient and was not open to competitive bids would be viewed as an earmark. It would not be included in appropriations measures. President Obama even stated in his 2011 State of the Union address that he would veto any legislation containing earmarks.

Various lawmakers in the House and Senate managed to circumvent the ban, often by less transparent means. As one account noted, lawmakers in both chambers "attempted to pack hundreds of special spending provisions into at least 10 bills" after "congressional leaders declared a moratorium on earmarks."[34] They were earmarks by another name. The techniques employed included "lettermarks," members writing to administrators to urge that home-based projects be funded; "phonemarks," calling executive officials to request money for projects in their states or districts; and "soft marks," simply "suggesting" to agency officials that money should be spent on the lawmaker's project.

In the nine-bill omnibus appropriations conference report mentioned earlier in this chapter, Senator Tom Coburn, R-Okla., asserted that it had "over $3.5 billion worth of phonemarks in it. We don't have earmarks anymore; they are all phonemarks."[35] Members also hiked the dollar amounts in broad budgetary accounts—rural development, procurement, and the like—and then strongly suggested to agency officials that some of the money be spent for lawmakers' projects back home. The political reality, as a lawmaker pointed out, is that "the agency knows who butters their bread, and who appropriates their money. And they're inclined, particularly when it's a powerful Member, to go along with the recommendation made."[36]

Members in both chambers and parties are unhappy with the informal ban on earmarks, which is why many continue to seek funds for favored projects. As Senate Appropriations Chair Daniel Inouye candidly stated: "I am going to do everything to reinstate earmarks—or whatever you want to call them—because the Constitution is clear and it was never intended to have the executive branch do all of that."[37] Or as GOP Senator Roger Wicker, Miss., expressed it: "What we agreed to do . . . was good policy" for the 112th Congress, but we should "revisit the issue" in the 113th Congress (2013–2015).[38]

Lawmakers also note that putting earmarks in spending bills is a lubricant that wins votes for measures and boosts members' reelection chances by bringing home the bacon.[39] Without the lubricant of earmarks, finding the votes to pass certain measures can be problematic. "When it comes to things like the highway bill that used to be very bipartisan, you have to understand it was greased to be bipartisan with 6,371 earmarks," explained Speaker Boehner. "You take the earmarks away, and guess what? All of a sudden people are beginning to look at the real policy behind it. So each one of these bills will rise or fall on their own merits."[40] Tellingly, the amount of money saved by banning earmarks is miniscule (around 1% to 2% of recent federal budgets that range from about $3.6 trillion to $3.8 trillion), and the funds saved are spent anyway by executive officials. Congress should minimize wrangling over earmarks, say earmark advocates, and instead focus on the big items that drive federal expenditures, such as Medicare, defense, and the like.

Proponents of the ban contend that the money saved may be small relative to the huge federal budget, but it is not an insignificant amount. Members "get millions for an earmark and end up voting for billions of dollars that [they] may oppose."[41] Wasteful pork-barrel politics also erode public confidence in the Congress and promote a larger, more intrusive government. Several lawmakers, concerned that many of their colleagues are "creatively trying to get around the ban, and talking openly about ending it," urged the Senate to make the moratorium permanent.[42] Senator Patrick Toomey, R-Pa., a major advocate of making the ban permanent, summed up the case against earmarks: "The earmarking system wastes taxpayers dollars, creates the appearance of corruption and undermines public confidence in the legislative process."[43] The Obama Administration also prepared a draft memo that would require all federal agencies to disclose publicly the letters they receive from members requesting funding of their projects. These lettermarking missives are to be "disclosed and searchable on the Internet within 30 days of their receipt by the agency."[44]

Spending Options of Appropriators. For each authorized program and agency subject to the annual appropriations process, the appropriations committees have three main options: (1) provide all the funds recommended in the previously approved authorization bill, (2) propose reductions in the amounts authorized, or (3) refuse to provide any funds. A newspaper headline declaring that Congress has just authorized, for example, a new $3 billion antidrug program means that the program officially exists on paper. However, the program still lacks money to operate until it receives an appropriation.

Congressional rules—which may not be observed—require authorizations to precede appropriations to ensure that substantive and financial issues are subject to separate and independent analysis. This procedure also permits almost every member and committee to participate in Congress's constitutional power of the purse. Numerous exceptions are made to this two-step model, despite House and Senate rules that encourage separation of the authorization and appropriations stages.

Constitutional Underpinning

The authorization–appropriation dichotomy is not required by the Constitution. It is a process that has been institutionalized by the rules of the House and Senate and in some cases by statute. Of the two steps, the appropriations stage is on firmer legal ground because it is rooted in the Constitution. An appropriations measure, which provides departments and agencies with authority to commit funds, may be approved even if the authorization bill has not been enacted. As long as "appropriations are enacted," wrote a budget scholar, "funds may be obligated by agencies, regardless of whether . . . authorizations have been enacted."[45] Informally, Congress has employed this division of labor since the beginning of the Republic, as did the British Parliament and the colonial legislatures. As U.S. Senator William Plumer of New Hampshire noted in 1806: "Tis a good provision in the constitution of Maryland that prohibits their Legislature from adding anything to an appropriation law."[46] Generally called supply bills in the early Congresses, appropriations measures had narrow purposes: to provide specific sums of money for fixed periods and stated objectives. Such bills were not to contain matters of policy (often called "legislation").

There were exceptions to this informal rule even during the early days, but the practice of adding **riders,** or extraneous policy provisos, to appropriations bills mushroomed in the 1830s. This practice often provoked sharp controversy in Congress and delayed the enactment of supply bills. "By 1835," wrote a parliamentary expert, the "delays caused by injecting legislation [policy] into these [appropriations] bills had become serious, and [then-Rep.] John Quincy Adams . . . suggested that they be stripped of everything save appropriations."[47] Two years later, the House adopted a rule requiring authorization bills to precede appropriations. The Senate later followed suit.

Separate Policy and Fiscal Decisions

Several major implications flow from Congress's efforts to separate policy from fiscal decision making—matters that usually are inextricably intertwined. Among the major implications are flexibility, bicameral differences, and committee rivalries.

Flexibility. The authorization–appropriations rules, like almost all congressional rules, are not self-enforcing. Either chamber can choose to waive, ignore, or circumvent them, or establish precedents and practices that obviate distinctions between the two. As one scholar has written:

> The real world of the legislative process differs considerably from the idealized model of the two-step authorization–appropriation procedure. Authorization bills contain appropriations, appropriation bills contain authorizations, and the order of their enactment is sometimes reversed. The Appropriations Committees, acting through various kinds of limitations, riders, and nonstatutory controls, are able to establish policy and act in a substantive manner. Authorization Committees have considerable power to force the hand of the Appropriations Committees and, in some cases, even to appropriate.[48]

Flexibility in the authorization–appropriations procedure allows it to accommodate stresses and strains. A failure to enact authorization bills does not bring the appropriations process (or an agency or federal program) to a halt. The Congressional Budget Office (CBO) reported that for fiscal year 2012 there were $261 billion of unauthorized appropriations.[49] Annual appropriations bills often become vehicles for extending or revamping existing laws that did not make it through the authorization process. Moreover, it is not uncommon for authorizers to ask appropriators to include their policy proposals in the annual appropriations bills. They want to hitch a ride on "must pass" appropriation bills heading to the White House. "Ideally, it's not great to use [appropriation] bills," remarked a House Financial Services chair. "But they may be the only vehicles we can use [for] some [authorization measures] where we're facing a veto or we have problems in the Senate."[50]

Bicameral Differences. Because the House and Senate are dissimilar, they have different rules governing the authorization–appropriations process. Table 2.1 compares the authorization and appropriations rules of the two houses. These differences reflect each chamber's fundamental nature: The smaller Senate permits greater procedural flexibility than the larger House.

The rules affect each chamber's legislative behavior and policy deliberations. The Senate, for example, sometimes gets off to a slower start on appropriations measures because, by tradition, the House originates those

TABLE 2.1   Authorization–Appropriations Rules Compared

House	Senate
No unauthorized appropriations are permitted except for public works in progress. The Appropriations Committee generally cannot report a regular appropriations bill unless there is an authorization law. However, this rule is commonly waived for a reported authorization bill.	Unauthorized appropriations are not permitted. Exceptions are if the Senate has passed an authorization during that session; if an authorization is reported by any Senate standing committee, including Appropriations; or if an authorization is requested in the president's annual budget.
No legislation (policy) is permitted in an appropriations bill.	No legislation is permitted in an appropriations bill unless it is germane to legislative provisions in the House-passed bill.
No appropriation is permitted in an authorization bill. Floor amendments that propose appropriations are not in order in authorization bills.	There is no equivalent rule. (Recall that the House initiates appropriations bills and objects to Senate efforts aimed at circumventing this arrangement.)

bills. Moreover, the multistage process creates numerous opportunities to shape issues. Policy debates may be resurrected again and again in different contexts in either chamber.

An issue of some concern to the House is the committee assignment practices of the Senate. In the House, for both parties, service on the Appropriations Committee is, with few exceptions, an exclusive assignment. Senators, by contrast, may serve simultaneously on both authorizing and appropriating committees. In some instances, the same senator chaired both the authorizing committee (or relevant subcommittee) and the comparable appropriations subcommittee. In the 113th Congress, for example, Senator Tom Harkin, D-Iowa, chaired both the Health, Education, Labor and Pensions Committee and the counterpart appropriations subcommittee (Labor, Health and Human Services, Education, and Related Agencies). Fundamental bicameral imbalances are created, said a House Science chair, when senators

> are permitted to serve on both Committees. Inevitably, Members will prefer to legislate in appropriations bills (or the accompanying reports), which by their nature and by the rules of both Houses, are more protected from debate, amendment, and perfection than are corresponding authorization bills.[51]

Committee Rivalries. Another consequence of the two-step system is that it breeds continuing conflict between the authorizing and appropriating committees. In the judgment of Senator McCain, "It has become standard practice around here to forgo the authorizing process and simply do everything on appropriations. That is wrong and it needs to stop."[52] Moreover, he exclaimed, a handful of appropriators and their unelected staff often contravene the decisions of the authorizers.[53] As a House authorizing chair said, "My panel plays second fiddle to the appropriators, which is where power and money is" joined.[54] Authorizers understand that if they cannot enact their bills in a timely fashion, they cede their policymaking prerogatives to the appropriators.

Blurring the distinction between authorizations and appropriations is what some budget analysts call "backdoor" spending by the authorizers. They avoid the appropriator's "front door" by passing legislation that permits mandatory spending—the legal authority to draw funds from the Treasury—for governmental programs. Three common forms of backdoor authorization are (1) borrowing authority (a federal agency, for instance, is authorized by law to borrow specific sums of money from the Treasury or the public, through commercial channels, to build low-cost homes or make student loans); (2) contract authority (for example, a federal agency is statutorily permitted to enter into contractual agreements with private companies for the construction of municipal sewage treatment plants, but appropriations must be provided in the future to honor these commitments); and (3) entitlement authority (federal programs, such as Social Security and Medicare, that allow eligible recipients to be automatically entitled to federal payments). Entitlements are the fastest growing part of the federal budget. Appropriators often suggest that various entitlement programs be taken off automatic pilot and subjected to annual appropriations review.

Some observers suggest that another fiscal area deserves greater legislative scrutiny: "tax expenditures," which are under the jurisdiction of the tax-writing House Ways and Means and Senate Finance Committees. Tax expenditures are revenue losses to the federal Treasury from various tax write-offs, credits, or deductions to encourage certain kinds of behavior, such as providing tax relief to developers so they have an incentive to build low-cost public housing units. Tax expenditures may be "viewed as spending programs channeled through the tax system."[55] In 2012, the total value of tax expenditures and discretionary spending were almost identical: just over $1 trillion. The comptroller general of the United States referred to tax expenditures as a form of backdoor spending. "If you can't achieve something through a direct spending program," he noted, "there's an incentive for people to create a tax incentive to get it off the books [and] outside the budget process, but it really does have an impact on the bottom line."[56] A former chief of staff to the Joint Taxation Committee observed that lawmakers find tax expenditures "irresistible." Members can provide voters with "a government benefit *and* get credit for lowering their tax bills," and "portray themselves as tax cutters rather than big spenders."[57]

Worth noting is that committees' jurisdictional rivalries also involve the House's tax-writing Ways and Means Committee. The House adopted a rule in 1983 stipulating that no committee except Ways and Means may report tax or tariff proposals. This rule was first used in that year on October 23, when the Ways and Means chair raised a point of order against a proposition in a general appropriations bill that concerned the duty-free entry of certain products from Caribbean countries. The presiding officer sustained the point of order by ruling that the provision was "a tariff in violation" of House rules. Just as authorizing committees may not report appropriations, appropriating and authorizing panels may not report tax and tariff proposals. Twenty years later, at the start of the 108th Congress (2003–2005), the House amended its rulebook to prohibit, for general appropriations bills, tax or tariff floor amendments that limit ("None of the funds. . . .") the administration of a tax or tariff.

Exceptions to the Rules

Legislative (or policy) provisions that change existing laws find their way into appropriations bills notwithstanding the strictures of the rules—for example, if no member raises a point of order against the practice or if either chamber waives its rules. The House, by precedent, also permits legislative riders and unauthorized programs to be included in CRs that provide interim funding for agencies whose general appropriations bills have not been enacted by the start of the fiscal year.

Senate rules, unlike those for the House, grant wide leeway to appropriators to authorize projects, programs, or activities. "I'm not about to start hunkering down and running like a scared rabbit because somebody says it's got to be authorized," said a Senate Appropriations chair. "If this committee wants to authorize demonstration grants, it has the authority."[58] As the precedents state in *Senate Procedure*, the chamber's volume on this topic, "There is no prohibition in the Standing Rules of the Senate or the precedents against making appropriations for a project or program in the absence of an authorization." Further, legislative amendments in the Senate can be added to a House-passed appropriations bill (see germaneness section, p. 68) if the House measure contains legislation.

Limitation Riders. Limitation riders are the chief device legislators use to insert policy in appropriations measures. These riders are provisions in general appropriations bills or floor amendments to those measures that prohibit the spending of funds for specific purposes. Always phrased in the negative ("None of the funds provided in this Act shall be used for . . ."), limitation riders are based on scores of House and Senate precedents that collectively uphold the position that because either chamber can refuse to appropriate funds for programs that have been authorized, the two bodies can also prohibit the use of funds for any part of a program or activity.

House members and staff aides, for example, devote a great deal of time to carefully drafting provisions that make policy in the guise of limitations. For guidance they turn to the House rulebook, which is replete with precedents that interpret permissible from impermissible limitations. There are three basic criteria for permissible limitations. Limitations cannot (1) impose additional duties or burdens on executive branch officials, (2) interfere with their discretionary authority, or (3) require officials to make judgments or determinations not required by existing law.

Legislators sometimes add riders to appropriations bills because the riders may not survive as freestanding bills. As "must pass" vehicles headed to the White House, appropriations measures often attract extraneous policy matters, as mentioned earlier. But they become difficult to pass when controversial riders trigger partisan disputes, bicameral controversies, lobbying battles, or veto threats. A good example involved abortion.

The 1977 antiabortion amendment remains a classic example of the important effect a limitation can have on policy. The appropriations bill for the Department of Labor and the Department of Health, Education, and Welfare (HEW, now the Department of Health and Human Services) contained a limitation on the use of funds "to perform abortions except where the life of the mother would be endangered if the fetus were carried to term." A point of order was raised and sustained against that provision on the ground that it was legislation in an appropriations bill. The limitation required officials in the executive branch to determine when the life of a pregnant woman would be endangered. The language was then amended to read: "None of the funds appropriated by this Act shall be used to pay for abortions or to promote or encourage abortions, except when a physician has certified the abortion is necessary to save the life of the mother." Again, a point of order was raised that the amendment was legislation in an appropriations bill. And again the chair ruled in favor of the parliamentary objection, this time on the ground that the federal government employed many physicians and that they would be required to make life-deciding judgments. Finally, the sponsor of the proposal, GOP Rep. Henry Hyde of Illinois, said he had no choice but to offer the following language: "None of the funds appropriated under this Act shall be used to pay for abortions or to promote or encourage abortions." There was no point of order, because the amendment required no judgments by executive officials. The Hyde amendment was then adopted.[59]

When the Labor–HEW bill, containing the Hyde amendment, reached the Senate, Edward W. Brooke, R-Mass., offered an amendment that permitted abortions "where the life of the mother would be endangered if the fetus were carried to term, or where medically necessary, or for the treatment of rape or incest." Barry Goldwater, R-Ariz., said the amendment was legislation in an appropriations bill and raised a point of order. The Senate has its own procedural devices to obviate such points of order, however, and Senator Brooke used them successfully on the abortion issue. Senator Brooke raised a "defense of germaneness" before the presiding officer had ruled on the Goldwater point of order.

Germaneness. Senate Rule XVI requires that amendments—either proposed from the floor or offered by the Appropriations Committee—to general appropriations bills be "**germane** or relevant to the subject matter contained in the bill." If a lawmaker raises a point of order against an amendment on the ground that it is legislation (or policy) in a general appropriations bill, the member who proposed the challenged amendment can raise—prior to the chair ruling on the point of order—the question, or defense, of germaneness. Under Senate rules, the issue is then submitted to the entire membership for resolution by majority vote and without debate. If the Senate decides that the proposed amendment is germane, the point of order automatically fails and the amendment may be considered. Conversely, if the Senate determines that the amendment is not germane, it also fails. In the abortion case, the Senate declared Brooke's amendment germane by a 74-to-21 vote. In such situations, senators are really voting on the policy issue and not on the procedural question. In short, technical objections can be waived to achieve preferred policy outcomes.

A 1979 precedent states that the defense of germaneness applies only when the House, which originates appropriations measures, "opens the door" by including legislative language to which a Senate amendment might conceivably be germane. The Senate then has an "inherent right" to amend the House-passed provision. Since the mid-1990s the defense of germaneness, which can be raised for committee or floor amendments, has generally not been in play. Today, the Senate Appropriations Committee typically sends its own original appropriations bill to the floor for debate and amendment—that is, it no longer reports to the Senate the House-passed appropriations bill with a series of discrete Appropriations Committee amendments. Because no House language is before the Senate, the defense of germaneness is no longer available to senators whose amendments are challenged on the floor as being neither germane nor relevant, and thus in violation of Senate rules.

However, even when the Senate takes up a House-passed appropriations bill for amendment purposes, the test for raising the defense of germaneness is low. Senators usually vet their proposed amendments with the parliamentarian, who commonly states that they pass the threshold test because the House has opened the door. There have been few recent instances of the defense when the Senate took up the House bill. Especially noteworthy is the defense of germaneness raised on October 4, 2005, when Armed Services Chair John Warner, R-Va., attempted to add the defense authorization measure, crafted as an amendment, to the defense appropriations bill. Senator Ted Stevens, R-Alaska, the chair of the Defense Appropriations Subcommittee, raised a point of order that the authorization violated Senate Rule XVI as nongermane legislation on an appropriations bill. Senator Warner immediately raised the defense of germaneness. The next day, the Senate voted 49 to 50 to reject the defense, and the Warner amendment fell.

The Senate and House Rein in Policy Riders on Appropriations Bills. On March 16, 1995, the Senate opened the floodgates on adding policy riders to appropriations bills. It voted to overturn the correct ruling by the presiding officer that an amendment offered by Senator Kay Bailey Hutchison, R-Texas, dealing with the Endangered Species Act, constituted legislation on an appropriations bill and violated Senate Rule XVI. (A precedent established in this manner trumps Senate rules.) Thus was born the Hutchison precedent, and with it came a greater proliferation of riders to appropriations bills, many of them sponsored to highlight partisan agendas. As a result, it became difficult to enact appropriations bills in a timely manner. Finally, the Senate voted on July 26, 1999, as the Senate majority leader noted, to "reinstate rule XVI which would make a point of order in order against legislation on an appropriations bill."[60]

The House experienced a rapid increase in the number of limitation riders—from 43 in 1979 to 74 in 1982. Many of those dealt with social issues—particularly school busing, school prayer, and abortion. When these controversial issues were repeatedly bottled up in the authorizing committees, members who wanted action on them turned increasingly to limitation riders as a vehicle for forcing House consideration. Frustrated by the sharp controversies and long delays these limitations were causing, the House changed its rules in 1983 to restrict the opportunities for members to offer limitation riders to appropriations bills. The change authorized limitation amendments only if the motion to rise (or exit) from the **Committee of the Whole** was either rejected or not offered after the regular amendment process was completed on an appropriations bill. (The Committee of the Whole House on the state of the Union is the special forum into which the House transforms itself to consider the most important measures. It is discussed in Chapter 4.)

When Republicans took control of the House in the mid-1990s, they again changed House rules by allowing the majority leader or a designee to have precedence in offering the motion to rise. "The intent of the rule is to permit the offering of limitation amendments at the end of the reading [for amendment], subject only to a motion to rise offered by the majority leader or a designee."[61] The effect of this change is to enhance the majority leadership's control over the offering of limitation amendments.

PRELUDE TO BUDGET REFORM

Congress's continuing struggle to control expenditures precipitated a comprehensive overhaul of its budgetary process. Titled the Congressional Budget and Impoundment Control Act of 1974, the law came about largely for three reasons. First, the Appropriations Committees gradually lost control of budget expenditures as the legislative, or authorizing, committees turned to backdoor financing techniques to accomplish their policy objectives. Congress thus lacked a central body to coordinate budgetary decisions, relate governmental revenue to expenditures, or calculate the effect of individual budget actions on the national economy. National fiscal policy reflected whatever emerged from Congress's excessively fragmented budget process. Second, the annual deficit had been on an upward spiral, and many lawmakers believed that a revamped budgetary process would enable Congress to gain better control of fiscal decisions. Third, presidents sometimes took advantage of Congress's piecemeal process. President Richard Nixon clashed with Congress over national spending priorities and impounded (refused to spend) monies at unprecedented levels for programs initiated by Democrats in Congress. "Far from administrative routine," wrote a budget scholar, "Nixon's impoundments in late 1972 and 1973 were designed to rewrite national policy at the expense of congressional power and intent."[62]

The combination of these three factors, along with growing public concern about the state of the national economy, led to enactment of the landmark 1974 budget law. That act established a congressional budget process that encouraged coordination and centralization and enabled Congress to review the budget as a whole. However, Congress did not institute this fiscal reorganization by abolishing the authorization, appropriations, or revenue processes. Such an attempt would have pitted the most powerful committees and members against one another and jeopardized any chance of realizing substantive budgetary changes. Instead, Congress added another budget layer to those already in place in the House and Senate.

The 1974 Budget Act

Passage of the 1974 Budget Act had a major institutional and procedural effect on the legislative branch. Many of the act's original requirements have been modified in response to new developments. However, almost five decades later, it is still worthwhile to describe the main features of the act because they remain generally intact—the institutional entities; the timetable for budget decisions; the concurrent budget resolution (a measure that establishes Congress's framework for considering revenue, spending, and budget-related legislation); controls on back doors and impoundments; reconciliation; and enforcement of the concurrent budget resolution. The Senate's "Byrd Rule," an amendment to the 1974 act, will also be examined. Recent political strains on the budget process will be noted selectively, because they exemplify how difficult it has become to adhere to the budgetary framework during a time of spending austerity and partisan polarization. Some lawmakers even assert that the legislative budgetary system is broken, citing such things as missed deadlines, government shutdown threats, and overreliance on CRs.

New Institutional Entities

The budget act created three new institutional entities: the House Budget Committee, the Senate Budget Committee, and the CBO. The two budget committees have essentially the same functions, which include preparing annually a concurrent budget resolution; overseeing the CBO, which reviews (or "scores") the impact of existing or proposed legislation on federal expenditures; monitoring the revenue and spending actions of the House and Senate; assembling, if necessary, a reconciliation bill; and proposing budget process reform legislation.

The two panels, however, are constituted differently. The House Budget Committee is required to have a rotating membership; most members may not serve more than 8 years during a period of six consecutive Congresses. The committee must be composed of members drawn mainly from other **standing committees**, including five each from the Appropriations and Ways and Means Committees, one from the Rules Committee, and a leadership member from each of the two parties. Although the rotation allows many lawmakers to serve over time on this panel, it also has the effect of inhibiting cohesion (members' loyalty is to other committees), making it difficult at times for committee members to reach consensus on issues. Furthermore, the committee's fundamental task remains critical, visible, and often sharply partisan: producing a concurrent budget resolution that reflects differing Democratic and Republican views on the role and priorities of the national government. By contrast, the Senate Budget

Committee is like the other standing committees: It has no restrictions on tenure, and its members are not required to come from other designated committees.

The nonpartisan CBO is Congress's principal official source for independent information and analysis that it needs to evaluate budget, tax, and spending proposals. Among other things, the roughly 250 staff members of the CBO analyze budget, economic, and policy issues and make fiscal projections for the House and Senate Budget Committees and other congressional panels. The director of the nonpartisan CBO is appointed to a 4-year term. The selection or reappointment of the director alternates between House and Senate leaders.

Because budgetary issues dominate much of the activity on Capitol Hill, the CBO's role in providing "scoring reports" and "cost estimates" to the House and Senate Budget Committees and other panels is especially significant. The CBO scorekeeping unit measures the budgetary effects of the spending and tax plans of appropriators, authorizers, party leaders, and presidents. In doing so, it tracks pending and enacted spending and revenue measures to assist Congress in ensuring that they are within the budgetary limits set by the concurrent budget resolution or other budget laws. CBO evaluates budget proposals against a baseline—an estimate of future spending and revenue projections for a fiscal year, assuming no change in existing laws. As a CBO report phrased it:

> The baseline is intended to provide a neutral, nonjudgmental foundation for assessing policy options. It is not "realistic," because tax and spending policies will change over time. Rather, the projections . . . reflect CBO's best judgment about how the economy and other factors will affect federal revenues and spending under existing policies.[63]

Baseline estimates, like any budget plan, are only as accurate as the assumptions (inflation, unemployment, or economic growth rates) used in their formulation.

Scoring can be controversial and opens the CBO to criticism from lawmakers of both parties who do not like the results. For example, if the CBO calculates that bills of top priority to either party cost more than expected, Democrats or Republicans can be subject to partisan political attacks for sponsoring such legislation. For example, President Obama and congressional Democrats suffered a setback during the developmental stages of their health care reform plans when the CBO director testified that their health care proposals would not reduce the escalating costs of health care—as the Democratic leaders promised—but, rather, would make the problem worse by adding to the federal deficit. As the CBO director told the Senate Budget Committee:

> In the legislation that has been reported [by the chamber's health panel] we do not see the sort of fundamental changes that would be necessary to reduce the

trajectory of federal health spending by a significant amount. And on the contrary, the legislation significantly expands the federal responsibility for health care costs.[64]

The director's testimony fomented great dismay among Democrats. Congressional Republicans quickly attacked the high-spending health care plan, putting Democrats on the defensive and sowing discord in their ranks. Democrats made adjustments in the health legislation so it would not add to the deficit, and in the end the health overhaul bill was enacted into law.

Timetable

To promote order and coordination in the budget process, Congress established a budgetary schedule. But the timetable, set out in Box 2.3, is periodically subject to change, and Congress commonly misses some of the target dates. For example, Congress is supposed to enact its concurrent budget resolution on or before April 15 of each year, but that does not always happen.

Disagreements over priorities and among the chambers, parties, and branches account, in addition to other factors, for the missed deadlines. In 1998 Congress failed for the first time to adopt a budget resolution. The House and Senate passed dramatically different resolutions, and the GOP leaders of each chamber could not agree on how to allocate funding. Four years later, also for the first time ever, the Senate could not adopt a budget resolution, in part because of partisan clashes. In 2004, for only the third time in 30 years, Congress could not adopt a budget resolution, in part because of policy disputes over tax policy. In 2006, Congress was unable to adopt a budget resolution, as also occurred in 2010, 2011, and 2012, either because of choice, bicameral conflicts, or other factors. On occasion, there is debate about whether a budget resolution is even necessary, especially if it does not contain reconciliation instructions (see the section below on reconciliation). "My sense is that it's not of overwhelming importance," remarked a House member, because the significant budget battles are joined "when the appropriations bills hit the floors."[65] There is no legal penalty if Congress fails to adopt a budget resolution. Politically, however, the opposition party often criticizes the majority for being incapable of fulfilling a fundamental governing responsibility.

Several reasons account for House–Senate difficulties in passing budget resolutions (one chamber or the other may adopt them, but, as noted, not both in recent years). First, the two parties substantially differ over how to curb the escalating fiscal deficits (more than $1 trillion in 2012), which compounds their ability to agree even on a budgetary framework. Democrats favor a mix of spending cuts and tax hikes to reduce the deficit. Republicans support tax cuts, not revenue hikes, and endorse deep spending cuts in programs favored by many Democrats. Forging majority consensus on how to reduce the deficit has been so controversial that it has led to budgetary gridlock.

BOX 2.3 Congressional Budget Process Timetable

Deadline	Action to Be Completed
First Monday in February	President submits budget to Congress
February 15	Congressional Budget Office submits economic and budget outlook report to Budget Committees
Six weeks after president submits budget	Committees submit views and estimates to Budget Committees
April 1	Senate Budget Committee reports budget resolution
April 15	Congress completes action on budget resolution
May 15	Annual appropriations bills may be considered in the House, even if action on budget resolution has not been completed
June 10	House Appropriations Committee reports last regular appropriations bill
June 15	Congress completes action on reconciliation legislation (if required by budget resolution)
June 30	House completes action on annual appropriations bills
July 15	President submits midsession review of administration's budget to Congress
October 1	Fiscal year begins

SOURCE: Section 301 of the Congressional Budget Act.

Second, budget resolutions reflect the priorities of the majority party. Commonly, minority party lawmakers unanimously oppose adoption of the budget resolutions, which means that votes for passage must come from the majority side. Vulnerable lawmakers up for reelection are unlikely to vote for a budget resolution that would cause them electoral grief back home, such as proposing cuts to Medicare. The "political thinking is," declared Senator Tom Coburn, R-Ok., "we don't want any of our members to have to be recorded on things that might affect the next election."[66] Thus, there are occasions when budget resolutions are voted down.

Third, in 2011, the Senate waited on the budget reduction plan that the top leaders of the House and Senate were negotiating with Vice President Joe Biden. The Biden group was unsuccessful, as was the 2010 commission created by President Obama, in achieving consensus on a "grand bargain" to reduce the deficit and debt. These leadership efforts led to delays in taking up budget resolutions. As Senate Budget Chair Kent Conrad, D-N.D. noted: "We ought to give [the Biden group] a chance before we pass a budget resolution that may be required to implement any plan they come up with."[67]

Fourth, in August 2011, Congress enacted the Budget Control Act (BCA; see the discussion below), which, in the judgment of many congressional Democrats, served as the functional equivalent of the concurrent budget resolution. Nonetheless, Republicans such as Senator Jeff Sessions, Ala., the ranking member on the Budget Committee, repeatedly castigated the majority Democrats for failing their legal duty to adopt a budget resolution for more than 1,000 days. "That is absolutely wrong," responded Budget Chair Conrad. "Have [Republicans] already forgotten the Budget Control Act? Didn't they know what they were voting on? The Budget Control Act contains the budget for this year [2012] and next."[68] Subsequently, the Senate Parliamentarian undermined that argument by ruling that enactment of the BCA did not obviate chamber consideration of a concurrent budget resolution. Under a 1983 precedent, "any Senator can force a vote [on a concurrent budget resolution] after April 1, and only 51 votes are needed" to call up the resolution on the floor.[69] Although a motion to proceed to a budget resolution is not subject to extended debate, a Senate majority could vote to reject such a motion. However, there could be numerous attempts to call up various budget resolutions, which minority party members could introduce and have placed on the legislative calendar. On the other hand, if budget resolutions reach the floor, the minority party could use the available debate time (50 hours) to force votes on scores of electorally volatile issues.

When the House or Senate are late in passing, or cannot produce, a budget resolution, either chamber may adopt what is called a "deeming resolution," which is a simple House (H. Res.) or Senate (S. Res.) resolution. Its functional equivalent may also be included in other legislation, such as the defense appropriations bill or in a special rule reported by the House Rules Committee. A deeming resolution may reflect the budget levels and enforcement procedures contained in a budget resolution adopted several months earlier by one chamber but not the other. Absent a deeming resolution, the multiyear budget levels adopted in the prior year's budget resolution remain in effect (except for discretionary spending levels for the upcoming fiscal year), but they may be "badly out of date, thereby undermining their value as a realistic basis for enforcement of present policies."[70]

The 1974 Budget Act prohibits the House and Senate from taking up budgetary measures before adopting the budget resolution for the upcoming fiscal year. However, the House permits appropriations bills to be taken up after May 15 even if legislators still have not agreed on a budget resolution.

The House can set aside the requirement by unanimous consent or majority vote; the Senate may also set aside this mandate by majority vote. In short, the budget timetable is often more aspiration than attainment.

Concurrent Budget Resolution

Congress's annual budget process commonly centers on the adoption of a concurrent resolution. This measure is formulated by the House and Senate Budget Committees, which consider the views and estimates of numerous committees and outside witnesses. The resolution (if there is one) addresses fiscal aggregates, such as total federal spending for a fiscal year, sets multi-year targets for these aggregates, and consists of five basic parts:

- The budget resolution estimates what the federal government will spend in the upcoming fiscal year, and in at least the 4 following fiscal years (at least 5-year projections are required). For each fiscal year, the spending is expressed in terms of both budget authority and outlays.
- The total aggregate spending is then subdivided among 20 functional categories, such as national defense, agriculture, or energy. For each category, the spending indicates what Congress expects to expend in those substantive areas. The national defense function, for example, "is not the same as the Department of Defense; the function also includes programs administered by the Department of Energy. In addition, some DOD-administered programs are listed in other functions because their primary purpose is something other than defending the country."[71]
- Next, the budget resolution stipulates the recommended levels of federal revenue needed to pay for the projected spending during each of the fiscal years.
- Because the federal government consistently runs deficits, the budget resolution identifies the estimated deficits (or surpluses, which occur infrequently).
- The total outstanding public debt (savings bonds, Treasury securities, etc.) permitted by law is also specified for at least the 5-year period. The debt represents the accumulation of deficits (more spending than revenues) over time. (In 2012, Congress raised the statutory debt ceiling to more than $16 trillion. See further discussion on p. 78 under the heading "Raising the Debt Limit.")

Various substantive and strategic factors influence the length in years of the budget blueprint. One is the accuracy of the fiscal estimates. Five-year projections are likely to be more reliable than 10-year calculations. Another is avoidance of partisan criticism. If economic forecasts indicate escalating long-term deficits without any prospect of a budget coming into balance, congressional budget makers may opt for a 5-year rather than a 10-year spending projection. A 5-year rather than a 10-year tax cut projection could obscure the magnitude of long-term revenue losses while keeping the costs of the tax cuts within the limits set by the budget resolution. Conversely, a 10-year rather than a 5-year projection might highlight significant reductions in the deficit because of revenue gains expected from a growing economy.

The budget resolution sets the overall level of discretionary spending for the upcoming fiscal year. That figure represents the "top line" that the appropriators cannot exceed, although emergency supplemental appropriations are exempt from the spending limit. (In August 2011, as mentioned earlier, the BCA superseded the spending caps for discretionary spending in the concurrent budget resolution that the House adopted 4 months earlier. With the caps in place, the Senate decided not to take up a budget resolution.) Budget resolutions may also include an optional process called reconciliation, which changes tax policy or entitlement programs. Congress develops reconciliation legislation to ensure that spending and revenue decisions comport with the policies set forth in the budget resolution.

The budget resolution, in sum, is a fiscal blueprint that establishes the context of congressional budgeting; guides the budgetary actions of the authorizing, appropriating, and taxing committees; and represents Congress's spending priorities. Because it is not submitted to the president, it cannot be vetoed and does not carry legal effect. As a senator explained, a budget resolution is

> analogous to an architect's set of plans for constructing a building. It gives the general direction, framework, and prioritization of Federal fiscal policy each year. Those priorities then drive the individual appropriations and tax measures which will support that architectural plan.[72]

Those priorities, it bears emphasizing, can be quite controversial substantively and politically. For example, the House's budget resolution for fiscal year 2012 called for a partial privatization of Medicare. Every Republican but four voted for the budget resolution. GOP strategists issued warnings to the lawmakers that senior citizens would oppose the proposed change in Medicare. Congressional Democrats blasted Republicans for supporting the plan and targeted vulnerable GOP lawmakers in the November 2012 elections. A House Republican who strongly backed the transformation of Medicare expressed the view of many of his party colleagues: "There's no way you attack the deficit in my lifetime without dealing with the growth of Medicare. Do we get a political benefit from proposing a legitimate solution to a major policy problem? That's an open question" to be decided in the next election.[73] (The GOP lost eight House seats in the November 2012 elections.)

House Consideration of Budget Resolutions. Although a budget resolution is "privileged" business in the House, which means it can interrupt other business to be called up as a priority matter, it is long-standing practice to consider the resolution under a rule issued by the Rules Committee. Typically, the Rules Committee limits House consideration only to amendments that propose alternative budget plans (i.e., amendments that are a complete substitute for the Budget Committee's reported product). For example, the Rules Committee may report three major substitute budget plans to the floor: one proposed by the minority party and two others recommended by informal groups in the House, such as the Republican Study Committee or the Congressional Black Caucus. Generally, the Rules chair points out that the order of consideration is important, "because if any one of these pass, then the debate immediately ceases and we go right to final passage."[74] (Parliamentary principles stipulate that it is not in order to re-amend something that has already been amended. A substitute budget plan, if adopted, would amend the entire text of the concurrent budget resolution, leaving nothing left to further amend.) Unsurprisingly, fiscal alternatives are turned down. The majority's budgetary blueprint prevails on party-line votes, because that document reflects the priorities of the party in control.

Raising the Debt Limit. The Constitution (Article I, Section 8) grants Congress the power "to borrow Money on the credit of the United States." The Treasury Department is assigned responsibility to conduct the sale of debt instruments (interest-bearing bonds, for example) when the government needs to borrow money to pay its bills for such things as building the Panama Canal, fighting world wars, stimulating the economy, or funding its legal obligations and policy priorities. There has often been controversy surrounding consideration of debt ceiling measures, but they were nonetheless regularly enacted into law. (From 1975 to 2011, debt ceiling bills became law more than 60 times, with seven occurring in 1990 alone.[75]) Rarely was there ever a serious threat to allow the government to default on its debts, which would roil the financial markets, affect the value of the dollar, and produce other adverse economic consequences. In the 112th Congress, many GOP lawmakers were willing to take that risk to compel the Obama Administration to accept their agenda of limited government, with its tax and spending cuts. (In 2012, the debt ceiling—the accumulation of annual deficits over time—exceeded $16 trillion, an amount larger than the nation's gross domestic product, or the total value of its goods and services.[76])

Voting to raise the debt ceiling is difficult for many lawmakers, especially in a polarized era. Minority members lay off voting for increases in the debt ceiling, forcing the majority members to bear the burden of passing the legislation. Those voting to hike the debt ceiling understand that the other party will attack them in the next election as "big and irresponsible spenders." For instance, a GOP challenger ousted a Democratic incumbent with a series of attack ads that said: "[The Democrat] promised to cut wasteful spending, but voted for $14 trillion in debt."[77] To insulate members from such criticism, the House devised a creative procedure for approving raises in the debt ceiling without voting directly on such legislation. Called the "Gephardt Rule" after Richard Gephardt, D-Mo., who originated the rule in 1979, it stated that after successful adoption of the budget resolution, the House would be "deemed" to have also enacted legislation increasing the statutory debt ceiling. The Senate requires its members to cast a direct vote on debt-ceiling legislation, which the House now emulates.

The GOP-controlled 112th House terminated the "deeming" rule. A key goal of Republicans was to cut spending dramatically, and consideration of a stand-alone debt ceiling bill gave them the leverage to achieve that objective. GOP lawmakers invoked the logrolling strategy: In exchange for their votes to raise the debt ceiling, the president must support deep spending reductions in federal programs and agencies. In sum, if the deficit ceiling was to be raised so the government could borrow more money to pay its debts, the terms would be set by congressional Republicans. When Treasury Secretary Timothy Geithner provided Congress with a firm deadline (August 2, 2011) for lifting the debt ceiling, the stage was set for another round of deadline brinksmanship.

President Obama and House Democrats urged Speaker Boehner to schedule floor action on a "clean" deficit ceiling bill—a $2.4 trillion increase in borrowing authority—with no other provisions embedded in the measure. For their part, House Republicans insisted that there must be a dollar in spending cuts for every dollar authorized for borrowing. To hammer home their leverage in raising the debt ceiling, Speaker Boehner complied with President Obama's request, and that of congressional Democrats, for a clean vote on raising the debt ceiling by $2.4 trillion. The vote occurred on May 31, 2011, in unusual circumstances. First, it was brought up under a procedure (suspension of the rules; see Chapter 4) that guaranteed its defeat; suspension procedure requires a two-thirds vote for passage. Second, GOP leaders urged their party colleagues to defeat the bill they introduced. Every Republican voted for rejection. Some GOP lawmakers seemed to relish a government default to dramatize the need for spending discipline. Third, Democrats who urged such a vote "assailed Republicans for bringing it up," calling their action a political stunt and warning that the measure's "certain defeat might unnerve the financial markets."[78] The vote for rejection was 318 to 97. That vote, said House Ways and Means Chair Dave Camp, R-Mich., underscores that our party is "making clear that Republicans will not accept an increase in our nation's debt limit without substantial spending cuts and real budgetary reforms."[79]

Subsequently, throughout June and July, there were extensive negotiations among the president, House leaders, and Senate leaders, as well as scores of debt reduction discussions within each party. For example, Speaker Boehner and President Obama tried unsuccessfully for a "grand bargain" of cuts in discretionary spending and entitlement programs, as well as the elimination of many tax expenditures; the House and Senate produced rival deficit reduction plans, such as the House-passed (July 19) "cut, cap and balance" legislation—cut $ 2.4 trillion over a decade, cap spending statutorily, and constitutionally require a balanced budget. The GOP bill would block action on a debt-limit measure until the House and Senate enacted a constitutional balanced budget amendment. Vice President Joe Biden also led a bipartisan, bicameral group of lawmakers who tried without success to reach a 10-year deficit reduction deal composed of spending cuts, entitlement reforms, and revenue increases.[80]

To break the impasse over raising the debt ceiling and to diminish the increasing fear of a default, Senate GOP leader McConnell, in early July, offered a creative and complex procedure that was incorporated in what became the Budget Control Act (BCA) of 2011. President Obama signed the BCA into law (P.L. 112-25) on August 2, just a few hours before the Treasury Department would lose its authority to borrow. Senator McConnell's rationale for the BCA was to give "Obama the authority to order necessary additions to the debt ceiling over the next year and a half and [let] Congress off the hook by not requiring congressional approval of any increase."[81] Congress, however, could enact a measure—a joint resolution of disapproval—rejecting the debt increase, which the president could veto. On August 1, the House passed (269 to 161) the BCA legislation (H.R. 365) that raised the debt ceiling; the Senate followed suit the next day (74 to 26). However, the weeks of partisan debate and gridlock aroused public dismay and fueled citizen disgust with the legislative branch. Its approval ratings fell to the low teens and even single digits. Moreover, Standard and Poors, a well-known financial rating agency, reduced the Triple A rating for Treasury bonds because "the deficit deal fell short of what was needed and that 'political brinksmanship' boded ill for the future."[82]

The Budget Control Act. This act consisted of four overlapping parts: raising the debt ceiling in three stages, subject to blockage if Congress enacted a joint resolution of disapproval and proved able to muster in each chamber the two-thirds vote required to override the expected presidential veto; imposing spending caps on discretionary spending, with sequestration (automatic spending cuts) as an enforcement mechanism; creating a Joint Select Deficit Reduction Committee; and requiring each chamber to vote on a balanced-budget amendment to the Constitution.

Debt Limit Increase. Under the BCA, a three-stage procedure—designed in part to keep deficit reduction in the public eye—was established to raise the deficit ceiling and reduce spending anywhere from $2.1 trillion to $2.4 trillion. Moreover, the more than $2 trillion increase that was agreed to made unnecessary another controversial vote on a debt increase bill prior to the November 2012 elections, a vote the president and various lawmakers wanted to avoid. The first stage occurred upon enactment of the act: The Obama Administration automatically received $400 billion in additional borrowing authority. As part of the default-avoidance law, the president was obligated for each of the three stages to issue a certification that the government was within $100 billion of exceeding its borrowing authority. The president issued the first certification when he signed the BCA into law.

The second stage was another automatic boost of $500 billion in the debt ceiling, unless both legislative chambers enacted a joint resolution of disapproval to prevent the increase. The GOP House, on September 14, 2011, did adopt (232 to 186) a disapproval resolution. The Senate, however, turned down (45 yeas to 52 nays) a comparable disapproval resolution.

With the debt limit hiked by $900 billion, the other $1.2 trillion increase was to occur in one of three ways: (1) congressional approval of a joint resolution of disapproval, subject to either chamber's unlikelihood of overriding President Obama's veto; (2) enactment of legislation reported by the joint panel (see p. 83) that would increase the debt ceiling and also reduce spending by an equivalent $1.2 trillion; and (3) legislative adoption of a constitutional balanced budget amendment (see p. 84). Of the three, only the first approach proved viable. Success in raising the statutory debt limit commenced on January 12, 2012. The president certified in a message to the Speaker and the president of the Senate (the vice president) that the debt limit would increase by $1.2 trillion to more than $16 trillion unless Congress enacted a disapproval resolution within 15 calendar days. Six days later, the GOP House, in a largely symbolic vote (239 to 176), denied President Obama the new borrowing authority. The Senate voted not to take up a companion disapproval resolution. Hence, the hike in the debt ceiling went into effect.

Statutory Spending Caps. A deficit reduction of $917 billion in discretionary spending over 10 years occurred upon adoption of the BCA. For each year, the law established limits on total discretionary spending, subject to various adjustments for purposes such as emergencies, disaster relief, or military activities. Recall that caps on discretionary spending, as noted earlier in this chapter, are part of the concurrent budget resolution process.

Enforcement of the spending caps is achieved mainly through sequestration (the cancellation of budget authority) and other means (points of order, which can be waived in either chamber, against legislation that exceeds the caps). Sequestration covers, as the law provides, "security" (defense, homeland security, intelligence, and the like) and "non-security" accounts (infrastructure, education, environment, and so on). A few mandatory spending programs, such as farm subsidies, are also subject to sequestration. Various programs are exempt from sequestration, such as Social Security, food stamps, and most of Medicare. Sequestration would occur if, as determined by the Office of Management and Budget, Congress exceeds the spending cap for a fiscal year. The consequence would be automatic across-the-board cuts in the security and non-security accounts within 15 calendar days after Congress adjourns for a session. (The failure of the Joint Select Deficit Reduction Committee, see p. 83, meant that sequestration would deal only with spending cuts, not revenue increases.)

Under the BCA, sequestration is not triggered until January 2, 2013 (after the 2012 elections). The threatened cutbacks have provoked the ire and concern of many in the broad defense establishment, among others. Defense Secretary Leon Panetta stated that a sequestration in the range of $600 billion, on top of reductions of $487 billion over 10 years achieved by the BCA's limits on discretionary spending, "would inflict severe damage to our national defense for generations."[83] House Armed Services Chair Buck McKeon, R-Calif., urged the delay or repeal of sequestration. Senate Armed Services Chair Carl Levin, D-Mich., supported the threat of sequestration for defense as a way to force a compromise on dealing with the escalating deficit. "The purpose of sequester is to force us to avoid a sequester," he said. "It's like a nuclear weapon. Totally useless. It can't be used except to . . . deter." He added that sequestration for defense is "totally unacceptable."[84] More generally, Treasury Secretary Timothy Geithner has said that if sequestration occurred, the spending cuts would be "damaging" and "arbitrary."[85]

Although the president threatened to veto legislation that derails sequestration, his own fiscal year 2013 budget proposed a mix of revenue increases and spending cuts to avoid the automatic cuts. And with opposition to sequestration in both chambers and parties, Congress might delay or modify the automatic cuts by finding cost savings in other governmental areas. Delay is not acceptable to various lawmakers, however. "A commitment was made, an agreement was reached [in the BCA] and I think it is wrong . . . to say we're just not going to honor the commitment," declared House Democratic leader Nancy Pelosi, Calif.[86] If Congress does not postpone or prevent sequestration before January 2, 2013, federal agencies will have to execute indiscriminate across-the-board spending cuts equally divided between domestic and defense programs, something that would no doubt require months of intensive work by federal personnel.

Noteworthy is that if Congress did nothing in 2012 to block sequestration or to extend the Bush-era tax cuts of 2001, 2003, and 2005, the "debt added over the next ten years will be reduced from a projected $11 trillion to about $3.7 trillion," a dramatic combination of spending cuts and tax hikes.[87] Neither is likely to occur, in part because either or both decisions might push a recovering economy into a recession. Thus, many of the fiscal issues that bedeviled Congress in the 112th Congress are set to return in the 113th Congress, such as raising the statutory debt ceiling and passing each of the dozen annual appropriations measures on time to avoid a massive CR. Whether Congress is able to act on these issues responsibly, with minimal acrimony, brinksmanship, and gridlock, is likely to depend on the outcome of the November 2012 elections. "The gridlock [in Congress] is as bad as it's ever been," exclaimed Paul Ryan, R-Wis., the chair of the House Budget Committee. "We need the American people to break it."[88] However, the electorate did not provide a message or mandate that was clear-cut rather than mixed and murky. Commentators suggested that the "lame duck" session following the November 2012 elections would produce a "perfect storm" of controversial fiscal issues: extending the Bush-era tax cuts, spending reductions under sequestration, acting on another omnibus CR, and raising the debt ceiling (see below). A "lame duck" session means that the members of the old 112th Congress will be the decision makers during this November–December 2012 time period, rather than the lawmakers who will compose the new 113th Congress starting in January 2013.

Joint Select Deficit Reduction Committee. The BCA established a 12-member bipartisan, bicameral Joint Select Deficit Reduction Committee. It had broad authority to deal with budgetary matters (revenue and spending) with the goal of producing a deficit reduction proposal over 10 years of at least $1.2 trillion, if not more. The panel's formation, dubbed a "super-committee" by pundits, underscored the inability of the regular legislative process to produce significant deficit reduction. The panel's product was to be considered under expedited procedures that restricted debate and amendment in both chambers. Its work was to be completed by November 23; a final report, with recommendations, issued by December 2; and the House and Senate required to vote on those recommendations by December 23, 2011.

On November 21, the co-chairs of the joint committee announced the panel's inability to achieve its goals. A consequence of failure was the automatic triggering of sequestration: $1.2 trillion in deficit reduction over 10 years with roughly $600 billion chopped from security accounts and $600 billion from non-security accounts. Various reasons were offered for the joint panel's dismal result, but one in particular concerned the GOP's reluctance to increase taxes and Democratic resistance to entitlement reforms. As Rep. Jeb Hensarling, R-Tex., the joint panel's co-chair, suggested: "We could not bridge the gap between two dramatically competing visions of the role [of] government."[89]

In the end, after President Obama and Speaker Boehner failed to reach a deficit accord, Senate GOP leader McConnell and Vice President Biden developed a compromise package to avert the so-called "fiscal cliff"—major tax increases to be triggered after December 31, 2012, with the expiration of the Bush-era tax cuts and, also at the start of the new year, indiscriminate across-the-board spending reductions in defense and domestic agencies and programs (called "sequestration"). Both actions would occur automatically unless barred by law. Technically, after midnight on December 31, 2012, Congress did go over the cliff. Two hours later, however, the Senate—on New Year's Day—passed the compromise package by an 89-to-8 vote. The House resisted for a time in agreeing to the Senate-passed product, but at 11 p.m. on January 1, 2013, it adopted the measure (257–166). Most Republicans (151) voted against the package, including Majority Leader Eric Cantor, Va., while most Democrats (172) voted for it.

The McConnell–Biden compromise, among other things, prevented tax increases for most Americans, except for individuals earning more than $400,000 and families earning more than $450,000. Tax rates on high earners also increased from 35% to 39.6%. Sequestration was also delayed for 2 months. As for an increase in the statutory limit on borrowing, the Treasury secretary informed Congress that the government reached its $16.4 trillion limit on December 31, 2012, but "signaled that he could juggle the books for about two [more] months before the nation runs out of cash to pay its bills."[90] In short, the 113th Congress confronts early in 2013 a series of critical deadlines: the debt-ceiling increase (in February, Congress extended the government's borrowing authority until later in 2013), sequestration (March 1), and the expiration (March 27) of a government funding law that, unless renewed by Congress, would trigger a government shutdown.

Balanced Budget Constitutional Amendment. The debt-avoidance law required both chambers to vote on a constitutional balanced-budget amendment between October 1 and December 31, 2011. This provision bolstered the support of conservative lawmakers for enactment of the BCA and placed members on record for political purposes in the upcoming November elections. Both chambers complied with the statutory requirement, but the proposal, even with the support of some Democrats, did not clear Congress. Constitutional amendments require a high threshold for congressional passage: a two-thirds vote from each chamber.

Senate Consideration of Budget Resolutions. Senate procedure for considering budget resolutions differs from that for other legislation in four major ways. First, floor action is regulated by the statutory requirements of the 1974 act, as well as by **unanimous consent agreements** negotiated by the party leadership. Second, concurrent budget resolutions are privileged, which means they can be taken up by a non-debatable motion to proceed to consideration. Because of their privileged character, budget resolutions are commonly taken up by unanimous consent.

Third, the 1974 act imposes a germaneness requirement on amendments to budget resolutions. The act permits the germaneness standard to be set aside, but it requires at least 60 votes, instead of a simple majority, to obtain the waiver. (The Senate, unlike the House, has no general germaneness rule. See Chapter 7 on Senate floor procedure.)

The chair of the Budget Committee watches for senators offering amendments outside the jurisdiction of the panel, which on their face are nongermane. Why the concern? Because if the Senate adopts what are termed "corrosive" amendments by the Senate parliamentarian, the budget resolution (and a related conference report)—as well as any reconciliation measure—is at risk of losing its privileged status (easy access to the floor, limits on debate, and so on). For example, a senator offered a detailed amendment to the budget resolution protecting middle-income taxpayers from tax increases. The Senate Budget chair pointed out that his panel lacks "the authority to tell committees of jurisdiction with specificity what they are to do," and if the amendment was adopted it would "put at risk the privileged status of the resolution itself." The presiding officer agreed, stating: "The Senator is correct."[91]

Fourth, budget resolutions carry a 50-hour statutory debate limitation, which means that they cannot be filibustered to death. Although debate is limited, *consideration* of the resolution is not. As a result, amendments can be taken up and voted on after the 50 hours, but without real debate. This circumstance often leads to so-called "vote-a-ramas" in which senators may over several days "cast back-to-back votes on a dizzying array of dozens of amendments," many designed to provide campaign ammunition (so-called "gotcha amendments") for the next election.[92]

> [One] vote-a-rama began at 11:15 a.m. [on] March 13 and continued until 2 a.m. March 14, with lawmakers on the floor for most of the session. Votes [by informal agreement] were separated by two minutes of "debate," with the sponsor having one minute to make his or her case and an opponent given one minute to respond.

Vote-a-rama amendments are generally nonbinding and germane "sense of the Senate" proposals. The overall number of amendments to budget resolutions has escalated over the years from an annual average of 21 during the first 20 years of the 1974 Budget Act to an annual average of nearly 80 during the next dozen years, with a peak of 106 in 1998.[93]

Another type of amendment—establishing "deficit neutral reserve funds"—has also proliferated in recent years, in part because various lawmakers have tried to discourage nonbinding "sense of the Senate" amendments. The deficit-neutral reserve fund amendments could allow authorizing committees with direct spending authority to report legislation that increases funding for various policy areas (transportation, education, and so on), provided the bills (1.) do not add to the deficit and (2.) the fiscal totals in the budget resolution are revised at the aggregate level (e.g., overall revenues) and for specific committees. As a senator explained:

> On the speculation that Congress may enact legislation on a particular issue— perhaps "immigration," "energy," or "health care"—a reserve fund acts as a "placeholder" to allow the Senate Budget Committee to later revise the spending and revenue levels in the budget so that future deficit-neutral legislation would not be vulnerable to budgetary points of order.[94]

The Budget Crosswalk. When the House and Senate pass budget resolutions that contain different aggregate and functional totals, which is normal practice, the disagreements usually have to be resolved by a conference committee. The conferees prepare a report that distributes the total agreed-on expenditures for the year among the relevant House and Senate committees with direct and discretionary spending authority. This allocation procedure is called a budget crosswalk. The crosswalk is necessary because Congress employs the functional category designations developed by the

White House's Office of Management and Budget. These designations do not correspond exactly to many House and Senate committees, with their overlapping jurisdictions.

Two allocation provisions of the 1974 Budget Act are especially important to the House and Senate Appropriations Committees and their dozen subcommittees. Section 302(a) provides the two appropriations committees with a spending allocation consistent with the amount recommended in the budget resolution. The two panels may not report appropriation bills that cumulatively exceed their overall aggregate allocations, enforceable through points of order on the floor (which may be waived, however). Under section 302(b), the House and Senate Appropriations Committees each subdivide their spending allocation among their 12 subcommittees. (If the concurrent budget resolution is not passed by the required April 15 date, informal allocations are made but are not enforceable, unless a deeming resolution has been adopted.) The subcommittee allocations are reported by the appropriations committees to their respective chambers. These allocations also are enforceable by members raising points of order against spending bills that exceed a subcommittee's assigned dollar amount. (These provisions can be waived in both chambers but require 60 votes in the Senate.)

When the GOP-controlled House adopted its budget resolution for fiscal year 2013, it provided $19 billion less for discretionary spending than stipulated in the BCA of 2011. The Democratic Senate adhered to the spending caps defined in the BCA. The result: The spending allocations assigned to the subcommittees of the House and Senate Appropriations Committees under the Section 302(b) requirement were not in general alignment. The House's decision to highlight how determined it is to reduce federal spending set the stage for a "conflict with the Senate over both the total spending level and how to distribute the funds."[95] This conflict increases the odds for both delay in the enactment of the regular appropriations bills and the need to approve one or more CRs.

Reconciliation

Reconciliation, as noted earlier, is an optional procedure that enables Congress to implement its comprehensive fiscal policy (as reflected in the budget resolution) by changing tax and entitlement laws. The two-step process is designed to reconcile the parts with the whole or, put differently, to bring existing law into conformity with the current budget resolution. In general, reconciliation is used to reduce spending, primarily through entitlement savings, and either to increase revenues or cut taxes. It does not address funding that is established in annual appropriations bills. The appropriations committees are bound by the discretionary spending limits set forth in the budget resolution (or the 2011 BCA). First employed in 1980, reconciliation is used more often than not because it has proven to be an effective device for achieving budgetary savings.

The first step in reconciliation calls for congressional approval of a budget resolution that instructs House and Senate committees to report by a certain date legislation making changes in spending, revenues, or a combination of the two (such as a certain amount of deficit reduction) on programs and agency operations. An example of House reconciliation directives is presented in Box 2.4. The panels' recommended budget changes, which are supposed to meet or exceed the amounts designated for each committee in the resolution if multiple committees are involved, are transmitted to the respective House and Senate Budget Committees. The second step involves the respective budget panels packaging the recommendations into an omnibus reconciliation bill, followed by floor action in each chamber. The budget committees cannot make substantive changes in the proposals received from each instructed committee. If only one committee is provided instructions, it reports its recommendations directly to the floor.

In a major and dramatic use of reconciliation, President Ronald Reagan in 1981 persuaded Congress to employ the procedure to achieve massive cuts in domestic programs (totaling about $130 billion over 3 years). Never before had reconciliation been employed on such a grand scale. The entire process was expedited in a manner that short-circuited regular legislative procedures. A highly charged atmosphere produced a legislative result (enactment of an omnibus reconciliation bill), wrote Howard H. Baker Jr., R-Tenn., then Senate majority leader, "that would have been impossible to achieve if each committee had reported an individual bill on subject matter solely within its jurisdiction."[96] Reconciliation forced nearly all House and Senate committees to make unwanted cuts in programs under their jurisdiction. Given their policymaking significance, these bills, not surprisingly, are shepherded through Congress by party leaders and key committee leaders.

The irony is that Congress's budget process, designed in 1974 to advance and reassert the legislative branch's power of the purse, was captured by the White House in 1981 and used to achieve President Reagan's objectives. However, reconciliation can be used by either branch or party provided it has the votes to implement its objectives. In 1995 the GOP-dominated Congress employed reconciliation to try to scale back the size of government, cut taxes, and balance the budget in 7 years. "Its efforts," observed one onlooker, "led to two historic federal government shutdowns, thirteen stopgap measures, several presidential vetoes, and ultimately failed to produce a meaningful fiscal agreement with the White House."[97]

On several occasions reconciliation directives provided for more than one reconciliation bill. In 1996, for cxample, the directive provided for a three-stage process in which a tax cut bill would be considered in conjunction with two measures drafted to achieve savings in Medicare, welfare, and other entitlement programs. In 2005, as another example, reconciliation instructions governed three measures: a spending bill, involving cuts in mandatory programs as part of the GOP's effort to demonstrate fiscal discipline;

BOX 2.4 House Reconciliation Directives

This excerpt from the concurrent budget resolution for fiscal year 2010 stipulates reconciliation instructions for three House committees. These standing committees are the principal House panels that deal with health care issues: Energy and Commerce, Ways and Means, and Education [and the Workforce]. The Speaker took the lead in melding their products into a nearly 2,000-page bill and mobilizing the votes to narrowly win passage of the landmark bill on a 220 to 215 vote.

SEC. 202. RECONCILIATION IN THE HOUSE.

(a) *HEALTH CARE REFORM.—*

(1) The House Committee on Energy and Commerce shall report changes in laws to reduce the deficit by $1,000,000,000 for the period of fiscal years 2009 through 2014.

(2) The House Committee on Ways and Means shall report changes in laws to reduce the deficit by $1,000,000,000 for the period of fiscal years 2009 through 2014.

(3) The House Committee on Education and [the Workforce] shall report changes in laws to reduce the deficit by $1,000,000,000 for the period of fiscal years 2009 through 2014.

(b) *INVESTING IN EDUCATION.*—The House Committee on Education and [the Workforce] shall report changes in laws to reduce the deficit by $1,000,000,000 for the period of fiscal years 2009 through 2014.

(c) *SUBMISSIONS.*—In the House, not later than October 15, 2009, the House committees named in subsections (a) and (b) shall submit their recommendations to the House Committee on the Budget. Upon receiving all such recommendations, the House Committee on the Budget shall report to the House a reconciliation bill carrying out all such changes without any substantive revision.

*****

SOURCE: House Report 111-89, Conference Report to accompany H. Con. Res. 13, *Concurrent Resolution on the Budget for Fiscal Year 2010* (March 27, 2009), 13–14.

---

a tax bill, concerning $70 billion in revenue cuts; and a bill to raise the debt limit. (Senate precedents stipulate that only three reconciliation bills—tax, direct spending, and debt limit—are in order. The House has no such precedent but observes the Senate's interpretation.)

Reconciliation in the House is considered under the terms of a rule from the Rules Committee. Procedurally, reconciliation bills are focused on the Senate because measures governed by this process are treated differently than are other bills and amendments under terms outlined in the 1974 Budget Act. They cannot be filibustered (there is a statutory time limit of 20 hours for debate), passage requires a simple majority, and amendments must be germane and deficit neutral (tax cuts or spending increases must be "offset" by equivalent revenue increases or spending reductions). It is not surprising that proposals likely to arouse controversy in the Senate are sometimes attached to filibuster-proof reconciliation bills.

Reconciliation aroused large controversy during President Obama's first year in office. A major overhaul of the nation's health care system was a top domestic priority. Congressional Democratic leaders successfully included reconciliation instructions in their budget resolution. The instructions specified that the relevant House and Senate committees would have until October 15, 2009, to report a health reconciliation bill, although this deadline is advisory rather than an enforceable date.[98] It is "a date that does not have legislative consequences," remarked Senate Budget Chair Conrad. "You can do reconciliation before Oct. 15. You can do reconciliation after Oct. 15."[99] (Absent reconciliation, Obama's health care overhaul measure would be subject to regular Senate procedures.)

Senate Republicans and several prominent Senate Democrats opposed the use of reconciliation for such major legislation. "If you're going to talk about reconciliation, you're talking about something that has nothing to do with bipartisanship," declared a GOP senator. "You're talking about the exact opposite of bipartisan. You're talking about running over the minority, putting them in cement, and throwing them in the Chicago River."[100] (Worth noting is that Republicans employed reconciliation to enact President George W. Bush's tax cut legislation when they were in the majority.) Senator Byrd, a principal author of the 1974 Budget Act, also expressed dismay that a procedure designed for deficit reduction could be used to enact major legislation. "We have seen one party, and then the other, use this process to limit debate and amendments on [partisan legislation] and non-budgetary provisions that otherwise may not have passed under the regular rules."[101]

Senate Republicans threatened to shut down the Senate through dilatory actions if Democrats employed reconciliation on President Obama's health care priority. Congressional Democrats decided not to use reconciliation on health care, but they recognized its leveraging potency. Speaker Nancy Pelosi, D-Calif., stated that "if bipartisanship did not yield health care reform, then we'll move to reconciliation."[102] On December 24, 2009, Senate Democrats mustered the 60 votes required to amend and pass the House's earlier enacted health reform bill (H.R. 3560). Seemingly, the landmark health care bill was destined soon to be enacted into law after both chambers resolved their differences on health care. However, on January

19, 2010, in a stunning special election upset in Massachusetts, Republican Scott Brown won the Senate seat held by Democrat Edward Kennedy. The result: Senate Democrats no longer could muster the 60 votes required to end filibusters solely from their own ranks. The fate of major health care reform quickly turned murky.

After weeks of negotiations among the Democratic leaders of both chambers and the White House, an agreement was reached in mid-March 2010 to use a "two-bill" strategy. The House would pass without any change H.R. 3590 as amended by the Senate and then immediately enact a second bill—a filibuster-proof reconciliation measure (H.R. 4872)—that would "correct" the amendments to H.R. 3590 agreed to by the Senate but strongly opposed by House Democrats. This approach avoided both a bicameral resolution process and any further action on H.R. 3590 in the Senate, where Senator Reid no longer had the 60 votes required to end a talkathon. Moreover, it was the fastest way to get comprehensive health reform to President Obama, who signed the bill into law on March 23, 2010. A week later, both chambers also enacted H.R. 4872, which was also when the president signed the reconciliation bill into law (March 30). During the health care strategy sessions, lawmakers from both chambers raised the issue of the Byrd Rule.

The Byrd Rule

The Byrd Rule, named after Senator Robert C. Byrd of West Virginia, was adopted on a temporary basis in 1985; 5 years later it became permanent as an amendment to the 1974 Budget Act. The rule states that reconciliation provisions must be consistent with the goals of the reconciliation instructions. Reconciliation requires committees with policymaking responsibilities—the tax-writing and authorizing committees—usually either to raise revenues or cut mandatory spending programs. However, these panels sometimes report policy provisions that have no effect on the budget, and may even worsen the deficit. Reconciliation has been used, for example, to expand Medicaid coverage, reinstate the broadcast fairness doctrine, and provide funds for the trade adjustment assistance program. Such provisions are inserted in reconciliation bills in part "because the budget committees are specifically prohibited from making any substantive changes in the recommendations from each committee."[103] Significantly, committees include these policies in reconciliation bills because they are considered under expedited procedures.

To underscore, the objective of the Byrd Rule is to exclude extraneous matter in reconciliation measures. Maximizing its potency, the rule can be waived only by a three-fifths vote of the Senate. Similarly, 60 votes are required to overturn a ruling of the Senate's presiding officer that a provision in a reconciliation bill (or a floor amendment to it) is extraneous.

What is extraneous, however, is not always easy to determine. The Byrd Rule itself provides six definitions of what is extraneous (and several exceptions to what is considered extraneous). The rule stipulates, for example, that a provision is extraneous if it does not produce a change in outlays or revenues or is outside the jurisdiction of the committee that recommended the provision for inclusion in the reconciliation measure. To apply such definitions in practical cases can be complex.

> The application of the [Byrd] rule can be tortuous. Take food stamps, for example. The House approved $7.3 billion in extra spending for food stamps in its reconciliation bill; the Senate did not. Conferees . . . agreed to include up to the House amount in the conference report, but [Senate] Republicans hope to strip it out, arguing that it violates the Byrd rule because it would force the [Senate Agriculture] committee to miss its deficit-cutting target. The Senate Agriculture Committee's target was $3.2 billion. [Senate] Democrats argued behind the scenes that it was impossible to apply the Byrd rule to a conference report. What was the relevant "committee?" House Agriculture? Senate Agriculture? The conference committee? The House's Committee of the Whole?[104]

In the end, the Senate parliamentarian agreed that the Byrd Rule could not be applied to this case. In doing so, he cleared the way for the food stamps provision to remain in the conference report. Needless to say, the Senate parliamentarian—an unelected congressional official—comes under enormous pressure from senators in both parties as he gives reconciliation bills a "Byrd bath," determining which provisions are extraneous and which are not.[105]

The constraints of the Byrd Rule gave some pause to Democratic leaders who decided to use, as noted earlier, reconciliation on Obama's health care overhaul plan. The Democratic leaders were worried that GOP senators might challenge numerous health care provisions as "Byrd droppings." A former staff director of the Senate Budget Committee explained:

> On something as massive as health care reform, there will be a number of provisions that don't have direct budgetary consequences. . . . Those Byrd violations [points of order] would be made and you'd end up making Swiss cheese out of the legislation.[106]

In the end, but to no avail, opponents of health care reform employed a number of other procedures (points of order, motions to return the health plan to committee, and the like), as well as employing a "vote-a-rama." After the statutory time limit of 20 hours expired on the follow-on health reconciliation measure (H.R. 4872), the Senate considered 42 amendments during a 2-day vote-a-rama.[107]

Because the Byrd Rule also applies to House–Senate conference reports, it is sometimes a source of conflict between the chambers. House committee chairs charge that the Byrd Rule, "by allowing Senators to rise on points of order and strike extraneous provisions [from conference reports], gives the Senate the power to dictate House actions."[108]

Controls on Impoundments

Title X of the 1974 Budget Act permits Congress to review executive impoundments of appropriated funds. The act divides impoundments into two categories—deferrals (a temporary delay in the expenditure of funds to achieve savings made possible through greater efficiencies or to provide for contingencies) and rescissions (the permanent cancellation of budget authority)—which are considered under separate procedures. Presidents are obligated to inform Congress of their proposed deferrals and rescissions and to set forth the reasons for them. The GAO is authorized to review these special messages to ensure that impoundments are not classified improperly.

To rescind budget authority, the president submits a message to Congress indicating the reasons for the rescission. Over the next 45 days of continuous session (days when Congress is in session, not calendar days), Congress may then pass a rescission bill that cancels all, part, or none of the amount requested by the president. If both houses fail to pass a rescission bill before the expiration of the 45-day period, the president must make the funds available for obligation. In short, inaction produces action: the release of appropriated funds. (The rescission procedure is seldom followed because the appropriations committees, after informal consultations with executive agencies, include the agreed-on rescissions in general appropriations bills.)

Enforcement of the Budget Resolution

The House and Senate enforce the goals and policies set forth in the budget resolution through devices such as scorekeeping; spending allocations to committees and subcommittees; reconciliation; budgetary information and analysis provided by the CBO and other relevant panels, including the Joint Taxation Committee, which scores revenue measures; the monitoring role of the Budget Committees; and raising points of order (parliamentary objections) on the House or Senate floor. Points of order under the 1974 Budget Act are either substantive or procedural in character. Substantive points of order are raised to ensure compliance with the budget resolution. For example, a lawmaker can challenge a floor amendment that would cause the appropriations committee to exceed its allocation of new discretionary spending authority. Procedural points of order are raised to ensure compliance with features of the 1974 Budget Act and companion legislation. The House and Senate permit waivers of any points of order. The House usually does this in a rule reported by the Rules Committee. The Senate, by contrast, must waive most points of order by a three-fifths vote of all senators. Senators, then, find themselves often in search of the 60 votes needed to set aside some feature of the budget act so they can accomplish a policy objective, especially when a broad consensus exists to pass a bill or amendment.

EVOLUTION OF THE BUDGET PROCESS

Congressional procedures and politics are forever changing, and the congressional budget process is no exception. In the mid-1980s and later, Congress enacted significant statutory changes in its budget process. These changes emerged from a new political climate: the politics of deficit reduction. After Ronald Reagan took office in 1981 the annual deficits soared. Reagan's objectives were clear and principally threefold: slash domestic spending, increase defense expenditures, and cut taxes. However, the revenue losses caused by the tax cuts, combined with rising defense expenditures and insufficient reductions in other areas, soon produced triple-digit deficits in the $200-billion-to-$300-billion range. Never before had the nation seen such huge deficits during peacetime and during an economic expansion—that is, the one that followed the 1982 economic recession. Congress acted to stem the river of red ink through legislation. (Needless to say, that river has turned today into an ocean of red ink.)

The 1985 Balanced Budget and Emergency
Deficit Control Act (Gramm-Rudman-Hollings)

As the national debt—recall that it is the accumulation of annual deficits—mounted after 1981, numerous proposals were put forth to deal with the escalating deficits. One notable initiative was put forth in the mid-1980s by senators Phil Gramm, R-Tex., Warren Rudman, R-N.H., and Ernest Hollings, D-S.C., and enacted into law. Its core feature was establishment of annual statutory deficit reduction targets that, if achieved, would over time lead to a balanced national budget. If Congress did not meet the targets, the president would have to sequester funds—that is, impose automatic across-the-board spending cuts evenly divided between defense and domestic programs. (The BCA of 2011 borrowed the idea of sequestration from this law.) The dire prospect of a "fiscal train wreck" was supposed to create an incentive for Congress and the president to decide how best to achieve deficit reduction. But, in the end, the plan did not work, and deficits continued to climb. Congress exempted 70% of the budget from sequestration, and budgetary gimmicks were employed to meet the statutory targets, at least on paper. In response, Congress enacted another major budgetary reform—the Budget Enforcement Act (BEA) of 1990, which was amended several times before it expired on October 1, 2002.

The Budget Enforcement Act of 1990

This act once again changed the fiscal procedures of Congress. The law was intended to shift Congress's attention from deficit reduction to spending control. Thus, it removed the threat of automatic, across-the-board reductions ("sequestration") if conditions beyond Congress's control—inflation, a worsening economy, or emergency funding for crises or disasters—pushed the deficit upward.

Two enforcement mechanisms undergirded the BEA. First, it set spending caps, or limits, for discretionary spending. The spending caps could be changed, but Congress and the president would have to agree to the modification. If Congress exceeded the spending limits, the law provided for across-the-board reductions to bring spending in line with the caps. However, a loophole in the law enabled Congress and the president to escape tight spending caps. If Congress and the president designated expenditures above the cap as "emergency" (a flexible term that implies something unforeseen or unpredictable) spending, they were exempt from the limits imposed by the BEA. When this law was negotiated in 1990 between congressional leaders and the first President George H. W. Bush, "some questioned the lack of flexibility to accommodate unforeseen natural or man-made disasters," so decision makers agreed to the safety valve of "emergency" spending. However, Congress and the president often viewed emergency spending as "free money" because "it is not controlled or offset vis-à-vis other federal spending."[109] For example, Congress used the emergency designation to finance the constitutionally required 2000 decennial census.

Second, the BEA subjected tax and entitlement programs to a new "pay-as-you-go" (PAYGO) procedure. Any tax reductions or any increases in direct spending (entitlement) programs had to be offset by tax hikes or reductions in other direct spending programs. The enforcement threat was across-the-board cuts in direct spending programs not exempt under BEA. As the chief counsel of the Senate Budget Committee explained: "The 'pay-as-you-go' label implies that Congress and the President may cut taxes or create [new direct spending] programs—that is 'go'—if they also agree to provide offsetting increased revenues or spending reductions—that is 'pay.'"[110] In short, lawmakers had to find "payfors" or offsets if they wanted to cut taxes or devise a new—or increase an existing—entitlement program.

The onset of a projected $5.6 trillion surplus era in the late 1990s uncapped a pent-up desire among many lawmakers to spend money on various programs and activities and cut taxes. Here was a case of fiscal projections driving policymaking, even though the money was not yet in the bank. The requirements of the BEA were either waived or ignored as the psychology of plenty took hold in Congress. Many lawmakers viewed the budgetary restraints embedded in the BEA as an out-of-date device for dealing with fiscal surpluses. As a result, in 2002 the law was allowed to expire.

However, under a so-called "elastic clause" provision (Section 301) in the 1974 Budget Act, each chamber's budget resolution may "require such other procedures, relating to the budget, as may be appropriate to carry out the purposes of this Act." Under Section 301, the Senate created its own PAYGO rule in 1993, which remains in effect today with various modifications. PAYGO rules were adopted as amendments to the House rulebook in the 110th and 111th Congresses. As a complement to the PAYGO rules of each chamber, President Obama successfully urged Congress in 2010 to pass a statutory PAYGO measure. "Emergency" spending, which triggered bicameral controversy in 2011 regarding offsets for disaster relief, as mentioned earlier, is not subject to the "payfor" requirements of PAYGO.

When the 112th Congress began in January 2011, the GOP-controlled House adopted rules that replaced PAYGO with a new CUTGO ("cut-as-you-go") rule. The new rule, like PAYGO, applies to direct (mandatory) spending (the purview of the authorizing committees) but not to discretionary spending, which is governed by the appropriations process. However, unlike PAYGO, which allows spending increases for mandatory programs to be offset (finding other budget savings) from spending cuts or revenue increases, CUTGO requires offsets for increases in mandatory programs to come from spending cuts only, not revenue increases. Thus, legislation cutting taxes—a key GOP principle—is not subject to the CUTGO rule even though the budget deficit could increase. Given heightened interest in a reexamination of the budgetary process (for instance, shifting to a 2-year budget cycle or converting the concurrent budget resolution into a joint resolution, giving it the force of law if signed by the president), what remains unclear is whether existing or proposed budgetary rules or laws—absent broad political and popular support—can curb the ever-increasing deficit and debt.

THE CHALLENGE AHEAD

Today, the nation confronts annual deficits of more than $1 trillion and a national debt that exceeds $16 trillion. Interest payments on the debt will continue to escalate into the hundreds of billions of dollars annually, and that translates into money that cannot be used for unmet domestic needs and other policy priorities. The country is on a dangerous, unsustainable path. Even after the fragile economy recovers fully, federal spending is projected to rise substantially faster than revenues and the government will be forced to borrow ever-increasing amounts. Without policy changes, federal debt will rise to unmanageable levels, which will push interest rates up, endanger our prosperity, and make us increasingly vulnerable to the dictates of our creditors, including nations whose interests may differ from ours.[111]

The director of the nonpartisan CBO added, "We as a society will either have to pay more for our government, accept less in government services and benefits, or both. For many people, none of these choices is appealing—but they cannot be avoided for very long."[112]

During this period of sharp partisan polarization in Congress, the choices outlined by the CBO director will not be easy to make. Both parties have fundamentally different views of the size and scope of the federal government. As broad generalizations, many Republicans state that federal deficits are the result of huge overspending, so governmental expenditures must be reduced significantly. Democrats contend that the deficits are largely due to the George W. Bush–era tax cuts, two unpaid-for wars (Afghanistan and Iraq), and the Great Recession. Hence, they advocate raising taxes on the wealthy. From the people's perspective, many favor limited government but strongly support the federal programs that benefit them. These and other complications underscore the challenge before Congress of finding the right balance between fiscal belt-tightening (e.g., terminating duplicative programs) and investing in programs (e.g., research and development) that promote the nation's future prosperity.

The nation's worrisome fiscal situation also comes at a time when an "entitlement revolution" is under way. "Call it government by ATM.," remarked an analyst. "You walk up, hit the buttons and the cash to which you're entitled pops out."[113] Seventy-six million baby boomers (those born between 1946 and 1964) are either starting to retire or fast approaching retirement. One think tank estimates that more than 10,000 baby boomers "will become eligible for Social Security benefits each day over the next two decades."[114] An aging and longer living population—thanks to new drugs and medical and technological developments—will produce an explosion of expenditures in the country's three major entitlement programs: Social Security, Medicare, and Medicaid. Already, projections show that in fiscal year 2013 the combination of Social Security and Medicare will exceed all discretionary spending.[115] Trustees of the Social Security Trust Fund reported that assets will be depleted by 2033, several years earlier than previous projections. After that, payroll tax revenues will cover about three-quarters of the scheduled benefits for seniors through 2085.[116]

Demographers project a smaller workforce, which means fewer workers contributing payroll taxes to cover the retirement needs of the elderly. There is a rough consensus that various options, albeit controversial, can effectively address the projected shortfall of money to cover the promised retirement benefits to retirees. They include such changes as raising the retirement age, increasing the payroll tax rate (in 2011 and 2012, the payroll tax rate was reduced to encourage more private spending and thus job creation), cutting benefits for future retirees, and reducing or eliminating Social Security benefits for the wealthy. To constrain the escalating cost of Medicare, Medicaid, and health care in general, however, is an even greater challenge because of its complexity, its significant impact on every family and the economy, and the controversy it engenders among so many individuals and entities—doctors, hospitals, insurance companies, the two political parties, employers, families, patients, and more. Meanwhile, the Medicare Trust Fund is projected to be solvent only until 2024, given the enrollment of more seniors in the program and the increase in expenditures for the beneficiaries.[117] As President Obama stated:

> Make no mistake: the cost of our health care is a threat to our economy. It's an escalating burden on our families and businesses. It's a ticking time-bomb for the federal budget. And it is unsustainable for the United States of America.[118]

In sum, given the government's long-term fiscal commitments and projections of rising deficits, Congress faces a serious dilemma in providing adequate funding for competing priorities (entitlements versus discretionary spending and, within the discretionary category, defense and homeland security versus domestic spending) and making higher interest payments on the ever-rising national debt. As an analyst for a nonpartisan think tank put it, "What we have done in the last several years is decide we can cut taxes, fight two wars, increase homeland security, expand government entitlement benefits, and leave the bill to future generations."[119] The government's overspending is funded to a large extent by borrowing from foreign nations, such as China and Japan, and there is no guarantee that this will continue indefinitely. Indeed, much of the discussion surrounding taxes, spending, debt, or deficits is crystallized by a question posed by Rep. Barney Frank, D-Mass.: "What is the appropriate level of public activity in our society?"[120] Or as Federal Reserve Chair Ben Bernanke put it: "The fundamental decision that Congress, the administration and the American people must confront is how large a share of the nation's economic resources to devote to federal government programs."[121] Democrats and Republicans provide different answers to this basic question. Kenneth Kies, a Washington-based tax expert, explained the partisan divide this way:

> Should we have a smaller federal government with lower taxes and fewer regulations that would leave people to largely take of themselves, as Republicans generally favor? Or should the federal government help prop up the elderly, the poor, and low-income workers as most Democrats believe?[122]

NOTES

1. Quoted in *Roll Call*, July 29, 2002, 4.
2. If the nation's economy is performing poorly with persistent joblessness, federal spending will also continue to spike as fewer federal taxes are collected and to pay for more unemployment and welfare expenditures.
3. House Committee on the Budget, *Congressional Control of Expenditures*, January 1977, 6. The study was prepared by Allen Schick.
4. There is no single "federal budget" document. Instead, the federal budget consists of the enactment annually of numerous budgetary measures, such as revenue and spending (appropriations) legislation. Collectively, the passage of these discrete bills constitutes the annual federal budget.
5. *Congressional Record*, April 4, 2000, S2055.
6. Michael Tomasky, "Washington: Will the Lobbyists Win?" *New York Review of Books*, April 9, 2009, 18.
7. *Congressional Record*, September 22, 2008, S9173.
8. *Congressional Record*, September 29, 2006, S10634.
9. Ibid., December 14, 2011, S8612.
10. David Ignatius, "Life in Budget Limbo," *Washington Post*, November 1, 2007, A21.
11. Russell Berman, "GOP Abandons Speaker's Plan to Split Funding Bills," *The Hill*, May 12, 2011, 12. Boehner's idea was also to split multiagency appropriations

bills, such as Labor and Health and Human Services, and allow the House to take up funding for each department separately.

12. Kerry Young and Sam Goldfarb, "House GOP Offers Three-Week CR," *CQ Weekly,* March 4, 2011, 582.

13. Ibid., "Shutdown Averted at 11th Hour," *CQ Weekly*, April 11, 2011, 806.

14. Ibid., "Funding Clears Despite Grumbles," *CQ Weekly*, April 18, 2011, 864.

15. *Congressional Record*, September 23, 2011, S5936.

16. See Don Wolfensberger, "A Debate Worth Having on Emergency Offsets," *Roll Call*, October 11, 2001, A-40.

17. Lisa Mascaro, "House Rejects Government Funding Bill as Shutdown Looms," *Los Angeles Times*, September 22, 2011, online edition.

18. Richard E. Cohen, "Senate Passes Compromise on CR," September 27, 2011, 4.

19. David Fahrenthold, "House Passes Budget Bill by Doing Nothing," *Washington Post*, September 30, 2011, A3.

20. Kerry Young, "House May Include CRs in 'Megabus,'" *CQ Today*, December 8, 2011, 6.

21. *Congressional Record*, November 17, 2011, H7746.

22. Stan Collender "Agony, Agita and Anguish Over Appropriations," *Roll Call*, October 4, 2011, 46.

23. Donald Marron, "Does Congress Thrive on Brinkmanship? Watch This Fall," *Christian Science Monitor*, September 19, 2011, 23.

24. Jake Sherman and Burgess Everett, "Republican Dysfunction Exhibit A: Highways," *Politico*, March 2, 2012, 15.

25. John William Ellwood, ed., *Reductions in U.S. Domestic Spending* (New Brunswick, NJ: Transaction Books, 1982), 21.

26. Eamon Javers, "Dirty Secrets of the 'Black Budget,'" *Business Week*, February 27, 2006, 41.

27. *Congressional Record*, February 9, 2006, S980.

28. Paul Singer, "CRS Finds Fewer Earmarks, Higher Cost," *Roll Call*, December 12, 2009, online edition.

29. Reid Wilson, "In Pitch for Bigger Tent, Barbour Calls on GOP to Accept Centrists," *The Hill*, May 21, 2009, 6.

30. *Congressional Record,* May 6, 2009, H5279. See also Susan Crabtree, "Flake Threatens New Assault on Earmarks," *The Hill,* July 16, 2009, 6.

31. Eric Lichtblau, "Lobbyist Helps a Project He Financed in Congress," *New York Times*, January 22, 2012, 18. See also T. W. Farnam, "Report: Ex-Lawmakers Lobbied for Groups That Got Earmarks," *Washington Post*, January 28, 2012, A16.

32. *Congressional Record,* July 6, 2009, S7133. House rules (Rule XXI, Clause 9) also require a statement from the appropriate committee that legislative matters do not contain a list of any congressional earmarks, limited tax benefits, or limited tariff benefits. For an example, see *Congressional Record,* July 15, 2009, H8185.

33. John Stanton, "Panel Lays Down Law: Earmarks Are Over," *Roll Call*, May 2, 2011, online edition.

34. Kimberly Kindy, "Lawmakers Try to Slip in Hundreds of Earmarks," *Washington Post*, November 30, 2011, A1.

35. *Congressional Record*, December 16, 2011, S8720. See also Scott A. Frisch and Sean Q. Kelly, *Cheese Factories on the Moon: Why Earmarks Are Good for*

America (Boulder, Colo.: Paradigm, 2011), and Ron Nixon, "Special Funds in Budget Called New Earmarks," *New York Times*, February 6, 2012, A13.

36. *Congressional Record*, July 9, 2009, H7909.
37. Humberto Sanchez, "Inouye Decries Partisan Fighting," *Roll Call*, October 4, 2011, 37.
38. Alexander Bolton, "Some in GOP Want Return to Earmarks," *The Hill*, February 9, 2012, 10.
39. Billy House, "The Case for Pork," *National Journal*, October 29, 2011, 46.
40. Jennifer Steinhauer, "The Formerly Routine Is Now the Tendentious," *New York Times*, March 24, 2012, A12.
41. Carl Hulse, "How Budget Battles Go Without the Earmarks," *New York Times*, February 27, 2011, 16. See also Burgess Everett, "Highways With No Earmarks? A Rough Road," *Politico*, January 25, 2012, 1.
42. Nancy Ognanovich, "Senators to Propose Permanent Ban on Practice of Congressional Earmarking," *Daily Report for Executives*, December 1, 2011, A-14. On February 4, 2012, the Senate voted down an amendment to make the earmark ban permanent. See also Paul Kane, "Minor Bill Is Transformed Into Major Reform Package," *Washington Post*, February 5, 2012, A7.
43. Bolton, "Some in GOP Want Return to Earmarks," 10. On February 7 and 8, 2012, *The Washington Post* carried two lengthy, front-page investigative stories by David S. Fallis, Scott Higham, and Kimberly Kindy about lawmakers who won earmarks that allegedly benefited their property holdings, as well as their immediate families. See, for example, "Public Projects, Private Interests," February 7, 2012, A1.
44. Kevin Bogardus, "Obama Administration Draft Memo Could Shed Light on 'Lettermarking,'" *The Hill*, November 9, 2011, 15. In 2008, President George W. Bush issued an executive order titled "Protecting American Taxpayers From Governmental Spending on Wasteful Earmarks." The president directed executive agencies to ignore nonstatutory earmarks, such as those contained in the committee reports of the House and Senate Appropriations Committees.
45. Richard Munson, *The Cardinals of Capitol Hill* (New York: Grove Press, 1993), 6.
46. Everett Somerville Brown, ed., *William Plumer's Memorandum of Proceedings in the United States Senate, 1803–1807* (New York: Macmillan, 1923), 490.
47. Robert Luce, *Legislative Problems* (Boston: Houghton Mifflin, 1935), 425–426.
48. Louis Fisher, "The Authorization–Appropriations Process in Congress: Formal Rules and Informal Practices," *Catholic University Law Review* (Fall 1979): 53.
49. Congressional Budget Office, "Unauthorized Appropriations and Expiring Authorizations," January 2011 (http://www.cbo.gov/publication/22004).
50. Quoted in Alan Ota, "Spending Bills May Be Democrats' Plan B," *CQ Today*, April 27, 2007, 8.
51. *Operations of the Congress*, hearing before the Joint Committee on the Organization of Congress, 103rd Cong., 1st sess., January 26, 1993, 70.
52. *Congressional Record*, July 29, 2005, S9368.
53. Ibid., September 21, 2011, S5798.
54. Corine Hegland, "Hyde-Bound It Isn't," *National Journal*, June 28, 2003, 2106.
55. See *Tax Expenditures: Compendium of Background Material on Individual Provisions* (Washington, DC: U.S. Government Printing Office, 2008). This

committee print is prepared by the Congressional Research Service for the Senate Committee on the Budget (S. Prt. 110-667).

56. Heidi Glenn, "Tax Expenditures Transparency Vital, Says Comptroller General," *Tax Notes*, March 6, 2006, 1038.

57. Lori Montgomery, "Tax Breaks Pile Up, Grow Most Costly," *Washington Post*, September 18, 2011, A14 (italics in the original). See also Jonathan Nicholson, "Do Tax Expenditures Really Work? Experts Say Not Enough Data to Tell," *Daily Report for Executives*, October 25, 2010, 1–6.

58. Jon Healey, "Lautenberg Moves to Reduce Transportation Earmarks," *Congressional Quarterly Weekly Report*, October 2, 1993, 2625.

59. Fisher, "Authorization–Appropriation Process in Congress," 74–75. The House considered the issue on June 17, 1977, and the Senate on June 29, 1977. See also Roger H. Davidson, "Procedure and Politics in Congress," in Gilbert Steiner, ed., *The Abortion Debate and the American System* (Washington, DC: Brookings, 1982), 30–46.

60. *Congressional Record,* July 26, 1999, S9171.

61. Ibid., January 4, 1995, H37.

62. Allen Schick, *Congress and Money* (Washington, DC: Urban Press Institute, 1980), 46.

63. Cited in Marc Labonte, "Baseline Budget Projections: A Discussion of Issues," *CRS Report*, February 3, 2006, 1.

64. Jonathan Nicholson, "CBO's Elmendorf Warns Health Reform Efforts May Not Reduce Costs or Lower Premiums," *Daily Report for Executives*, July 17, 2009, A-14. See also Suzy Khimm, "Little CBO Packs an Authoritative Punch," *Washington Post*, July 29, 2011, A7; Stan Collender, "Gingrich Wants to Kill the CBO Messenger," *Roll Call*, November 15, 2011, 34; Philip Joyce, *The Congressional Budget Office* (Washington, DC: Georgetown University Press, 2011); and Erik Wasson, "Questions Sparked on CBO Reform," *The Hill*, October 19, 2011, 1.

65. David Baumann, "Does a Budget Really Matter?" *National Journal*, April 15, 2006, 39.

66. *Congressional Record*, May 26, 2011, S3408.

67. Ibid., May 25, 2011, S3316.

68. Ibid., January 24, 2012, S63–S66 (Sen. Sessions), S60 (Sen. Conrad).

69. Meredith Shiner and Steven Dennis, "Senate Democrats Wary of Budget Fights," *Roll Call*, April 9, 2012, online edition.

70. Stan Collender, "Budget Battles: The Future Is Now," *NationalJournal.com*, January 21, 2003, 2–3.

71. *Congressional Record*, March 2, 2000, S1050.

72. *Congressional Record*, March 2, 2000, S1050.

73. Glenn Thrush and Jake Sherman, "House GOP Budget Still Explosive," *Politico*, May 23, 2011, 18.

74. *Congressional Record*, May 17, 1995, H5107.

75. See *Fiscal Year 2012 Historical Tables* (Washington, DC: U.S. Government Printing Office, 2010), 143–144.

76. The nation's debt consists of two parts: the public debt, which is "the sum of the Treasury securities held by individuals, financial institutions, and foreign governments," and intragovernmental debt. This is the "sum of Treasury bonds held by agencies of the federal government, principally the Social Security Trust

Fund." See John Steele Gordon, "A Short Primer on the National Debt," *Wall Street Journal*, August 29, 2011, A17.

77. Gregory Korte, "Paying Price of Debt-Limit Votes," *USA Today*, July 18, 2011, 4A.

78. Jackie Calmes, "Pressing Obama, House Bars Rise for Debt Ceiling," *New York Times*, June 1, 2011, A1.

79. Humberto Sanchez and Billy House, "Debt Vote Marked by Political Theater," *National Journal Daily*, June 1, 2011, 7. See also Russell Berman, "Debt Vote Set to Trap Democrats," *The Hill*, May 25, 2011, 1.

80. See, for example, Paul M. Krawzak, "Uneasy Next Steps on Deficit," *CQ Weekly*, November 28, 2011, 2504–2507; Joseph J. Schatz and Sam Goldfarb, "No Grand Bargain on Debt Ceiling," *CQ Weekly*, July 25, 2011, 1628–1631; and Bob Woodward, *The Price of Politics* (New York: Simon & Schuster, 2012).

81. John Cranford and Joseph J Schatz, "In Whose Hands?" *CQ Weekly*, July 18, 2011, 1546.

82. *CQ Weekly*, January 9, 2012, 29.

83. Charles Hoskinson, "Panetta Plan Cuts $259B From DOD Budget by 2017," *Politico*, January 27, 2012, 6.

84. Sara Sorcher, "Levin: Sequester Cuts Can't Be Split to Exclude Defense," *NationalJournal.com*, January 26, 2012, 11.

85. Nancy Cook, "Hard Promises," *National Journal*, March 17, 2012.

86. Jared Serbu, "GOP Plan Cuts Fed Pay, Workforce to Save DoD From Sequestration," *FederalNewsRadio.com*, February 3, 2012, 2.

87. Judd Gregg, "Autopilot Is Driving US to Ruin," *The Hill*, February 13, 2012, 27. Gregg is a former chair and a ranking member of the Senate Budget Committee who voluntarily retired from the Senate at the end of the 111th Congress.

88. John Aloysius Farrell, "Divided We Stand," *National Journal*, February 24, 2012, 13.

89. "The Last Best Hope," *The Economist*, November 26, 2011, 39.

90. Lori Montgomery and Paul Kane, "Senate Continues Marathon Push to Avoid Cliff," *Washington Post*, December 30, 2012, A8.

91. Mark Preston, "'Vote-a-Rama' Keeps Wearing Senate Down," *Roll Call*, March 26, 2003, 1.

92. John Stanton, "Specter Seeks to Tame 'Bedlam,'" *Roll Call*, April 2, 2008, 20. For data on the number of amendments offered after the expiration of debate time, see "Vote-a-Rama Begins," National Journal's *CongressDailyAM*, April 3, 2009, 8.

93. Senator Arlen Specter, *Testimony Before the Senate Budget Committee*, February 9, 2009, 4.

94. Senator Arlen Specter, *Testimony Before the Senate Budget Committee*, February 9, 2009, 4.

95. Anne L. Kim, "House Panel Sets Fiscal 2013 Spending Cap at $19 Billion Less Than Senate," *CQ Today*, April 26, 2012, 15.

96. Anita Krishnakumar, "Reconciliation and the Fiscal Constitution: The Anatomy of the 1995–96 Budget Train Wreck," *Harvard Journal on Legislation* (Summer 1998): 489.

97. Paul Krawzak and Bart Jansen, "Reconciliation Deadline Not So Drop-Dead After All," *CQ Today*, September 23, 2009, 1.

98. Steven T. Dennis and Tory Newmyer, "Another Day, Another Deadline Missed," *Roll Call*, October 14, 2009, 1.

99. Jonathan Nicholson, "Budget Chairmen Both Leery of Using Reconciliation for Cap-and-Trade Legislation," *Daily Report for Executives*, March 18, 2009, A-24.

100. Robert C. Byrd, *Testimony Before the Senate Budget Committee*, February 9, 2009, 3.

101. David Clarke and Paul Krawzak, "Negotiators Face Post-Recess Quandary on How Aggressively to Move," *CQ Today*, April 3, 2009, 3.

102. Alex Wayne, "Health Care Plans Stuck in Legislative Limbo," *CQ Today*, February 8, 2010, 1.

103. George Hager, "The Byrd Rule: Not an Easy Call," *Congressional Quarterly Weekly Report*, July 31, 1993, 2027.

104. Walter Alarkon, "Healthcare Reform's Fate Lies in the Hands of Parliamentarian," *The Hill*, April 23, 2009, 3.

105. Peter Cohn, "Hill Veteran Sees Pitfalls in Using Budget Reconciliation," *CongressDailyPM*, March 6, 2009, 3.

106. Karen Foerstel, "Byrd Rule War Erupts Once Again," *Roll Call*, February 24, 1994, 13.

107. Kathleen Hunter, "Republicans Prepare Amendments, Budget Points of Order," *CQ Today*, March 4, 2010, 27.

108. Robert Keith, "The Budget Reconciliation Process: The Senate's 'Byrd Rule,'" July 2, 2010, 1.

109. Gail Russell Chaddock, "War Costs Irk the Congress," *Christian Science Monitor*, February 21, 2006, 11. See also John Cranford, "The Defense Deceit," *CQ Weekly*, January 30, 2006, 262.

110. Brian Riedl, "PAYGO Is an Unworkable Gimmick," *Washington Times*, June 23, 2009, A4.

111. Senator Pete Domenici and Dr. Alice Rivlin, *Testimony Before the Senate Budget Committee*, March 15, 2011, 1.

112. Lisa Mascaro and Christi Parsons, "Congress Returns, and So Does the Partisan Budget War," *Los Angeles Times*, September 5, 2011, online version.

113. Matthew Miller, "The Big Federal Freeze," *New York Times Magazine*, October 15, 2000, 5.

114. See Jon Ward, "Public 'Scared' of Overtaxing System," *Washington Times*, August 11, 2009, B1. The think tank is the Peter G. Peterson Foundation, a bipartisan, nonprofit entity.

115. David Harrison, "Rise in Entitlement Spending Draws New Focus," *CQ Today*, February 28, 2012, 1.

116. Kristen Ricaurte Knebel, "Social Security Trustees' Report Moves Projected Insolvency Up Three Years, to 2033," *Daily Report for Executives*, April 24, 2012, G-7. See also David Harrison, "Trustees Report on Entitlement Funds Give GOP Boost in Debt Debate," *CQ Today*, May 16, 2011, 4.

117. Steve Teske, "Medicare's Hospital Trust Fund Solvent Until 2024, Trustees' Report Says," *Daily Report for Executives*, April 24, 2012, A-21.

118. Theodore R. Marmor and Jonathan Oberlander, "Health Reform: The Fateful Moment," *New York Review of Books*, August 13, 2009, 69.

119. Gail Russell Chaddock, "GOP's Family Feud Over Spending," *Christian Science Monitor*, May 22, 2006, 10.
120. *Congressional Record*, July 16, 2002, H4749.
121. Michael Barone, "Big Government Becomes the Battle-Line Issue," *Washington Examiner*, August 12, 2009, 12.
122. Nancy Cook, "The 51 Percent," *National Journal*, February 11, 2012, 14.

CHAPTER 3

Preliminary Legislative Action

I NTRODUCING A BILL when the House or Senate is in session is a deceptively simple procedure. House members drop their bills into the hopper, a mahogany box near the clerk's desk at the front of the chamber. Senators generally submit their proposals and accompanying statements to clerks for printing in the *Congressional Record*, or they may introduce their bills from the floor. Various assumptions are associated with the introduction of many bills, such as that a problem exists and action is required by the national government to address it rather than leaving the matter to the states or private sector to resolve. Further, lawmakers introduce legislation with different motives (policy, electoral, constituent, and so on) in mind. With gasoline prices on the increase, House and Senate members will typically introduce hundreds of bills on energy-related issues, in part for parochial reasons. Woe to lawmakers who return to their district or state and cannot answer this question from voters: "So, what have you done about energy costs?"[1] A disarming response: "I have introduced a bill on that very topic!" Members, too, introduce partisan legislation as a way to draw contrasts with the other party's policy approach or to activate and energize supporters in their electoral base.

But it is one thing to introduce a bill and quite another to move it through the lawmaking process. For that reason, lawmakers contemplate a variety of pre-introductory considerations, especially for major bills, which are subject to the most scrutiny and debate. Timing is important. Should a controversial bill be introduced early or late in a legislative session? For example, a bill likely to be filibustered in the Senate might be introduced early to allow plenty of time to overcome any talkathon. Naming the legislation might also be important. Upset with the large bonuses received by Wall Street executives whose firms received federal bailout funds, Vermont Senator Bernie Sanders introduced a bill named the "Stop the Greed on Wall Street Act."[2] An attractive title, such as the Freedom of Information Act, the American Dream Restoration Act, or an acronym such as USA-PATRIOT Act—"Uniting and Strengthening America by Providing Appropriate Tools Required to Intercept and Obstruct Terrorism"—could bring a bill useful media attention. "People are recognizing that interesting bill names can help bills get noticed and remembered," noted a House staffer.[3] In what might be a first for Congress, Don Young, R-Alaska, a former chair of the House Transportation and Infrastructure Committee, named a transportation bill after his wife Lula, titling the measure the Transportation and Equity Act: A Legacy for Users, or TEA-LU.[4]

The political reality today is that a cottage industry of people devotes considerable time to crafting catchy acronyms for legislation. To cite a few more: the JOBS Act (Jump Start Our Business Startups), the REINS Act (Regulations From the Executive in Need of Scrutiny), and the SWEEP Act (Stop Waste by Eliminating Excessive Programs). Bill titles are also used for clearly partisan message sending, such as the Reducing Barack Obama's Unsustainable Deficit Act, or Reversing President Obama's Offshore Moratorium Act. As an analyst pointed out, "If Republicans can take a silly name like Repealing the Job-Killing Health Care Law Act and make it stick, they've helped communicate its meaning and importance to audiences they're trying to reach."[5] GOP critics of the Violence Against Women Act noted that it was a difficult measure to oppose because of the title. "Obviously, you want to be for the title," remarked Senator Roy Blunt, R-Mo. "If Republicans can't be for it, we need to have a very convincing alternative."[6]

Opponents of legislation also play the name game in an attempt to attach an unattractive label to a measure. For example, legislation to revamp the Defense Department's personnel system was called the "civil service destruction act" by the House minority whip.[7] Disputes involving the taxation of estates led proponents of estate tax abolishment to dub it the "death tax," while opponents of abolition called it the "Paris Hilton Benefit Act."[8] Eric Cantor, R-Va., the House majority leader, unveiled a measure that consisted of six bills, four of which the chamber had previously passed by huge margins. The other two also enjoyed wide support. Cantor's bill was entitled the aforementioned JOBS Act. House minority whip Steny Hoyer, D-Md., mocked Cantor's acronym by labeling it "Just Old Bills."[9]

Another strategic consideration: Should companion bills (identical legislation) be introduced concurrently in the House and Senate to expedite legislative action? How many cosponsors (members who join together to introduce a bill) should be sought, and who should they be? As Senator Edward M. Kennedy, D-Mass., once said about conservative Senator Strom Thurmond, R-S.C., during their service in the Senate: "Whenever Strom and I introduce a bill together, it is either an idea whose time has come or one of us has not read the bill."[10] There is no limit to the number of House or Senate members who may cosponsor legislation. A large number of cosponsors—or if ideological opposites join together as did Kennedy and Thurmond—might encourage committee chairs to take some action (hearings, for example) on the measure. Electoral considerations also influence cosponsorship. Senator Claire McCaskill, D-Mo., for example, faced a tough November 2012 reelection. Part of her strategy for winning was to cosponsor bills with GOP colleagues "as a means to build credibility with [her] states' conservative voters."[11] In a technological and participatory departure, House GOP leader Eric Cantor, Va., released an app dubbed "Citizen Cosponsor" that allows individuals to indicate support for legislation by their electronic "cosponsorship."[12]

Worth noting is that the 112th House amended its rules on opening day to require all representatives to attach to every bill or joint resolution they introduce a signed "statement citing as specifically as practicable the power or powers under the Constitution authorizing the enactment of that bill or joint resolution."[13] The purpose of this rules change, according to GOP lawmaker Greg Walden of Oregon, is to ensure that "Congress respects the limits imposed on it by the founding document."[14] The House clerk is not to accept for introduction any bill or joint resolution that lacks a constitutional authority statement. These statements are printed in a separate section of the *Congressional Record* (see Box 3.1) and made available electronically to the public. A study conducted by the conservative House Republican Study Committee found that many of these statements are vague and short. The GOP group established that in 2011, of the more than 3,000 measures introduced, 616 simply listed "Article I, Section 8," which enumerates Congress's powers and duties. The vagueness of so many justifications prompted Speaker Boehner's spokesperson to say, "The statements of constitutional authority are a start, and only a start, towards reestablishing the proper place for the federal government in American life."[15]

Considerable pre-introductory jockeying on major bills also may take the form of behind-the-scenes battles between or among committees. Because committees' jurisdictional mandates overlap, several panels may want to lay claim to bills on significant topics, such as health care or communications technology, because doing so boosts the political clout of members who serve on the winning committees and garners them campaign contributions. As one scholar explained: "Committee jurisdictions are akin to property rights [over issues], and few things in Washington are more closely guarded or as fervently pursued."[16]

BOX 3.1   Constitutional Authority Statement

Pursuant to clause 7 of rule XII of the Rules of the House of Representatives, the following statements are submitted regarding the specific powers granted to Congress in the Constitution to enact the accompanying bill or joint resolution.

By Mr. Latham: H.R. 6690. Congress has the power to enact this legislation pursuant to the following: Article 1, Section 8 of the Constitution of the United States.

By Mr. Scott of Virginia: H.R. 6691. Congress has the power to enact this legislation pursuant to the following: Clause 1 of Section 8 of Article I of the Constitution.

Source: *Congressional Record*, December 20, 2012, H7424. See also Stephen Dinan, "Defenders of Constitution Don't Always Use It for Law," *Washington Times*, January 15, 2013, A1.

The complexity and interconnectedness of many contemporary issues almost guarantee that more than one committee will share jurisdiction over legislation, called a "multiple referral" (see the section on p. 115, "Referral to Several Committees," and Box 1.2). Furthermore, lawmakers recently have made wider use of so-called megabills, measures that are hundreds of pages long. The average number of pages per law increased from 2 1/2 in the 1950s to more than 15 in the 2000s.[17] The contemporary Congress may pass fewer laws than before, but they are considerably larger.

The act of introducing a bill sets off a complex and variable chain of events that may or may not result in final passage. Although thousands of pieces of legislation are introduced in every Congress, only a small number become law. For example, of the 10,569 public bills and joint resolutions introduced during the 112th Congress (2011–2013), only 238 (2.3%) became public law, about a third of them simply naming post offices or federal buildings. More public laws were enacted in earlier Congresses: for example, 640 in the 90th (1967–1969) and 550 in the 99th (1985–1987). Part of the general decline can be explained by the use of omnibus or megabills. The decline may also stem from widespread congressional sentiment that more laws may not be the answer to the nation's problems. But the decline may also reflect political stalemate resulting from the complexity of issues, the intensity of partisanship, divided government, or legislative–executive and bicameral conflicts.

CATEGORIES OF LEGISLATION

Committees are the primary graveyard for most bills that die in Congress. From the vast number of introduced measures, committees select those they believe merit further consideration. The winnowing process that occurs in committee suggests that the thousands of **bills introduced** in each Congress can be broken down into roughly three categories: bills that have so little support that they are ignored and die in committee; noncontroversial bills that are expedited through Congress; and major bills that generate so much debate that they occupy the major portion of Congress's time. Legislative proposals take four forms: **bill, joint resolution, concurrent resolution**, and **resolution**.

Bills Lacking Wide Support

Bills that have little support are usually introduced with no expectation that they will be enacted into law. Members introduce such bills for a variety of reasons: to go on record in support of a given proposal, to satisfy individual constituents or interest groups from the member's district or state, to convey a message to executive agencies, to publicize and provoke debate on an issue, to attract media attention, to fend off criticism during political campaigns, or to lay the groundwork for possible action in the next Congress. Once a member has introduced a bill, he or she can claim action on the issue and can blame the committee to which the bill has been referred for its failure to win enactment. Most of the bills introduced in each Congress fall into this category. To be sure, the ideas embedded in various bills can be "added as amendments to a larger bill or negotiated into a markup or conference report."[18]

Noncontroversial Bills

Noncontroversial bills make up another large segment of the measures introduced. Examples are bills that authorize construction of statues of public figures, establish a university program in the memory of a senator, rename a national park, or name federal buildings after former members of Congress. Committees in both chambers have developed rapid procedures for dealing with such measures. Generally, these bills are passed on the floor rather quickly and without much debate.

Major Legislation

Bills taking up the largest percentage of a committee's time have some or all of the following characteristics: They are prepared and drafted by key committee leaders, the political parties, executive agencies, or major pressure groups; they are initiated by committee chairs or other influential members of Congress; they are supported by the majority party leadership; or they deal with issues on which a significant segment of public opinion and the membership of Congress believe some sort of legislation is necessary, such as revamping health care or modernizing the nation's infrastructure.

Bills having such characteristics do not necessarily become law. They also are unlikely to become law in the form in which they were originally introduced. Indeed, sentiment may be so sharply divided that they do not even emerge from committee. Nevertheless, these are the major bills before Congress each year. They may affect the wage earner's paycheck (taxes and Social Security) and the consumer's pocketbook (health insurance and electricity deregulation), and they may be brought up repeatedly at presidential news conferences, legislative floor debates, and covered in the electronic and print media. Overall, Congress devotes the largest portion of its committee and floor time to these bills, which account for perhaps only a hundred or so of the thousands introduced in each Congress.

Executive Branch Bills. The president's leadership in the initial stages of the congressional process is pronounced. The administration's major legislative proposals are outlined in the president's annual State of the Union address, which is televised nationally during prime time and delivered before a joint session of Congress. In the weeks and months after the address, the president sends to Congress special messages detailing his proposals in specific areas, such as defense, education, energy, and health. Bills containing the administration's programs are drafted in the executive agencies.

Members of Congress, usually committee chairs, are asked to introduce them simultaneously as companion bills in both chambers. It is customary in both chambers for the words "by request" to appear in the *Congressional Record* by the sponsor's name to flag the measure as an administration initiative. Introducing one such bill, Senate Armed Services Chair Carl Levin, D-Mich., explained:

> As is the case with any bill that is introduced by request, [I] introduce this bill for the purpose of placing the administration's proposals before Congress and the public without expressing [my own view] on the substance of these proposals.[19]

(Members may also introduce measures "by request" for constituents, lobbyists, or state and local officials, for example.) Only representatives and senators, not the president or executive officials, may introduce legislation in Congress. Of course, there are many occasions when presidents and executive officials cooperate with lawmakers in the initial development of legislation, especially when the same party controls the House, the Senate, and the White House.

Influential Members' Bills. On June 26, 2009, the House passed a major global climate control measure. The key reasons: It had the strong support of Speaker Nancy Pelosi, D-Calif., who called it her "signature" issue, the relevant committee and subcommittee chairs, and other Democratic leaders. She even took the bill to the floor, uncertain if she had the votes to pass the comprehensive bill. According to one account, as the vote took place, Speaker Pelosi "stood at the rear rail [in the chamber] with two 'if needed' yea votes at her side. They were needed. In the end, she prevailed by a vote" of 219 to 212.[20] The legislation died in the Democratic Senate, in part because majority party leaders could not attract the 60 votes (see Chapter 6) to enact the climate control bill. Informally called the "cap and trade" bill for its complex procedures for reducing carbon emissions, opponents called it the "cap and tax" bill, arguing that homeowners' electricity costs would go up every time they turned on a light switch.

The "policy window" that opened for global warming in the 111th House and that closed in the Democratic Senate remained firmly shut during the 112th Congress (2011–2013). Various reasons accounted for this development, including the skepticism of many lawmakers who doubted the validity of the climate science and the GOP takeover of the House following the November 2010 midterm elections. The key proposed policy solutions for addressing climate change—taxing and regulating greenhouse gas emitters, along with spending on renewable energy—were anathema to most Republicans. Absent the dearth of influential champions in the 112th Congress urging legislative action on global warming, any future push for such legislation remains problematic until, or if, the policy window opens again.

Must-Pass Legislation. As lawmakers, members of Congress may not want to deal with controversial public issues such as abortion, gun control, immigration, or Social Security reform. But as politicians who must answer constituent mail, respond to inquiring lobbyists and journalists, and face reelection, they may not be able to ignore them. Because members who are in basic agreement that legislation must be enacted to deal with a controversial problem often disagree sharply about the solution, they must seek a legislative compromise to avoid adverse consequences. Money bills also fall into the category of must-pass legislation, such as the 12 general appropriations bills, as well as bills to address major crises or emergency events.

BILL REFERRAL PROCEDURE

Once a bill is introduced, it receives an identifying number. Measures introduced in the House are identified by the letters "H.R." (for House of Representatives) and an accompanying number; Senate bills are identified by the letter *S* and a number. Usually, bills are assigned numbers according to the chronological order in which they are introduced. Occasionally, however, members will ask the bill clerk to reserve a particular number. For example, H.J. Res. 51 might admit the District of Columbia as the 51st state. S. 25 might ban .25 caliber bullets. S. 1040 (after the federal tax form) might replace the current tax system with a flat tax. To be sure, bill numbers can also be used to criticize legislation. H.R. 1000, a pension security measure, "has an appropriate number," exclaimed Rep. Loretta Sanchez, D-Calif., "because it will make employees 1,000 times worse off than they are today."[21]

Bill numbers also may be assigned for political purposes. Customarily, majority party leaders of the House and Senate reserve the first several numbers for measures that reflect the majority party's priority agenda items. In the 108th Congress (2003–2005), the largest expansion of Medicare ever—providing a prescription drug benefit for the elderly—was designated by each chamber's GOP leaders as H.R. 1 and S. 1 to underscore the measure's political and substantive significance. Since the 106th Congress, the House has adopted an order on its opening day that states: "The first ten numbers for bills (H.R. 1 through H.R. 10) shall be reserved for assignment by the Speaker to such bills as she may designate when introduced during the first session."[22] The 112th House adopted a new rule that reserved "the second ten numbers (H.R. 11 through H.R. 20) for assignment by the Minority Leader."[23] Sometimes, the first 5 or 10 numbers in the Senate would be used by the majority leader and the next 5 or 10 by the minority leader.

Some measures are assigned the same number for several Congresses. This is often done to avoid confusion among legislators and others who have grown accustomed to referring to a proposal by its bill number.

Rep. John Dingell, D-Mich., the longest serving House member in history, regularly introduces a national health insurance plan his father first introduced in 1943 and receives "the number H.R. 15, for his district."[24] Informally, many bills receive names from journalists ("Cash for Clunkers," for example) or come to be known by their sponsors, such as the McCain–Feingold (after Senators John McCain, R-Ariz., and Russell Feingold, D-Wis.) Campaign Reform Act of 2002 (significantly undermined by the Supreme Court's 2010 decision in *Citizens United v. Federal Election Commission*). And then there was the artfully titled "Abraham–Lincoln" bill (after former Senators Spencer Abraham, R-Mich., and Blanche Lincoln, D-Ark.), intended to create a task force to recommend an appropriate way to recognize the slave laborers "who helped build the north wing of the Capitol during the 1790s."[25] (The slave laborers were recognized when the new Capitol Visitors Center opened in December 2008. A law passed the previous year named the Great Hall of the Visitors Center the "Emancipation Center" to honor and recognize the contribution of slaves in building the Capitol.)

With few exceptions, bills are referred to the appropriate standing committees.[26] The job of referral is formally the responsibility of the Speaker of the House and the presiding officer of the Senate, but usually this task is carried out on their behalf by the parliamentarians of the House and Senate, who provide expert parliamentary advice to the members and staff of their respective chambers.[27] (The House parliamentarian is named by the Speaker, and the Senate majority leader has the authority to appoint or dismiss that chamber's parliamentarian.) Precedent, public laws, memoranda of understanding between committee chairs, turf battles, and the jurisdictional mandates of the committees as set forth in the rules of the House and Senate determine which committees receive what kinds of bills.

The vast majority of referrals are routine. Bills dealing with farm crops are sent to the House Agriculture Committee and the Senate Agriculture, Nutrition, and Forestry Committee; tax bills are sent to the House Ways and Means Committee and the Senate Finance Committee; and bills dealing with veterans benefits are sent to the Veterans Affairs committees of each chamber.[28] Thus, referrals generally are cut-and-dried decisions. (House and Senate standing committees are listed in Box 3.2.)

Yet committees can and do clash over their jurisdictional prerogatives. Irate that the House Ways and Means Committee chair objected on turf grounds to a provision in an appropriations bill, the Democratic leader of the House Appropriations Committee declared: "Ways and Means is the biggest octopus not only in this Capitol, but any capital in the world. Once in a while, something ought to escape its jurisdiction."[29] A Senate Democrat on the Commerce Committee said of the Banking Committee chair's expansionist instincts: "He does everything in the world to come in on our jurisdiction."[30] Jurisdictional border wars influence the expansion or

---

BOX 3.2 **Standing Committees, 113th Congress (2013–2015)**

Senate

Agriculture, Nutrition, and Forestry	Finance
Appropriations	Foreign Relations
Armed Services	Health, Education, Labor, and Pensions
Banking, Housing, and Urban Affairs	Homeland Security and Governmental Affairs
Budget	Judiciary
Commerce, Science, and Transportation	Rules and Administration
Energy and Natural Resources	Small Business and Entrepreneurship
Environment and Public Works	Veterans' Affairs

House

Agriculture	House Administration
Appropriations	Judiciary
Armed Services	Natural Resources
Budget	Oversight and Government Reform
Education and the Workforce	Rules
Energy and Commerce	Science, Space and Technology
Ethics	Small Business
Financial Services	Transportation and Infrastructure
Foreign Affairs	Veterans' Affairs
Homeland Security	Ways and Means

---

contraction of committees' authority. Some committees even have "staffers called 'border cops,' whose jobs involve protecting turf and looking for new areas to conquer."[31]

In the House, a member is not permitted to appeal referral decisions to the entire membership except in rare instances of erroneous referral. However, by modern practice, unanimous consent is used to correct an erroneous referral. Similarly, in the Senate, the rules allow an **appeal** to the full Senate by majority vote, but in practice such appeals do not take place. Disputes over referral in the Senate are resolved informally by unanimous consent.

Senate (and House) party leaders often request that committees with overlapping responsibility work together and reach a consensus on how their respective issues should be addressed in draft legislation. Party leaders may then assume responsibility for putting the different pieces together. For example, the Democratic leaders in the House and Senate actively encouraged the committees with health jurisdiction to work together on what is probably President Obama's major domestic priority success of his first term: signing into law a comprehensive overhaul of the health care system (the Patient Protection and Affordable Care Act, dubbed "Obamacare" by opponents of the law—a term the president now embraces).

In the House, three committees—Education and the Workforce, Energy and Commerce, and Ways and Means—have primary responsibility for this subject area. The chairs of the panels wrote to President Obama and pledged to develop a single health care measure and report that to the House: "As chairs of these committees and veterans of past health reform debates, we have agreed to coordinate our efforts. Our intention is to bring similar legislation before our committees and work from a harmonized approach to ensure success."[32] The Speaker closely managed their activities, holding numerous closed-door meetings among the full committee and subcommittee chairs with health care expertise.[33] The House majority leader described the coordination between the party leaders and committee chairs:

> It's very nice to consider something in committee, but it has to come to the floor, so the committee has to have an idea of what will happen to it on the floor, and the leadership has to have an idea that we can get something from committee that [we] can have success with on the floor.[34]

In the Senate, two committees have primary jurisdiction over health: the Finance Committee and the Health, Education, Labor, and Pensions (HELPS) Committee. Majority Leader Reid granted both committees wide leeway in developing their health reform measures. For example, in more than a year of preparation, Finance Chair Max Baucus, D-Mont., "largely developed a new model for writing complex legislation, bringing an array of interest groups, lobbyists and other experts to lay out issues and options for senators and aides."[35] Later, in an effort to craft a bipartisan health care reform bill, Senator Baucus convened a group of three Finance Democrats (he was one of the three) and three Finance Republicans—the so-called "Gang of Six"—to try (unsuccessfully) to formulate a bill that would attract significant support from both parties. In the end, Majority Leader Reid decided what must be in the controversial health measure if it was to pass the Senate.[36] He was successful.

Legislative Drafting, Referral Strategy

Bill sponsors often try to draft legislation in such a way that it will be referred to a committee likely to act favorably on it instead of one whose members are known to be less sympathetic. Lawmakers, in brief, often engage in venue shopping during this lawmaking stage. One technique is to word the measure ambiguously so it can fall legitimately within the jurisdiction of more than one committee. The Speaker or the presiding officer of the Senate (i.e., the respective parliamentarians) then has some options in making the referral. (In the House and Senate, the full-time professional staff of each chamber's Office of Legislative Counsel is skilled at converting members' ideas for laws into legislative language.[37]) Or members may opt for another technique—introducing legislation that amends statutes over which their committees have jurisdiction. To lay claim to Internet legislation and avoid referral of their bill to the Commerce Committee, two House Judiciary Committee members drafted their measure to amend the Sherman Antitrust Act, which is within their panel's exclusive jurisdiction, and not the Telecommunications Act of 1996, which falls under the Commerce Committee. Artful drafting connecting eminent domain with rural development allowed the House Agriculture Committee to receive a bill dealing with eminent domain—the seizure of private land for economic development—even though the House Judiciary Committee would typically handle the issue. As the House parliamentarian stated: "The bill involved the Committee on Agriculture's jurisdiction because of the way it defined the term 'federal economic development program.'"[38] In the Senate, as noted earlier, the Finance and HELPS Committees claim jurisdiction in the area of health care. Finance members can obtain health care legislation by addressing health issues in the context of changing relevant provisions of the tax code; HELPS members could write bills that focus on employer-sponsored health plans.

Knowledge of precedents is also important in influencing the referral of legislation. Typically, references to taxes in measures mean that the bills will be sent to the tax-writing committees (House Ways and Means or Senate Finance). To avoid referral of his bill barring taxation of Internet commerce to the House Ways and Means Committee, a Commerce Committee member took advantage of precedents stating that "so long as the bill is limited to the taxing powers of state and local governments, it is the domain of the Judiciary or Commerce Committees."[39]

The House and Senate parliamentarians regularly provide congressional staffers with general advice on what language or terms to include in legislation so their measures will be referred to particular committees. (The parliamentarians even receive briefs from lobbyists on bill referrals.) According to the Senate parliamentarian,

> A great deal of our time in the office is spent dealing with drafts of bills, the committee to which they would be referred, advising staff on what to include and what to delete if in fact they have a preference in terms of committee referral.[40]

These bill-drafting techniques and others are the exceptions and not the rule for how bills are referred to committees. Committees guard their jurisdictional turfs closely, and the parliamentarians know and follow the precedents. Only instances of genuine jurisdictional ambiguity provide opportunities for the legislative draftsman and referral options for the

Speaker and the presiding officer of the Senate to bypass one committee in favor of another.

Referral to Several Committees

When a bill cuts across the jurisdictional lines of several committees, a common occurrence, referral may sometimes prove difficult. At the start of the 109th Congress (2005–2007), the House created a new standing committee on homeland security, a broad issue area—as well as a large cabinet department—that overlaps the jurisdiction of several other standing committees. To ensure that the legitimate interests of the existing committees were protected, a statement of legislative history was inserted in the *Congressional Record* to clarify the reference of homeland security legislation. According to the statement, for example, the new Homeland Security Committee would have primary jurisdiction over "transportation security" while the Transportation and Infrastructure Committee would retain its jurisdiction over "transportation safety."[41] As the Rules chair, one of the principal proponents of the new panel, stated: "We envision a system of purposeful redundancy. By that, we mean that more than one level of oversight and an atmosphere in which the competition of ideas is encouraged."[42]

Like homeland security, the jurisdictional mandates of other committees often are ambiguous or overlap in various policy domains. For example, House rules assign the Committee on Foreign Affairs jurisdiction over international economic policy; Commerce handles foreign commerce generally; and Ways and Means considers reciprocal trade agreements. To facilitate action, committees often share jurisdiction—formally or informally. For example, to minimize clashes on referrals, the chairs of the House Armed Services and the House Transportation and Infrastructure Committees developed a memorandum of understanding that explained how matters involving the merchant marine would be divided between them. As the chairs wrote: "In general, matters relating to merchant marine activities will be referred to the [Armed Services] Committee if the national security aspects of the matter predominate over transportation and other merchant marine aspects."[43] This type of informal intercommittee referral agreement will be honored by the parliamentarian unless or until the Speaker declares that "it shall no longer provide jurisdictional guidance."[44]

There are three types of multiple referral: joint referral of a bill concurrently to two or more committees; sequential referral to one committee, then a second, and so on; and split referral of various parts of a bill to different committees. Split referrals are rarely used, because the interlocking character of bills makes them difficult to divide into parts. Sometimes, multiple referrals are used in combination—after committees report a multireferred bill, another panel might obtain a sequential referral, typically for a designated time period. Multiple referrals are common in the House, less so in the Senate.

The Senate makes infrequent use of multiple referrals, largely because all senators have opportunities to offer nongermane amendments to pending legislation. Majority Leader Reid noted: "We have a procedure—it does not happen often—where you have a joint referral."[45] Measures and nominations normally are sent to a single committee based on the parliamentarian's determination as to which panel either has jurisdiction over the nomination or the "subject matter which predominates," the referral criterion specified for legislation in the Senate by the Legislative Reorganization Act of 1946. Multiple referrals can be implemented either by unanimous consent or upon a joint motion made by the majority and minority leaders (to date, this latter technique has never been employed). Here is a Senate example of a multiple referral unanimous consent request:

> Mr. President, I ask unanimous consent that when the [Homeland Security and Governmental Affairs] Committee reports S. 1977, the bill then be sequentially referred to the Committee on Finance for a period of up to 45 days during which the Senate is in session. I further ask unanimous consent that if the bill is not reported by the end of that period, it be discharged from the Finance Committee and placed back on the calendar.

If no senator objects, the sequential referral request is binding on the Senate. The Senate normally grants such requests because senators who offer them usually have worked out an agreement previously with all interested parties—committee chairs, party leaders, and other members concerned about the bill. By the time the bill is introduced, the appropriate bases have been touched, and so no senator is likely to object to the multiple referral.

Until 1975, House precedents dictated that the Speaker refer a bill to only one committee. That year, flexibility was injected into the bill referral process by two changes in the rules. First, Speakers are permitted to refer a bill to more than one committee through joint, sequential, or split referral. Multiple referrals augment the power of Speakers by enabling them to delay (by sending a bill to several panels) or expedite (by fixing committee reporting deadlines) action on legislation. Second, Speakers, subject to House approval, are permitted to create ad hoc committees to consider measures that overlap the jurisdictions of several committees. (In 1977, the Speaker gained formal authority to impose time limits on committees' consideration of legislation: upon initial referral or during subsequent sequential referral of a bill to other panels. This Speaker's prerogative, although seldom used, strengthens leadership influence over committees by encouraging the timeliness of their decision making.)

Speakers have seldom employed their prerogative of establishing ad hoc panels. Speaker Thomas P. "Tip" O'Neill Jr., D-Mass., exercised this option in 1977, for instance, to create an Ad Hoc Energy Committee to expedite action on the Carter Administration's top priority: enactment of a complex array of energy proposals. The ad hoc committee was composed of members selected from the five committees to which various parts of the energy proposal initially had been referred.[46] In 2002, the Speaker initiated the formation of the Select Committee on Homeland Security to report a comprehensive bill creating a new Department of Homeland Security after reviewing the recommendations of the dozen standing committees with some jurisdiction over homeland security issues. Every member of the nine-member select panel (five Republicans, four Democrats) held a leadership position in their party's hierarchy. Chaired by the majority leader, the select panel was modeled on the ad hoc energy panel. As the Rules chair said, the process for considering the new department is "similar to the one that was used a quarter of a century ago by Speaker Tom O'Neill in addressing the energy crisis."[47] The Senate has no formal rule providing for the creation of ad hoc committees by party leaders. However, Senate (and House) party leaders may create on their own authority partisan or bipartisan task forces or other ad hoc devices for considering legislation.

In 1995, the new House Republican majority abolished joint refer-rals (retaining sequential and split references) and added to House rules the requirement that the Speaker shall "designate a committee of primary jurisdiction upon the initial referral of a measure to a committee."[48] This change was designed to achieve greater committee accountability for legis-lation, while retaining significant flexibility for the Speaker in determining whether, when, and how long additional panels will receive the legislation. The House parliamentarian refers to this new form of multiple referral as an "additional initial referral." Such referrals occur in this way:

> H.R. 4169. A bill to require the development of a comprehensive strategy to end serious human rights violations in Sudan, to create incentives for govern-ments and persons to end support of and assistance to the Government of Sudan . . . , and for other purposes; to the Committee on Foreign Affairs, and in addition to the Committees on Financial Services, Oversight and Government Reform, and the Judiciary, for a period to be subsequently determined by the Speaker, in each case for the consideration of such provisions as fall within the jurisdiction of the committees concerned.[49]

For H.R. 4169, the Committee on Foreign Affairs is the primary com-mittee of jurisdiction; the other three committees obtain the measure on an additional initial basis. Secondary panels can consider measures before the primary committee, but their action does not force action on the part of the primary committee. However, once the primary committee files its report on a bill, the Speaker imposes time limits for action on the other panels. Committees jockey to be named "primary" on major bills, because that designation gives panel members a large say in shaping significant legislation; more panel members are also named to the conference com-mittee. In addition, the primary designation often enhances the ability of panel members to raise campaign funds from outside groups interested in the legislation.

Jurisdictional conflict over health care issues in the early 2000s between the Committees on Energy and Commerce and Ways and Means prompted the majority Republicans to again amend the multiple referral rule on the opening day, January 7, 2003, of the 108th Congress, which subsequent Congresses have retained. To minimize turf disputes, they permitted the return of joint referrals without any designation of a primary committee. (Republicans disliked joint referrals when Democrats ran the House because the Republicans viewed joint referrals as a formula for stalemate.) However, the Rules chair emphasized that the change is "meant only as a minor deviation from the normal requirement under rules for the designation of one committee of primary jurisdiction and should be exercised only in extraordinary jurisdictionally deserving instances."[50] Committees may also waive their right to consider a measure, or particular sections of the measure, in the interest of expediting legislation and without their decision constituting a referral precedent when comparable measures are subsequently introduced on the topic (see Box 3.3).

Several observations may be made about multiple referrals:

- Because contemporary problems tend to have repercussions in many areas, more and more of the major bills coming before Congress—particularly those in new problem areas such as homeland security—will be candidates for multiple referrals.
- To the extent that a multiple referral is chosen as an option, the decentralized nature of congressional decision making is reinforced.
- Every time another committee is added to the legislative process, additional opportunities arise for delay, negotiation, compromise, and bargaining.
- Multiple referrals may promote effective problem solving because several committees are bringing their expertise to bear on complex issues.
- On the one hand, when the Speaker designates a panel as primary, he or she knows which committee to call to get action. On the other hand, multiple referrals sometimes require the Speaker to get involved in mediating and resolving jurisdictional claims or disputes between or among committees.
- Multiple referrals are commonplace in today's House—that is, "one bill, one committee" no longer applies to the extent it once did. Many committees, including multiple subcommittees within the parent committees, review legislation.
- To accommodate the interests of several panels, multiple referrals often require more complex debate and amendment arrangements on the floor and in the selection of conference committees created to resolve bicameral differences on legislation. However, the centralization of authority in the contemporary speakership means that multiple referral issues are typically mitigated by the Speaker's control of the Rules Committee and his or her rule-based right to name conferees.

BOX 3.3 **An Example of Jurisdictional Accommodation**

House of Representatives,
Committee on Armed Services
Washington, DC, July 31, 2012

Hon. DARRELL E. ISSA,
Chairman, Committee on Oversight and Government Reform, House of Representatives, Washington, DC.

DEAR CHAIRMAN ISSA: I am writing to you concerning the bill S. 300, Government Charge Card Abuse Prevention Act of 2011, as amended. This legislation includes provisions that deal with the Department of Defense policies regarding government charge cards which fall within the Rule X jurisdiction of the Committee on Armed Services.

Our committee recognizes the importance of S. 300, and the need for the legislation to move expeditiously. Therefore, while we have a valid claim to jurisdiction over this legislation, the Committee on Armed Services will waive further consideration of S. 300. I do so with the understanding that by waiving consideration of the bill, the Committee on Armed Services does not waive any future jurisdictional claim over the subject matters contained in the bill which fall within its Rule X jurisdiction. I appreciate your willingness to work with the Committee on Armed Services to incorporate modifications requested by the Office of the Secretary of Defense to the legislation to be considered in the House. I request that you urge the Speaker to name members of this committee to any conference committee which is named to consider these provisions.

Please place this letter and your committee's response into the Congressional Record during consideration of the measure on the House floor. Thank you for the cooperative spirit in which you have worked regarding this matter and others between our respective committees.

Sincerely,
HOWARD P. "BUCK" McKEON,
Chairman.

House of Representatives,
Committee on Oversight and Government Reform,
Washington, DC, July 31, 2012.

Hon. HOWARD P. "BUCK" McKEON,
Chairman, Committee on Armed Services, House of Representatives, Washington DC.

Dear Mr. Chairman: Thank you for your letter regarding the Committee on Armed Services' jurisdictional interest in S. 300, the "Government Charge Card Abuse Prevention Act of 2011," and your willingness to forego consideration of S. 300 by your committee.

(Continued)

BOX 3.3   (Continued)

I agree that the Armed Services Committee has a valid jurisdictional interest in certain provisions of S. 300 and that the Committee's jurisdiction will not be adversely affected by your decision to forego consideration of the bill. As you have requested, I will support your request for an appropriate appointment of outside conferees from your Committee in the event of a House–Senate conference on this or similar legislation should a conference be convened.

Finally, I will include a copy of your letter and this response in the Congressional Record during the floor consideration of this bill. Thank you again for your cooperation.

Sincerely,

DARRELL ISSA,

Chairman.

CONSIDERATION IN COMMITTEE

Once a bill has been referred, the receiving committee has several options. It may, for example, consider and **report** (vote out) the bill, with or without amendments or recommendations, for possible floor action by the full House or Senate. The receiving committee may rewrite the bill entirely, reject it, or simply refuse to consider it. Failure of a committee to act on a bill is often equivalent to killing it. When a committee does report a bill and it is taken up in the House or Senate, its main thrust is often accepted even when the chamber amends the bill on the floor.[51]

Lawmakers defer to the committees' decisions for several reasons. For one thing, committee members and their staffs have a high degree of expertise on the subjects within their jurisdiction, and a bill undergoes its sharpest congressional scrutiny at the committee stage. Therefore, a bill that has survived examination by the experts will probably be given serious consideration on the floor by the generalists of the House and Senate.

A committee's decision not to report a bill is generally respected by the chamber as a whole. After all, if the experts have decided not to approve a bill, why should their decision be second-guessed? Furthermore, the rules in both chambers—particularly those of the House—are designed to "protect the power and prerogatives of the . . . committees . . . by making it very difficult for a bill that does not have committee approval to come to the floor."[52] Formal procedures are in place for overturning committee decisions or even bypassing committees, but these procedures are employed infrequently and are seldom successful. Other ways are also available for circumventing committees, such as the formation of partisan task forces to draft legislation.

When a committee decides to take up a major bill, the full committee may consider it immediately. But more often, the chair assigns the bill to a subcommittee for study and hearings. The subcommittee usually schedules public hearings on the bill, inviting testimony from interested witnesses in both the public and private sectors. Or the subcommittee may decide not to schedule hearings if executive branch officials, interest groups, or others (the so-called "stakeholders") strongly oppose the legislation. After the hearings, the subcommittee meets to mark up the bill—that is, to consider the bill's specific language line by line and section by section—before sending it to the full committee. The subcommittee may approve the bill unaltered, amend it, rewrite it, or block it altogether. The panel reports its recommendations to the full committee.

When the full committee receives the bill, it may repeat the subcommittee's procedures in whole or in part, or it may simply ratify the subcommittee action. If the committee decides to report the bill to the House or Senate, it justifies its actions in a written statement called a report, which must accompany the bill. (The Senate has no formal requirement that a written report must accompany legislation, but it is informally observed in most cases.)

On a major legislative proposal, the entire committee process may stretch over several Congresses, with a new bill containing identical or similar provisions introduced at the beginning of each Congress. For example, the struggle to enact controversial legislation dealing with immigration reform, clean air, gun control, or health care can take several consecutive Congresses. Decades may pass before some bills become public law. For other legislation, the process can be compressed into a very short time, especially during times of crisis such as the terrorist attacks of September 11, 2001, or the Wall Street financial meltdown 7 years later.

THE COMMITTEE CHAIR'S ROLE

To a large extent, the options available to a committee in dealing with a bill are exercised by the chair, who has wide discretion in establishing the committee's legislative priorities. Among the chair's sources of authority are control of the committee's legislative agenda, referral of legislation to the subcommittees, management of committee funds, hiring and firing of committee staff, use of committee facilities, and designation of majority party conferees. As one House chair observed, the "real power" of the chair is "to set the agenda, mark the course and lead."[53]

The chair usually has had a long period of service on the committee and is likely to be better informed than most other members on the many issues coming before the committee. Moreover, the chair is often privy to the leadership's plans and policies, especially the Speaker's or the Senate majority leader's legislative objectives. Chairs can use these and other resources to delay, expedite, or modify legislation.

A chair who opposes a bill may simply refuse to schedule hearings on it or allow hearings to drag on until it is too late to finish action on the bill during that session. Or the chair could instruct the committee staff to stack the witness list so most testify against the bill, ask witnesses holding favorable views to submit statements instead of appearing in person, or try to exclude some proponents of the legislation from testifying. A staff aide for Catholic Charities described how the organization had to "fight to testify" on a welfare reform bill, and when they did, "it was 8 o'clock at night after almost all the members and all the press had gone."[54]

During markup, chairs who oppose measures may recognize panel members who are likely to raise dilatory questions, offer "poison-pill" amendments, or employ other obstructive tactics before others. Through control of committee funds and the power to hire and fire most staffers, the chair can block action on a bill by directing the staff to disregard it.[55]

A chair who favors a bill can give it top priority by mobilizing staff resources, compressing the time for hearings and markups, and, in general, encouraging expeditious action by committee members. Chairs sometimes bypass the public hearing stage entirely and proceed directly to full committee markup. They typically are the chief agenda setters of committees. They employ this prerogative to powerfully influence the form in which bills are reported to the House or Senate, as well as the timing of floor action on their bills. Committee chairs are also active in molding public and legislative opinion on behalf of their objectives.

The ranking minority party member on a committee also has certain prerogatives. These prerogatives include hiring and firing of minority staff aides; recommending minority party conferees; acting as the minority side's spokesperson to the press and media; influencing, depending on his or her relationship with the committee leader, the panel's agenda of activities; and designating the minority floor manager for legislation reported by the committee. Like committee chairs, ranking members devise parliamentary strategy, anticipate amendments, ensure the attendance of their members, offer proposals that divide the majority party, mobilize winning coalitions, and coordinate their approach to markups with their central party leaders.

Committee Chairs in Perspective

The general picture that had persisted during half of the 20th century of a committee chair as an almost omnipotent figure underwent modification during and since the 1970s. Until then, committee chairs were the central figures in the legislative process, holding power equaled only by a few party leaders of great influence, such as Speaker Sam Rayburn, D-Texas (House, 1913–1961; Speaker, 1940–1947, 1949–1953, 1955–1961), or Senate Majority Leader Lyndon B. Johnson, D-Texas (Senate, 1949–1961; majority leader, 1955–1961). The chairs' power was gradually trimmed under pressure from newly elected members and from some senior members who wanted to equalize the distribution of power. During the 1970s, when Democrats were in charge of the House, they approved several fundamental changes that ended the nearly absolute authority enjoyed by committee chairs, such as ending their unilateral power to create subcommittees; to name the majority members, including the subcommittee chair; and to determine whether subcommittees would have any resources to function (staff and budget, for instance) or even a defined jurisdiction.

These important chairmanship changes came when both parties decided to modify the seniority system, specifically the practice of automatically selecting as chair the majority party member with the longest continuous service on the committee, regardless of ability or receptivity to new ideas. Seniority meant that chairs normally came from safe congressional districts, were repeatedly reelected, and served until their retirement or death. Because many safe districts during the 1950s and 1960s were in the conservative Democratic South, chairs often were sharply at odds with Democratic presidents, congressional leaders, and northern Democrats. Nevertheless, as seniority was then practiced, the chairs could not be removed. The chairs were able to use their entrenched positions to block civil rights and social welfare legislation proposed by Democratic administrations. Today, because of party rules and other changes made by Democrats and Republicans in each chamber, all committee chairs (and ranking minority committee members) are subject to secret ballot election within the confines of their party caucus or conference. Chairs and ranking minority committee members are now accountable for their actions to at least a majority of their party's caucus or conference.

With the GOP takeover of Congress in the mid-1990s after four decades of Democratic control (1955–1995), the House amended its rules to impose a 6-year term limit on committee and subcommittee chairs to prevent them from accumulating too much power. The Democratic 110th House deleted term limits from the chamber's rulebook but reinstituted it for the 111th House. House Republicans, however, retained term limits as a party rule during the 4 years that Democrats ran the House. The GOP-controlled 112th House reinstated term limits as a rule of the chamber and retained them for the 113th. Senate Republicans emulated the GOP House's term-limit idea but imposed it as a party rule, starting in 1997—a 6-year term limit for their committee and subcommittee chairs. Senate Democrats have no rule imposing term limits on their members. Legislative experience with term limits reveals that on occasion it has led to the retirement of knowledgeable and experienced committee leaders. Term limits also made committee leaders "lame ducks" during their final 2 years. It also placed a premium on party fundraising for those seeking to become committee chairs. On the other hand, term limits also infused flexibility in the committee structure by allowing other, often younger, members a chance to head committees.

When Newt Gingrich, R-Ga., took over as Speaker (1995–1999), he ignored seniority and named several committee chairs who were ideologically in sync with the leadership's views and agenda. J. Dennis Hastert, R-Ill., who took over as Speaker in 1999, employed an unprecedented interview process to determine who would replace term-limited chairs. GOP contenders for open chairs appeared before the GOP's committee assignment panel (the Steering Committee). They were asked to respond to questions such as, How much money had they raised for the party? Did they have a communications strategy for advancing GOP priorities? When Democrats took control of the 110th Congress (2007–2009), Speaker Pelosi's committee assignment panel followed seniority in designating the chairs of the various standing committees, which was also the practice in the 111th Congress. In the 112th House, Speaker Boehner ensured that the term-limit rule was followed. Two former committee chairs who had reached the 6-year limit— one on Appropriations and the other on Energy and Commerce—wanted the party's assignment panel to grant them a waiver so they could continue as leaders of those panels. Speaker Boehner rejected their requests for waivers. He did the same in the 113th with one exception, Paul Ryan continued as Budget chair.

Since at least the mid-1990s, committee chairs take more direction from assertive party leaders, especially in the House, and there are potential costs if chairs buck their leadership.[56] A recent example of leadership message-sending to committee chairs—party power over committee power— occurred at the start of the 109th Congress (2005). House GOP leaders ousted Veterans Affairs Chair Christopher Smith of New Jersey, who was in the fourth year of his 6-year term, as the committee's leader and also removed him from the panel. Smith's outspoken advocacy for more spending for veterans benefits angered Speaker Hastert and other party leaders. In the 113th, Speaker Boehner stripped four GOP members from their coveted committee assignments, apparently because of their inability to work well with their Republican colleagues.[57] The Speaker and minority leader also name either the majority or minority members of three standing committees: Ethics, House Administration, and Rules.

Upon assuming the speakership, Representative Boehner's preference was to devolve authority to the committee chairs, as noted in Chapter 1, and implement a more participatory and bottoms-up approach to lawmaking. The Speaker would articulate general policy principles and let the committee chairs produce the bills that comported with those guidelines. His decentralized approach to policymaking did not always work as anticipated, and Speaker Boehner on those occasions had to provide more centralized direction to House decision making. On the Speaker's 2012 signature surface transportation issue, he relied on the Transportation chair to produce a surface transportation measure acceptable to at least 218 lawmakers. Instead, the Transportation Committee produced a flawed bill that numerous lawmakers, including the Speaker, viewed as too costly and too partisan to pass the House. As a result, Speaker Boehner took charge of the bill to try to clear away various roadblocks to its passage. A senior staff aide explained that the austere budget climate, combined with the ban on earmarks to woo votes, means that the "leadership has had to play a bigger role" on the transportation measure and other bills as well.[58] Moreover, more important legislation was brought to the floor without committee consideration in the Boehner-led House than in the Democratic 110th and 111th Houses, a sign that Boehner, like Speaker Pelosi, will assert centralized direction when occasions demand.[59]

Committee chairs remain crucial figures in the legislative process despite the shift toward centralized leadership control. Because Congress functions primarily through its committees, the person who heads a committee has considerable influence over the advancement or defeat of legislation. Their authority is bolstered by a number of factors, such as committee rules, procedural knowledge and substantive expertise, agenda-setting prerogative, coalition-building skills, access to leadership plans, and, fundamentally, the willingness of at least a majority of committee members to follow their lead. The rarity of committee "revolts" against committee chairs underscores the deference committee members typically afford their leaders.

COMMITTEE HEARINGS

The decision to hold hearings is the fundamental prerogative of committee chairs. They may be influenced by a variety of internal and external factors—requests from party leaders, colleagues, administration officials; the need to act on expiring legislation; and so on. Ultimately, however, it is the chairs who determine their committees' hearing schedule, setting the date, place, and subject matter of any hearing. Although committee hearings serve a variety of purposes, they are certainly important as fact-finding and educative instruments. Witnesses from the executive branch, concerned members of Congress, interest group spokespersons, academic experts, celebrities, and knowledgeable citizens appear before the committee to give members their opinions about the merits or pitfalls of a given piece of legislation. From this encounter, the committee members gather the information and analysis they need to act as informed lawmakers. Hearings also aid members in determining whether new laws are needed or whether changes in the administration of existing laws will be sufficient to resolve problems. "Legislation need not always be the answer," remarked a senator. "In many areas, the most important missing ingredient is attention, and an elevated awareness of the problem can be a very successful outcome of hearings."[60] Committee members are sometimes more interested in making opening statements or engaging colleagues in discussions, especially at high-profile hearings, than in listening to witnesses. From the witnesses' perspective, such sessions might be called "listenings" rather than hearings. Conversely, witnesses may be there because angry lawmakers are more interested in lambasting them for their misdeeds, wrong policies, or incompetence than in listening to their testimony.

Much information is available to committee members long before the hearings take place. Major bills usually have been the subject of public debate and media coverage. The positions of the administration and the special-interest groups are well known, and, in all likelihood, executive branch officials and pressure-group lobbyists have already presented their views to committee members and staff aides. Because the members themselves likely have strong partisan positions on the legislation, they may have little interest in whatever additional information emerges from the hearings.[61] In general, hearings are often poorly attended by committee members, and interruptions are common because of floor votes or quorum calls.

Hearing Formats

Committees regularly utilize five main hearing formats—traditional, panel, joint, field, and high-tech—when they conduct legislative (focusing on a particular bill or set of related measures), oversight, investigative, or confirmation hearings. For each hearing type, staff research and preparatory work precede the committee hearings. Committee aides may, for example, interview witnesses in advance, compile research and documentary materials, and prepare notebooks for committee members to use at the hearings. These notebooks may list the questions—and the answers—used in probing the witnesses. A committee staff director explained:

> We write the question. Under the question we write the answer. This is the answer we expect to get on the basis of the staff research that has gone before. The Member who asks the question knows what the witness has told us in the weeks and weeks of preparation; and he knows he should get the same information. If he does not get that information, then he has the answer in front of him and he can ad lib the questions that solicit that information or refute it.[62]

Some committees even hold prehearings to assess privately issues that witnesses will discuss later during the public sessions. For example, a House Financial Services Subcommittee on Capital Markets, Insurance, and Government-Sponsored Enterprises held six private dinners and forums to learn more about those issues with guests such as Treasury Secretary Timothy Geithner and Paul Volcker, former Federal Reserve chair. Several outside groups, however, criticized the private "hearing" sessions, contending that they should have been open to the public.[63] Committees sometimes organize public "roundtable" hearings with outside witnesses and members sitting together around a table, with the chair acting as moderator. A witness may present a brief summary of her views, and then a free-flowing discussion would ensue among the other witnesses and committee members.

Hearings can be perfunctory, particularly where similar legislation has been before the committee for several years in succession. Witnesses usually read or summarize from prepared texts, while the committee members present may listen intently, feign interest, or simply look bored until the statement has been presented. Once the formal testimony is completed, each committee member, usually in order of seniority and alternately between the parties, asks the witness questions. House rules allot at least 5 minutes per member to question witnesses. House rules also provide that the chair or ranking minority member may designate specific committee members or staff to conduct extended questioning of up to 30 minutes per side, per witness. Senate rules have no such provisions. Each committee establishes its own rules governing internal procedures. For example, the rules of the Senate Energy and Natural Resources Committee give each member 5 minutes to question witnesses until all members have had an opportunity to ask questions. (Several comparable House and Senate rules that govern the hearings process for most committees are presented in Box 3.4.)

Committees also conduct joint hearings (with other panels or with the other house), field hearings (away from Capitol Hill), and panel sessions where two or more witnesses of similar or divergent views are arrayed at a table in front of the committee members. Microsoft's Bill Gates testified before the Senate Judiciary Committee in a panel setting with other chief executive officers of computer companies who were hostile to Gates's alleged monopolistic practices. To foment rhetorical fireworks and win publicity for their aims, the committee staff deliberately placed Gates next to his chief antagonist. Congress is also increasing its use of high-tech or interactive hearings, during which witnesses located around the United States or around the world can testify before House or Senate committees via, for example, videoconferencing. The House Agriculture Committee was "the first congressional panel to broadcast its proceedings in live audio format over the Internet."[64] An astronaut appeared before the House Science Committee and became the first person in history to testify from space. He told lawmakers "what it was like to spend months aboard the space station and how such experience could be valuable in planning missions to Mars and beyond."[65] (House rules require committees to "make [their] publications available in electronic form to the maximum extent feasible" and to "provide audio and video coverage of each committee hearing or meeting and maintain recordings that are easily accessible to the public." Senate hearings are available on committee's web sites.)

Purposes of Hearings

Despite their limitations, hearings remain an integral part of the legislative process. They provide a permanent public record of the positions of committee members and various interest groups on a legislative proposal. In fact, the executive agencies and interest groups give high priority to preparation of congressional testimony. Above all, hearings are important because members of Congress believe them to be important. The decision to hold hearings is often a critical point in the life of a bill. Measures brought to the floor without first undergoing the scrutiny of hearings will likely receive sharp criticism. (Policies not subject to hearings often become public law, however. Offering legislative proposals as floor amendments, incorporating them into conference reports, or burying them in megabills are among the techniques for bypassing committee hearings.) The importance of the committee stage is based on the assumption that the experts—the committee

---

BOX 3.4   Selected Formal Rules Governing Hearing Procedures

Although House and Senate committees have wide latitude in how they organize and conduct hearings, formal rules in each chamber regulate these proceedings. Several of the most important rules for committee hearings are described here.

Notice. The committee chair shall publicly announce the date, place, and subject matter of a committee hearing at least one week before commencement of the hearing. House rules permit this rule to be waived either with the concurrence of the chair and ranking minority member or by majority vote of the committee. Senate rules permit the notice rule to be waived if the committee determines that good cause exists to begin a hearing at an earlier date.

Openness. Hearings shall be open to the public and the media. Each chamber has provisions that enable committees or subcommittees to close the hearings, but only for certain enumerated reasons such as endangering national security, compromising sensitive law enforcement information, or defaming or disgracing an individual.

---

members—carefully scrutinize a proposal, and hearings provide a demonstrable record of that scrutiny.

Hearings are perhaps the most orchestrated phase of policymaking and usually are part of any overall strategy to get bills enacted into law. Committee members and staff typically plan with care who should testify, when, and on what issues. Consumer advocate Ralph Nader's testimony before several congressional committees on his 1965 best-selling book, *Unsafe at Any Speed,* led to passage of the Traffic Safety Act of 1966. The testimony of celebrity witnesses, such as movie stars, television personalities, or professional athletes, is a sure-fire way to attract national attention to issues. As a senator put it: "Quite candidly, when Hollywood speaks, the world listens. Sometimes when Washington speaks, the world snoozes."[66]

Witnesses who have experienced issues or problems firsthand and can tell their stories to lawmakers are especially sought after, because they put a human face on public problems.

Speaking to a congressional committee [considering the issue of child care], a 10-year-old girl whose parents could no longer afford day care said, "Some things scare me when I'm alone—like the wind, the door creaking, and the sky getting dark fast. This may not seem scary to you," she told the committee of adults, "but it is to young people who are alone."[67]

During Senate Finance Committee hearings about the Internal Revenue Service (IRS) abuses of taxpayers, not only did ordinary taxpayers recount

Quorum. House rules stipulate that committees may fix the number of members who must be present to take testimony, but it may not be less than two. Senate rules allow committees to set any number who may be present to take testimony, even if just one senator.

Witness Requirements. Witnesses are required, unless there is good cause for noncompliance, to submit in advance copies of their written testimony to the committee. House rules also require nongovernmental witnesses to file a curriculum vitae and to disclose the amount and source of any federal grant or contract they might have received during the current year and preceding 2 years.

Broadcasting. House rules state that whenever any committee or subcommittee hearing is open to the public, those proceedings shall be open to coverage by radio or television or both. Senate rules provide that any public hearing of a committee or subcommittee may be broadcast under the terms specified in committee rules.

Minority Party's Right to Call Witnesses. The minority party on a committee is entitled, upon a request made to the chair by a majority of the minority members before the completion of the hearing, to call witnesses of its choosing to testify on the subject of the hearing for at least one day.

---

their "horror stories" of tax collection efforts by the IRS, but IRS employees "disguised behind screens, with altered voices for some witnesses," provided high drama to the proceedings.[68] Committees often want witnesses who will provide a broad coalition of endorsements for their predetermined position and promote political and public support for this course of action.

Hearings serve other functions as well. They may be used to assess the intensity of support or opposition to a bill, to gauge the capabilities of an executive agency official, to publicize the role of politically ambitious committee chairs and members, to allow citizens to express their views to their representatives, to promote new ideas or agendas, to assert the jurisdictional reach of committees, to encourage productive discussions among committee members, or to build public support for an issue. Added House Financial Services Chair Barney Frank, D-Mass.: "So you have hearings to pressure people. People don't like to be embarrassed. You have hearings to send messages. So they can have an impact. Sometimes they're a waste of time."[69]

In carrying out its constitutional duties, the Senate holds hearings on advising and consenting to treaties and presidential nominations to the executive and judicial branches. The Judiciary Committee's televised hearings on Supreme Court nominations—such as Robert H. Bork in 1987, Clarence Thomas in 1991, John Roberts and Samuel Alito in 2005, Sonia Sotomayor in 2009, and Elena Kagan in 2010—involve extensive preparation by both the nominee and committee chair. The nominees often participate in mock hearings called "murder boards" to get ready for the tough questions they may face. Judge Roberts "participated in some 10 mock hearings of two to three hours each at the Department of Justice, where administration lawyers and a revolving cast of Judge Roberts's colleagues and friends baited him with queries" anticipated from Democratic members of the Judiciary Committee.[70] The Judiciary chair may prepare by participating in mock videotaped questioning of someone playing the role of the nominee.

Congress also uses oversight and investigative hearings to explore problems and issues and assess program performance. These hearings serve several purposes. They promote efficient program administration, secure the information needed to legislate, and inform public opinion. American households watched on television the unfolding drama of the 1954 Army-McCarthy hearings; the 1957 hearings into corruption of the Teamsters Union; the Senate Foreign Relations Committee's hearings during the 1960s on the Vietnam War; the Watergate hearings of the 1970s; the 1987 Iran-contra hearings; the late 1990s presidential impeachment hearings; the 2006 hearings on the recommendations of the Iraq Study Group on how to end the chaos in Iraq and improve the prospects for security and stability in that troubled country; the 2009 hearings on the financial bailout of Wall Street firms by the government's Troubled Asset Relief Program; and the 2012 hearings on the terrorist attack on the American consulate in Benghazi, Libya, that killed U.S. Ambassador Chris Stevens and several other Americans. Investigative hearings often prompt the drafting of legislation to deal with the problems that were uncovered and subsequently lead to more hearings on the legislation itself. On occasion, individual members initiate and conduct informal investigative hearings of their own.

House and Senate rules allow a majority of the minority members on a committee, before the completion of a hearing, to request in writing to the chair that they have a day in which to call witnesses of their choosing to testify on the measure or matter before the panel. (Usually, the chair will informally accommodate the minority's requests that certain witnesses be invited to testify, unless the recommendations trigger partisan disagreement.) The formal rule, if invoked, still leaves the chair in the driver's seat, because the rule neither defines when the hearing is to occur nor the meaning of the word *day* (an hour, two, or more, for example). In 2005, the then-minority Democrats on the House Judiciary Committee invoked the minority witness rule. The chair scheduled the session for a Friday, when most lawmakers are in their district, and at "the very unusual congressional starting time of 8:30 a.m."[71] Furthermore, after listening to repeated criticisms of the Bush Administration by the minority's witnesses, the chair gaveled the hearing to a close, ordered the microphones turned off, and stopped transcription of the testimony.[72]

In a somewhat similar circumstance, House Minority Leader Pelosi was quite angry that the Oversight and Government Reform Committee held a hearing in 2012 on contraception, birth control, and religious freedom with all-male witnesses. A female Georgetown University law student was excluded from the all-male panel. The result: Minority Leader Pelosi used the Democratic Steering and Policy Committee to conduct an unofficial ad hoc hearing on those topics, with the Georgetown law student as the featured witness.[73]

THE MARKUP

After the conclusion of the hearings, the committee or subcommittee may meet to mark up, or amend, the bill (thus, the word *markup*, which refers to the session at which committee members debate and propose changes to a bill before it might be reported out). At this session, committee members decide whether the legislation should be rewritten, either in whole or in part. The chair's task is to keep the committee moving, getting unanimous agreement on as many sections of the bill as possible, trying to resolve differences through compromise, sensing when to delay or speed up matters, or forcing action on issues through party-line voting. Committee chairs regularly line up leadership backing for their committee's bill, negotiate privately with wavering committee members, insert special provisions in legislation to win members' support, or accommodate interest groups or agency officials by soliciting their comments on a draft markup proposal or permitting them to make presentations during committee markup. Because the chair is likely to be responsible for managing the bill on the floor, he or she will try throughout markup to gather as much support within the committee as possible. A sharp split among the committee members may seriously damage chances of passing the bill in the House or Senate.

Overview

The markup is where committee members redraft portions of the bill, attempt to insert new provisions and delete others, bargain over language, and generally determine the final committee product. The different kinds of markups used by committees reflect committee traditions and customs as well as the nature of the legislation—that is, how controversial it may be. Chairs sometimes schedule informal, private pre-markup sessions for committee members, either on a partisan or bipartisan basis, to discuss possible revisions of major legislation and to develop a consensus on the bill. On an overhaul of the Clean Air Act, for example, the Senate Environment and Public Works Committee chair "scheduled several seminars prior to the formal markup, to educate the members on the major issues and to try to develop a consensus among the members on the issues."[74] In other preparatory actions, committee chairs or ranking minority members might develop markup summaries (analyses of the bill, a list of which members or outside groups support or oppose it, and so on), organize briefings for the legislative staff of individual committee members, anticipate possible amendments and develop responses to them, devise party strategy, and ascertain which members will be in attendance and where absent members can be reached.

BOX 3.5   Selected Procedures Governing Markup

Notice. Chamber and committee rules require public notice of markup sessions.

Quorum. Chamber and committee rules set a quorum for markups at one third of the membership of the panel.

Markup Vehicle. The chair selects and lays down the vehicle to be considered for markup.

Opening Statements. The committee chair, often in consultation with the ranking minority member, determines if all or only some panel members will make opening statements and for what length of time.

Reading for Amendment. In the Senate, the text is considered as read and open to amendment at any point. In the House, there is a requirement that the measure must be read in its entirety, but this can be avoided by a nondebatable

---

Some committees closely adhere to formal parliamentary procedures; others conduct conceptual markups in which committee members agree generally on broad ideas or principles, and staff then draft the legal language for later review by the members; and still other panels operate informally, largely by consensus, and in a bipartisan manner. The rules of the Senate Foreign Relations Committee even state: "Insofar as possible, [markup] proceedings of the Committee will be conducted without resort to the formalities of parliamentary procedure and with due regard for the views of all members." Overall, some markups are sedate affairs, while others are torn apart by partisan or substantive controversies.

Senate markups typically occur at the full committee level rather than in subcommittees. By contrast, House markups could occur at both the subcommittee level and full committee level. A key reason for this bicameral difference is that senators are subject to greater workload and time pressures than the average House member. For example, senators serve on about a dozen committees and subcommittees; House members sit on about a half dozen panels.

Whether in the House or Senate, markups are generally characterized by a greater degree of personal and parliamentary informality than proceedings in the chamber. As smaller entities, committees simply need less formality in their markup meetings. Moreover, in neither chamber are official parliamentarians assigned to the committees to assist in interpreting the rules. Committee and subcommittee chairs often use their own experience and judgment in enforcing the rules, or, if a particularly knotty procedural issue arises, they may request the advice of a majority committee staff aide knowledgeable in parliamentary matters or seek the counsel of the House or Senate parliamentarian.

motion to waive the reading if printed copies of the text are available to the members. Typically, the markup vehicle is read section by section, and after each section is read, the bill is open to amendment. A House committee, by unanimous consent, may agree to read the bill by title or that it be open to amendment at any point.

Amending Process. In general, the same amending rules apply during markup as apply on the House or Senate floor. In the Senate, there are ordinarily no limits on either debate or the number of amendments that senators may offer. In the House, amendments are considered under the **5-minute rule**. A member seeks recognition from the chair to speak for 5 minutes on the pending amendment(s).

Voting. Proxy voting is prohibited in the House; it is permitted in the Senate under limitations stated in chamber and committee rules. In both chambers, voting is by voice, division (show of hands), or roll call.

Reporting the Measure. Both chambers require that a majority of the panel's membership must be physically present to report, or vote out, the legislation.

Rarely are points of order made on the floor against a bill's consideration on the grounds of defective committee procedure. For example, unless a committee violated an explicit House rule, House precedents stipulate that the rules or procedures of committees are for those committees to interpret. Even if a committee directly violates a House rule, the Rules Committee can obviate points of order by waiving the relevant chamber rule. The more flexible Senate has a "cleanup" rule, which states that if a committee follows proper procedure in reporting a bill to the floor—a quorum of panel members who vote in open session and in person—then challenges against consideration of the bill for violating other markup rules (holding secret sessions as a matter of convenience, for example) will not be upheld. Box 3.5 summarizes selected markup procedures.

COMMITTEE MARKUP PROCEDURES

House and Senate rules each distinguish between a quorum for markups (one third of the committee membership) and a quorum to report legislation (a majority of the membership). Several other procedural issues suffuse House and Senate markups, such as the choice of vehicle, or document, to be used for markup purposes; the amendment process; the openness of markup sessions; and the conduct of votes.

Committee and subcommittee chairs typically decide what document will be used for markup purposes. The choices include the bill as introduced and referred to the committee, a subcommittee-prepared product, the administration's proposal, a staff draft, or a legislative draft that is commonly called the "chair's mark," containing the chair's idea of what the committee members should focus on. The selection is important for both substantive and procedural reasons. Substantively, the markup vehicle frames and shapes the policy discussion among the committee members. Procedurally, keeping items in the markup document is often easier than striking provisions from it, which can arouse public debate and controversy. As a senator noted: "Everybody knows that . . . it is much more difficult to get something out of a committee bill than it is to put something into the committee bill."[75] Some committees make their markup document available on their panel's Internet home page and also publish transcripts of the proceedings. The 112th House added additional transparency rules for markups. They include the following: The vehicle to be marked up is to be available in electronic form at least 24 hours before the meeting; any record vote is to be publicly available in electronic form within 48 hours of the vote; and the text of any adopted amendment is to be similarly available within 24 hours of the markup.

Once the markup vehicle is before the committee—the chair simply presents it to the panel members—and after the chair and members make brief opening statements, the committee is ready to consider amendments (proposals to change the text of the markup document) that it will recommend to either the House or Senate. (Committees merely recommend amendments, because only the full House or Senate has the authority to amend the text of legislation.) In the House, the committee amendment process tracks closely the amendment process in the chamber at large. For example, the markup vehicle is commonly read (the reading is usually waived by unanimous consent) section by section, and members are recognized to offer their amendments once a section is pending before the panel. Members are accorded 5 minutes to discuss amendments, and the chair alternates between the majority and minority side in recognizing members to offer amendments or to debate the pending proposals. In the Senate, committee members can offer amendments to any part of the bill, and few restrictions are made on debate. Dilatory actions in Senate markups are often harder to stop than in the House, because senators in most committees can filibuster either by talking at length or by offering scores of amendments, even requiring that they be read in full. Furthermore, to stop markups from continuing, senators sometimes invoke a Senate rule, which is usually routinely waived, that forbids markups after the Senate has been in session for 2 hours and in no case beyond 2 p.m.

Most House and Senate markups are conducted in open session. Senate Rule XXVI even stipulates that open markup meetings shall be "publicly available through the Internet [as] a video recording, audio recording, or a transcript . . . not later than 21 business days after the meeting occurs." House and Senate committee reports accompanying legislation also contain the names of members voting for and against any amendments and motions to report the bill. To be sure, important measures (tax or appropriations, for example) may still be discussed in private without much protest from the media or others. Even proponents of openness admit that members can reach compromises and make tough decisions more easily when they are away from the glare of lobbyists sitting in the audience. Moreover, because of the scores of journalists and media representatives covering Capitol Hill, the results of closed sessions become quickly known once the committee opens its doors. "Closed sessions don't necessarily mean bad legislation and sunshine doesn't guarantee good laws," remarked a journalist. "Openness just makes the process and the results slightly easier to discern."[76]

During markup, House and Senate committees decide issues by **voice vote**, a show of hands, or a roll call vote. Senate committee chairs may collect proxy votes to win key issues—often to the chagrin of the minority committee members who are in attendance. Proxy voting permits a committee member to cast a vote for an absent colleague, but proxy voting is prohibited on the House or Senate floor. As one account of a Senate markup noted:

> [The subcommittee chairman's] preparation paid off. The committee had been in session for more than five hours and about half the members had left. But when the vote was taken, [the chair] could supplement the eight votes he had in the room with nine proxies. The vote was 17–12.[77]

In 1995 the GOP-controlled House banned proxy voting in committees and subcommittees. During their 40 consecutive years in the minority, Republicans had long chafed under a system where their members attended committee markups yet were always outvoted by the handful of Democrats present because the chair voted the proxies of absent colleagues. Abolishing proxy voting was intended to promote member participation in markups. However, lawmakers with multiple committee assignments often had to sprint back and forth to cast votes in committees **marking up bills** simultaneously or run back and forth from committee markup sessions and the floor to cast votes. Their participation in markups was minimal. Furthermore, some GOP chairs discovered midway through a markup that they had suddenly lost control of the proceedings. For example, 20 Republican absences in one committee "allowed Democrats to win adoption of a GOP-opposed amendment."[78]

To prevent this from happening, Republicans adopted a House rule in 2003 that permitted committee chairs to postpone votes and to reschedule them when they were certain of majority support. Representative Dingell, D-Mich., who viewed the change as a subterfuge, pointed out that

> by permitting votes to be postponed to a time certain, Members will no longer have to attend committee markups while important amendments are being debated. Instead, they will merely have to show up at a specified time to vote. It sounds an awful lot like proxy voting to me.[79]

The ban on proxy voting and the provision allowing chairs to postpone votes remain part of today's House rulebook.

Strategies During Markup

Committee chairs and members use various strategies during the markup. To accelerate action on major legislation, chairs can, for example, schedule marathon markups that go on for days or weeks and that meet daily from early morning until late at night. Or chairs might hold abbreviated markups to speed legislation to the floor. One ploy, sometimes used by opponents of a bill, is to add amendments to strengthen the measure. For example, during markup of a gun control measure by the House Judiciary Committee, the National Rifle Association (NRA), the major lobbying group opposed to gun control, told its supporters in Congress that it would be easier to defeat a strong firearms proposal. "The way we look at it," said an NRA lobbyist, "the stronger the bill that comes out of committee, the less chance it has of passing on the floor."[80] Conversely, proponents of a strong bill might try to weaken it in committee so that it stands a better chance of winning majority support on the floor. Supporters can then try to persuade the other chamber or the House–Senate conference committee to strengthen the measure.

Another approach used by a bill's opponent is to offer a flurry of amendments to make a bill complicated, confusing, and unworkable for the executive branch agencies that would be responsible for administering the law. Moreover, offering scores of amendments, or offering one huge amendment and insisting that it be read—slowly—in full, may stall the markup and grant opponents additional time to lobby against the legislation. For example, a senator once sought to delay markup of a federal employees bill "by reading—slowly and deliberately—a lengthy statement explaining his opposition. He then offered seven amendments" and launched into a long explanation of each.[81] Sometimes minority committee members boycott markup sessions to delay or prevent these meetings from proceeding for lack of a quorum (one third of the panel's membership, as mentioned earlier, is the standard requirement in both chambers).

Mobilizing grassroots support, crafting a public relations strategy ("message" sending), and targeting the states or districts of key committee members are often critical to the outcome of markups. During markup by Congress's tax-writing panels, special interests work diligently to shape the thinking of these committees. As one account noted:

> For several months, the lobbyists have been working behind the scenes trying to influence the outcome by personally talking with members and aides of the tax committees in both chambers and getting members of their lobbying coalitions to write and phone their Congressmen. To bolster their arguments, the lobbyists have hired independent research firms to produce analyses that show the impact of the proposed tax changes, and they have tried to mold public opinion through press releases and advertising campaigns.[82]

To win over opponents or skeptics, chairs often willingly accept numerous amendments from their committee colleagues. In this way, these members develop a stake in the legislation and may stand united behind it on the House or Senate floor. The reverse strategy is to load down a bill with scores of costly add-ons so the legislation possibly sinks of its own weight. "We might just as well kill the president's [health reform] bill with kindness" by adding costly and untenable amendments, said an opposing lawmaker during a markup of the House Education Committee.[83]

An important factor affecting markup strategies in the Senate is the smaller size of its panels. One senator wrote that to get an amendment adopted by his Senate subcommittee he needed "only two other votes of the five-member subcommittee. In the House, subcommittees with more than 20 members are common."[84] One consequence: Greater effort may be needed to forge winning coalitions.

Compromise during the committee markup—or at any stage of the legislative process—is more likely when the members recognize that some sort of legislation is necessary. The outcome of markups, with their trade-offs, compromises, and complexities, may not be perfect, but it does reflect what attracted at least a majority vote of the panel members. As a House Ways and Means chair said after a tax markup: "We have not written perfect law. Perhaps a faculty of scholars could do a better job. A group of ideologues could have provided greater consistency. But politics is an imperfect process."[85] Another legislator emphasized this point in describing coalition building on a controversial measure: "Our goal is to find something that's 60 percent acceptable to 52 percent of the members and I think we have a 75 percent chance of doing that."[86] Once committees conclude their markups, members often mobilize to achieve their objectives, such as lobbying colleagues and organizing pep rallies on Capitol Hill. Table 3.1 lists several major differences between the House and the Senate in the introduction, referral, and committee consideration of legislation.

THE REPORT

Assuming that major differences have been ironed out in the markup, the committee then meets to vote on reporting the bill out of committee. House and Senate rules require a committee majority to be present for this purpose; otherwise, a point of order may be made on the floor that will force the bill to be returned to committee. Bills voted out of committee unanimously stand a good chance on the floor. A sharply divided, party-line committee vote presages an equally sharp dispute on the floor. A bill is rejected if the committee vote is a tie.

Committees have several options when they vote to report, or approve, a bill. They may report the bill without any changes, with various discrete amendments, or with a complete substitute amendment that is the functional equivalent of a new bill. Or a committee that is proposing to amend a bill extensively may instruct the chair to incorporate the modifications

TABLE 3.1   Procedural Differences at Preliminary Stages of the Legislative Process

House	Senate
Bills are usually introduced before committee or floor action can proceed.	Committees may originate their own bills without first having measures sent to them.
No effective way to challenge the Speaker's (parliamentarian's) referral decisions.	Referrals are subject to appeals from the floor, but unanimous consent is used to correct erroneous referrals.
The Speaker is granted authority by House rules to refer bills to more than one committee.	Multiple referrals occur by unanimous consent, although the majority leader and minority leader can jointly offer a motion to that effect.
The Speaker is authorized, subject to House approval, to create ad hoc panels to consider legislation.	Neither the majority leader nor the presiding officer has authority under Senate rules to create ad hoc panels to process legislation.
Generally difficult to bypass committee consideration of measures.	Bypassing committee consideration of measures occurs more easily.
Floor action is sometimes less important for shaping policies than is committee action.	Floor action is as important as committee action in decision making.

in a new measure, known as a **clean bill**. This bill will be reintroduced, assigned a new bill number, referred back to the committee, and reported by the panel.

The clean bill procedure is employed for various reasons, such as expediting floor consideration of legislation. Another factor for the House is the germaneness rule. Provisions already in a bill are by definition considered to be germane and, therefore, are protected in the House against points of order. Germaneness rules apply to proposed free-standing amendments, committee, or pre-filed floor amendments. In the Senate, committees may report a clean bill to avoid running afoul of Senate Rule XV. The thrust of this rule states that it is not in order for the Senate to consider any proposed committee amendment "which contains any significant matter not within the jurisdiction of the committee proposing such amendment."[87] Finally, a clean bill may reflect negotiated agreements between key committee members and executive officials.

Committees may take other actions besides favorably reporting a bill. They may report out a bill adversely (unfavorably), recommending that the bill not be passed by the full chamber, or they may report legislation without a formal recommendation, allowing the chamber to decide the bill's merits. In either case, the bill may be sent to the full chamber and scheduled for floor action. Committees adamantly opposed to a measure may decide not to take any action at all, thereby blocking further consideration except through special procedures.

After the bill is reported, the committee chair instructs the staff to prepare a written report. (House rules require a written committee report to accompany legislation; Senate rules do not, but committees commonly issue a written committee report.) The report describes the purposes and scope of the bill, explains the committee revisions, notes proposed changes in existing law, and usually includes the views of the executive branch agencies consulted. Committee members opposing the bill often submit dissenting, or minority, views. Any committee member may file minority, supplemental, or additional views, which are printed in the committee report. House and Senate rules also require committee reports to contain certain information, such as 5-year cost estimates, oversight findings, and regulatory impact statements. Measures are open to points of order on the floor if their committee report fails to contain this material. On an omnibus measure, a report may be more than 1,000 pages long.

Reports are directed primarily at House and Senate members and seek to persuade them to endorse the committee's recommendations when the bill comes up for a floor vote. The reports are the principal official means of communicating a committee decision to the entire chamber. Committee reports are also used by executive officials to fathom legislative intent when they are interpreting ambiguous statutory phrases. Federal judges, too, examine committee reports and other aspects of legislative history (hearings, floor debates, and conference reports) when laws are challenged in court. Some federal justices, most notably Supreme Court Justice Antonin Scalia, argue that legislative history should be minimized in the interpretation of ambiguous statutes. Instead of examining the committee hearing record or staff-written committee reports to determine what Congress intended, Justice Scalia argues, judges should consider only the exact text of the statute, because lawmakers vote on that and not on legislative history. Disparaging the value of committee hearings as legislative history, Justice Scalia noted that testimony often occurs before "an undetermined number of likely somnolent congressmen."[88] Supreme Court Justice Stephen G. Breyer, by contrast, answers "that no one claims that legislative history is in any strong sense 'the law,' but rather that it is useful in ascertaining the meaning of words in the statute."[89]

Reports are numbered, by Congress and the chamber, in the order in which they are filed with the clerk of the House or Senate. Thus, in the 113th Congress the first House report was designated as H. Rept. 113-1 and the first Senate report as S. Rept. 113-1. The first page of a report is shown in Figure 3.1. Both the committee-reported bill and its accompanying report are then assigned to the appropriate House or Senate calendar to await scheduling for floor action.

112TH CONGRESS ⎱
   2d Session   ⎰ HOUSE OF REPRESENTATIVES ⎰ REPT. 112–513
                                               Part 1

MIDNIGHT RULE RELIEF ACT OF 2012

JUNE 1, 2012.—Committed to the Committee of the Whole House on the State of
the Union and ordered to be printed

Mr. ISSA, from the Committee on Oversight and Government
Reform, submitted the following

REPORT

together with

MINORITY VIEWS

[To accompany H.R. 4607]

[Including cost estimate of the Congressional Budget Office]

The Committee on Oversight and Government Reform, to whom
was referred the bill (H.R. 4607) to ensure economy and efficiency
of Federal Government operations by establishing a moratorium on
midnight rules during a President's final days in office, and for
other purposes, having considered the same, report favorably thereon without amendment and recommend that the bill do pass.

CONTENTS

19–006

FIGURE 3-1   House Committee Report

BYPASSING COMMITTEES

Party leaders are not reluctant to circumvent committee consideration of priority legislation or to propose changes in legislation if circumstances warrant after committees report their handiwork. During the 112th Congress, when different parties controlled the House and Senate, many major bills "emerged not from the traditional process of committee members debating and marking up bills, but from backroom negotiations among party leaders."[90] Lawmaking by brinksmanship and deadlines prompted this development. Both parties and chambers waited "until the last possible moment to reach agreement on major bills, a habit that short-circuits the committee process in favor of direct negotiations between House and Senate leaders."[91]

Committees in the House or Senate may be bypassed in various ways, such as attaching legislative riders to appropriations bills, having the House Rules Committee bring bills to the floor without committee hearings or markups, offering to pending legislation on the Senate floor nonrelevant amendments that embody bills pigeonholed in committee, or adding new propositions to conference reports during bicameral negotiations on legislation.

Various overlapping reasons account for the tendency to circumvent committees, but five are among the most important. The first is time. Two classic examples are the 1995 House Republican Contract with America and the 2007 Democratic "100-hour" legislative agenda. In both cases, party leaders believed that committees had insufficient time to conduct hearings and markups and issue reports on their agenda items before the promised time period of 100 days or hours for action ticked away. Party leaders, too, may rush to the floor measures that are popular with the public or that lawmakers want to consider quickly, such as President Obama's economic stimulus plan (the American Recovery and Reinvestment Act).

A second reason is partisanship. Majority party leaders may want to avoid review by a committee divided by sharp partisan disagreements. In their estimation, the minority party should not be provided two opportunities—in committee and on the floor—to frustrate the majority and to showcase its agenda. The partisan infighting associated with committee consideration of a politically potent issue and the negative media coverage it will generate is something the majority leadership prefers to avoid. Party leaders may also want to circumvent committee consideration to force a floor vote on a so-called "wedge" issue (something that energizes one party but divides the other) that can be used in the next election against members of the other party.

A third factor is committee gridlock. Factional disputes within the majority party, combined with strong resistance from the minority party, may prevent committees from reaching agreement on measures deemed important to the majority party. As a result, party leaders will intervene to bypass the stalled committee stage and bring the legislation to the floor. Occasions also may arise when committees are substantively out of sync with the policy preferences of their party or with political imperatives that require the House or Senate to act expeditiously on legislation.

A fourth reason is electoral salience. Certain compelling issues are of such political importance to the majority party in terms of their appeal to the general public or to their party's core supporters that the leadership will circumvent the committee process to keep tight control of them. The Speaker, for example, will use her authority over the House Rules Committee to have her preferred version of a bill sent to the floor under debate and amendment procedures that advantage the majority party. The Senate majority leader might convene closed-door drafting sessions or invoke a procedure (Rule XIV) that places a measure directly on the legislative calendar, preventing it from being referred to committee.

A fifth factor is consensus: The relevant committee of jurisdiction, and perhaps a majority of the membership or at least the majority party, supports circumvention. Committees may waive consideration on the grounds that they have conducted hearings and markups on the legislation for several successive Congresses. Some proposals, too, may be debated year after year by the House and Senate so lawmakers are familiar with the pros and cons of the legislation. "This bill [heading directly to the floor] is pretty straightforward," remarked a House member. "I don't know that it needs much scrubbing by a committee."[92]

When a bill has been reported from committee, it is ready to be scheduled for floor action. Like the winnowing process that occurs in committee, scheduling involves budgeting congressional time. Important political choices must be made in determining the order in which bills will be considered on the floor, how much time will be devoted to each measure, and to what extent the full chamber will be permitted to reexamine a committee decision.

NOTES

1. Michael Janofsky, "Scent of Ballots Is in Air, and Energy Bills Are Blooming," *New York Times*, June 20, 2006, A11.
2. Lisa Lerer, "Senate Embraces Sanders' Pay Cap," *Politico*, February 9, 2009, online edition.
3. Chrissie Long, "Lawmakers Turn to Catchy Names for Bills," *The Hill*, April 21, 2005, 6.
4. "The Final Word," *CongressDailyPM*, March 9, 2005, 9.
5. Richard Simon, "Congress Turns Bill Titles Into Acts of Exaggeration," *Los Angeles Times*, June 19, 2011, online edition.
6. Jonathan Weisman, "Women Figure Anew in Senate's Latest Battle," *New York Times*, March 15, 2012, A22.
7. *CongressDailyAM*, May 20, 2003, 3.
8. David Francis, "Estate Tax Fight Hinges on Money, Morality," *Christian Science Monitor*, July 13, 2005, 2.

9. Jonathan Strong, "Time for Election Year Agendas," *Roll Call*, February 29, 2012, 12.
10. Julie Rovner, "Senate Committee Approves Health Warnings on Alcohol," *Congressional Quarterly Weekly Report*, May 24, 1986, 1175.
11. David Drucker, "Bipartisanship Is McCaskill's Election Strategy," *The Hill*, May 18, 2011, 6.
12. "Hoyer-Cantor, Round XXIVX," *Roll Call*, March 22, 2012, 16.
13. *Congressional Record*, January 5, 2011, H13. In addition to this provision to the House rulebook, the chamber also repealed an earlier rule, adopted in 1997, that required committee reports accompanying bills and joint resolutions to include a constitutional authority statement.
14. Ibid., H21.
15. Daniel Newhauser, "Authority Statements Are Often Vague," *Roll Call*, April 10, 2012, 11. The Republican Study Committee tracks each statement and distributes a "Questionable Constitutional Authority Statement of the Week."
16. David C. King, *Turf Wars: How Congressional Committees Claim Jurisdiction* (Chicago: University of Chicago Press, 1997), 11.
17. See Norman J. Ornstein, Thomas E. Mann, and Michael J. Malbin, *Vital Statistics on Congress, 2008* (Washington, DC: Brookings Institution Press, 2008), 127.
18. Paul Singer, "More Bills, More Lawyers for Leg Offices," *Roll Call*, March 28, 2007, 22.
19. *Congressional Record*, March 31, 2008, S2234.
20. Ronald M. Peters Jr. and Cindy Simon Rosenthal, *Speaker Nancy Pelosi and the New American Politics* (New York: Oxford University Press, 2010), 181.
21. *Congressional Record*, May 14, 2003, H4021.
22. *Congressional Record*, January 7, 2003, H13.
23. *Congressional Record*, January 5, 2011, H15.
24. Nicole Duran, "Dingell's Valentine Wish: A Record," *Roll Call*, August 1, 2005, 13.
25. Allison Stevens, "House Revisits Capitol Slave Labor Issue," *CQ Weekly*, July 12, 2003, 1723.
26. On occasion, a member introducing a bill may ask unanimous consent that the bill be passed. Unanimous consent can be granted in the Senate and the House but only on a noncontroversial measure or one on which all members agree that immediate action is required.
27. Article I, Section 3, of the Constitution provides that the vice president is president of the Senate, but vice presidents preside over that body infrequently. The Constitution also provides for a president pro tempore. By custom, that position is held by the most senior member of the majority party. Usually, however, junior members designated by the majority leader preside over the daily sessions of the Senate. Each chamber has a parliamentarian, who is an expert on rules of procedure. During a session, the parliamentarians or one of their assistants is present to advise the chair on all points of order and parliamentary inquiries.
28. Committee structure and jurisdiction are not identical in the House and Senate, but they are broadly parallel.
29. *CongressDailyPM*, May 4, 1998, 6.
30. *CQ Daily Monitor*, March 1, 2000, 8.

31. David C. King, "The Nature of Congressional Committee Jurisdictions," *American Political Science Review* (March 1994): 49.
32. Alex Wayne, "House Chairmen Promise to Move Similar Health Care Overhaul Bills," *CQ Today,* March 12, 2009, 16.
33. Richard E. Cohen and Brian Friel, "The Big Lift," *National Journal,* July 4, 2009, 28.
34. Edward Epstein and Catharine Richert, "Committee Chairmen Set for a Busy Year as They Tackle Several Big Issues," *CQ Today,* March 16, 2009, 7.
35. David Herszenhorn, "Baucus Grabs Pacesetter Role on Health Bill," *New York Times,* June 24, 2009, A16.
36. Emily Pierce, "Reid Committed to Health Care Timeline, Has Plan for Forthcoming Bill," *Roll Call,* July 16, 2009, online edition.
37. Lawrence E. Filson, *The Legislative Drafter's Desk Reference* (Washington, DC: CQ Press, 1992). The legislative counsel's office also reviews drafts prepared for lawmakers by various entities or groups. As the head of the House Office of Legislative Counsel stated: "It is clear that the number of outside groups striving to design and control the details of legislative language is growing." See also Billy House, "Counsel's Office Flooded With Outside Bills," *CongressDailyPM,* May 29, 2006, 6.
38. Michael Sandler, "Not a Job for Judiciary Committee? House Ag Handles Eminent Domain Bill," *CQ Today,* August 8, 2005, 7.
39. *CongressDailyPM,* April 24, 1998, 6.
40. "Senate Parliamentarian Can Control Course of Bills," *C-Span Update,* January 14, 1990, 6.
41. *Congressional Record,* January 4, 2005, H26.
42. Ibid., H14.
43. *Congressional Record,* January 30, 1995, H849. When the 110th Congress convened, chairs of the House Committees on Homeland Security and Transportation and Infrastructure signed a memorandum of understanding clarifying their respective jurisdictions over the Federal Emergency Management Agency and the Coast Guard. See *Congressional Record,* January 4, 2007, H15–H16.
44. See Speaker J. Dennis Hastert's "jurisdictional issues" statement on the opening day of the 109th Congress, *Congressional Record,* January 4, 2005, H35.
45. *Congressional Record,* December 14, 2007, S15580.
46. See Bruce I. Oppenheimer, "Policy Effects of U.S. House Reform: Decentralization and the Capacity to Resolve Energy Issues," *Legislative Studies Quarterly* (February 1980): 5–30; and David J. Vogler, "Ad Hoc Committees in the House of Representatives and Purposive Models of Legislative Behavior," *Polity* (Fall 1981): 89–109.
47. *Congressional Record,* June 19, 2002, H3694.
48. *Congressional Record,* January 4, 1995, H36.
49. *Congressional Record,* March 8, 2012, H1303.
50. *Congressional Record,* January 7, 2003, H11.
51. All Senate committees have the authority to draft an original bill and report it out without referral of the measure back to the committee after its introduction by the committee chair. In the House, only a small number of committees, such as the Appropriations Committee, have the authority to report original legislation.
52. Randall B. Ripley, *Congress: Process and Policy* (New York: Norton, 1975), 75.

53. *Congressional Record*, May 9, 1994, H3181.

54. *Washington Post*, May 21, 1995, A4.

55. Members of Congress rely heavily on committee staff for assistance in organizing hearings, selecting witnesses, and drafting bills, as well as for many other key support functions. The chair's control of committee staff, therefore, is an important resource in his or her control of the legislative process.

56. Senate party leaders can also exert influence over committee chairs. For example, Majority Whip Richard Durbin, D-Ill., underscored that there is "a close working relationship between committee chairs and the leadership. We meet regularly to discuss our agenda," he said. Then Durbin added: "The committee chairs . . . understand that if [majority party leaders] are not going to create special committees and special task forces [to craft policies] that it means they have a greater burden" to act on party-preferred priorities. See also Epstein and Richert, "Committee Chairmen Set for a Busy Year as They Tackle Several Big Issues," 7–8.

57. Jonathan Allen, "The A-Hole Factor," *Politico*, December 13, 2012, online edition.

58. Dan Friedman and Fawn Johnson, "Boehner Threatens to Move Senate Bill," *National Journal*, March 7, 2012, 12.

59. Don Wolfensberger, "Weak Committees Empower the Partisans," *Roll Call*, November 8, 2011, 26.

60. *Wall Street Journal*, April 11, 1986, 54.

61. Members unable to attend a committee session frequently assign committee staffers to attend the meeting and brief them later. Staff aides can ask questions of witnesses if authorized by committee rules or by the chair.

62. *Workshop on Congressional Oversight and Investigations*, 96th Cong., 1st sess., 1979, H. Doc. 96-217, 25.

63. Alan Ota, "Closed Doors Keep Out Sunlight at Subcommittee Soirees," *CQ Today*, July 21, 2009, 1, 9.

64. *Washington Post*, September 23, 1998, A23.

65. Warren Leary, "When Astronauts Brief Congress, a Little Levity Goes a Long Way," *New York Times*, June 15, 2005, A16.

66. Bob Pool, "Survivors Take Stock of Gains Against Cancer," *Los Angeles Times*, May 30, 1997, B1. See also Linda J. Demaine, "Navigating Policy by the Stars: The Influence of Celebrity Entertainers on Federal Lawmaking," *Journal of Law and Politics* (Spring 2009): 83–143.

67. *Christian Science Monitor*, November 27, 1985, 28. See also Barbara Vobejda, "Children Show Congress Scars of Gun Violence," *Washington Post*, March 11, 1993, A16.

68. Jackie Calmes, "New Round of Senate Hearings on IRS Risks Overkill," *Wall Street Journal*, March 31, 1998, A24.

69. Jeffrey Toobin, "Barney's Great Adventure," *New Yorker*, January 12, 2009, 46.

70. Elizabeth Bumiller, "Lengthy Practices Prepare Court Nominee for His Senate Hearings," *New York Times*, September 11, 2005, A11.

71. Keith Perine, "It's Not Used Much, but House Democrats Invoke Rule 11 to Get Extra Exposure on Gitmo," *CQ Today*, June 10, 2005, 12.

72. Mike Allen, "Panel Chairman Leaves Hearing," *Washington Post*, June 11, 2005, A4.

73. Billy House, "Remote Control," *National Journal*, February 25, 2012, 3.

74. *State Government News*, April 1982, 4.
75. *Congressional Record*, July 20, 1983, S10430.
76. *Washington Post*, May 6, 1984, F5.
77. Ronald Elving, "Smoking Ban for Short Flights Likely to Ignite Senate Scrap," *Congressional Quarterly Weekly Report*, October 3, 1987, 2409.
78. *CQ Daily Monitor*, March 21, 2000, 1.
79. *Congressional Record*, January 7, 2003, H18.
80. *Washington Post*, February 6, 1976, A6.
81. Elizabeth Palmer, "Roth's Parliamentary Moves Halt Hatch Act Reform," *Congressional Quarterly Weekly Report*, March 7, 1992, 534.
82. *New York Times*, October 15, 1985, D25.
83. Dana Priest and Spencer Rich, "Key Hill Committees Take Up Health Care Legislation," *Washington Post*, May 19, 1994, A23.
84. Paul Simon, "Trying on the Senate for Size," *Chicago*, November 1985, 150.
85. *Washington Post*, November 25, 1985, A4.
86. *Washington Post*, February 24, 1988, A22.
87. Senate Rule XV is seldom invoked, in part because a committee amendment ruled out-of-order could be transformed into a floor amendment and offered to the committee-reported bill.
88. Joan Biskupic, "High Court Opinions Anything but Brief," *USA Today*, June 13, 2011, 6A.
89. Robert A. Katzmann, "Justice Breyer: A Rival for Scalia on the Hill's Intent," *Roll Call*, May 30, 1994, 5. See Joan Biskupic, "Congress Keeps Eye on Justices as Court Watches Hill's Words," *Congressional Quarterly Weekly Report*, October 5, 1991, 2863–2867; and Joan Biskupic, "Listening In on the 'Conversation' between Court and Congress," *Washington Post*, May 1, 1994, A4. See also Michael Koby, "The Supreme Court's Declining Reliance on Legislative History: The Impact of Justice Scalia's Critique," *Harvard Journal on Legislation* (Summer 1999): 369–395; and Michael Slade, "Democracy in the Details: A Plea for Substance over Form in Statutory Interpretation," *Harvard Journal on Legislation* (Winter 2000): 187–236.
90. Stacy Kaper, Nancy Cook, and Jim Tankersley, "Congressional Committees, RIP: 1789–2011," *NationalJournalDaily*, December 19, 2011, 1. Also see Manu Raju, "How Hill Leaders Sow Dysfunction," *Politico*, December 20, 2011 1.
91. Ibid., "Congressional Committees, RIP: 1789–2011," 1.
92. *CongressDailyAM*, May 12, 1999, 11.

CHAPTER 4

Scheduling Legislation in the House

"THE POWER of the Speaker of the House is the power of scheduling," observed Thomas P. "Tip" O'Neill Jr., D-Mass., who served as Speaker for more consecutive years (1977–1987) than any of his predecessors.[1] Setting the House's agenda and scheduling floor action on that agenda is fundamentally the prerogative of the Speaker. To paraphrase a former president, the Speaker is "the decider," but the Speaker consults with numerous colleagues and weighs many factors that influence agenda-setting decisions: House rules, budgetary timetables, bicameral considerations, election-year activities, the administration's programs, the pressures of national and international events, the majority leadership's policy and political preferences, and the actions of the House Rules Committee. Speakers understand that the politics and strategies of scheduling can strongly influence a bill's fate. Determining when (if at all), what, how, and in which order measures are brought to the floor is part of the arsenal of legislative considerations that the majority leadership uses to produce winning coalitions, provide political protection to members, mobilize bipartisan support, engineer a record of accomplishment, or advance its own partisan agenda.

Scheduling is a complex process that involves juggling a wide range of considerations, demands, and pressures. Like his recent predecessors, Speaker John Boehner, R-Ohio (2011–) relies on the majority leader (Eric Cantor of Virginia) to help draft and manage the agenda after consulting with the committee chairs, rank-and-file lawmakers, majority-party leaders, and others. Bicameral coordination and consultation can also be a factor in scheduling. During the 112th Congress, Speaker Boehner and Senate Minority Leader Mitch McConnell, R-Ky., regularly consulted about the scheduling of issues. The two chambers' **recess** schedules sometimes became a matter of institutional and political significance. To constrain the president's constitutional recess appointment authority—preventing the chief executive from installing in federal posts nominees opposed by Republicans—the two GOP leaders adopted a simple formula: no congressional recesses, no recess appointments by the president. (See Chapter 6 for additional details on this matter.)

Under the Constitution (Article I, Section 5), neither chamber shall adjourn for more than 3 days without the consent of the other house. The GOP-controlled House refused to adopt these normally routine concurrent adjournment resolutions of more than 3 days, forcing both chambers to convene in pro forma session every third day. The goal of the GOP leaders'

147

scheduling plan: to delay or prevent President Obama from making recess appointments—bypassing the Senate's "advice and consent" prerogative—under the chief executive's constitutional authority (Article II, Section 3) "to fill up all Vacancies that may happen during a Recess of the Senate." Despite legislative breaks of a week or more, the House and Senate remained technically open for business, if only for a few seconds, thwarting the president's ability to make recess appointments. However, in the case of a specific controversial nomination—for the chair of the new Consumer Financial Protection Bureau, whose approval was blocked for months by Senate Republicans—President Obama broke precedent. He recess appointed the chair of the bureau even though both chambers were technically not in recess and were able to conduct official business. Precedent dictated that a recess or adjournment must be longer than 3 days (more like 10) before the president can use his recess appointment authority. The president's action set off numerous protests from Senate Republicans and led to several legal challenges.[2]

Both parties in each chamber also organize periodic partisan retreats where they focus in part on what their agenda priorities should be going forward. House Republicans even surveyed citizens, online activists, national party leaders, and their own colleagues to get input on their agenda priorities. As part of that initiative, the House GOP instituted the "You Cut" program that allowed the public each week to go to Majority Leader Cantor's website and "select one of three government programs to cut. The proposal with the most votes will be introduced as a bill, with the public able to track its progress on the website."[3] Scheduling, in brief, is a collective and consultative activity that involves at least five major concerns.

First, the majority leadership sets out the daily, weekly, monthly, and annual agenda of the House. This activity involves such matters as advance planning of annual recesses (district work periods) and adjournments, coordinating committee and floor action, trying to provide a predictable weekly agenda of business, and regulating the flow of bills to the floor during slack or peak periods. Plainly, scheduling can be a challenge, especially if the House and Senate observe their often "Tuesday-through-Thursday" workweek (lawmakers depart for their constituencies Thursday evening or at least by midday Friday and return by late afternoon on Monday).

Second, scheduling can become a campaign issue. Congressional Democrats criticized Republicans in the November 2006 elections for having kept the House in session that year fewer days (103) than did the "do-nothing" GOP-controlled 80th Congress (110 days) targeted by Harry Truman during his 1948 presidential campaign. One-upping Truman, congressional Democrats called the GOP-controlled 109th House the "do-less-than-do-nothing" Congress. Thus, when Democrats took over the 110th House (2007–2009), Majority Leader Hoyer said that most weeks the House would come in "Monday at 6:30 p.m. and be working on Fridays, as we used to do, until about [2 p.m.] to give people time so they can get home" to their districts.[4]

Four years later, with Republicans in charge of the House, the majority leadership instituted a schedule markedly different from that of the previous Democratic majority. The GOP instituted a "two weeks on, one week off" schedule for 2011 and 2012, with more breaks in the election year. Under the majority leader's plan, members would be in Washington for 2 weeks, followed by 1 week in their respective districts. To provide committees with uninterrupted time to conduct hearings and meetings, votes in the chamber would occur daily no earlier than 1 p.m. Moreover, the last vote would occur no later than 7 p.m. Cantor's schedule also provided that on Mondays, when members were returning to Washington from their districts, votes would begin at 6:30 p.m. On Fridays, no votes would occur after 3 p.m., to facilitate members' travel plans.[5]

Many House members welcomed the new schedule. Democratic leaders, however, castigated it for two overlapping reasons. First, the House ignored coordinating its schedule with that of the Democratic Senate. With their out-of-sync **calendars**, it was harder to get bicameral work done and to push legislation to enactment. One chamber might be in session while the other was not. Second, legislative productivity was down. "We've conducted legislative business a mere 111 days [in 2011]," exclaimed Minority Whip Hoyer, "nearly equal to the 104 days spent either in recess or in pro forma business."[6] Where the Democratic House in 2010 considered 986 measures, the next year under GOP management the number fell to around 200, largely because of gridlock between the parties and chambers, divided government, and the ban on commemorative legislation in the House.[7] Majority Leader Cantor contended that the schedule produced positive results; Democrats asserted that the GOP's ineffective management hampered the House's ability to address the nation's pressing problems.

Third, a host of strategic considerations influence scheduling. For example, with an eye toward upcoming elections, the majority leadership schedules legislation designed to energize and activate the party's electoral supporters. Even if those measures fail, they draw sharp interparty policy contrasts. During presidential election years, congressional leaders work with their party's nominee to coordinate agendas and messages. "Wedgislation" is also popular in election years because various measures—immigration reform, same-sex marriage, flag burning, and so on—unify one party and promote discord in the other. Forcing votes on "hot-button" measures provides campaign ammunition to opposition challengers back home.

Legislation may be scheduled for floor action at specific times—for instance, a constitutional amendment to ban flag burning just before July 4 or tax reform legislation on or around April 15—to maximize public attention on the issue. "Deadline lawmaking" is common on major bills. Party leaders will inform the rank and file that before the House can adjourn for a scheduled recess, it must stay in session until it considers a certain measure or set of measures. Calendar deadlines are important leadership devices for moving legislation. The Speaker, too, may organize the schedule to highlight party themes or priorities—such as "make it in America week," "cybersecurity week," or "energy week"—that unify party colleagues around a set of domestic or international policies. For its part, the opposition might label the majority's "energy week" as "dirty air week." This day, exclaimed a minority lawmaker, the House will consider "legislation to cut the heart out of the Clean Air Act."[8] One chamber, too, may refuse to consider a measure until the other body takes up a bill it has passed.

Fourth, the Speaker tries to balance the House's workload requirements with lawmakers' family or personal obligations. "Family-friendly" scheduling aims to achieve better balance in the public and private lives of members. A GOP champion of the House's "two-and-one" schedule said: "We have given members the certainty of time back home for their families and constituents."[9]

Finally, scheduling even involves some mystery as majority leaders assess whether the political climate is favorable for bringing a bill to the floor. As Jim Wright, D-Tex., who served as Speaker from 1987 to June 1989, once noted:

> In scheduling the program for the Congress one must be constantly aware of the importance of maintaining a little suspense. I learned this from Agatha Christie. Always hold something back and keep people guessing a little bit. And that is what we are doing with this bill, quite frankly. We are maintaining a little suspense in the schedule [while we determine the best time for taking up this legislation].[10]

Needless to say, the best time for the majority leadership to bring up priority measures is when it believes it has the votes. A Speaker who finds that a bill lacks the support to pass may delay in taking it up or yank it off the floor if it is already under consideration. There are occasions when measures will be taken up despite uncertainty about whether they will be enacted. Asked if a bill would pass the House, a majority leader replied: "Who knows? We're writing the bill on the floor."[11]

When Nancy Pelosi was Speaker (2007–2011)—a historic figure as the first female Speaker—she stated that Democrats "came to the floor when we had consensus." She added: "You'll have to make sure the [legislative] design has 218, certain people one time, and other people another time."[12] Similarly, GOP Speaker Dennis Hastert (1999–2007) explained that it was

> always important to get 218 before we brought a bill to the floor, especially if it was a partisan bill. . . . There weren't many times that we took to the floor without knowing what our whip count was.[13]

Unlike his two predecessors, and for at least two reasons, Speaker Boehner encountered greater difficulties in mobilizing GOP votes to pass legislation. First, he chose a role that emphasized open, steady, and collegial party leadership, compared with the "top-down, carrots-and-sticks" approach of Pelosi and Hastert. One result is that many rank-and-file Republicans are not afraid to oppose the Speaker's plans, in part because the imposition of sanctions is unlikely. (Recall that, prior to the start of the 113th Congress, Boehner removed four wayward GOP members from their key House committees.) Second, Boehner's party contains numerous GOP lawmakers who often reject the idea of compromise and who challenge and criticize, sometimes publicly, attempts at bipartisan bargaining by the Speaker. These members' policy and political self-interests commonly trump support for the Speaker's agenda.

The minority party also advocates and advertises its agenda of legislative priorities. The minority's agenda is often geared toward sending a message for the next election. For example, to demonstrate to voters that they are the party of new ideas, the minority may advocate an "Innovation Agenda" that includes, for example, more investment in basic research and development. Minority agenda items are often a counterpoint to majority proposals. However, in a closely divided and highly partisan chamber, majority party leaders are unlikely to permit consideration of politically attractive minority initiatives, and only if they have a compelling alternative and the votes to reject the minority's idea. Despite its general powerlessness in agenda setting, the minority party articulates an agenda to energize its electoral supporters, attract public attention, foment legislative debate, and demonstrate that it has a vision of what to do if it wins control of the House.

The procedures for managing the flow of bills to the floor have evolved throughout the history of Congress and still undergo frequent change. At first glance, they may appear needlessly complex and cumbersome, but they have an internal logic and serve the needs of the House.

THE HOUSE LEGISLATIVE CALENDARS

The House maintains four legislative calendars, which aid in the scheduling of floor action. All measures reported from committee are assigned, in chronological order, by the clerk of the House to the Union Calendar, the House Calendar, or the Private Calendar. In addition, measures may be placed on the Discharge Calendar.

Legislation dealing with raising, authorizing, or spending money is assigned to the **Union Calendar** (technically, the Calendar of the Committee of the Whole House on the state of the Union). Nonmoney measures, such as proposals to amend the Constitution, are put on the **House Calendar**. Bills of a private nature ("for the relief of")—that is, those not of general application and usually dealing with individuals or specific entities—are assigned to the **Private Calendar**. The **Discharge Calendar** lists bills removed from committees through special, and infrequently successful, procedures.

When the House is in session, members receive a daily document, the *Calendars of the United States House of Representatives and History of Legislation,* which lists all House and Senate measures that have been reported from committee (see Figure 4.1). Not every measure listed is called up and considered by the House.

Regardless of the legislative calendars, any lawmaker can request unanimous consent at almost any time the House is in session to pass legislation. However, since the mid-1980s, all Speakers on the opening day of a new Congress have announced that they will confer recognition ("For

ONE HUNDRED THIRTEENTH CONGRESS

FIRST SESSION { CONVENED JANUARY 3, 2013

SECOND SESSION {

CALENDARS

OF THE UNITED STATES
HOUSE OF REPRESENTATIVES

————AND————

HISTORY OF LEGISLATION

LEGISLATIVE DAY 7   CALENDAR DAY 7

Tuesday, January 22, 2013

SUSPENSIONS

HOUSE MEETS AT 10 A.M.

FOR MORNING-HOUR DEBATE

SPECIAL ORDERS

(SEE NEXT PAGE)

www.HouseCalendar.gov

PREPARED UNDER THE DIRECTION OF KAREN L. HAAS, CLERK OF THE HOUSE OF REPRESENTATIVES:
By the Office of Legislative Operations

The Clerk shall cause the calendars of the House to be distributed each legislative day. Rule II, clause 2(e) *Index to the Calendars will be included on the first legislative day of each week the House is in session*

U.S. GOVERNMENT PRINTING OFFICE: 2013   29–038

FIGURE 4.1   Calendars of the U.S. House of Representatives and History of Legislation

what purpose does the gentlelady rise?") for "unanimous consent requests only when assured that the majority and minority floor leadership and the committee and subcommittee chairmen and ranking minority members have no objection." The Speaker's recognition power is an unchallengeable prerogative of the chair.

MINOR AND NONCONTROVERSIAL MEASURES

As with many legislative assemblies, the House has different procedures for handling minor and noncontroversial measures compared with major bills.[14] Legislation on the Private Calendar is in order only during certain days of the month. The House also processes noncontroversial measures that are on the Union or House Calendars under procedures that grant them privileged access to the floor during certain designated days of the week or month. These include measures brought to the floor under the widely used suspension of the rules procedure and the few bills dealing with the District of Columbia. Most of the legislation that comes before the House is considered under suspension procedure—more than 1,500 measures each in the 110th and the 111th Congresses.[15]

Suspension of the Rules

The principal legislative shortcut and increasingly utilized source of agenda control by the Speaker—sometimes for important as well as minor public bills, resolutions, and conference reports—is **suspension of the rules** ("I move to suspend the rules and pass H.R. 1234."). Until the 108th Congress (2003–2005), the suspension procedure was in order every Monday and Tuesday and during the last 6 days of a session of Congress. On an experimental basis, the GOP-controlled 108th House added Wednesday as another suspension day. When the 109th Congress began, Rules Chair David Dreier, R-Calif., explained that Wednesday now would be a permanent suspension day "after the very successful experiment we had with suspensions on Wednesday in the 108th Congress."[16] Democrats also kept Wednesdays as a suspension day when they won majority control of the 110th and 111th Congresses, as did Republicans when they took charge of the 112th and 113th Houses (2011–2015). Informally, the GOP leadership also required that suspension measures must be publicly available in electronic form for 3 days prior to their consideration by the House. This party protocol can be waived in exigent circumstances by the majority leader.[17] (The Rules Committee sometimes reports resolutions, subject to House approval, that authorize the Speaker to entertain motions to suspend the rules on days other than Monday, Tuesday, and Wednesday.) Lawmakers often refer to measures on the "suspension calendar" even though there is no formal calendar for this purpose.

Three key rules govern suspension procedure and limit its use on most occasions to noncontroversial measures that enjoy broad bipartisan support, such as naming post offices after deceased lawmakers. First, debate on suspension bills is limited to 40 minutes, evenly divided between proponents and opponents. Second, the motion to suspend the rules and pass a bill may include amendments, but only if they are stipulated in the motion offered by the majority floor manager ("I move to suspend the rules and pass H.R. 1234, with an amendment"); otherwise, amendments from the floor (as well as any points of order) are not permitted. Third, the final and only vote on the measure is both to suspend the rules and to pass the bill—by a two-thirds vote, a quorum (218) being present. Bills that fail to gain the necessary two-thirds support may be considered again under regular House procedures (i.e., a special rule granted by the Rules Committee or, far less likely, even another suspension attempt). Sometimes majority party leaders schedule bills they dislike for suspension procedure because the two-thirds requirement makes them easier to defeat.

To accommodate lawmakers' constituency and legislative activities, the House instituted a cluster voting rule. The Speaker announces that **recorded votes** on a group of bills considered under the suspension procedure will be postponed until later that day or within the next 2 days. The bills then are brought up in sequence and disposed of without further debate. On the first clustered vote in a series, members have a minimum of 15 minutes in which to vote; on the remaining votes, the Speaker may reduce the time on each one to a minimum of 5 minutes. Cluster voting is a convenience for members, to minimize their having to run back and forth to the chamber scores of times throughout the day to vote on issues.

The Speaker is in complete charge of measures considered under the suspension procedure through the discretionary recognition prerogative. Committee chairs, usually with the concurrence of their ranking minority colleagues, write the Speaker requesting that certain bills be taken up via the suspension route. Typically, these bills were reported by committee. But any measure—reported or not, previously introduced or not, including conference reports and constitutional amendments—can be brought to the floor under suspension of the rules if the Speaker chooses to recognize the representative offering the suspension motion. Speaker O'Neill, for example, brought a constitutional amendment, the Equal Rights Amendment (ERA), to the House floor in 1983 under suspension procedure to prevent opponents from offering controversial floor amendments on abortion and the military draft. However, the ERA failed to attract the required two-thirds vote, in part because even its supporters objected to taking up such a significant issue under procedures that limited debate and prevented amendments. The House's majority leadership might also use the suspension route to determine if they have the required two-thirds vote to override a president's veto.

The majority Republicans have guidelines that govern the consideration of measures under the suspension method. Under Republican Conference rules, there are provisions that state, for example, that the Speaker will not schedule measures for suspension procedure that are opposed by more than one third of the committee members reporting the bill, that fail to include a cost estimate, and that have not been cleared by the minority. The majority leadership "does not ordinarily schedule bills for suspensions unless confident of a two-thirds vote."[18] In the 112th House, however, the first two bills scheduled for suspension went down to defeat. The losses, said GOP leaders, occurred because of their inexperience in managing the floor; the defection of GOP newcomers who believed the measures were taken up without adequate review; and the unexpected loss of support from the Democratic minority. In the view of Majority Leader Cantor, "It's very easy, when you bring things up under suspension, if the minority wants to take it down, they can. We used to do that . . . so that was kind of a learning day for us."[19]

The suspension procedure enables the House to bypass normal floor procedures and quickly approve legislation that can attract an overwhelming voting majority. Committee chairs generally support the suspension of the rules because the procedure protects their bills from floor amendments and points of order. Party leaders may use the suspension route to expedite emergency legislation. At times, the minority party gets upset with the majority leadership for not scheduling enough of their bills via suspension procedure. To protest, minority party members may vote against suspension bills until more of their routine measures are taken up on the floor. They may also castigate the majority leadership for using suspension-of-the-rules procedure on bills that in their estimation merit more debate than 40 minutes and require the offering of stand-alone amendments.[20] As a minority member exclaimed:

> The suspension calendar is meant as a vehicle to name post offices or to honor sports teams or to do things that are noncontroversial. Yet here we're transferring $8 billion from the general fund to bail out the Highway Trust Fund. Under rules of suspension, that simply doesn't seem right. That is not responsible legislating.[21]

The use of suspension procedure has been on the increase, although it declined during the first year of the GOP-controlled 112th House. Majority Leader Cantor noted that "the percentage of bills that have come to the floor under suspension of the rules has dramatically declined from [over] 80 percent [in 2010] to 55 percent this year."[22] Part of the reason is the GOP's goal of focusing the House's deliberations on major issues involving deficit reduction and shrinking the role of government. Moreover, a polarized House finds it harder to approve legislation requiring a two-thirds vote for passage. Despite the decline in 2011 of the number of measures taken up by the suspension procedure, the general trend has been toward greater use of the device. Donald Wolfensberger, a congressional scholar and former staff director of the House Rules Committee, noted that of the measures that became law during the 107th Congress (2001–2003), nearly "eight out of every 10 bills enacted into law were brought to the House floor under the procedure. Two decades ago, roughly a third of enacted laws were brought to the House floor under the same process."[23] He also noted that "69 percent of laws enacted [thus far] for the 112th Congress . . . passed the House under suspension of the rules."[24]

Two other purposes are also served by having numerous suspension votes, which regularly occur at predetermined dates and times: (1) boosting lawmakers' voting percentages over the 90% mark, inoculating them against campaign attacks on their attendance record, and (2) ensuring lawmakers' presence in the chamber, thus enabling party whips to solicit their views and votes on upcoming priority measures.

Occasionally, minority party members will contend that noncontroversial bills that could easily pass by suspension instead are brought up with an open rule—granted by the Rules Committee—that provides for more than 40 minutes of debate and allows floor amendments. As a minority member of the Rules Committee exclaimed, "[I] would very much like to see these good, well-crafted utterly noncontroversial bills where they belong, and that is on the [informal] suspension calendar," where they can be passed quickly without wasting the House's time by employing open rules. Minority party lawmakers also assert that majority leaders want to use open rules for routine bills so they can claim credit for protecting minority rights. A minority member stated:

> Equating a suspension of the rules procedure which allows only 40 minutes of debate and no amendments with an open rule denigrates the democratic process. . . . Very often the questions are not whether the bill will pass ultimately or not, but in what form.[25]

During the hectic last days of a congressional session, suspension of the rules is used more frequently—and even on important measures. Dozens of bills may be scheduled daily for suspension votes. The parliamentary situation also is somewhat different during this period. Members who at an earlier time in the session might have voted against a bill brought up under suspension, because they had no opportunity to offer amendments to it or because it was a major bill, might vote for the same legislation during the end-of-the-session crunch, rationalizing that it is that version or nothing. The minority party's role is also enhanced during this pressure-packed, rush-to-adjourn time, because suspension votes virtually always require some bipartisan support.

District of Columbia Legislation

The federal capital is a unique governmental unit. Residents of the District of Columbia have no voting representation in Congress. (They have a nonvoting delegate in the House and no representation in the Senate.) Periodically, efforts are made to grant the District voting representation in the House of Representatives, but these initiatives have been unsuccessful to date.[26]

In a rules change initiated by D.C. delegate Eleanor Holmes Norton, the 103d Congress (1993–1995) permitted Norton, the three territorial delegates (Guam, Samoa, and the Virgin Islands) and the one resident commissioner

(Puerto Rico)—all Democrats—to vote in the Committee of the Whole (see Chapter 5). However, if their votes determined the outcome of an amendment, an automatic revote would be taken in the House without their participation. Republicans vehemently protested granting the delegates and resident commissioner the right to vote in the Committee of the Whole. In a good example of the majority rule principle in action, they dropped this provision from the House's rulebook when they took control in the 104th Congress.[27] Democrats reinstated this rule for all nonstate representatives when they took control of the 110th House and retained it in the 111th House. Republicans terminated the rule when they won majority control of both the 112th and 113th House. (Worth a brief mention is that a new delegate entered the 111th House for the first time to represent the Northern Marianas.)

Despite home rule for the capital, the House exercises control over the District of Columbia principally through two committees, Appropriations and Oversight and Government Reform. House rules set aside the second and fourth Mondays of each month for District of Columbia legislation reported by the Oversight and Government Reform Committee. District bills are typically considered in what is called "the House as in Committee of the Whole"—a hybrid entity that combines procedural features of the House and the Committee of the Whole. For example, general debate is not permitted, but debate and amendment may occur under the 5-minute rule. Appropriations bills for the District of Columbia do not come up during those special days. Instead, they are considered under the privilege (access to the floor) given to legislation reported by the Appropriations Committee.

Worth mention is that the 112th Congress saw a resurgence of interest in granting budget autonomy to the District of Columbia. A key advocate in the House was the chair of the Oversight and Government Reform Committee and in the Senate, the chair of the Homeland Security and Governmental Affairs Committee, the two authorizing panels with policy responsibility for the District of Columbia. The Obama Administration also backed budget autonomy. As the president's 2013 budget stated: "Consistent with the principle of home rule, it is the administration's view that the District's local budget should be authorized to take effect without a separate annual Federal appropriation bill." Delegate Norton declared that it is long past the time for the District to make its own fiscal decisions without having "to bring its own local funds to a national legislature, which had nothing to do with raising those funds, for approval to spend them."[28] However, the 112th Congress did not enact this legislation.

The Private Calendar

Private bills are designed to provide legal relief to specified persons or entities adversely affected by laws of general applicability. The constitutional basis for private bills rests on the right of the people, under the First Amendment, "to petition the Government for a redress of grievances." Most private bills deal with immigration and naturalization cases and claims against the federal government. For example, general immigration requirements may be waived or expedited to permit foreign-born athletes to join the U.S. Olympic team, to allow a Philadelphia woman to marry a man who is a Greek citizen, or to enable an undocumented worker to remain in the United States with his family. Most private bills are referred to the House and Senate Judiciary Committees for review, and, like other bills, private bills passed by both chambers are sent to the president for signature or veto.

Under House procedures, the Speaker is required to call private bills on the first Tuesday of each month (unless the rule is dispensed with by a two-thirds vote, or unanimous consent is obtained to transfer the call to some other day of the month) and, at the Speaker's discretion, on the third Tuesday as well. Because few lawmakers have the time to review private bills, the Private Calendar Objectors Committee is assigned that task. The panel is composed of three members of each political party appointed by the majority and minority leaders.[29]

Bills must be placed on the Private Calendar 7 days before being called up to give the objectors time to screen them for controversial provisions. (Committee reports on private measures must also be available to the objectors for 3 calendar days.) The objectors attend House sessions on Private Calendar days to answer any questions about the pending measures. If two or more members of the House object to a bill on the first Tuesday, it automatically is sent back to the committee that reported it, although at the request of a member it may at this time be "passed over without prejudice" for later consideration. Generally, private bills are not subject to lengthy consideration and are disposed of by voice vote.

The number of private bills introduced each Congress has declined sharply. From the 1,269 private claims bills introduced during the 80th Congress (1947–1949), the number fell to 132 in the 109th Congress (2005–2007). In the 82nd Congress (1951–1953), Congress cleared 1,023 private bills that became private law; in the 103d Congress (1993–1995), 8; in the 104th, only 4; in the 107th and 108th, only 6 each; in the 109th, 1; in the 110th and 111th, zero; and 1 in the 112th. Several factors account for the drop-off. Scandals were associated with the introduction of private bills for pay. For example, in the so-called Abscam scandal of 1980, FBI agents dressed as Arab sheiks paid several lawmakers to introduce private immigration bills for them. These scandals led to stricter procedures for the consideration of such bills. Second, Congress authorized administrative agencies and the U.S. Court of Claims to handle the bulk of these cases. Third, private bills often require an enormous amount of time to handle, and in the end the claims can prove to be incorrect or fraudulent. Fourth, congressional staff aides have suggested that legislators feel uncomfortable approving private claims bills that benefit only a few people when so many other programs affecting larger numbers of people are being cut.[30] Finally, some lawmakers want a comprehensive immigration reform bill to be enacted into law before they introduce private bills.

PRIVILEGED LEGISLATION

Under House rules, five standing committees have direct access to the floor for selected bills. The Appropriations and Budget panels report measures to finance the operations of the government; the Ethics Committee deals with matters involving the public reputation of the House; the House Administration panel handles necessary housekeeping proposals; and the Rules Committee plays a major role in determining which measures the House considers. The committees and types of legislation eligible to be called up for immediate debate are listed in Table 4.1.

Unlike the other standing committees, which act only on legislation referred to them, these panels have the authority to originate, or initiate, specific measures. The bills may be called up when other matters are not already pending on the House floor. Despite the privilege, most of these bills cannot be considered for at least 3 days so that members have time to read the committee reports. (Observance of these rules can be set aside via waivers granted by the Rules Committee.) Special rules from the Rules Committee must lay over only one day, whereas reports on budget resolutions must be available to members for 10 days. (A few other matters, such as declarations of war, are exempt from the 3-day layover rule.) Privileged measures are matters of special import to the House as an institution or to the federal government.

Even privileged measures are subject to points of order (parliamentary objections that any member may raise at an appropriate time) on the grounds that they violate certain rules of the House. If upheld, such points of order return the measure to the committee that considered it. Committees with privileged access, therefore, will usually ask the Rules Committee to waive points of order against their bills. The Appropriations Committee, for example, may violate House rules banning unauthorized appropriations or

TABLE 4.1 Committees With Direct Access to the Floor for Selected Legislation

Committee	Legislation
Appropriations	General appropriations bills; continuing appropriations resolutions if reported after September 15
Budget	Budget resolutions and reconciliation bills under the Congressional Budget and Impoundment Control Act of 1974
Ethics	Resolutions recommending action with respect to the conduct of a member, officer, or employee of the House
House Administration	Matters relating to enrolled bills, contested elections, and House expenditures, including committee funding resolutions
Rules	Rules of the House and the order of business

SOURCE: Compiled from the House rulebook.

legislative provisions (policy provisos) in general appropriations bills and will protect the panel's bills from points of order by persuading the Rules Committee to issue waivers.

There are a few occasions when the Appropriations Committee will bypass the Rules Committee. Instead, a majority committee member will ask and receive the unanimous consent of the House to define the procedural framework for debating and amending an appropriations bill.[31] If consideration of an appropriations bill is regulated by a special rule—which is common practice—unanimous consent can still be used during the bill's consideration to expedite floor action on the legislation. Such unanimous consent requests are harder to obtain given today's heightened polarity between the two political parties.

MAJOR LEGISLATION

Most major bills do not go automatically from committee to a calendar and then to the House floor. Simply put, most major bills lack "privilege." **Privilege** is a parliamentary term that grants certain legislative business precedence "over the regular order of business. It is business that can supersede or interrupt other matters that might otherwise be called up or pending before the House."[32] The House has a rule outlining the daily order of business, but most of the time the chamber operates by means of "privileged interruptions," such as adoption of special rules from the Rules Committee. (Unanimous consent and suspension procedure are other examples of privileged interruptions that set aside the daily order of business established by Rule XIV.) The main routes to the House floor are shown in Figure 4.2.

Recall that only a few matters, such as general appropriations bills, are accorded privilege by the House rulebook. In addition, the House rulebook makes certain measures (suspension and private bills) privileged for floor consideration during specified days of the week or month. Most major bills are *not* accorded privileged access to the floor by the House rulebook. Thus, the route to the floor for major legislation is through the Rules Committee. It can grant privilege to measures that lack this special status by giving them rules (procedural resolutions designated H. Res. and numbered).

Brief Overview

The Rules Committee is among the oldest of House panels. The First Congress in April 1789 appointed an 11-member rules body to draw up its procedures. With a few early exceptions, each succeeding Congress has done the same, although for nearly a century the Rules panel was a select (temporary) committee that prepared procedures for the incoming Congress and then went out of existence.

In 1858 the Speaker became a member and leader of the Rules Committee. In 1880 the Rules Committee became a standing (permanent) committee, and in 1883 it initiated the practice of reporting special orders, or rules,

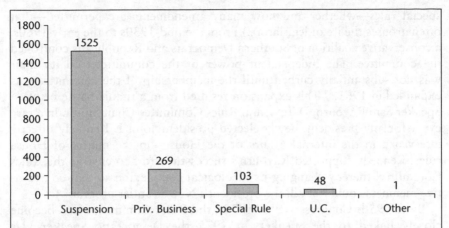

SOURCE: Christopher Davis, congressional expert, Congressional Research Service.

NOTES: Chart reflects initial House consideration of all legislation, regardless of legislative form. "Other" category is made up of one measure passed under the "automatic procedures" of House Rule XXVII as adopted in the 111th Congress, a rule commonly called the "Gephardt Rule." The GOP 112th House dropped the Gephardt procedure from the chamber's rulebook. Figure represents initial House consideration.

FIGURE 4.2   Procedures Used to Bring Measures to the House Floor

which, when agreed to by majority votes of the House, controlled the amount of time allowed for debate on major bills and the extent to which they could be amended from the floor.

Speakers during and after the 1880s permitted the Rules Committee to acquire authority over the House's agenda and the order of business. Speaker Joseph G. Cannon, a Republican from Illinois who was Speaker from 1903 to 1911, abused his agenda-setting and other powers, with the result that the House revolted in 1910 and removed the Speaker from the Rules Committee. The House majority leadership, however, retained—and still retains, in cooperation with the Rules Committee—fundamental control over the flow of legislation reaching the floor.

A notable exception was Rules Committee Chair Howard W. Smith, D-Va. (1931–1967), who presided over the committee with an iron hand from 1955 to 1967. Smith was no traffic cop simply regulating the flow of bills to the floor. He firmly believed the committee should "consider the substance and merits of the bills," and he often blocked measures he disapproved of and advanced those he favored, sometimes thwarting the will of the majority.[33]

Although the Rules Committee lacks authority to amend bills, the Smith-led panel bargained with committee leaders for changes in legislation in return for granting rules. (During the Smith era, frustration with the panel stemmed from its refusal to issue rules; today, it is the character of special rules—whether and how many amendments are permitted—that often arouses the ire of legislators.) From the mid-1930s to the early 1960s, a conservative coalition of Southern Democrats and Republicans controlled the committee. The independent power of the committee and its chair was not substantially curbed until the membership of the committee was expanded in 1961.[34] This expansion resulted from a titanic battle between Speaker Sam Rayburn, D-Tex., and Rules Committee Chair Smith. In a rare event for any president, newly elected president John F. Kennedy directly intervened in the internal affairs of the House—in the matter of House rules. Kennedy supported Rayburn's successful effort to enlarge the Rules Committee, thereby changing its ideological complexion so that conservative members could not kill the president's New Frontier program.

By the 95th Congress (1977–1979), the Rules Committee had become closely linked to the Speaker. In 1975 the Democratic Speaker was authorized by his party caucus to appoint, subject to party ratification, all majority party members of the Rules Committee. In 1989 House Republicans authorized their leader to name all the GOP members of the Rules Committee. The committee's composition in the 113th Congress (2013–2015) was nine Republicans and four Democrats. Thus, in the 113th Congress, Speaker Boehner named the chair (Pete Sessions of Texas) and the other eight Republican members, and Minority Leader Nancy Pelosi, Calif., as ranking minority member, appointed the four Democratic members, including Louise Slaughter, N.Y. (Traditionally, the panel has a disproportionate partisan ratio to ensure majority control.) Today, the committee is one of the few centralizing panels in a decentralized House. It is the "Speaker's Committee" and functions to implement the program of the majority party. Its rule-writing responsibilities mean that it has the job of ensuring that legislation brought before the House is considered in a coherent and systematic manner and under procedural ground rules that advantage the majority party. As former Speaker Jim Wright, D-Tex. (1987–1989), stated:

> The Rules Committee is an agent of the leadership. It is what distinguishes us from the Senate, where the rules deliberately favor those who would delay. The rules of the House, if one understands how to employ them, permit a majority to work its will on legislation rather than allow it to be bottled up and stymied.

The leader of the GOP Conference expressed the same idea: "It's the committee that makes the difference between the House and Senate. It's the committee that makes the House more efficient."[35] A Rules vice chair expressed the common view of the panel's relations with the Speaker: "How much is the Rules Committee the handmaiden of the Speaker? The answer is, totally."[36] That view requires some modification for the 112th House, however.

Speaker Boehner allowed the Rules Committee greater leeway in structuring floor consideration of major legislation. More openness is the Speaker's preference, and the Rules Committee delivers when it can. Speaker Boehner's "touchstone is openness," noted a Rules Republican. "He really errs on giving all sides an opportunity" to offer amendments. A Rules Democrat acknowledged that Rules Republicans "have tried to be open when they can, and closed when they can't."[37] The somewhat larger independence accorded Rules, along with Speaker Boehner's desire for a more open amendment process, has sometimes led to lengthy and contentious debate on the floor. "Allowing members to work their will can be more cumbersome, and it's not efficient. But it's more democratic," explained a Rules Republican.[38]

In brief, the Rules Committee's power should not be underestimated. The Speaker cannot track every major and minor bill or issue instructions constantly to the panel. The history of the Rules Committee is "one of the committee's accommodating the leadership on the one hand and seeking independent status on the other."[39] The 112th Congress has witnessed more independence for Rules, but, fundamentally, it "acts according to the Speaker's interests," observed a Rules Democrat.[40]

Role of the Rules Committee

The power of the Rules Committee lies in its scheduling responsibilities: its so-called "traffic cop" role. Besides deciding whether to grant a rule, the committee must craft rules to accomplish diverse purposes, such as providing for orderly review of major policy alternatives on the floor, protecting partisan objectives, focusing House debate on the main proposals in contention, and expediting consideration of priority measures.

As public bills are reported out of committee, they are entered in chronological order on one of the two main calendars, the Union Calendar or the House Calendar. All revenue bills, general appropriations bills, and measures that directly or indirectly appropriate money or property (including all authorization measures) are placed on the Union Calendar; all remaining public measures, such as constitutional amendments or rules from the Rules Committee, go on the House Calendar. If all measures have to be taken up in the order in which they are listed on the calendars, as was the practice in the 19th century, many major bills would not reach the House floor before Congress adjourns. Instead, major legislation reaches the floor in most instances because it has been granted precedence through a special order (a rule) obtained from the Rules Committee. Recall that a rule is a simple resolution (H. Res.). A written request for a rule is usually submitted to the Rules Committee chair by the chair of the committee reporting the bill. The Rules Committee then holds a hearing on the request—witnesses are limited to lawmakers—and debates the nature of the special rule in the same manner that other committees consider legislative matters. One congressional scholar has called hearings the "dress rehearsal" function of the Rules Committee.

Rules members comprise the first audience for a piece of legislation outside the narrow confines of the committee and subcommittee that reported it. As such, the hearing on a rule request serves as the "dress rehearsal" for bill managers before they take the legislation to the House floor. The hearing on a rule is an opportunity for the members to present their case and test the reaction from Rules members.[41]

After the hearings, Rules members of the majority party, with the aid of the House parliamentarian's office, craft their rule and vote it out of committee. (In a rare occurrence involving a bill to establish the Department of Homeland Security, the special rule "governing consideration of this legislation [was] jointly recommended by the GOP Speaker and the Democratic leader and then brought to the Committee on Rules.")[42] Once reported by the panel, the rule is considered on the House floor as a privileged matter, which essentially means that after it is read in full it is subject to 1 hour of debate and no amendments, and it is voted on in the same manner as regular bills. (See the section below on "Adoption of the Rule.") In effect, a rule provides a tailor-made procedure for floor consideration of a measure—that is, it is a departure from the procedures provided in the standing rules of the House. A rule, then, serves several important purposes:

- It bumps a bill up the ladder of precedence, eliminating the waiting time that would be needed if chronological order were observed. The Rules Committee, in effect, shuffles the Union and House Calendars by holding back rules for some bills and reporting them for others.
- It governs the length of general debate on the bill as opposed to allowing any member to speak for up to 1 hour on it.
- It usually dispenses with the first **reading of the bill** and the reading of amendments that are preprinted in the Congressional Record or in the report of the Rules Committee accompanying the rule.
- It usually limits the number of amendments that may be offered and the time for debate on any amendment, as opposed to allowing any member to offer and debate as many germane amendments as he or she wants. (The committee commonly requires lawmakers who want to offer amendments to pre-file them with the panel by a specified date and time.)
- It orders the **previous question** on the measure being granted privileged status by the rule—that is, debate ceases, no amendments are permitted, and the House votes immediately on the matter—as opposed to allowing the House to further amend and debate the bill after it has been reported from the Committee of the Whole.

In blocking or delaying legislation from reaching the floor, the Rules Committee is not necessarily playing an obstructionist role. It may be providing political cover by drawing fire away from the leadership, certain committees, and individual members. Representatives sometimes request that the Rules Committee prevent unwanted bills or amendments from reaching the floor. As Speaker O'Neill once said, "It takes the heat for the rest of the Congress, there is no doubt about that."[43] Three other functions of the panel merit review.

First, the committee acts as an informal mediator of disputes among House committees and members. For example, a committee may report a measure that trespasses on the authority of another. In such a case, the Rules Committee may resolve the jurisdictional dispute by authorizing the second committee to offer amendments to the measure or by refusing to waive points of order on the floor, thus giving members of the second committee an opportunity to delete offending matter.

Second, the Rules Committee plays a jurisdictional arbitration role on multiply referred legislation. As a precondition for a rule, the committee may urge or require competing committees to agree on the vehicle—one of the committee's reported bills, some consensus product, or something else— for floor debate and amendment. This practice limits floor fights among rival committees, simplifies floor decision making, expedites the processing of legislation, and avoids putting the Rules Committee in the position of deciding which panel's bills to use for floor deliberation.

Third, the Rules Committee has substantive (or original jurisdiction) responsibilities. It has developed and reported out such major measures as the Legislative Reorganization Act of 1970, the Congressional Budget and Impoundment Control Act of 1974, and resolutions providing for the creation of a permanent Select Intelligence Committee and the televising of House floor sessions. As part of its jurisdiction over the rules of the House, the panel regularly recommends during every new Congress a variety of procedural changes that affect the way the House conducts its business.

Worth a brief mention is the panel's role as a central and public repository for many important legislative documents, such as major legislation, conference reports, and the text of amendments filed with the committee or made in order for floor consideration. Its website contains a plethora of useful information and reports on House processes and procedures. Moreover, its hearing room in the Capitol is now equipped for television, and all committee proceedings are streamed live and archived on the panel's website.[44]

Traditional Types of Special Rules

The Rules Committee has traditionally granted three basic kinds of rules: open, closed, and modified. The distinctions among them go solely to the question of the amendment process. All three types almost always provide a fixed number of hours for general debate. In addition, any of these types may contain waivers of points of order. An example of an open rule from the Rules Committee, with an explanation of its basic features, is shown in Box 4.1.

BOX 4.1 Reading a Special Rule

H. Res. 289

[Report No. 106-317]

Original Text of the Resolution

Resolved, That at any time after the adoption of this resolution the Speaker may, pursuant to clause 2(b) of the rule XVIII, declare the House resolved into the Committee of the Whole House on the state of the Union for consideration of the bill (H.R. 1655) to authorize appropriations for fiscal years 2000 and 2001 for the civilian energy and scientific research, development, and demonstration and related commercial application of energy technology programs, projects, and activities of the Department of Energy, and for other purposes.

> EXPLANATION: *Authorizes the Speaker to transform ("resolve") the House into the Committee of the Whole House to consider the measure after adoption of the special rule.*

The first reading of the bill shall be dispensed with. General debate shall be confined to the bill and shall not exceed one hour equally divided and controlled by the chairman and ranking minority member of the Committee on Science.

> EXPLANATION: *Dispenses with the first reading of the bill. (Bills must be read three times before being passed.) Sets the amount of general debate time—one hour—and specifies which members control that time—in this instance, the chair and ranking minority member of the Committee on Science. Specifies that debate should be relevant to the bill.*

After general debate the bill shall be considered for amendment under the five-minute rule.

> EXPLANATION: *Sets reading for amendment one section at a time (or one paragraph at a time for appropriations bills), and provides that each member can speak for five minutes on each amendment. Because this special rule sets no limitations on amendments that can be offered, it is an open rule. Nonetheless, amendments still must comply with the House's standing rules, such as germaneness.*

It shall be in order to consider as an original bill for purposes of amendment under the five-minute rule the amendment in the nature of a substitute recommended by the Committee on Science now printed in the bill. Each section of the committee amendment in the nature of a substitute shall be considered as read.

> EXPLANATION: *Identifies text to be open to amendment in the Committee of the Whole. A special rule can provide that a committee-reported substitute be considered as an original bill for the purpose of amendment. Allowing a full-text*

substitute to be considered as an original bill is usually done to permit second-degree amendments to be offered. (The Rules Committee may also allow, as in the case of concurrent budget resolutions, only full-text substitutes to measures. This type of rule could be called a "substitute-only rule.")

During consideration of the bill for amendment, the Chairman of the Committee of the Whole may accord priority in recognition on the basis of whether the Member offering an amendment has caused it to be printed in the portion of the Congressional Record designated for that purpose in clause 8 of rule XVIII. Amendments so printed shall be considered as read.

EXPLANATION: *Determines recognition order for offering amendments. Open rules customarily grant the chair of the Committee of the Whole discretion to give priority recognition to members who submitted their amendments for preprinting in the* Congressional Record. *Absent this provision, the chair would follow the custom of giving preferential recognition to members, based on seniority, who serve on the reporting committee, alternating between the parties.*

The Chairman of the Committee of the Whole may: (1) postpone until a time during further consideration in the Committee of the Whole a request for a recorded vote on any amendment; and (2) reduce to five minutes time for electronic voting on any postponed question that follows another electronic vote without intervening business, provided that the minimum time for electronic voting on the first in any series of questions shall be 15 minutes.

EXPLANATION: *A special rule that allows amendments to be offered might allow the chair of the Committee of the Whole to postpone votes on amendments, as shown here. The chair may reduce to two minutes the time for electronic voting on a postponed question, provided that the voting time on the first in any series of questions is not less than fifteen minutes. (The 112th House amended its rules to allow the chair of the Committee of the Whole to use two-minute voting when there are a series of back-to-back votes.)*

At the conclusion of consideration of the bill for amendment the Committee shall rise and report the bill to the House with such amendments as may have been adopted.

EXPLANATION: *Provides for transformation ("to rise") back to the House from the Committee of the Whole. This provision eliminates the need for a separate vote on a motion to rise and report.*

Any Members may demand a separate vote in the House on any amendment adopted in the Committee of the Whole to the bill or to the committee amendment in the nature of a substitute.

(Continued)

BOX 4.1   (Continued)

EXPLANATION: *Enables separate votes to occur in the House on each first-degree amendment approved by the Committee of the Whole. House rules require the House to vote on each first-degree amendment approved by the Committee of the Whole.*

The previous question shall be considered as ordered on the bill and amendments thereto to final passage without intervening motion except one motion to **recommit** with or without instructions.

EXPLANATION: *Expedites final passage. By automatically imposing the "previous question," intervening debate and the offering of motions is precluded. The only motion allowed is a motion to recommit.*

SOURCE: Michael L. Koempel and Judy Schneider, "Reading a Special Rule," in *Congressional Deskbook 2005–2007* (Alexandria, Va.: TheCapitol.Net, 2005), 258–259. www.thecapitol.net. Reprinted with permission. The author has made a few updates to this explanation.

Open Rules. Open rules were common for most bills until around the 101st Congress (1989–1991), when there were more restrictive rules issued (55%) compared with open rules (45%). This pattern, with a few exceptions, was observed in subsequent Congresses (see Table 4.2).[45] Under an open rule, germane amendments to a bill may be offered from the floor so long as they comply with the 1974 Budget Act and House rules and precedents, such as the requirement that amendments must be in writing at the time they are offered. Amendments may be simple or complex. For example, an amendment may extend the funding of a program from 2 to 4 years or it may rewrite whole sections of a bill. Some committees, such as Science, Space and Technology, customarily request the Rules Committee to grant an open rule for their legislation.

Although open rules permit germane amendments, they do have a downside in the length of time it may take to complete action on legislation, particularly if the House is operating under a tight schedule. Opponents of a measure might conduct a "filibuster by amendment." If consideration of legislation stretches into days, the majority floor manager may seek unanimous consent to restrict the number of amendments and impose time limits on their debate. Or the majority leadership will direct the Rules Committee to report another special rule that limits the amending process. Moreover, an open amendment process can be unpredictable in terms of the proposals that might be offered. The minority

TABLE 4.2   Open Versus Restrictive Rules, 103rd to 112th Congresses, 1993 to 2012

Congress		Open Rules		Restrictive Rules	
		Number	Percentage	Number	Percentage
103rd	(1993–1995)	46	44	58	56
104th	(1995–1997)	83	58	59	42
105th	(1997–1999)	74	53	66	47
106th	(1999–2001)	91	51	88	49
107th	(2001–2003)	40	37	67	63
108th	(2003–2005)	34	26	99	74
109th	(2005–2007)	24	19	101	81
110th	(2007–2009)	23	14	140	86
111th	(2009–2011)	1	1	110	99
112th	(2011–September 21, 2012)	25	18	110	82

SOURCE: Donald Wolfensberger, resident scholar, Bipartisan Policy Center, Washington, DC, March 30, 2012. In this table, open and modified open (a preprinting and/or a time cap on the amendment process) are classified as "open rules"; structured (amendments are specified in the rule or in the report on the rule), modified closed (only one amendment allowed), and closed (no amendments except proposed by the reporting committee or contained in the motion to recommit with instructions; see Chapter 5) are all categorized as "restrictive rules."

party, for example, might craft amendments designed to eviscerate the majority's legislation, stall action on it, or create electoral grief for majority party members by forcing them to vote on "hot button" campaign-inspired issues.

Significantly, open rules raise the important question of where the fundamental deliberations on legislation should take place: in the committee setting among a relatively small number of lawmakers who specialize in the subject area or on the House floor with the entire membership having a say in policy formulations. Further, can a House of 435 members function effectively without some limits on debate and amendments during floor action on major and controversial bills? (See the discussion on p. 180 on "Promises of Openness.")

Closed Rules. Closed rules prohibit floor amendments, except, at times, those offered by the reporting committee or committees. Recent years have seen an increase in the number of closed rules that require a bill to be considered in the House and not in the Committee of the Whole under procedures that limit general debate to 1 hour, for example, and restrict or prohibit amendments. The rule also automatically orders the previous question on the bill. For example, a major domestic initiative (H.R. 1, the Medicare Prescription Drug and Modernization Act of 2003) was considered in the House and not the Committee of the Whole to expedite its consideration. Language in the special rule stated that the "previous question shall be considered as ordered on the bill and any amendment thereto to final passage without intervening motion," except for 3 hours of debate on the bill and one amendment if offered by Rep. Charles Rangel, D-N.Y., or his designee. As noted earlier, "ordering the previous question" means that, unless a special rule provides exceptions such as for H.R. 1, debate ceases, no amendments are permitted, and the House votes immediately on the issue at hand.

Critics say closed rules (also called "gag" rules) hamper the legislative process and violate democratic norms. A House Democrat put it this way:

> In most cases, closed rules say that we as individual Members are willing to allow a small portion of the whole to decide what information we need to consider, what complexities our minds are able to master, and from what alternatives we should choose. Furthermore, many times closed rules indicate either an arrogance on the part of the proponents of a bill or an insecurity about the bill's merits or abilities to stand up against competing ideas.[46]

Supporters of closed rules state that they are needed for complex measures that are subject to intense lobbying. In addition, legislation related to a national emergency sometimes must be expedited by the closed rule procedure.

Tax bills provide a good illustration of the pressures surrounding closed rules. For decades and even today, the House considers tax measures under closed rules, agreeing with the argument of Wilbur D. Mills, D-Ark. (1939–1977), chair of the Ways and Means Committee from 1958 to 1974, that tax legislation was too complex and technical to be tampered with on the floor. If unlimited floor amendments were allowed, Mills argued, the Internal Revenue Code would soon be in shambles and at the mercy of pressure groups. The Rules Committee may permit complete substitutes—the functional equivalent of an alternative bill—to be offered to Ways and Means–reported tax bills.

Modified Rules. This third category of special rules comes in two versions—modified open rules and modified closed rules—but these designations are somewhat subjective. A modified open rule might indicate that all parts of a bill are open to amendment except a specific title or section. Or it might mean, as a majority Rules member stated, "This [modified open rule] makes in order all amendments that were preprinted in the *Congressional Record* and which otherwise comply with the rules of the House."[47]

Worth mention: Whichever party is in the minority may declare that modified open rules are not truly open rules. Why? If there is a preprinting requirement for amendments, common to modified open rules, critics lament that "as the legislative process proceeds," it "may spark an idea for an amendment."[48] A preprinting requirement prevents spontaneous amendment opportunities.

A modified closed rule could state that an entire bill is closed to amendment except a certain title or section. The distinction between the two is based on the number of amendments allowed by the Rules Committee. Fundamentally, modified open rules provide more amendment opportunities than modified closed rules. During the early 2000s, the special rule of choice on major bills for the then GOP majority leadership, operating with a small majority, was the modified closed rule. This rule typically permitted the minority party only one amendment—a complete substitute for the underlying bill—or a limited number of amendments.

Sharp Democratic criticism of the GOP's management of the House, particularly the curtailment of amendment opportunities for the minority, led to an informal development in the 109th Congress (2005–2007). Republicans, but not the minority Democrats, no longer mentioned "modified closed" rules. Instead, Rules Republicans characterized modified closed as "structured" rules. (See the discussion on "Structured Rules.") This change in terminology is a mini-example of the contemporary emphasis on language in framing political communication. *Closed* implies exclusion, whereas *structured* suggests a fair and systematic procedure for taking up amendments. Whichever party is in the majority, *structured* is the preferred term rather than *modified closed* to describe a special rule that imposes specific restrictions on amendments.

Waiver Rules. Waivers of formal House rules appear in open, closed, modified, and other types of special rules. They set aside specific House rules so points of order cannot be raised against the legislation being made in order for floor consideration. Without such waivers, measures in technical violation of House procedures could be blocked from floor consideration or important parts of bills could be deleted for technical reasons during floor debate. "If we went strictly by the House rules," remarked one House member, "I am sure this body would have a very difficult time operating."[49]

The sole purpose of some rules is to waive points of order against the consideration of certain matters that are privileged, such as conference reports, because they have violated various House rules. Even the Rules Committee needs waivers to avoid contravening chamber rules. For example, the Rules Committee may issue a "same-day" (also called "martial law") rule. The purpose of this special rule—typically employed when the House is trying to wrap up its end-of-session business quickly—is to allow the Rules Committee to bring priority legislation to the floor on the same day the panel approves a special rule. The House rulebook specifies that special rules brought to the floor on the same day they are approved by the panel require a two-thirds vote for adoption instead of the usual majority vote for approving a rule. A martial law or same-day rule, which the House adopts by majority vote, waives the two-thirds requirement.

Generally, waivers are of two types: (1) exemptions from specific House rules and procedures or (2) blanket waivers of all points of order against pending legislation. For example, the Rules Committee may waive the House rule requiring committee reports on legislation to be available to lawmakers for at least 3 calendar days (excluding Saturdays, Sundays, and legal holidays) before the House can take up a measure. House Rule XIII requires the Rules Committee to specify waivers in its committee reports on special rules providing for the consideration of a measure, to the maximum extent feasible, "the object of any waiver of a point of order against the measure or against its consideration." The report of the committee accompanying the special rule contains an explanation of the points of order waived by the rule. Regardless of which party is in charge, waivers are granted to advance party and substantive objectives. Sometimes, members refer to "open plus" rules, which mean an open amendment process with the added benefit of having waivers that provide protection for certain amendments against valid points of order.

The panel, however, cannot waive points of order against earmarks or unfunded mandates—unpaid-for federal obligations placed on the states. For example, if a rule waives all points of order against a bill, a lawmaker could raise a point of order against the special rule because, in his or her estimation, the bill does contain an earmark(s) or an unfunded mandate(s). The House then debates the point of order for 20 minutes, equally divided between the two sides, and decides by separate majority vote the "question of consideration"—should the chamber consider the measure made in order by the special rule notwithstanding the point of order? Thus, at the expiration of the 20 minutes of debate, the Speaker will state: "Will the House now consider the resolution [from the Rules Committee]?" Uniformly, this is a party-line vote won by the majority party. If the House voted against consideration, it would mean the rejection of the special rule and the delay or defeat of the bill itself. Minority lawmakers often raise earmark and unfunded mandate points of order to get debate time so they can castigate the majority's priorities. For example, a minority member who raised an unfunded mandate point of order exclaimed: "Sadly, we're here once again with my Republican colleagues who are trying to ram through this fat-cat tax extenders legislation, providing mere crumbs from the master's table for working people."[50]

The Rules Committee may also establish informal practices of its own with respect to waivers. Although general appropriations bills are privileged under House rules, these measures are commonly regulated by special rules that waive appropriate points of order. When Republicans took control of the House in 1995, the GOP leadership established a protocol relating to waivers of unauthorized programs and legislative language (policy) in general appropriations bills. As the Rules Committee chair explained:

> Under this protocol, the Committee on Rules would provide the necessary waivers to enable the bill to come to the floor if the authorizing committee chairmen did not object to them. If the authorizing chairmen objected to the waivers, then under the leadership's protocol, the Committee on Rules would leave the specific language in question exposed to a point of order on the floor.[51]

Today, this informal policy is regularly observed by both parties when either is in the majority.

Creative Rules for the House

Fundamental changes in the workings of the House that began during the 1970s and continue into the 2000s triggered the rise of "creative rules." The House witnessed a dramatic redistribution of internal influence from powerful, seniority-chosen committee chairs to scores of individual lawmakers, including subcommittee chairs, faction leaders, and rank-and-file members. Party leaders, especially the Speaker, gained large influence, in part because their partisan followers support centralized leadership. The Democratic Caucus and the Republican Conference were allowed to approve (or disapprove) committee chairs (or ranking minority members). Party polarization also enveloped the House, as did the intensity of outside pressures, such as the rise of partisan, 24/7 media outlets, and intense and extensive special-interest involvement in lawmaking and campaigning.

Substantive and procedural complexity triggered the need for creative rules as well. Not only did measures become bigger and more complex, but also new procedures—multiple referrals, the requirements of the 1974 budget act, and various statutory provisions providing special procedures for certain bills—required the Rules Committee to sort through the complications and devise an orderly procedure for debating and amending legislation. The House also amended its formal rules in ways that encouraged lawmakers to ask for more recorded votes. The House permitted recorded votes in the Committee of the Whole in 1971 (previously votes had been unrecorded in this main amending forum), and electronic voting was authorized 2 years later.

All these changes produced a basic shift in the political culture of the House. It moved from the "to-get-along, go-along" spirit of Speaker Rayburn's era to an entrepreneurial and participatory style within which even freshmen lawmakers are accorded many opportunities to voice their views and exert their influence in all phases of lawmaking. The Rules Committee responded to the new climate during most of the 1970s by providing members with wide-open amending opportunities on the floor.

As one scholar pointed out:

> Fewer than 900 amendments were offered in the 91st Congress (1969–1970) and fewer than 800 were offered in the 92nd Congress (1971–1972), but over 1,400 were offered in the 93rd Congress (1973–1974) and nearly 1,400 were offered in the 94th (1975–1976). In the 95th, floor amendments peaked at nearly 1,700. Clearly, the incentive to put oneself or one's opponents on the record helped to stimulate more amending activity. . . . [Further, a] group of Republicans—John Ashbrook of Ohio, Robert Bauman of Maryland, and John Rousselot of California—deliberately badgered Democrats with many amendments and requests for recorded votes.[52]

By the end of the 1970s, Democratic leaders and lawmakers wanted the Rules Committee to exert greater control over floor procedures and produce greater certainty in an environment grown more conflict-ridden and unpredictable. The open amendment process produced longer sessions, disruptions in members' schedules, more dilatory tactics, and numerous challenges to committee-reported measures that often undercut the carefully crafted compromises negotiated in advance of floor consideration. When President Jimmy Carter's proposal to create a Department of Education went to the floor in June 1979, "Republican opponents prepared nearly 200 amendments, for the express purpose of delaying a final vote and blocking passage."[53] GOP lawmakers also proposed floor amendments designed, as noted earlier, to embarrass Democrats and to supply Republican House challengers with campaign ammunition.

In response to these diverse circumstances, the Democratic-controlled Rules Committee (and later the GOP-controlled panel, 1995–2007; the period starting in 2011 was somewhat more open) tightened opportunities for floor amendments and devised a variety of innovative and procedurally creative rules, which remain available today. Several principal aims of creative rules are to expedite floor decision making, protect party programs by limiting or blocking minority amendments, focus member attention on the major policy alternatives, enhance partisan goals, and strengthen committee prerogatives. Among these creative procedures— which can be used separately or in combination and are commonly used—are structured rules, self-executing rules, multiple-stage rules, time-structured rules, and bifurcated rules. Each of these rules will be discussed next, in no special order.[54]

Structured Rules. Structured rules are the most widely used of special rules. They limit the number of floor amendments to those specified in the special rule or, more typically, in the report of the Rules Committee accompanying the rule. The parliamentary language that characterizes a structured rule is as follows:

> No amendment to the bill shall be in order except those printed in part A of the report of the Committee on Rules accompanying this resolution. Each such

amendment may be offered only in the order printed in the report, may be offered only by a Member designated in the report, shall be considered as read, shall be debatable for the time specified in the report equally divided between and controlled by the proponent and an opponent, shall not be subject to amendment, and shall not be subject to a demand for division of the question in the House or in the Committee of the Whole. All points of order against such amendments are waived.[55]

Structured rules, in short, promote predictability, vote mobilization, and the preservation of time. However, they prevent spontaneity in members' ability to offer free-standing proposals to the amendments identified in the committee report of the Rules Committee (Part A, as noted above). With a scripted amendment process, there is simply no opportunity for lawmakers to propose unanticipated ideas that might strengthen achievement of the measure's objectives. If the Rules Committee anticipates reporting a structured rule, notice is given to the House membership by, for example, a "Dear Colleague" letter from the Rules chair or by a 1-minute statement made on the House floor by a majority member of the panel. (See Box 4.2 for an example of a "Dear Colleague" letter sent by the chair to all members of the House.)

Structured rules may require as well that all amendments be published in the *Congressional Record* prior to floor action on the legislation or be submitted in advance to the Rules Committee so they can purposefully plan for the debate on the floor. Although structured rules restrict members' general right to offer floor amendments—something that frequently arouses the ire of minority party members—they also can expand the range of policy options put before the membership. Issues that are not eligible under normal parliamentary procedures can be made eligible for floor consideration, such as nongermane amendments or legislation stuck in committee.

These rules could also script the sequence of action on amendments, which could influence the ultimate outcome. For example, the majority leadership might decide to allow a costly initiative to be offered as well as a less expensive one advocated by the minority leadership. The Rules Committee could fashion a structured rule that permits votes on only three policy alternatives: the costly version; the less costly version; and a compromise midway between the two, advanced by the majority leadership and designed to attract broad support. Members who opposed both the budget-buster and the inexpensive alternative could then say that they voted for the reasonable and responsible amendment.

Self-Executing Rules. This kind of rule embodies a two-for-one procedure—that is, when the House adopts a rule, it also automatically agrees to dispose of a separate matter, which is specified in the rule itself. Self-executing language in the special rule often states something like the following: "The amendment printed in [Section 2 of this resolution or in

---

BOX 4.2   "Dear Colleague" Letter

Dear Colleague:

The Committee on Rules may meet the week of May 23rd to grant a rule that could limit the amendment process for floor consideration of H.R. 1745, the Jobs, Opportunity, Benefits, and Services Act of 2011. The bill was ordered reported on May 11th by the Committee on Ways and Means.

Any Member wishing to offer an amendment must submit an electronic copy of the amendment and description via the Committee's website. Members must also submit 30 hard copies of the amendment, one copy of a brief explanation of the amendment, and amendment login form to the Rules Committee in room H-312 of the Capitol **by 10 a.m. on Wednesday, May 25, 2011.** Both electronic and hard copies must be received by the date and time specified. Members should draft their amendments to the text of the manager's amendment in the nature of a substitute offered by the Chairman of the Committee on Ways and Means. Both the text of the manager's amendment in the nature of a substitute and the text of the bill as reported are available on the Rules Committee website.

Members should use the Office of Legislative Counsel to ensure that their amendments are drafted in the most appropriate format. Members should also check with the Office of the Parliamentarian, the Committee on the Budget, and the Congressional Budget Office to be certain their amendments comply with the rules of the House and the Congressional Budget Act. If you have any questions, please contact myself or Adam Jarvis of the Committee staff at extension 5-9191.

Part 1 of the report of the Committee on Rules accompanying this resolution] shall be considered as adopted in the House and in the Committee of the Whole." Thus, a self-executing rule may stipulate that a discrete policy proposal is deemed to have passed the House and been incorporated in the bill to be taken up. The effect is that neither in the House nor in the Committee of the Whole will lawmakers have an opportunity to amend or to vote separately on the self-executed provision. For example, to minimize a floor battle with tobacco-state lawmakers, the House adopted a rule that automatically incorporated into the text of the bill made in order for consideration a provision that prohibited smoking on domestic airline flights of 2 hours or less.

A self-executing rule saves the time of the House by avoiding multiple subsequent votes, and it allows members to escape a direct recorded vote on a controversial and/or unpopular issue. Such rules can also assist party leaders in constructing winning coalitions. Post-committee revisions to reported legislation strengthen proponents' vote-mobilization efforts. For example, after the Ways and Means chair reports a tax bill, he may learn that there are not enough votes to pass the legislation because of concerns raised by outside groups and non-committee members. An option for the chair is to address those concerns by proposing modifications to the tax bill that are attractive to many wavering lawmakers. The privately negotiated tax changes would be submitted by the chair to the Rules Committee with a request that they be self-executed into the tax measure. Upon adoption of the rule, the substantive revisions to the committee-reported measure would be automatically adopted, or self-executed, into the text of the tax bill made in order for House consideration.

Multiple-Stage Rules. At times, the Rules Committee will issue several rules for the same bill, often to facilitate coherent consideration of issues or to expedite action on legislation. A common type of multiple-stage rule is one that separates general debate from the amendment process. For example, the initial rule on a defense measure may govern the terms of general debate. This rule is intended to focus House deliberation on the major issues and to apportion debate fairly among the interested parties. A second rule will govern the amendment process on the principal military issues. All relevant amendments might be grouped together and debated in sequence under specific time limits. There could even be a third or fourth rule to regulate how all the remaining amendments will be considered by the membership. The time lapse among multiple-stage rules can be hours, days, or weeks.

A variation of the multiple-stage rule occurs when a bill has bogged down on the floor because of dilatory actions. Failing actions to end the stalling activity, the committee in charge of the legislation, with the support of the majority leadership, will request the Rules Committee to issue a "shutdown" rule that imposes debate and amendment restrictions during further consideration of the bill.

Another multistage permutation is a several-part rule (whether open, structured, etc.) that makes in order several discrete bills and specifies whether amendments are in order, or not, to each measure. For example a special rule made three disparate bills in order (outlined in Sections 1, 2, and 3 of the procedural resolution) and specified that one bill would be closed to amendments and the other two would follow a structured amendment process. A fourth section of the rule allowed suspension procedure to occur on days beyond Monday, Tuesday, or Wednesday but only for the consideration of a railway labor bill.[56]

Time-Structured Rules. To expedite floor action, the Rules Committee may issue rules that establish time limits on the entire amendment process. The procedural resolution will include a provision something like the following: "After general debate, the bill shall be considered for amendment under the five-minute rule for a period not to exceed three hours." Critics contend that such rules are not genuinely open, because the time for debating and voting on amendments is counted against the cap. A 3-hour restriction may leave, for example, only 2 hours for considering discrete amendments. Time limits, Democrats said, encourage dilatory tactics by the majority party. Recorded votes may be called on amendments that could pass by voice vote "in order to consume time allotted for considering amendments."[57] Republicans responded that Democrats should consult in advance with their leaders to identify priority amendments that need to be offered inside the time cap.

Bifurcated Rules. Bifurcated rules make at least two separate bills in order for back-to-back consideration in the chamber. Under bifurcated rules, the House first debates, amends, and passes one bill, and then proceeds to consider another related but different bill. These actions can occur on separate days. Once the House agrees to the second measure, the rule provides that the two bills will be combined into one measure and sent to the Senate. A separate vote is not taken on the combined legislation. Among the principal purposes of bifurcated rules are to provide political cover for majority party members when the minority party has the momentum on an issue and to mobilize winning coalitions on majority party priorities. Both parties utilize bifurcated rules when they control the House. Two examples from the GOP years illustrate these purposes.

In the 106th Congress (1999–2001), the GOP leadership opposed the idea of raising the minimum wage—a key priority of nearly every House Democrat. However, the Republican leadership recognized that some moderate Republicans strongly supported raising the minimum wage and that the combination of the two blocs—Democrats and moderate Republicans—made it a winning coalition. The GOP leaders thus faced a potential revolt within their ranks if they did not bring minimum wage to a vote on the floor. They also realized that without a vote on minimum wage some of their vulnerable moderates could be hurt in the November elections.

The Rules Committee crafted a bifurcated rule designed to neutralize the issue's campaign potency in Republican-held districts where organized labor's influence remains strong. The rule first permitted consideration of a bill providing $122 billion in tax cuts over 10 years, which appealed to both GOP moderates and conservatives and took the sting out of the wage hike for the Republican-leaning business community. No amendments were permitted to the tax bill—a closed-rule process. The second bill, raising the minimum wage, was then taken up and debated under a modified closed-rule procedure (two amendments were made in order). The House passed both bills by a separate vote. Then, under the bifurcated rule, they were combined into one measure (in this instance, the wage hike was added to the tax cut bill) and sent to the Senate without ever having been voted on as a single piece of legislation. Combining two bills into a single package presents a potential problem, however, if the combined bill is sent to the president. If the chief executive favors one proposal but not the other, a veto ends up killing both.

As another example, the 112th House employed a bifurcated rule to consider two measures back-to-back with the requirement that if each was agreed to by the House, they would then be combined into a single package. As the pertinent section of the bifurcated rule (H. Res. 448) stipulated: "In the engrossment of H.R. 674, the Clerk shall add the text of H.R. 2576, as passed by the House, as new matter at the end of H.R. 674." An **engrossed bill** means that the clerk prepares an accurate and official copy of the measure as it passed the House. The engrossed bill is then sent to the Senate for its consideration.

In this instance, the bifurcated rules imposed a closed amendment process for both measures, because each amended the Internal Revenue Code. Measures that affect the tax code are typically brought to the floor, as noted earlier in this chapter, with closed rules. The bifurcated rule was necessary to provide the required offset (a "payfor") for the main bill (H.R. 674). This bipartisan measure, endorsed by President Obama, would repeal a federal rule "that requires federal, state, and local governments to withhold 3 percent of some payments to contractors."[58] Both parties viewed the bill as a job creator, because it would leave more money in the hands of contractors so they could hire additional workers. However, the repeal would decrease federal revenues by more than $11 billion over 10 years and add to the deficit, something the two parties wanted to avoid.[59] Hence, the need to pass H.R. 2576: It offset the lost revenue by making savings in Medicaid.

As this array of innovative special rules demonstrates, the majority on the Rules Committee displays considerable procedural imagination. "Instead of choosing from among a few traditional patterns," wrote two congressional scholars, "the Rules Committee has demonstrated their willingness to create unique designs by recombining an increasingly wide array of elements, or by creating new ones as the need arises, to help leaders, committees, and members manage the heightened uncertainties of decision making on the House floor."[60] Today, the Rules majority can select a number of discrete elements—waivers, self-executing provisions, and the like—and package them into a structured rule. The goal: Skew the procedural playing field to ensure that measures that reach the floor are considered under terms that advantage the majority's preferred outcomes.

To sum up, the increased use of complex creative rules reflects several trends. Among them are wider use of multiple referrals, which requires Rules to play a larger coordinative role in arranging floor action on legislation; the rise of omnibus bills—hundreds of pages in length—containing priorities the Speaker does not want picked apart on the floor; the desire of majority party leaders to exert greater control over floor proceedings; members' restlessness with dilatory tactics by minority party members; lawmakers' demands for greater certainty and predictability in floor decision making; the political necessity of protecting vulnerable members from casting difficult votes; and efforts by committee and party leaders to keep unfriendly amendments off the floor. The heightened polarization in the Congress is another factor and merits separate discussion in the context of procedural promises made by Republicans and Democrats when they won control of the House.

PROMISES OF OPENNESS BY THE MAJORITY PARTY

When Robert Michel, R-Ill., ended his 38-year career in the House, the last 14 (1981–1995) as minority leader, he lamented that during his time as GOP leader the majority Democrats "clamped down on the granting of open rules, making it more and more difficult for Members to offer amendments to legislation."[61] Given their frustrating and even embittering experience with rules that restricted their right to offer amendments, Republicans promised a new era of openness, deliberation, and fairness when they took control of the House following the earthquake election of November 1994. GOP leaders promised more amendment opportunities for all lawmakers. Their intentions proved short-lived. Open rules were rather scarce during much of the 12 years of Republican control.

Minority Democrats complained loudly about the lack of democracy in the institution. Democratic Rules Committee member James McGovern, Mass., urged his House colleagues to examine a specific open rule "very closely, study it, because it is a very, very rare specimen." He added: "Whenever an issue is the least bit contentious, whenever there is a hint of disagreement about a bill, the majority clamps down on its Members, chokes debates, and forces a closed rule."[62] Republicans responded to Democratic complaints by citing, among other things, that they are fairer to the minority than when Democrats ran the House, that the electorate made the GOP the governing majority and it expects Republicans to advance their agenda, and that the minority is more interested in making political points and undermining GOP goals than engaging in bipartisan policymaking.

Fast-forward to Democratic control of the House following the November 2006 elections. Speaker Pelosi and other Democratic leaders vowed that the 110th House would be run in a different manner. The Speaker articulated several principles for managing the House in a civil and bipartisan manner, such as protecting minority rights and consulting regularly with the minority leadership.[63] However, right from the opening day of the 110th Congress, the promise of fairness on rules was not observed. Instead, Democrats opted for structured rules that restricted amendments— or prevented them entirely—to advance their agenda. Repeatedly during the 110th House, Republicans castigated Democrats for reneging on their promises. As a Rules Republican declared:

> When it comes to shutting down debate, silencing ideas, restricting minority rights, ignoring rules they themselves wrote, and running the House in a top-down, shut-up, sit-down manner, this Democrat majority has no peer. . . . They have passed more closed rules that block all amendments and debate than any House in history.[64]

Responding to the GOP criticisms, Democrats such as Rules Chair Slaughter charged that Republicans "have a lot of nerve complaining about how the House has been run" given the procedural abuses Democrats suffered when the GOP ran the House.[65]

Again in charge of the 111th House, the Democratic Rules Committee continued to use structured or closed rules, although some rank-and-file party members complained early on about leadership circumvention of the regular order, such as amendment restrictions that affected all lawmakers regardless of party. Bitter partisan clashes reached a boiling point when Democrats brought all 12 general appropriations bills to the floor under structured rules. Traditionally, appropriations measures are considered under open rules. "What they wanted to do," stated Representative Dreier, the senior Rules Republican, "is they want to avoid tough votes [by their vulnerable Democrats] on appropriations bills."[66]

In protest, Republicans engaged in numerous dilatory tactics, such as forcing repeated 15-minute roll call votes and submitting hundreds of amendments to the Rules Committee for possible floor action. Rep. (now Senator) Jeff Flake, R-Ariz., set a new Rules record by requesting the panel to make 552 amendments in order for House debate.[67] During the June 19, 2009, consideration of the Commerce, Justice, Science appropriations bill (H.R. 2847), Republicans forced a record-setting 53-vote marathon.[68] Democrats claimed that the goal of Republicans was simply to delay and extend debate on the bills, that when Republicans ran the House they also utilized structured rules on appropriations measures, and that Republicans were engaging in political "theatrics."[69]

When Republicans captured control of the 112th House, Speaker Boehner promised a return to a more open floor amendment process, especially for appropriations measures. Given demands by rank-and-file Republicans, particularly the Tea Party–endorsed freshmen, to cut spending and shrink the government, the Rules Committee accommodated their party colleagues by issuing open and modified open rules. Significantly, appropriations bills were taken up with open rules. In the view of a scholar of House procedures, for the most part, "Republicans have been fairer to their minority counterparts on amendments than Republicans had been treated when in the minority" in the Democratic 111th House.[70]

Judgments about the openness of special rules based on one Congress, however, are problematic. Rules Democrats continue to castigate the unfairness of the GOP-crafted special rules. As Louise Slaughter, the ranking Rules Democrat, exclaimed with respect to a rule on H.R. 1, a full-year continuing resolution:

> [While] this rule may have the word "open" in the title, I assure [my colleagues] that this is not an open process. Through last-minute changes convoluted parliamentary maneuvers and a pre-printing requirement, the Republican majority has provided an extremely convoluted and restrictive process.[71]

The bottom line: Regardless of which party controls the contemporary House, the fundamental objective of the majority is to maximize the achievement of its policy and political goals, even if that minimizes or prevents entirely the minority party's opportunity to amend legislation. No longer is it the case, as it once was, that lawmakers have ample opportunities to offer and debate amendments under open rules. Today, members' ability to offer amendments is a privilege—not a parliamentary right—granted them by the political majority on the Rules Committee. An open amendment process clashes with a fundamental tenet of the governing party: Enact priority measures even if that means restricting lawmakers' amendment opportunities.

Thus, a "new normal" has taken hold in the House. Where the House once spent days or weeks debating and amending important legislation, such as a defense authorization bill, it now typically spends a day or two. Many factors account for this change, including the burgeoning agenda of complex and often time-sensitive issues and the large time and workload demands on members. One trend is important to underscore because it suffuses so much of House activity: the often acrimonious relationship between the two parties. Why? The reasons include such developments as the large ideological chasm between the two parties—one largely liberal and the other mainly conservative—which makes bipartisan compromises hard to achieve on many issues; the intense electoral competition between the parties to hold or reclaim majority control (members of both parties understand that being in the minority is not much fun); and the significant policy differences that divide the parties. It is little surprise that House majority leaders aggressively deploy procedural and political resources to enact their agenda, protect electorally vulnerable party colleagues from casting "hot-button" votes, and disallow minority amendments that could undermine the carefully laid plans of the majority party. In today's partisan-charged environment, promises of openness and fairness are hard to keep, as are efforts by majority leaders to win minority party cooperation in passing consequential legislation. Noteworthy, however, is Speaker Boehner's willingness to have appropriations measures taken up in the 112th House with open rules, a marked departure from the actions of other recent Speakers.

Adoption of the Rule

All rules must be approved by a majority vote of the House. Rules are reported to the House by the Rules Committee and are debated for a maximum of 1 hour, with the time equally divided by custom for purposes of debate only—preventing any attempt at this stage to amend the rule—between the Rules chair, or a designee, and the ranking minority member of the committee, or a designee. The hour rule is the basic rule of floor debate in the House. Theoretically, it permits each member 1 hour of debate on any question. The hour rule is never followed in practice, however.

A member who controls the debate time under the hour rule, in this case the Rules chair or the chair's designee, always moves the previous question at the end of this hour (or before the full hour is used if no member seeks time for debate). Adoption of this motion by majority vote, as noted earlier, stops all debate, prevents the offering of amendments, and brings the House to an immediate vote on the main question—the rule itself, in this context.

The main strategy, then, for a member wishing to amend a rule is to defeat the previous question, a rare occurrence. (Recall that adoption of the previous-question motion terminates debates, prevents the offering of amendments, and brings the House to a vote on the main question: the special rule.) "I am urging my colleagues to vote against the previous question on this rule so that we can offer a substitute rule" is a common refrain from members who oppose the rule. Under House precedents, the member who led the fight against approval of the previous question is recognized by the Speaker to propose a substitute rule. The significant vote often is not on adoption of the rule but on approval of the previous question. The majority and minority party often disagree about the import of the previous question: Is it a vote on policy, or is it a vote on procedure? Often, the answer to each question depends on a party's majority or minority status. If in the majority, party leaders call the vote "procedural"; if in the minority, party leaders tell their partisans it is a "policy" vote.

If there is no controversy, rules are adopted routinely by voice vote after a brief discussion. Under a 1977 procedural change, the Speaker may postpone votes on rules and permit them to be voted on at 5-minute intervals later in the day or any time within the next 2 days. The procedure is similar to cluster voting under suspension of the rules and is for the convenience of lawmakers and to promote the workload efficiency of the House.

The House seldom rejects a rule proposed by the Rules Committee. Speaker O'Neill once remarked, "Defeat of the rule on the House floor is considered an affront both to the Committee and to the Speaker."[72] The Rules Committee generally understands the conditions the House will accept for debating and amending important bills. Furthermore, the majority expects party-line support for rules, and deviations from this behavioral norm could be held against a lawmaker when, for example, plum committee assignments are handed out. The record number of rules defeated during the 103d Congress—seven—highlighted the fissures within Democratic ranks that doubtlessly contributed to their loss of the House in November 1994 after 40 years of continuous control. (Six rules were rejected in the 100th Congress, three in the 101st, none in the 102nd, one in the GOP-run 104th, five in the 105th, none in the 106th, two in the 107th, and none in the 108th, 109th, 110th, 111th, and 112th.) There are occasions, too, when the majority leadership will either not take up a rule or will yank it off the floor if the House appears likely to turn it down. This usually occurs because of divisions within the majority party.

LEGISLATION BLOCKED IN COMMITTEE

What happens when a standing committee refuses to report a bill that many members support, or when the Rules Committee fails to grant a rule to legislation having substantial support? Several procedures are available to bring such legislation to the floor, and the procedure used depends on the nature of the legislation. Suspension of the rules is appropriate if the measure is relatively noncontroversial or minor. If a major bill is being blocked, extraordinary procedures can be employed to spring the bill from committee. These procedures are difficult to implement, but if the House is determined, committees can be compelled to yield legislation.

The Discharge Petition

The discharge procedure, adopted in 1910, provides that if a bill has been before a standing committee for 30 **legislative days** (that is, days on which the House met), any member can introduce a motion to relieve the panel of the measure. A clerk of the House then prepares a discharge petition, which is made available for members to sign when the House is in session. If the requisite number of members (218) signs the petition, this procedure permits a majority of the House to bring a bill to the floor even if it is opposed by the committee that has jurisdiction over the measure, the majority leadership, and the Rules Committee. This procedure is difficult to use in part because majority party leaders often urge their partisan colleagues not to sign petitions.

Until the early 1990s, House precedents prohibited public disclosure of the names of lawmakers who signed discharge petitions until the required 218 signatures were obtained. Then the names were published in the *Congressional Record*. Critics of this procedure successfully changed House rules in 1993 to require the signers' names to be made public as soon as a discharge petition is introduced instead of when a majority is achieved. The sponsor, James M. Inhofe, R-Okla. (House, 1987–1994; Senate, 1994–), and backers such as 1992 Reform Party presidential candidate H. Ross Perot, conservative talk show hosts, the *Wall Street Journal,* and freshmen lawmakers, including Democrats, argued that the change would help eliminate secrecy and hypocrisy by ending the practice whereby House members introduce, cosponsor, or publicly proclaim support for bills but then refuse to sign discharge petitions that might facilitate getting those same measures to the floor. Without public disclosure, they said, party and committee leaders could pressure members either not to sign or to remove their names if they had signed a discharge petition. The House amended its rules in 1995 to require weekly publication in the *Congressional Record* of members who have signed a discharge petition and daily availability in the clerk's office of the cumulative list of signers.

When 218 members have signed the petition, the motion to discharge is put on the Discharge Calendar. After 7 legislative days on the calendar, it becomes privileged business on the second and fourth Mondays of the month (but not during the last 6 days of a session). Any member who signed the petition may be recognized to offer the discharge motion. When the motion is called up, debate is limited to 20 minutes, divided between proponents and opponents. If the discharge motion is rejected, the bill is not eligible again for discharge during that session. If the discharge motion prevails, any member who signed the petition can make a motion to call up the bill for immediate consideration. It then becomes the business of the House until it is disposed of. A vote against immediate consideration assigns the bill to the appropriate calendar, with the same rights as any bill reported from committee.

Few measures are discharged from committee. From 1931 through 2011 (which roughly coincides with the period during which the modern version of the rule has been in effect), 628 discharge petitions were filed, but only 47 attracted the required signatures and only 19 bills were discharged and passed by the House (see Table 4.3).[73] Of those, only three became law: the Fair Labor Standards Act of 1938, the Federal Pay Raise Act of 1960, and the Bipartisan Campaign Reform Act of 2002.

Several factors account for the general failure of the discharge procedure. Members are reluctant to second-guess a committee's right to consider a bill. The discharge rule violates normal legislative routine, and even members who support a bill blocked in committee may refuse to sign a discharge petition for this reason. Committees, too, may nullify the discharge attempt by reporting the bill. Because it no longer has the measure, the committee cannot be discharged.

TABLE 4.3   Proceedings Under the House Discharge Rule, 2005 Through 2011

Congress and (Years)	Discharge Petitions Filed	Discharge of Motion		Underlying Measure	
		Entered	Called Up	Committee Discharged	Passed House	Received Final Approval
109 (2005–2007)	18	0	0	0	0	0
110 (2007–2009)	18	0	0	0	0	0
111 (2009–2011)	13	0	0	0	0	0
Totals (2005–2011)	49	0	0	0	0	0
Totals since 1931	628	47	31	26	19	4

SOURCE: House Final Calendar for the Congress indicated. Compiled by Christopher Davis, Congressional expert, Congressional Research Service.

Legislators also are reluctant to write legislation on the House floor without the guidance and information provided in committee hearings and reports. Particularly for complicated legislation, many members want committee interpretation. Then, too, obtaining 218 signatures is not easy. Finally, members are hesitant to employ a procedure that one day may be used against committees on which they serve.

But for all its limitations, the discharge rule serves important purposes. It focuses attention on particular legislative issues, and the threat of using it may stimulate a committee to hold hearings or report a bill or the majority leadership to schedule floor debate on an issue. Discharge petitions also provide a way for the minority party to gain some visibility for its key agenda items, and contrast their ideas with the majority party's. Discharge efforts are "part of our message strategy, not our legislative strategy," remarked a minority party aide.[74] However, if the minority party fails to attract sufficient discharge signatures for its priority items, it can undermine any message of party unity. "How do you say the [minority] caucus is united—that we want this [bill] on the floor—with only 140 signatures?" said an exasperated minority aide.[75] Discharge petitions can also serve campaign objectives. Vulnerable House members can be subject to attack ads for failing to sign a discharge petition supported by many voters in their respective districts.[76]

Rules Committee's Extraction Power

The Rules Committee has an extraordinary authority that it seldom exercises: It can introduce rules for bills that the committee of jurisdiction does not want to report. The power of extraction is based on an 1895 precedent, which the committee has rarely invoked. Extraction, a highly controversial procedure, evokes charges of usurpation of other committees' rights.

On one of the rare occasions when extraction was used, the Education and Labor Committee refused on February 9, 1972, to approve a dock strike measure, but the Rules Committee reported a rule for floor action on the bill. Despite the vigorous opposition of Speaker Carl Albert, D-Okla. (1947–1977), the House adopted the rule by a 203-to-170 vote, thus springing the bill from the committee. The House then passed the bill.

The threat of extraction by the Rules panel in itself can break legislative logjams. In 1967 the Judiciary Committee balked at reporting an anti-riot bill. Rules Committee Chair William M. Colmer, D-Miss., announced that his committee would soon hold hearings on a rule for the bill. This was enough to prompt the Judiciary Committee to report the legislation.[77]

A Rules Committee chair can try to make any measure in order for floor action, even if it has not received committee consideration. In 1988, Chair Claude Pepper, D-Fla., "used his position to circumvent Ways and Means and clear his home-care health bill for floor action without hearings, debate, or markup in the committee of jurisdiction—a rare use of the Rules Committee's chairman's power."[78]

In 1995, when the GOP-controlled Government Reform Committee rejected legislation changing the federal retirement system, the Rules Committee included the change as part of a major tax bill. "In what is clearly an extraordinary departure from usual procedures," declaimed the ranking minority member on the Government Reform panel, "the Rules Committee has chosen to take a course of action which negates the very existence of the authorizing committees."[79] Despite that protest and those of others, the House agreed with the action of the Rules Committee.

Discharging the Rules Committee

The discharge rule also applies to the Rules Committee. The main reason a discharge petition is usually filed on a special rule is to control the terms of debate and amendment on the bill the special rule would make in order. (Absent a rule governing floor consideration, a discharged bill could be subject to extensive debate and unlimited germane amendments.) The bill itself must still have been pending for at least 30 legislative days before a standing committee. A motion to discharge the Rules Committee is in order 7 legislative days—instead of 30—after a special rule has been referred to the panel.

Because the Rules Committee reports rules as a matter of original jurisdiction, members who wish to discharge a rule (making the stalled bill in order) have to draft and introduce one of their own so there will be something to discharge. (This introduced rule, according to the House rulebook, can neither allow for nongermane amendments nor make more than one bill in order.) Then, once the rule has been pending before the Rules Committee for 7 legislative days, House precedents state it is in order to bring before the House "a measure pending before a standing committee for 30 legislative days." If the Rules Committee determines that a discharge attempt might be successful, it can report its own special rule for considering the bill on which discharge is sought. As congressional scholar Richard Beth has noted:

> Increasingly often in recent years, the Committee on Rules has responded to discharge efforts by reporting its own special rules for considering the measures involved. It often does so even when the petition is not completed, especially for petitions filed on special rules, rather than on the measures themselves. Since 1967, measures on which this form of petition was filed have had over twice as much chance of reaching the floor . . . as when the petition was filed on the measure itself. Perhaps as a result, this form of discharge has become more popular, amounting to almost 70 percent of petitions filed during the past decade (1993–2002).[80]

Calendar Wednesday

Under House procedures, every Wednesday is reserved for standing committees to call up measures (except privileged bills) that have been reported but not granted rules by the Rules Committee. Under a 111th Congress amendment, House Rule XV now requires "the Clerk to read only those committees where the committee chair has given notice to the House on Tuesday that he or she will seek recognition to call up a bill under Calendar Wednesday." This change replaces the former requirement that "the Clerk read the list of all committees, regardless of whether a committee intends to utilize the rule."[81]

The **Calendar Wednesday** rule was adopted to circumvent Speaker Joe Cannon's (1903–1911) control of the legislative agenda. Today, it is seldom employed and usually dispensed with by unanimous consent. During the 98th Congress (1983–1985), however, a group of Republicans led by Representative Gingrich objected regularly to dispensing with Calendar Wednesday proceedings. Their purpose was to generate political heat on the majority leadership to schedule nonprivileged measures (a constitutional balanced budget amendment, school prayer measures, criminal code reform, and so on). Republicans called their list of priority measures the Agenda of the American People (precursor of the Contract with America). In 1984 the House even adopted an agriculture bill under its Calendar Wednesday procedure.[82] Objections to dispensing with Calendar Wednesday soon ended because of the inherent limitations of the procedure.

Since 1943 fewer than 15 measures have become law under Calendar Wednesday proceedings.[83] House consideration of the 1984 agricultural measure was the first time the procedure had been used in a quarter-century. Four factors account for the limited use of this procedure: (1) Only 2 hours of debate are permitted, one for proponents and one for opponents, which may not be enough for complex bills; (2) a bill not completed on one Wednesday is not in order the next Wednesday unless two thirds of the members agree; (3) the procedure is subject to dilatory tactics because the House must complete action on the same day; and (4) only the chair or a member authorized by the committee may bring up a bill under Calendar Wednesday.

FINAL SCHEDULING STEPS

After a bill has been granted a rule, the majority party leaders decide when the measure will be debated. The leadership prepares daily and weekly schedules of floor business and adjusts them according to shifting legislative situations and demands. A bill the majority has scheduled for consideration may be withdrawn if it appears to lack sufficient support. Nothing in the House rules requires the majority leadership to provide advance notice of the daily or weekly legislative program. However, as a matter of long-standing custom, majority party leaders make announcements about prospective floor action at the end of each week, often in response to a query from the minority whip, as Box 4.3 shows. The legislative program for the next day for both chambers also is published in each issue of the *Congressional Record*, in a section called the "Daily Digest." The *Friday Record* contains a section called the "Congressional Program Ahead," which lists the next

---

BOX 4.3   A Scheduling Ritual

This typical exchange between House minority whip Steny Hoyer, D-Md., and majority leader Eric Cantor, R-Va., on scheduling legislation for the following week appeared in the *Congressional Record*.

Legislative Program

(MR. HOYER asked and was given permission to address the House for 1 minute.)

MR. HOYER. Madam Speaker, I yield to the gentleman from Virginia, the majority leader, for the purposes of inquiring about the schedule for the week to come.

MR. CANTOR. I thank the gentleman from Maryland, the Democratic whip, for yielding.

Madam Speaker, on Monday, the House is not in Session. On Tuesday, the House will meet at noon for morning-hour and 2 p.m. for legislative business. Votes will be postponed until 6:30 p.m. On Wednesday and Thursday, the House will meet at 10 a.m. for morning-hour and noon for legislative business. On Friday, the House will meet at 9 a.m. for legislative business. Last votes of the week are expected no later than 3 p.m.

Madam Speaker, the House will consider a number of bills under suspension of the rules, a complete list of which will be announced by the close of business tomorrow.

In addition, the House will consider H.R. 5872, the Sequestration Transparency Act, sponsored by Congressman Jeb Hensarling. . . .

Finally, and in keeping with funding our national security, the House will consider H.R. 5856, the Department of Defense Appropriations Act, sponsored by Congressman Bill Young. . . .

MR. HOYER. I thank the gentleman for that scheduling information.

SOURCE: *Congressional Record,* July 12, 2012, H4855.

---

week's legislative agenda and the dates for which floor action has been scheduled.

Each party also maintains a website that lists daily and for each week the expected schedule of legislation to be considered on Monday, Tuesday, and so on, along with convening times of the House and other relevant information. Moreover, whips in both parties have an array of ways to keep lawmakers informed about the schedule. They utilize e-mails, social media, and apps that provide real-time updates on what is happening on the floor. There are daily, weekly, and nightly whip notices that highlight the floor schedule: when the House will meet, when the first vote is likely, when the last vote is predicted, and what is currently pending on the floor. Staff in member, committee, and party offices constantly monitor floor activities so they can keep their bosses informed of significant developments. Text messages and telephone recordings also announce the daily and weekly program, legislative actions taken on the floor, and changes in the schedule. Moreover, the 112th House modified its rules to permit members to use mobile electronic devices on the floor so long as they do not impair decorum. These devices assist lawmakers in keeping up-to-date on the House's schedule. In short, lawmakers have an array of ways to learn about the floor schedule: current and projected.

Another agenda-setting device requiring mention is so-called "fast-track" procedures. Fast-track procedures are specified in various statutes to expedite the processing of certain legislation. Known as rulemaking provisions, these statutory procedures are enacted under Congress's constitutional authority to "determine the rules of its proceedings." They are equivalent to the formal rules of each chamber, which also means they can be set aside if either body chooses to follow another procedure. Examples of fast-track procedures are (1) timetables established in law for committees to report measures, including automatic discharge if they fail to report; (2) privileged access to the House and Senate floor for such matters; (3) the prohibition of floor amendments of any type; (4) the imposition of strict debate limits; and (5) automatic hookup of companion legislation from the other chamber so it can be voted on promptly with little or no debate, thus avoiding the need for a conference committee or the amendment exchange procedure to resolve bicameral differences (see Chapter 8 on resolving House–Senate differences on legislation).

Traditionally, trade laws contain fast-track provisions. They are designed to expedite House and Senate committee and floor consideration of trade agreements negotiated by the president and follow-on implementing legislation. Under these laws, Congress delegates trade negotiating authority to the president with the explicit requirement that the president must consult with Congress during the negotiations. The two committees of principal trade jurisdiction—House Ways and Means and Senate Finance, and perhaps other panels—may conduct informal hearings and markups of the trade agreement and the draft implementing legislation sent to Congress by the White House. These "mock" sessions allow lawmakers to raise issues and suggest changes to both the trade agreement and the draft implementing legislation. When the trade agreement and implementing legislation are formally submitted to Congress, fast-track procedures prohibit any amendments by the House or Senate and impose a timetable for committee and floor action. "The goal of fast track," wrote an analyst, "is to prevent U.S. trade agreements from being amended in Congress in ways that might be unacceptable to the other nation or nations that are parties to the agreements."[84]

Party leaders, in sum, consider many factors and circumstances to advance their agenda-setting objectives. Bills may be scheduled to correspond with well-known dates (back-to-school legislation), or the House floor may be used as a campaign platform to highlight partisan agenda items (message politics), especially as the November elections draw nearer. Party leaders may advocate agendas of interest to selected groups or interests, such as the business or labor communities. Legislation may be scheduled for action late at night to minimize public attention. And party leaders take advantage of various work or electoral cycles and deadlines to facilitate action on legislation.

NOTES

1. *Congressional Record*, November 15, 1983, H9856.
2. During a 2-week adjournment in April 2012, President Obama agreed not to make any recess appointments during this period. For their part, Senate Republicans agreed to approve more than 60 of Obama's stalled nominees. As a result, the House and Senate took a real recess without the need to convene in pro forma sessions at least every 3 days. See Stephen Dinan, "Congress Puts Obama Recess Power to the Test," *Washington Times*, April 2, 2012, A3.
3. Sean Longell, "GOP Revives 'You Cut' Program," *Washington Times*, May 12, 2011, A3. See also Jackie Kucinich, "GOP Surveys Itself on New Agenda," *Roll Call*, July 6, 2010, online version.
4. Jennifer Yachnin, "Hoyer: House to Work Monday–Friday in 110th," *Roll Call*, December 6, 2006, 1.
5. See Molly K. Hooper, "Two Weeks On, One Week Off in 2011 House Schedule," *The Hill*, December 9, 2010, 1; Sean Lengell, "GOP Schedule Plans to End 4-Day Weekend," *Washington Times*, December 9, 2010, A3; and John Stanton, "'12 House Schedule Looks Familiar," *Roll Call*, October 27, 2011, 4.
6. Pete Kasperowicz, "House Schedule Too Light, Say Democrats," *The Hill*, October 28, 2011, 8.
7. Stanton, "'12 House Schedule Looks Familiar," 4.
8. *Congressional Record*, September 22, 2011, H6377.
9. Richard E. Cohen, "New House Calendar Criticized as Stoking Conflict, Reducing Productivity," *CQ Today*, October 24, 2011, 24.
10. *Congressional Record*, July 2, 1980, H6106.
11. Andrew Taylor, "Budget Enforcement Legislation Founders in the House," *CQ Today*, June 24, 2004, 1.
12. Jake Sherman and Marin Cogan, "Boehner Governs at Expense of the Right," *Politico*, April 15, 2011, 9.
13. Ibid.
14. When Newt Gingrich became Speaker in 1995, he won adoption of a House rule banning the introduction of so-called commemorative legislation: "Ice Cream Month," "National Dairy Goat Awareness Week," "National Save for Retirement Day," and the like. House Rule XII, Clause 5, stated that a "bill or resolution, or an amendment thereto, may not be introduced or considered in the House if it establishes or expresses a commemoration." Gingrich believed that consideration of these types of bills, some of which became

law with the president's signature, wasted the House's time and taxpayer dollars. Members continued to introduce bills or joint resolutions that, if passed and signed into law, would name post offices and other federal facilities after prominent individuals, such as the Ronald Reagan Post Office. Seventy post-office–naming laws were enacted during the 111th Congress (2009–2011). House Republican rules for the 112th Congress (2011–2013) directed the Speaker not to schedule commemorative measures under suspension of the rules. Moreover, the GOP's rules tightened the definition of what constitutes a commemoration compared with the rather brief text contained in House Rule XII, Clause 5.

15. Data provided by Christopher Davis, congressional expert, Congressional Research Service.
16. *Congressional Record*, January 4, 2005, H13.
17. See "Leadership Protocols for the 112th Congress," February 23, 2011. The protocols can be found on Majority Leader Eric Cantor's website (http://www .majorityleader.gov/protocols).
18. Martin Gold, Michael Hugo, Hyde Murray, Peter Robinson, and A. L. "Pete" Singleton, *The Book on Congress* (Washington, D.C.: Big Eagle, 1992), 124.
19. Paul Kane and Karen Tumulty, "House GOP Trips Over Another Vote," *Washington Post*, February 10, 2011, A3.
20. *Congressional Record*, December 17, 2005, H12057.
21. *Congressional Record,* June 14, 2008, H5867.
22. Kasperowicz, "House Schedule Too Light, Say Democrats," 8.
23. Damon Chappie, "House Caught in a State of Suspension," *Roll Call*, January 27, 2003, 22. This article was based on a study of the suspension procedure by Donald R. Wolfensberger, director of the Congress Project, Woodrow Wilson Center, Washington, DC.
24. Jonathan Nicholson, "Congress on Pace to Enact Fewest Laws In Post-War Era, BNA Analysis Shows," *Daily Report for Executives*, April 16, 2012, B-3.
25. *Congressional Record,* February 28, 2007, H1986.
26. See, for example, D.C. delegate Eleanor Holmes Norton's statement in the *Congressional Record*, January 7, 2009, E26–E27, and Tim Craig and Paul Kane, "D.C. Vote Supporters Defer Fight in Congress," *Washington Post*, June 10, 2009, B1.
27. See Justin Gelfand, "Members Without a Vote Are Raising Their Voices on Hill," *The Hill*, July 23, 2003, 6.
28. *Congressional Record*, April 19, 2012, H2022. The quote from the president's budget was also cited by Delegate Norton in her April 19 statement (H2023). See also Emma Dumain, "Push for D.C. Budget Autonomy Grows," *Roll Call*, April 17, 2012, 3.
29. See "The Private Calendar," *Congressional Record,* March 31, 2011, E586.
30. Jeffrey S. Hill and Kenneth C. Williams, "The Decline of Private Bills: Resource Allocation, Credit Claiming, and the Decision to Delegate," *American Journal of Political Science* (November 1993): 1017.
31. *Congressional Record*, July 14, 2003, H6655.
32. William Holmes Brown and Charles W. Johnson, *House Practice: A Guide to the Rules, Precedents, and Procedures of the House* (Washington, D.C.: Government Printing Office, 2003), 657.
33. *Nation's Business*, February 1956, 103.

34. See, for example, Charles O. Jones, "Joseph G. Cannon and Howard W. Smith: An Essay on the Limits of Leadership in the House of Representatives," *Journal of Politics* (September 1968): 617–646; Robert L. Peabody, "The Enlarged Rules Committee," in *New Perspectives on the House of Representatives*, 2d ed., eds. Robert L. Peabody and Nelson W. Polsby (Chicago: Rand McNally, 1969); and James A. Robinson, *The House Rules Committee* (Indianapolis, Ind.: Bobbs-Merrill, 1963).

35. Jonathan Allen, "What's the Deal With the House Rules Panel Usually Meeting Late at Night?" *CQ Today*, May 22, 2003, 6.

36. *New York Times*, April 2, 1995, 20.

37. Richard E. Cohen, "Boehner Keeps Reins Loose on Rules Panel Despite Risks of Trouble on Floor," *CQ Today*, March 5, 2012, 3.

38. Ibid.

39. *New York Times*, December 18, 1987, A34.

40. Cohen, "Boehner Keeps Reins Loose on Rules Despite Risks of Trouble on Floor," 3.

41. *A History of the Committee on Rules*, 97th Cong., 2d Session (Washington, D.C.: U.S. Government Printing Office, 1983). See also Bruce I. Oppenheimer, "The Changing Relationship Between House Leadership and the Committee on Rules," in *Understanding Congressional Leadership*, ed. Frank H. Mackaman (Washington, D.C.: CQ Press, 1981). Professor Oppenheimer also wrote the history of the committee.

42. *Congressional Record*, June 19, 2002, H3696.

43. Spark Matsunaga and Ping Chen, *Rulemakers of the House* (Urbana: University of Illinois Press, 1976), 2.

44. See *Survey of Activities of the House Committee on Rules for the First Session of the 112th Congress*, H. Rept. 112-357, December 30, 2011, 5–7.

45. Stanley Bach and Steven Smith, *Managing Uncertainty in the House of Representatives* (Washington, D.C.: Brookings, 1988), 50.

46. *Congressional Record*, December 15, 1987, H11436.

47. Ibid., March 20, 2012, H1408.

48. Ibid., February 15, 2011, H806.

49. Ibid., July 14, 1987, H6282.

50. Ibid., December 13, 2011, H8746.

51. Ibid., July 10, 1997, H5049.

52. *Floor Deliberations and Scheduling, Hearings Before the Joint Committee on the Organization of Congress* (Washington, D.C.: Government Printing Office, 1993), 216–217.

53. Alan Ehrenhalt, "O'Neill Studying Moves to Counter GOP 'Obstructionism,'" *Washington Star*, August 5, 1979, A3.

54. There are many other types of special rules, such as "King of the Hill" and "Queen of the Hill." For an excellent article on these procedural resolutions, see James V. Saturno, "Toppling the King of the Hill: Understanding Innovation in House Practice," in Jacob R. Strauss, *Party and Procedure in the United States Congress* (New York: Rowman & Littlefield, 2012), 35–60.

55. *Congressional Record*, February 15, 2012, H740. A divisible amendment means a proposition that consists of two separable proposals—each able to stand alone so that if one is voted down, the other remains as a distinct proposal. See Chapter 5 for a discussion of the Committee of the Whole.

56. *Congressional Record*, November 30, 2011, H7949–H7950.
57. Ibid., February 27, 1995, H2235.
58. Richard E. Cohen, "Aides Say Offset to Revenue-Reducing Bill Not Indicative of Republican Shift," *CQ Today*, October 26, 2011, 7.
59. Ibid.
60. Bach and Smith, *Managing Uncertainty in the House of Representatives: Adaptation and Innovation in Special Rules* (Washington, D.C.: Brookings Institution, 1988), 27.
61. Bob Michel, "Beyond the Political Wilderness: Reforming 40 Years of One-Party Rule," *Common Sense* (Fall 1994), 56.
62. *Congressional Record*, June 5, 2003, H4986.
63. John Bresnahan, "Democrats Vow Fairness on Rules," *Roll Call*, November 2, 2006, 3.
64. *Congressional Record*, May 14, 2008, H3824.
65. Ibid.
66. Andrew Taylor, "Democratic Leaders in House Keep Debate Short, Liability Low," *Washington Times*, July 17, 2009, A7. See also "Opportunities Lost, the End of the Appropriations Process," a July 2009 report of Republicans on the Rules Committee. The report is available on the Rules Republican website.
67. *Congressional Record*, July 29, 2009, H8977.
68. Keith Perine and Seth Stern, "GOP Protest Impedes First Spending Bills," *CQ Weekly*, June 22, 2009, 1448–1449.
69. Walter Alarkon, "GOP Holds Second Protest during Spending Bill Debate," *The Hill*, June 25, 2009, 4, and Nancy Ognanovich, "Hoyer Says Democrats to Consider Time Frames for Spending Bill Debates," *Daily Report for Executives*, June 22, 2009, A-14.
70. Donald R. Wolfensberger, "First Session of 112th Congress: More Than Disappointing," January 11, 2012, 4. Available at http://www.bipartisanpolicy.org/blog
71. *Congressional Record*, January 15, 2011, H805. Also see Daniel Newhauser, "Closed CR Reignites Criticism," *Roll Call*, September 21, 2011, 1.
72. "Switched Votes for Gas Bill," *Congressional Quarterly Weekly Report*, February 14, 1976, 313.
73. Richard S. Beth, the foremost expert on the discharge procedure, kindly provided the information. See also Beth, "The Discharge Rule in the House: Recent Use in Historical Context," *CRS Report 97-856*, April 17, 2003; Beth, "The Discharge Rule in the House: Principal Features and Uses," *CRS Report 97-552*, November 26, 2008; and Kathryn Pearson and Eric Schickler, "Discharge Petitions, Agenda Control, and the Congressional Committee System, 1929–76," *Journal of Politics*, October 2009, 1238–1256.
74. Richard E. Cohen, "A Strong Sense of Entitlement," *National Journal*, April 27, 2002, 1226.
75. Ethan Wallison, "House Democrats Split on Strategy," *Roll Call*, February 17, 2000, 28.
76. David Sands, "Short Session Likely Partisan," *Washington Times*, September 10, 2008, A13.
77. Matsunaga and Chen, *Rulemakers of the House*, 25.
78. Julie Kosterlitz, "Still Going Strong," *National Journal*, January 2, 1988, 15.
79. *Congressional Record*, April 5, 1995, H4204.

80. Beth, "The Discharge Rule in the House," *CRS Report 97-856*, April 17, 2003.
81. *Congressional Record,* January 6, 2009, H11.
82. *Congressional Record,* January 25, 1984, H126–H139.
83. Information compiled by Richard Beth, congressional specialist, Government Division, Congressional Research Service, Library of Congress.
84. Bob Benenson, "Removal of 'Fast Track' May Put GATT in the Fast Lane," *Congressional Quarterly Weekly Report*, September 17, 1994, 2561. Also see I. M. Destler, *American Trade Politics*, 2d ed. (Washington, D.C.: Institute for International Economics, 1992), 71–76.

CHAPTER 5

House Floor Procedure

VISITORS TO the House gallery may be surprised by what they observe on the House floor. For one thing, the floor activity appears quite disorganized. People come and go in an endless stream. Motions are offered, amendments are proposed, and points of order are raised. Amid all this activity, representatives on the floor may display little interest in what is going on. Legislators talk in small groups or read various materials while their colleagues make speeches. Furthermore, attendance is often sparse during floor debates. Members may be in committee sessions, meeting with constituents, or attending to numerous other tasks. Members can reach the floor quickly, however, to respond to quorum calls, participate in debate, or vote.

The House chamber itself is divided into two levels. Above the floor are the galleries for visitors, diplomats, reporters, and other observers. Visitors sit on either side of the chamber or facing the Speaker's rostrum; the press sits above and behind the rostrum. Unlike senators, representatives have no desks in the chamber. Seats, which are unassigned, are arranged in semicircular rows in front of the Speaker. Aisles divide groups of seats, and a broad center aisle divides the majority and minority parties (see Figure 5.1). Informally, groups of lawmakers congregate and often sit with the same people every day. For example, there is a "Pennsylvania Corner" in the chamber where that state's Democratic lawmakers gather to meet.[1]

While in session, the House normally convenes daily, except Saturdays and Sundays, at noon or earlier.[2] Buzzers ring in committee rooms, members' offices, and in the Capitol, summoning representatives to the floor. Rules and informal practices set the daily order of business: an opening prayer, approval of the *Journal* (a record of the previous day's proceedings as required by the Constitution), the Pledge of Allegiance, receipt of messages from the Senate or the president, **1-minute speeches,** and other routine business. Monday through Thursday, a morning-hour debate is held prior to the start of formal legislative business. The House convenes from an hour to an hour and a half earlier to accommodate lawmakers who want to discuss various issues of the day. The time is equally divided between the two parties.

With the escalation of partisanship, each party has established a theme team or message group to coordinate and orchestrate the daily speeches during the morning hour, 1-minute, and special-order debate periods: the three basic types of so-called nonlegislative debate. On one occasion, for

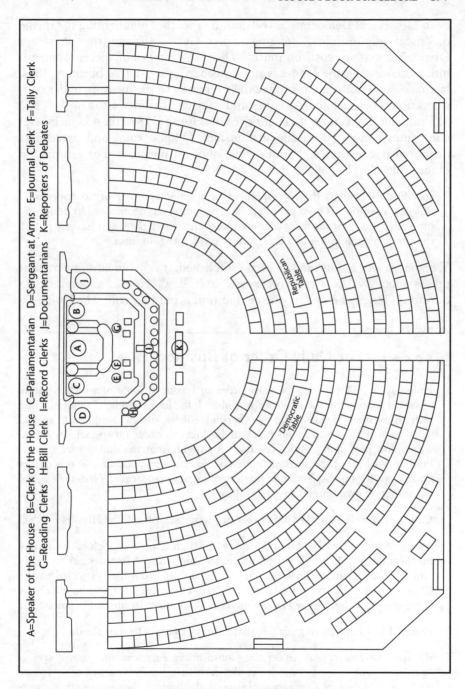

A=Speaker of the House B=Clerk of the House C=Parliamentarian D=Sergeant at Arms E=Journal Clerk F=Tally Clerk
G=Reading Clerks H=Bill Clerk I=Record Clerks J=Documentarians K=Reporters of Debates

FIGURE 5-1   Floor Plan of the House of Representatives

example, several Democrats gave 1-minute speeches highlighting the theme of "fiscal responsibility," refuting earlier GOP criticisms that President Obama's initiatives cost too much.[3] These three types of speech opportunities occur when the House is not considering legislative business; thus, lawmakers do not need to confine their remarks to the measure under consideration. They can address issues and subjects that interest them.[4]

Under the Constitution, a majority of the House (218 of the 435 members) constitutes a quorum to conduct business. House rules and precedents define what constitutes "business" for quorum purposes. For example, a House rule

> specifically prohibits the entertainment of a point of order of no quorum unless a question has been put to a vote. The House has determined by adopting such a rule that the mere conduct of debate, where the Chair has not put the pending proposition to a vote, is not "conducting business."[5]

Whether or not a quorum has been established, it is assumed to be present unless officially discovered otherwise. In today's House, a point of no quorum is largely limited to when a question is put to a vote. The House, in

---

BOX 5.1   The Daily Order of Business

House Rule XIV sets out the daily order of business, some of which is rarely observed (correcting the reference of public bills, for example). Commonly, the order of business is superseded by other procedures, such as adoption of special rules from the Committee on Rules or business in order on special days (e.g., suspension procedure). Rule XIV itself highlights that the daily order is non-binding, with this parenthetical: "unless varied by the application of other rules and except for the disposition of matters of higher precedence." Nonetheless, the usual routine on a normal day is as follows:

Call to Order. The Speaker or Speaker pro tempore will call the House to order.

Morning-Hour Debate. From Monday through Thursday, before legislative business begins, there is a period of debate, limited to 5 minutes per majority and minority member. Each member is recognized from lists provided to the Chair by the majority and minority leaders. Following morning-hour debate, there is a recess before the House convenes to conduct its normal business.

Prayer. The Chaplain, or guest Chaplain, offers a prayer to start the day.

Approval of the Journal. Under the Constitution, each chamber must "keep a Journal of its Proceedings," which includes the official legislative action of the House (or Senate). Unlike the *Congressional Record*, the Journal does not contain a generally verbatim transcript of the debates. The Speaker may announce his approval of the Journal—the record of the previous day's proceedings—or any lawmaker can

brief, frequently operates with far fewer members than a majority physically present in the chamber.

While in session, the House usually convenes Monday through Friday. Mondays are reserved mainly for routine legislation. The workload on Fridays is generally light because many members want to return to their home districts on weekends. (Recall from Chapter 4 that the last vote on Fridays in the 112th House commonly occurred no later than 3 p.m.). Most major business is usually conducted from Tuesday through Thursday. Other scheduling arrangements are sometimes employed at different times, such as around-the-clock daily sessions during the hectic last days of a legislative session. The House has also tried for years to make its schedule more predictable and therefore more family friendly, but that is hard to accomplish because the legislative job is not a 9 a.m. to 5 p.m. routine. Typically, the House meets fewer days during the second session (an election year) than the first session to accommodate lawmakers who want to get home to campaign.

Although no one day on the House floor is the same—some days the House meets only briefly, while other times it meets all night, for example—a recurring pattern of daily activity has emerged, as noted in Box 5.1.

---

request a vote on the Journal. If that occurs, the vote is typically postponed until later in the day. This vote is sometimes used by party leaders to lobby their colleagues as they come to the floor to win their support for priority issues; the Journal vote is sometimes called by members upset with House proceedings.

Pledge of Allegiance to the Flag. A majority and minority lawmaker alternate each day the House is in session in leading the members in the pledge.

One-Minute Speeches. Typically, the Speaker will recognize members from each side of the aisle to make a limited number of 1-minute speeches on virtually any topic. This period is essentially a time for "free speech."

Legislative Business. The conclusion of the 1-minute period typically begins action on the substantive business of the day, as scheduled by the majority leadership. This might be bills taken up under suspension of the rules procedure or a special rule from the Rules Committee making in order a bill for chamber consideration.

Special Orders. At the conclusion of the day's legislative business, there is a period for special-order speeches. Members may be recognized for up to 1 hour, alternating between the two parties. Members who belong to various informal groups (the Congressional Black Caucus or the Republican Study Committee) often reserve an hour to spotlight their policy views to the C-SPAN viewing audience. This period does not extend beyond 10 p.m.

Adjournment. When the special-order speeches are concluded, a member will be recognized and say something like: "I move that when the House adjourns today, it stand adjourned to meet at [a certain time] on [a certain day]." This motion is routinely adopted by unanimous consent or voice vote.

In considering major bills, the House usually follows the steps listed below. Each merits some discussion.

1. Adopt the rule granted by the Rules Committee.

2. Resolve the House into the Committee of the Whole.

3. Proceed with the general debate.

4. Undertake the amending process, if permitted.

5. Consider any motions to recommit.

6. Take final action (full House).

ADOPTION OF THE RULE

The first step in bringing a major bill to the floor is House adoption of a special rule issued by the Rules Committee. A rule sets the conditions under which a measure will be considered, decreeing whether floor amendments will be permitted and how much debate will be allowed.

The House rarely rejects a rule, as noted in Chapter 4, largely because it normally receives overwhelming support from majority party members. Majority party leaders make it clear to partisan colleagues that procedural votes are party-line votes. Their advice is regularly followed, but not always. For example, freshmen Republicans who represent moderate districts carried by President Obama want at times to demonstrate their independence from their more conservative party leaders by casting votes against procedural resolutions or motions. As one account explained about conservative Democrats who represent GOP-leaning districts, they "try to put distance between themselves and leadership on social and spending issues because they come from competitive districts where looking independent can help with voters skeptical of [the liberal] Democratic leaders."[6]

More typically, House members of the majority party usually vote for rules. They realize that at some point in the future they may need a rule from the Rules Committee for one of their own bills, and so challenging the committee is unwise. In general, when a rule is rejected, it usually reflects sharp divisions in the House; disagreements within the majority party; heavy lobbying by pressure groups, the president, or federal agency officials; or broad agreement that the reporting committee did a poor job of drafting the bill.

Voting down a rule is often a procedural kill. As one House leader stated, it enables members "to get rid of the bill without putting their fingerprints on the trigger."[7] Such actions demonstrate how procedural matters can have a critical impact on policymaking. Without favorable action on a rule, often because of splits in the majority party, the House may lose the chance to consider a measure and face subsequent delays in taking it up. A special rule rejected by the House underscores this legislative dynamic.

As the 107th Congress (2001–2003) headed for final adjournment, GOP leaders suffered a rare defeat on a rule when they decided to take up a bankruptcy conference report. The House voted down 172 to 243 the rule making the conference report in order for floor consideration.[8] The rule's rejection, even with Speaker Dennis Hastert, R-Ill. (1999–2007), casting a vote in favor, sounded the death knell for bankruptcy reform. Action was blocked on the conference report by an unusual coalition of Democrats and religiously oriented conservative Republicans. Democrats opposed the conference agreement because they viewed it as anticonsumer and pro-credit card companies; conservative Republicans rebelled against a provision in the conference report that prohibited antiabortion protesters from filing for bankruptcy to avoid paying court-ordered fines for blocking abortion clinics. Republican defections were encouraged by antiabortion Christian groups that "flooded Republican offices with phone calls and e-mails . . . railing against the bill and splitting the [GOP] Conference between business-friendly Republicans and social conservatives."[9]

COMMITTEE OF THE WHOLE

After the House votes to adopt a rule, the Speaker declares the House resolved into the Committee of the Whole. The Committee of the Whole is the House in another form. Its basic purposes are to expedite action on legislation and to promote debate by the members. Every legislator is a member. House rules require all revenue-raising or appropriations bills to be considered first in the Committee of the Whole. The staff director of the House Rules Committee once wrote that, with its special authority for revenue and spending bills, the Committee of the Whole "is the very essence of the House exercising its special [fiscal] powers and prerogatives under the Constitution."[10]

Technically, there are two such bodies. One is the "House as in Committee of the Whole," which is a forum that can be used for considering private bills and District of Columbia legislation.[11] The other and more important body is the Committee of the Whole House on the state of the Union, commonly shortened to Committee of the Whole, which considers public measures. The Committee of the Whole has its origins, like many congressional practices, in the British Parliament. During the 17th century, the Parliament and the Crown regularly clashed over finances and taxes. To ensure that all members of the House of Commons participated in debates involving the expenditure of money, Parliament established the Committee of the Whole to review and check the financial proposals made by parliamentary committees, which were sometimes stacked with the king's or queen's supporters. A further elaboration of the Committee of the Whole's origins is provided by a scholar and former member of the House of Representatives, De Alva Stanwood Alexander, R-N.Y. (1897–1911):

> It originated in the time of the Stuarts, when taxation arrayed the Crown against the Commons, and suspicion made the Speaker [of the House of Commons] a tale-bearer to the King. To avoid the Chair's espionage the Commons met in secret [in a Committee of the Whole], elected a chairman in whom it had confidence, and without fear of the King freely exchanged its views respecting [financial] supplies.[12]

The Committee of the Whole uses rules different from those of the House; they are designed to speed up floor action and facilitate debate. Table 5.1 sets out several rules or customs that distinguish the conduct of business in the full House from proceedings in the Committee of the Whole.

First, a quorum is only 100 members in the Committee of the Whole; 218 members constitute a quorum in the House. Second, by custom, the Speaker does not preside over the Committee of the Whole. Instead, the Speaker appoints a colleague, who is also a member of the majority party, to fill that role—a practice that can be traced to English precedent. The Speaker is permitted to remain in the chamber and take part in debate but seldom participates except to make closing remarks on tightly contested

TABLE 5.1   Major Characteristics, House and Committee of the Whole

House	Committee of the Whole
Mace raised	Mace lowered
Speaker presides	Chair presides
More than half the House (218) is a quorum	One hundred is a quorum
One-hour rule for amendments	Five-minute rule for amendments
Previous question in order	Motion to limit debate on amendments, but not the previous question motion, in order
Forty-four members, or one fifth of the House quorum of 218, trigger a recorded vote	Twenty-five members trigger a recorded vote
Motion to recommit in order	Motion to recommit not in order

SOURCE: Adapted from *Manual on Legislative Procedure in the U.S. House of Representatives*, 6th ed., 99th Congress, prepared under the auspices of the House Republican leader, May 1986.

major bills. When Nancy Pelosi, D-Calif., was Speaker (2007–2011), she was an exception. As one account noted, few Speakers "have spoken so much."[13] By tradition, the Speaker usually does not vote in the Committee of the Whole (or the House), except to break a tie. (Speaker Pelosi was also an exception in this regard, voting more than her immediate predecessors or her successor.) Third, it is in order in the Committee of the Whole to close or limit debate on sections of a bill by unanimous consent or majority vote of the members present; the prime debate-ending motion in the House is the previous question. Fourth, various motions that are in order in the House are not permitted in the Committee of the Whole, such as the previous question motion or motions to recommit, adjourn, or reconsider the vote by which an amendment was agreed to or rejected. Fifth, amendments to bills are introduced and debated under the 5-minute rule in the Committee of the Whole, not under the hour rule as in the House.[14] Sixth, in the Committee of the Whole, 25 members can trigger a recorded vote; in the House, 44 members (one fifth of a quorum) can do so.

Finally, the position of the mace, a 46-inch column of ebony rods bound together by silver and topped by a silver eagle, indicates whether the House is in the Committee of the Whole. The mace, symbol of the authority of the sergeant at arms, is carried by the sergeant at arms if called on to enforce order on the floor. The mace rests on a pedestal on a table at the right of the Speaker's podium. It is taken down from the table when the Speaker hands the gavel to the chair of the Committee of the Whole. When the committee rises (dissolves) and the Speaker resumes the chair, the mace is returned to its place.[15]

GENERAL DEBATE

The first order of business in the Committee of the Whole is general debate on the entire bill under consideration, equally divided between the majority and minority parties.[16] For most bills, 1 hour is authorized; for complex and highly significant legislation, as many as 10 or more hours may be scheduled. The chair of the Committee of the Whole presides over the proceedings and wields the gavel to maintain order and fairness. "It's an art form," said a lawmaker. "It takes an ability to sense the mood of the House, track the chemistry of what is going on the floor, apply the gavel lightly or hard, depending on what is warranted."[17]

Each party has a floor manager from the committee of original jurisdiction who controls time, allotting segments to supporters or opponents, as the case may be. (On multi-referred measures, there may be two or more pairs of floor managers.) Almost without exception, the floor manager for the majority party is the spokesperson for the bill. When both sides favor passage of a bill, both floor managers rise in support. During debate on controversial legislation, both floor managers may declare their support for the bill's aims but have differences of opinion on specific sections or amendments.

The term *general debate* can be misleading, as most members deliver prepared speeches and engage in a minimum of give-and-take. Because committees and subcommittees shape the fundamental character of most legislation, only a limited number of representatives participate in the debate, and those who do are usually members of the committee that drafted the legislation. Yet general debate has an intrinsic value that is recognized by most House members and experts on the legislative process.

Because of its large size and workload, the House imposes strict debate limits on lawmakers. Nearly every second of debate time (the hour rule, the 5-minute rule, 40 minutes for suspensions, and so on) is regulated by some rule or practice. The House did experiment with three Oxford-style floor debates in 1994 on agreed-on national issues—health, welfare, and trade—where teams of lawmakers engaged each other in sustained discussions of these topics. This British format has not taken hold in the House, because lawmakers prefer debate to be tied directly to specific legislation.[18]

Purposes of General Debate

General debate is both symbolic and practical. It assures both legislators and the public that the House makes its decisions in a democratic fashion, with due respect for majority and minority opinion. "Congress is the only branch of government that can argue publicly," noted a House Republican some years ago. "Debate appropriately tests the conclusions of the majority."[19] General debate forces members to come to grips with the issues at hand; offers a forum for explaining difficult and controversial sections of a bill; alerts constituents and interest groups to a measure's purpose through press coverage of the debate; gives floor leaders an opportunity to assess member sentiment; builds a public record, or legislative history, for administrative agencies and the courts, indicating the intentions of proponents and opponents alike; allows legislators to take positions for reelection purposes; and, occasionally, influences fence-sitters. General debate also permits Republicans and Democrats, especially in election years, to raise issues that are of concern to their respective electoral constituencies. In the judgment of a senior lawmaker, when the House in 1979 began televised coverage of its proceedings, "We've lost out a lot with the camera . . . because it emphasizes combat and drama rather than a thoughtful analysis of issues."[20]

Some legislators doubt that debate can change views or affect the outcome of a vote. But debate, especially by party leaders just before a key vote, can change opinion. For example, a House member noted that an address by the Speaker marked "one of the few times on the House floor when a speech changed a lot of votes."[21] The Speaker and minority leader, by custom, are granted extra time to address the House even though they are yielded only a few minutes by their respective floor managers. As the minority leader at the time, GOP leader John Boehner, Ohio, spoke for an hour on a climate change bill after being yielded 2 minutes. His speech, dubbed a "fili-Boehner," was so energized that it was viewed more than 70,000 times on YouTube.[22] Robert H. Michel, R-Ill., House minority leader from 1981 to 1995, highlighted the importance of having informed and persuasive speakers take part in floor debates.

> A classic example ... occurred during our debate on the nuclear freeze in 1983. A Democratic colleague challenged my Illinois colleague, [Republican] Henry Hyde, who had just criticized a prominent woman advocate of the freeze. The Democrat said: "Yes, she is, as you say the mother of the freeze. But President Reagan, through his lack of arms control progress, is the father of the freeze." And, without missing a beat, Henry Hyde shot back: "And that makes you a son of a freeze." The debate went our way after that.[23]

Reasoned deliberation is important in decision making. Lawmaking consists of more than logrolling, compromises, or power plays. General debate enables members to gain a better understanding of complex issues, and it may influence the collective decisions of the House. The dilemma members often face, said one House member, "is to know what is right, and to make the right decisions" even though information may be skimpy, incomplete, or simply unavailable.[24] This was certainly the case in 1991 when the House debated authorization for President George H. W. Bush to use military force against Iraq's invasion of Kuwait. The legislation amounted to a declaration of war, said Speaker Thomas S. Foley, D-Wash., and general debate on it was "the longest in the modern history of the House of Representatives, extending over 20 hours."[25] Similarly, in 2002 House members debated for 20 hours over the joint resolution authorizing President George W. Bush to launch a preemptive military strike against Iraq. "Just as in 1991," said Rules Committee Chair David Dreier, R-Calif., "every single Member will have a chance to be heard" on the White House's view that the Saddam Hussein–led regime poses a serious terrorist threat to the United States.[26]

A decade later, while Iraq and Afghanistan remain topics of often contentious debate, fiscal issues (entitlements and the rising deficit and debt discussed in Chapter 2) and the role of the federal government (its size and scope) dominate deliberations on Capitol Hill, not to mention ways to promote economic growth. For example, the two congressional parties disagree strongly over taxes, and the debate between them is often intense and clearly demarcated. As an astute commentator phrased it: "Republicans don't want to raise taxes on anyone, and Democrats don't want to raise taxes on almost anyone [only those who are viewed as wealthy]."[27] Debate alone is unlikely to end this partisan standoff without some external stimulus, such as huge citizen outcry at the loss or decline of public services. Still, debate has the potential to help resolve the many procedural and substantive differences endemic to Capitol Hill's environment.

Floor Managers' Role

Long-standing customs govern much of the action on the House floor, but the floor managers direct the course of debate on each bill. The manager for the majority side is often the chair of the committee that reported the bill or an appointed committee colleague. The ranking minority committee member, or an appointed surrogate, is usually the floor manager for the minority party. Floor managers generally can count on support from their party leadership.

During the debate, the floor managers sit at long tables near the center of the chamber, with the main aisle separating the Democratic side from the Republican side. They also are permitted to have up to five of their committee's staff members on the floor during debate, ready to research rules and precedents, draft amendments, answer technical questions about the bill, or prepare statements.

In guiding their bill through final disposition by the House, the floor managers principally inform colleagues (and by inference the general public and media) about the contents of the bill; explain the issues in controversy and why the committee made the decisions it did; and provide lawmakers with reasons to vote for the legislation and to reject alternatives. In addition, they must

- plan strategy and parliamentary maneuvers to meet changing floor situations;
- respond to points of order;
- attempt to protect the bill from amendments the majority considers undesirable;
- alert supporters to be on the floor to vote for or against closely contested amendments;
- advise colleagues on the meaning and importance of the amendments;
- judge when amendments of committee members should be offered or deferred;
- inform party leaders of member sentiment and the mood of the House toward their bill;
- control the time for general debate and, if necessary, act to limit debate on amendments, sections, or titles of the bill, or on the entire measure;
- arrange the sequence of speakers on major amendments to ensure that the best supporting orators are matched against those of the opposition; and
- mobilize outside support to build winning coalitions on the floor.

The fate of much legislation depends on the skill of the floor managers. Effective floor management increases the chances for smooth passage. For example, enactment of the landmark Congressional Budget and Impoundment Control Act of 1974 was credited in large part to its skillful floor manager, Rep. Richard W. Bolling, D-Mo. (1949–1983).

Floor managers are given several advantages over their colleagues. They customarily lead off debate in the Committee of the Whole and therefore have the first opportunity to appeal for support. During the debate, they receive priority recognition from the chair. Floor managers may take the floor at critical moments ahead of other legislators to defend or rebut attacks on the bill, or they may offer amendments to coalesce support for the measure. And floor managers, who are entitled, by custom, to close the debate on an amendment, have the last chance to influence sentiment. As a result of committee hearings, discussion, and markup, the managers have a reservoir of knowledge about the technical details of a measure and are in a good position to judge which amendments to accept and reject, and the best arguments to employ for or against them.

Delaying Tactics

Despite the generally tighter rules on debate in the House than in the Senate, representatives have various ways to prolong or delay proceedings. They may raise numerous points of order, make scores of parliamentary inquiries, or offer trivial amendments. For example, during consideration of a bill creating the Department of Education, an opponent offered two unsuccessful but dilatory amendments. One would have changed the department's name to the Department of Public Education (DOPE), the other to the Department of Public Education and Youth (DOPEY).[28] Members may also demand recorded votes on every amendment and motion; ask unanimous consent to speak for additional minutes on each amendment; make certain that all time for general debate is used; appeal rulings of the chair; or offer a priority motion, unless special rules provide otherwise, that the Committee of the Whole rise. To prevent dilatory use of the motion to rise, special rules commonly include language that the presiding officer may entertain such motions only if made by the appropriate committee chair.

Often the purpose of delaying tactics is to stall action on a measure to allow more time to gather support (if those using such tactics favor the bill) or to kill it (if they are opposed). At times, delay is intended to force action and other times to prevent it. In today's polarized House, delay is often employed by the minority party for a number of reasons: to protest the heavy-handed actions of the majority, to attract publicity for their agenda, to energize or rally their electoral supporters, to extract policy concessions, or to promote party unity. A few recent examples of dilatory activities by minority Democrats during the 1995-to-2007 period, the minority Republicans' tactics during 2007 to 2011, and then the minority Democrats' stalling tactics (2011–2013) illustrate how traditional rules and practices can be turned into partisan procedural devices. These examples highlight something akin to a parliamentary law of emulation that is operative in today's polarized House. When a party loses the House, it emulates the dilatory tactics used against it when the opposition ran the chamber; moreover, the new minority often adds to the repertoire of dilatory procedures.

Democrats (1995–2007). In the minority from 1995 to 2007, Democrats employed many of the parliamentary guerrilla warfare tactics used by Republicans when they were the minority for decades, such as raising procedural objections; clashing verbally with lawmakers on the other side of the aisle; demanding roll-call votes; forcing votes on the motion to adjourn the House, to **reconsider a vote** by which a measure was just agreed to, or to reconsider the vote by which engrossment (preparation of the official copy of the bill as passed by the House) and third reading (the obligatory reading of the bill, by title, just before the vote on final passage) is ordered; and offering floor amendments (if the special rule allows) designed to foment reelection difficulties for members of the opposing party who must vote against them. "The job of the minority is to make trouble for the majority," remarked a GOP majority leader, "and they are doing a very good job of this."[29]

Democrats also added to the array of stalling tactics, as illustrated by these two examples. First, House Democrats, including the minority leader, employed questions of privilege in a systematic manner.[30] **Questions of privilege** involve the rights of the House collectively, its safety, dignity, and the integrity of its proceedings. This kind of question is brought before the House as a resolution, and it has precedence over every other motion except a motion to adjourn. (The Speaker determines whether these resolutions constitute legitimate questions of privilege.) In addition, the resolution must be read in full (its verbiage is designed to portray the majority negatively), and it can interrupt most pending business because of its privileged character. Any lawmaker may offer this privileged resolution after providing one day's notice on the House floor of the resolution's language. The Speaker then has up to 2 days to schedule it for floor consideration and also to rule on its legitimacy. The majority leader and the minority leader are exempt from these requirements and may offer privileged resolutions at almost any time. If the resolution is not immediately tabled (or killed), and after the Speaker states that it does present a question of the privileges of the House, the resolution is debated under the 1-hour rule equally divided between the proponent and an opponent.

Minority leader Pelosi, D-Calif., used questions of privilege a number of times to castigate Republicans on their management of the House and to spotlight what she called the GOP's "culture of corruption"—a campaign theme that proved to be an important key to Democratic success in the 2006 House elections. Although most were immediately tabled on a party-line vote, Pelosi got Republicans on record as voting against electorally salient issues, such as an inquiry into the ethical conduct of Majority Leader Tom DeLay, R-Tex.; the creation of a bipartisan ethics task force; the Iraq War and the lack of committee oversight of the executive branch; the 3-hour roll call on the Medicare prescription drug bill; and an investigation of the lawmakers and staff implicated in the criminal activity of lobbyist Jack Abramoff.[31] Questions of privilege, according to a congressional expert, are "helping the minority to document their case and rally their troops against Republican rule."[32]

In the second example, Democrats walked en masse to the chamber when they learned that the Ways and Means chair had earlier in the day called the Capitol Police to evict Democratic members of the panel from the committee's library. Angry at the chair's behavior, Democratic leader Pelosi marched to the floor with her party colleagues to introduce a privileged resolution reprimanding the Ways and Means chair for his extraordinary action. The result was a bitter debate between the two parties.

Republicans argued that the chair had called the police to restrain the only Democrat on the committee who remained in the room with the other GOP members during a markup. The Republicans alleged that the Democrat was about to start a fight with a Republican member of the panel. Democrats disputed the allegation and contended that the chair had called the police to oust them from the library, where they had gone to plan strategy on a pension reform bill that was slated to be marked up that day. "I want to focus on how the chairman can call upon the Capitol Police to evict Members at his whim from the committee space," exclaimed Pelosi. "We cannot let this stand. We cannot let this go unchallenged."[33] In the end, the House voted down Pelosi's resolution, but 5 days later the chair apologized to the House and admitted his mistake in calling the police on the Ways and Means Democrats.

Democrats, however, were not mollified by the apology. They remained angry at the GOP majority for not permitting them much say in policymaking, especially over a child-care tax credit proposal. Pelosi threatened disruptions during the week preceding the chamber's traditional August recess. "I say this as a promise not a prediction: This will be a week from hell for Republicans," declared Pelosi. "We will be disruptive on the floor until we get a child tax credit."[34] Democrats then proceeded to employ various parliamentary tactics to stall House action, such as offering motions to adjourn and forcing votes on usually noncontroversial procedural matters. During debate on the special rule making in order a GOP-sponsored bill (H.R. 2210) revamping the preschool Head Start program, Rules Democrat Alcee Hastings, Fla., yielded to 23 Democrats to make unanimous consent requests to revise and extend their remarks; all the requests were granted by the House. In their remarks, every Democrat said virtually the same thing, such as "Mr. Speaker, H.R. 2210 would cynically dismantle Head Start, so I rise in opposition," or "Mr. Speaker, H.R. 2210 will dismantle the successful Head Start program," or "Mr. Speaker, H.R. 2210 will dismantle Head Start and rob single moms of the best early childhood education for their children."[35] The bill passed the House by one vote.

Republicans (2007–2011). During the GOP's return to minority status (2007–2011), their members employed a wide range of parliamentary and political tactics to frustrate and foil the 110th and 111th Democratic majority. A comment made by Democratic majority leader Steny Hoyer, Md., when his party was in the minority (1995–2007), captures accurately the viewpoint of the then Republican minority toward the Democratic majority: "We are certainly going to frustrate their efforts to run the House because we are being shut out by the arrogance of the [majority] leadership."[36] The following were among the GOP's array of stalling maneuvers.

Questions of Privilege. Republicans employed questions of privilege more frequently than Democrats did when they were the minority party. Because these resolutions are read to the House (and the C-SPAN viewing audience) in their entirety, Republican drafters sometimes included more than 60 "whereas clauses" designed to criticize and embarrass Democrats—such as, "Whereas 'Republicans yelled in protest as Democrats held the 15-minute vote open for 27 minutes while Democratic leaders urged holdouts in the party to support the party position.'"[37] Questions of privilege end with "Now, therefore, be it resolved" that something should be done that is anathema to Democrats, such as stripping a party member of his Ways and Means chairmanship.[38] If the Speaker determines that the resolution qualifies as a question of privilege, a majority Democrat would quickly move to **table** (kill) the resolution so it would not be subject to debate under the 1-hour rule. Immediately, a minority member would request a recorded vote on the tabling motion knowing full well that it would be agreed to. Yet the public record of how Democratic incumbents voted provided potentially useful campaign material to GOP challengers. Moreover, should the Speaker correctly determine that a resolution is not privileged under House Rule IX, that decision would be appealed ("I appeal the ruling of the Chair") by a minority party member. The GOP appeal would then be tabled by the Democratic majority.

Appeal Correct Rulings of the Chair. Appeals of the chair's rulings were once rare. After more than 40 years as House parliamentarian (1927–1974), Lewis Deschler wrote that "there have been only eight appeals from decisions of the Speaker."[39] In 2008 alone, there were 13 appeals; a year later there were 17. Moreover, unlike the Deschler period, the tabling votes on appeals (and questions of privilege) are now transformed into campaign fodder. Here is how the process plays out: The minority party will offer a question of privilege that they know is out of order to force a fight and a vote on appealing the Speaker's ruling. The GOP's goal is to "raise an issue and put [vulnerable] first-term" Democrats in a difficult electoral situation.[40] The freshmen Democrats realize that their tabling vote will be framed not as a simple procedural vote upholding the correct ruling of the chair but as a vote on a substantive matter (guns, taxes, or national security) backed by many of their constituents.

Motions to Recommit. Republicans were especially skilled during the 110th Congress in using the motion to recommit (returning a bill to committee) to frustrate Democratic leaders. This motion is the prerogative of the minority party (guaranteed under House rules to the minority leader or his designee), and is usually voted down by the majority party because it is, after all, a minority party motion. However, in the 2007-to-2008 period, Republicans artfully crafted recommit motions to attract support from Democrats elected from conservative districts. The result: They won adoption of the recommit motion 25 times compared with only 14 agreed to over the dozen years when Democrats were the minority.[41] (The Republican's use of the word *promptly* rather than the customary *forthwith* was an important feature for their success with recommit motions. The difference between the two words is discussed below in a separate section.)

Republicans often employed a series of back-to-back stalling actions on their recommit motions. For example, the GOP would knowingly offer a motion to recommit a bill to committee with instructions that it report back a nongermane Republican substitute. Motions to recommit must be germane to the pending bill that is before the membership. A Democrat would raise a point of order against the GOP's motion, and the Speaker would correctly rule the GOP's policy alternative out of order. A minority member would appeal the chair's ruling, which Democrats would vote to table. Once Republicans lost the vote on appeal, they would then offer a germane recommit motion: obtaining two back-to-back votes on issues of their choosing. Motions to recommit are not provided in advance to members, and they often contain hard-to-address political and policy surprises for the majority leadership.

Calendar Wednesday. Republicans reprised Calendar Wednesday as a dilatory tactic, used by Newt Gingrich, R-Ga., in the mid-1980s to pressure Democrats to take action on their legislative proposals. Every Wednesday a nonprivileged bill reported by a committee that is on the Union or House Calendar could be called up by a committee chair or authorized committee member. On several Wednesdays, Rules Republican Pete Sessions, Tex., used this procedure to blame Democrats and then Speaker Pelosi for the escalating gasoline prices. Sessions would repeatedly make parliamentary inquiries of the chair on various Wednesdays asking whether various committee chairs could have called up a number of energy bills that "would help the Speaker to implement her secret plan by reducing the demand for gasoline prices and bringing down the prices that have skyrocketed under this Democratic leadership."[42] Answering the parliamentary inquiries, the

Speaker would note that only an authorized committee member could call up Calendar Wednesday business. Unsatisfied with that response, a minority member sometimes moved to adjourn the House ("Mr. Speaker, I move that the House do now adjourn.") The vote on the adjournment motion would lose, but it consumes valuable time and can disrupt other legislative activities as members rush to the floor to cast their ballot. To prevent Calendar Wednesday's use as a delaying and messaging device, Democrats amended the House rulebook at the start of the 111th Congress (2009–2011) to make Calendar Wednesday in order only if a committee chair or other authorized committee member "has announced to the House a request for such a call on the preceding legislative day." (Republicans have retained this rule for 112th and 113th Congresses.)

Voting to Delay. Requiring the House to vote on an array of procedural motions is a sure-fire way to frustrate the majority party and delay floor action. As mentioned in Chapter 4, the House conducted a record 53 roll call votes that consumed nearly 8 hours of consecutive voting. The minority Republicans were furious that an appropriations bill was being considered under a structured rule. (Traditionally, open rules are granted to appropriations bills.) An innovative way that GOP members further delayed proceedings was to line up "to vote manually with colored cards [indicating either yea or nay] rather than using the electronic voting system."[43] Once the chair closes the voting stations in the chamber but has not announced the final result, members can still vote manually through the use of the colored cards at the desk handed to lawmakers by the appropriate clerk. Forgetting or not using their personal voting cards, numerous GOP lawmakers would stand in a long line to vote manually.

Reading of Amendments. Minority members asked that amendments or motions be read in full. (Generally, the reading requirement is set aside by a special rule or by unanimous consent.) For example, on a lengthy motion to recommit, Republicans required a House clerk to spend nearly an hour reading it. Then the GOP member who offered the recommit motion withdrew it and submitted another to be read. This dilatory tactic aroused the ire of the Appropriations chair, who asked:

> "Why on Earth, if we're supposed to take this motion seriously, were we required to listen through the reading of a 55-page amendment, witness it being withdrawn, and then have [the GOP member] introduce an amendment which is virtually the same in an identical form?"[44]

Democrats charged that the reading tactic was used so Republicans could attend Minority Leader Boehner's annual fundraiser (the "Boehner Beach Party"). A Boehner spokesperson disputed that interpretation. Instead, we "forced the reading to protest un-democratic rules the Democratic leadership is insisting on for the appropriations process."[45]

Democrats Again in the Minority (2011–   ). Four years in the majority (2007–2011) ended rather quickly for Democrats, which underscores how rapidly party control of the contemporary House can change. Minority Democrats knew they had a panoply of tried-and-true procedural ways to frustrate the Republican majority of the 112th House (2011–2013). Still, they added a few "new" ones—at least new for them—to foil temporarily the GOP majority. Two examples make the point. First, angry that Republicans included 39 anti-environment riders in an Interior-Environment appropriations bill and with more pending as amendments, Democratic leaders took action. They "prevented consideration of [unwanted] amendments for hours by organizing their members 'to strike the last word,' a procedural motion that gives a member five minutes to speak."[46] Rep. Steven LaTourette, R-Ohio, a close ally of Speaker Boehner's, dubbed the Democratic tactic a "mini-filibuster."[47]

Second, when Republicans took up their budget resolution on the floor, the Rules Committee made in order for consideration—as is customary— several major alternatives to the fiscal plan proposed by Budget Chair Paul Ryan, Wis. One of the budget alternatives was sponsored by the conservative Republican Study Committee (RSC). Their plan advocated far deeper program spending cuts than wanted by the GOP leadership, including Ryan. As expected, Democrats initially voted against the RSC's budget alternative. However, a number of conservative GOP lawmakers voted "present" rather than "yea" or "nay" to avoid angering party colleagues and constituents who believed that the cuts were either too deep or not deep enough. Many Republicans believed that an overwhelming number of Democrats, along with many GOP lawmakers, would vote against the RSC budget, giving them a "free vote" to please their Tea Party supporters. Suddenly, Democrats began switching their votes on the RSC's amendment from "nay" to "present" to lower the threshold required to enact the conservative's budget plan and thus embarrass the GOP leadership. (Voting "present" does not count in the final tally of whether an amendment is adopted or rejected. As long as a quorum, or 218, of the House votes either for or against a proposition, that tally is determinative of whether a proposal is agreed to or not.) In the end, many GOP members who voted "present" were persuaded to change their votes to "no" to prevent passage of the RSC's budget, which was rejected (199 nays to 136 yeas). Rules Chair David Dreier, R-Calif., called the Democratic gambit "great theater."[48] Democratic whip Hoyer noted, "We learned from [you]."[49]

THE AMENDING PROCESS

The complex amending process is the heart of decision making on the floor. Amendments can be (1) categorized by form—whether they add or insert language, take out or strike matter, or do both, strike and insert;

(2) differentiated by their degrees (described later in this chapter); and (3) distinguished by type, how much they change a bill or a pending amendment. A "perfecting amendment" (here *perfecting* does not mean improving in the dictionary sense) modifies less of the language open to amendment than a "substitute amendment," which replaces the entire text (every word) of a pending first-degree amendment. An alternative for an entire bill is called "an amendment in the nature of a substitute" (see the discussion on p. 219 on substitute amendments). Amendments—which are policy alternatives—determine the final shape of bills passed by the House. At times, they are more important or controversial than the bills themselves. (Remember that lawmakers' opportunities to amend measures are determined by the character of the special rules reported by the Rules Committee.)

The 5-Minute Rule

House rules require that all bills and joint resolutions be read three times to give members every opportunity to become familiar with the measures they are considering. In practice, though, bills are not read word-for-word. The first "reading" occurs when a measure is introduced and referred to committee. The bill is not read aloud; the bill's number and title are published in the *Congressional Record*. The second reading occurs in the Committee of the Whole. And the third, by title (the name of the bill only), is held just before the vote on final passage.

Bills are considered, or read for amendment, as specified in the rule from the Rules Committee, usually section by section. The Rules Committee might specify a reading by title instead of by section to permit larger, interrelated parts of the measure to be open to amendment. Customarily, general and supplemental appropriations measures are read for amendment paragraph by paragraph. The Rules Committee can define how amendments will be taken up; infrequently, members agree to a unanimous consent request to utilize another approach.

At the end of general debate, a bill is read for amendment under the 5-minute rule. Under this House rule, any member "shall be allowed five minutes to explain the amendment, after which the Member who shall first obtain the floor shall be allowed to speak in opposition to it. There shall be no further debate thereon."[50]

Actual practice differs from the rule. Amendments are regularly debated for more than the 10 minutes allowed. Members gain the floor by offering **pro forma amendments**, moving to **strike the last word (or the requisite number of words)**. Although technically these are amendments, no alteration of the bill is contemplated by the sponsors; their purpose is to extend the debate. (Pro forma amendments are not in order under a closed rule.) In addition, members may ask for unanimous consent to speak longer than 5 minutes.

Debate on amendments cannot extend forever, however, and a floor manager can move that discussion be terminated at a specified time or there is no unamended text left to change. Time limits on amendments can be critical to the fate of legislation. For example, a time limit on debate on a Labor–Health and Human Services (HHS) appropriations bill, engineered by the chair of the HHS Appropriations Subcommittee, effectively prevented amendments from being offered on sensitive social topics such as abortion.

Amendments are in order as soon as the section to which they apply has been read, but they must be proposed before the clerk starts to read the next section. If the clerk has passed on to a succeeding section, a member must be granted unanimous consent to offer an amendment to the previous section. In addition to being timely, amendments must be germane to the bill, the section under consideration, or to a pending amendment. Reading by section or title helps structure rational consideration of complex bills, but on noncontroversial measures the floor manager usually asks unanimous consent that the entire bill be considered as read. In that case, the entire measure is open to amendment at any point. Thus, under the regular (customary) order, as explained by the Rules Committee:

> As each section is read, any amendments recommended by the reporting committee are automatically considered first without having to be offered from the floor. Quite often a special rule will provide that if the committee amendment is adopted, it becomes part of the base text for the purpose of further amendment so as not to block other members from amending that portion of the bill. Traditionally, the Chair next recognizes other members with amendments to that section. If two or more Members seek recognition, the Chair gives priority to Members of the committee(s) of jurisdiction over the bill, taking account of their seniority. Members of the primary committee of jurisdiction are recognized before secondary committee Members. The Chair will alternate between the parties in recognizing Members to offer amendments.[51]

House rules permit a nondebatable motion to be made in the Committee of the Whole to dispense with the reading of an amendment if it was either published in the *Congressional Record* or printed in the bill reported by a committee. The reading of amendments may also be dispensed with by unanimous consent or, commonly, by special rule. Indeed, the Rules Committee often requests (or requires) that lawmakers have their proposed amendments to bills printed in advance in the amendment section of the *Congressional Record*. The special rule will then state that the "amendments so printed are to be considered as read." Rules may also require that lawmakers submit their amendments to the panel by a specific deadline, so they can determine which and how many of them will be made in order.

In general, the prenotification of amendments strengthens the reporting committee's role on the floor by enabling it to prepare advance arguments, alternatives, or modifications to each prenoticed change. Advance notice of amendments also provides some degree of predictability in floor decision making, an objective favored by the floor managers and the majority leadership.[52] On the other hand, minority party members may object to the prenotification of amendments on at least two grounds: It eliminates the spontaneity of the amending process and prevents their ability to modify and improve proposals if only preprinted amendments are made in order for floor consideration.

Scripted Amendment Process

On major bills, it is common for the Rules Committee to sift through 100 or more proposed amendments before the majority members decide, after consultation with the Speaker and other key actors, which, when, and how many amendments will be made in order for floor consideration. It is this political–procedural process that determines the restrictiveness of the amendment process on priority legislation. A bill governed by a scripted (i.e., structured) process is easy to recognize. The special rule will include boiler-plate language that includes such procedural features as these: (1) Only those amendments printed in the written report of the Rules Committee accompanying the special rule are in order; (2) the amendments may be offered only in the order printed in the report; (3) they may be proposed only by the lawmaker named in the report; (4) they are considered as read; (5) they shall be debatable only for the time specified in the report, equally divided between the proponent and an opponent; and (6) they shall not be subject to amendment.

A scripted amendment process governs floor consideration of numer-ous consequential measures. From the majority party's perspective, the substantive and political risks are too high and the benefits too low to per-mit an unfettered amendment process. A narrowly divided House, com-bined with the reality that few if any minority party members are likely to vote with the majority to enact their priority issues, are among the factors that contribute to the clampdown on amendment opportunities for lawmakers. From the minority's perspective, the limitation on amend-ments prevents them from defining their policy differences with the major-ity party and offering alternative solutions to problems that may attract bipartisan support.

Rationale for Amendments

Amendments serve diverse objectives. Some are offered in deference to pres-sure groups, executive branch officials, or constituents; others are designed to attract public notice, to stall the legislative process, to demonstrate con-cern for an issue, to test sentiment for or against a bill, and, of course, to alter the pending bill; and still others are politically motivated in that they are designed to force controversial votes and thus provide electoral ammu-nition to congressional challengers, and to energize a party's core electoral supporters. "I want the Republicans on record having endorsed all these shortfalls in key programs the public wants, for education, veterans, housing, the environment," declared a House Democrat.[53] Some amendments are more technical than substantive; they may renumber sections or titles of a bill or correct typographical errors.

Committees, as noted in Chapter 3, do not have final authority to amend bills or measures during their markups. Only the full House has the authority to approve or disapprove of proposed changes to legislation. Committee amendments, then, are recommendations to the full House, where they are granted priority consideration ahead of amendments proposed by individual lawmakers. Committee amendments may be subject to amendment and are disposed of before amendments from the floor are taken up. Committee amendments, floor amendments, and substitutes are different types of amendments that merit some mention, along with the House's requirement that amendments must be germane.

Committee and Floor Amendments. House precedents grant priority to amendments recommended by the reporting committee(s). These precedents state: "Committee amendments to a pending section are normally considered prior to amendments offered from the floor."[54] This condition is another example of the parliamentary advantage accorded committees by House rules and precedents. Committees receive most of the bills introduced in the House, influence the kind of rule their bills receive from the Rules Committee, and control general debate on the floor.

Until the 1970s or so, the House was inclined to defer to the committees' recommendations, but that changed. The committee monopoly over policymaking diminished as the Capitol Hill environment became more permeable to outside influences. Now committees may be bypassed in whole or in part by various means, such as informal or leadership task forces established to draft legislation. The multiple referral of measures to several committees also undercuts jurisdictional monopolies. The trend away from committee autonomy has been reinforced by partisan actions that further consolidate power in the office of the Speaker and the majority party caucus.

With most committees open to greater challenges on the floor (subject to the character of the rule), chairs not surprisingly may look to the suspension procedure as a way to protect their measures from floor amendments. Or the Rules Committee may make it clear that if legislation gets bogged down during an open amendment process, the panel will reconvene and report a shutdown rule that limits amendments and expedites action on the bill.

Germaneness. Amendments that are extraneous to the subject matter of a bill are far more common in the Senate because House rules require amendments to be germane or relevant to the pending matter. Any member can question the relevance of a proposed amendment by raising a point of order, on which the chair must rule. (The point of order must be made in a timely manner: after the amendment is proposed but before debate on it has begun.) A lawmaker whose amendment is challenged on germaneness grounds is automatically considered "guilty" and must marshal arguments to prove that the amendment is relevant to the bill or pending amendment. Such points of order are not always raised, however, either because the rule from the Rules Committee may waive them, or because members are in general agreement with the provision. "I don't make points of order on all [nongermane amendments]," a member once observed, "because some may be necessary due to changing conditions."[55] The House's strict rule requiring that committee and floor amendments be germane is not self-enforcing.

A fundamental objective of the germaneness rule ("no motion or proposition on a subject different from that under consideration shall be admitted under color of amendment") is to focus the House's attention on one subject at a time. In addition, the rule facilitates majority party control of the agenda—by preventing, for example, the minority party from offering unrelated amendments—and bolsters the role of committees. Although brief, the germaneness rule, which applies to all amendments (committee and individual), is difficult and complex to apply. For example, if an amendment is proposed to a pending amendment, is the proposed change supposed to be germane to the pending amendment, to the bill, or to both? (The answer is, to the pending amendment.)

House members use scores of precedents and tests to defend their amendments from germaneness points of order, some of which are listed in Box 5.2. A dilemma for lawmakers is that these tests and "precedents do not set down perfectly distinct guidelines for analysis."[56] Nonetheless, if you fail one of the tests, the amendment will be ruled nongermane. Two brief examples illustrate the point. Take a bill to cut taxes reported from the Ways and Means Committee. An amendment to increase taxes meets the subject matter and committee jurisdictional tests noted in Box 5.2. However, it fails the fundamental purpose test because the amendment proposes to raise rather than further cut taxes. An amendment challenged on germaneness grounds must meet all the tests if it is to be ruled in order.

As another example, Rep. John Conyers Jr., D-Mich., offered an amendment to add crimes of fraud and deception to a bill addressing crimes of violence against children, the elderly, and other vulnerable persons. A germaneness point of order was successfully lodged against Conyers' amendment on the grounds that it did not deal with crimes of violence. Immediately, Conyers offered another amendment—to add environmental crimes (the pollution of the environment) to the underlying bill. Again, a successful germaneness point of order was raised and sustained by the chair, who ruled that Conyers's amendment was "not confined to the subject of crimes of violence" as defined in the U.S. criminal code. Quickly, Conyers proposed a third amendment—to include environmental crimes as a subset of crimes of violence under the appropriate section of the U.S. criminal code.

BOX 5.2 Some Tests of Germaneness

When a Representative raises a germaneness point of order, the burden of proof rests with the sponsor of the amendment to establish its germaneness.

1. *Fundamental Purpose.* A basic test of germaneness is that the fundamental purpose of an amendment must be germane to the fundamental purpose of the bill. In determining this purpose, substantial reliance should not be placed upon the title of the bill as the title need not state the fundamental purpose of the bill, either as introduced or later amended. One must look rather to the text of the bill as the principal tool in determining purpose.

2. *Subject Matter.* The amendment must relate to the subject matter under consideration. One must determine "what is the subject matter under consideration?" Once it is clear just what the subject matter is, the next element is whether or not the amendment relates to that subject matter.

3. *Committee Jurisdiction.* The jurisdiction of a committee is not necessarily controlling as to the germaneness of an amendment. When an argument has been advanced that the subject matter of an amendment lies within the jurisdiction of a committee other than the committee reporting the bill, the Chair has ruled that the germaneness of an amendment is based upon its relation to the bill in its amended form. In short, the subject matter of the bill is the controlling factor, not the description in the Rules of the House of the various committees' jurisdiction.

SOURCE: Excerpted from *Manual on Legislative Procedure in the U.S. House of Representatives,* 6th ed., 99th Congress, prepared under the auspices of the Republican leader, May 1986.

A germaneness point of order was raised, but the chair overruled it on the grounds that Conyers's amendment was confined to the subject of violent crimes against vulnerable persons.[57]

Substitute Amendments. There are two kinds of substitutes, as briefly noted earlier: a **substitute amendment** and an **amendment in the nature of a substitute.** The first type is an amendment that deals with part of a bill. For example, when an amendment is made to change part of a bill, a substitute amendment offers alternative language for the entirety of that pending amendment. By contrast, a perfecting amendment seeks to change, but not replace completely, the language in the first offered amendment.

This distinction goes to form rather than substance. This means, as an example, that a first-degree perfecting amendment might simply change a date (from August 27 to August 28) in a section of the bill. A substitute replaces all the language ("in lieu of the matter") in the pending first-degree amendment, but its sole objective is to accomplish the same purpose as the first-degree amendment (perhaps by using similar but not identical language). Strategically, if an unfriendly second-degree perfecting amendment has been offered to the first-degree amendment, the limb available for a friendly amendment is the substitute branch (see Figure 5.2).

The second kind of substitute recommends new language for the entire bill. Amendments in the nature of substitutes are commonly reported by the standing committees. They have increased in importance in recent years, in part because of the complexity and interrelatedness of contemporary issues and in part because of multiple referrals. For example, committees that consider the same bill may report dissimilar versions of it. Sometimes, such differences are resolved through intercommittee cooperation. Members and

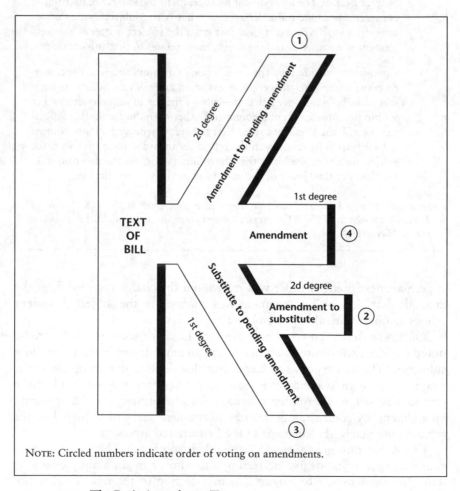

NOTE: Circled numbers indicate order of voting on amendments.

FIGURE 5.2   The Basic Amendment Tree

staff from each panel might blend their products into a consensus bill that will be offered on the House floor as an amendment in the nature of a substitute for the bill as originally introduced. Usually, the Rules Committee will accommodate the committees by giving such a substitute special status by making it, instead of the original bill, the vehicle for House debate and amendment. The rule typically states that the consensus or substitute text will be considered an "original bill for the purpose of amendment."

Degrees of Amendments

A basic parliamentary principle permits only two degrees of amendments: an amendment and an amendment to it. Any further motion to amend is a third-degree proposal (an amendment to an amendment to an amendment) and is out of order. "The line must be drawn somewhere," Thomas Jefferson wrote, "and usage has drawn it after the amendment to the amendment."[58]

When a bill is open to revision in the House, only four amendments may be pending simultaneously: (1) a first degree amendment to the bill itself, (2) a second degree amendment to the first amendment, (3) a first degree substitute amendment, and (4) a second degree amendment to the substitute amendment. Once an amendment to a bill has been offered (the first degree), the other three may be offered and be pending simultaneously. Once either of the second degrees is adopted or rejected, another may be offered until there is no unamended text left to change in the pending alternatives (the first-degree perfecting and the first degree substitute for it). If a substitute is adopted, its effect is to replace the language of the original first-degree proposal and any second-degree changes to it that might have been adopted.

The four amendments, with the degrees that are permissible and the order of voting on each, are depicted in Figure 5.2. This representation of the common amendment tree has two first-degree amendments—the amendment to the text and the substitute amendment—and two amendments in the second degree. House Rule XVI states:

> When a motion or proposition is under consideration a motion to amend and a motion to amend that amendment shall be in order, and it shall also be in order to offer a further amendment by way of a substitute, to which one amendment may be offered.

Second-degree amendments are voted on first, and the second-degree amendment to the original amendment to the bill is voted on before the second-degree amendment to the substitute. A short-hand way to remember the voting order is this: Perfect the amendment, perfect the substitute, vote on the substitute, and then vote on the original amendment, as or if modified. The first degree is the last voted on to give lawmakers ample opportunity to perfect it before they decide whether to adopt it. Thus, a lawmaker faces a series of binary voting choices: on the first vote, do I like the original amendment as is or do I prefer the amended version? On the second vote, do I prefer the substitute or the alterations to it? On the third vote, do I favor the amendment first offered (no doubt as amended) or the substitute, possibly as amended? On this vote, if the substitute prevails, it replaces all the language in the original amendment. In this case, it is plain that this is the preferred option of most lawmakers. Finally, the last vote, which is likely to be pro forma, amounts to this choice: Accept the first amendment offered (as or if modified) or stay with the language in the original bill.

There is no necessarily "right" place on the amendment tree. Members understand that the initial first-degree amendment is likely to be the target for change by either a first-degree substitute or one or more second-degree perfecting amendments. If proponents of the first-offered amendment have the votes, they can defeat any of the proposed changes and prevail in the end. If they lack the votes, the proponents could end up voting against their own proposal because it was amended with unwanted changes. Lawmakers often want the first vote—the second-degree perfecting amendment—because it cannot be further amended (that would be a third-degree proposal). So a lawmaker whose amendment occupies this slot gets a "clean" vote on his or her proposition.

Strategically, the amendment procedure can be critical to policy formulation. Either side of an issue may be aided by the voting sequence—whether the amendment is voted on first or last. During House consideration of a nuclear freeze proposal, the proponents wanted the House to vote first on their policy recommendation. As a result, they waited for opponents to offer a first-degree amendment before they countered with a second-degree amendment to their liking. This approach gave backers of the freeze the opportunity "to formulate the final version of any amendment."[59] The first vote, therefore, was on the freeze backers' alternative amendment to the opponents' amendment revising the text of the freeze resolution. The strategy of "fighting fire with fire" means that "threatening amendments by opponents are . . . met with counteramendments" by proponents.[60] The reverse approach is to arrange for a colleague to offer a "friendly" second-degree amendment to the first-offered proposal so as to block opponents from trying to undermine the original amendment with poison-pill changes. (Useful to emphasize again is that the Rules Committee, subject to House approval, can establish a unique amendment tree— the scripted version—for major legislation, setting aside the traditional amendment process.)

Maneuvering for Advantage: Common Tactics

Proponents and opponents of bills constantly seek to advance their policy objectives through the amending process. Skillful use of various motions, dilatory tactics, or shrewd drafting of the wording of amendments can influence which side carries the day. Customarily, the minority party has self-appointed floor watchdogs who seek to protect party interests and stymie majority steamrollers by raising points of order or making parliamentary inquiries. Timing, too, is all-important to the success of many floor maneuvers, especially preferential motions and amendments to sweeten bills.

Strike the Enacting Clause. Certain motions from the floor take preference over other House business. One is the motion to strike the **enacting clause**—"Be it enacted by the Senate and House of Representatives of the United States of America in Congress assembled, . . ." This clause, which opens every House and Senate bill, makes a bill an operative law once the bill is approved by Congress and signed by the president. Under House rules, approval of a motion to strike the enacting clause is equivalent to rejecting the measure. A motion to strike the clause is in order at any time during the amending process. The preferential motion is phrased as follows: "I move that the Committee [of the Whole] do now rise and report the bill to the House with the recommendation that the enacting clause be stricken out." This **privileged motion** must be disposed of before the House takes up any further business on the bill. Debate on the motion is limited to 10 minutes, 5 for and 5 against. The motion is in order only once, unless the bill is materially changed by adoption of major amendments, a determination the chair makes if a point of order is raised against a second motion to strike. In procedural "hardball" circumstances, the Rules Committee can include a provision in a special rule that states, "The Chair may not entertain a motion to strike out the enacting clause of the bill."[61]

Sweeteners. Members can make measures considered unpalatable more acceptable by proposing changes—that is, sweetening the measures—to attract broader support. Changes might include amendments granting members more staff or additional office allowances, or pork-barrel provisions for the construction of dams, highways, port facilities, airports, and the like in various congressional districts. Because lawmakers and others have criticized pork-barrel (or "earmark") spending, amendment sweeteners that reduce spending, streamline federal regulations, or cut bureaucratic red tape may also appeal to voters.

Poison Pills. Killer or poison-pill amendments aim to turn a majority against the legislation.[62] For example, adoption of an amendment to include primaries in a congressional public financing bill is almost certain to kill the legislation, because many House incumbents, particularly those from safe and one-party districts, oppose any measure that aids party challengers. Or, as a recent Speaker said to proponents of an amendment he strongly opposed, "If that is your goal, if you just want to find a cynical way to burden down the committee bill and make it unpassable, then you might want to vote for the [amendment]."[63]

Importance of the Amending Process

Subject to the character of the special rule from the Rules Committee, lawmakers try to amend controversial bills when they are considered in the Committee of the Whole. The amending process is a critical—and complex—stage for any bill. To summarize, some of the main features of the process under an open rule are as follows:

- Amendments in the Committee of the Whole are usually offered section by section under the 5-minute rule.
- All amendments must be offered from the floor in written form.
- Amendments may not be repetitious. When an amendment is rejected, a member may not offer exactly the same proposal later.
- Any amendment may be challenged on a point of order before debate on the amendment has begun.
- Committee amendments are considered before those introduced by other legislators.
- Pro forma amendments ("Mr. Chairman, I move to strike the last word") enable members to discuss the bill under consideration for 5 minutes, even though no change is intended.
- Amendments must be germane to the subject under consideration. Occasionally, nongermane amendments may slip by, either because members generally agree on their intent or because the Rules Committee has barred points of order against them.

The amending process is a key feature of lawmaking. Yet it is important to emphasize again that in today's polarized House there are fewer opportunities compared with earlier eras for members to propose changes to legislation. The combination of wider use of the suspension procedure—which prohibits free-standing amendments—and greater use of structured or modified closed rules on major bills means that lawmakers regularly confront a restrictive amendment environment, although Speaker Boehner has aspired to permit more amendment opportunities for rank-and-file lawmakers. Not all Democrats agree, however. As a Rules Democrat exclaimed: "This is a bill written only by Republicans which only Republicans can amend. . . . This is the new and improved open House that they promised. Open House my foot, Mr. Speaker."[64]

VOTING

The House uses a variety of methods for voting, and many of its votes take place in the Committee of the Whole. (The methods are listed in Box 5.3.) A significant change in voting occurred on January 23, 1973: Electronic voting was introduced. In electronic voting, which was authorized by the

Legislative Reorganization Act of 1970, members insert a personalized card about the size of a credit card into one of the more than 40 voting stations located on the House floor and press one of three buttons: "yea," "nay," or "present." Each member's vote is displayed behind the Speaker's desk and on the wall panels over the press gallery. The system is also used to establish quorums. If electronic voting malfunctions, traditional methods are used. GOP House leader Michel (1981–1995) was not a fan of electronic voting because it quickened the pace of the House:

> It eliminates the time for informal chats with other members. C-SPAN is even more of a problem. Members now follow the affairs of the House from their offices, rushing to the floor to vote only at the last minute. Again, valuable face-to-face contact is gone.[65]

These technological changes have placed additional pressures on the floor managers. Electronic voting cut balloting time in half, from about 30 minutes under the traditional roll call method to no less than 15 minutes. The chair has discretionary authority either to close the vote after the expiration of 15 minutes or to keep the vote open, allowing additional time for lawmakers to vote or more opportunities for party leaders to persuade reluctant members to vote their way. The voting period ends when the chair announces the final result. Recent changes in the rules have permitted the Speaker to postpone votes and schedule votes in clusters on matters such as passing bills or agreeing to suspension of the rules motions. The Speaker may reduce to 5 minutes the minimum time allowed for electronic votes under House rules, provided the first vote in a series is a 15-minute vote. Sometimes the time for votes is reduced to 2 minutes. The chair of the Committee of the Whole reduces votes to no less than 2 minutes on a series of questions that have been postponed, provided that the first vote in the series is a minimum of 15 minutes.

From the floor managers' standpoint, the electronic voting system has advantages and disadvantages. Managers have computer display terminals that allow them to easily track the progress of a vote. In doing so, they can quickly spot problems such as the absence of one member or the unexpected vote switch. Absent members can be summoned to the floor, and vote switchers can be approached by persuasive members of the party. Managers have less time, however, to evaluate opposition to proposals and line up votes. Today, floor managers must work harder to build support before bills reach the floor.

House rules also permit what are called "live" **pairs**, a rarely used procedure. The practice of live pairs is an informal agreement

> between one Member who is present and voting and another on the opposite side of the question, who is absent. . . . By agreement, the voting Member withdraws his vote and records himself as 'present' by submitting an amber "present" card.[66]

BOX 5.3 Methods of Voting

In the House. There are four ways of voting in the House: voice, division, yea and nay votes, and recorded votes. A voice vote means that lawmakers call out "yea" or "nay" on one side or the other when a question is put by the presiding officer, and the chair decides the result. A **standing vote** (or **division vote**) means that those in favor of a proposal and then those opposed stand up while the chair takes a head count. Only vote totals are announced; there is no record of how individual members voted. Yea and nay votes are provided for by the Constitution and are obtained "at the Desire of one fifth of those present" regardless of how few lawmakers are in the chamber. House rules also provide for an "automatic," publicly recorded vote. To obtain an automatic vote, a member says, "I object to the vote on the ground that a quorum is not present, and I make a point of order that a quorum is not present." The actual vote will then determine both issues simultaneously: the presence of a quorum and the vote on the pending question. A recorded vote under House rules is obtained when a lawmaker states, "Mr. Speaker, I demand a recorded vote." If at least one-fifth of a quorum (44 of 218) stand and support the request, then the recorded vote will be taken by electronic device. (There are back-up procedures if the electronic voting system malfunctions.) Recall that the distinction between recorded votes and the **yeas and nays** goes to the number of lawmakers required to support each request: *one fifth of a quorum* (44 of 218) for a recorded vote and *one fifth of those present* for the yeas and nays. Members employ the automatic method when they might not be able to get the support of either a fifth of those present or a fifth of a quorum.

In the Committee of the Whole. Three methods of voting are available in this forum: voice, division, and recorded. The constitutional yea and nay votes are not permitted in this forum. A request for a recorded vote in the Committee— where a quorum is 100 members—is obtained when it is supported by at least 25 lawmakers (the member who asked for the recorded vote counts as part of the tally). If there are few members in the chamber, a member may say, "Mr. (or Madam) Chairman, I request a recorded vote and, pending that, I make a point of order that a quorum is not present." Once the chair determines that a quorum is not present, there is an immediate quorum call and the member who requested the recorded vote can ask 24 other colleagues to support his request as they come onto the floor.

A live pair subtracts one vote, yea or nay, from the final tally and could influence the outcome of closely contested issues. Although rarely used, a live pair was in play when the House passed a major Medicare reform bill (H.R. 1) by a 216-to-215 vote in June 2003.[67] House Appropriations Committee Chair Bill Young, R-Fla., attended the funeral of an army sergeant who died from wounds suffered in Iraq.

But Young made sure his absence . . . would not affect the vote. He made arrangements to "pair" the vote he would have cast for the bill with that of Rep. Ernest Istook, R-Okla., who opposed the bill but voted "present."[68]

Pairs are not counted in tabulating the final results of recorded votes, but they are printed in the *Congressional Record* and announced before the vote is finally declared. As Representative Istook stated: "Mr. Speaker, on my vote just recorded I voted 'no.' I have a pair with the gentleman from Florida, Mr. Young, who is at a funeral, and desire to change my vote and be recorded as 'present.'"

Factors in Voting

On any given day, legislators may be required to vote on measures ranging from foreign aid to abortion, from maritime subsidies to tax reform. It is nearly impossible for a member to be fully informed on every issue before the House. As one lawmaker said, "The sheer volume of votes is so great that there's no way you can weigh each and every issue."[69] Many lawmakers, as a result, follow the "rational ignorance" principle. They rely on cue givers for guidance on matters beyond their special competence. These may be committee or party leaders, members of the state congressional delegation, trusted colleagues, staff aides, or floor managers.[70] "You want to know how Members are voting on an issue," a representative said, "you want to know how Members from your delegation vote, and you want to know how Members who always vote the opposite of you are voting."[71]

Party loyalty, constituency interests, electoral concerns, and individual conscience are primary factors in determining a member's vote on any issue, but they are not the only factors. Members sometimes vote for proposals they oppose to prevent enactment of something worse or in the expectation that somewhere along the line the proposal will go down to defeat. Members might vote one way on an authorization bill and another on the corresponding appropriations measure. And lawmakers use their votes as trading material. In exchange for voting yea or nay on an issue, they may receive some project or favor that benefits their district.

On controversial and divisive issues, it is not easy to mobilize winning coalitions. A classic example is the Medicare prescription drug bill (H.R. 1). Sponsored by GOP Speaker Hastert, the top domestic priority of President George W. Bush, and the largest expansion of an entitlement program for seniors since Medicare, the legislation was viewed as "must win" by Republicans, but enactment was enormously difficult for two main reasons. First, around two dozen small-government, deficit-minded Republicans opposed the measure as overly expanding a government entitlement program. Second, Minority Leader Pelosi worked diligently to promote party unity, arguing that the GOP plan would weaken Medicare and undermine the party's "ownership" of the issue and encourage more seniors to vote Republican. The GOP faced an uphill challenge to find the votes to pass the prescription drug bill. (The same uphill challenge confronted House Democrats in November 2009 when they succeeded in passing—by the narrow margin of 220 to 215, with nearly 40 Democratic defections and the support of only one Republican, Joseph Cao of Louisiana—President Obama's controversial health care reform plan, which he signed into law in 2010.)

To expedite action on the prescription drug conference report, the House on November 21 adopted a special rule waiving the requirement that a two-thirds vote is necessary to take up a rule on the same day it is reported from the Rules Committee. Rules Democrat Louise Slaughter objected to the same-day rule for various reasons, including the exclusion of Democratic conferees from the bicameral negotiating sessions (see Chapter 8) and the lack of time for lawmakers to read the conference report, which was close to 700 pages long. (The report was filed at 1:17 a.m. on November 21; House rules state that conference reports are to be available 3 legislative days prior to floor action.) The chair of the GOP Conference responded that the conference report was available on the respective websites of the Committees on Rules and Ways and Means, and "anyone is free to look it up and read it at their leisure."[72] The House first adopted the same-day rule and then another rule waiving all points of order against the conference report and its consideration.[73]

The conference report was taken up on November 21, but GOP leaders were uncertain whether they had enough votes to adopt it. When the tally began at 3 a.m. on November 22, it was evident to GOP leaders that they lacked the votes for passage. Thus, the vote was held open for nearly 3 hours (about an hour into the vote, the tally was 216 for and 218 against) as GOP leaders and executive branch officials used a combination of promises and threats to persuade several lawmakers to switch their votes from "nay" to "yea." They were successful. The conference report was agreed to by a 220 to 215 vote. "A vote is a pressure cooker sometimes," stated Speaker Hastert. "It just took that amount of time to get people to change their minds."[74] Democratic leaders were outraged at the extraordinary length of the vote. However, Rules Chair Dreier pointed out: "This was in complete compliance with the rules of the House. Members have a minimum [not a maximum] of 15 minutes to vote."[75]

The Medicare vote illustrates a theme prevalent in the contemporary House: Regardless of party, majority leaders go all out to win their paramount policy priorities. As a spokesperson for Speaker Hastert put it: "We are not going to play unless we play to win. We want to have a public discourse and debate, but we want our position to prevail."[76] Of course, majority party leaders prefer to know in advance through their whip system that a winning coalition has been forged to pass priority measures, but even if not, the majority leadership may not be reluctant to bring major legislation to the floor under dicey circumstances. The combination of tailor-made special rules—artfully constructed to restrict minority amendments—and the persuasive "carrot-and-stick" abilities of party leaders is generally enough to bring about chamber passage of party-preferred agenda items.

Speaker Boehner, however, is not as fortunate as Speakers Gingrich, Hastert, or Pelosi in mobilizing 218 votes before bringing legislation to the floor. Boehner confronts a more unruly party than his recent predecessors. Many Republican members do not routinely follow Speaker Boehner's lead and vote for the agenda items he schedules for floor action. As a result, Speaker Boehner has seen House rejection of major bills because of GOP defections. Two key strategic choices confront Speaker Boehner: He can reach out to Democrats to push bills over the finish line, but the minority party may demand policy concessions sure to offend many among the GOP rank and file. If Speaker Boehner made the changes wanted by Democrats to win their votes, he might not remain Speaker for long. Second, Speaker Boehner can reject deal making with Democrats, avoiding political backlash from Tea Party adherents in GOP ranks. His choice, then, is to accommodate the Tea Party Republicans and win their support before he brings legislation to the floor. Ohio GOP Representative LaTourette, a Boehner confidant, highlighted the dilemma that confronts the Speaker.

> He's not ruling the [GOP] conference with an iron fist; he's letting people do what they need to do, based on what their constituents want. That's refreshing—it hasn't happened up here in a while. But the bad part is that every time we have mass defections on the budget or the [continuing resolution] when they're in negotiations [with the Senate and White House], I think it weakens him as a negotiator, because the other side knows he might not have everyone in his pocket.[77]

A conservative faction in GOP ranks often refused to support Speaker Boehner's legislative recommendations. More than a dozen Republicans even opposed Boehner's reelection as Speaker of the 113th Congress. Boehner won reelection by a 220 to 192 vote, "the closest any Speaker has come to not securing a first-ballot victory since Newt Gingrich's narrow reelection in January 1997, following an ethics admonishment."[78]

The voting records of members can become a campaign issue. For example, Democratic newcomers who represent GOP-leaning or coal-producing districts and who voted for a controversial global warming measure found themselves under political attack at home via media ads and automated telephone calls paid for by the Republican congressional campaign committee.[79] Representatives who miss numerous votes may have to explain their spotty congressional attendance record. Many interest groups contribute campaign funds to legislators whose votes are in accord with the groups' views. "If I cast a vote, I might have to answer for it," said a House member. "It may be an issue in the next campaign. Over and over I have to have a response to the question: Why did you do that?"[80] Another lawmaker put it this way: "If you don't like fighting fires, don't be a fireman . . . and if you don't like voting, don't be a congressman."[81]

When voting on all amendments has been concluded, the Committee of the Whole rises (dissolves) and reports the bill back to the full House. (Special rules from the Rules Committee provide that the Committee of the Whole rises automatically at the end of the amending process.) Then the chair hands the gavel back to the Speaker, who resumes his or her place at the podium. The mace is returned to its pedestal on the table next to the podium, and a quorum becomes 218 members (a majority of the House). As prescribed in the rule, a standard sequence of events takes place prior to the vote on final passage of a bill.

FINAL PROCEDURAL STEPS

After taking the chair, the Speaker announces that "under the rule [from the Rules Committee], the previous question is ordered." This means that no further debate is permitted on the measure or on amendments, no amendments other than those reported by the Committee of the Whole may be considered, and previously adopted amendments are not subject to further amendment. Then members, sitting as the House, consider the decisions taken in the Committee of the Whole.

The Speaker asks all the members to identify amendments on which they want separate recorded votes. (Only first-degree amendments adopted in the Committee of the Whole are eligible for a revote.) The remaining amendments are decided en bloc by voice vote, after which the contested amendments are voted on individually. Separate recorded votes are not usually requested on amendments adopted in the Committee of the Whole unless the earlier votes were very close and the amendments highly controversial. On occasion, the House rejects amendments adopted in the Committee of the Whole.[82] If the majority party expects a series of minority-instigated "nuisance votes" on the amendments reported from the Committee of the Whole, the Rules Committee will include a provision in the special rule prohibiting a separate vote on each amendment. Instead, the House will vote once on all the amendments as a package (*en gros*).

After all floor amendments are disposed of, two more steps remain before the final vote on passage. The first is engrossment and third reading. "The question is on engrossment and third reading of the bill," the Speaker declares. This is a pro forma question, which is commonly approved quickly by voice vote. House rules provide that the bill be read by its title. (Before 1965, any legislator could demand that the bill be read in full, but the rules were changed to prevent this dilatory tactic.) Recall that engrossment is the preparation of a final and accurate version of the bill by an enrolling clerk for transmission to the Senate. This can be a complicated process, particularly if numerous amendments were adopted.

Next is the motion to recommit, mentioned earlier in this chapter, which provides a way for the House to return (recommit) a bill to the committee that reported it. The motion is provided for in the rule from the Rules

Committee. There are two forms of the motion: the rarely used "straight" motion to return the measure to committee (which effectively kills it) and a motion to recommit with instructions—these contain the minority party's policy alternative and must be germane to the bill—that the committee reports "forthwith," which means the bill never leaves the floor. If this motion to recommit is adopted, the committee chair immediately reports back to the House in conformity with the instructions, and the bill, as modified by the instructions, is automatically before the House again. The committee chair states: "Madam Speaker, pursuant to the instructions of the House on the motion to recommit, I report the bill, H.R. 1234, back to the House with an amendment." The House votes separately on this amendment, and, if adopted, then again on the pro forma engrossment and third reading questions, and finally on passage of the bill. An example of a motion to recommit can be found in Box 5.4.

By precedent, either form of the motion is made by a minority party member who opposes the legislation. A minority member will say, "I have a motion to recommit at the desk." And the Speaker will ask: "Are you opposed to the bill?" The minority member's response to qualify is: "In its present form I am." The Speaker will then ask the clerk to report the motion. As Box 5.4 highlights, often these motions are artfully drafted by the minority party to create electoral fodder to be used against the opposition party. Majority members who vote against a motion to recommit such as the one in Box 5.4 might see campaign ads stating that they favor federal tax benefits for pornography and prostitution. Majority leaders are quite successful in mobilizing party-line votes against these motions, arguing that they are simply procedural and not policy motions.

Straight or forthwith motions to recommit are not usually successful because they are considered an opposition party device, but they do serve to protect the rights of minority members by granting them an opportunity to reshape the measure. When Republicans took majority control in 1995, they amended House rules to guarantee the minority leader or the leader's designee the right to offer a motion to recommit with instructions. Although the Democrats retained this guarantee following their election victories in 2006 and 2008, they did change two specific features of the rule on the opening day of the 111th Congress, which still remain in effect.

One change eliminated the word *promptly* in favor of the traditional *forthwith* in the instructions. In the 110th House (2007–2009), Republicans increasingly used the word *promptly* rather than *forthwith* in their instructions. Democrats viewed recommit motions containing the word *promptly* as a GOP plan to kill the bill. Republicans disputed that notion and argued that the committee could meet and report the bill back to the House.[83] In the minority, Democrats occasionally used the word *promptly* in their recommit motions, but nowhere near the GOP's usage. Republicans used the motion to recommit more aggressively than Democrats had in the minority, said a spokesperson for GOP leader Boehner, "to make

---

BOX 5.4 **Motion to Recommit**

MR. DEUTCH. Mr. Speaker, I have a motion to recommit at the desk.

THE SPEAKER PRO TEMPORE. Is the gentleman opposed to the bill?

MR. DEUTCH. I am opposed.

THE SPEAKER PRO TEMPORE. The Clerk will report the motion to recommit.

The Clerk reads as follows:

Mr. Deutch moves to recommit the bill H.R. 9 to the Committee on Ways and Means with instructions to report the same back to the house forthwith with the following amendments:

At the end of paragraph (2) of section 200(C) of the Internal Revenue Code of 1986, as proposed to be added by section 2 of the bill, add the following:

"(C) DENIAL OF THE DEDUCTION FOR CERTAIN BUSINESSES.—The term 'domestic business gross receipts' shall not include any gross receipts attributable to any of the following:

"(i)   ILLEGAL ACTIVITES.—Any illegal activity, including trafficking in illegal drugs and prostitution.

"(ii) PORNOGRAPHY.—Any property with respect to which records are required to be maintained under section 2257 of title 18, United States Code.

"(iii) DISCRIMINATORY GOLF COURSES AND CLUBS.—Golf courses or clubs that discriminatorily restrict membership on the basis of sex or race."

THE SPEAKER PRO TEMPORE. Pursuant to the rule, the gentleman from Florida is recognized for 5 minutes in the support of his motion.

SOURCE: *Congressional Record*, April 19, 2012, H2008.

---

vulnerable Democrats choose every day between Speaker Pelosi and their constituents."[84] And they were successful on a number of occasions. Democratic leaders would sometimes request Republicans to accept a word change in their motion: substitute *forthwith* for *promptly*. The GOP turned down those offers, causing angst among Democrats who would either have "to cast uncomfortable votes [gun control, immigration, and the like] or make unwelcome changes to the bill."[85] One response of Democratic leaders was to yank the bill off the floor to rethink their next moves.

To end these procedural headaches, the Democratic majority on January 6, 2009, amended the House rulebook to forbid the minority party from offering "promptly" motions. In the majority, Republicans have retained this House rule. Now, only "forthwith" motions to instruct are in order:

"Mr.___ moves to recommit the bill, H.R. 5678 to the Committee on Ways and Means with instructions to report the same back to the House forthwith with the following amendment."

In a second change, House rules were further amended to permit 10 minutes of debate, equally divided, on the straight motion to recommit. Previously, this motion was not subject to debate. Now minority lawmakers have the opportunity to explain why they want to return a bill to committee for an indefinite and unspecified period of time.

Although recommittal motions are seldom successful, as noted earlier, much depends on the size of the minority party in the House and the political circumstances. Probably the most dramatic recommittal motion in recent Congresses occurred on September 25, 1984 (only a few weeks before national elections), when the Comprehensive Crime Control Act was enacted via the recommittal route. A GOP lawmaker offered the recommittal motion with instructions containing the recodification of the criminal code, debated it for 5 minutes, and urged members to pass a crime package that "has been languishing here in the House since March of this year."[86] A Democratic opponent of the recommittal motion then took the floor and urged rejection of the motion in his 5 minutes.

To the surprise of nearly everyone, the recommittal motion was passed by a 243-to-166 vote. Then the continuing resolution to which the crime bill was attached was approved by the House. Democratic leaders were chagrined that the crime package had passed in this manner. Speaker O'Neill declared that it was the "wrong way" to pass major crime legislation—after only 10 minutes of debate.[87] When the next Congress convened, the House changed its rules, which continue in force today, to permit the majority floor manager—but not the minority floor manager—to request up to an hour of debate, equally divided, on a motion to recommit with instructions. This is a good example of the majority rule principle that undergirds House operations.

If the recommittal motion is rejected, the Speaker moves to the third step, the final vote on the whole bill. "The question is on the passage of the bill," says the Speaker. Normally, final passage is by a recorded vote. If the outcome is obvious and the members are eager to be done with it, the measure may be passed by voice vote. When the results of the final vote have been announced, a pro forma motion to reconsider is made and laid on the table (postponed indefinitely) to prevent the bill from being reconsidered later. House rules state that a final vote is conclusive only if an opportunity was provided to reconsider it on the same legislative day (a day on which the House is in session) or the succeeding legislative day.

NOTES

1. Josephine Hearn, "Win a Seat—Then Pick a Seat," *Politico*, November 8, 2007, 16–17.
2. During the 95th Congress (1977–1979), the House developed a regular system of scheduling floor sessions in response to the desires of members, committees,

and party leaders, which has been followed since that time. Members complained about problems in arranging their personal schedules and their inability to make firm commitments for meetings in their districts; committees wanted more time early in the session to work on legislation without being interrupted by floor meetings; and party leaders sought to better synchronize committee and floor action and use session time more effectively. As a result, the House varies its starting time over the course of a year. See *Congressional Record*, January 3, 2013, H24.

3. *Congressional Record,* May 19, 2009, H5717.

4. At the start of each new Congress, the Speaker announces the policies with respect to certain legislative matters, including 1-minute speeches and special-order speeches. See *Congressional Record,* January 3, 2013, H26. Morning hour debates and 1-minute speeches typically occur at the start of the day; special-order speeches occur at the end of the day, either for periods of 5 minutes or an hour. Special-order speeches may not extend beyond 10 p.m.

5. William Holmes Brown, Charles W. Johnson, and John V. Sullivan, *House Practice: A Guide to the Rules, Precedents, and Procedures of the House* (Washington, DC: Government Printing Office, 2011), 744.

6. David Clarke and Kerry Young, "'Blue Dogs' and Freshmen Rebelled Against Restrictions," *CQ Today,* August 4, 2009, 9.

7. Jeffrey H. Birnbaum and Alan S. Murray, *Showdown at Gucci Gulch* (New York: Random House, 1987), 163.

8. *Congressional Record*, November 14, 2002, H8742–H8757.

9. Susan Crabtree, "Hastert Asserts His Authority," *Roll Call*, November 18, 2002, 18. Also see Jennifer Dlouhy, "Yet Another Blow to Bankruptcy Rewrite," *CQ Weekly*, November 16, 2002, 3021–3022.

10. Donald R. Wolfensberger, "Committees of the Whole: Their Evolution and Functions," *Congressional Record*, January 5, 1993, H31.

11. The "House as in Committee of the Whole" is a hybrid body that combines several procedures employed in the House and in the Committee of the Whole. The principal features of this hybrid entity are that there is no general debate, bills are open to amendment at any point under the 5-minute rule, the previous question is in order, a quorum is half the House plus one, and the Speaker may preside over the proceedings.

12. De Alva Stanwood Alexander, *History and Procedure of the House of Representatives* (New York: Burt Franklin, 1916), 257.

13. John Bresnahan, "The Speaker Likes to Speak," *Politico*, June 3, 2008, 15.

14. In the House sitting as the House, an hour is permitted for debate on amendments. "No member," the rule states, "shall occupy more than one hour in debate on any question in the House." Technically, then, all matters could be debated for 441 hours—1 hour each for the 435 representatives, 5 delegates (from the District of Columbia, the Virgin Islands, American Samoa, Guam, and the Northern Mariana Islands), and 1 resident commissioner (from Puerto Rico). In practice, measures are debated for only 1 hour in total and then are voted on.

15. For a description of the 17th century English origins of the Committee of the Whole, see Alexander, *History and Procedure of the House of Representatives*, 257–258.

16. Technically, the first order of business in the Committee of the Whole is the reading of the bill. But this step is usually dispensed with either by unanimous consent or by the terms of the rule, which is the ordinary practice today.

17. Lizete Alvarez, "Taking a Job That Others Would Not," *New York Times*, December 19, 1998, B2.

18. Sometimes the special-order period at the end of the legislative day is organized to permit both sides to participate in debate on a policy issue. See *Congressional Record*, July 14, 2008, H6456.

19. *U.S. News and World Report*, August 20, 1984, 30.

20. David Rogers, "Obey Surveys the House Then and Now," *Politico*, July 23, 2010, 8.

21. *Washington Post*, October 22, 1983, A19.

22. Molly K. Hooper, "Boehner's Climate Speech Is Seen as One for the Ages," *The Hill*, July 1, 2009, 7.

23. *Congressional Record*, September 12, 1989, E3001.

24. *Congressional Record*, May 24, 1983, H3257.

25. *Congressional Record*, January 12, 1991, H441. See also Joseph M. Bessette, *The Mild Voice of Reason: Deliberative Democracy and American National Government* (Chicago: University of Chicago Press, 1994).

26. *Congressional Record*, October 8, 2002, H7178.

27. Ezra Klein, "Washington's Dangerous Consensus on Taxes," *The Washington Post*, April 14, 2012, A2.

28. *Congressional Record*, June 11, 1979, H14213–H14215.

29. Nancy Roman, "Disaster Measure Doubles in Its Cost," *Washington Times*, June 5, 1997, A3.

30. See Donald R. Wolfensberger, "Questions of Privilege in the House: Minority Party Tools for Unity, Accountability, and Reform" (paper prepared for the annual meeting of the American Political Science Association, September 1–4, 2005). Mr. Wolfensberger is the director of The Congress Project at the Woodrow Wilson Center for International Scholars and a former staff director of the House Rules Committee.

31. See *Congressional Record*, July 18, 2003, H7148; July 23, 2003, H7336; October 8, 2004, H8993; March 15, 2005, H1435; April 14, 2005, H1992; June 9, 2005, H4318; November 3, 2005, H9566; December 8, 2005, H11264; February 16, 2006, H351; and April 5, 2006, H1513.

32. Wolfensberger, "Questions of Privilege in the House," 26.

33. *Congressional Record*, July 18, 2003, H7149.

34. Mark Wegner, "Pelosi Threatens 'Week from Hell' Absent Vote on Child Tax," *CongressDailyAM*, July 22, 2003, 16.

35. *CongressDailyAM*, July 24, 2003, H7519–H7521.

36. Hans Nichols, "House Dems Ratcheting Up Guerrilla War," *The Hill*, June 17, 2003, 1.

37. *Congressional Record*, March 12, 2008, H1543.

38. *Congressional Record*, February 10, 2009, H1128.

39. *Congressional Record*, June 27, 1974, 21590.

40. David Rogers, "Party of One," *Politico*, June 4, 2008, 1.

41. Jackie Kucinich, "Republicans Wage Floor Games," *Roll Call*, July 27, 2009, 15.

42. *Congressional Record*, May 7, 2008, H3114. See also *Congressional Record*, April 18, 2007, H3481; March 12, 2008, H1542.

43. Seth Stern, "House Passes Spending Bill After GOP Employs Procedural Delaying Tactics," *CQ Today*, June 19, 2009, 10.

44. *Congressional Record*, July 23, 2009, H8680.

45. Steven T. Dennis, "Republicans Force Lengthy Bill Reading During Boehner Fundraiser," *Roll Call*, July 23, 2009, online edition.

46. Lauren Gardner, "House Girds for Long Debate as GOP Criticizes Democratic 'Mini-Filibuster,'" *CQ Today*, July 26, 2011, 28.

47. Ibid.

48. John Stanton, "Democrats Tweak GOP on RSC Budget in High-Drama Move," *Roll Call*, April 15, 2011, online edition. Interestingly, two Pennsylvania Democrats—Jason Altmire and Mark Critz—faced off in a 2012 Democratic primary because of redistricting. Altmire ran a television ad castigating Critz for not standing up to the Tea Party by voting against, rather than "present," on the RSC's budget proposal. House Democratic leaders publicly sprang to Critz's defense. As a House Democrat explained, the "present" vote was a strategy vote to highlight the RSC's "radical policies." "We shouldn't use Hill strategy votes against each other. That's just not cool." Cameron Joseph, "Altmire Ads Unfair, Say Colleagues," *The Hill*, April 19, 2012, 1, 5. Critz won the Democratic primary contest.

49. Alan K. Ota, "Not Wanting to Gift-Wrap Votes, Democrats Plan to Be 'Present,'" *CQ Today*, May 2, 2011, 16.

50. *Constitution, Jefferson's Manual, and Rules of the House of Representatives*, 111th Congress, 2009, H. Doc. 110-162, 768.

51. "Amendment Procedure in the Committee of the Whole: A Brief Synopsis," Parliamentary Outreach Program, Committee on Rules, June 3, 1997.

52. The Legislative Reorganization Act of 1970 provided that amendments published in the *Congressional Record* at least 1 day prior to their consideration in the Committee of the Whole are guaranteed 10 minutes of debate time, regardless of any committee agreements to end debate on the bill. The objective is to prevent arbitrary closing of debate when important amendments are pending. The Rules Committee can waive this requirement.

53. Peter Cohn, "Obey's FY04 Strategy: Get Republicans 'on the Record,'" *CongressDaily*, August 7, 2003, 2.

54. *Procedure in the U.S. House of Representatives*, 97th Cong., 4th ed. (Washington, DC: Government Printing Office, 1982), 526.

55. Richard F. Fenno Jr., *The Power of the Purse* (Boston: Little, Brown, 1966), 74.

56. Martin Gold, Michael Hugo, Hyde Murray, Peter Robinson, and A. L. "Pete" Singleton, *The Book on Congress* (Washington, DC: Big Eagle, 1992), 226.

57. See *Congressional Record*, May 7, 1996, H4482–H4484. For other examples of germaneness points of order, see *Congressional Record*, March 10, 2011, H1687–H1698.

58. *Constitution, Jefferson's Manual, and Rules of the House of Representatives*, 235.

59. Pat Towell, "After 42 Hours of Debate: Nuclear Freeze Resolution Finally Wins House Approval," *Congressional Quarterly Weekly Report*, May 7, 1983, 869.

60. Barry R. Weingast, "Fighting Fire With Fire: Amending Activity and Institutional Change in the Postreform Congress," in *The Postreform Congress*, ed. Roger H. Davidson (New York: St. Martin's Press, 1992), 165.

61. *Congressional Record*, June 24, 2009, H7167.

62. See James M. Enelow and David H. Koehler, "The Amendment in Legislative Strategy: Sophisticated Voting in the U.S. Congress," *Journal of Politics* (May 1980): 396–413; and James M. Enelow, "Saving Amendments, Killer

Amendments, and an Expected Utility Theory of Sophisticated Voting," *Journal of Politics* (November 1981): 1062–1089.

63. *Congressional Record*, May 25, 1982, H2824. The amendment was not adopted.
64. Ibid., April 18, 2012, H1928.
65. Donnie Radcliffe, "Many Hits, One Era," *Washington Post*, March 9, 1994, C4.
66. Brown and Johnson, *House Practice*, 926.
67. *Congressional Record*, June 27, 2003, H5256.
68. *CongressDaily*, July 1, 2003, 5.
69. *New York Times*, June 29, 1983, A14.
70. On factors influencing votes, see, for example, John W. Kingdon, *Congressmen's Voting Decisions* (New York: Harper and Row, 1973); and Donald P. Matthews and James A. Stimson, *Yeas and Nays* (New York: Wiley, 1975).
71. *Congressional Record*, July 16, 1986, H4558.
72. *Congressional Record*, November 21, 2003, H12176.
73. Ibid., H12230–H12246.
74. Jackie Koszczuk and Jonathan Allen, "Late-Night Medicare Vote Drama Triggers Some Unexpected Alliances," *CQ Weekly*, November 29, 2003, 2958.
75. Robert Pear and Robin Toner, "Sharply Split, House Passes Broad Medicare Overhaul; Forceful Lobbying by Bush," *New York Times*, November 29, 2003, 21.
76. Isaiah J. Poole, "Two Steps Up, One Step Down," *CQ Weekly*, January 9, 2006, 82.
77. Jake Sherman and Marin Cogan, "Boehner Governs at Expense of the Right," *Politico*, April 15, 2011, 9.
78. Paul Kane, "Boehner Narrowly Wins 2nd Term as House Speaker," *Washington Post*, January 4, 2013, A4.
79. Erin McPike, "Warming Vote Brings Heat at Home," *CongressDailyAM*, July 9, 2009, 1.
80. *New York Times*, May 13, 1986, A24.
81. Jack Anderson and Michael Binstein, "Synar Stands His Ground," *Washington Post*, August 22, 1993, C7.
82. See, for example, Martha Bridegam and Pat Towell, "'Goodwill Games' Spark Sharp Exchange," *Congressional Quarterly Weekly Report*, June 27, 1987, 1386.
83. *Congressional Record*, July 10, 2008, H6375.
84. Mike Soraghan, "House Dems Grapple With Their Rebels," *The Hill*, March 19, 2008, 4.
85. Kathleen Hunter, "GOP Continues to Vex Democrats on Procedure," *CQ Today*, November 7, 2007, 30.
86. *Congressional Record*, September 25, 1984, H10129.
87. See Charles R. Wise, *The Dynamics of Legislation* (San Francisco: Jossey-Bass, 1991).

CHAPTER 6

Scheduling Legislation in the Senate

REPRESENTATIVES AND SENATORS work long days, not only on the floor and in committee but also in meetings with executive branch officials, constituents, interest groups, and the media. Moreover, they must maintain contact with the diplomatic community, party leaders, and state and local officials. And then there are the periodic trips home to attend important political functions, meet with constituents, or appear at campaign fundraising events. As a senator pointed out, "A big part of the job is taking the pulse of our constituents."[1]

Of legislators in the two houses of Congress, senators lead the more harried existence. The legislative and committee workload is as heavy in the Senate as in the House, but it must be carried out by fewer lawmakers (100 senators compared with 435 House members), and in most cases senators represent a larger number of constituents. Senators are more often in the public eye and are called on more frequently to comment on national and international policy. Senators not uncommonly are expected to be in two or more places at the same time. In such a situation, a senator must select the top-priority event to attend in person and delegate staff members to cover the rest or rely on a fellow senator to recount what took place. (See Box 6.1 for a senator's daily schedule.)

Because of the role senators must play, the time restraints on them, and the smaller size of the Senate, the chamber's legislative scheduling system is much more flexible than that of the House, and its deliberative process is more informal (see Table 6.1). The Senate has formal rules dictating floor procedure, but they are routinely set aside. Instead, the chamber relies on unanimous consent agreements. Senators also have significant parliamentary prerogatives, especially with respect to their ability to stymie floor action, and senators are not reluctant to wield these prerogatives to achieve individual or partisan objectives. As a result, floor decision making can be an uncertain or unsettled affair. And, unlike the House, where the majority party led by the Speaker is in charge of scheduling, the majority and minority leaders in the Senate consult regularly about the institution's program and agenda. "I will be working with my friend, the majority leader," said the minority leader. "I mean we work together every day."[2] The majority leader, however, is ultimately responsible for setting the Senate's schedule of business.

In response to the manifold pressures on members, the Senate has evolved a highly adaptable and flexible legislative scheduling system that responds

---

BOX 6.1   A Tuesday in 2012 for Senator Jon Tester, D-Mont.

9:15 a.m.	Press interview
10:15 a.m.	Meet with Richard Bassuk, Howard Friedman, Iris Langman, and Elliot Lepler
11 a.m.	Meet with former Vice President Walter Mondale, Senator Baucus, and University of Montana President Royce Engstrom
11:15 a.m.	Senate floor session
11:30 a.m.	Preside over the Senate floor
12:30 p.m.	Democratic Caucus meeting
2:15 p.m.	Meet with Amanda Lott (Helena, MT), with the Arthritis Foundation
2:30 p.m.	Meet with George Trishman (Twin Bridges, MT) and Joe Helle (Dillon, MT), with the Montana Stockgrowers Association and Montana Public Lands Council
2:45 p.m.	Meet with Jay Skoog (Helena, MT), Bill Lloyd (Helena, MT), Robert J. Morrison (Helena, MT), and Gary Simonich (Butte, MT), with the American Council of Engineering Companies
3 p.m.	Meet with Mike Fiebig and Scott Bosse, with the campaign for Montana's Headwaters
3:15 p.m.	Meet with Charlie Briggs (Helena, MT), with Goodwill Industries
3:30 p.m.	Call students at Big Sky High School (Missoula, MT)
4 p.m.	Meet with students from Bentley University
4:15 p.m.	Press interview
6:30 p.m.	Attend the 2012 Spring Real Estate Roundtable Meeting and Policymakers Reception

---

to the needs of the individual members, as well as to the needs of the institution. The system bears little resemblance to what the formal rules specify and rests largely on usage and informal practice. Senators' frustration with delays and uncertainty in scheduling sometimes prompts changes that may be observed at different times, depending on legislative workload and

Table 6.1 House and Senate Scheduling Compared

House	Senate
Important role for the Rules Committee	No equivalent body; instead, unanimous consent agreements often govern floor action on measures
Majority party leaders, especially the Speaker, are the predominant force in scheduling	Majority party leaders control the flow of legislation to the floor in close consultation with minority party leaders
More formal process	Less formal process
Only key members are consulted in scheduling measures	Every reasonable effort is made to accommodate the scheduling requests of all senators
Elaborate system of formal calendars and special days for calling up measures	Heavy reliance on informal practice and personal accommodation in scheduling (Senate has only two calendars)
Party leaders can plan a rather firm schedule of daily and weekly business	Party leaders regularly juggle several measures to suit events and senators
Noncontroversial measures usually considered via suspension of the rules procedure	Noncontroversial measures passed by unanimous consent

political circumstances, such as when the Senate is scurrying to move a backlog of business.

Different Options

To try to pass the 12 general appropriations bills and a few other key legislative priorities during an election year when a third of the membership is busy campaigning, majority leaders may plan several 5-day workweeks with votes on Mondays and Fridays so as to complete action on "must-pass" measures.[3] The two chambers may strive to coordinate their schedules so both are usually in session at the same time and able to make progress in lawmaking. For a brief period, the Senate tried a scheduling system that called for 3 weeks in session each month followed by 1 week off to give "Senators some predictability, to schedule their trips back home to their constituencies, or to catch up on committee work here or other work here," said Robert C. Byrd, W.Va., the Senate Democratic leader who instituted the change.[4] Senators did not, however, adhere regularly to the 3-week–1-week system, and so it soon lapsed as they reverted to the usual Tuesday-to-Thursday work pattern.

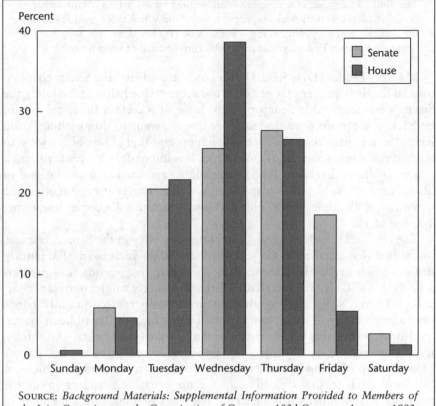

SOURCE: *Background Materials: Supplemental Information Provided to Members of the Joint Committee on the Organization of Congress,* 103d Congress, 1st sess., 1993, 1092.

FIGURE 6.1 Distribution of Senate and House Votes, 102nd Congress, by Day of Week

Many electorally vulnerable lawmakers wanted to be in their states to campaign for reelection.

Figure 6.1 depicts the concentration of Senate floor activity in the Tuesday-to-Thursday period during the 102nd Congress (1991–1993) and contrasts the Senate pattern with that of the House. This several-decades-old pattern generally remains typical of senatorial activity today. As a recent account noted, "most weeks the chamber works late on Thursday nights so members can catch [Friday] morning flights back home."[5]

The subject of scheduling improvements comes up perennially, such as suggestions to reinstate the aforementioned 3-week–1-week plan. The fundamental goals of these proposals is to strive to ensure certainty and predictability in the chamber's day-to-day work. This is a difficult task, however. As one Senate majority leader explained:

The ability of any Senator to speak without limitations makes it impossible to establish total certainty with respect to scheduling. When there is added to that the difficult and very demanding schedules of 100 Senators, it is very hard to organize business in a way that meets the convenience of everybody.[6]

Majority Leader Harry Reid, D-Nev., once mused after the Senate chaplain offered the daily prayer that he could use some divine help in scheduling the Senate's business. "One Senator has to leave at a certain time, one has to be back at a certain time, and another doesn't want to do anything," said Reid. "So it is hard to make everyone happy, and that is one of my jobs: to try and make everyone happy. Sometimes it is impossible."[7] Senator Patrick Leahy, D-Vt., underscored Reid's scheduling predicament when he said of his colleague: "He has the worst job in America, trying to accommodate the schedules of 99 other people, plus his own, which usually comes in number 100 out of 100."[8]

The best-laid scheduling plans can always go awry in the Senate, because individual senators have the capacity through various parliamentary devices to frustrate plans for moving the legislative agenda in a predictable fashion. Given the individualistic and increasingly partisan character of today's Senate, Republicans and Democrats commonly battle over agenda control. Understandably, a Democratic or Republican majority leader wants the Senate to focus on his party's agenda; the minority leader wants, by contrast, the opportunity to advance his party's priorities by offering nonrelevant amendments to whatever vehicle or bill lends itself to that objective. In the majority, one senator said, "the majority leader must show he's running the calendar, not a member of the minority."[9]

Major Scheduling Considerations

Scheduling involves a host of significant strategic, political, personal, policy, and procedural considerations in determining the chamber's agenda of business: coordinating floor action with the Speaker of the House—which chamber should go first or second, for instance—facilitated when both are of the same party; responding to crises; heeding the policy suggestions of state and local officials; and much more. Regularly, both parties present dueling agendas at the start of every Congress and throughout the 2-year life of a Congress. There are occasions when the majority party's top priorities are identified by the first few bill numbers, such as S. 1 through S. 10. For instance, Majority Leader Reid introduced S. 1 (the American Recovery and Reinvestment Act) on the opening day of the 111th Congress (2009–2011); it was a fiscal stimulus bill designed to revive the ailing national economy. Sometimes when the House and Senate are controlled by the same party, the respective chamber leaders will coordinate and assign the same bill number (H.R. 1 and S. 1) to the party's top priority for that Congress. Among several interconnected elements that majority leaders take into account when making scheduling decisions are the following.

Strategic. Numerous overlapping factors are subsumed by the term *strategic* in scheduling the Senate's business. For example, if the Senate is in gridlock over a measure because of various stalling tactics, the majority leader may threaten to make members work long days, through the weekend, and even through a planned recess until the impasse is resolved. Majority Leader Reid kept the Senate in session for 25 days straight—including rare Saturday and Sunday sessions with votes held in the middle of the night (1 a.m., for instance) and on Christmas Eve (the first time since 1895 that a roll-call vote was held on that day)—to enact President Obama's landmark health care reform plan (the Patient Protection and Affordable Care Act). Alternatively, if senators agree on a date for a final vote on controversial legislation, the majority leader might extend a scheduled Senate recess for another week. Or the majority leader might set a difficult vote just before a recess. A majority leader, for instance, "scheduled the politically tough vote [raising the nation's debt ceiling] on the last day before Congress adjourns for a weeklong St. Patrick's Day recess."[10] If the Senate failed to enact this "must-pass" measure and thus put the government in default, the Senate would likely have remained in session until it did pass, scrambling the senators' travel and other recess plans.

Strategic scheduling is also part of deadline or end-game politics. Legislation may be scheduled during the closing weeks of a Congress to maximize political pressure for action. Party leaders recognize that members are often willing to wait until the end of a Congress, "believing that he, she, or they will have maximum leverage at the end of the tunnel."[11] (Recall from Chapter 2 that recent years have witnessed bitter battles between the House GOP majority and President Obama over raising the statutory borrowing limit.) Or real or contrived crises can be generated as certain deadlines approach—the start of the fiscal year or the traditional August recess. The sense of urgency can heighten the pressure and the stakes, so lawmakers will act before the clock or calendar runs out. Each party or chamber may hold off acting on "must-pass" measures until the last moment—the brinksmanship strategy—to demonstrate steadfastness to their electoral base. Majority leaders will also schedule floor action on politically treacherous issues months before the November elections to avoid the risk of "fighting them out in the weeks before" voters go to the polls.[12]

Electoral/Campaign. The political and electoral ramifications of scheduling loom large in election years. Democratic and Republican leaders will work to bring measures to the floor with limited chance of passage but large potential in rallying the party's electoral supporters and promoting fundraising efforts. To energize conservative voters, GOP leaders may call up constitutional amendments to prohibit gay marriage or flag burning. GOP minority leader Mitch McConnell, Ky., even promised that if his party captured control of the Senate in the November 2012 elections and he became the majority leader, repealing "Obamacare" would be "the first item on the agenda in the Senate."[13] (McConnell did not achieve his goal, however.) Many GOP lawmakers and voters across the country continue to oppose President Obama's Patient Protection and Affordable Care Act. Senate Republicans wanted to draw sharp policy contrasts with Democratic priorities to provide their incumbents and challengers with a "message agenda" they can highlight in their campaigns.

Similarly, Democratic leaders want "red-meat" legislation brought to the floor that appeals to their base (union workers and females, for example), such as measures protecting women against violence. To score political points in the lead-up to the 2012 elections, Senate Majority Leader Reid repeatedly scheduled votes on legislation blocked by GOP senators but backed by voters across the country, such as a bill to protect women against violence, a measure to prevent an interest-rate increase for student loans, and the so-called "Buffett Rule" (named after billionaire Warren Buffett, who pointed out that his tax bracket is lower than his secretary's). The Buffett Rule, contained in the Paying a Fair Share Act, would hike taxes on millionaires to at least 30%. Democrats realized they could not win passage of the millionaires tax, but their objective was to rally "middle-class and working-class voters behind them" in the lead-up to the November elections.[14] Reid's plan was a "win-by-losing" strategy. GOP leader McConnell rebuffed the Democrats' initiative by contending that it is wrongheaded to raise taxes "on the very people we're counting on to create the jobs we need to get us out of a jobs crisis."[15]

Stalemates in processing legislation can be a campaign issue as the majority party blames the minority for obstructing the chamber's business. The majority leader, for example, could schedule several votes on a motion to proceed to a bill, knowing full well that he lacks the votes to overcome dilatory tactics by the minority. His goal: to put minority members on record as "obstructionists." For their part, minority members would castigate the majority for managing a "do-nothing" Senate or suggest an unappealing alternative to the Senate's majority leader. On the student loan bill mentioned above, Senator McConnell urged Senator Reid to consult with Speaker Boehner to get the legislation moving. McConnell favored the House-passed measure, not the Senate's version. Instead, Senator Reid urged Mitt Romney, the GOP's presidential nominee, to telephone McConnell and persuade him to back the Senate's student loan bill.[16] Political point-scoring is the objective of such back-and-forth rhetorical salvos.

Campaign fundraising also affects scheduling. Senate majority leaders are mindful that their colleagues must devote considerable time and effort to "dialing for dollars." As a result, they provide "windows" in the schedule that are free of scheduled votes so senators can engage in money-raising activities. Windows can occur in the morning, afternoon, or evening. They will not occur if the majority leader determines that the chamber must continue to work on a bill until it is completed. "It does not matter what events are going on around town, we are going to work and finish this bill," declared Senator Reid. "There will be no windows."[17]

The President. Presidents can influence the Senate schedule in numerous ways, as these examples illustrate. They often act as the nation's "chief legislator" by presenting their legislative program to Congress in the annual State of the Union address and in other messages to the House and Senate. President Obama's ambitious agenda for the 111th Congress (2009–2011) reflected both his 2008 campaign promises and the huge problems he inherited. Both chambers addressed a wide range of consequential presidential initiatives, such as health care reform, a $787 billion economic stimulus package to revive an ailing economy, and financial regulatory reform. Various analysts even worried that President Obama was overloading the legislative circuits. Senate Democratic leaders generally worked in tandem with the Obama Administration to advance these priorities. By contrast, the 112th Congress, with a Republican House and Democratic Senate, was noted more for gridlock and partisan acrimony than productivity in lawmaking. Of course lawmakers sympathetic to the Tea Party philosophy of smaller government and less spending would view the low productivity of laws as a virtue and not a vice.

On the campaign trail for a second term, President Obama confronted a number of reelection challenges, such as a sluggish economy and slow job creation. As a result, the president urged Congress to pass his five-point program, which he referred to as a "Congress To-Do List" (job creation and mortgage relief, for example).[18] He even invited the bipartisan congressional leadership to the White House to discuss job creation. It was dubbed the "hoagie summit" after the sandwich the president served to the House and Senate leaders.[19] "We have a 'to stop' list for him," remarked Senate GOP Policy Committee Chair John Thune, S.D., who castigated the president for advocating job-killing legislation.[20] To be sure, Senate Democrats worked with the president to advance a "Jobs First" agenda. If Republicans blocked their legislative plans, President Obama would blast the GOP as "obstructionists." Thus, the Senate Democratic floor agenda's purpose is "less to make law than to buttress Obama's charge that Republicans are obstructing measures that would benefit the economy."[21] Republican leader McConnell, of course, was dismayed that the Senate floor had become an extension of the Obama campaign. The Senate, he declared, "has ceased to be a place where problems are resolved and has become instead a place where Democrats produce campaign material" and "show votes" for political gain.[22] Common to both parties is that they raise issues and force votes in the chamber not to make laws but to provide material for campaign attack ads, to promote fundraising, and to energize their outside supporters.

For their part, Republicans supported Senator McConnell's goal of making Obama a one-term president. GOP leaders coordinated floor actions with the campaign agenda of Mitt Romney, their presidential nominee. Senator McConnell, for example, named Senator Ron Johnson, Wis., to develop a legislative agenda with House Republicans that meshes with the priorities of the Romney campaign.[23] Senator Roy Blunt, Mo., served as Romney's chief liaison to Congress. A former House GOP leader, Blunt was strategically positioned to help coordinate and develop a congressional Republican message agenda at variance with Democratic priorities. The Senate floor would then be used to advance Romney's presidential campaign themes. In election years, campaigning by legislating routinely suffuses congressional activities.

Presidents have the constitutional authority to call one or both houses into special session "on extraordinary Occasions" (Article II, Section 3). The most recent example is when President Harry S. Truman in July 1948 called the GOP-controlled Congress into special session to pass legislation on civil rights, housing policy, and other issues. These measures did not pass the Congress. As a result, Truman campaigned against the "do-nothing 80th Congress" and surprised pollsters by winning in November.

Presidents also submit diplomatic, judicial, and high executive branch nominations to the Senate under the Constitution's "advice and consent" clause (Article II, Section 2). As Alexander Hamilton wrote in *The Federalist* No. 66, the Senate "cannot themselves CHOOSE—they can only ratify or reject the choice [the president] may have made." The Senate can approve, reject, or stall action on the president's nominees. As presidents often do in periods when their party controls the Senate, they urge their majority leaders in election years to schedule rapid action on the White House's nominees before the traditional Labor Day kickoff to the November campaign season. "If the [minority party in the Senate] believes it's going to be in the majority the next Congress, they may not see a lot of incentive to cooperate," said the White House's chief Senate liaison. "The closer we get to the election, the harder it will be to move these nominations," especially judicial appointments with lifetime tenure.[24]

During periods of divided government, there may be a marked lack of trust between the president and the opposition party in charge of the Senate, which affects the appointments process. Under the Constitution (Article II, Section 2), when the Senate is in recess, the president can make temporary (or recess) appointments to fill vacant diplomatic, judicial, or executive positions, bypassing the Senate's confirmation prerogative.

President George W. Bush sometimes took advantage of Senate recesses to name controversial individuals unlikely to win Senate confirmation as recess appointees. To prevent this from happening, the Senate may meet in brief (less-than-a-minute) pro forma session during various chamber recesses to discourage the president from making recess appointments. The Senate, remarked Majority Leader Reid, "will be coming in for pro forma sessions during the Thanksgiving holiday to prevent recess appointments" by President Bush.[25] (Substantive business is typically not conducted during pro forma sessions, and presiding officers sometimes "compete to see who can most quickly gavel the Senate in and out of business. The record belongs to former Senator Robert Byrd (D-W.Va.): 0.06 seconds."[26])

Ironically, Senator Reid encouraged President Obama to make recess appointments to fill numerous administrative vacancies. The reason: to circumvent dilatory tactics by Senate Republicans that blocked the confirmation of many of Obama's nominees. The president took Reid's advice. On January 4, 2012, after a long series of pro forma sessions starting in mid-October 2011, the president recess-appointed Richard Cordray as head of the Consumer Financial Protection Bureau—created as part of the 2009 Wall Street reform law—along with three members of the National Labor Relations Board (NLRB). Senate GOP objections to the NLRB nominees left that entity without a quorum to function and the new consumer bureau without an official leader. Senate Republicans stated that their price for allowing a vote on the Cordray nomination, the most controversial of the recess appointments, was to amend the Wall Street statute and "replace the single Director [Cordray] with a board of directors."[27] The official historian of the Senate noted that the GOP's block on Cordray appeared unprecedented. He "could not remember a similar instance when a minority blocked presidential nominees because of opposition to the agency's very existence or out of a desire to change the law establishing the agency."[28]

Instead, President Obama ignored the pro forma session gambit and made the four recess appointments. The Justice Department's Office of Legal Counsel advised the president that if no business is conducted during pro forma sessions, he could exercise his recess-appointment power. Obama's decision set off a firestorm of protest among Senate Republicans and many others.[29] Senators asserted that business was conducted during these pro forma sessions, citing Senate approval on December 23, 2011, of a temporary payroll tax measure. Moreover, senators made clear that the Senate determines when it is in session to conduct business, not the president. At this juncture, the president's recess appointment authority remains an unsettled area of both legal jurisprudence and legislative challenge.

Family-Friendly Schedules. The demands and pressures on senators and the Senate are not particularly conducive to family life. Late-night sessions, constant meetings, or evening committee markup sessions can sometimes cause stress and strife in families. Majority leaders are sensitive to this reality. Many try to make the Senate a family-friendly institution by accommodating senators' personal obligations. As a majority leader stated: "I had an inquiry this afternoon on when the votes will occur on Monday. One of our colleagues on this side is attending a Little League baseball tournament where his son is involved and he cannot be back until 3:00 p.m., so he will be accommodated."[30]

To balance institutional obligations with individual requests is no easy assignment for majority leaders. For example, a roll-call vote at 5 p.m. on Thursday "means GOP Senator Kay Bailey Hutchison can make an evening flight [to Texas] to be with her two newly adopted children. A 6:30 p.m. vote means she can't depart until Friday."[31] Sensitive to family concerns, Majority Leader Reid stated that the Senate is "becoming a place where there is an obligation people have with their families," which means that the Senate cannot always work "the long weeks we have in the past."[32] However, if Majority Leader Reid believes it is imperative to finish action on a bill, such as health care reform, he is not reluctant to keep the Senate in continuous session for many days. The Senate even "set a modern record [during the health care debate]—for the most number of weekends spent at work."[33]

Procedure and Time. Majority leaders are constantly aware of the need to use the time of the Senate effectively if they are to process its growing workload. Too much time spent debating one measure means less time available for floor action on other matters. Committee chairs, dozens of bipartisan lawmakers, and individual senators often "lobby" the majority leader to schedule floor time for their bills and amendments or to permit more floor debate on priority measures. Thus, majority leaders are creative in employing various Senate procedures to "manufacture" that most precious commodity of senators and the Senate: time.

Take the use of cloture as an example (see Chapter 7 for detailed discussion). **Cloture** is a Senate rule (XXII) whose principal aim is to end extended debate (the **filibuster**). Under Rule XXII, once a cloture motion to end debate is filed by the majority leader, there is a lapse of two additional days before the Senate votes on invoking cloture (closure of debate). A constitutional three fifths of the Senate (60 if there are no vacancies) is required to invoke cloture. Under recent practice, the majority leader may file cloture on the motion to proceed to a specific bill, withdraw that procedural motion, and then move to other business for the Senate's consideration.[34] Meanwhile, cloture on the motion to proceed remains pending for a vote 2 days later unless the majority leader and minority leader negotiate an agreement in the interim that obviates the vote on cloture. An upshot of this course of action: the majority leader, by withdrawing the motion to proceed, can focus the Senate's time and attention on other priority measures, such as a defense authorization bill. Time management is fundamental to the job of the majority leader. (At the beginning of the 113th Congress, the Senate adopted filibuster reforms designed to mitigate dilatory action on the motion, see Box 7.4.)

Moreover, unlike House members, all senators have an opportunity to participate in scheduling legislation for floor action. Robert J. Dole, R-Kans., who was majority leader from 1985 to 1987 and from 1995 to mid-1996, once reported: "The Senate leadership convened a special meeting this morning for all 100 Senators—81 Senators attended to discuss [the schedule for] wrapping up the year's business before adjournment."[35] On determining when President Obama's signature health care reform measure might be completed in the 111th Congress, Majority Leader Reid stated:

> We will see what the mood of the Senate is. Everybody should be alerted that unless Senator McConnell [the GOP leader] and I and the other 98 Members can work something out, we may have to be here this weekend.[36]

Scheduling reflects the key role of the two party leaders in accomplishing the Senate's business and the power that every member has under senatorial rules. "One person can tie this place into a knot," said a senator. "And two can do it even more beautifully."[37] Senators have the "ability to burn time, to drag out debate in ways that can grind legislative business to a halt and leave the Senate caught in an interminable purgatory."[38] Partisan wrangling over the schedule of business, a common occurrence in recent Congresses, compounds the Senate's difficulty in raising and completing action on legislation and nominations.

Minor or noncontroversial bills are expedited to save time for major and controversial measures. Action on important bills, insofar as possible, is scheduled to suit the convenience of members and to minimize conflicts with legislative activity taking place off the Senate floor. "The Senate operates largely on the basis of unanimous-consent agreements, comity, courtesy, and understanding," said Senator Byrd, the longest serving member ever in either chamber.[39] To be sure, these features of the Senate are often less in evidence in recent years given the partisan and policy divide between Democrats and Republicans.

Classifying Measures

The Senate's system for classifying measures for floor debate is simpler and more informal than the House system. In contrast with the House and its three calendars, the Senate has only two calendars: the Calendar of General Orders and the **Executive Calendar**. All legislation, major or minor, public or private, is placed on the former; treaties and nominations under the Senate's advice and consent authority are placed on the latter.[40]

Within the course of a single day, the Senate may consider measures on both the General Orders and Executive Calendars. It may go from executive session to legislative session before finishing pending items on the Executive Calendar. (The motion to enter or exit an executive session is not debatable; however, the nomination or treaty to be taken up can be filibustered.)

Treaties are referred to the Foreign Relations Committee, and presidential nominations are sent to the appropriate committee of jurisdiction. Unlike nominations or regular legislation, treaties do not die at the end of a Congress. For example, the Genocide Treaty was ratified by the required two-thirds vote in 1986, 37 years after being submitted by President Harry S. Truman in 1949. The 1994 Law of the Sea Treaty, which governs nations' use of the world's oceans, won the approval of 161 nations but not that of the United States. The Foreign Relations Committee twice approved the treaty during the George W. Bush Administration, but it did not attract the required two-thirds vote of the Senate. In 2012, the Senate panel again considered the Law of the Sea Treaty, but it was not ratified by the Senate.[41] By contrast, presidential nominations must be acted on in a session or they die, and as Senate Rule XXXI states, they must "again be made to the Senate by the President."

Relatively noncontroversial legislation in the House comes up under suspension-of-the-rules procedure or by unanimous consent. Specific days of the month are designated for consideration of legislation on the Private Calendar. The Senate has no comparable procedures. Formal Senate rules for calling up legislation—both controversial and noncontroversial—are cumbersome and consequently are generally ignored. One of these rules, for example, requires a daily calendar call, with measures brought up and debated in the order in which they appear on the calendar. An example of the Senate Calendar of Business for Thursday, January 3, 2013, appears in Figure 6.2. Were the Senate to follow that rule, it would lose virtually all flexibility in processing its workload.

At the start of each day, the majority leader often presents an overview of the Senate's floor agenda for that day, an example of which is provided in Box 6.2. Similarly, the majority leader, or a designee, announces the program for the next day or subsequent days at the conclusion of the daily session. Periodically, the leader indicates what the legislative agenda looks like for longer periods of time. Senators are kept informed of the legislative program through a variety of means, such as weekly whip notices (issued more frequently and as needed by each party) listing the measures likely to be considered during the week. The Senate's whip notices are less detailed than those of the House, because Senate rules limit predictability in scheduling. Like the House, the Senate has electronic ways to keep senators apprised of the floor schedule and changes to it.

SENATE OF THE UNITED STATES
ONE HUNDRED THIRTEENTH CONGRESS

FIRST SESSION $\{$ CONVENED JANUARY 3, 2013 $\}$ DAYS OF SESSION 1

CALENDAR OF BUSINESS

Thursday, January 3, 2013

SENATE CONVENES AT 12:00 NOON

PREPARED UNDER THE DIRECTION OF NANCY ERICKSON,
SECRETARY OF THE SENATE

By KATHLEEN ALVAREZ TRITAK, LEGISLATIVE CLERK

www.SenateCalendar.gov

29–015

FIGURE 6.2   Senate Calendar of Business

BOX 6.2 Setting the Daily Schedule

Mr. REID. Mr. President, we are on the motion to proceed to S. 3414, which is the cybersecurity bill. This is postcloture. At 4:30 p.m., the Senate will proceed to executive session to vote on the nomination of Robert Bacharach, of Oklahoma, to be a U.S. circuit judge for the tenth Circuit. This likely will be our last vote on a circuit judge for this Congress. I hope we can be successful. This is a person whom I will talk about a little bit, and he is certainly well qualified. He came out of committee unanimously.

At 5:30 p.m., today, there will be a cloture vote on the Bacharach nomination. If cloture is not invoked on the Bacharach nomination, the Senate will resume legislative session and begin consideration of the cybersecurity bill following the vote.

SOURCE: *Congressional Record*, July 30, 2012, S5631.

NONCONTROVERSIAL BILLS

Practically all noncontroversial measures are called up by use of unanimous consent agreements and enacted without debate.[42] In fact, Senator Byrd has estimated that "easily 98 percent of the [noncontroversial] business of the Senate is called up by unanimous consent."[43] The leaders and staff aides in both parties check with senators to clear minor or noncontroversial legislation before such measures reach the floor, because a single dissent will hold up floor action until the roadblock is cleared away. Once cleared, minor and noncontroversial bills generally take from several seconds to a few minutes to pass. "Locomotive velocity may develop at this point, as bills come up and pass through with no objection," Byrd has noted.[44] Typically, these measures are considered at the end of the daily Senate session, during the wrap-up period (see Box 6.3).

The Senate's small size, flexibility, and tradition of cooperation mean that the majority and minority leaders frequently can schedule noncontroversial legislation on a daily basis. Through informal floor discussions or colloquies, each examines the calendar to be sure that noncontroversial bills have been cleared by senators interested in those bills. The measures then are passed quickly by voice vote.

Minor and noncontroversial measures also may reach the Senate floor on a motion by any senator. However, the majority and minority leaders normally try to reach agreement in advance on the floor schedule and are likely to oppose action that will bring bills to the floor without prior clearance from them. The leaders' prerogative of receiving preferential recognition from the presiding officer—first the majority leader, followed by the minority leader—enables them to control the agenda of activities on the floor. As Senator Byrd explained:

> A majority leader has enormous power when it comes to the schedule of the Senate, the scheduling of bills and resolutions and the programming of the Senate schedule. The majority leader has the first recognition power and that is a big arrow in his arsenal. . . . Nobody can get recognition before the majority leader.[45]

Members of both parties, even in today's polarized Senate, recognize that it is the majority leader's prerogative to schedule the Senate's agenda of business. As a Senate Republican whip said about Majority Leader Reid: "The majority leader has two great powers that no one else in the Senate has. One is the right of first recognition by the Presiding Officer and the other is the power to set the schedule."[46]

MAJOR LEGISLATION

Once major Senate bills are reported from committee, the majority leader must consider several questions. First, what measures should be called up? Here the majority leader, after receiving input from numerous sources, such as committee chairs, the minority leader, the White House, and the rank and file, identifies both the must-pass and must-not-pass bills. Second, absent an emergency or deadline-driven situation, when should the legislation be taken up? In a workload-packed Senate, time is always a factor. "I want to see the votes," said a majority leader. "And I want to see an outline of what the parliamentary situation will be, because time is a consideration around here."[47] Finally, how can legislation be positioned so it can be taken up? Some bills can be considered without sparking any procedural or substantive wrangling. For other measures, substance is at issue. And for yet other legislation, controversy rages over procedure and substance, which is the most difficult scenario for getting a bill called up.

Once the majority leader determines which measure to call up from the legislative calendar, it can take one of two main routes to the floor: through unanimous consent or by motion ("I move to take up S. 1234"). Before these stages are reached, however, the legislation may be subject to the 1-day rule, the 2-day rule, or to "holds."

One-Day and Two-Day Rules

The 1-day rule states that bills and reports must lie over on the calendar for 1 legislative day before they are eligible for floor consideration. This rule is seldom enforced and commonly is waived by unanimous consent. To speed up action, the majority leader states, "I ask unanimous consent that [these bills] be considered as having been on the calendar 1 legislative day for the purpose of the rules of the Senate."[48] Rarely is an objection heard to the request.

---

box 6.3 Wrapping Up the Senate's Day

It took just a few minutes for the Senate to act on some 150 nominations and a handful of bills early in the morning of November 21 as work wound down for the session. But getting to that point was a long, long process.

"It can consume a lot of time," said Secretary of the Majority David Schiappa.

Each nomination and measure Majority Leader Bill Frist, R-Tenn., rattled off for final action required hours, even days, of behind-the-scenes work by the majority and minority cloakrooms. Every senator's office had to be contacted to win agreement. Objections led to negotiations, trades, and promises as Senate leaders and cloakroom staff sorted out the bills individually.

Every day when Congress is in session, the majority and minority cloakrooms update the inventory of the legislation awaiting floor action. Such measures are known as "hotlined" bills, and Senate offices learn which ones they are from an actual telephone hotline.

"We may be seeking unanimous consent for the following bills," those calls customarily begin. After that, according to interviews with people involved in the process, the outcome relies on a combination of moxie and modern-day electronics.

Staff assistants e-mail hotline lists to appropriate legislative staff. Staff, in turn, must make hasty evaluations of whether their bosses might have a problem with or a strategic reason to try to slow down anything on the list.

Senators' staffs, bill sponsors, and cloakroom personnel then start negotiating. Sometimes, the leadership intervenes. Bills that remain problematic are dropped

---

The 2-day rule requires that printed committee reports accompanying legislation reported by a committee be available to members for at least 2 calendar days before those proposals are eligible for floor action. (Chapter 7 discusses the difference in the Senate between legislative and calendar days.) This rule, too, may be waived by unanimous consent or by joint motion of the majority and minority leaders. However, in procedural hardball circumstances, setting aside the 2-day rule can be difficult, as this example illustrates.

In 1987, two strong-willed Senate leaders—Byrd and Dole—engaged in a classic game of "tit-for-tat" over the 2-day rule. That year, the Senate was considering President Ronald Reagan's controversial nomination of Robert H. Bork to the Supreme Court, and Majority Leader Byrd wanted to facilitate floor action on the nominee. He repeatedly asked GOP leader Dole to join him in waiving the two-day rule. "Would the distinguished Republican leader indicate whether or not he is willing to join with me in waiving the 2-day rule?" asked Byrd. "I regret that I am not in a position now to waive the 2-day rule," answered Dole.[49] The discussion surrounding the 2-day rule involved jockeying by both parties as they tried to expedite or stretch out debate on the proposed, and ultimately unsuccessful, Bork judgeship.

from the list of measures that can be passed by voice vote—without most senators present—via a unanimous consent request.

The wrap-up list typically is dominated by Post Office namings, congratulatory resolutions, and other measure that are noteworthy only in one locality.

"It's not that they are big things," said one Democratic aide, "but they can mean big things back home." Nominations to executive branch boards, judicial posts, commissions, and offices can be particularly difficult to hotline.

A case in point was the long list of executive nominations that went through the Senate November 21. The quest of Senator Harry Reid, D-Nev., to get one of his staffers, Gregory Jaczko, nominated and confirmed to the Nuclear Regulatory Commission began more than a year ago. Reid declared he would block all nonmilitary executive nominations until Jaczko got the seat reserved for a Democrat.

Talks to confirm Jaczko, or to let some other nominations through without his confirmation, were on and off again. Nominations stacked up. It was not until October that a package began to take shape.

The final package was worked out late on November 20 before the senators went home for Thanksgiving. Reid settled for the promise of a 2-year Jaczko recess appointment with some strings attached, and the White House saw erased, overnight, its huge bottleneck of unconfirmed nominees.

SOURCE: Adapted from Daphne Retter, "The Road Leading from 'Hotline' to Senate Wrapup is Not Necessarily a Short Trip," *CQ Today*, November 29, 2004, 3.

During the 104th Congress (1995–1997), when Dole was majority leader and Byrd was the Senate's senior Democrat (he had voluntarily relinquished his party leadership role at the start of the 101st Congress), Dole hoped to act quickly on legislation curbing unfunded federal mandates (when the costs of national programs are passed on to state and local governments). To hasten floor action on the unfunded mandates bill, Dole requested the two committees with jurisdiction (Budget and Governmental Affairs) not to submit committee reports with the measure. He did not want the bill delayed by the 2-day rule or the Senate rule granting committee members 3 calendar days to file supplemental, additional, or minority views for inclusion in the report. (Unlike the House, the Senate has no formal rule requiring committee reports to accompany legislation. Senate committees, however, usually file committee reports.) Despite protests from each committee's Democratic members, neither panel issued a formal committee report. Instead, the two GOP committee chairs filed substitute statements in the *Congressional Record*.[50]

Senator Byrd quickly made a floor issue of the speed with which the bill whizzed through committee. "The Senate is not up against a deadline," he said. "We're not up against an adjournment *sine die*." (**Adjournment** *sine die* is the opposite of **adjournment to a day certain.**) The measure, he argued, needed a thorough examination on the floor. He underscored the importance of formal committee reports, noting, for example, their value "to any court in determining what the legislative intent is with regard to a particular bill."[51] Then for 2 weeks, Senator Byrd led the Democratic effort to delay action on the GOP proposal. "We have what we know as 'Byrd-lock,'" quipped Majority Leader Dole.[52] After 59 hours of debate on the bill and 44 roll-call votes, the Senate finally enacted the legislation.[53]

Holds

Holds are an informal custom unique to the Senate. They permit any number of senators—individually or in clusters—to stop (sometimes permanently, sometimes temporarily) floor consideration of legislation or nominations simply by making requests of their party leaders not to take up such matters. As a senator explained, a hold is "a notice by a Senator to his or her party leader of an intention to object to bringing a bill or nomination to the floor for consideration."[54] Party leaders can move ahead anyway, but then they face the daunting prospect of overcoming various dilatory tactics. Nonetheless, it is ultimately the decision of the majority leader whether to honor a hold and, if so, for how long. Unlike filibusters, which are ostensibly educational and occur in full view of everyone, holds require no public utterance and often occur in shrouded circumstances. (Various senators have a policy of publicly announcing in the chamber that they have placed holds on measures or nominations. If so, they are exempt from the procedures mentioned below purporting to end secret holds.) Sometimes called the "silent filibuster," they are especially effective on limited or special-purpose measures that attract little public or political attention. Must-pass legislation, such as continuing resolutions, will not be killed by holds. Only senators can place holds, but they may do so at the request of House members, lobbyists, or executive branch officials. In some instances, factional leaders place holds on behalf of their senatorial colleagues.[55] Holds may take various forms.

> There are "rolling" holds, a group sport in which one senator after another steps in to keep a measure from coming to the Senate floor. There are also "hostage" holds, where a senator may hold up a nomination, for example, to force concessions on something else. Then there are what have come to be known as "Mae West" holds: a come-hither message for senators to stop by and work something out.[56]

There are also "political holds." In an election year, senators in tight races will discover that holds are placed on their bills by opposition party members. The objective of these holds is to prevent senators in competitive races from claiming credit and reaping favorable publicity back home for winning enactment of legislation. "Blanket holds" occur when a senator's aim is to prevent action on a large category of measures or nominations, such as all nominees to the independent regulatory agencies (see Box 6.3 for an example).

Relatively little is known about holds even among insiders in Washington.[57] There is no current or comprehensive public record of who places holds, how they are done (often by letter to the party leader), how many holds are placed on any bill, or how long they are honored by the leadership. Senator Byrd once noted that most holds are used so senators "might be assured that they will be informed or contacted so they can be present when the matter is called up, or have an opportunity to offer an amendment."[58] A list of the Democratic and Republican senators who have holds on various measures is kept by the respective leaders of each party, but this information is restricted and closely held. To be sure, an advantage of holds for party leaders is that they serve as an "early warning" system, indicating which members or factions have scheduling concerns that could provoke dilatory actions and who needs to be consulted to craft a unanimous consent agreement. In practice, party leaders often consider "holders" as members who formally or informally object to consent requests to call up measures or matters.

Holds can forestall floor action because they are linked to the Senate's tradition of extended debate and unanimous consent agreements. Party leaders understand that to ignore holds can precipitate objections to unanimous consent requests or filibusters, which require 60 votes to break. During the rush to Senate adjournment, holds can be fatal. "At this stage in the year, you have a finite amount of time and an infinite amount of legislation. Either the hold goes away, changes are made to the legislation or the person with the hold wins," observed a Senate GOP leadership aide.[59] Holds are also used during the end-of-session rush when members are searching for must-pass bills to which they can attach their favorite amendments. For example, one senator placed a hold on the Export Administration Act so he could try to attach his home equity loan amendment to it.[60]

Holds are a more prominent feature of today's Senate because assertive senators operating in a polarized environment recognize the partisan and policy potential of this extra-parliamentary practice. Holds "have come into a form of reverence which was never to be," exclaimed one senator.[61] Periodically, party leaders assert that senators cannot put indefinite or anonymous holds on matters, but it seems the practice still continues because senators recognize the tactical benefits.

The Senate did address secret holds in 2007 when it passed the Honest Leadership and Open Government Act (S. 1), which President George W. Bush signed into law. Although the measure established a procedure for ending anonymous holds, it did not achieve that goal. A senator, for example, had 6 session days to decide whether to formally place a public hold. If so, the member would inform by letter the majority or minority leader, as the case may be. Then that member's name would be publicized in the *Congressional Record* and listed in a special section ("Notice of Intent to

NOTICE OF INTENT TO OBJECT

When a notice of intent to object is given to the appropriate leader, or their designee, and such notice is submitted for inclusion in the Congressional Record and the Senate Calendar of Business, or following the objection to a unanimous consent to proceeding to, and, or disposition of, a measure or matter on their behalf, it shall be placed in the section of the Calendar entitled "Notice of Intent to Object".
(S. Res. 28, 112th Congress)

NUMBER	TITLE	DATE AND SENATOR
H.R. 359	An act to reduce Federal spending and the deficit by terminating taxpayer financing of presidential election campaigns and party conventions.	Feb. 14, 2011.—Mr. Kyl.
H.R. 359	An act to reduce Federal spending and the deficit by terminating taxpayer financing of presidential election campaigns and party conventions.	Feb. 14, 2011.—Mr. DeMint.
H.R. 359	An act to reduce Federal spending and the deficit by terminating taxpayer financing of presidential election campaigns and party conventions.	Feb. 14, 2011.—Mr. Paul.
S. 520	A bill to repeal the Volumetric Ethanol Excise Tax Credit.	June 7, 2011.—Mr. Grassley.
S. 530	A bill to modify certain subsidies for ethanol production, and for other purposes.	June 7, 2011.—Mr. Grassley.
S. 871	A bill to repeal the Volumetric Ethanol Excise Tax Credit.	June 7, 2011.—Mr. Grassley.
S. 1057	A bill to repeal the Volumetric Ethanol Excise Tax Credit.	June 7, 2011.—Mr. Grassley.
S. 1145	A bill to amend title 18, United States Code, to clarify and expand Federal criminal jurisdiction over Federal contractors and employees outside the United States, and for other purposes.	June 28, 2011.—Mr. Grassley.
S. 618	A bill to promote the strengthening of the private sector in Egypt and Tunisia.	June 29, 2011.—Mr.Coburn.
S. 1385	A bill to terminate the$1 presidential coin program.	Oct. 17, 2011.—Mr. Coburn.
S. 1014	A bill to provide for additional Federal district judgeships.	Nov. 2, 2011.—Mr. Grassley.
S. 1793	A bill to amend title 28, United States Code, to clarify the statutory authority for the longstanding practice of the Department of Justice of providing investigatory assistance on request of State and local authorities with respect to certain serious violent crimes, and for other purposes.	Nov. 17, 2011.—Mr. Grassley.

FIGURE 6.3 Notice of Intent to Object

Object to Proceeding") of the Senate's Calendar of Business (see Figure 6.3). However, if a senator foregoes sending the letter, then for at least 6 session days there is a secret hold in effect. Furthermore, a senator could arrange for a number of like-minded colleagues, near the expiration of each 6-day period, to place a hold (so-called "rolling" or "rotating" holds). Even if Senate Democrats had the required votes to break the hold, they may not have the time to do so because, as Majority Whip Richard Durbin, D-Ill., noted, the Senate would have to "put a lot of our important work aside. We've got our hands full."[62]

The ineffectiveness of the 2007 change in ending secret holds prompted the Senate at the start of the 112th Congress (2011–2013) to try again. The Senate adopted a standing order on January 27, 2011, that kept many features of the 2007 reform—for example, public disclosure in the *Congressional Record* and the legislative calendar. Revisions were made, however, and two merit mention. First, senators must make their holds public within 2 session days—down from the previous 6. This change aims to minimize use of "rotating" holds. Second, as before, a hold is presumed to have occurred when a member objects to a unanimous consent request to proceed to a measure or nomination. However, if no senator comes forward and submits a "hold" letter to the appropriate leader within 2 session days, then whoever made the initial objection would be recorded as the "holder." The objective of this change is to ensure that some member is publicly accountable for placing the hold.

To date, it is unclear whether or to what extent the revised procedure is working to curb anonymous holds. An early review found the two parties in disagreement over "hotline" inquiries made to Democratic and GOP member offices by, respectively, the majority and minority leadership. Hotlines commonly seek the consent of senators to call up measures or nominations (see discussion of unanimous consent agreements, below). If a senator objects to a hotline inquiry, is this considered a "hold" under the 2011 change? Many Democrats and Republicans interpret the standing order "as not applying to hotline-request objections."[63] However, these pre-floor objections appear to some as the equivalent of secret holds. Enforcement of the standing order largely rests with the two party leaders. They may prefer to let party colleagues "informally slow bills" and nominations without requiring them to file written notices.[64] In the view of Majority Leader Reid, "We tried to do something on secret holds, but that hasn't helped [the nominations process] much at all."[65]

Holds encourage bargaining not only among senators but also between the Senate and the executive branch. Senators regularly place holds on diplomatic and other nominations to extract concessions from the State Department and other federal agencies. Hostage holds, as noted earlier, enable senators to gain leverage to achieve other objectives. For example, a senator placed a hold on a number of Department of Energy nominations to force the Senate's energy committee to hold a hearing on a public lands bill important to his state.[66] As a senator said about holds: "The only way you get compromise sometimes is by stopping the trains and making people listen."[67]

Holds have become so common for presidential nominations that a Democratic leader said jokingly that nominees should feel lonely if they're not subjected to a hold.

> You know, who's your holder? That seems to be the question of every nominee. It's almost a status symbol among senators. "I have no holds. I'm going to have to pick out a nominee to get to know him or her a lot better." It works that way. . . . "Hello, I'm your holder. Come dance with me."[68]

UNANIMOUS CONSENT AGREEMENTS

If the Senate strictly observed every rule, it would become mired in a bog of parliamentary complications. Instead, the chamber frequently dispenses with its formal rules and follows negotiated agreements submitted to the Senate for its unanimous approval. The objectives are to expedite work in an institution known for extended debate, to impose a measure of predictability on floor action, and to minimize dilatory activities. Any senator can object to a unanimous consent agreement. As Majority Leader George Mitchell, D-Maine (1989–1995), once said,

> I regularly propound unanimous-consent requests on the floor, and . . . when Senators object we hear within seconds—within seconds. Frequently when I am in the middle of a sentence, the phone rings and staff comes running out to say, "Senator so and so objects."[69]

Senator Tom Coburn, R-Okla., for instance, informed the other 99 senators that he would object to any attempt to pass a measure increasing the debt ceiling by unanimous consent.[70]

GOP and Democratic leaders "hotline" requests for unanimous consent agreements to all senators' offices via special telephone lines. Senators are provided with a specific time frame in which to object; otherwise, the measure or matter will come to the floor and pass by unanimous consent. As Senator Jeff Sessions, R-Ala., explains:

> What is a hotline? In each Senate office there are three telephones with hotline buttons on them. Most evenings . . . these phones begin to ring. The calls are from the Republican and Democratic leaders to each of their Members, asking consent to pass this or that bill—not consider the bill or have debate on the bill but to pass it. Those calls will normally give a deadline. . . . If the staff miss the hotline, or do not know about it or were not around, the Senator is deemed to have consented to the passage of some bill.[71]

Unanimous consent agreements are often the product of intensive and extensive negotiations, with drafts of agreements (even letters between the two party leaders) exchanged on and off the floor among concerned senators; once an accord is reached among the key actors, each side will try to sell the unanimous consent agreement to their other colleagues. Sometimes unanimous consent agreements can take months to negotiate. A classic example occurred in the 109th Congress (2005–2007). The majority leader and minority leader negotiated for nearly a year trying to work out an accord to permit the Senate to vote on a controversial but bipartisan House-passed stem-cell bill authorizing federal funding for research. Many conservative senators opposed action on the legislation, viewing stem-cell research as akin to abortion; supporters urged action on the research bill because of its potential to produce cures for diseases such as Alzheimer's. (President Reagan suffered from the disease before his death in 2004, and his wife, Nancy, is a strong advocate of stem-cell research.)

Under an artful unanimous consent agreement negotiated by the two sides, a package of three stem-cell bills (the House-passed measure and two others) would be brought to the floor for a combined 12-hour debate equally divided between the two sides. No amendments would be permitted to any of the bills, and each must pass by 60 or more votes (obviating the threat of any filibuster). Minority Leader Reid asked the majority leader: "If any one of these three bills or all of them receive 60 votes, they would be passed." The response: "That is correct. Each of these bills will have a 60-vote threshold."[72] The unanimous consent agreement further provided that the Senate would not consider any amendment or bill relating to stem-cell research during the remainder of that Congress. In 2007, President George W. Bush vetoed a stem-cell research bill (S. 5), which the Democratically controlled 110th Congress could not override. President Bush imposed strict limits on stem-cell research because of ethical concerns of using federal funds to conduct research that destroys living embryos. In March 2009, President Obama signed an executive order reversing the previous administration's stem-cell restrictions by allowing federal funding of such research under new guidelines.[73]

Unanimous consent agreements also have a political dimension. The stem-cell unanimous consent agreement was a "win-win" for both parties. From a Republican perspective, despite the initial reluctance of many GOP senators to go along with the accord, they recognized that Democrats would offer stem-cell research amendments at every opportunity and force vulnerable Republicans in an election year to cast votes on an issue supported, according to polls, by the general public. And with three bills to be voted on, many Republicans who opposed destroying life in any form could vote for a bill "that promotes stem-cell research methods that don't destroy embryos."[74] From a Democratic perspective, proponents would likely win Senate passage of a bill that expands federal funding for stem-cell research. Senate Democrats "are convinced that a presidential veto of stem-cell research legislation would provide their candidates with an effective wedge issue to exploit in the mid-term elections this fall."[75]

The Senate, in brief, is fundamentally a unanimous consent institution. Every day the Senate is in session, there are scores of routine and complex consent requests. As one senator stated:

> The way the Senate conducts its business hour after hour, day after day, week after week, and year after year, is Senators voluntarily waive the rights which they possess under the rules. I would guess in the course of a typical week we probably enter into anywhere from 10 to 200 unanimous consent agreements, literally, where Senators by unanimous consent, with 100 Senators agreeing to yield some right that they may have—the right to debate, to offer amendments, the right to do this, that or the other thing—waive their rights so that the body may proceed in a way that seems expeditious.[76]

Once accepted, unanimous consent agreements are as binding on the Senate as any standing rule and may be set aside or modified only by unanimous consent, as underscored by this consequential example. In October 1999 the Senate agreed to a unanimous consent agreement that set a final date for a vote on the Comprehensive Nuclear Test Ban Treaty, a top priority of President Clinton. However, the administration quickly realized that it lacked the required two-thirds vote for approval and wanted to put off the vote. Intensive negotiations then began on how to gracefully avoid a showdown on the floor. But, as Connecticut Senator Joseph I. Lieberman pointed out, "the interesting procedural trick is that you need unanimous consent" to postpone the vote.[77] In the end, several conservative GOP senators refused to accept any change in the unanimous consent agreement, and the treaty went down to defeat. The vote "marked the first time an arms control agreement has been rejected by the Senate and only the sixth time in history that senators rejected any treaty."[78]

Overview

Two general types of unanimous consent permeate Senate operations: simple and complex. Senators can use both types to set aside the rules, precedents, and orders of the Senate. A single objection ("I object") blocks a unanimous consent request. The two types share a general purpose: to do things on the floor that could not be done without unanimous consent. However, the complex form has large procedural and policy implications.

Simple Unanimous Consent Agreements. Simple unanimous consent requests are made from the floor by any senator; these almost always deal with routine business or noncontroversial actions. For example, senators regularly ask and receive permission for staff members to be present on the floor during a debate ("I ask unanimous consent that my legislative fellow, Jane Doe, be granted floor privileges during consideration of the bill S. 1234"). Simple unanimous consent requests also may be submitted to rescind quorum calls, add senators as cosponsors of bills, insert material in the *Congressional Record,* or dispense with the reading of amendments. From its beginning, the Senate provided an environment conducive for simple unanimous consent. Its small size, few rules, and informality encouraged the rise of this practice. Several of the Senate's early rules even incorporated unanimous consent provisions to speed the Senate's routine business. For example, a Senate rule adopted on April 16, 1789, stated:

> Every bill shall receive three readings to its being passed; and the President [of the Senate] shall give notice at each, whether it be first, second, or third; which readings shall be on three different days, unless the Senate unanimously directs otherwise.

Complex Unanimous Consent Agreements. Complex unanimous consent agreements establish a tailor-made procedure for handling virtually anything considered on the Senate floor: bills, joint resolutions, simple resolutions, concurrent resolutions, amendments, nominations, conference reports, and treaties. Fundamentally, the Senate operates much differently with them than without them. As two Senate parliamentarians wrote: "Whereas the Senate Rules permit virtually unlimited debate, and very few restrictions on the right to offer amendments, these agreements usually limit time for debate and the right of Senators to offer amendments."[79] In effect, unanimous consent agreements are a form of voluntary cloture, as Table 6.2 shows. Senators generally accept the debate and amendment restrictions common to most unanimous consent agreements largely for

TABLE 6.2 Purposes and Features of a Complex Unanimous Consent Agreement

Broad Purposes	General Features
Impose time limits on debate	Is a negotiated contract accepted by all senators
Expedite scheduling the Senate's workload	Can be changed only by another unanimous consent agreement
Establish predictability and permit flexibility	Is comprehensive or partial in character
	Limits debate on measures and any motions related thereto
	Structures the amendment process
	May require the relevancy of amendments
	Waives points of order

two overlapping reasons: They facilitate the execution of the Senate's workload, and they serve the interests of individual senators because they make floor scheduling more predictable. In truth, so many variations of complex agreements exist today that they cannot be distinguished adequately.

Unanimous consent agreements are based on trust. Majority leaders request and receive unanimous consent to modify unanimous consent agreements if any senator believes he or she was misinformed or ill-informed about its terms. As a majority leader said on one occasion:

> The agreement was reached in good faith, but I am now advised that due to a misunderstanding and an inadvertent error, a Senator's right to make a point of order was not protected and included in the agreement. That was an honest mistake. And since becoming majority leader, I have taken the position that whenever an agreement is reached that includes a provision placing a Senator at a disadvantage as a result of an inadvertent error or mistake, either by a Senator or staff, that the disadvantage should be removed and the agreement modified to reflect the circumstances which should have existed when the agreement was adopted.[80]

Senator John Kerry, D-Mass. (now Secretary of State), also underscored the comity that suffuses these accords at a time when he might have won quick Senate approval of a unanimous consent request:

> Mr. President, I am going to be asking unanimous consent to proceed forward on the bill, but I am not going to do that until someone is here from the other side. And I know they are going to object.[81]

Unanimous consent agreements are proposed orally—usually by the majority leader—and often after protracted negotiations among other party and committee leaders and key senators.[82] Once agreed to, they are formally recorded in the *Congressional Record,* the daily *Calendar of Business,* and the *Senate Journal.* Such agreements may establish the order in which measures will be taken up, pinpoint when measures will reach the floor, and set the rules for debate, including time limitations and, frequently, a requirement that all amendments be relevant to the bill under consideration. For example, a unanimous consent agreement could specify that the amendment offered by Senator A will have a time limit of 20 minutes equally divided between the two opposing sides or that the amendment cosponsored by Senators B and C will have a time limit of 30 minutes equally divided and controlled in the usual form—that is, between the mover of the amendment and an opponent.

Party leaders are sometimes able to negotiate only partial, or incremental, unanimous consent agreements (covering parts but not the entire bill) before they call up the bill for floor action. Many piecemeal unanimous consent agreements—limiting debate on specific amendments or deciding when to call up a measure—are hammered out on the floor. Party leaders and floor managers take what they can get when they can get it and work from there to more embracing unanimous consent agreements. It is "so hard to get these agreements," said one majority leader. "I find it is somewhat better to do them a little bit at a time."[83] Or as a congressional scholar wrote: "A dozen or more complex agreements are no longer uncommon for complicated contentious measures."[84]

The primary objective of unanimous consent agreements is to limit the time needed to dispose of controversial issues in an institution noted for unlimited debate. These agreements, therefore, expedite action on legislation and structure floor deliberation. Numerous precedents have evolved over time to govern unanimous consent agreements. Typically, agreements impose time limitations on every debatable—and thus delaying—motion, including amendments and final passage, points of order, or appeals from the rulings of the presiding officer. These agreements, however, may allow an unlimited number of amendments to be offered, thereby permitting what a senator dubbed a "time agreement filibuster."

A unanimous consent agreement could ban or restrict the number and types of amendments or place time limits on them, preventing a time agreement filibuster. Thus, depending on what the circumstances warrant, party leaders can craft highly detailed, complex, and creative unanimous consent agreements to accommodate the diverse procedural contingencies that might arise on the floor. Their fundamental problem is winning consent from senators reluctant to waive any of their procedural prerogatives. As Senator Byrd once said: "The leader is the prisoner of Senators, and always has been. Any Senator can object to time agreements, they can make it difficult for every other Senator."[85]

Complex unanimous consent agreements usually specify which senators from opposing sides of the issue will control the time for debate on the bill and all amendments. Common, too, is the requirement that amendments be relevant. Senate rules do permit nongermane floor amendments, but unanimous consent agreements may limit their number or prohibit them to prevent extraneous issues from being taken up. Some agreements may also set the date and time for the vote on final passage of the measure. In an institution noted for procedural flexibility and sparseness, as compared with the House, unanimous consent agreements underscore the Senate's recognition that it needs to voluntarily impose additional rules on itself to expedite its business.

Complex unanimous consent agreements generally impose limitations on two of the most significant prerogatives associated with being a member of the Senate: the right of unlimited debate and the right to offer an unlimited number of floor amendments, even if they are nonrelevant. The irony of unanimous consent agreements is that, on the one hand, if they are accepted by everyone, the Senate can do almost anything it wants (one exception, for example, is that unanimous consent agreements cannot waive the constitutional requirement that veto overrides occur by recorded vote). On the other hand, if even one senator objects, then the Senate has difficulty accomplishing anything.

In today's Senate, whose paramount contextual features are individualism, ideological polarization, and partisanship, party leaders have to work harder to negotiate unanimous consent agreements that accommodate the partisan and individual interests of senators. Party leaders understand that the business that comes before the Senate attracts varying degrees of interest and support from lawmakers. This situation creates opportunities for bargaining when fashioning unanimous consent agreements. Senators, for instance, may make it clear to party leaders that their consent to a unanimous consent agreement hinges on whether they receive expeditious floor action on another measure or nomination.

Senate Leadership and Unanimous Consent Agreements

The majority leader generally has an important scheduling ally in the minority leader. In contrast to the House, where scheduling is the sole prerogative of the majority leadership, Senate scheduling traditionally involves the leaders of both parties. The Senate system derives not merely from equity but also from necessity, because Senate rules confer on each individual member formidable power to frustrate the legislative process, including the right to object to any unanimous consent request. The majority and minority leaders constantly consult with each other and with their top aides, other senators, executive officials, lobbyists, and key staff members on legislative scheduling.

Since the post–World War II period, all party leaders have relied extensively on unanimous consent agreements to process the Senate's workload. During the majority leadership of Lyndon B. Johnson (1955–1961), these agreements were often comprehensive in scope, identifying, for example, when a measure was to be taken up, when it was to be voted on for final passage, and everything in between. Two subsequent majority leaders— Democrats Mike Mansfield of Montana, who held the post longer than any other senator (1961–1977), and Robert Byrd (1977–1981; 1987–1989)— were largely responsible for refining and extending the use of unanimous consent agreements. During their tenure, unanimous consent agreements became more complicated and governed floor action on a larger number of measures.

The personal style of other majority leaders and the political context in which they served (the size of the majority party, for example, or whether their party occupied the White House) also influenced how they employed unanimous consent agreements. For example, Howard H. Baker Jr., R-Tenn., majority leader from 1981 to 1985, brought measures to the floor without first obtaining comprehensive agreements. With the Senate and White House in GOP hands, the Democrats were reluctant to enter into broad agreements restricting their floor options because they had little idea what amendments might surface. Thus, narrower agreements were often negotiated on the floor, typically regulating the consideration of a particular amendment or series of amendments.

Today, in a period of sharp partisanship, unanimous consent agreements tend to be quite specific in terms of their purposes, such as limiting the number of amendments, including nonrelevant amendments, and specifying how long each amendment and the bill itself can be debated. In the view of a knowledgeable Senate aide, unanimous consent agreements increasingly lean toward the comprehensive rather than the incremental. Comprehensive unanimous consent agreements "are now used to manage the decision-making process on the Senate floor to an unprecedented degree."[86]

Reaching Agreement

The Senate's tradition of individual and minority rights means that strategic considerations often permeate the use and shape of unanimous consent agreements. Three examples highlight their use, for example, as devices to force action on measures and to achieve partisan and substantive purposes. In today's polarized Senate, partisan clashes over unanimous consent agreements routinely occur over how many amendments may be offered, whether nonrelevant amendments may be offered, and the vote required to enact amendments or the bill itself. In today's polarized Senate, it is common for unanimous consent agreements to impose a 60-vote requirement for adoption of amendments and passage of the bill, as or if amended.

A Classic Action-Forcing Unanimous Consent Agreement. Two weeks prior to the scheduled mid-August 1986 recess of the Senate, Majority Leader Robert Dole, R-Kans., circulated a unanimous consent agreement outlining how he planned to juggle floor action on four major measures: a Defense Department authorization bill, a debt ceiling extension measure, economic sanctions against South Africa, and aid to the contras (a paramilitary group) in Central America. The controversy between the parties involved the last two bills. Broad bipartisan support existed for economic sanctions against South Africa because of its policy of apartheid (racial separation), with Democrats urging a final vote by Friday, August 15. Aid to the contras, a priority of the Reagan Administration, attracted only a bare majority of the Senate, almost all from GOP ranks.

After lengthy negotiations with Minority Leader Byrd and other senators, a unanimous consent agreement was reached that took Majority Leader Dole nearly an hour to read and that consumed three pages of the *Congressional Record*.[87] In fact, the agreement was "so complicated that senators admitted they could not understand it even after two or three readings."[88] Strategically, Dole's unanimous consent agreement forged an interdependent link between the two bills.

The unanimous consent agreement required the Senate to consider the contra aid package before South Africa sanctions. At Dole's insistence, a key clause had been added to the unanimous consent agreement. As Dole explained the provision, "unless cloture is invoked on both items, meaning

South Africa and Contra aid, then this agreement is null and void, with the proviso . . . that as much of the August recess, as necessary, be null and void in order to complete action" on both proposals.[89] Not only did Dole threaten to delay the Senate's long-awaited August recess if these two issues were not resolved, but he also effectively choked off any Democratic incentive to filibuster the contra aid package. Furthermore, the agreement headed off dilatory action by senatorial opponents of South Africa sanctions.

On August 13, the Senate invoked cloture on both measures, thus ensuring a final vote on each bill. Under the unanimous consent agreement, a cloture vote was to be taken first on contra aid. It failed on a 59-to-40 vote (60 votes are needed). The unanimous consent agreement then required a cloture vote on sanctions against South Africa. Despite the Reagan Administration's opposition to sanctions, cloture was overwhelmingly approved 89 to 11. Then another cloture attempt occurred on contra aid, because the unanimous consent agreement explicitly required cloture to be invoked on both measures. On the second attempt, cloture was invoked (62–37).

Partisan Disagreements: Number and Character of Amendments. Both parties and individual senators assess the political and policy costs and benefits of going along with a unanimous consent agreement. Position taking, electoral advantage, member preferences, media coverage, and partisan advantage are among the many factors that influence Senate acceptance of these compacts. The controversy associated with a measure may have little or no bearing on when or whether an accord is reached.

Majority Leader Reid and Minority Leader McConnell have had their disputes over unanimous consent agreements, as these two examples illustrate. Both address a common occurrence: disputes over the number and type of amendments that may be offered to legislation. On a measure assisting workers, homeowners, and businesses (H.R. 3548) that enjoyed wide support in both parties, a dispute occurred over the number and type of amendments that each side could offer to the bill. Majority Leader Reid wanted to limit amendments to six in his unanimous consent request. McConnell preferred eight, including several politically charged proposals. Reid objected. He said with respect to one of the GOP-suggested amendments: "I see no reason that we have to do immigration on this bill; that is what E-Verify is about." Senator McConnell disagreed and again requested unanimous consent to proceed to the bill with only eight amendments made in order. Senator Reid objected and expressed his frustration at not being able to move legislation extending unemployment benefits. Senator McConnell replied, "We have two competing consent agreements: one with six amendments and one with eight. Either one would move the process along." Senator Reid responded that "these are not competing unanimous consent agreements." He then asked unanimous consent to "pass H.R. 3548 with no amendments." Senator McConnell objected, noting that "cutting people off and not allowing any amendments at all is not an acceptable approach."[90] In the end, Senator Reid brought the bill to the floor without a unanimous consent agreement. Cloture was easily invoked on both the motion to proceed to consider H.R. 3548 and on the bill itself, which passed the Senate (98–0), the House (403–12), and was signed into law (P.L. 111-92).

On a bill (S. 1789) to reform the postal system, controversy also erupted over the number and type of amendments that senators could offer. Senator Reid asked unanimous consent that only relevant amendments be offered to the postal reform measure. Senator Rand Paul, R-Ky., objected. He wanted a vote on his amendment to reduce aid to Egypt by $2 billion. Senator Reid remarked that he was sympathetic to Senator Paul's amendment but underscored the necessity and urgency of acting on postal reform. He restated his unanimous consent request. Senator Paul again objected. Reid responded by mentioning how important it was to deal with the approaching bankruptcy of the Postal Service, that a "standard of relevance merely asks that we stay on the subject," and that Paul's action left Reid with "no alternative but to fill the amendment tree," thus blocking all amendments until it might be possible to reach an accord how to proceed on S. 1789.[91] (Chapter 7 discusses "filling the amendment tree.")

Other senators joined the debate. Senator Lamar Alexander, R-Tenn., urged Reid to respect Senator Paul's right to offer his Egypt amendment and to work with Senator McConnell to produce a unanimous consent agreement that would allow relevant amendments. Other members made similar arguments in a discussion that went on for several hours. Senator Lieberman, the floor manager of the postal reform bill, informed the members: "It is my understanding that both caucuses now are hotlining a request to Senate offices that if Senators have an amendment they want to introduce on this postal reform bill, to let their respective cloakrooms know so that we can see what the universe is and then when we can see if we can work on an agreement" that improves the chances that we can enact the bill.[92]

The next day, April 18, 2012, Senator Reid stated that it is "a shame" that the Senate could not move forward on postal reform. Majority Whip Durbin stressed that the postal reform bill should not be used to debate foreign aid to Egypt. GOP Senator Jerry Moran of Kansas urged the party leaders and all senators to reach a unanimous consent agreement on the postal bill but also to protect the right of Senator Paul and other members to offer their amendments. Peer pressure, the importance of the bill, a deadline of mid-May when the Postal Service planned to close thousands of post offices to save money, and intensive private negotiations led Senator Reid to state on April 19 that the two parties were close to an agreement. "The main issue now is whether there will be a 50-vote hurdle or 60-vote hurdle" to adopt amendments and the bill itself.[93]

Later that day, Senator Reid propounded a unanimous consent agreement that was accepted by the Senate. The two leaders and all senators, said Reid, "decided we were going to have an amendment process. Maybe it is not as far as everyone wants to go, but it is a step in the right direction" with a broad relevance standard for amendments. Thirty-nine amendments were made in order, including seven by Senator Paul (but not his Egypt amendment), with all roll-call votes on amendments and the bill, as amended, subject to an affirmative 60-vote threshold for adoption.[94] Senator Paul did ask unanimous consent to call up his Egypt amendment. Floor manager Lieberman objected, stating: "It is irrelevant to the subject matter of the Postal Service."[95] The Senate passed the postal bill by a 62-to-37 vote.[96]

In short, scheduling involves numerous considerations. Party leaders must balance their interest in planning the Senate's business on a daily, weekly, and annual basis with (1) the needs of committees, which require concentrated periods of time, particularly early in the session, to process legislation assigned to them; (2) the needs of senators, who prefer some degree of predictability and certainty so they can schedule their time most efficiently; and (3) the needs of their party, which means considering an agenda that facilitates their continued majority status. Moreover, they must respond to demands and requests of presidents, individual senators, outside events, and the special interests. These various imperatives mean that no matter how carefully Senate leaders plan the legislative agenda—the times and dates measures will be scheduled, and in what order they will be considered on the floor—they still must juggle bills to satisfy senators, take account of external events and political circumstances, and, where possible, influence policy outcomes in the interests of their own party.

THE TRACK SYSTEM

Another device used at times for scheduling purposes is the track system. The track system was instituted in the early 1970s by Majority Leader Mike Mansfield, D-Mont., the longest serving majority leader ever (1961–1977), with the concurrence of the minority leadership and other senators. It permits the Senate to have several pieces of legislation pending on the floor simultaneously by designating specific periods during the day when each proposal will be considered. The system is particularly beneficial when many important bills are awaiting floor action or when a protracted floor debate is taking place on a bill.

Democratic Senator Alan Cranston, Calif. (1969–1993), who served as his party's whip, found that with the two-track system the Senate could "continue to work on all other legislation on one 'track' while a filibuster against a particular piece of legislation is . . . in progress on the other 'track.'"[97] Dual tracking aims to facilitate consideration of "must-do" legislation. A majority leader said that he preferred to move to a dual-track process "that will divide the chamber's daily sessions between appropriations bills and reauthorizations."[98] An acting Democratic leader announced:

> Madam President, we are trying something in the Senate that we have tried on a number of other occasions. . . . We are going to do two bills at one time. It is dual tracking. We are going to take up the Interior Appropriations bill in the morning and go until 12 noon on that legislation. At 12 o'clock, we will have an hour of morning business, and then we will go back to the Homeland Security bill. We will do the same thing on Thursday.[99]

Majority Leader Reid and Minority Leader McConnell discussed dual tracking, moving "other bills while health care soaks up the lion's share of floor time."[100] Reid also stated that he was planning a two-track strategy to allow the Senate to daily debate an omnibus appropriations bill as well as a nuclear arms treaty with Russia.[101]

Use of the track system is implemented by the majority leader after obtaining the unanimous consent of the Senate. Or the different tracks can be put into place by agreement between the majority leader and the minority leader. Infrequently, the Senate may operate on triple or quadruple tracks.

The use of unanimous consent agreements and the track system imposes a measure of discipline on the Senate. Formerly, senators could arrive in the midst of a debate on a banking bill, for example, obtain recognition from the chair, and launch into a lengthy discussion of the wheat harvest prospects. Today, complex agreements and the track system prevent that from happening. Now, senators generally know what measure will be considered on a specific day and at what time, when they are scheduled to speak on that bill, and how long they will have the floor.

SCHEDULING PROCEDURES COMPARED

The Senate has nothing that compares with the scheduling function of the House Rules Committee.[102] That panel regulates the flow of major bills to the floor, specifies the time for general debate, stipulates whether amendments can be offered, and decides if points of order are to be waived. The legislative route in the House is clearly marked by firm rules and precedents, but that is not so in the Senate. "Rules are never observed in this body," a president pro tempore observed long ago in an overstatement. "They are only made to be broken. We are a law unto ourselves, and it is entirely immaterial in my judgment whether we have a code of rules or not."[103]

Nonetheless, the Senate's unanimous consent agreements and the special rules drafted by the Rules Committee are similar in several respects, as Table 6.3 shows. Each waives the rules of the respective chamber to permit timely consideration of important measures and amendments. Each must be approved by the members—in the Senate by unanimous consent of all senators and in the House by majority vote of the representatives. Each

TABLE 6.3   Comparison of the House Special Rule and Senate Unanimous
Consent Agreement

House Special Rule	Senate Unanimous Consent Agreement
Specifies time for general debate	May specify time for debating the bill and amendments offered to the bill
Permits or prohibits amendments	Often restricts the offering of nonrelevant amendments
Formulated by Rules Committee in public session	Formulated by party leaders informally in private sessions; also on the Senate floor
Approved by majority vote of the House	Agreed to by unanimous consent of senators
Adoption generally results in immediate floor action on the bill	Adoption is sometimes aimed toward prospective floor action
Covers many aspects of floor procedure, including final passage of legislation	Geared primarily to debate and amendment restrictions and to limits on other debatable motions
Does not specify date and exact time for vote on final passage	May set date and exact time for vote on final passage, which could include a 60-vote adoption requirement
Effect is to waive House rules	Effect is to waive Senate rules

effectively sets the conditions for debate on the legislation in question and on all proposed amendments. And special rules and unanimous consent agreements are formulated with the involvement of party leaders, although such participation in the House is generally limited to the majority party.

Among the more important differences between special rules and unanimous consent agreements are that rules are considered in public session by a standing committee, whereas unanimous consent agreements are often negotiated privately by senators and staff aides. Measures given a rule in the House are commonly taken up almost immediately, but unanimous consent agreements sometimes involve prospective action on bills.

The amendment process in each house also makes for important differences. Procedural resolutions from the Rules Committee may limit the number of permissible amendments or prohibit them altogether. Senate unanimous consent agreements, except those prohibiting nonrelevant amendments, do not usually limit or forbid floor amendments. Senate practices regard an amendment as relevant—even when it is not relevant to a bill—if it is specifically enumerated in the unanimous consent agreement.

Finally, procedural resolutions from the Rules Committee specify almost every significant floor procedure that will affect consideration of the bill. Complex agreements in the Senate focus on two points in particular: (1) setting limits on the debate time to be allowed for amendments, motions, points of order, and appeals from the rulings of the chair, and (2) structuring the amendment process. In general, procedural experimentation is easier to accomplish in the smaller Senate than in the 435-member House.

NOTES

1. Adam Graham-Silverman, "Senators Leave Piles of Work to Take the Pulse Back Home," *CQ Today*, October 6, 2003, 6.
2. *Congressional Record*, November 30, 2011, S8012.
3. Mark Preston, "Lott Wants Five-Day Workweek," *Roll Call*, May 11, 2000, 1.
4. *Congressional Record*, December 9, 1987, S17474.
5. Rachel Leven, "In Senate, Thursday is the New Friday," *The Hill*, November 17, 2011, 1.
6. Ibid., July 20, 1990, S10183.
7. Ibid., February 26, 2008, S1149.
8. Ibid., January 22, 2008, S58.
9. Helen Dewar, "Senate Battle on Child Health Care Symbolizes Kennedy-Lott Power Struggle," *Washington Post*, May 23, 1997, A9.
10. Grete Wodele, "Partisan Rhetoric Rises as Senate Nears Debt Limit Vote," *CongressDailyPM*, March 10, 2006, 4. See also Walter Alarkon, "Senate Faces Vote to Raise Debt Ceiling Beyond $12 Trillion," *The Hill*, September 8, 2009, 13.
11. Norman Ornstein, "Let the End Games Begin," *Roll Call*, September 12, 1994, A23.
12. Carl Hulse, "With Flurry of Deals, and Eye on Calendar, Congress Clears Decks," *New York Times*, June 21, 2008, A11.
13. Major Garrett, "Leading From Behind," *National Journal*, June 11, 2011, 45.
14. Susan Ferrechio, "Senate Democrats Seek Political Edge With Tax Vote," *The Examiner*, April 9, 2012, 16.
15. Dan Friedman, "Schumer's Strategy," *National Journal*, November 5, 2011, 44.
16. Humberto Sanchez, "Political Upside to Stalled Student Loan Bill," *Roll Call*, May 9, 2012, 6.
17. *Congressional Record*, October 15, 2007, S12853.
18. David Nakamura, "Obama Pushes Congress to Back Five-Point 'To-Do List,'" *Washington Post*, May 9, 2012, A3.
19. Steven T. Dennis and Meredith Shiner, "Hoagies Only Topic of Agreement at 'Summit,'" *Roll Call*, May 17, 2012, 1.
20. Steven T. Dennis, "New Obama Jobs Plan Gets Same GOP Rebukes," *Roll Call*, May 9, 2012, 4.
21. Dan Friedman, "Reid's New Electoral Strategy," *National Journal*, January 14, 2012, 32.
22. See *Congressional Record*, May 8, 2012, S2934, and May 10, 2012, S3052.
23. Manu Raju, "GOP Unity Elusive as Hill Preps Agenda," *Politico*, March 27, 2012, 15.
24. Erin Billings, "Bush Puts Focus on Nominees," *Roll Call*, May 30, 2006, 17.

25. *Congressional Record,* November 16, 2007, S14609.
26. Rosalind S. Helderman, "Two Senators, 26 Seconds: FAA Is Back in Business," *Washington Post,* August 6, 2011, A3.
27. *Congressional Record,* December 8, 2011, S8422.
28. Ben Weyl, "GOP's Procedural Blockade," *CQ Weekly,* September 12, 2011, 1846.
29. Office of Legal Counsel, *Lawfulness of Recess Appointments During a Recess of the Senate Notwithstanding Periodic Pro Forma Sessions,* January 6, 2012, 22.
30. *Congressional Record,* July 26, 1989, S8870.
31. Shailagh Murray, "On Daschle's Agenda: Getting the Senate to Show Up," *Wall Street Journal,* April 12, 2002, A4.
32. *Congressional Record,* June 4, 2009, S6136.
33. "Weekend Work a Record," *CQ Weekly,* December 28, 2009, 2927.
34. See Richard S. Beth, Valerie Heitshusen, Bill Heniff Jr., and Elizabeth Rybicki, "Leadership Management Tools in the U.S. Senate" (paper prepared for delivery at the annual meeting of the American Political Science Association, Toronto, Canada, September 3–6, 2009). This material was developed by Dr. Beth.
35. *Congressional Record,* November 17, 1989, S15948.
36. *Congressional Record,* October 30, 2007, S13531.
37. *New York Times,* May 21, 1987, B10.
38. David M. Herszenhorn, "Threat and Parry on the Senate Floor," *New York Times,* November 22, 2009, E3.
39. *Congressional Record,* March 21, 1980, S2789. Senator Byrd, who wrote a multivolume Senate history, is widely regarded as the premier authority on the chamber's rules and precedents.
40. Each calendar is printed separately. There are also separate executive and legislative journals. The General Orders Calendar is found in the Senate's Calendar of Business, which is printed each day the Senate is in session. Measures on the calendar are assigned a calendar order number. The Senate's Executive Calendar appears whenever there is executive business.
41. Emily Cadel, "Senate Panel Turns to Law of the Sea Treaty," *CQ Today,* May 17, 2012, 8.
42. *Congressional Record,* January 26, 1973, 2301. According to Senate rules, "Any rule may be suspended without advance notice by unanimous consent of the Senate."
43. *Congressional Record,* August 5, 1987, S11293.
44. Ibid., April 8, 1981, S3618.
45. Ibid., January 4, 1995, S39.
46. Ibid., December 21, 2009, S13669.
47. *CQ Daily Monitor,* June 10, 1996, 5.
48. *Congressional Record,* December 10, 1982, S14345.
49. Ibid., October 14, 1987, S14197.
50. Ibid., January 9, 1995, S646; January 11, 1995, S783.
51. Ibid., January 12, 1995, S858–S859.
52. Edwin Chen and Melissa Healy, "Byrd Dogs Republicans With Stall on GOP Proposals," *Los Angeles Times,* January 18, 1995, A5.
53. David Hosansky, "Chipping Away at Opposition, Senate Passes Mandates Bill," *Congressional Quarterly Weekly Report,* January 28, 1995, 276.

54. *Congressional Record*, April 17, 2002, S2850.
55. Lawrence Evans, testimony before the Senate Committee on Rules and Administration, June 17, 2003, 3. Evans is a professor of political science at the College of William and Mary.
56. Helen Dewar, "For Senators, Soul-Searching About the Rules," *Washington Post*, June 23, 2003, A19.
57. Scholarly interest in holds seems to be on the increase. See C. Lawrence Evans, Daniel Lipinski, and Keith Larson, "The Senate Hold: Preliminary Evidence From the Baker Years" (paper presented at the annual meeting of the Midwest Political Science Association, Chicago, April 2003), and the June 17, 2003, testimony of several political scientists and others before the Senate Rules and Administration Committee. The panel was considering a resolution (S. Res. 151) to eliminate secret holds.
58. *Congressional Record*, February 24, 1986, S1512.
59. *CQ's Daily Monitor*, October 4, 1994, 5. For an informative study of holds, see Toby McIntosh, "Senate 'Holds' System Developing as Sophisticated Tactic for Leverage, Delay," *Daily Report for Executives* (No. 165), Bureau of National Affairs, August 26, 1991, C1–C5.
60. *Congress DailyAM*, October 5, 1994, 5.
61. *Congressional Record*, December 5, 1985, S16916.
62. David Ingram, "Six Months and Waiting for Johnsen," *Legal Times*, July 13, 2009, 1.
63. Dan Friedman, "Secret Holds Are Dead; Long Live Secret Holds," *NationalJournal.com*, March 31, 2011, online version.
64. Ibid.
65. Meredith Shiner and Humberto Sanchez, "Senators Shy From Obama Filibuster Reform," *Roll Call*, January 26, 2012, 10.
66. Lynn Garner, "Sen. Kyl Places Hold on Nominees to Force Hearing on Land Exchange," *Daily Report for Executives*, May 14, 2009, A-32.
67. Charles Hurt, "Resolution Seeks to End Holds on Bills," *Washington Times*, June 18, 2003, A5.
68. Lawrence Goodrich, "Congressional Journal," *Christian Science Monitor*, November 28, 1997, 4.
69. *Congressional Record*, August 6, 1992, S11692.
70. Ibid., September 20, 2007, S11777.
71. Ibid., March 28, 2006, S2454. Senators sometimes object to clearing legislation by use of the hotline. For example, Senator Tom Coburn, R-Okla., said: "The problem with hotlining bills is they don't get due deliberation. . . . Most of the Senate had never read the bills, didn't know what was in the bills." *Congressional Record*, November 15, 2007, S14451. See John Stanton, "Without Time for Review, Coburn Will Block Bills," *Roll Call*, December 6, 2007, 3.
72. *Congressional Record*, June 29, 2006, S7170.
73. See Rob Stein, "Obama's Order on Stem Cells Leaves Key Questions to NIH," *Washington Post*, March 10, 2009, A1.
74. Sarah Lueck, "Amid Veto Threat, Senate Poised to Weigh Trio of Stem-Cell Bills," *Wall Street Journal*, July 12, 2006, A4.
75. Greta Wodele, "Dems See Political Gain in Stem-Cell Veto," *CongressDailyAM*, July 12, 2006, 1.
76. *Congressional Record*, September 25, 1990, S13803.

77. CQ *Daily Monitor*, October 13, 1999, 2.

78. Ibid., October 14, 1999, 5.

79. Floyd Riddick and Alan Frumin, *Senate Procedure: Precedents and Practices* (Washington, DC: Government Printing Office, 1992), 1311.

80. *Congressional Record*, February 4, 1992, S872.

81. Ibid., September 19, 2002, S8899.

82. Unlike simple requests, which are formulated orally, complex unanimous consent agreements are formalized in writing and easily reported to senators by means of the *Congressional Record*, the front page of the daily Calendar of Business, and in party whip notices.

83. *Congressional Record*, September 13, 1994, S12793.

84. Steven S. Smith, *Call to Order* (Washington, DC: Brookings, 1989), 115.

85. *Congressional Record*, June 1, 1989, S5939.

86. James Wallner, "The Death of Deliberation: Party and Procedure in the Modern United States Senate," in Jacob Strauss, ed., *Party and Procedure in the United States Congress* (Lanham, Md.: Rowman & Littlefield, 2012), 155. For an example of a detailed unanimous consent agreement, see *Congressional Record*, February 17, 2011, S824–S825.

87. *Congressional Record*, August 9, 1986, S10952–S10955.

88. John Felton, "Senate's Climate of Partisanship Yields an Agreement of Unusual Complexity," *Congressional Quarterly Weekly Report*, August 16, 1986, 1878.

89. *Congressional Record*, August 9, 1986, S10952.

90. See Ibid., October 26, 2009, S10712–S10713.

91. Ibid., April 17, 2012, S2356–2357.

92. Ibid., S2382.

93. Ibid., April 19, 2012, S2535.

94. Ibid., S2538.

95. Ibid., April 25, 2012, S2684.

96. Ron Nion, "Senate Passes Plan to Give Postal Service Fiscal Relief," *New York Times*, April 26, 2012, A13.

97. *Congressional Record*, January 21, 1975, 928.

98. Ethan Wallison, "Frist Plans Dual Track," *Roll Call*, May 1, 2003, 1.

99. *Congressional Record*, September 3, 2002, S8138.

100. Edward Epstein and Alan K. Ota, "Workload, Senate Republicans Complicate Democrats' Wish List," *CQ Today*, December 1, 2009, 6.

101. Emily Cadel, "White House, Democrats Still Have New START on Their Shopping Lists," *CQ Today*, December 13, 2010, 3.

102. The Senate Rules and Administration Committee has jurisdiction over internal Senate matters but is not involved in scheduling bills for floor debate.

103. *Congressional Record*, December 18, 1876, 266.

CHAPTER 7

Senate Floor Procedure

A VISITOR WHO moves from the House gallery to the Senate gallery is struck immediately by the contrast in atmosphere. The Senate chamber is more sedate, it is quieter, and business is conducted at a more relaxed pace. The chamber is smaller and more intimate. Given their higher visibility and fewer numbers, senators are more easily recognizable than their House counterparts. Typically, only a handful of senators are present on the floor. The remainder are busy in committee meetings or occupied with constituent or other legislative business. All senators, however, generally arrive on the floor quickly in response to buzzers announcing roll-call votes or quorum calls.

The Senate chamber is ringed by an upper level of galleries for the press, visitors, and dignitaries. Figure 7.1 shows a map of the Senate floor with desks arranged in four semicircular tiers. Each of the 100 senators has an assigned desk, complete with snuffbox and open inkwell. A broad aisle separates the Republicans, sitting on the right (facing the podium), from the Democrats, on the left. Depending on the makeup of the Senate, more seats may be on one side than the other. The Senate has no electronic voting machines; each senator responds aloud as his or her name is reached during a roll call. Both the Senate and the House employ microphones on the floor, but, unlike representatives, each senator has a microphone.

On the raised platform, the constitutional president of the Senate—the vice president of the United States—presides on expected close votes crucial to administration policy. He may vote only to break a tie. The record is held by Vice President John Adams (1789–1797), who cast 29 tie-breaking votes.[1] The vice president usually does not preside, however.[2] The Constitution provides for a Senate president pro tempore, elected by that body, to preside in the vice president's absence. (Sometimes, the Senate establishes the post of deputy president pro tempore as well.) The president pro tem by modern practice is the most senior senator of the majority party. (In the 113th Congress, Senator Patrick Leahy, D-Vt., is the president pro tempore.) In practice, each day's session is chaired by several temporary presiding officers—often freshman majority-party senators chosen by the president pro tem to serve on a rotating basis for about an hour or so.[3]

Neither the president pro tem nor the presiding officer is analogous to the Speaker of the House, in part because neither possesses the political resources to exert such wide-ranging influence in the Senate. (One consequence is that rulings of the presiding officer occasionally are appealed and *overturned*

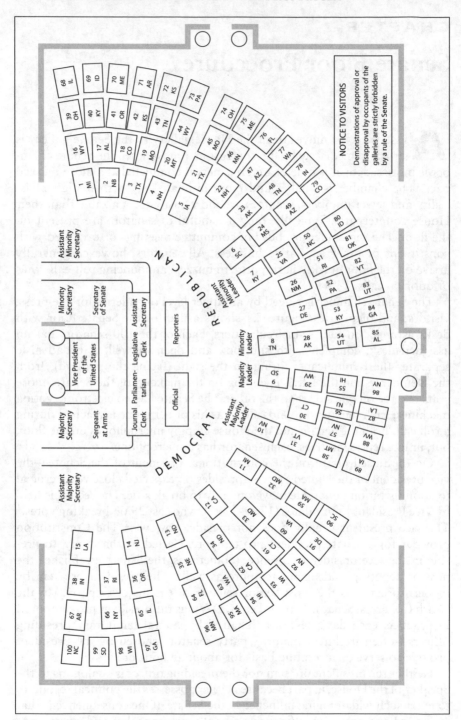

Figure 7.1 Senate Floor Plan and Seating Chart

by the Senate; in the House, as noted in Chapter 4, appeals have become a partisan tactic, but the Speaker's rulings are virtually never overturned.) The president pro tempore "has never been able to establish his authority as a party leader to the extent of the Majority Leader," said Senator Byrd, the longest serving House or Senate member in history. (Byrd served as majority leader 1977–1981 and 1987–1989. He was minority leader 1981–1987. Byrd also wrote a four-volume history of the Senate.) "This is partly the result of the President pro tempore's irregular appointments and uncertain tenure over the years while serving in the absence of the Vice President."[4]

The principal elective leaders of the Senate are to be found at the two front desks on the center aisle, those assigned to the majority and minority leaders. Next to the majority leader and next to the minority leader sit the party whips, second in command in the Senate party hierarchy. These party leaders, or their designees, customarily remain near or on the floor at all times to protect their party's interests.

The leadership and individual senators are in frequent contact. To a much greater extent than in the House, each member has the power to influence the course of the legislative process on a daily basis. Any senator can disrupt the Senate's consideration of a bill more easily and with more telling effect than any one representative in the House. That this does not always occur, especially in a Senate that today is often filled with partisan conflicts, is a tribute to the operation of the Senate's system of unanimous consent, the skill of party leaders, and the long tradition of trust, colleagues working together, and reciprocal courtesy among members, which has survived periodic lapses into hard-line partisanship and confrontation.

LEGISLATIVE AND CALENDAR DAYS

The Senate, unlike the House, regularly distinguishes between a calendar day and a legislative day.[5] "Calendar day" is the commonly understood notion of what constitutes a day—the 24-hour period of time. "Legislative day" refers to the period when the Senate convenes after an adjournment and ends when it next adjourns. Recesses and adjournments determine the sequence of legislative days and calendar days. If the Senate adjourns at the end of a daily session, the legislative day ends with that calendar day. If, however, it chooses to recess, the legislative day is carried over to the next calendar day. For example, if the Senate recesses on May 3 and continues that practice for several calendar days, the legislative day remains May 3 even if the calendar day is May 21. However, once the Senate adjourns after a series of recesses, the legislative day and calendar day become the same.

The distinction between the types of days is important because many of the Senate's rules are tied to the legislative day. For example, according to Senate precedents, the "word 'day,' as used in the rules, unless it is specified as a calendar day, is construed to mean a legislative day."[6] The decision to adjourn or recess is made either by **unanimous consent** (the usual way) or by majority vote (rare) on a motion made by the majority leader. The majority leader's decision to ask for a recess or an adjournment can influence whether legislation comes before the Senate (see "Placing Measures on the Calendar" later in this chapter). Senate rules prescribe a daily order of business, but it may be followed only when the Senate begins a new legislative day.

DAILY ORDER OF BUSINESS

Under resolutions adopted at the start of each Congress, the Senate generally convenes each day at noon. On the opening day of the 113th Congress, for example, the Senate adopted S. Res. 3, which stated: "Resolved, That the daily meeting of the Senate be 12 o'clock meridian unless otherwise ordered." The leadership, by a unanimous consent request or motion, may modify the time on a day-to-day basis to stay abreast of the Senate's workload. An average day in the Senate commonly follows this pattern of activities.

- *The Call to Order*, as in the House, is followed by the *Prayer* and then the *Pledge of Allegiance*.
- *Presiding officer*. A letter from the president pro tempore is read to the Senate appointing a majority party member to perform the duties of the Chair. (The pro tempore seldom presides, as is the case with the president of the Senate, the vice president of the United States.)
- *Leader time*. By standing order, 10 minutes are reserved each session day to the majority leader and the minority leader. The majority leader, for example, might review the schedule for the day or make a statement about a substantive matter. If neither leader wants to use his guaranteed time during these opening proceedings, it is reserved to each for use later that day.
- *Morning business*. It is usual for each session day to have "morning business" (more on this below). This is a period of time where senators, by unanimous consent, can make brief statements on any matter.
- *New or unfinished business*. The majority leader might bring new business before the Senate through use of the two fundamental methods for this purpose: requesting unanimous consent ("I ask unanimous consent to call up S. 1234") or making a motion ("I move to call up S. 1234"). The Senate, too, might resume consideration of unfinished business from the previous session day.

Like the House, the Senate must keep and approve a Journal of the previous day's activities. The Journal usually is "approved to date" by unanimous consent when the Senate adjourns or recesses at the end of each day. Any senator could object to the Journal's approval and propose amendments to it, but this is an exceedingly rare occurrence. (In 1986, the Senate amended its rules to permit a nondebatable motion for the Journal's approval. Previously, reading the Journal was sometimes used as a filibustering device.)

At the start of a new legislative day, the first 2 hours of Senate activity are traditionally called the morning hour—even if this period occurs in the afternoon. (The morning hour is rarely invoked, and recent Senates have not observed it, typically deeming this period expired by unanimous consent.) Morning business occurs by unanimous consent nearly every day the Senate is in session. Technically, morning business is conducted during the morning hour; it includes the receipt of messages, reports, and communications from the president, the House, and heads of executive branch departments. Bills and resolutions are introduced and referred to committee, committee reports filed, statements inserted in the *Congressional Record,* and brief speeches delivered. As Senator Robert C. Byrd, D-W.Va., summarized:

> "Morning business" and the "morning hour" do not mean the same. The morning hour is the first two hours after the Senate convenes following an adjournment. Morning business is that period within the morning hour during which senators may introduce resolutions, bills, petitions, or memorials; committees may report matters, and certain matters come over from the previous day.[7]

Senators may speak during morning business only by unanimous consent, which is why the majority leader usually receives unanimous consent that a period be set aside for the transaction of routine morning business and that each senator be allowed to speak therein for 5, 10, or more minutes. "One of the great opportunities that comes with having been elected a Member of the U.S. Senate is to participate . . . in what we call here morning business," said Connecticut Senator Joseph I. Lieberman. "I have always seen [it] as the people's forum," he added, "an opportunity to speak on the events of the day, both public and, in some senses, those that are more personal."[8]

The leadership may restrict or change morning business by unanimous consent. (Sometimes, a single calendar day has several morning business periods or an entire day could be consumed by morning business.) Both parties are increasingly using morning business to highlight their partisan agenda and goals. Each party has their communications "war room" and rapid response team to refute partisan attacks.[9]

During the morning hour, a nondebatable motion to proceed to any item on the legislative calendar also is in order. Rarely is such a motion made during this period. However, if the Senate is in a procedural "hardball" situation, the majority leader may adjourn, rather than recess, the Senate, so he can employ the rarely used morning hour to call up a measure or matter and obviate at least one filibuster—on the motion to proceed to a measure. Even if the majority leader recessed the day before, when the Senate next convened he could adjourn the Senate for 1 minute, create a new legislative day, and use morning hour to offer the nondebatable motion to take up a measure. (See Box 7.4 for changes to the motion to proceed.)

After these preliminaries, the Senate may proceed, as briefly noted earlier, to new or unfinished business—legislation pending from a previous day. If there is no unfinished business, the majority leader or the leader's designee requests unanimous consent or offers a motion to take up a new measure that the leadership, after consultation with the minority leader and other interested senators, has scheduled for floor action. This is a critical juncture in the proceedings, for opponents of the bill could employ dilatory tactics, such as a filibuster, to delay or prevent consideration of the legislation.

DEBATE IN THE MODERN SENATE

In the early Congresses, the Senate was characterized by protracted debates and great orators: by Daniel Webster, John C. Calhoun, and Stephen A. Douglas on slavery, and later by Henry Cabot Lodge and others on the League of Nations. Today, senators are so busy, and the legislative agenda so crowded, that extended give-and-take among numerous senators is the exception rather than the rule. "In this United States Senate it is rare indeed to have one-third of the members present to hear debate," observed a senator. "There is dialogue and debate, but most of it does not take place on the floor under public scrutiny."[10] In the view of freshman Senator Rand Paul, R-Ky., "The Senate floor stands nearly empty, senators come in to speak with no one listening; we vote and move on."[11]

Debate still serves to publicize issues, address constituencies, critique executive policies, identify areas of consensus, and influence Senate votes. After one spirited floor session, a senator declared, "I was really undecided on the pending amendment, but [the] Senator so ably presented his case that I will join him" in opposing the amendment.[12] Or as Senate Democratic leader Harry Reid, Nev., stated after listening to a discussion between two senators: "Mr. President, people wonder if debate helps. This is a perfect example of how. This debate has helped resolve a very contentious issue."[13] However, not all speeches are so persuasive. As another senator said, "There almost never is a mind changed by debate on the floor of the Senate because, for the most part, no one is ever listening." Or senators have already committed themselves before debate begins.

Great debates can capture national attention and mobilize national sentiment on critical issues such as civil rights, terrorism, health care, national defense, or Social Security. Debate, too, is used to reshape a party's public image on issues ostensibly owned by the other party or to inoculate a party against campaign attacks. During debate on an education bill, remarked a senator, both parties were "rehearsing political attack lines in the event" the education bill failed to pass.[14] On another occasion, a lull in the Senate's scheduling of top-tier issues provided the chamber's Republican minority with an opportunity to "road test" their message agenda for the November elections. The sparse schedule "certainly gives us the ability to talk about a range of issues, and not just what's on the floor," remarked a senior GOP leadership aide. He added that "we've been able to be much more proactive than just responding" to what Senate Democrats and the Obama Administration are doing.[15]

Debate in the modern Senate often consists of prepared speeches perfunctorily read (or inserted in the *Congressional Record* without having been formally delivered before a largely empty chamber).[16] "I am surprised by the lack of deliberation in the World's Greatest Deliberative Body," remarked then–freshman Senator Barack Obama, D-Ill.[17] He further elaborated, "Each of us is speaking to an empty floor and to C-SPAN [the Cable Satellite Public Affairs Network] giving stock speeches."[18] Another senator added that debate "generally just boils down to simple talking points and sound bites, rather than really immersing ourselves in the substance and complexities of any given issue."[19]

When intensive debate does occur, it is often among only a handful of senators with special interest in the legislation. To minimize personality clashes, the Senate (like the House) forbids first-person references during debate. "One of the reasons for the rule that a Senator must address another Senator through the Chair and not in the first person," explained Senator Byrd, "is to avoid casting aspersions, and causing acridness in debate and hurt feelings."[20]

Although the Senate is known for its principle of unlimited deliberations, debate can be restricted on four occasions. First, unanimous consent agreements typically limit debate on, for example, bills, amendments, and various motions. Second, when the Senate invokes cloture (or Rule XXII), post-cloture debate is limited to a specific number of hours (30). Third, the motion to table is nondebatable and is often used by floor managers to stop debate on and kill floor amendments simultaneously. Rarely is a motion to table made on the bill itself, because if the motion were agreed to, it would kill the measure. Fourth, various statutes have built-in debate-limiting features. The Congressional Budget and Impoundment Control Act of 1974, for example, is replete with restrictions on debate, such as a 2-hour limit on any amendment to the concurrent budget resolution and a 10-hour limit on the budget conference report.

Unlike the House, where the Speaker's recognition power is discretionary ("For what purpose does the gentlelady rise?"), the Senate presiding officer (addressed as either "Mr. President" or "Madam President") must recognize the first person seeking to speak unless the majority leader, minority leader, or one of the two floor managers is seeking recognition at the same time. Then Senate precedents stipulate that one of the four in the order mentioned has priority. Once a lawmaker is recognized, however, Senate precedents say that the senator may hold the floor for as long as he or she chooses. When senators yield the floor, others may be recognized to speak. Sometimes a unanimous consent agreement will stipulate the order in which senators may speak and for what period of time. The presiding officer may not put the pending measure or matter to a vote if senators are still seeking recognition to speak.

As in the House—even though only a scattering of members are on the floor—a quorum technically is present in the Senate until a member suggests otherwise. Any senator may suggest the absence of a quorum. When this occurs, the presiding officer is obligated to direct the clerk to call the roll of members. In contrast to House practice, the presiding officer may not first count the senators present to determine whether a quorum exists, except during post-cloture proceedings. To ascertain the presence of a quorum, the calling of the roll prior to a vote on cloture—a formal procedure to end lengthy debate—is mandatory unless it is dispensed with by unanimous consent.

Quorum calls are commonly employed to give senators time to work out procedural arrangements (positive delay, as opposed to negative delay), such as a unanimous consent agreement, or to give a member scheduled to speak time to reach the floor. (A reading clerk calls the roll of senators very slowly.) "What I would like to do is suggest the absence of a quorum," said a senator, "so that the parties involved here might sit down in the quiet of some room to see exactly how we can get this particular [amendment] to a point where we can vote up or down."[21] Once this is done, further calling of the roll to establish a quorum is dispensed with by unanimous consent. When Lyndon B. Johnson was majority leader (1955–1961), he

> would ask for a quorum call and wait, sometimes for close to an hour, while the reading clerk droned slowly through the names. Then, when Johnson was ready for the Senate to resume, he would suspend the calling of the roll.[22]

Cumulatively, the Senate spends considerable time on quorum calls. A study by C-SPAN found that in 2011 the Senate "spent more than 32 percent of its time in quorum calls. That's more than in any comparable period dating to 1997."[23]

Quorum calls to delay proceedings temporarily are to be distinguished from live quorums. For the latter, a senator insists that at least a majority of the members come to the chamber and answer to their names. It can be a time-consuming process. As one senator observed, "It took almost one hour to round up fifty-one Senators to respond to their names."[24] The two types of quorum calls are distinguished by the different number of bells ringing in members' offices and Senate committee rooms. By modern practice, it is the majority leader who typically announces that he is requesting a live quorum. Senate Rule XXII, as noted earlier, requires a live quorum call prior to a cloture vote, but this is usually dispensed with by unanimous consent.[25]

If the Senate officially discovers that it lacks a quorum, it has two options: (1) It adjourns (recesses if there is a previous order to that effect), or (2) it votes to instruct the sergeant at arms to request (compel) the attendance of senators—"Mr. President, I move to instruct the Sergeant at Arms to request the attendance of absent Senators."

Television and Debate

In 1986, after years of consideration, the Senate authorized gavel-to-gavel coverage of its floor proceedings, which are carried over C-SPAN. Television has brought about some change in floor debate and activity. Speeches are more numerous, but they are better organized and livelier than before. Senators "are making better speeches," said Senator Byrd. "They are using more gestures and rhetorical flourishes, and it seems to me that overall, the debate has improved from a substantive point of view."[26]

The staff members of senatorial offices regularly monitor the floor debate so they can alert their bosses when issues are being discussed that require their attendance. Senators also watch floor proceedings from their offices, and what they observe may prompt them to go to the floor. "I came here to talk about this amendment," said Senator Reid, because "I watched with interest from my office." He continued: "I was especially impressed with, and was able to watch, the remarks of my colleague."[27] Senators, too, are using more props, graphs, and charts to illustrate their policy and partisan ("chart wars") points. Moreover, as more Americans embrace widescreen televisions, "senators of all political stripes are figuring out that visual messaging is more compelling than . . . droning on from prepared texts."[28] Some senators, to attract local media coverage, wait to offer floor amendments until it is prime time back home.

Floor Managers' Role

Floor managers have the major responsibility for guiding legislation to final passage. "I lean on the manager of the bill and the ranking [committee] members to carry the load" on the floor, Senator Byrd once observed.[29] Usually, two floor managers (one from each party from the reporting committee) are assigned per measure, usually the chair and ranking minority member of the reporting committee. In the infrequent case of multiply referred legislation, several majority and minority floor managers might be designated.

Senate floor managers, like their House counterparts, have varied responsibilities. For example, they identify favorable times to schedule their legislation; they negotiate time-limitation agreements on amendments, work to efficiently dispose of them, or develop a manager's package comprising scores of discrete amendments that can be agreed to by unanimous consent; they may offer amendments to strengthen their bills as well as to counter proposed weakening amendments; they have to respond to any points of order raised against language in the legislation; and they must alert proponents when their support is needed on the floor.[30]

There are occasions, too, when the majority and minority floor managers will work together to defeat amendments that jeopardize enactment of legislation reported from their committee. A good example is when Tom Harkin, R-Iowa, the chair of the Health, Education, Labor and Pensions Committee (HELPS), and Mike Enzi, R-Wyo., the ranking minority member, and their staffs worked for more than a year on a bipartisan basis to craft the Food and Drug Administration Safety and Innovation Act of 2012. The two created bipartisan working groups to craft consensus policy proposals, invited the staff of noncommittee members to participate in the discussions, engaged the outside stakeholder community, and involved the administration and the public in developing the legislation. Both successfully opposed nonrelevant amendments that "have nothing to do with the bill," as well as proposals geared more to presidential-year politics than passage of important legislation.[31] The two floor managers "led opposition to all of the amendments that came up for a vote, and all were defeated."[32] The measure (S. 3187) passed the Senate by a vote of 96 to 1.

In brief, strategic calculations are a manager's stock in trade, such as deciding when to offer an amendment at an advantageous time, who to enlist to propose friendly amendments, how to combat unfriendly amendments, or whether to raise a point of order. Points of order can be raised at any time a bill, amendment, or motion is pending before the Senate. The principal exception occurs when the Senate is debating an amendment under a time constraint imposed by a unanimous consent agreement. All time must expire or be yielded back before a point of order can be made.

BILLS CONSIDERED BY UNANIMOUS CONSENT

Unanimous consent agreements, often the product of extensive negotiations, are crucial to the efficient operation of the legislative process in the Senate. "We aren't bringing [measures] to the floor unless we have [a unanimous consent] agreement," exclaimed a senator. "We could bring child-care legislation to the floor right now, but that would mean two months of fighting. We want to maximize productive time by trying to work out as much as we can in advance [of floor action]."[33] There are times, to be sure, when the two party leaders will offer "dueling" consent agreements. Each leader will ask unanimous consent to call up a measure knowing full well that the other side will object. Their respective objective: to blast the other party as "obstructionists," stalling important legislation. Box 7.1 shows a typical example of a unanimous consent agreement specifying the bill's number and the terms of its consideration.

The complex agreement in Box 7.1, like many others controlling floor action on legislation, reflects several general procedures common to many of these accords. First, the majority leader determines, following consultation with the minority leader, when to proceed to the consideration of the defense authorization bill (S. 1390). Second, an amendment (Levin–McCain) is to be debated for 2 hours, with the time equally divided between Senator Carl Levin, D-Mich., the chair of the Armed Services Committee, and Senator Saxby Chambliss, R-Ga., a member of the panel. No amendments are in order to the Levin–McCain proposal. Once debate time has been used or yielded back, the Levin–McCain amendment is voted on. Finally, the unanimous consent agreement stipulates that when the Senate resumes consideration of the bill the next day, debate will continue on an amendment proposed by GOP Senator John Thune of South Dakota. Thune's

---

BOX 7.1   Unanimous Consent Agreement

S. 1390 (Order No. 89)

Ordered, that at 10:00 a.m. on Tuesday, July 21, 2009, the Senate resume consideration of S. 1390, an original bill to authorize appropriations for fiscal year 2010 for military activities of the Department of Defense, for military construction, and for defense activities of the Department of Energy, to prescribe military personnel strengths for such fiscal year, and for other purposes; provided, that the Senator from Michigan (Mr. Levin) be recognized to offer the Levin–McCain amendment relating to the F22 and that the amendment be limited to 2 hours of debate with the time equally divided and controlled between the Senator from Michigan (Mr. Levin) and the Senator from Georgia (Mr. Chambliss) or their designees; provided further, that upon the use or yielding back of time, the Senate proceed to vote on the amendment, with no amendment in order thereto prior to a vote.

Ordered further, that on Wednesday, July 22, 2009, when the Senate resumes consideration of S. 1390 and Amdt. No. 1618, offered by the Senator from South Dakota (Mr. Thune), the time until 12 noon be for debate with respect to the amendment, with the time equally divided and controlled between the Senator from South Dakota (Mr. Thune) and the Senator from Illinois (Mr. Durbin), or their designees; provided, that no amendments be in order to Amdt. No. 1618 during its pendency; provided further, that at 12 noon, the Senate proceed to vote in relation to the amendment, with the adoption of the amendment requiring an affirmative 60 vote threshold; provided further, that if the amendment achieves that threshold, then it be agreed to and the motion to reconsider be considered made and laid upon the table; further, that if it does not achieve that threshold, then the amendment be withdrawn.

SOURCE: Senate of the United States, 111th Congress, *Calendar of Business*, July 21, 2009, 2.

---

amendment is to be voted on at noon. Further, as many unanimous consent agreements increasingly direct, the Thune amendment must receive 60 votes, rather than a simple majority, to be adopted.

Bipartisan trust is essential to the use of unanimous consent agreements. For example, in an admittedly infrequent occurrence, all 100 senators

> signed off on an unusual [consent] agreement that turned the normal legislative process on its ear by allowing 20 amendments to be adopted en bloc to the annual defense authorization bill (S. 1390) in the late hours of July 23 [2009]—after the Senate had already passed the measure and most senators had left the building.[34]

Senators were exhausted from working late into the evening and entrusted the two floor managers—Armed Services Chair Levin and ranking member McCain—to screen and approve the outstanding amendments. Trust and bipartisanship continued under these two committee leaders into the 112th Congress as they succeeded once again in winning enactment into law of the annual defense authorization measure. In the 113th Congress, under the Senate GOP's 6-year term limit rule for chairs or ranking members, Senator James Inhofe, Okla., replaced McCain as the ranking member on Armed Services.

Occasionally, however, hard feelings can be generated over expectations or interpretations associated with unanimous consent agreements. An especially contentious case involving a major GOP priority occurred soon after Republicans won control of the Congress in the mid-1990s. Many senators expected to vote on February 28, 1995, on final passage of a constitutional amendment to balance the budget (H. J. Res. 1), a major plank in Speaker Newt Gingrich's, R-Ga., "Contract with America" (10 major proposals all to be considered during the first 100 days of the 104th House). To the chagrin of opponents, Majority Leader Robert J. Dole, R-Kans., recessed the Senate because he was one vote short of the 67 (or two thirds) needed to pass a constitutional amendment. "I thought a deal was a deal," complained Minority Leader Tom Daschle, D-S.D.[35] Senator Byrd harshly condemned Dole's decision to block the final vote, but it was permitted under the terms of the consent agreement.

> The stalling move . . . was technically allowed under the unanimous consent agreement that governed the last several days of the debate. The agreement only promised a final roll call "following the stacked votes" on proposed changes to the amendment on Feb. 28. It did not specify precisely when thereafter the final vote would occur, giving Dole the loophole he needed to claim extra time to search for the 67th vote needed to approve H. J. Res. 1. In addition, a majority leader is traditionally recognized when he calls for the Senate to go into recess.[36]

Dole was unable to find another vote, and the Senate defeated the centerpiece of the GOP's Contract with America. (When the outcome was plain, Senator Dole switched his vote from "yea" to "nay" and entered a motion to reconsider to comply with Senate rules requiring members to be on the prevailing side to be eligible to offer that motion, thus giving the Senate another chance to review and revote on the issue at some time in the future. Dole suggested he would call for another vote if he could round up one more supporter, but he never did.) Although relations between the parties remained tense for some time, the two party leaders of necessity continued to cooperate in crafting unanimous consent agreements.

Measures governed by unanimous consent agreements are commonly called up by the majority leader or the majority floor manager. Customarily, the presiding officer recognizes the bill's floor manager, usually the chair of the committee or subcommittee that handled the bill, for a short description of the legislation and its intent. The floor manager is followed by the ranking minority committee or subcommittee member, who presents similarly brief opening remarks. The Senate then is ready to consider and debate amendments to the bill.

THE AMENDING PROCESS

The Senate's amending process provides lawmakers with an opportunity to make changes in the text of a measure or a pending amendment during floor consideration. Although the amending process can be complex, it is subject to certain conditions and principles. These conditions or principles, however, can be waived by unanimous consent of the membership.

Like the House, the Senate distinguishes among types (perfecting or substitute), degrees (first degree or second degree), and forms (motions to strike, to insert, or to strike and insert) of amendments. Furthermore, certain factors affect any senator's eligibility to offer floor amendments. One factor is *spatial*. Are there any limbs (or places) left on the amendment tree? The Senate's volume of precedents, *Senate Procedure: Precedents and Practices*, presents four charts that depict the number of amendments that may be pending at the same time. (The House effectively functions with only one amendment chart.) Which chart (or "amendment tree") is in use on the Senate floor depends on whether the first amendment is a motion to insert (Chart 1); an amendment to strike (Chart 2); an amendment to strike and insert (Chart 3); or a complete substitute—an amendment that replaces the entire text of the pending bill (Chart 4). The simplest tree (Chart 1), used later for illustrative purposes, permits a maximum of three amendments; the most complex tree (Chart 4) allows as many as 11 amendments to be pending simultaneously (a rare occurrence).

Another factor that influences the amending stage is *time*. Is the amending process regulated by a time-limitation agreement that may specify when or in what order amendments are to be offered and limits debate on each one? Still another factor is *contextual*. For example, are there formal (the imposition of cloture, for example) or informal (the floor managers want to limit amendments to their bill) circumstances that impinge on the amending process?

Unlike the House, the Senate has neither a Committee of the Whole nor a 5-minute rule for debating amendments. The Senate has no closed rules. Any measure is open to virtually an unlimited number of amendments unless a unanimous consent agreement specifies otherwise. Worth noting is that senators may "file" (hand to a Senate clerk for printing) as many amendments as they want, but they must be called up, or "pending," to be considered in the Senate. The Senate must dispose of all pending amendments, but not those filed but never called up for floor consideration. A recent trend is that hundreds of amendments are often filed on major bills. A knowledgeable congressional journalist explains why.

> Senators and their staffs have become quite adept at stymieing major bills by raising—or threatening to raise—scores or even hundreds of amendments. Senators can use this little-noticed tool to jam the legislative gears without ever resorting to the musty and old-fashioned filibuster.[37]

Senators also file "placeholder" amendments that lack formal text ("Byrd relevant," for example), which gives them the right to call up their specific proposals to a bill.

Senators, unlike House members in the Committee of the Whole, can modify their own amendments without the need for unanimous consent or the majority approval of the chamber. A senator, for example, might propose an amendment that the floor manager will support if the language is discretionary, not mandatory. The senator can make the change on his or her own authority—"Madam President, I send to the desk a modification of my amendment No. 1450 to S. 1234"—and perhaps improve the amendment's chances of being adopted by the Senate. These modifications are permissible until the Senate takes some "action" on the amendment, such as agreeing to take a vote on it or arranging a unanimous consent agreement limiting debate time. Senators sometimes quickly ask for action on their amendments because, even though they lose the right to modify them, they gain the right to offer amendments to their own amendments should the need arise.

Senators must be recognized by the presiding officer before they can offer amendments. Officially reported committee amendments automatically take precedence over those offered by other members from the floor. Committee amendments are subject to further amendment from the floor.

Senators can propose amendments at any time to any section of a bill. This approach differs from the more orderly routine followed by the House, where the rules specify that each part of a measure be considered in sequential order, usually section by section. Senate custom gives individual senators greater leeway in offering and amending legislation. This flexibility means that a senator can eventually force virtually any issue to the floor through amendments and displace the best-laid agenda of any majority leader. To avoid having senators offer their favorite bill as an amendment to other measures or amendments, a majority leader may promise lawmakers a specific time when the Senate will consider and vote on their bill.

Amendments must be read by the Senate clerk, but this usually is dispensed with by unanimous consent unless an attempt is being made to delay the bill. Opposed to a bill, a senator said he planned to offer continuous and very long second-degree amendments to the bill and require that each be read in full. "It was a good old-fashioned filibuster," remarked a Senate aide.[38] During the 2009 debate on health care reform, GOP senators objected to the usually routine request to dispense with the reading of two lengthy amendments. In one instance, Senator Tom Coburn, R-Okla., insisted on a line-by-line reading of Senator Bernie Sanders's, I-Vt., 767-page amendment creating a single-payer (government-run) health care program. After 3 hours of reading by Senate clerks, Senator Sanders withdrew his amendment, but not without a controversy as to whether Sanders could interrupt the reading and withdraw his proposal. The presiding officer, on advice from the Senate parliamentarian, ruled that Sanders could withdraw his amendment.[39] In another case, Minority Leader Mitch McConnell, R-Ky., demanded that Majority Leader Reid's 383-page manager's health care amendment be read word-for-word. Senator McConnell thanked the clerks for having "to read for the last 7 or 8 hours."[40] Worth noting is that at the start of the 112th Congress, the Senate amended its rules to prevent the reading of amendments if they have been available to senators for 72 hours. (For several general House–Senate differences in the amending process, see Table 7.1.)

TABLE 7.1 Selected Bicameral Differences in the Amendment Process

House	Senate
Measures read for amendment section by section or title by title	Measures open to amendment at any point, unless a unanimous consent agreement states otherwise
Strict germaneness rule	No general germaneness rule
Amendment rights of members commonly limited by the Rules Committee	Unlimited freedom for senators to offer amendments, unless unanimous consent agreement stipulates otherwise
Third-degree amendments prohibited	Third-degree amendments prohibited but can still be offered by unanimous consent
Five-minute rule for discussing amendments	No debate limit for amendments unless imposed by a unanimous consent agreement
Points of order against amendments must be raised after an amendment is read but before debate on it has begun	Points of order against amendments can often be raised at any time
Representatives have no right, in the Committee of the Whole, to modify or withdraw amendments on their own authority	Senators have the right to modify or withdraw their amendments unless action (such as a call for a vote on the amendment) has been taken on it by the Senate

Principle of Precedence

An important concept that shapes the Senate's amending process is precedence. The basic idea is that something, such as a motion, of lower priority cannot displace something of higher priority, but something of higher priority can be offered while something of lower priority is pending. Fundamentally, the principles of precedence determine (1) the number of amendments that may be pending simultaneously and (2) the order in which those amendments will be voted on. To be sure, amendment theory does not always comport with the realities or practicalities of floor decision making. For example, despite the prohibition against third-degree amendments, third-degree amendments might be made in order by unanimous consent. Further, the Senate might have dozens of amendments pending simultaneously on the floor. This situation occurs because senators ask and receive unanimous consent to set aside the pending amendments so they can offer theirs. Recall from earlier in this chapter that pending amendments must be disposed of by the Senate, typically by rejecting, tabling, approving, or withdrawing them.

Two principles of precedence merit review because they provide useful insight into amendment procedure. The first principle: A second-degree amendment (an amendment to the first degree) is voted on before the first degree. The second principle: A perfecting amendment takes precedence over a substitute amendment. These principles determine which type of amendment (perfecting or substitute) may be offered when others are pending and the order in which those amendments are voted on. A perfecting amendment, unlike a substitute, is one that alters some but not all of the language in a part or portion of a bill or pending amendment. A substitute, by contrast, seeks to replace new text for the *entirety* of the pending proposal. Perfecting amendments (which are always motions to strike, to insert, or to strike and insert) have precedence—or priority—over substitutes (always a motion to strike and insert). Thus, if Senator A offers a perfecting amendment to a bill (a first-degree amendment to insert) and Senator B then proposes a second-degree perfecting amendment to it, no other amendments are in order until the second-degree proposal is disposed of. And if the latter is adopted, other second-degree amendments—perfecting or substitute—may be offered until there are no unamended parts to alter.

Alternatively, as depicted in Figure 7.2, Senator B may offer a second-degree substitute for Senator A's amendment to add something to the bill. Then Senator C, under the Senate's principles of precedence, can propose a second-degree perfecting amendment to Senator A's amendment, which would be voted on before the substitute. The order of offering amendments is the inverse of the order of voting. Thus, the last offered amendment is the first to be voted on.

Lawmakers often calculate where they would like to be on the amendment tree depending in part on whether they want the first or last vote. Knowing that the first amendment is likely to be the target of many

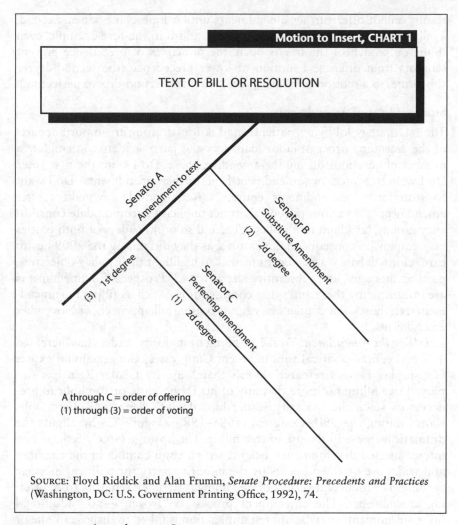

FIGURE 7.2 Amendment to Insert

amendments, a senator may draft his or her amendment as second-degree perfecting so it will be voted on first. If a senator believes she has the votes to fend off any attempts at change, she might opt to offer her idea as a first-degree amendment. Predicting the optimal place on the amendment tree can be difficult because much will depend on broader political dynamics and the kinds of ongoing substantive changes that amendments typically undergo on the floor.

The concept of filling the amendment tree has two meanings. First, as illustrated by the actions of Senator C in Figure 7.2, every available branch (or limb) of the tree is filled according to the chart in play. Senators, as a result, cannot offer further amendments until a limb comes open. Second, as illustrated by the actions of Senators A and B in the first example, even though a branch of the tree is open, the principles of precedence prevent senators from offering a motion of lower precedence (the second-degree substitute) to a motion of higher precedence (the second-degree perfecting).

Strategic Uses of Amendments

Timing, strategy, lobbying, patience, and skillful drafting are important parts of the amending process. Floor managers and party leaders contemplate a number of questions during the amending phase: Do I want the first vote? Do I want to protect my amendment from further amendments? Do I want to stop further amendments entirely? (Rank-and-file lawmakers offer amendments for various purposes: attract publicity, accommodate constituency groups, lay claim to a policy idea, and so on.) Leaders of both parties may employ on consequential measures, as they did during the 2009 health care reform debate, "amendment teams" to highlight their policy objectives, partisan messages, and substantive alternatives.[41] Prospects for amendments are influenced by these and other considerations, such as filling the amendment tree, the second-degree strategy, the poison-pill approach, or November amendments.

Filling the Amendment Tree. Tree filling by majority leaders has increased as a procedural–political tool in recent Congresses. Congressional expert Christopher Davis's research reveals that Majority Leader Reid has employed tree filling far more that any of his Democratic or Republican predecessors since the majority leadership of GOP Senator Robert Dole, Kans., during the 99th Congress (1985–1987). Figure 7.3 highlights the dramatic increase in the use of tree filling. The upsurge largely reflects two interconnected developments: heightened partisan conflict in the chamber and wider use of amendments by the minority party for political message sending. The immediate effect of tree filling is to block senators from offering amendments. The amendment process is "frozen"—no "additional floor amendments may be offered until action is taken to dispose of one or more of those already pending."[42]

Any senator can fill the amendment tree, but the majority leader has special advantages if he chooses to use this parliamentary tactic. The majority leader is able to fill the tree easily because Senate precedents grant the majority leader preferential recognition. Thus, despite other precedents stating that senators lose the floor when they propose an amendment, the majority leader is able to offer amendment after amendment until the tree is filled. The ultimate or full tree is achieved when the majority leader also fills a separate tree on the motion either to recommit (when a committee has reported a bill) or commit (when a proposal has not been reported from a committee) a bill to the pertinent committee with instructions. In the House, this is a preferential motion for the minority party. In the Senate, however, the motion to commit, or recommit, is higher on the

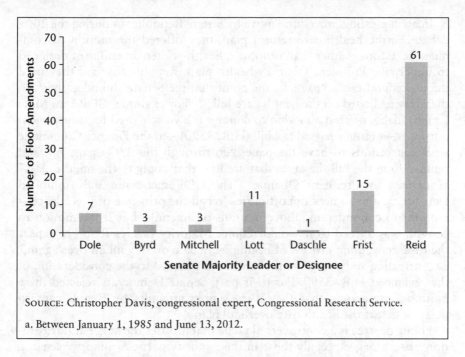

SOURCE: Christopher Davis, congressional expert, Congressional Research Service.

a. Between January 1, 1985 and June 13, 2012.

FIGURE 7.3 Floor Amendments Limited by Majority Leader Filling the Amendment Tree: 99th–112th Congresses

precedence ladder than motions to amend. (Senate Rule XXII, best known for outlining the procedure for cloture, also defines the chamber's priority of motions. Motions to amend rank last in priority.) Thus, the majority leader may fill the tree on a bill and then immediately offer a motion to recommit (or commit) the measure to close off every possibility for minority party amendments. As a frustrated senator stated when the majority leader filled the tree:

> I checked with the Parliamentarian about the procedural status we are in this morning. I am informed this is the status: We have S. 2062, which is this bill to reform class action [legal] procedures. There is an amendment offered to that by [the majority leader], a perfecting amendment [to insert]. There is a second-degree perfecting amendment offered to that. There is a motion to commit that has been made by [the majority leader]. [Note: The amendment tree for a motion to commit is identical to the chart in Figure 7.2.] There is a [leader] perfecting amendment to the motion to commit, and there is a [leader] second-degree perfecting amendment to the first-degree perfecting amendment to the motion to commit. So the obvious question I put to the Parliamentarian is, what is there that is in order for us to offer at this time for the Senate to consider? The answer is, nothing. Nothing is in order. The tree is full . . . and nothing can be offered.[43]

In an interesting procedural move by Senate Republicans during the 2009 debate on the health care reform plan, they offered the motion to commit several times rather than propose a health-related amendment designed to undermine President Obama's health plan. Republicans said they used the procedural tactic "to make the point that the Senate should go back to the drawing board on the health care bill."[44] For example, GOP Sen. Mike Crapo, Idaho, offered a motion to commit the vehicle used for amendment purposes—a House-passed tax bill (H.R. 3590)—to the Finance Committee with instructions to have the panel "go through the 2,074-page bill and remove from the bill the taxes that are in it that apply to the middle class" as defined by President Obama.[45] The GOP tactic not only inhibited Democratic amendment opportunities (recall the principle of precedence— motions to commit rank above motions to amend)—but if the motion to commit was agreed to it would require Majority Leader Reid "to repeat the time-consuming process of beginning debate on the bill all over again," i.e., attracting sixty votes on the motion to proceed to the consideration of the revamped H.R. 3590. For their part, Senate Democrats rejected these motions, contending that they were simply attempts by Republicans to delay or defeat the health care overhaul plan.

Filling the tree is a controversial tactic that arouses the anger and frustration of senators, especially those in the minority party. A minority senator, for example, proposed a Senate rules change to block the majority leader from offering back-to-back first- and second-degree amendments. "If a first-degree amendment were pending, the only second-degree amendment that would be in order would be one offered by the opposing party."[46] Tree filling is not an everyday occurrence but one that is used to achieve different purposes, such as stopping the minority from offering policy alternatives that can attract public attention away from the majority's priorities; safeguarding a bill from divisive amendments that might fracture support for the legislation; protecting vulnerable party colleagues from casting votes that may jeopardize their reelection chances; expediting Senate decision making by restricting the number of floor amendments; allowing the majority leader to pre-clear amendments in advance of floor consideration, opening a "branch" on the amendment tree if the proposals are acceptable to him; or fostering negotiations between the two party leaders to work out an agreement on how many amendments each side may offer, especially if hundreds have been filed. As a senator pointed out:

> Sometimes, after the tree has been filled, there will be extensive negotiations among Senators to agree on a limited number of specified amendments that both sides are willing to vote on. In part, this is done to limit the time it will take to finish the bill. More often, it is done to eliminate the tough votes where Senators will have to take positions on controversial issues which could be used against them in future campaigns, including 30-second television spots.[47]

A classic example of tree filling illustrates its policy-affecting potential. It occurred in 1997 on a campaign finance reform bill (S. 25) opposed by most Republicans but advocated by Senate Democrats and a handful of Republicans. Given a threat by President Bill Clinton to call the Senate into special session if it adjourned without voting on campaign finance reform, Majority Leader Trent Lott, R-Miss., brought the bill to the floor and quickly filled the tree on the bill and on the motion to recommit.[48] Each amendment, dubbed "paycheck protection," was virtually identical to all the others, and all were anathema to Senate Democrats and their outside union supporters. Lott's proposal would require labor union officials to get prior consent via signed statements from their workers permitting their dues to be used for campaign purposes. The goal: to reduce labor's clout in electoral politics. Tellingly, Lott's successful stratagem required Democrats to filibuster a campaign reform measure they supported because they vehemently opposed paycheck protection. "They're going to be filibustering, not us," said Lott.[49] In the end, the Senate never acted on the legislation. Not until 2002 did changing political conditions—the election of more campaign reform-minded senators, for example—permit Congress to pass a major overhaul of campaign spending, which the president signed into law (the Bipartisan Campaign Reform Act).

At the beginning of the 112th Congress (January 27, 2011), the two Democratic and Republican leaders reached an informal accord dubbed the "gentlemen's agreement." Its overlapping purposes were several: ease partisan tensions in the chamber, promote bipartisan comity and cooperation, enhance the productivity of the Senate, and weaken initiatives by reform-minded senators to change filibuster rules. Majority Leader Reid agreed to provide more amendment opportunities for Republicans, using tree-filling "infrequently." For his part, Minority Leader Mitch McConnell pledged that Republicans would employ their "procedural options with discretion," particularly their ability to block measures from reaching the floor by filibustering the motion to proceed to legislation.

Both parties have had their complaints with the informal accord. "The spirit of the agreement was they'd get amendments and we would get bills done," exclaimed Senator Charles Schumer, D-N.Y. "The way it's turned out, they are getting their amendments, but the bills are still getting blocked."[50] Republicans lament that Democrats avoid bringing bills to the floor to protect vulnerable Democrats from voting on GOP amendments. "The less votes the Democrats cast, the less they can be challenged in the next election. It's no way to run a railroad," said GOP Senator Charles Grassley of Iowa.[51] Moreover, the gentlemen's agreement did not apply to other dilatory tactics that could delay or prevent a final vote on legislation, such as a "filibuster" by amendment strategy. In short, the gentlemen's agreement did not achieve its objectives.

Second-Degree Strategy. The second-degree strategy is relatively easy to employ by any senator but especially by the majority leader, because of that leader's priority of recognition. The idea behind this approach is that every time a senator offers a first-degree amendment, another senator comes after to propose a second-degree amendment that undermines the intent of the first-offered amendment. Recall that under the principles of precedence, second-degree amendments are voted on before first-degree amendments, and, if adopted, they may replace or wipe out the first-degree proposition. Second-degree amendments are employed for various political and substantive reasons, such as fending off unwanted propositions or providing political cover to senators. For example, a Democratic Senator offered a first-degree amendment to create a new position—assistant secretary for civil rights—in the Department of Agriculture. Quickly, a GOP senator proposed a second-degree amendment that said before new administrative positions are created, the Senate should act on nominations reported by committees and awaiting action by the full Senate, citing a controversial nominee by name. The Democratic senator withdrew his amendment.

Senators understand that second-degree amendments can eviscerate the intent or purpose of the first-degree proposal. To counter this tactic, according to a Senate procedural expert, minority lawmakers since the mid-1990s began to insist that second-degree amendments be transformed into two first-degree amendments so senators could get a "clean" vote on each of their first-degree proposals.[52] Senators often call this approach a "side-by-side" amendment process, with unanimous consent agreements often including this procedure. As Senate Democratic leader Harry Reid explained:

> The reason we have considered these side by side on a number of occasions is the person offering the amendment initially wants a vote on his amendment. The second degree usually wipes out that amendment, which they have a right to do. It has been discovered in the past that we are much better off considering them side by side right off the bat rather than doing the parliamentary skirmishing.[53]

Even if both first-degree amendments are adopted and they contradict each other, no Senate rule or precedent prohibits inconsistent amendments. These kinds of conflicts are typically resolved in conference with the other chamber.

Poison-Pill Approach. One strategy of a bill's opponents is to load down the legislation with controversial amendments, possibly sparking a filibuster and jeopardizing Senate passage. "Overweight the plan, sabotage it with an unrealistic amendment," and that will ensure defeat of the legislation, noted a senator.[54] Another senator said about a bill he opposed, "If this amendment worsens it a little more, then I'm for it."[55] This was the exact strategy of a conservative, anti-union Republican senator who voted *for* a successful labor-endorsed amendment sponsored by a Democratic colleague. "He voted for the amendment to kill the bill," said a GOP senator.[56] Another senator explained that the way you kill a bill is with "nongermane amendments that are called killer amendments or poison pills, because they are political amendments one side or the other does not want."[57]

During Senate debate in 2009 on health care reform, the chair of the Finance Committee, Max Baucus, D-Mont., labeled a GOP-sponsored amendment designed to protect Medicare a "killer amendment." Baucus contended that it would "kill the tax cuts in the bill, kill assistance for copays, kill the Medicaid expansion for the lowest income Americans, kill additional funding for the Children's Health Insurance Program."[58] The Senate rejected the GOP amendment on a 43-to-56 vote. (Worth noting is that under a previous order of the Senate, adoption of that amendment required 60 votes.) But as in the House, senators also employ amendments as "sweeteners" to entice colleagues to vote for their legislation.

November Amendments. Senators turn up the political heat on their colleagues as the November elections draw closer. A senator pointed out that amendments were being offered to one measure

> with only one and only one purpose in mind. Let us be realistic. [This] is an opportunity for Senators on either side of the aisle, whether it be Democrats or Republicans, to develop ammunition to be used in some 30-second spot ad in the next political campaign. These votes are not about substance. They are strictly about politics, positioning, window dressing, and so forth.[59]

The reverse approach is to prevent votes on troublesome amendments. A minority leader complained that the majority leader was protecting his members who had close November election contests from having to cast votes on issues that might cost them support back home. "They don't want to have votes on anything but naming airports," declared the minority leader. The majority leader's spokesman replied: "The [opposition is] just frustrated because we aren't voting on the things they want to vote on. Welcome to the minority."[60] Both parties allow senators in tight election contests to offer popular amendments that could win votes for them back home.

November amendments are particularly important in the contemporary Senate because party control of the chamber can flip rather quickly. As a result, majority and minority leaders craft amendment strategies whose basic purposes are, if in the majority, to hold power by demonstrating the capacity to govern effectively, or, if in the minority, "to build a political case against the majority's legislative program" and majority members up for reelection.[61] Democratic Senator Claire McCaskill of Missouri, who faced a tough but successful 2012 reelection, exclaimed: "For the past two years [Minority Leader] Mitch McConnell has been trying to figure out what amendments he could put on the floor to make my life miserable. There have been so many gotcha votes." McConnell has been trying, she said, to devise "some way to put something on the floor that would get me to vote against my own mother."[62]

Voting on Amendments

The Senate has three types of voting: voice, division (standing), and roll call. Voice and division voting are similar to House procedures, but the Senate has nothing comparable to the electronic voting procedures of the House. But the system of buzzers that summons senators to the floor for a vote is much like that of the House.

During a roll call, members respond "yea" or "nay" as their names are called alphabetically. The Senate establishes the length of time for roll-call votes at the start of each Congress. When the 113th Congress convened on January 3, 2013, the Senate agreed by unanimous consent

> that for the duration of the 113th Congress, there be a limitation of 15 minutes each upon any roll call vote, with the warning signal to be sounded at the midway point, beginning at the last 7 1/2 minutes, and when roll call votes are of 10-minute duration, the warning signal be sounded at the beginning of the last 7 1/2 minutes.

When votes are grouped back-to-back, referred to as *stacking*, the second and succeeding votes often occur, by unanimous consent, at 10-minute intervals or less. It is not uncommon that prior to a vote in a stacked sequence, each side customarily is allowed at least 1 minute to explain what the issue is about.

Party leaders and floor managers make every effort to ensure that their supporters are on the floor when needed for a vote. "My experience convinces me," commented Senator Byrd, that voting "is the most critical step in the legislative process. . . . [The leaders and the floor managers must] have the right members at the right place and at the right time."[63] As President Lyndon Johnson told advocates pressing for legislation from Congress: "You can get anything you want if you've got the votes. How many votes have you got?"[64]

Recorded votes in the Senate usually can be obtained easily; only a sufficient second—one fifth of the senators present—is needed, with a minimum of 11 as required by the Constitution. (Article I states that "a Majority of each [House] shall constitute a Quorum to do Business," and the "Yeas and Nays" of either chamber shall occur on any question "at the Desire of one fifth of those present.") If the minimum number is not on the floor at the time the request is made, a senator can summon other colleagues through a quorum call, try get their support, and then renew the request for a roll-call vote. As Senator Byrd explained:

> If any Senator wants a roll-call vote around here, he will ultimately get it. If he does not get it at first, he will put in a quorum and he will not let us call off the quorum. So we have to have a live quorum or give him the yeas and nays.[65]

Most roll calls occur on amendments.

Worth mention is that voting brings senators to the chamber, and many stay for a time to converse with colleagues on both sides of the aisle. A senator emphasized the value of these exchanges. "A tremendous amount of business is transacted. In a sense there is a certain aspect of a social event," he said, "but a lot of business is transacted. There are a lot of accommodations and a lot of learning about the personalities and how to come together on issues."[66]

Casting Procedural Votes. On controversial amendments, members often maneuver for procedural, instead of substantive, votes. A vote to table (kill) amendments or other motions is a classic ploy to avoid being recorded directly on politically sensitive policy issues. Senator Byrd has explained the difference:

> A motion to table is a procedural motion. It obfuscates the issue, and it makes possible an explanation by a Senator to his constituents, if he wishes to do so, that his vote was not on the merits of the issue. He can claim that he might have voted this way or he might have voted that way, if the Senate had voted up or down on the issue itself. But on a procedural motion, he can state he voted to table the amendment, and he can assign any number of reasons therefor, one of which would be that he did so in order that the Senate would get on with its work or about its business.[67]

If a procedural vote can be arranged to kill or delay a controversial bill, it is likely to win the support of senators who may prefer to duck the substantive issue. Moreover, senators generally support the party leadership on procedural votes. As one senator has pointed out, on a procedural vote, members "traditionally stick with the leadership."[68] There are no guarantees, however. Senate Majority Whip Richard Durbin, D-Ill., urged party unity on procedural votes in the 111th Congress (2009–2011), especially on priority measures such as health care reform. "We're just urging our members to stick with us when it comes to procedural votes," said Durbin. The response by some of his Democratic colleagues: "I didn't come here to be told what to do by someone else."[69]

Part of members' consideration in casting procedural or substantive votes involves the role of such votes in political campaigns. Senate GOP leader McConnell made it clear that lawmakers who cast a procedural vote on the motion to proceed to the health care reform bill were really voting in favor of the bill. "Anyone who votes 'aye' tonight" on the motion to proceed, said Senator McConnell, "is voting for all these [negative] things:" higher taxes on almost everyone, hikes in health insurance premiums, and massive cuts in Medicare.[70] Senator Ben Nelson, D-Nebr., even had to purchase a 30-second television ad during the Holiday Bowl featuring University of Nebraska's football team to explain and defend his crucial 60th vote supporting consideration of the health care reform legislation.[71] Of course, any senator who voted for the motion to proceed could be attacked politically for casting the

60th vote. Sometimes it is publicly known that a certain lawmaker did in fact cast the deciding ballot.[72]

Votes are not used simply to make decisions or as trading material; they also are used by interest-group organizations, who select issues of concern to them to characterize legislators as heroes or zeroes, depending on how members voted on the groups' legislative priorities. Votes are also used to test sentiment for or against amendments or legislation. A key test vote might occur on a motion to table (kill) an amendment or to take up a bill. A lopsided vote for an amendment might provide the momentum required to get it through the House. Some votes are also considered "free" by various senators, because even if the measure is enacted by the Senate, it is unlikely to pass the House. For example, Senator Bob Corker, R-Tenn., considered Senate action on a Chinese currency bill a "message vote, meaning that 'yes' votes are safe because the House is not likely to take up the bill."[73]

Since at least the 1990s, the Senate increasingly includes in unanimous consent agreements a 60-vote requirement for the adoption of measures or matters. Two unanimous consent agreements in the 104th Congress contained the supermajority standard compared with more than 50 in both the 110th and 111th Congresses.[74] This development serves a number of purposes. The 60-vote standard saves the time of the Senate by expediting floor decision making. The formal procedure for ending a talkathon—called "cloture," which requires 60 votes to invoke (see the discussion below)—is a time-consuming process that can extend over several days, lessening the Senate's opportunity to deal with other matters. A 60-vote "adoption threshold," wrote congressional scholar Valerie Heitshusen, "can significantly expedite Senate business without asking opponents to give up the procedural rights that (if their number exceed forty) would allow them to prevent adoption."[75] And, as congressional researcher Megan Lynch stated, a 60-vote threshold "has the effect of bypassing the procedural vote [on cloture] to grant Senators a direct vote on the policy issue at hand."[76]

Like the House, the Senate permits vote pairing, either live or dead pairs. In a live pair, one senator is present on the floor during the vote. The practice is for the senator to cast a vote, "yea" or "nay," then withdraw it and announce, "I have a pair with the senator from [naming the state]. If he were present and voting, he would vote ['yea' or 'nay']. If I were at liberty to vote, I would vote ['yea' or 'nay']." In a dead pair, both senators are absent from the floor. Their positions are published in the *Congressional Record* after each roll call. Live and dead pairs are not tabulated on roll-call votes, but a live pair can affect the outcome of a vote. Explained Senator Byrd:

> The arranging of pairs has been decisive from time to time on very close votes, because it is possible to pair off enough present Senators to affect the outcome of the vote and perhaps make a difference of 1 or 2 votes which, had the Senators present not been paired, would have decided the issue opposite to the outcome that resulted.[77]

Senators generally will not agree to give a live pair except on the condition that the outcome is not changed by virtue of the pair given.[78]

Final Action on a Bill

"When no Senator seeks recognition," Senator Byrd explained, "the Chair automatically puts the question of adoption of amendments and passage of bills."[79] Unlike the House, which has procedures for bringing measures to a final vote, so long as any senator wishes to be recognized to discuss a debatable proposition, a vote on final passage cannot occur. Typically, once the amending process is completed, the Senate proceeds to a vote on final passage, unless a unanimous consent agreement has been made setting a later date and time for the final vote. The floor manager may announce that no further amendments are pending. He or she then requests a third, and final, reading of the bill. The presiding officer orders the bill engrossed—put in the precise form in which it emerged from the Senate's amending process—and read a third time (the title of the bill only), a procedure that takes only a few seconds. Then the question is put on final passage of the measure.

The final vote is not over until the chair announces the outcome. Senate rules prohibit "any Senator from voting after the Chair has announced the decision," Senator Byrd pointed out. Senate rules provide "that the Chair cannot even entertain a unanimous consent request to suspend this rule."[80] Senators, like House members, may change their vote during the regular 15-minute voting period, which is a minimum and not the maximum time allowed. For example, during an unusually lengthy Senate roll call, dozens of senators switched their votes and defeated a proposal offered by a senator. "I just want to announce that Dr. Cary's in his office for everyone whose arm is out of socket," exclaimed the senator.[81] (Dr. Freeman Cary was the Senate physician.)

After the result of the final vote on the bill has been announced, one more parliamentary step is required before Senate action is complete. This step is available only to the side that prevailed on the final vote. If the bill is passed, a senator who voted for the bill, or who did not vote, makes a motion to reconsider the vote. (The motion is in order that day or the next 2 days of session. Sometimes the majority leader, per the earlier Dole example, will "enter" a motion to reconsider, which means that he can determine when, or if, he may try at some future date during that Congress to trigger a revote on the measure or matter.) Immediately after the motion to reconsider is offered, another proponent of the bill moves to table it. By this procedural device, Senate rules protect the bill from further consideration. Rarely does the motion to table fail. This procedure also is used after votes on amendments. The House procedure is basically identical, except for the idea of "entering" the motion to reconsider. (Entering a motion to reconsider is not employed in the modern House.)

BILLS WITHOUT UNANIMOUS CONSENT

Sometimes party leaders are unable to achieve unanimous consent agreements. This may happen for a variety of reasons: intense opposition to the bill by certain senators, a general desire for unrestricted debate and amendment, commitments by some senators to protect the interests of absent colleagues, or personal pique of some senators against party leaders. Passage of legislation then becomes a much more difficult task. Debate can be extensive and amendments numerous. Operating under the Senate's rules, this can be extremely time-consuming. Moreover, if one or more senators are intensely opposed to a bill, the well-known device of the filibuster may be threatened (like holds, the threat is another version of the silent filibuster) or actually used.[82] In the days leading up to scheduled recesses or at the end of legislative sessions, the threat or use of filibusters is especially effective. (Under Senate rules, if no member is speaking, a senator who is recognized by the presiding officer can hold the floor for as long as he or she is able.) In the contemporary Senate, extended debate—the filibuster—is *not* typically employed to educate or enlighten colleagues but, rather, to block or defeat legislation or nominations.

Determining when extended debate becomes a filibuster can be difficult, because a senator does not make a motion to filibuster a bill. Extended debate may occur because the issue warrants lengthy discussion. Extended debate also may occur because senators intend to stall action on measures. Determining senators' intent during debates is often not an easy task. Senator Byrd once said, "I will be able to perceive one, because I know one when I see it."[83] There are a lot of senators, he added, "who wouldn't know a filibuster if they met one on the way home ... or if they met it in the middle of the road."[84]

Long viewed as the tool of last resort, today the threat of a filibuster is part of the Senate's daily life. Lengthy or around-the-clock filibusters are largely a thing of the past. As a former Senate parliamentarian noted,

> there is very little distinction between a filibuster and a threat to filibuster. Any credible threat to filibuster is treated as if it were a filibuster because the Majority Leader, who has limited time in which to move his party's agenda, must regard it as such. Thus, the filibuster is largely silent, invisible, and relatively painless to the minority.[85]

Or, as a senator put it, "you don't have to talk to filibuster."[86]

Filibuster threats send signals to the majority leadership that 60 votes (to invoke cloture) may be needed to pass legislation. The Senate, unlike the House, is a supermajoritarian institution, because 60 votes—three fifths of the membership—are commonly required to enact major and controversial legislation. The political reality often is, as a majority leader observed, that "everything in this Senate needs 60 votes."[87] Another senator said: "It isn't good enough to have the majority. You've got to have 60 votes."[88] Freshman

Senator Jeff Merkley, D-Ore., added: "It's not a filibuster anymore. It's a supermajority requirement. And when that becomes commonly used, it's a recipe for paralysis."[89]

Little surprise that many commentators call it the "sixty-vote Senate." A supermajority vote is now the "new normal" for enacting virtually all types of measures or matters. In fact, the 60-vote requirement appears to have become an institutionalized norm, an accepted aspect of today's senatorial decision making. Why? Because the filibuster (real or threatened) provides any senator or party leader with a significant source of procedural and policy leverage. "The power to block the other person's bill gives you the power to influence the content," noted Senator Thad Cochran, R-Miss.[90] To be sure, the likelihood of filibusters influences the majority leader's decision as to when or whether to bring debatable—and almost everything is in the Senate—measures or matters to the floor, such as bills, resolutions, conference reports, nominations, and treaties. "I think there's some feeling that you don't spend time on the floor trying to figure out if you've got 60 votes," noted Commerce, Science, and Transportation Chair Jay Rockefeller, D-W.Va. "You have to understand before you go to the floor that you have 60 votes."[91]

The Filibuster

Generally characterized in the public mind as a nonstop speech, a filibuster in the fullest sense employs every parliamentary maneuver and dilatory motion to delay, modify, or defeat legislation. Asked for filibustering pointers by a colleague, one senator said: "If it takes unanimous consent, object. If not, you make a little speech, suggest the absence of a quorum, then . . . use parliamentary procedures[,] . . . motions to adjourn, motions to recess." He added: "You have to have the floor protected 100 percent of the time."[92] As Senator Pat Roberts, R-Kans., explained: "You can always shut down the Senate by simply putting the Senate in a quorum call and objecting to any unanimous consent [to dispense with the call] to go back to business."[93] It could take an hour or so, as mentioned earlier, for a quorum of at least 51 senators to arrive in the chamber. For the contentious debate on President Obama's health care reform initiative, Senator Judd Gregg, R-N.H., prepared an outline of procedures that minority party members could employ to protect their parliamentary rights and insist on full and lengthy consideration of the various reform proposals for health care. In the judgment of Majority Whip Durbin, Gregg's outline "largely includes the rights to slow down and stop the activity of the Senate."[94]

More has been written about extended debate in the Senate than about any other congressional procedure. Hollywood even glamorized the filibuster in the 1939 movie *Mr. Smith Goes to Washington,* starring Jimmy Stewart. The filibuster permeates virtually all senatorial decision making. Measures might not be reported from committee or scheduled for floor action because senators are threatening a filibuster. "In many instances, it's the threat of a filibuster that keeps a bill from coming up," observed Senator Byrd.[95] "The modern filibuster," said another senator, "requires only a threat and no talking."[96] Threatened filibusters usually mean that the public is unaware of which senators are promising to hold up Senate action.

The filibuster has long been part of the Senate, but unrestricted debate aroused little concern during much of the 19th century. The number of senators was small, the workload was limited, and lengthy deliberations could be accommodated more easily. Since Rule XXII (cloture) was adopted in 1917, the number of filibusters has varied over time. Scholars have identified three broad filibuster periods.

> The first lasts from roughly 1917 to 1937, in which the number of filibusters per Congress averages about 4.1. That period is followed by a quiet period between 1937 and 1968, where the mean number of filibusters is 2.1. In the 1970s, however, filibustering reaches new levels, before mushrooming in the 1980s and 1990s. Indeed, over the past twelve [89th to 101st] congresses, the number of filibusters has averaged 17.6.[97]

Congressional scholar Barbara Sinclair compiled data showing that filibusters or filibuster threats occurred during the 91st Congress (1969–1971) on 10% of major legislation. By the 105th Congress (1997–1999), 53% of major measures encountered actual or threatened talkathons, and in the decade of the 2000s, that number rose to 70% of major measures.[98]

Defenders of the filibuster say it is needed to prevent bad bills from becoming law, to protect minority rights against majority steamrollers, to ensure thorough analysis of legislation, to dramatize issues for the public, and to encourage the due deliberation that can lead to a better result. Democratic Senator Daniel Inouye of Hawaii supported the filibuster because, "as someone representing a small state, it was a tool I needed to ensure we were not pushed aside."[99] Senator Byrd added:

> One of the things that makes the United States Senate the unique upper body that it is is the ability to talk at great length. And there have come times when the protection of a minority is highly beneficial to a nation. Many of the great causes in the history of the world were at first only supported by a minority. And it's been shown time and again that the minority can be right. So this is one of the things that's so important to the liberties of the people. As long as a people have a forum in which members can speak at length, the people's liberties will be safe.[100]

Opponents argue that the filibuster thwarts majority rule, delays or kills legislation, brings the Senate into disrepute, and permits small minorities to extort unwarranted concessions in bills supported by Senate majorities. Exasperated by the blocking actions of a dozen filibustering senators near the close of a session, a majority leader declared in frustration, citing an earlier test vote: "Only in the United States Senate and only in the last few days of a session can 85 Senators vote one way: Yes, for this bill; 12 Senators vote another way: No, against the bill—and the no's prevail."[101] As another senator said on a separate occasion, "The only thing it's easy to do in the Senate is slow things down. The Senate is 100 human brake pads."[102] Senators also say that filibuster threats—often implicit in objections to unanimous consent requests made by the majority leader—are simply over-used in today's Senate.

These pro and con arguments highlight a dilemma: how to strike a balance between the right to debate and the need to decide. There is no easy answer. (Analysts sometimes suggest that the Senate gives too much weight to minority prerogatives while the House overemphasizes majority rule.) What is apparent is that the filibuster is a powerful bargaining and blocking device. Even the possibility of its use can force compromises in committee or on the floor. Senators of widely diverse viewpoints have resorted to it from time to time or have threatened to use it to influence legislation.

Measures or matters may face at least two primary or "double" fili-busters: the first on the motion to take up the legislation and the second on consideration of the bill itself. Important to note is that the Senate on January 24, 2013, adopted procedural changes that would effectively end filibusters on the motion to proceed. How these changes (discussed below) will work in practice is yet to be determined, which means that the "double filibuster" might remain a procedural option for a minority. Some matters, such as conference reports, have "privilege" under Senate proce-dures. This means they are not subject to a double filibuster because the motion to proceed to these matters is nondebatable. The 1964 civil rights bill filibuster consumed 16 days on the motion to take up the measure and 57 days on the legislation itself. Those filibusters were unique in that they marked the first time the Senate had ever voted to end an extended debate on a civil rights bill. (Strom Thurmond of South Carolina set the filibuster record when he was a Democrat by talking for 24 hours and 18 minutes against the 1957 civil rights bill.)

For years, Majority Leader Reid has filed cloture regularly on what he calls "these senseless motions to proceed that I have to file cloture on" and which consume a large amount of the Senate's time. "It takes us a week to get on a bill because we have to file motions to invoke cloture every time we proceed to a bill."[103] He added, "It is what we do every time because the Republicans demand that."[104] Needless to say, Senate Republicans put the onus on the majority leader for the increased use of cloture on motions to proceed, blaming Senator Reid for restricting their right to offer relevant and nonrelevant amendments. "Never in the history of the Senate," declared GOP Senator Coburn, "did we give up our rights to allow the majority leader to decide what amendments will be voted on or offered."[105] Thus, the response of Republicans is to make it difficult for the majority leader to call up measures or matters unless and until the two party leaders agree on a reasonable number of amendments to legislation for each side. (See below for data on the hike in cloture on the motion to proceed.)

Wider Use of Filibusters. Before the 1970s, conservative senators—often Southern Democrats who used extended debate to defeat or delay civil rights measures—were almost the only users of filibusters. Recent decades witnessed an increase in the overall number of filibusters, including those conducted by moderate and liberal senators in each party. The filibuster is a "parliamentary tool available to liberals and conservatives who wish to dramatize issues in the only forum of our national government that provides for thorough analysis and unhurried consideration of proposed public laws."[106]

Furthermore, filibusters (and threats of filibusters) are occurring on issues of great national importance and visibility as well as on a wide range of less momentous topics. "We filibuster everything," remarked Senator Durbin, "even bills that are bipartisan, which everybody agrees on."[107] Lamented a majority leader:

> Not long ago the filibuster or threat of a filibuster was rarely undertaken in the Senate, being reserved for matters of grave national importance. That is no longer the case.... The threat of a filibuster is now a regular event in the Senate, weekly at least, sometimes daily. It is invoked by minorities of as few as one or two Senators and for reasons as trivial as a Senator's travel schedule.[108]

Several factors account for the increase in filibusters. First, there are senators (some of whom may be former House members socialized by rough partisan politics) who prefer to push their own agendas even if the Senate's institutional activities grind to a halt. On occasion, one senator noted, senators are "determined to follow [their] own perspective even to the perversion, the distortion, and the destruction of the [legislative] process."[109]

Second, filibusters have enhanced potency in an institution that is workload packed and deadline driven. Insufficient time is available to accommodate the manifold claims on the Senate's agenda. Thus, senators who simply indicate their intention to filibuster can exercise significant leverage. In addition, the tactic of ending filibusters by exhaustion is no longer a realistic option in today's Senate. The time demands on senators are too large for them to wait out the filibusterers. "Electoral demands are quite severe, both in terms of senators' need to spend time in their home states as well as the perpetual drive to raise campaign funds."[110]

Third, the internal incentives (the "get-along, go-along" approach, for example) that fostered deference to seniority and party leaders are gone. Richard F. Fenno Jr., a noted congressional scholar, has studied how the 1950s Senate evolved from a "communitarian" institution, where senators were expected to use extended debate sparingly and only for high-stakes national issues, to today's "individualistic" Senate. He found that with "more openness, more media visibility, more candidate-centered elections," more interest groups, more political obligations, and more staff, Senate newcomers are independent entrepreneurs unwilling to submerge their personal and political objectives "to the norms of any collectivity."[111] Senators have increased incentives for obstructive behavior, such as from specialized groups that may encourage members to launch or threaten filibusters in exchange for campaign funds and support. When Lyndon B. Johnson was majority leader, he exercised tight control over floor proceedings, including use of the filibuster.

> While Johnson went to great lengths to avoid filibusters, once they had begun . . . he tended to regard filibusters as a personal challenge to his stewardship. Instead of making an end run around the combatants . . . he often preferred to break the filibuster by keeping the Senate in session for long hours, even around the clock, and forcing the minority ultimately to give up in exhaustion.[112]

By contrast, contemporary party leaders may accommodate filibustering senators who have meetings to attend back home.

Fourth, partisanship has contributed to gridlock and stalemate in the Senate. According to two scholars, "As the two parties became internally more cohesive and the differences between them grew larger, holding together a party-backed filibuster became significantly easier."[113] The threat of partisan filibusters is common in today's Senate, and cloture votes regularly follow party lines. For instance, the political reality that Majority Leader Reid confronted during debate on health care reform meant that he could not obtain any votes from a united Republican party to reach the threshold to invoke cloture, forcing him to mobilize the 60—often many times—by winning the support of all 58 Democrats and the 2 independents (Vermont's Bernie Sanders and Connecticut's Joseph Lieberman). As a congressional scholar sums up, "In a party-polarized chamber where the Senate minority party demonstrates the sort of disciplined opposition that one sees in parliamentary out parties, a Senate majority party has extraordinary difficulty either recruiting bipartisan support or governing alone."[114]

Ending a Filibuster. Besides mistakes (e.g., disorderly language) that could cause filibustering senators to lose the floor, two interrelated and broad methods of ending a filibuster are by informal compromise or by the only formal Senate procedure—called cloture (Rule XXII)—used to terminate debate.[115] Frequently, cloture cannot be obtained unless compromises are made. Party leaders sometimes try "shuttle diplomacy" between the two sides to avoid full-scale filibusters.[116]

Informal Compromise. The threat of filibusters can encourage policymaking compromises. During a filibuster, senators may meet in the cloakroom—off the Senate floor—or in the offices of the party leaders to conduct negotiations, which can go on day and night. The process may take several days or even weeks, depending on how controversial the bill is. If compromise fails, the odds increase that opponents of the legislation will win the battle and thus sidetrack the bill indefinitely. Alternatively, proponents may invoke cloture.

Cloture. After decades of determined resistance by many senators, the Senate in 1917 adopted Rule XXII, which gave the Senate the formal means—cloture—to end extended debate. Until that time, debate could be terminated only by unanimous consent, unlikely in the face of a filibuster, or exhaustion. In 1893, Senator Orville Platt, R-Conn., stated:

> There are just two ways under our rules by which a vote can be obtained. One is by getting unanimous consent—the consent of each Senator—to take a vote at a certain time. Next comes what is sometimes known as the process of "sitting it out," that is for the friends of a bill to remain in continuous session until the opponents of it are so physically exhausted that they cannot struggle any longer.[117]

Unanimous consent and exhaustion have been the hardy perennials of Senate procedure. "Exhaustion is always the way to build bipartisan consensus," declared Senator Mark Kirk, R-Ill.[118]

What finally prompted the Senate to adopt Rule XXII was a filibuster that killed a bill to arm U.S. merchant ships against attacks by German submarines. President Woodrow Wilson strongly criticized the filibuster and called a special session of the Senate, which adopted the cloture rule on March 8, 1917, five weeks before war was declared.

Under Rule XXII, a cloture motion signed by 16 senators first must be filed with the presiding officer (see Boxes 7.2 and 7.3). (A senator who is holding the floor can be interrupted by a colleague so he or she can present the cloture motion. The motion must be presented when the bill or amendment to which it is directed is pending before the Senate.) Two session days later (e.g., a cloture motion submitted on Monday is acted on by Wednesday) and 1 hour after the Senate convenes, the presiding officer, as noted earlier, must ascertain (often waived by unanimous consent) whether a quorum is present. That having been established, the presiding officer is obliged to ask, "Is it the sense of the Senate that the debate shall be brought to a close?" A vote is held immediately.

If three fifths of the entire Senate membership (60 of 100 members) vote in favor, cloture is invoked. Thereafter, there is an additional 30 hours of consideration, with senators permitted to speak for no more than 1 hour on a first-come, first-served basis. (The procedural changes adopted in 2013 reduced the time for post-cloture debate in several instances, as discussed below.) At the expiration of the 30 hours, which can be shortened by unanimous consent, the Senate votes on the question addressed in the cloture motion. Rule XXII also stipulates that first-degree amendments must be filed by 1 p.m. on the day following the filing of the cloture petition; second-degree amendments also must be filed in a timely manner—until 1 hour prior to the cloture vote. Before 1975, when the current three-fifths rule

---

BOX 7.2   A Cloture Motion

MR. REID. Mr. President, I have a cloture motion at the desk.

THE PRESIDING OFFICER. The cloture motion having been presented under rule XXII, the Chair directs the clerk to read the motion.

The bill clerk read as follows:

Cloture Motion

We, the undersigned Senators, in accordance with the provisions of rule XXII of the Standing Rules of the Senate, hereby move to bring to a close debate on the motion to proceed to Calendar No. 341, S. 2237, the Small Business Jobs and Tax Relief Act.

Harry Reid, Kent Conrad, Tom Harkin, Richard Blumenthal, Jeff Bingaman, Carl Levin, Al Franken, Daniel K. Inouye, Richard J. Durbin, Benjamin L. Cardin, Max Baucus, Charles E. Schumer, Jeff Merkley, Patty Murray, John D. Rockefeller IV, John F. Kerry.

SOURCE: *Congressional Record*, September 30, 2009, S9975.

---

was adopted, a two-thirds majority of those senators present and voting was required to invoke cloture. (The two-thirds requirement still applies to proposals to amend the Senate's rules.)

No limit has been placed on the number of times cloture can be sought on a single piece of legislation. Majority Leader Reid, for example, had to win in 2009 three key cloture votes on health care reform to achieve the measure's passage and to deny the GOP's goal of preventing the bill's enactment before Christmas on the theory that citizen protests over the holidays would weaken Senate Democratic support for the health care reform bill. A summary of why the Senate voted cloture three times on health care overhaul is useful to review. First, Senator Reid knew that the Senate's health proposal would contain tax provisions; however, the Constitution requires the House to originate revenue-raising measures. To comply with the Constitution, Reid took a House-passed tax bill (H.R. 3590) and used a "shell bill" strategy to win passage of the Senate's version of health reform legislation. Once the two Senate panels of jurisdiction (the Finance and the Health, Education, Labor, and Pensions Committees) reported their health care reform bills, Senator Reid melded their products into an alternative proposal (called a "complete substitute"). He then deleted the text contained in H.R. 3590 (keeping the bill number) and replaced it with his

---

BOX 7.3   Ending a Senate Filibuster

Cloture

Day 1: Motion signed by 16 members.

Day 2: First-degree amendments are to be filed by 1 p.m.

Day 3: Second-degree amendments are to be filed until 1 hour before the cloture vote.

A constitutional three-fifths vote (or 60 votes) is required to invoke cloture in the 100-member chamber. A two-thirds vote is required to invoke cloture on proposals to change Senate rules.

Post-Cloture

- Thirty-hour debate limit with time counted for votes, quorum calls, and other matters.
- Amendments must be germane.
- One-hour debate per senator.
- Presiding officer can rule out dilatory motions on his or her own initiative without waiting for a point of order.
- The measure on which cloture has been invoked remains the unfinished business of the Senate, to the exclusion of all other business.

---

health plan. Various Democratic senators, however, had major concerns with Reid's complete substitute. As a result, Reid made changes and concessions to win the support of all the wavering Democrats. Senator Reid then incorporated the compromises in a manager's amendment that he offered to the complete substitute. Thus, the three cloture votes: first on the manager's amendment, then on the complete substitute, and, finally, on the bill (H.R. 3590) itself, as amended by the Democrats' health care plan. (Worth noting is that once cloture is invoked, the Senate remains on the clotured matter until it is disposed of.)

Procedurally, it is important to emphasize that the three cloture votes were required not just to stop a filibuster on each proposition but because once cloture is invoked, there is a strict post-cloture germaneness requirement for amendments. (See the section below on nongermane amendments.) Because H.R. 3590 addressed tax assistance to servicemen purchasing homes, Reid's health substitute was plainly nongermane to the purposes of H.R. 3590. His manager's amendment was also nongermane to language in the complete substitute. This procedural scenario set up the three votes. First, invoking cloture on the manager's amendment (and its subsequent approval) made it a germane part of the complete substitute. Second, the same procedure was followed on the complete substitute: Invoke cloture on the complete substitute (now modified by the manager's amendment); run out the 30-hour post-cloture clock; and then adopt the complete substitute, making it part of and thus germane to H.R. 3590. Third, cloture was required on the bill itself (H.R. 3590, as amended) to block a filibuster on it and to move the legislation to final passage.

The record for cloture votes is eight, which occurred during the 100th Congress on a bill to limit campaign expenditures for Senate general election races. Majority Leader Byrd had made the spending-limit measure a priority, but Senate action was stymied by a 3-month, GOP-led filibuster. Seven cloture votes were held in 2003 on a controversial federal circuit court nomination—Miguel Estrada—before he withdrew his name from consideration.

Today, cloture is often used for purposes unrelated to ending talkathons. (Thus, counting the number of cloture votes is not a good indicator of how many filibusters occur in any year. However, the surge in filibusters or their threats has triggered a corresponding increase in the use of cloture.) It was not unusual for a majority leader—to expedite action on Senate business—to file a cloture petition on the motion to proceed and then immediately withdraw that motion. The majority leader would then bring other matters to the floor, leaving the clotured motion to proceed in a state of parliamentary limbo (not subject to debate or amendment) until cloture ripens 2 days later and the Senate votes on whether to invoke Rule XXII. A minority leader railed against this practice. "There is a time and a place for cloture," he said on one occasion, "but that time and place is not as soon as the bill is laid down."[119] On another occasion, he lamented: "I am reminded, again, as we file cloture, that the motion to invoke cloture is a motion to end debate. I am always amused by that phrase, 'end debate.' How do you end debate that you haven't even started?"[120] If cloture is invoked, then the motion to proceed becomes the pending business subject to the terms of Rule XXII. If cloture is defeated, the Senate will turn to other matters.

There are some occasions when the minority leader or a minority senator will file a cloture petition. This is unusual because it is typically the majority party that is trying to invoke cloture on the dilatory actions of the minority leader and his partisan colleagues. However, minority leaders or members may file a cloture petition to force votes on issues of political and substantive significance. Senator Tom Coburn, R-Okla., filed a cloture petition to force an unsuccessful cloture vote on his amendment to end tax subsidies for corn ethanol producers.[121] Or members of the minority party may overwhelmingly support cloture on the motion to proceed to a bill they oppose to force debate on germane "November" amendments. By a vote of 92 to 4, with only one GOP lawmaker voting against cloture, the Senate agreed to proceed to a controversial bill repealing tax breaks for the oil industry. Minority Republicans said they backed cloture to focus the Senate's attention on a Democratic bill that, they argued, would result in higher gasoline prices. Moreover, they wanted Democrats to vote on a number of amendments "that could force [them] to take some uncomfortable positions."[122] Conversely, the majority leader might schedule a series of cloture votes on bills unlikely to pass and then blame the minority party for being obstructionists.

In a Senate closely divided by party, the majority leader is unlikely to attract the required 60 votes, but this may set the stage for continued negotiations between the two sides on how to structure the floor amendment process. Cloture, too, is used to test sentiment for or against a measure, expedite action on legislation, permit party position-taking on issues, or, if it is invoked, keep nongermane amendments off the floor.

Recent Senates have also seen an increase in the majority leader "entering" a motion to reconsider a failed cloture vote—"Mr. President, I enter a motion to reconsider the vote by which cloture was not agreed to on S. 1234"—providing him additional time to round up the required votes, if he can. It is common for the majority leader to switch his vote on cloture to be on the prevailing side, as required by Senate rules, so he is eligible to offer the motion to reconsider at a later date. Entering the motion to reconsider a cloture vote also saves the Senate's time and enables the majority leader to better orchestrate floor proceedings. As congressional scholar Richard Beth explained:

> If the Majority Leader had instead chosen to offer a second cloture motion, the requirements of Rule XXII would have bound the Senate to a vote on the motion two days later. . . . By entering a motion to reconsider instead, the Majority Leader not only [avoids] being bound to a two-day layover period, but also [gains] the ability (at any point when sufficient support was available) to call up the motion to reconsider, bring the Senate to an immediate vote on cloture, and automatically bring the [measure or matter] back before the Senate under the restrictions of cloture.[123]

A marked increase in attempts to invoke cloture has characterized recent Congresses. For example, the decade from 1961 through 1971 saw 5.2 cloture votes per Congress,[124] whereas during the 107th Congress (2001–2003) alone, there were 61 cloture votes. The 110th Senate broke all records when the chamber voted on 112 cloture motions, "twice the number in the previous Congress and more than double the average number over the previous twenty years."[125] In Majority Leader Reid's judgment, what "we are seeing [this Congress] from Republicans is not ordinary obstruction. It is obstruction on steroids."[126] When the number of cloture motions for the 110th, 111th, and 112th Congresses are totaled, they approach 400. Senate Republicans, such as Lamar Alexander, Tenn., insist that the "real obstructionists have been the Democratic majority which for an unprecedented number of times, have used their majority advantage to limit debate, not allow amendments and bypass the normal committee consideration of legislation."[127]

An increase occurred as well in the number of cloture petitions filed on a subset of all cloture motions: on the leader's motion ("I move to take up

S. 1234") to proceed to legislation or nominations. Only two cloture petitions were filed on motions to proceed during the 96th Congress (1979–1981). Since the mid-1990s and continuing through the end of the 112th Congress (2011–2013), cloture on the leader's motion to proceed was always in the double digits. The current record was set in the 110th Congress (2007–2009) when "cloture was sought on the motion to proceed to consider 53 measures, 78 percent of all items of business on which cloture was attempted."[128]

In testimony presented to a 1993 congressional joint reorganization committee, a majority leader highlighted the obstacle course that legislation then had to complete if opposition to it was strong (see Box 7.4 for recent changes).

> When a filibuster occurs or is threatened, a cloture motion to terminate debate must be filed. The vote on that motion cannot occur until two days after it is filed. So if a cloture motion were filed today, Tuesday, the vote on it would occur on Thursday. If three-fifths or more vote to invoke cloture, there are still up to thirty hours of debate on the motion, post-cloture, or effectively two more days. So right now under Senate rules, cloture could be required up to six separate times on a single bill: on the motion to proceed to the bill, on the committee substitute, on the bill itself, and then . . . three times to get to conference with the House—[on the motions (1) to insist on Senate amendments, or disagree to House amendments; (2) to request a conference with the House; or (3) to authorize the chair to appoint conferees].[129]

Periodically, frustration with dilatory tactics gives rise to attempts to change Rule XXII, which has been amended a half-dozen times since 1917. In 1979, for example, Rule XXII was amended to allow, before a final vote on the measure or matter, 100 hours of post-cloture consideration; in 1986, the 100-hour cap on post-cloture consideration dropped to 30 hours. A filibuster reform advocated by various senators "would have declining cloture requirements of 60, 57, 54, 51, and then a simple majority on successive cloture votes."[130] Among other proposals are imposing debate limits (e.g., 2 hours) on the motion to proceed to consider a measure or matter; providing for majority cloture; reducing post-cloture debate on certain nominees from 30 hours to 2 hours; requiring senators who oppose a bill or nominee to take the floor and engage in a "talking filibuster" rather than just threatening extended debate; limiting to 2 hours debate on a motion to convene a conference (see Chapter 8) with the House; or providing "a mechanism by which the majority leader under certain circumstances could move the Senate to an immediate vote on cloture before the [2-day] layover period has expired."[131]

Various senators have urged an informal approach to improve Senate operations. "If the minority members would allow the majority leader to bring a bill to the floor without the 60-vote process, the legislation would be open to all relevant amendments but not to nonrelevant amendments."[132] In fact, a few weeks after the start of the 112th Congress, the two party leaders announced a nonbinding "gentlemen's agreement." For his part, GOP leader McConnell said that Republicans would restrict filibusters on motions to proceed to consider legislation. Democratic leader Reid stated that he would exercise restraint in filling the tree to block GOP amendments. In the end, these leadership commitments were not fulfilled. At the start of the 113th Congress, the two leaders did reach an agreement to modify filibuster procedures—while maintaining the 60-vote threshold for measures and nominations—that the Senate adopted on January 24, 2013. Although various senators viewed the changes as modest and incremental, Senators Reid and McConnell avoided use of two controversial methods to revise the cloture rule: by creating a new precedent or by majority vote of the Senate at the start of a new Congress (see below).

BOX 7.4   A Summary of New Filibuster Changes, 2013

The Senate adopted two bipartisan packages of new filibuster changes—one permanent (S. Res. 16) and the other temporary (S. Res. 15)—negotiated by the two party leaders: Majority Leader Reid and Minority Leader McConnell. Among the fundamental objectives of the changes are to expedite Senate action on legislation by minimizing the threat of a filibuster on the motion to proceed by allowing a simple majority to take up a bill, if amendment opportunities are guaranteed to the majority and minority parties, thus inhibiting "filling the tree"; collapsing into a single debatable motion, rather than three, the process for taking a bill to conference with the House, although that single motion is still subject to a filibuster; and shortening post-cloture debate time on certain nominations. In addition, Senators Reid and McConnell agreed that each would insist that senators who object to unanimous consent requests or threaten to filibuster must come to the floor and engage in debate; that the presiding officer could call for the question (a vote) under certain circumstances if no senator is seeking recognition to debate; and that the regular order (committee review, for example) would be followed during the 113th Congress for any further procedural changes.

A number of senators and outside groups criticized the changes for not going far enough. For example, some wanted to invoke cloture by majority vote rather than the 60-vote requirement for most measures and matters. (Recall that a two-thirds vote of those present and voting is required to end debate on Senate rules changes. A standing order has the same status as a Senate rule, but debate on it can be ended by 60 votes because formal Senate rules are not amended by it.) Others advocated a rules change that would require a "talking filibuster," akin to movie actor Jimmy Stewart's role in the classic movie *Mr. Smith Goes to Washington*. However, the incremental approach to change avoided a parliamentary meltdown if the "nuclear option"—changing Senate rules with majority support—had been used by Senator Reid; moreover, Senator Reid understood that Democrats would one day be in the minority and need the filibuster when the GOP controlled the Senate. Furthermore, use of the nuclear option was viewed as a "slippery slope" that any majority could use at any time to change Senate rules. The Senate might then become more like the majoritarian House.

A large difficulty in revising Senate procedures is the filibuster itself. Recall that to end extended debate on a proposal to change Senate rules requires a two-thirds cloture vote of those present and voting. (If cloture is invoked on a rules change, the revision then can be adopted by a simple majority vote.) The two-thirds voting threshold, combined with heightened partisanship in the Senate, makes procedural change difficult unless enough members from both sides support the modification of Senate rules. Two interconnected routes to procedural reform that would bypass the two-thirds hurdle require brief mention because they are often advocated by Senate reformers. One is the creation of a new Senate precedent, and

---

I. Permanent Changes (S. 16, adopted 86 to 9)—Amending Senate Rules

Motion to Proceed. Creates a bipartisan cloture motion to call up measures if signed by the majority leader and the minority leader and seven members from each party. The cloture vote will occur the day after a cloture motion is filed— thus eliminating a day's wait— and if cloture is invoked, the vote will occur on the motion to proceed without further debate.

Conference Committees. Allows one debatable motion to convene a conference with the House. If cloture is required to end debate, that motion is subject to 2 hours of debate, equally divided. If cloture is invoked by three fifths of the Senate (or 60 votes if there are no vacancies), the motion to take a bill to conference is voted on without further debate.

II. Temporary Changes (S. Res. 15, adopted 78 to 16)—Standing Order (Expires With the 113th Congress)

Motion to Proceed. Debate on a motion to proceed is limited to 4 hours, equally divided, in exchange for two amendment opportunities for each party. Specifically, if the motion to proceed is agreed to, then the first amendments in order shall be a first-degree minority party amendment, followed by a majority party amendment, then another minority party amendment, and then a majority party amendment. Each relevant or non-relevant and debatable amendment cannot be amended, and each must be disposed of before the next amendment in order can be offered. Disposition might include tabling, for example. The amendments, if cloture is filed, are subject to timely filing requirements. Moreover, if cloture is invoked on the measure, and a guaranteed amendment is ruled nongermane (recall that cloture imposes a germaneness requirement on amendments), the amendment "shall not fall upon that ruling, but instead shall remain pending and shall require 60 votes in the affirmative to be agreed to."

Nominations. If cloture is invoked to end debate on a nominee to be a federal district judge, post-cloture debate is limited to 2 hours, equally divided, rather than 30 hours. Post-cloture debate on lower-level federal appointments is limited to 8 hours, equally divided. Supreme Court and federal circuit court nominees, as well as cabinet-level positions are not affected by this change.

the other emphasizes the Senate's constitutional rulemaking authority at the start of a new Congress.

A New Precedent. In 2005, Majority Leader Bill Frist, R-Tenn., contemplated a parliamentary "nuclear option" (also called a "constitutional option") to end the partisan stalemate over judicial nominations by forcing their approval by majority vote. Frustrated by Democratic filibusters against several of President George W. Bush's judicial nominees, Frist planned to establish a new precedent that would change Senate procedure without amending Rule XXII by ending the requirement for a supermajority vote to end filibusters on judicial nominees. Under one version of this parliamentary maneuver, Frist would raise a point of order that further debate on a judicial nominee was dilatory and out of order and a vote on the judicial nominee should occur within a certain number of days or hours. The presiding officer would sustain the point of order, thereby setting aside and disregarding the Rule XXII (or 60-vote) procedure for ending the talkathon. No doubt a Democratic senator would appeal the ruling of the presiding officer, and Frist would then move to table (or kill) the appeal. (Motions to table are nondebatable.) Senate approval of the tabling motion would set a new and authoritative precedent for ending judicial filibusters by majority vote.[134] In the end, an ad hoc group of senators—seven Democrats and seven Republicans—came up with a compromise that avoided use of the nuclear, or constitutional, option. The so-called "gang of fourteen" signed a memorandum of understanding on judicial nominations, a key part of which stated that the seven Republicans would not support use of the nuclear option and the seven Democrats would not filibuster judicial nominees except under "extraordinary circumstances," an ambiguous phrase that was not defined.[135]

The Senate's Rulemaking Authority. The Constitution (Article I, Section 5) states: "Each House may determine the Rules of its Proceedings." Under the Senate's constitutional rulemaking authority, champions of filibuster reform have contended that the Senate, like the House, can change any of its rules by majority vote when a new Congress convenes. Rule XXII and not the entire Senate rulebook was the target for revision by the reformers of the 1950s, 1960s, 1970s, and, most recently, in 2011 and 2013. Opponents strongly disagreed with the reformers' approach. They argued, for example, that the Senate is a "continuing body"—only one third of its membership is up for reelection every 2 years, unlike the House—and thus has a quorum to conduct business. Moreover, its standing rules carry over from one Congress to the next unless they are amended by observing the chamber's rules. Significantly, Senate Rule V declares: "The rules of the Senate shall continue from one Congress to the next Congress unless they are changed as provided in these rules." In short, proponents of the rulemaking approach confront a "Catch-22" situation: The Constitution permits a majority, even a simple majority, to change Senate rules at any time—not just at the beginning of a new Congress—but opponents of procedural change contend that reformers are required to employ Rule XXII (with its two-thirds threshold) to stop filibusters against proposals to revise chamber rules.

If cloture is invoked, filibusters by amendment broken, and other delaying tactics ended, the Senate proceeds to a final vote on the bill under consideration. If obstructionist tactics cannot be stopped, the leadership may withdraw the bill and proceed to other business. While frustrating floor action is relatively easy, Senate rules make it difficult to bottle up measures in committees and prevent them from reaching the floor.

PROCEDURES TO CIRCUMVENT COMMITTEES

Bypassing committees, while not an everyday occurrence in the Senate, is easier to accomplish in that chamber than in the House. House members have access to various procedures for bringing to the floor bills that are blocked in committee, including the **discharge petition**, the power of extraction by the Rules Committee, and the suspension of the rules procedure. Yet, except for suspension, which generally is used for relatively noncontroversial bills, these procedures are seldom employed and rarely successful.

In the Senate, at least four techniques are available: (1) proposing nonrelevant amendments, also sometimes known as riders; (2) placing House-passed and Senate-introduced bills immediately on the Calendar of General Orders; (3) suspending Senate rules; and (4) implementing the discharge procedure. The first two are the most effective. The third was seldom used until recently, and then triggered a new Senate precedent. The fourth is rarely employed.

Technically, there is yet one other way to bypass a Senate committee: by unanimous consent. The Senate can do almost anything it wants by unanimous consent. However, unanimous consent will not be obtained if a single member—presumably a member of the committee that would be bypassed—objects. (It is common practice for the Senate to discharge measures from committees by unanimous consent—meaning with the committee's permission.)

Nongermane Amendments

Unlike the House, the Senate has never had a rule requiring that all amendments be germane to pending legislation. This feature probably ranks just below the filibuster as one of the Senate's most distinctive characteristics. "Amendments may be made," wrote Thomas Jefferson, "so as totally to alter the nature of the proposition."[136] A classic case occurred in 1965 when Senator Everett McKinley Dirksen, R-Ill. (1951–1969), tried to add a proposal for a constitutional amendment on legislative reapportionment to a joint resolution designating August 6 to September 6 as National American Legion Baseball Month. Dirksen's amendment had been blocked by the Judiciary Committee. An opponent of the proposal called the senator's attempt a "foul ball."

Periodically, the Senate has considered rule changes that would permit it to impose a germaneness requirement on floor amendments. Proponents argue that such a requirement would improve efficiency, expedite the workload, enhance relations with the House (which has a strict germaneness requirement), strengthen committees as centers of policymaking, and promote predictability in scheduling. Opponents contend that the right of senators to offer nonrelevant amendments serves as a safeguard against capricious committee actions, permits any senator to raise important issues, and enables the Senate to respond quickly to new developments. "What is at stake [in the ability of senators to offer nongermane amendments] is the right of a minority—even a tiny minority, even one Senator—to raise an issue," declared one senator.[137]

Germaneness sometimes has been a vexing issue for the Senate. On the one hand, the lack of a general prohibition on extraneous riders permits senators to raise and debate popular and unpopular issues and lessens the opportunity for arbitrary committee action. On the other hand, some senators complain that the practice wastes the Senate's time by permitting contentious debate on matters unrelated to the fundamental purpose of a pending bill.

Senate Prohibitions. Although the Senate does not have a general germaneness rule, the chamber requires germane amendments to pending legislation in four situations:

1. For unanimous consent agreements containing a requirement that amendments be germane (today, the term *relevant* is often employed because it is less restrictive)

2. For amendments to general appropriations bills

3. When cloture has been invoked

4. During consideration of certain measures governed by law, such as reconciliation bills

When the Senate operates under a germaneness requirement, its tests for determining whether amendments are germane are stricter than those in the House. A Senate report noted that "a legislative amendment is germane if, and only if, it proposes to strike out or to change a number or date, or if its effect would be to restrict the scope of the measure or the powers it grants."[138] A presiding officer once noted, if an "amendment expands the effect of the bill or introduces new subject matter it is not germane."[139] Thus, if a farm bill dealt with five items—barley, wheat, rice, cotton, and soybeans—and a senator sought to amend the measure by adding a sixth item to the list, a germaneness point of order could be made against the amendment. Sense-of-the-Senate (or sense-of-Congress) amendments, which are nonbinding and generally symbolic in intent, and amendments to strike language are considered germane in most circumstances. (In 2000, the Senate agreed that 60 votes are needed to add sense-of-the-Senate amendments to budget resolutions.)

In the mid- to late 1980s, the Senate so narrowed its meaning of what constituted a germane amendment that when the germaneness requirement was in effect, it prevented consideration of "policy alternatives that are highly pertinent but nonetheless nongermane because they expand the coverage of the bill or the powers it conveys."[140] The Senate needed a broader term to permit subject-related amendments to be offered to pending measures when they were governed by the germaneness stricture. Beginning in the mid- to late 1980s, the Senate began to employ the term *relevancy*. The test for relevancy is defined by Senate precedent:

> When relevancy of amendments is required by a unanimous consent agreement, that test is broader than the germaneness test as it is a subject matter test, and amendments that deal with the subject matter of the bill to which this requirement attaches are in order, provided they do not contain any significant matter not dealt with in that bill.[141]

Periodically, the question of the relevancy of amendments provokes sharp controversy on the Senate floor.[142] In a rare occurrence, a unanimous consent agreement stipulated that the two floor managers, rather than the Senate parliamentarian advising the presiding officer, "will be the arbiters of relevancy."[143]

On occasion, once cloture has been invoked—which triggers the stricter germaneness standard—a unanimous consent agreement has permitted selective relevant amendments to be offered post-cloture. As a majority leader noted after cloture was invoked, "Under an additional consent, relevant trade amendments are in order in addition to the germaneness requirement under rule XXII."[144]

Placing Measures on the Calendar

When bills or joint resolutions are introduced in the Senate or passed by the House and sent to the Senate, they customarily are referred to a committee. According to Senate Rule XIV, all measures, including House-passed bills, must be read twice on different legislative days before they can be referred to committee. If an objection is raised after the first reading, the second reading cannot occur until the next legislative day. After the second reading, the bill or joint resolution is sent to the appropriate committee. However, if an objection to further consideration of the bill is raised at the second reading, the measure is placed directly on the legislative calendar (see Box 7.5). Placing a bill on the calendar gives the leadership the option of calling up the House-passed measure or, if one exists, the Senate committee-reported version.

Rule XIV has been used increasingly in recent years.[145] Although it is not used for the vast majority of measures, Rule XIV is often employed on party issues of high priority. The majority leader may employ it to bypass committees because no time is available for lengthy committee review, some senators fear a bill might get stuck in committee, the Senate wants to vote quickly on a measure, or the majority leader wants an issue on the legislative calendar ready to be called up at his discretion.

BOX 7.5 Measure Placed on the Legislative Calendar

Measure read the first time—H.R. 436, June 11, 2012

MR. MENENDEZ. MR. President, I understand there is a bill at the desk, and I ask for its first reading.

The PRESIDING OFFICER. The clerk will read the bill by title for the first time.

The legislative clerk read as follows:

A bill (H.R. 436) to amend the Internal Revenue Code of 1986 to repeal the excise tax on medical devices.

MR. MENENDEZ. MR. President, I now ask for a second reading and, in order to place the bill on the calendar under the provisions of rule XIV, I object to my own request.

The PRESIDING OFFICER. Objection having been heard, the bill will be read for the second time on the next legislative day.

Measure placed on the calendar—H.R. 436, June 12, 2012.

MR. REID. MR. President, H.R. 436 is at the desk, and due for a second reading.

The ACTING PRESIDENT PRO TEMPORE. Without objection, the clerk will read the bill by title for the second time.

The legislative clerk read as follows:

A bill (H.R. 436) to amend the Internal Revenue Code of 1986 to repeal the excise tax of medical devices.

MR. REID. I now object to proceeding further on this matter at this time.

The ACTING PRESIDENT PRO TEMPORE. Objection having been heard, the bill will be placed on the calendar.

SOURCE: *Congressional Record,* June 11, 2012, S3929-S3930; June 12, 2012, S931.

For instance, a majority leader, concerned about the pace of deliberation in the Judiciary Committee on an immigration reform measure, said he
would use Rule XIV to place his alternative immigration measure on the legislative calendar. (Instead, he asked and received unanimous consent to place
his bill on the calendar.) The majority leader also threatened to bring his bill
directly to the floor, bypassing Judiciary, unless the panel reported its version
of immigration reform in 11 days.[146] Judiciary met the deadline. Sometimes
a majority leader will both introduce a bill and have it referred to committee,
and also use Rule XIV to place a virtually identical measure on the legislative
calendar. In this way, if the committee is unable to act on the bill, the majority leader has it positioned to be called up at his discretion. (House-passed
measures are held at the desk when similar Senate bills are pending on the
calendar or are expected to be reported shortly out of committee.)

The majority leader's ability to recess or adjourn the Senate can be used strategically to prevent a senator's use of Rule XIV. Recall that when the Senate recesses at the end of a calendar day (August 28, for instance) the Senate continues in that legislative day—even though it could extend for several calendar days—until the Senate adjourns. Majority Leader Reid, for example, twice recessed the Senate to prevent Senate Republicans from introducing legislation (the Semper Fi Act) denying $2 million in federal funds to Berkeley, California, until the Marine Corps could continue its recruitment efforts in that city.

> Instead of adjourning at the end of a day as usual, the Senate "recessed" twice, a move that, under Senate rules, slows the process of adding new bills to the calendar. Majority Leader Harry Reid (D-Nev.) did not adjourn until Friday, effectively pushing back floor consideration on the GOP bill until Tuesday— the same day that the [Berkeley] city council is likely to tone down its call for the Marine Corps recruiters to leave town.[147]

In the end, the Berkeley city council affirmed the right of the Marine Corps to recruit in Berkeley, and the Senate did not take up the Semper Fi Act.

Suspension of the Rules

Senate rules can be suspended provided there is one day's written notice and the terms of the suspension motion are published in the *Congressional Record*. Senate rules are silent on the number of votes needed to suspend. Precedents require two-thirds of those present and voting, a quorum being present, to approve suspensions. Customarily, suspension motions were employed by senators who wanted to offer, contrary to Senate rules, policy amendments to general appropriations measures. The procedure was rarely successful, largely because it represented a challenge to the Appropriations Committee—a powerful Senate panel—and the voting requirement to suspend is high.

> Mr. President, in accordance with rule V of the Standing Rules of the Senate, I hereby give notice in writing that it is my intention to move to suspend paragraph 4 of rule XVI for the purpose of proposing to the bill, H.R. 2862, the Science, State, Justice, Commerce appropriations bill, the following amendment: [establishing a commission in the legislative branch].[148]

Quite suddenly, 2010 and 2011 witnessed a spike in motions to suspend the germaneness requirement for amendments stipulated in Rule XXII. (Most of the motions were noticed by senators Jim DeMint, R-S.C., and Tom Coburn, R-Okla.) In 2010, for example, the number of suspension notices aimed at Rule XXII "more than doubled (from 17 total in the previous 30-year period to 32 in 2010 alone," and the number actually offered on the floor "more than quadrupled (from a total of 4 between 1979 and 2009 to 18 in 2010 alone)."[149] The next year, the number of notices of intent jumped to 41, but the number offered dropped for various reasons, such as cloture not being invoked.[150]

In short, use of suspensions to circumvent cloture prohibitions was a new tactic, mainly employed by minority senators. Angry at the majority leader for filling the tree, as he did on various measures, minority senators employed the suspension tactic to force votes on their party-preferred, and nongermane, amendments during and even after the 30-hour post-cloture period. None of the post-cloture suspension motions were adopted in either year. But their often dilatory purpose and more frequent use triggered a response from the Democratic majority.

On October 6, 2011, the Senate established a new precedent that apparently disallows any suspension motions during the post-cloture stage. The Senate on that day was considering a bill (S. 1619) that addressed China's unfair manipulation of its currency to gain a trade advantage for its products in the world marketplace. The majority leader had filled the amendment tree on the bill pre-cloture, which angered Republicans who wanted an opportunity to debate their unrelated amendments, such as one advanced by Senator McConnell to force a vote on President Obama's jobs bill that would show weak Democratic support. The Senate voted (62 to 38) to invoke cloture on the currency bill, but GOP senators anticipated this result. A day earlier, on October 5, they noticed in the *Congressional Record* nine motions to suspend Rule XXII's germaneness requirement for amendments post-cloture, including Senator McConnell's.

Negotiations between the two party leaders—Democrat Reid and Republican McConnell—on devising a unanimous consent agreement broke down over how many and which motions to suspend would be allowed. Senator Reid exclaimed, "We have offered seven, but it is not the seven the minority leader wants." In response, Senator McConnell declared that we would "like to be able to pick our amendments [embedded in the motions to suspend] and not have him pick them."[151] This standoff led to a new procedural precedent banning post-cloture suspension motions.

First, Senator Reid pointed out that "since the Senate amended Rule XXII in 1979, cloture has been a process to bring Senate consideration to a close. The fundamental nature of cloture is to make consideration of the pending measure finite." He further emphasized that unless

> the Senate votes to change precedents today, we will be faced with an endless series of motions to suspend the rules after the Senate has voted overwhelmingly to bring consideration to a close, and that is a result that a functioning democracy cannot tolerate.[152]

Second, the majority leader called up Senator Coburn's suspension motion relating to foreign aid. Immediately, Senator Reid made a "point of order that the motion to suspend is a dilatory motion under rule XXII." The presiding officer, following the advice of the parliamentarian, said: "The point of order is overruled." (The chair's ruling was based on earlier precedents that stated, "When the Senate is operating under cloture, it is in order to move to suspend the rules.") Senator Reid quickly appealed the ruling of the chair (appeals are nondebatable once cloture is invoked), who the put this question to the Senate: "Shall the decision of the Chair stand as the judgment of the Senate?" The Senate answered "no"—48 senators voted to uphold the chair's ruling, and 51 voted against, thus sustaining Reid's point of order and creating the new Senate precedent.

Under the Senate's new precedent, "it will now be against the rules to seek the 67 votes needed to suspend the cloture rules and bring up an amendment that is non-germane, or unrelated, to the bill in question after a successful cloture vote."[153] Reid's action set off a debate on whether he had invoked the "nuclear option," similar to what Majority Leader Frist planned to do in 2005 to end judicial filibusters. Some said yes and some said no.[154] Only time will tell whether the precedent will be long lasting, modified, or reversed by some future Senate. In the judgment of a congressional scholar, "clamping down on efforts to offer non-germane amendments post-cloture was consistent with this general pattern [since 1979] of trying to make the Senate hew more closely to the intent of the cloture."[155]

Another perspective was provided by reform Senator Tom Udall, D-N.M., who characterized Reid's action as the "majority option," citing Senator Byrd's observation that "at any time that 51 Members of the Senate are determined to change [a] rule . . . and if the leadership of the Senate joins them . . . that rule will be changed."[156] At issue is whether Reid's relatively minor procedural tweak might tomorrow encourage a frustrated majority to overturn the chair's decisions to establish more significant precedents that foil dilatory actions by minority opponents.

Discharge Petition

The formal process to discharge a bill from a committee under Rule XVII has taken place only 14 times in the history of the Senate. It was last employed successfully in 1964. More recently, in 2003, Majority Leader Frist, seeking to demonstrate his determination to force action on several of President Bush's controversial judicial nominations, introduced several resolutions to discharge these nominees from the Judiciary Committee.[157] His **discharge resolutions** were placed on the Executive Calendar and received no further action.

The prevailing sentiment in the Senate is that the discharge procedure undercuts the committee system and also that the rules governing its use are cumbersome. The discharge motion can be made by any senator but only during the morning hour, which has fallen into disuse in today's Senate, and it must remain at the clerk's desk for one legislative day. Majority party leaders can forestall discharge motions for days or weeks by recessing, thus keeping the Senate in the same legislative day. If debate on the motion is not concluded within the morning hour, the motion is placed on the calendar where it faces the threat of a series of filibusters. A vote to **discharge a committee** of a bill requires a simple majority vote unless cloture must be invoked to stop a filibuster.

NOTES

1. During his service as vice president, John Adams (1789–1797) "cast 29 tie-breaking votes, more than any of his [45] successors in that position." *Congressional Record*, April 21, 1987, S5204.
2. For Cheney, see Steven Dennis, "Democrats' Procedural Gambit Sends Budget Savings Bill Back to the House," *CQ Today*, December 22, 2005, 6.
3. Erin Mershon, "Presiding Loses Its Prestige in Senate," *Roll Call*, August 2, 2011, 1.
4. *Congressional Record*, May 21, 1980, S5674.
5. On November 17, 1982, for the first time since 1793, the House had two legislative days in the same calendar day. It adjourned at 1:19 p.m. (the first legislative day) and then reconvened at 4 p.m. (the second legislative day). Sharp partisanship stimulated the Democratic leadership to employ this rare tactic.
6. *Senate Procedure: Precedents and Practices,* 97th Congress, 1st sess., 1982, S. Doc. 97-2, 565.
7. *Congressional Record*, March 26, 1987, S3927.
8. Ibid., February 27, 1998, S1175.
9. See Patrick Sellers, *Cycles of Spin, Strategic Communication in the U.S. Congress* (New York: Cambridge University Press, 2010).
10. *Congressional Record*, April 16, 1985, S4256.
11. Dan Friedman, "Rand Paul Makes Overture to Democrats," *National Journal Daily*, October 6, 2011, 3.
12. *Congressional Record*, June 9, 1977, 18179.
13. Ibid., June 21, 2004, S7086.
14. Kenneth Cooper, "Battle May Be Brewing on Hill Over Renewal of Education Act," *Washington Post*, May 14, 2000, A10.
15. John Stanton, "Senate GOP is Pushing a Message," *Roll Call,* April 28, 2009, 1, 3.
16. A Senate rule requires 3 hours of germane discussion at the beginning of each day's debate on a measure. Called the Pastore Rule after its sponsor, Senator John O. Pastore, D-R.I. (1950–1976), its purpose is to confine debate to pending business.
17. Kirk Victor, "Reason to Smile," *National Journal*, March 18, 2006, 22.
18. Kathy Kiely, "Fresh Faces in Congress Stress Cooperation," *USA Today*, June 6, 2005, 10A.
19. "Outspoken: A Conversation With Olympia Snowe," *Washington Post*, October 18, 2009, B2.
20. *Congressional Record*, January 21, 1986, S8.
21. Ibid., May 21, 1987, S6979.
22. Rowland Evans and Robert Novak, *Lyndon B. Johnson: The Exercise of Power* (New York: New American Library, 1966), 115.
23. David Fahrenthold, "In Senate, Clerk's Droning Means Lot of Nothing Going On," *Washington Post*, June 10, 2011, A15.
24. Joseph S. Clark, *Congress: The Sapless Branch* (New York: Harper & Row, 1964), 247–248.
25. Senate Rule XII also requires a live quorum call to precede acceptance of a unanimous consent agreement that sets "the taking of a final vote [on passage of a bill or joint resolution] on a specified date." This rule is observed rarely.

26. *New York Times*, June 8, 1986, E5.
27. *Congressional Record*, September 27, 1993, S12550.
28. Alexis Simendinger, "Chart Wars," *National Journal*, December 19, 2009, 43.
29. *Congressional Record*, October 28, 1977, 5857.
30. Ibid., May 17, 2012, S3265–S3266; May 21, 2012, S3304–S3307.
31. Ibid., May 21, 2012, S3305.
32. Brett Norman, "Senate Swiftly Passes FDA User Fee Reauthorization," *Politico*, May 25, 2012, 16.
33. Susan Rasky, "With Few Bills Passed or Ready for Action, Congress Seems Sluggish," *New York Times*, May 14, 1989, 24.
34. Kathleen Hunter, "Deals and Midnight Meetings in Senate Are a Matter of Trust," *CQ Today*, July 31, 2009, 1.
35. *Wall Street Journal*, March 2, 1995, A16.
36. *CQ Daily Monitor*, March 2, 1995, 5.
37. Richard Cohen, "Amendment Mania," *National Journal*, November 1, 2003, 3335.
38. John Bresnahan, "Democrats Angered by Senate Maneuvering on FEC," *Roll Call*, August 3, 1998, 3.
39. *Congressional Record*, December 16, 2009, S13290, S13309, S13311.
40. Ibid., December 19, 2009, S13479.
41. Carrie Budoff Brown, "Senate Debate Begins as Dems Look for a Deal," *Politico*, November 30, 2009, 15.
42. Christopher M. Davis, "Filling the Amendment Tree in the Senate," *CRS Report* RS22854, April 2, 2008, 2.
43. *Congressional Record*, July 8, 2004, S7785.
44. Emily Pierce, "GOP Quickly Goes to War," *Roll Call*, December 2, 2009, 1.
45. *Congressional Record*, December 11, 2009, S13004.
46. Emily Pierce, "Specter Wants Changes To Rules for Debate," *Roll Call*, February 6, 2007, 16. Also see *Congressional Record*, May 6, 2008, S3753–S3756.
47. *Congressional Record*, September 24, 2008, S9379. See also Christopher M. Davis, "Filling the Amendment Tree in the Senate," *CRS Report for Congress*, RS22854, February 2, 2011, 2–3.
48. *Congressional Record*, September 29, 1997, S10103–S10114.
49. *Congressional Quarterly Almanac, 1997* (Washington, DC: Congressional Quarterly, 1998), 1–27.
50. Steven T. Dennis, "Rocky Road for Senate Comity," *Roll Call*, June 16, 2011, 1.
51. *Congressional Record*, June 29, 2011, S4206.
52. Martin B. Gold, *Senate Procedure and Practice* (Lanham, Md.: Rowman & Littlefield, 2004), 91–92.
53. *Congressional Record*, June 21, 2004, S7062.
54. Ibid., November 5, 1985, 30522.
55. *Washington Post*, July 24, 1991, A1.
56. Robert D. Novak, "Dorgan's Poison Pill," *Washington Post*, June 14, 2007, A27.
57. *Congressional Record*, July 8, 2004, S7785.
58. Ibid., December 7, 2009, S12599.
59. Ibid., May 20, 1996, S5339.
60. *Congress DailyAM*, May 11, 2000, 5.
61. Frances E. Lee, "Party Politics, Public Relations, and Changes in Senate Floor Politics, 1959–2008," Paper Prepared for Presentation at the Congress and

History Conference, University of California, Berkeley, June 10–11, 2010, 7. Frances Lee is a political science professor at the University of Maryland.

62. Quoted in "Final Word," *National Journal Daily PM Update*, June 5, 2012, 4.

63. *Congressional Record*, January 26, 1973, 2301.

64. Colbert King, "Democrats Are on the Wrong Battlefield," *Washington Post*, July 23, 2005, A17.

65. *Congressional Record*, December 9, 1987, S17476.

66. Ibid., March 29, 2007, S4221.

67. Ibid., September 23, 1975, 29814.

68. Ibid., June 23, 1987, S8442.

69. "Durbin Wants Dems to Stick Together," *CongressDailyPM*, July 7, 2009, 6. See also Emily Pierce, "Leaders Press Case for Unity," *Roll Call*, July 8, 2009, 1.

70. Emily Pierce and John Stanton, "Lincoln's Saturday Timing Puzzles Colleagues," *Roll Call*, November 21, 2009, online edition.

71. David M. Drucker, "Nelson Scrambles to Defend Health Vote," *Roll Call*, December 30, 2009, online edition.

72. Senator Blanche Lincoln, D-Ark., waited until she was the last lawmaker to vote on the motion to proceed to health care reform and "arguably became the decisive vote that put the Democratic bill over the top." Pierce and Stanton, "Lincoln's Saturday Timing Puzzles Colleagues." See also Manu Raju and Chris Frates, "Lincoln's Long Walk to 60th Senate Vote," *Politico*, November 23, 2009, 1.

73. Rachel Boehm and Aaron Lorenzo, "Senate Passes Bill to Pressure China on Foreign Exchange Rate Policy," *Daily Report for Executives*, October 12, 2011, EE-15.

74. Data and analysis on the heightened use of the supermajority requirement in unanimous-consent agreements was developed by Valerie Heitshusen of the Congressional Research Service.

75. Ibid., 23.

76. Megan Suzanne Lynch, *Unanimous Consent Agreements Establishing a 60-Vote Threshold for Passage of Legislation in the Senate*, CRS Report RL34491, May 12, 2009, 5.

77. *Congressional Record*, April 8, 1981, S6874.

78. Ibid., S3618.

79. Ibid., July 22, 1983, S10701.

80. Ibid., October 10, 1985, S13114.

81. *New York Times*, December 21, 1982, D29.

82. The word *filibuster* derives from the Dutch word *Vrijbuiter*, meaning "freebooter." Passing into Spanish as *filibustero*, the term was used to describe military adventurers from the United States who in the mid-1800s fomented insurrections against various Latin American governments. For an account of William Walker, filibusterer of the 1850s, see *Smithsonian*, June 1981, 117–128. The first legislative use of the word is said to have occurred in the House in 1853, when a representative accused his opponents of "filibustering against the United States." By 1863, the word *filibuster* had come to mean delaying action on the floor, but the term did not gain wide currency until the 1880s.

83. *Congressional Record*, July 18, 1983, S10216.

84. Ibid., November 12, 2002, S11034.

85. Robert B. Dove, "Senate Rule XXII: The Good, the Bad, and the Ugly," *Roll Call*, November 13, 2003, 20.

86. *Congressional Record*, July 8, 2004, S7789.
87. Ibid., July 20, 1995, 19662.
88. Doug Obey, "Alaska," *The Hill*, July 10, 1996, 27.
89. Ezra Klein, "After Health Care, We Need Senate Reform," *Washington Post*, December 27, 2009, B2.
90. *Washington Post*, February 20, 1994, A13.
91. Geof Koss, "Climate Unchanged on Energy Bill," *CQ Today*, June 11, 2010, 6.
92. *New York Times*, December 12, 1982, 4E.
93. Josh Rogin, "Reports Renew Guantánamo Fight," *CQ Today*, August 5, 2009, 2.
94. *Congressional Record*, December 16, 2009, S13312–S13313.
95. *Washington Times*, November 17, 1987, A6.
96. *Congressional Record*, December 21, 2010, S10854.
97. Sarah Binder, Eric Lawrence, and Steven Smith, "Explaining Senate Change: The Rise in Filibustering, 1917–1996" (paper presented at the annual meeting of the Midwest Political Science Association, Chicago, April 10–12, 1997), 3.
98. Ezra Klein, "The Rise of the Filibuster: An Interview With Barbara Sinclair," *Washington Post*, December 26, 2009, online edition, and Barbara Sinclair, *Unorthodox Lawmaking*, 2d ed. (Washington, DC: CQ Press, 2000), 99.
99. "Take Five, Q&A," *Roll Call*, April 17, 2012, 27.
100. *CongressDailyAM*, November 10, 1993, 1, 7.
101. *Congressional Record*, October 5, 1992, S16577.
102. "Democrats to Forgo Control in Brief Edge," *Washington Times*, November 29, 2000, A4.
103. *Congressional Record*, June 13, 2012, S4126.
104. Ibid.
105. Ibid.
106. Ibid., February 26, 1979, 3232.
107. Ibid., May 8, 2012, S2954.
108. *Operations of Congress: Testimony of House and Senate Leaders*, hearing before the Joint Committee on the Organization of Congress, 103d Congress, 1st sess., January 26, 1993, 50.
109. *Congressional Record*, September 27, 1984, S12137.
110. Gregory J. Wawro and Eric Schickler, *Filibuster: Obstruction and Lawmaking in the U.S. Senate* (Princeton, NJ: Princeton University Press, 2006), 260.
111. Richard F. Fenno Jr., "The Senate Through the Looking Glass: The Debate Over Television," *Legislative Studies Quarterly* (August 1989): 316.
112. *Congressional Record*, March 3, 1986, S1915.
113. Sarah Binder and Steven Smith, *Politics or Principle? Filibustering in the United States Senate* (Washington, DC: Brookings, 1997), 15.
114. Frances E. Lee, "Senate Deliberation and the Future of Congressional Power," *PS*, April 2010, 227.
115. One example of a mistake filibustering senators can make that will lose them the floor is violation of the two-speech rule, which forbids members from making a third speech on the same question in the same legislative day. For a contentious debate on the two-speech rule, see *Congressional Record*, September 25, 1986, S13687–S13710, and *Washington Post*, October 1, 1986, A17. Further, senators who use objectionable or offensive language might, under Senate Rule XIX, lose their right to the floor. Rarely is this rule invoked.

116. *Washington Post,* June 11, 1982, A11.

117. *Congressional Record,* September 21, 1893, 1636.

118. Kerry Young, "Senate Hopes to Complete Second 'Minibus' Before Thanksgiving Recess," *CQ Today,* November 10, 2011, 3.

119. *Congressional Record,* July 7, 1998, S7565.

120. Ibid., March 28, 2000, S1832.

121. Steven Mufson, "Ethanol Subsidy Fight Not Over," *Washington Post,* June 16, 2011, A18.

122. Olga Belogolova, "Senate Sets Up Energy Debate—and Key Votes," *National Journal Daily,* March 27, 2012, 14.

123. Beth et al., "Leadership Tools for Managing the U.S. Senate," 7.

124. David Baumann, "The Collapse of the Senate," *National Journal,* June 3, 2000, 1759.

125. Eve Fairbanks, "Tough Reid," *The New Republic,* April 15, 2009, 14.

126. *Congressional Record,* December 12, 2007, S15158.

127. Ibid., January 27, 2011, S322.

128. Beth et al., "Leadership Tools for Managing the U.S. Senate," 6.

129. *Operations of Congress,* 116.

130. *Congressional Record,* June 27, 2003, S8844.

131. Christopher M. Davis, Valerie Heitshusen, and Betsy Palmer, "Proposals to Change the Operation of Cloture in the Senate," CRS Report R41342, July 27, 2010, 8.

132. Carl Levin and Lamar Alexander, "Model for Self-Restraint in Senate," *Washington Post,* April 27, 2012, A15.

133. *Congressional Record,* January 3, 2013, S9.

134. See Martin B. Gold and Dimple Gupta, "The Constitutional Option to Change Senate Rules and Procedures: A Majoritarian Means to Overcome the Filibuster," *Harvard Journal of Law and Public Policy* (Fall 2003): 206–271. Senator Robert C. Byrd refuted claims by Gold and Gupta that Byrd as majority leader established precedents that justify the nuclear option. See *Congressional Record,* March 20, 2005, S3100–S3103. See also Sarah A. Binder, Anthony J. Madonna, and Steven S. Smith, "Going Nuclear, Senate Style," *Perspective on Politics,* December 2007, 729–740.

135. The memorandum is printed in the *Congressional Record,* May 24, 2005, S5830–S5831.

136. *Constitution, Jefferson's Manual, and Rules of the House of Representatives,* 102d Congress, 2d sess., H. Doc. 102-405, 233.1.

137. *Congressional Record,* February 26, 1986, S1663.

138. Senate Committee on Rules and Administration, *Report on Senate Operations,* 1988, 100th Congress, 2d sess., September 20, 1988, S. Print 100-129, 55.

139. *Congressional Record,* February 9, 1982, S599.

140. Ibid.

141. Floyd Riddick and Alan Frumin, *Senate Procedure: Precedents and Practices* (Washington, DC: Government Printing Office, 1992), 1362–1363.

142. See, for example, *Congressional Record,* May 21, 2003, S6827–S6828.

143. *Congressional Record,* June 21, 2002, S5882.

144. Congressional Record, November 2, 1999, S13632. See Richard Cohen, "Amendment Mania," *National Journal,* November 1, 2003, 3334–3338.

145. C. Lawrence Evans and Walter J. Oleszek, "Message Politics and Senate Procedure," in *The Contentious Senate*, Colton Campbell and Nicol Rae, ed. (Lanham, Md.: Rowman & Littlefield, 2001), 107–127.

146. Jonathan Weisman, "Frist Pushes for Quick Vote on Immigration," *Washington Post*, March 17, 2006, A4.

147. Manu Raju, "Reid's Move Delayed Rap on Berkeley," *The Hill,* February 12, 2008, 13.

148. *Congressional Record*, September 8, 2005, S9800.

149. These data were kindly provided by CRS congressional expert Elizabeth Rybicki. Along with two other congressional authorities—Richard Beth and Valerie Heitshusen—Rybicki is working on a draft report on the Senate's use of suspension motions during post-cloture periods.

150. Ibid.

151. *Congressional Record,* October 6, 2011, S6314–S6315. Useful to note is that the tree remained filled post-cloture, which was confirmed by the chair. As Senator McConnell inquired of the chair: "At the end of cloture, would it require consent to offer motions to suspend?" The chair responded, "Once an amendment slot is available [on the filled tree], the motion to suspend is in order." These statements are found on page S6314.

152. Ibid.

153. "Reid Sets Procedural Precedent; Senate Minority Rights at Stake," *CQ Weekly*, October 10, 2011, 2103.

154. See Marc A. Thiessen, "Harry Reid's Nuclear Blunder," *Washington Post*, October 8, 2011, A19, and the majority leader's rebuttal, Harry A. Reid, "A Return to Order in the Senate," *Washington Post*, October 11, 2011, A23.

155. Sarah Binder, "Did the U.S. Senate Just Go Nuclear?" *Brookings: The Monkey Cage* (Professor Binder's Blog), October 7, 2011, 2. For a detailed review of cloture and the limitation of debate in the Senate, see *Senate Cloture Rule*, Senate Committee on Rules and Administration, S. Prt. 112-31 (Washington, D.C.: U.S Government Printing Office, 2011).

156. *Congressional Record,* October 11, 2011, S6375.

157. Ibid., July 7, 2003, S8893.

CHAPTER 8

Resolving House–Senate Differences

UNDER THE CONSTITUTION, before measures can be sent to the White House for presidential consideration, they must pass the House and Senate with exactly the same bill number and legislative text.[1] House- and Senate-passed versions of the same bill frequently differ, sometimes only slightly but often on critical points. But whatever the differences, the two versions must be reconciled by mutual agreement. Whenever possible, this reconciliation is undertaken informally through negotiations between the relevant actors of each chamber. However, a fair percentage of all bills passed by both chambers require action by the most prominent of the bicameral reconciliation methods: the formation of a House–Senate conference committee, an ad hoc joint committee composed of members selected by each chamber to resolve differences on a particular bill in disagreement.[2] Major and controversial legislation usually requires conference committee action, although recent Congresses have seen a decline in their use (discussed later in this chapter).

Conference committees are called the "third house" of Congress. Here the final version of a bill is written, often by a small number of lawmakers, who sometimes are only majority party members. A senator who taught college government courses underscored the key role of conference committees.

> I used to teach political science classes. . . . You know, I feel guilty. I need to refund tuition to students for those 2 weeks I taught classes on the Congress. I was so off in terms of a lot of the decision making.
>
> I should have focused on the conferences committees as the third House of Congress, because these folks can do any number of different things. And the thing that drives me crazy is you can have a situation where the Senate did not have a provision in the bill, and the conference committee just puts it in the bill. Then it comes back for an up-or-down vote. No opportunity to amend.
>
> Or you can have a situation where the Senate and the House pass bills with provisions in them and the conference takes it out. It is, I think, the least accountable part of decision making in Congress.[3]

OBSCURITY OF THE PROCESS

The conference committee process is older than Congress itself. State legislatures used conference committees before 1789 to reconcile differences between the chambers of their bicameral legislatures. The conference committee system was taken for granted when the first Congress convened, and it has been in use ever since.[4] Nevertheless, for many citizens the conference committee is a little-known or little-understood entity compared with the other aspects of the legislative process.

Until the mid-1970s, conference committees almost always met in secret sessions with no published record of their proceedings. The conference committee reports they produced revealed the results of the secret negotiations, but the bargaining and deliberations that led to these results were not formally disclosed.

In one of the most significant reforms of congressional procedure, both chambers in 1975 adopted rules requiring open conference committee meetings unless a majority of the conference members (called conferees or managers) from either chamber voted in public to hold secret sessions. In 1977 the House went a step further, adopting a rule requiring the full House to vote to close a conference. Closure usually occurs on legislation dealing with national security. For example, the head of the House conference delegation will offer the nondebatable motion to close the conference committee "to the public at such times as classified national security information is under consideration."[5]

Conferees still conduct much of their important business in secret, however. As the late Senator Russell B. Long, D-La. (who voluntarily retired at the end of the 99th Congress after 38 years of service), once noted in a statement that holds true today:

> The Senator knows when we started the openness thing we found it more and more difficult to get something agreed to in the conferences, it seemed to take forever. So what did we do? The Senator knows what we did. We would break up into smaller groups and then we would ask our chairman . . . to see if he could not find his opposite number on the House side and discuss this matter and come back and tell us what the chances would be of working out various and sundry possibilities.[6]

Relatively few complaints have been raised about closed sessions. Political commentators and others recognize the value of candid exchanges (away from the glare of special interest groups) in informal closed meetings. Furthermore, reporters are usually kept well informed of the results of closed conferences. In today's open and Internet politics era, "secret" does not mean what it used to on Capitol Hill. On occasion, conference negotiating sessions have been televised over the Cable-Satellite Public Affairs Network (C-SPAN). Televising conferences, which is usually the prerogative of the overall conference committee chair, might even be part of the strategy to influence conference decision making. Televising an energy conference, remarked a senator, "might help public opinion" sway reluctant conferees to support more domestic oil production given rising gasoline prices.[7] (For a mini-case example of conference committee proceedings, see the appendix to this chapter, which provides an overview of the 2012 surface transportation conference.)

The conference committee is one of the most critical points in the legislative process. For several reasons, however, members of Congress may try to avoid this stage and resolve House–Senate differences on legislation without recourse to the conference committee process. First, pressure exists to approve the legislation quickly. Second, the House may be concerned that members of the other chamber will filibuster the conference report on legislation. For example, on a nuclear waste storage bill, the House leadership "decided to go with the Senate version in an attempt to avoid a filibuster threatened by Nevada's [the proposed nuclear waste storage site] senators on any conference report to the legislation."[8] Third, a conference committee could become deadlocked—particularly in the weeks and days before the final adjournment of Congress. Failure of the conferees to reach agreement before the end of a Congress means that the bill dies. Sometimes lawmakers from each chamber may not want to officially create a conference until they get a sense through private negotiations that a compromise can be worked out. In these cases, creation of a conference committee "will be more an indication that a deal is done than a forum to find one."[9]

Another reason why a conference would not occur is because the House believes that the Senate-passed legislation violates the origination clause of the Constitution by including revenue-raising provisions in its bill.[10] For example, the House and Senate each passed their own version of legislation reauthorizing the Violence Against Women Act (P.L. 103-322). The House GOP leadership stated they would not go to conference on the Senate-passed bill "because it contained a little-noticed revenue provision that raises fees on certain kinds of visas for immigrants." In such cases, the House uses a "blue slip" to return to the other body the Senate measure on the ground that the legislation invaded the constitutional prerogatives of the House. Senate Majority Leader Harry Reid, D-Nev., disagreed strongly with the House Republican leadership, urging them to "abandon their hypertechnical objections and join us in conference."[11] The House did not agree, upending bicameral action on the legislation.

AGREEMENT WITHOUT A CONFERENCE

There are two ways of achieving bicameral ignition—that is, each chamber approving the same bill—without a conference. First, one chamber can adopt verbatim the version of the bill produced by the other. This route is taken most frequently in lawmaking because most of the legislation agreed to is noncontroversial, such as measures to name post office buildings after prominent individuals. However, there are occasions when the "rubber-stamp" route is tried on controversial measures. The "rubber-stamp" approach may also involve informal consultation before or after passage of the bill by lawmakers and staff of one chamber with their counterparts in the other body. For instance, House and Senate members and their staff aides consult informally prior to a bill's introduction in one chamber to facilitate its approval without amendment by the second-acting chamber.

Sometimes one chamber will adjourn and put the other chamber in a "take-it-or-leave-it" position. On the popular "Cash for Clunkers" automobile trade-in program, the House adopted the bill (H.R. 3435) on July 31, 2009, replenishing the program's depleted funds. The House then left town for the traditional month-long August break. With large public interest in the popular program, Senate advocates preferred not to wait until after Labor Day to consider the bill. They successfully urged their colleagues to approve the House-passed bill without change. "If we leave here without adopting the House Bill," exclaimed Senator Carl Levin, D-Mich., "it is the end of the most successful [economic] stimulus package to date."[12]

Second, the two houses may send measures back and forth several times, amending each other's amendments, before they agree to identical language on all provisions of the legislation. "This method is frequently used in the closing days of a Congress to save time," wrote a congressional journalist. "Bills may be sent back and forth on an hourly basis until there is a meeting of the minds, or one side backs down, or the two chambers give up in failure."[13] The "ping-pong" approach may also be employed in combination with conference committee negotiations. The chambers, for instance, may start out using the ping-pong approach but then convene a conference committee to reconcile the remaining matters in disagreement. Or the reverse could occur: The chambers might create a conference committee, resolve most of the matters in disagreement, enact a partial conference report, and resolve the outstanding amendments in disagreement via the exchange of amendment procedure. Table 8.1 presents data on how often different procedures for reaching bicameral agreement were used in selected Congresses.

House and Senate committee staff, as well as the lawmakers, communicate regularly on legislation of mutual interest. Drafts of measures are exchanged for comment and consistency, companion bills are studied, and strategies are devised to facilitate passage in each chamber. Executive branch officials and lobbyists often participate in these informal strategy sessions. This kind of prior consultation, as noted earlier, frequently helps clear away obstacles to passage—allowing legislation to be approved by both houses in identical form, thus avoiding the need for a conference.

Informal bicameral discussions were instrumental in the passage of the landmark Congressional Accountability Act (H.R. 1), applying federal workplace safety and antidiscrimination laws to the legislative branch. The House acted first on the bill and sent it to the Senate, where members wanted to make some changes. After consultations with the House sponsors of the legislation, the Senate passed S. 2, its version of the accountability act, and sent that measure to the House. To avoid the need for a conference committee, House leaders decided to take up S. 2 under suspension of the

TABLE 8.1   Methods of Bicameral Resolution on Public Laws, 1993 to December 2011

Congress	Public Laws	Simple Adoption by One Chamber of the Version Sent to It by the Other	Amendments Between the Houses	Conference*
103rd (1993–1994)	465	291 (63%)	1,112 (24%)	62 (13%)
104th (1995–1996)	333	234 (70%)	55 (17%)	44 (13%)
105th (1997–1998)	394	278 (71%)	77 (20%)	39 (10%)
106th (1999–2000)	580	436 (75%)	106 (18%)	38 (7%)
107th (2001–2002)	377	289 (77%)	55 (15%)	33 (9%)
108th (2003–2004)	498	406 (82%)	57 (11%)	35 (7%)
109th (2005–2006)	482	396 (82%)	60 (12%)	26 (5%)
110th (2007–2008)	460	371 (81%)	80 (17%)	9 (2%)
111th (2009–2010)	385	293 (76%)	78 (20%)	12 (3%)
112th, first session (to December 20, 2011)	73	58 (79%)	13 (18%)	2 (3%)

Source: Elizabeth Rybicki, Congressional Research Service expert on resolving bicameral differences.

*If both chambers appointed conferees, the measure was included in the count of conference committee, even if some differences were resolved through amendment exchange.

rules, and the measure was passed by more than the two-thirds vote (390–0) required under that procedure. The House action cleared the legislation for presentation to President Bill Clinton, who signed the measure into law.

Worth underscoring is that House and Senate members often look to allies in the other body for assistance in advancing legislation. For example, GOP senators in the 112th Democratic Senate looked to their Republican colleagues "in the House to move bills in that chamber and urge House leaders to press the Senate to consider the measures."[14] House and Senate leaders of the same party, as well as their top staff aides, consult frequently on strategies to advance their priorities through each chamber. In short, a diverse array of informal bicameral interactions permeates congressional policymaking.

More on Amendment Exchange Between the Chambers

Given wider use in recent Congresses of the amendment exchange procedure, three points about ping-ponging amendments back-and-forth between the houses are useful to note. First, a technical limit exists to the number of times measures may be shuffled between the chambers. The third-degree amendment prohibition applies to amendments between the House and

Senate. Each chamber gets two shots at amending the amendments of the other body.

> In short, after each chamber has passed the same bill for the first time (for example, the House passes a House bill and the Senate passes the House bill with Senate amendments), each chamber may have one opportunity to amend the amendments of the other chamber.[15]

Like many legislative procedures, the two-degree principle can be waived, ignored, or overturned. (The House sets aside this principle by special rule, suspension of the rules, or unanimous consent; the Senate, usually by unanimous consent.) The Consolidated Omnibus Reconciliation Act of 1985 bounced between the chambers a record-setting nine times.

Second, the back-and-forth procedure is usually employed intentionally to avoid conferences or when circumstances warrant its use. For example, a House chair may ask the chamber to concur in the Senate amendment to the House amendment to the Senate-passed bill. House approval is "appropriate parliamentary procedure, which allows us to avoid the trouble of a conference when faced with such small [bicameral] differences."[16] The House in this case agreed to the Senate amendment, which cleared the bill for the president. Lack of time also can prevent formation of conference committees and necessitate use of the back-and-forth approach. Or procedural and political conditions require its use as the only feasible option for resolving bicameral differences on legislation.

Finally, recent Congresses, especially the 110th (2007–2009) and the 111th (2009–2011), witnessed greater use of the ping-pong method on controversial and consequential legislation because of the Senate's difficulty in getting to conference (see section in this chapter titled "Requesting a Conference"). The Senate's tradition of extended debate and the exclusion of minority-party conferees from participating in the bicameral bargaining process led to the heightened importance of the ping-pong approach. Several consequences flow from the greater use of the exchange of amendment procedure for resolving bicameral differences on major legislation.

First, the exchange of amendment procedure bolsters the negotiating role of the Speaker and Senate majority leader. They are strategically positioned, along with selected key lawmakers, to fashion compromises through amendment exchanges with sometimes little input from rank-and-file members, the committees of original jurisdiction, or the minority party. On a children's health bill, for example, the majority leader of the House stated that if the Senate was unable to convene a conference because of blocking actions by various senators, they would meet informally with their Senate leadership counterparts to negotiate a compromise bill. As one account noted, the top House and Senate majority leaders "met for nearly two hours" working "to reach a final agreement on compromise [children's health] legislation."[17] The greater prominence of the ping-pong procedure reflects the gradual institutionalization of a leadership-influenced bicameral bargaining process that has been evolving for several years.

Second, use of the ping-pong procedure on major bills can minimize the role of committee leaders and members. On a major energy bill (H.R. 6) that was signed into law, as many as 40 committee members with energy expertise criticized the secret bicameral process by which the compromise measure was jointly assembled by each chamber's majority leaders. As the House Energy and Commerce chair exclaimed:

> H.R. 6 is not the product of a formal conference, but rather the result of amendments being passed between the House and Senate as a means of resolving the differences between their respective bills. I have noted in the past, and will continue to note, that I find this manner of legislating to be unsatisfactory and unwise. Given the difficulty experienced by the Senate in going to conference on this bill this year, however, this process is the best that we can hope for under the circumstances. . . . One of the reasons this [ping-pong] process is inferior to that of a formal conference is the lack of a conference report and, thus, the lack of a written legislative history detailing why certain policies were adopted and others excluded.[18]

Third, minority party members also may be excluded from these bicameral negotiating sessions unless their input is sought by the leaders (the Speaker and Senate majority leader) in charge of the back-and-forth amendment procedure. Such participation is more likely to involve minority-party senators than minority House members. The contributions of minority-party senators might be important in devising a product that can attract not only a majority but the supermajority often required to enact legislation in the Senate. From the majority leadership's perspective, they may ask why they should create a bipartisan conference committee when minority party conferees are likely to oppose and stall whatever the majority tries to do.

Fourth, a number of formal House and Senate rules that apply to conference reports are avoided by using the exchange of amendment procedure. For example, as noted above by the House Energy chair, there is no joint explanatory statement that accompanies the amendment exchange procedure unless the negotiators include some explanatory material in the *Congressional Record*. A majority of House and Senate conferees must sign the conference report; no such public requirement exists for those involved in ping-pong negotiations. Points of order can be raised if a new matter not considered in either chamber is included, or "air dropped," in a conference report. This prohibition does not apply to amendment exchanges. For example, a House amendment to a Senate amendment to the House-passed bill may reflect a major new policy proposal that was negotiated in secret by a handful of House and Senate members and crafted to attract sufficient votes to pass each chamber. Conference reports cannot be amended, which is fundamental to the amendment exchange procedure. Conference reports must be made available to House and Senate lawmakers in advance of floor consideration. There is no such requirement for the ping-pong method, unless each chamber's leaders decide otherwise.[19]

A recent development: Senate majority leaders, using their priority of recognition from the presiding officer, have started to fill the tree (back-to-back, first- and second-degree proposals, for instance) on motions to dispose of a House amendment(s) to a Senate-passed measure. At this stage of legislative proceedings, which is prior to the formal "stage of disagreement" (one chamber asks for a conference, and the other agrees to that request), motions to dispose of House amendments receive preference in three ways. Top priority is given to motions that further amend measures—that is, motions to concur (agree) to the House amendment *with a Senate amendment*. Second in priority are motions to concur to the House amendment to the Senate-enacted measure, which sends the measure to the White House. Lowest in priority at this phase of the bicameral process are motions to disagree to the House amendment to the Senate bill. (Motions to disagree often lead to the convening of a conference committee once the House formally insists on its amendment to the Senate measure.)

The tree-filling objectives of party leaders are usually to expedite floor decision making, to promote inter- or intraparty negotiations, and, importantly, to prevent opponents from offering unwanted amendments. The first motion to dispose of the House amendment commonly reflects the majority leader's preference. For example, if the majority leader wants to alter the House amendment to the Senate bill, he will offer first the highest priority motion: to concur (agree) to the House amendment *with a Senate amendment*. The majority leader's amendment, importantly, could be the product of a privately negotiated compromise drafted and designed by key House and Senate members to pass both houses. Because the leader's amendment is subject to further amendments, to promote its adoption the majority leader will block undesirable amendments by filling the tree by offering a second-degree perfecting amendment. With the tree filled, the stage might now be set for bargaining and vote counting by proponents and opponents of the Senate amendment. To be sure, a variety of procedural complexities (cloture, motions to refer with instructions, amending the instructions, etc.) could occur with this procedure, as noted below.[20]

Tree filling on motions to concur to House amendments apparently was first used in the 109th Congress (2005–2007), when the majority leader (GOP Senator Bill Frist of Tennessee) employed it twice. Majority Leader Reid employed the procedure seven times in the 110th Congress and eight in the 111th Congress, according to congressional scholar Elizabeth Rybicki and her colleagues.[21]

Now part of the parliamentary tool kit of majority leaders, it is useful to highlight its application. Senator Reid employed the procedural tactic in 2009 to advance President Barack Obama's landmark health care reform plan, but he used it on a different bill that he had to call up. Senate Republicans, who were united in their opposition to the president's health care reform plan, decided to stall consideration of the "must-pass" defense appropriations bill (H.R. 3326), funding military operations in Iraq and Afghanistan, paying soldiers' salaries, and fulfilling many other important purposes. Customarily, most Senate Republicans are strong supporters of military-spending bills, but not this time. They decided to stall action on H.R. 3326 to delay action on the health care reform bill. A GOP senator and member of the Appropriations Committee explained why he backed dilatory action on H.R. 3326: "I don't want health care."[22] With little time to try to convene a conference committee so late in the session, bicameral differences on the defense measure took the ping-pong route.

Accordingly, Senator Reid requested the presiding officer to lay before the Senate the House's "message" with respect to H.R. 3326—that chamber's amendment to the Senate's amendment to the House-passed defense measure. Reid immediately offered a motion to concur (agree) to the House amendment—the bicameral agreement worked out informally and privately by each chamber's relevant actors—to the Senate amendment. Second, he filed cloture on the debatable House amendment to stymie any talkathon. Third, the majority leader filled the tree on the motion to concur to the House amendment to block unwelcome GOP amendments. Then, in an uncustomary procedural move, Senator Reid offered a motion to refer H.R. 3326 to the Appropriations Committee with instructions—designed to embarrass Senate Republicans—to report back a study on the impact on service members' families of delaying approval of the defense-spending bill. Senator Reid also filled the tree on the motion to refer with instructions.

Two noteworthy points with respect to the motion to refer merit mention. Motions to refer are higher in precedence than motions to amend (and debatable), so the majority leader on the defense bill needed to block Senate Republicans from offering the referral motion. The referral instruction, moreover, is subject to amendment. Senator Reid filled the tree on the motion to refer with instructions to prevent Republicans from offering amendments that suited their political and policy aims. In the end, the Senate voted to invoke cloture (63–33) on Reid's motion to concur—three GOP senators, Susan Collins and Olympia Snowe of Maine and Kay Bailey Hutchison of Texas, voted for cloture. (With an agreement on cloture, the motion to refer automatically fell, because Senate Rule XXII stipulates that if cloture is invoked on a measure or matter, it "shall be the unfinished to the exclusion of all other business until disposed of.") Following post-cloture debate (much of it on the health care reform bill), the Senate voted 88 to 10 to concur to the House amendment, clearing the measure for presidential consideration.[23] President Obama signed the defense-spending bill into law.

The Senate returned to health care reform which passed the Senate (60 to 39) as a complete substitute amendment to H.R. 3590 on Christmas Eve with Vice President Biden presiding. Press accounts reported that Senator Reid planned to take the required steps to convene a conference, but Senate Republicans objected.[24] As a result, the Democratic majority leaders in each chamber turned to the amendment exchange procedure to resolve their differences. The top Democrats in each chamber met privately at the White House to develop a compromise (the *House amendment* to the Senate amendment to H.R. 3590) satisfactory to Speaker Nancy Pelosi, Senate Majority Leader Reid, and President Obama that could attract majority support in the House and 60 votes in the Senate.

The surprise victory in the January 2010 Massachusetts special Senate election of Republican Scott Brown (who replaced Democratic Senator Edward Kennedy) dramatically changed the political landscape and policy dynamic in Congress and the White House. With Brown becoming the 41st GOP senator, Senate Democrats lost their filibuster-proof majority and could no longer muscle health care reform through their chamber. Senator Brown's victory upset the plans of congressional Democrats and President Obama to move health care reform to enactment. In the end, congressional Democratic leaders used a "two-bill" strategy to enact the landmark overhaul of the health care system.

First, a reluctant House—many lawmakers opposed provisions in the Senate's product—adopted unchanged the Senate's version of health reform (Senator Reid's amendment, which was equivalent to a separate health bill), clearing the H.R. 3590 for President Obama's signature (P.L. 111-148). This approach avoided further Senate action where Senator Reid no longer had 60 votes to stop a filibuster, and it was the fastest way to get the health reform legislation to the president. Second, the Democratic leaders of the House and Senate agreed to use the filibuster-proof reconciliation process to enact a second reconciliation bill H.R. 4872 that amended provisions in Senator Reid's complete substitute to H.R. 3590. It, too, was signed into law (P.L. 111-152).

PRECONFERENCE CONSIDERATIONS

It is often clear from the outset that controversial measures will end up in conference. Members plan their floor strategy accordingly. They make floor statements that emphasize their unyielding commitment to their own chamber's positions. In advance of a "House–Senate conference," noted one senator, "it is not unusual for the respective [chambers] to stake out positions for themselves and even to utter statements about their absolute intransigence, that sometimes does not always prevail when the conference convenes."[25]

Members frequently add expendable amendments to use as bargaining chips in conference. Such amendments can be traded away for other provisions considered more important. Members who sponsor floor amendments are mindful of the bargaining chip ploy. As one senator remarked:

> I have been in this body long enough to beware of the chairman of a committee who says in an enticing voice, "Let me take the amendment to conference," because I think that is frequently the parliamentary equivalent of saying, "Let me take the child into the tower and I will strangle him to death."[26]

With conference committees presumptively open, or at least subject to some public review, conferees sometimes must put up a fight for such amendments before dropping them. Conferees understand, too, that some bargaining chips are more influential than others. Before these amendments are dropped, conferees will consider the implications of offending powerful members. Even though she was not a conferee, Senator Diane Feinstein, D-Calif., worked successfully behind the scenes to ensure that her proposal banning a controversial chemical from various products was not viewed as "trading bait" by House–Senate negotiators.[27]

Another preconference tactic is for one chamber to deliberately keep out of its bill something it knows the other chamber wants. During a conference, the House conferees may give in to the Senate and accept their favorite provision, but only in return for Senate acceptance of something wanted by the House. For these reasons, counting the number of times one house appeared to give in to the other is not a good indication of the winners and losers in conference.[28] It is difficult to identify chamber "winners" or "losers," in any case, without knowing the goals and motives of the respective conferees.

House and Senate floor managers also consider whether they want recorded votes on certain amendments when they are debated in their chamber. For example, one senator's strategy on an amendment he opposed was to seek a recorded vote on it

> to beat the amendment, and beat it good, burying the issue in the Senate once and for all, and also putting him in a position to tell a Senate–House conference on the bill that the proposal was resoundingly defeated in the Senate.[29]

Alternatively, floor managers sometimes prefer not to draw attention to amendments they oppose (or favor)—and thus hope to avoid taking roll-call votes—on the assumption that it will then be easier to drop (or advocate) them in conference.

Members, too, are sensitive to the overall contours of their bill and the margin of support for its passage on the floor. A large vote on passage of legislation in either chamber may generate political pressure on the other house to embrace the measure. "A strong vote for final passage [of this tax cut bill] will certainly strengthen our hand [in conference]," said Senator Max Baucus, D-Mont., "and we did receive a strong vote of 62 Senators."[30]

In an unusual preconference move, then-Speaker Dennis Hastert, R-Ill. (1999–2007), directed the chairs of the several committees with jurisdiction over a major immigration reform bill to conduct field hearings around the country in 2006 to build support for the House's bill, which emphasized on border security. The legislation also made it a felony for illegal aliens to live in the United States. The Senate's version, backed by President George W. Bush and agreed to after the House passed its bill, also addressed border security, but it included a pathway to citizenship for the estimated 12 million illegal immigrants living in the country. House Republicans lambasted the Senate's bill as providing "amnesty" to illegal aliens. They "decided to focus on strengthening their bargaining position [if and when the two sides meet in conference] through public hearings."[31]

Not to be outdone, the chair of the Senate Judiciary Committee, the panel with jurisdiction over immigration reform, announced that his committee would also hold field hearings to generate public backing for the Senate's broader and more moderate immigration reform package. The dueling hearings underscore not only the controversial and complex nature of the issue but also the fractiousness within party ranks as House Republicans were pitted against Senate Republicans and President Bush. Congress has yet to pass comprehensive immigration reform as President Obama's second term in office begins. Immigration reform is a top Obama priority, however.

CONFERENCE COMMITTEE PROCESS

The five major steps in the conference committee process, setting aside the requirement that both chambers must act on legislation carrying the same bill number, are (1) one house requesting a conference and the other chamber agreeing to it, the so-called stage of disagreement; (2) selecting and, as a possibility, instructing conferees; (3) bargaining in conference, including negotiating objectives and procedural issues; (4) filing the conference committee report; and (5) taking final House and Senate action on the conference committee version of the bill.

Requesting a Conference

When the House passes a bill that is then amended by the Senate and returned, the House has several options. It may refuse to take further action, in which case the measure dies; it may approve an entirely new version of the bill and send it to the Senate; it may agree to the Senate's amendments, negating the need for a conference; it may amend the Senate's amendments and return the measure once again to the Senate; or it may request a conference.

Occasionally, the Speaker will refer the Senate amendments—especially if they are nongermane to the House-passed measure—to the standing committee that has jurisdiction over the subject matter of the amendments. More commonly, though, on major legislation, a member will ask and receive unanimous consent for the House to disagree to the Senate's amendments and request a conference with the Senate. The Speaker usually recognizes an appropriate committee member to make the unanimous consent request to go to conference on the bill. "Mr. Speaker, I ask unanimous consent to take from the Speaker's table the bill H.R. 1234 with the Senate amendments thereto, disagree to the amendments of the Senate, and ask for a conference with the Senate." (Senate amendments are not "privileged" in the House. This means they lack the right to be called up by interrupting the chamber's regular order of business.)

If any representative objects to the unanimous consent request, the legislation can get to conference in three other ways. First, the House can suspend its rules (an action that requires a two-thirds vote) by adopting, for example, the following motion: "Mr. Speaker, I move to suspend the rules and take from the Speaker's table the bill H.R. 1234 with the Senate amendments thereto, disagree to the amendments of the Senate, and ask for a conference with the Senate." If the legislation is controversial, this procedure is unlikely to be employed because of its supermajority requirement.

Second, the Rules Committee can report a rule sending a measure to conference. Today, this is the customary way for measures to reach the conference stage. On occasion, the Rules Committee will report a rule that not only specifies how a House measure will be debated and amended but also provides for an automatic Senate hook-up following completion of floor action on the bill. A hook-up provision in a special rule permits a companion Senate-passed measure to be immediately called up and the House-passed version inserted after the Senate's bill number. Technically, the House and Senate have passed the same numbered measure. The practical effect is that conference committee negotiations will involve two versions (the House's and the Senate's) of the same numbered bill.

Third, representatives can invoke House Rule XXII to get a measure to conference. This rule permits legislation to reach conference by majority vote of the House if a member of the committee of jurisdiction, typically the chair, is authorized by his or her panel to offer the motion. Under Rule XXII, this motion "shall be privileged in the discretion of the Speaker if offered by direction of the primary committee and of all reporting committees that had initial referral of the proposition." Typically, the pertinent committee chair will be immediately recognized by the Speaker to offer the Rule XXII motion: "Mr. Speaker, by direction of the Committee on _____, I move to take from the Speaker's table the bill H.R. 1234, with a Senate amendment thereto, disagree to the Senate amendment, and agree to the conference asked by the Senate." This motion is subject to debate under the 1-hour rule.

When the situation is reversed and a Senate-passed bill is amended by the House and returned to the Senate, it is "held at the desk and almost always subsequently laid before the Senate by the Presiding Officer upon request or motion of a Senator," usually the majority leader.[32] Recall that House amendments are "privileged" in the Senate, which means the request to call them up—by unanimous consent or motion—is not subject to a filibuster.

The House amendment or amendments may be dealt with in four ways by the Senate: (1) by adopting a motion to refer the amendment(s) to the appropriate standing committee, (2) by further amending the House amendments, (3) by agreeing to the House amendments (thus clearing the bill), or (4) by disagreeing to the House amendments, in which case a conference is commonly requested.

The usual way for the Senate to get to conference on a House-passed bill is for the majority leader or majority floor manager to ask unanimous consent or move to call up the House measure. Then the majority leader or floor manager would say: "Mr. President, I move to strike all after the enacting clause of H.R. 1234 and insert in lieu thereof the text of the Senate bill, S. 567." After adoption of this motion (virtually always by consent), the Senate would then pass H.R. 1234, as amended. (S. 567 would be returned to the legislative calendar.) At this point, the House and Senate would have passed the same bill (H.R. 1234), but there would be two different versions of it.

Next, the majority leader would make this three-part request: "Mr. President, I move that the Senate insist on its amendments, request a conference with the House on the disagreeing votes thereon, and that the Chair be authorized to appoint conferees." Alternatively, the majority leader would say something like this: "Mr. President, I move that the Senate disagree to the House amendment to the Senate bill, request a conference with the House, and authorize the presiding officer to name conferees." The normal routine for the Senate is to agree to the three-part proposal—insist (or disagree to the House amendment), request, and authorize—by unanimous consent. As Robert B. Dove, the former parliamentarian of the Senate, noted:

> The three steps are usually bundled into a unanimous consent agreement and done within seconds. But if some senators do not want a conference to occur and if they are determined, they can force three separate cloture votes to close debate [on each of the discrete parts], and that takes a lot of time. It basically stops the whole process of going to conference.[33]

In a precedent-making move, GOP senators opposed to sending a campaign finance bill to conference during the waning days of the 103rd Congress (1993–1995) launched filibusters against each part of the triple proposal. "In the 210 years in the history of the United States Senate, never—until last week—has there been a series of filibusters on taking a bill to conference," stated Majority Leader George J. Mitchell, D-Maine (1989–1995).[34] With GOP expectations high for recapturing control of the Senate after the November 1994 elections, Republicans wanted to block action on this largely Democratic initiative. They were successful on both counts.

By the early 2000s, given an environment of sharper partisan conflict, what had been precedent shattering to Majority Leader Mitchell in 1994 became a fairly common occurrence in the Senate. Minority-party senators often blocked the Senate from going to conference with the House. The triggering cause was the exclusion of the then-minority Democrats from conference committee negotiations, even though they had been officially appointed as conferees by the Senate. As Senator Richard Durbin, D-Ill., exclaimed,

> I have been appointed to conference committees in the Senate in name only, where my name will be read by the [presiding officer] and only the conference committee of Republicans goes off and meets, adopts a conference report, signs it, and sends it back to the floor without even inviting me to attend a session.[35]

With the two parties at loggerheads, stalemate is often the order of the day. The Senate minority lambasted the other party for abusing its power and suggested greater use of preconference methods to achieve bicameral agreement on legislation. Majority members countered that minority conferees were unwilling to negotiate in good faith with the other body. Majority members also noted that minority conferees are invited to participate in conferences if they are constructive negotiators who share the majority's policy goals. On occasion, the majority will play procedural "hardball" and file, or threaten to file, cloture on the various motions to proceed to conference with the other body. Their objectives are twofold: to encourage the minority to reach a deal on forming a conference and thus avoid a vote on cloture and, if cloture fails, to blame the minority for stymieing action on an issue of vital importance to the public.

This impasse, like so many in the Senate, is usually resolved on a case-by-case basis when the frustration level rises so high that each side is willing to hammer out a mutually acceptable accord. The minority stops their blocking actions and receives assurances from the majority that their conferees will be full participants in the House–Senate negotiating sessions. Both chambers and parties, moreover, took steps to defuse clashes involving the participation of minority conferees in the conference process. The House adopted a rule stating that their conferees

> should endeavor to ensure that meetings for the resolution of differences between the two Houses occur only under circumstances in which every manager [conferee] on the part of the House has notice of the meeting and a reasonable opportunity to attend.

Similarly, the Senate included protocols in the Honest Leadership and Open Government Act of 2007 recommending that conference committees should hold regular meetings of all conferees, that all Senate conferees be given adequate notice of meetings, and that all conferees should be afforded an opportunity to participate in these bicameral negotiating sessions.

In January 2013, the Senate adopted a series of filibuster reforms (see Box 7.4). One reform addressed the three-part motion to convene a conference committee. The change collapsed the tree parts into a single motion. This motion can be filibustered, but one—rather than three—successful cloture vote of 60 would end the talkathon.

Selecting and Instructing Conferees

Bicameral differences must be reconciled before legislation can be sent to the White House, and this assignment falls to the conferees selected from each chamber.

Selecting Conferees. The selection of conferees is governed in both chambers by rules and precedent. Each time a bill is sent to conference, the Speaker and the presiding officer of the Senate formally appoint the respective conferees. In practice, both chambers usually rely on the chair and ranking minority member of the committee that originally considered and reported the bill to recommend the selections. Sometimes, chairs will delay in naming conferees to signal displeasure with the other chamber and to apply "leverage on the other body [and encourage it to] cave in on . . . key issues" even before a conference is formally convened.[36] Other factors, too, may slow the appointment of conferees. For example, as a form of hostage politics, senators may block the appointment of conferees on a bill they oppose until conferees are named on a measure they support. Or the Speaker may delay naming conferees, seeking, for example, to first ensure that the soon-to-be-named conferees will include what the Speaker wants in the conference report or to pressure the other body to concede to the House on certain provisions.

The Speaker may also delay in appointing conferees to prevent the minority party from offering repetitive motions to instruct (see the section in this chapter on "Instructing Conferees"), thus avoiding votes on politically charged issues that party colleagues would be hard-pressed to vote against. House and Senate leaders may also delay in naming conferees because they need more time to develop their strategy for dealing with significant measures heading to conference. Strategic considerations are often critical when time is at a premium and the majority leadership is working to formulate an "end game" that effectively wraps up action on priority business as the first or second session of a Congress comes to a close.

The Speaker and the Senate presiding officer typically appoint conferees from the list given them in advance by the committee leaders, who select members of their own committees. (The Speaker, after the original appointment, also has the authority to remove managers or name additional conferees.) A member of another committee may be appointed when he or she has special knowledge of the subject matter or if the bill is of particular interest to the member's state or district. (Members not named conferees are sometimes invited to attend the bicameral meetings because of their specialized knowledge.) When a bill has been referred to several committees (multiple referral), it is common to have conferees from all the committees that handled it. Party ratios on conference committees generally reflect the party membership in the House and Senate.

House and Senate party leaders get actively involved in naming conferees on issues of fundamental importance. In a virtually unprecedented decision, GOP Speaker Newt Gingrich (1995–1999) in 1995 named a Democratic member, Gary A. Condit of California, as a conferee on unfunded mandates legislation. Condit, who ranked 10th in seniority on the committee of jurisdiction (Oversight and Government Reform), was supporting GOP efforts to inhibit congressional passage of bills that imposed financial costs on state governments. However, he could not persuade either the ranking Democrat on the Government Reform panel or the minority leader to appoint him as a conferee. (Under party rules at the time, the "Democratic Leader shall make recommendations to the Speaker of all Democratic Members who shall serve as conferees.") Speaker Gingrich was amenable to the idea and appointed Condit to one of the designated GOP conferee slots. As a result, the House conference delegation was bipartisan: four Republicans and four Democrats. (Condit belonged to a conservative Democratic group called "The Coalition," whose support Gingrich sought to help pass GOP legislation.)[37]

House rules state that the Speaker shall "appoint no less than a majority [of conferees] who generally supported the House position as determined by the Speaker," those "who are primarily responsible for the legislation," and, to the fullest extent possible, include "the principal proponents of the major provisions of the bill" passed by the House. Clearly, this language grants wide discretion to the Speaker in appointing conferees and allows him or her the opportunity to "stack" a conference with majority-party members who favor his or her position on the legislation. For example, after the House adopted a major amendment opposed by GOP Speaker Hastert (1999–2007), he chose not to name the GOP authors of the amendment as conferees. Instead, most of the conferees he appointed opposed the amendment; they did, however, support the House position on the overall bill "as determined by the Speaker." Lamented one of the GOP authors of the amendment, "Is that stacking the deck, is that trying to subvert the will of the House, or what?"[38] (Seniority used to be a nearly inviolable criterion in the appointment of conferees, but freshman members in both chambers are now selected, as are vulnerable lawmakers whose designation as conferees may boost their reelection prospects.)

Conferee selection in the Senate sometimes arouses controversy over both the number of managers and the ratio of majority to minority members. For example, a major pension reform bill was stalled in getting to conference over these issues. "There is a dispute over whether the conference should have seven Republicans or eight Republicans," exclaimed Democratic leader Reid. "I need an extra Senator. I need 8 to 6."[39] The GOP leader insisted on a 7-to-5 ratio. Finally, after nearly a 3-month delay, a unanimous consent agreement authorized the presiding officer to appoint conferees at a ratio of 9 to 7. As the GOP leader explained:

> We had originally requested 7 to 5. As my colleagues know, the Democratic leader insisted on an 8 to 6 ratio. The 9 to 7 ratio we agreed to allows us to have equal representation from the Finance and HELP Committees. As I repeatedly insisted, it is important we not stack the deck in favor or against either committee. Through mutual agreement, we have reached that objective.[40]

There are occasions when House and Senate party leaders are named as conferees—a sign that they want to direct conference negotiations on high-stakes issues important to each party. The House majority leader often serves on important tax conferences. "The House has a special sense of its constitutional obligation to initiate tax bills," said a majority leader. "We always felt we wanted a strong statement from our leadership, protecting our institution."[41] During the 108th Congress (2003–2005), a conference on a major expansion of Medicare—to provide a prescription drug benefit to the elderly—included the leadership of the Senate (Majority Leader Frist and Minority Leader Tom Daschle, D-S.D.). Both also served on the Senate committee of jurisdiction (Finance). However, as Senate leader Frist explained:

> I could have stayed off the [conference] committee and sat back with Speaker Hastert to help make some of the fundamental decisions. But I wanted to be involved in the process, to fully understand, to listen to the debate on both sides and to be in the best position to help make some of the major decisions that inevitably are going to have to be made.[42]

Speaker Hastert named Majority Leader Tom DeLay, R-Tex., whom he dubbed his "super conferee," to be a lead negotiator for the House on the Medicare measure. When top majority-party leaders of either chamber are appointed conferees, it signals both the importance of the measure and that the negotiating session will be, as one senator declared, a "majority-party [leadership] driven" conference.[43] To be sure, on major issues, party leaders exert significant influence on conference negotiations whether they are named conferees or not (see the appendix to this chapter for an example).

The House, less so the Senate, often appoints both "general" conferees, who are authorized to negotiate all matters in bicameral disagreement, and "limited" conferees, who are responsible for negotiating differences on certain provisions or sections of the legislation. Importantly, one chamber cannot outvote the other by appointing more conferees, because each house votes as a unit. Each house, in effect, has one vote ("yea" or "nay") to cast. Large conference delegations, especially for the House, are not uncommon. Multiple committee consideration of comprehensive bills that crosscut the jurisdiction of several panels is the driving force behind big conferences. Large conference delegations affect the mechanics of conference decision making. They often divide into smaller groups called subconferences.

The largest conference in congressional history involved the 1981 omnibus budget reconciliation bill. "Over 250 Senators and Congressmen met in 58 [subconferences] to consider nearly 300 issues" in disagreement, noted Senate Majority Leader Howard H. Baker Jr., R-Tenn.[44] The use of subconferences enables bicameral negotiators to proceed on several fronts simultaneously and to expedite what is inherently (because of numbers) a more complex process.

The nature of the issues in disagreement may account most for the length of conferences. But large conference delegations invariably require more time to iron out bicameral differences; the diversity of views that need to be harmonized affects the pace of deliberations. Finally, the larger the number of conferees, the easier it is for lawmakers who are not conferees, interest groups, and executive officials to have access to the negotiations. (Many conferences involve multilateral instead of bilateral negotiations, because scores of outside actors and interests can influence conference outcomes.) If large conferences become unwieldy even if they divide into subconferences, they often break down into smaller and smaller groups. This process was followed during a huge savings and loan conference, which embraced nearly one quarter of the House, including every member of the House Financial Services Committee. As one House conferee put it:

> One hundred and two conferees were appointed and no progress was made until the four principals [the House Financial Services and Senate Banking chairs and ranking minority members] went behind closed doors. And I'm not complaining. If [the House Financial Services chair] had not reduced the conference from 102 members to four, we would still be there arguing over this bill. He should get an Oscar for his starring role in, "Honey, I shrunk the conference."[45]

Instructing Conferees. After either chamber has agreed to go to conference but before the conferees have officially been named, the House (see Box 8.1) or Senate may adopt motions instructing their conferees, for example, to sustain the majority position of the chamber on a particular amendment or provision. A member of the minority party is granted priority in the House to offer the motion to instruct, and only one can be made at this stage.[46] (Instructions are in order before, during, and after a conference.) Senators may offer several successive instruction motions prior to the naming of conferees, which are debatable and, therefore, subject to a filibuster. In each chamber, conferees cannot be instructed to do that which is not within their authority (delete text that both chambers have agreed to, for instance) or, in the case of the House, the motion to instruct may not include argumentative language.

Instructions place additional political and moral pressure on the conferees and may strengthen their position in conference committee bargaining. "We need to give the House conferees some backbone to stand up to the Senate on this issue," declared a House member in support of a motion to instruct conferees.[47] However, instructions adopted by either chamber are not binding. (The practice is more common in the House than the Senate, because it appears unseemly to instruct senators and these motions are mainly symbolic.) As a result, conferees may disregard the instructions, particularly when they feel the need for room to maneuver or compromise. The full House and Senate still have an opportunity to accept or reject the conference committee report on the bill, and a new conference may be requested if either house feels that its conferees have grossly violated their instructions or authority. For example, conferees from both chambers are obligated by rule and precedent to address only the matters in bicameral disagreement and not introduce new matters that have not been considered in either chamber (see the appendix for this chapter).

During the early 1990s, when Democrats controlled the House, Republicans began to use the instruction motion to bring their issues before the chamber. In 1993, it was used 11 times; the next year, more than

---

BOX 8.1   Instruction of Conferees

MOTION TO INSTRUCT CONFEREES ON H.R. 4348, SURFACE
TRANSPORTATION EXTENSION ACT OF 2012, PART II

Ms. HAHN. Madam Speaker, I have a motion at the desk.

THE SPEAKER pro tempore. (Ms. FOXX). The Clerk will report the motion.

The Clerk read as follows:

Ms. Hahn moves that the managers on the part of the House at the conference on the disagreeing votes of the two Houses on the Senate amendment to
the bill H.R. 4348 be instructed to agree to the freight policy provisions in
Sec. 1115, Sec. 33002, Sec. 33003, and Sec. 33005 of the Senate amendment.

THE SPEAKER pro tempore. Pursuant to clause 7 of rule XXII, the gentlewoman from California (Ms. HAHN) and the gentleman from California
(MR. DENHAM) each will control 30 minutes.

SOURCE: *Congressional Record*, June 27, 2012, H4151.

---

double that number. Only one motion to instruct can be offered prior to
the appointment of conferees, as noted earlier, and this motion is reserved
to the minority. However, if a conference during this era could not reach
agreement within 20 calendar days, House rules permitted lawmakers to
offer (with 1 day's notice) an unlimited number of instruction motions.
During a 1994 crime conference that ran more than 20 days, for example,
Republicans offered "nine motions to instruct conferees on, among other
things, provisions regarding 'racial justice,' prison construction, and the
death penalty."[48]

Democrats did the same thing when they were in the minority: They
offered instruction motions to force votes on their election-year and
political priorities.[49] To constrain this practice, the majority party modified House rules at the start of the 108th Congress (2003–2005). The
change, which still remains in effect, retained the 20-calendar-day period
but added 10 legislative days to boot. This modification is designed to give
the conference committee a chance to enter into serious negotiations before
motions to instruct are in order. For example, under the old rule, a conference committee might officially convene only a few times before Congress
adjourned for the traditional August recess. Once the House returned in
early September, multiple motions to instruct would be in order even though
conferees hardly had time to meet and greet one another, let alone resolve
bicameral disagreements. The addition of 10 legislative days ensures that
conference committees have 2 or more weeks to resolve interchamber differences before instruction motions are in order. House leaders may delay in

naming conferees to avoid triggering the "20-10" rule, which can tie up the floor with debates on politically motivated motions to instruct. A delay still allows "unofficial" House conferees to conduct preconference negotiations with colleagues from the other chamber.

To sum up, party and committee leaders often devote considerable time to who is named a conferee and who is passed over. Regularly, lawmakers lobby committee or party leaders to be chosen as conferees, because they are then strategically positioned to advance their substantive and political goals. On bills of great partisan and substantive importance, the top leaders of the House (by custom, the Speaker is not a conferee) or the Senate, including the majority leader, are named conferees.

Bargaining in Conference

Before the conferees officially convene, informal preconference negotiations are usually held. These negotiations commonly involve only key House and Senate staff aides but may also include committee members, party leaders, and others. Preconference sessions are used, among other things, to differentiate between minor and major matters in disagreement, to identify the administration's position on significant issues, and to try to forge a unified position on important matters before beginning the formal negotiations. These private preconference sessions may involve only majority (or minority) party members and staff aides.

No formal rules, such as quorum or proxy voting requirements, govern internal conference committee bargaining. The only stipulation is that the conferences must meet formally at least once in open session (unless they have taken the appropriate steps to meet in private). The lack of rules is deliberate to foster an informal give-and-take environment conducive to reaching bicameral compromises, especially when the chambers have passed starkly different measures. As a Ways and Means chair said of trying to meld major bicameral differences on a health care reform bill, "It's akin to mating a Chihuahua with a Great Dane."[50]

A conference chair is selected in an ad hoc fashion, because there are no House or Senate rules that govern the procedure. On recurring measures that go to conference annually, such as appropriations and revenue bills, custom dictates that leadership rotates between the two houses. The chair, usually in consultation with his counterpart from the other chamber, plays an influential role in the conference process, arranging the time and place of meetings, the agenda of each session, and the order in which disagreements are negotiated. The chair also has charge of the official "papers"—the House and Senate versions of the measure in conference and other relevant communications between the chambers. As Rep. John Dingell, D-Mich., pointed out, "Whoever controls the papers gets to control the final product the conference votes on."[51]

The chair also sets the pace of the bargaining (often meeting in private to hammer out deals), proposes compromises, and recommends tentative agreements. At a major energy conference, the Senate chair of the conference stated that he would first start out with the least controversial provisions and then "work up to the more difficult questions . . . trying to build momentum" for an eventual bicameral accord.[52] Or the conference chair, to facilitate bargaining flexibility, may suggest observance of a common negotiating practice: "Nothing is agreed to until everything is agreed to."

On occasion, disputes arise as to which chamber's turn it is to chair. Institutional pride, ego, public attention, and more are factors that give rise to these disputes. The chairs of the two tax-writing committees have sometimes been at odds over who should chair conference committees. For example, one might work to avoid going to conference on a bill of little public visibility because it is his turn to chair the next conference and it is on a major tax bill. The other chair, however, might add controversial matters to a relatively noncontroversial measure, trying to force a conference so it will be his turn to chair the major tax conference. Indeed, the party leaders of both chambers are at times

> called upon to help settle disputes between the two chairmen, who regularly jockey for the right to chair conference committees and are rumored to have resorted to a variety of ploys to prevent the other from presiding over high-profile House–Senate negotiations.[53]

Staff members, too, play an important role in conference deliberations. They draft compromise amendments, negotiate agreements, provide advice to members, and prepare the conference reports. Aides played a particularly important role during a complex conference on an omnibus budget reconciliation bill. According to the executive director of the House Budget Committee,

> The role of the staff has been not only to explore where there may be areas of agreement, but also to make the deal. How else are you going to get hundreds of issues resolved in a couple of weeks unless you give the staff some kind of license?[54]

Conference committee bargaining, like bargaining throughout the legislative process, is subject to outside pressure. Even before the sunshine rules of the mid-1970s that required open conference meetings, conferees were lobbied heavily by special-interest groups, executive agency officials, and sometimes even the president, who will invite conferees to the White House for a "pep talk" on what the administration expects from the negotiations. The president or presidential aides "write letters to conferees; . . . administration personnel show up at conference meetings; and the president freely threatens to use his veto unless conferees compromise."[55] Conservative and liberal members in the respective chambers will write letters to the conferees warning that they will not vote for the conference report unless certain provisions are contained in the final package. A bipartisan group of 10 nonconferee senators formed a "working group" to monitor "the conference committee negotiating the details of the [Medicare] prescription drug legislation in an effort to ensure [that] a final product reflects the bipartisan backing won by the Senate bill."[56] When many minority party senators were excluded from participating in an energy conference, a senator declared that if minority-party views were ignored, floor consideration of the conference report could trigger the "procedural nuclear weapon"—the Senate filibuster.[57]

The party leaders of Congress, as noted earlier, also get directly involved— brokering compromises or urging conferees to meet a certain timetable or objective. Occasions also arise when the real negotiators are not the conferees but the top congressional leaders and administration officials who convene privately to resolve the issues in disagreement. Their decisions are then implemented by the conferees.

Bargaining Objectives and Tactics. Three key—and conflicting—objectives underlie the bargaining and informal give-and-take at conference sessions: (1) Conferees usually want to sustain the position of their respective chambers on the bill, (2) they want to achieve a result acceptable to a majority of each chamber's conferees, and (3) they want to craft a compromise product that is acceptable to a majority of the membership of both chambers and one that the president will sign. These objectives cannot be upheld consistently. "We caved so quickly to the House side, it was like watching water go over a waterfall," declared a senator about a conference on an antiterrorism measure.[58]

The conferees may be able to reach compromises quickly on their differences. For example, splitting the difference on bills appropriating funds for federal programs is often relatively painless. As one senator said, if the Senate bill contains a number, "say it is 200, and the House number is 100, if we cannot get together, we would say 'Let's make it 150. Let's split the difference.'"[59] Or logrolling may occur, with House conferees agreeing to certain Senate-passed provisions to gain leverage to win acceptance of House-passed provisions elsewhere in the bill that are strongly supported by members of their own chamber. Offers and counteroffers are part of the often-exhausting conference process.

Conferees also employ other techniques and tactics during the bargaining process. For example, if conferees chair subcommittees, they may convene hearings while the conference is under way to generate outside pressures on conference decision making. Senators may say that they cannot accept a House compromise offer because it would generate a filibuster in the Senate. Similarly, House conferees may say that a Senate offer is unacceptable because it violates House rules. One side may even fight hard for a position on which it plans to yield so the conferees can tell their parent chamber that they put up a good battle but the other side would not relent.

The bargaining skills of individual conferees can produce favorable results for his or her chamber's position. One House staff aide reflected on the skill of certain conferees during marathon bargaining sessions: "You're talking about a poker game," he said. "There are people with an enormous degree of patience who will just wait and wait and wait until the other side either slips or collapses or falls asleep."[60]

Sometimes, to break a deadlock, the conferees of one chamber will threaten to break off negotiations and return to their chamber for instructions— thereby reinforcing their position when negotiations resume. A House member once described this ploy as follows:

> Last year there was a difference of about $400 million between the House and Senate versions of the foreign aid appropriations [bill]. The chairman of the House delegation in the conference took a very firm position that we had to end up with slightly less than 50 percent of the difference as a matter of prestige. It was the day we [Congress] were to adjourn. We were in conference until about 10:30 p.m., and the Senate [conferees] wouldn't give in. I think the difference between conferees was only five or ten million dollars. The Senate was fighting for its prestige, and our chairman for his. At 10:30 he started to close his book [staff papers prepared for the conference] and he got up saying he would get instructions from the House. All the rest of our [House] conferees did the same. That prospect was too much for the senators. They capitulated.[61]

This example illustrates some of the factors in conference bargaining: the importance of timing and leadership; the influence of certain members on the negotiations; the effect of threats to convene another series of protracted meetings after one side receives instructions; the role fatigue can play in resolving hotly contested issues; and the political and professional investments of senators and representatives in upholding the prestige of their respective chamber and committees.

Another Approach Once Used for Appropriations Conferences. Today, appropriations measures in bicameral disagreement follow the procedure observed by the other House and Senate standing committees when they meet in conference to reconcile interchamber disagreements on their counterpart bills. Recall from Chapter 2 that appropriations measures, by custom, originate in the House. Thus, when the Senate calls up House-passed appropriations bills, it follows the contemporary and usual procedure for reaching the conference stage. The Senate will strike out everything after the enacting clause of the House-passed bill and insert its own appropriations measure in the form of an amendment in the nature of a substitute. The procedural effect of the Senate's action is that when the two chambers meet in conference, they are dealing with only one amendment in disagreement. In such cases, the conference committee can consider the products of both houses (in effect, two separate bills) and draft a third rendition of the legislation, provided it is a germane modification of the House and Senate versions. This approach gives the conferees maximum bargaining flexibility and discretion in drafting a bicameral accord.

Traditionally and until the mid-1990s, the resolution of bicameral differences on appropriations measures observed the combination approach: A conference committee would be created to work out most of the matters in disagreement; they would be included in a partial conference report that each chamber would pass. Then the outstanding issues would be considered separately from the partial conference report by each chamber as a series of numbered Senate amendments in disagreement. These matters would be resolved through the ping-pong approach. All these matters needed to be resolved before the bill could be sent to the White House.

Under the combination approach, appropriations conferees enjoyed less latitude in arriving at compromises because of the targeted nature of the remaining items in bicameral disagreement. Relating House provisions to the corresponding Senate amendments (numbered, as noted, for ease of comparison) was not difficult to accomplish. Also, appropriations bills deal with amounts of money for programs and agencies, making it easy to compare the two chambers' resource allocations. Until relatively recently, then, appropriations legislation took a two-pronged approach to achieve bicameral reconciliation: First agree to a partial conference report and then use the ping-pong approach to resolve the outstanding amendments in bicameral disagreement. Why the change?

When Republicans won control of Congress in the mid-1990s, their leadership decided to expedite bicameral action on appropriations measures as a way to advance their cost-cutting agenda. Too much floor time was consumed by acting on both a partial conference report and numerous amendments in disagreement when other pressing measures required chamber consideration. Moreover, the House Rules Committee started to waive all points of order against conference reports. No longer was there the earlier concern that if amendments in disagreement that violated House rules were included in the partial conference report, a point of order could result in rejection of the partial accord. To be sure, the House and Senate could return at any time to their former way of handling appropriations bills sent to conference, but, to date, that has not occurred.

Procedural Limits on Bargaining

Theory and practice often diverge on whether the formal rules of either chamber inhibit the bargaining discretion of the conferees. Scope and germaneness are important procedural constraints—points of order can be raised against the conference report if either of these constraints is violated.

Scope. *Scope* is a complex technical term embedded in the rulebook of each chamber. It essentially means the conferees are not to add new matter, reopen provisions that both chambers agreed to, or exceed the range of the matters in disagreement committed to them—that is, conferees are not to write new law not previously considered and adopted by either body. If the House, for example, authorizes $5 million for a program and the Senate authorizes $10 million, precedents state that the agreement must be sought within these high and low figures, which represent the scope of the bicameral disagreement. (Splitting the difference—$7.5 million, in this case—is a common compromise device.) However, when words, not numbers, are in disagreement, judging whether a policy provision reworded by the conferees meets scope requirements is usually harder.

House. In the House, it is customary that special rules waive points of order against the conference report and its consideration in the House, thus setting aside scope violations.[62] However, lawmakers may raise points of order against the consideration of conference reports (and their accompanying joint explanatory statements) if they fail to include a list of earmarks in these documents. It is not in order for the Rules Committee to waive earmark violations in their special rule, as Chapter 4 noted. The House rulebook states that the chair will "put the question of consideration with respect to the [special] rule" on the conference report. The question is then subject to 20 minutes of debate, equally divided between the member who raised the point of order and an opponent. Needless to say, the vote on the question of consideration is uniformly decided affirmatively on a party-line vote; otherwise, a negative vote defeats the rule and action on the underlying conference report.

A similar procedure, also mentioned in Chapter 4, is observed when a lawmaker makes a point of order against a special rule for a conference report if it contains an unfunded mandate (federal obligations imposed on states, for example) or if it violates pay-as-you-go principles. For instance, a lawmaker will state that the special rule violates the Unfunded Mandates Reform Act of 1995 (referencing a section of the 1974 Congressional Budget Act) because it contains a waiver of all points of order against the conference report. Next, the Speaker will say something like: "The [lawmaker] has met the threshold burden to identify the specific language in the resolution on which the point of order is predicated. Such a point of order shall be disposed of by the question of consideration," which triggers a 20-minute debate equally divided.[63] In this polarized era, the debate is less about procedural technicalities and more about minority-party criticisms of majority-party actions.

Senate. Rule XXVIII of the Senate addresses conference reports and contains this prohibition against scope violations: "Conferees shall not insert in their report matter not committed to them by either House, nor shall they strike from the bill matter agreed to by both Houses." This rule is not self-enforcing, however. Senators (like House members) must raise points of order if they believe conference reports have contravened the rule. Of course, it sometimes occurs that only after a conference report is agreed to in each chamber and signed into law that lawmakers learn new language was added or identical House and Senate text was deleted.

When the Senate passed the Honest Leadership and Open Government Act of 2007, it enhanced enforcement of Rule XXVIII by prohibiting the "airdropping" of items in conference reports. "Air drops" are measures or matters inserted into conference reports without first being enacted by the House or Senate. Under the previous Rule XXVIII, a scope point of order would kill the conference report. Under the revised Senate rule, sustaining a point of order against an airdropped item does not result in the rejection of the conference report. The offending material is deleted and the remaining matter can be returned to the House for its consideration using the exchange-of-amendment procedure. Another conference might also be convened.

When a Rule XXVIII point of order was raised for the first time under the new procedure, it was sustained by the presiding officer. He then stated: "Under the rule, the Senate now considers the question of whether the Senate should recede from its amendment to the House bill and concur with a further amendment [the conference report minus the offending material]."[64]

Important to note is that Rule XXVIII can be waived by a constitutional three-fifths vote of the Senate (60 if there are no vacancies). Senator John McCain, R-Ariz., raised a Rule XXVIII point of order against a conference report dealing with appropriations for the legislative branch. As he stated, conferees took the "opportunity to airdrop into the bill's conference a 'continuing resolution' to continue funding the operations of the government through October 31, having, obviously—certainly not according to the rules of the Senate—any relation to the appropriations bill."[65] The Senate voted 61 to 39 to waive McCain's point of order and agreed to the conference report (see the appendix for this chapter).

The Senate also created a new rule (Rule XLIV), which focuses on earmarks. (Recall that the 112th Congress banned earmarks.) Before a conference report can be considered, sponsors of earmarks must be identified through lists, charts, or other means and made publicly available on a congressional website for at least 48 hours. The majority leader or appropriate committee chair must certify (in a statement on the Senate floor, for example) that these requirements have been met before it is in order to vote on a conference report. Senators may raise points of order against alleged earmark provisions in the conference report. If the points of order are sustained, then the offending material is dropped from the conference report and the Senate then proceeds to address whether it will use the ping-pong procedure.

Rule XLIV, like Rule XXVIII, is also subject to a 60-vote waiver requirement. For both rules, the motion to waive is debatable for 1 hour. If a three-fifths vote of the Senate is obtained, debate on the conference report continues. If not, the presiding officer rules on the point of order. Any appeals from rulings of the presiding officer are debatable for 1 hour; 60 votes are required to sustain the appeal.

Worth mention is that Senate precedents are quite broad for judging whether new and extraneous provisions are included in conference reports. A precedent still on the books is that matters not "entirely irrelevant" to the subject matter of the conference report are allowed. More recently, the Senate employs a "reasonably related" standard rather than the entirely irrelevant criterion. Either principle could be difficult to apply when one chamber passes a bill and the other replaces the entire text of the measure with a complete substitute. In this case, as noted earlier, the conferees have wider leeway to write a third version of the legislation as long as it is "germane to the provisions of one or the other passed bills."[66]

Germaneness. The Senate is able to add amendments to House-passed measures that are considered nongermane under House rules. For years, House conferees were faced with a take-it-or-leave-it proposition—accept the nongermane Senate amendments or lose the bill in its entirety, including the House-passed provisions, given that conference reports are not open to amendment. Members of the House expressed frustration over this recurring dilemma. The House finally acted against the Senate practice by adopting a 1972 rule change permitting separate votes on the nongermane portions of conference reports. The rule was designed to accommodate the Senate's right to offer nongermane amendments while protecting the procedural prerogatives of the House.

Any House member may make one or more points of order against a conference report when it is called up for final approval on the ground that it contains nongermane material. The member simply says, "Mr. Speaker, I make a point of order under House Rule XXII that the last section of the conference report contains nongermane material." Typically, special rules are obtained from the Rules Committee to protect the conference report against such points of order. Assume there is no rule, and the Speaker sustains the point of order. The representative who raised the objection on the floor will then move to reject the nongermane conference matter. Forty minutes of debate, equally divided between those who support and those who oppose the motion, are permitted under this procedure, after which the House votes on the motion to reject. If it is adopted, the nongermane material is deleted, and the pending question before the House is disposition of the remaining conference material minus the nongermane portion. Defeat of the motion permits the House to keep the nongermane matter in the conference report. Seldom is this rule invoked in the House.

Filing the Conference Report

When a majority of the conferees from each chamber have reached agreement and added their signatures to the conference report, they instruct committee staff aides to prepare a conference report, which embodies their negotiated recommendations on the matters in bicameral disagreement. Figure 8.1 provides an example of a conference report. Conference reports must be accompanied by a joint explanatory statement. This statement is prepared by the conferees (and appropriate staff) of both houses so the explanation of what was decided on will not be different in the two houses and thus subject to differing interpretations. The conference report contains statutory language while the joint explanatory statement provides a more readable summary of the conferees' decisions. An appropriate conferee will submit, or file, the conference report for printing to the chamber that requested the conference (customarily, only the House prints the conference report and joint explanatory statement).

A majority of the conferees from each house—sometimes they are only from the majority party—must sign the conference report for it to be sent back to the House and Senate. When conferences end, the conferees sometimes scatter quickly, forcing staff members clutching official signature pages to track down managers for both houses in their offices or in elevators, hallways, or restaurants. The parliamentarians will not accept photocopied signatures or other facsimiles.[67] After the necessary signatures are obtained, the conference committee has concluded its work. (Unlike reports of standing committees of each chamber, conference reports are prohibited by precedent from containing minority or additional viewpoints.) Sometimes the official filing of conference reports is delayed for strategic reasons, such as the need to make changes to pick up votes or to encourage lawmakers to support another measure.

During the 109th Congress, House GOP leaders delayed the filing of a highway conference report because they were uncertain if they had the votes to pass the Central America Free Trade Agreement (CAFTA). The highway conference report was replete with projects for many lawmakers, and the GOP leadership implied to its members that their position on CAFTA could affect the fate of their highway projects. As the House GOP whip explained: "It's certainly not beyond the realm of possibility that members come and say, 'Gee, how am I doing with my projects in the highway bill?' And we're probably not beyond saying, we'll check and see how you're doing" on CAFTA.[68] Both measures passed the House.

Party leaders can stir sharp controversy if they add or delete material after a conference committee has officially concluded its work. This type of action rarely occurs; however, a conference committee on a defense appropriations bill had new matter added after the negotiators had signed and issued the bicameral accord and announced it to the public. Technically, the conference was over. No further changes were permitted to be made to the defense conference report unless the conference committee was reconvened

112TH CONGRESS 2d Session	HOUSE OF REPRESENTATIVES SENATE	REPORT 112–557

MAP–21

CONFERENCE REPORT

TO ACCOMPANY

H.R. 4348

JUNE 28, 2012.—Ordered to be printed

FIGURE 8.1 Conference Report

for that purpose. As David Obey, Wis., the Democratic leader on the House Appropriations Committee, exclaimed:

> After the conference was finished at 6 p.m., Senator Frist marched over to the House side of the Capitol about 4 hours later and insisted that over 40 pages of legislation, which I have in my hand, 40 pages of legislation that had never been seen by conferees, be attached to the bill. The Speaker joined him in that assistance so that, without a vote of the conferees, that legislation was unilaterally and arrogantly inserted into the bill after the conference was over in a blatantly abusive power play by two of the most powerful men in Congress.[69]

To prevent this from happening again, the House adopted new rules stating that conference reports are "inviolate to change" unless all the House conferees have a chance to reconsider their decisions. In addition, it is not in order for the House to consider a conference report whose substantive content does not reflect the decisions of the conferees on all the differences between the two chambers.[70]

Conference reports must be published in the *Congressional Record* before they are brought before the House or Senate for final action. House rules require a 3-day layover for conference reports, which must be available in printed or electronic form to all members for reading at least 2 hours prior to floor consideration. Senate rules state that conference reports must be available on each senator's desk before they can be taken up on the floor. These rules also state that conference reports must be available to senators and the general public (via publicly accessible legislative websites) at least 48 hours before they are voted on. In each chamber, these rules can be set aside, usually by a rule from the House Rules Committee and in the Senate by unanimous consent or, in the case of the 48-hour requirement, a 60-vote waiver of that rule, and by joint agreement of the majority leader and minority leader if there are significant Internet disruptions.

Final Floor Action on Conference Reports

Once the conference report is agreed to and filed with the House and Senate, the report must be acted on by both chambers before it is cleared for the president. Customarily, the chamber that requests a conference acts last on the conference report, but only if the papers are in its possession. The papers, as mentioned earlier, are the official documents, such as the bill as originally passed by one chamber and the amendments added to it by the other chamber. Normally, the papers are held by the chamber that agreed to go to conference; that house, then, would be the first to consider the conference report. However, the papers may be transferred to the other chamber by agreement of the conference committee, or one house may simply walk out with them.

Policy outcomes sometimes are influenced by which chamber acts first or last on the conference report. For example, the chair of the committee that reported legislation creating the Department of Education got the House in 1979 to ask for a conference with the Senate. He wanted the House to act last on the conference report so the parliamentary options available to the bill's opponents—who were more numerous in the House—would be limited.

The first chamber to act on a conference report has three options: adopt, reject, or recommit (return it to the conferees for further deliberation). When the first chamber to act adopts the conference report, however, this automatically dissolves the conference committee, and the other chamber is faced with a "yes" or "no" vote on the report. The chair's strategy worked in the case of the Department of Education bill. After intense lobbying by the White House and various education groups, the House agreed to the conference report establishing the new department.

Conference reports are privileged and may be brought up at almost any time the House and Senate are in session, subject to each chamber's requirement for the availability of conference reports and typically with the prior approval of the leadership. The senior majority and minority conferees from each house's delegation normally act as the floor managers of the conference version. Both chambers require conference reports to be accepted or rejected in their entirety; they are not open to amendment. However, conference reports can be changed via adoption by both chambers of a concurrent resolution authorizing either the Clerk of the House or the Secretary of the Senate to correct language in a conference report during the enrollment process (see below). Another option is to enact a separate bill to change the text and intent of a conference report.

In the Senate, conference reports are usually brought up by unanimous consent at a time agreed to by the party leaders and floor managers, as shown in Box 8.2. Because conference reports are privileged, if any senator objects to the unanimous consent request, the majority leader (or a proponent) can offer a nondebatable motion to take up the conference report: "Mr. President, I move to proceed to the conference report to accompany S. 1234." The conference report itself, however, can be filibustered. Commonly, conference reports are debated under a time-limitation agreement.

In the House, there are three main routes to the floor for conference reports, which because of their privileged character can be called up at almost any time. First, conference reports may be considered under the 1-hour rule, with the time divided equally between the majority and minority floor managers. In 1985, the House changed its rules to permit one third of the time to be assigned to a member who opposes the bicameral accord if both the GOP and Democratic floor managers support it. Second, suspension of the rules is sometimes used to bring conference reports to the floor, but this is not a preferred procedure because it involves a severe requirement: a two-thirds instead of majority vote for adoption. Third, it is usual practice for a waiver rule, as mentioned earlier in this chapter, to be obtained from the Rules Committee, an example of which can be seen

---

BOX 8.2   Calling Up a Conference Report: Unanimous Consent Agreement

CONFERENCE REPORT TO ACCOMPANY H.R. 2112

MR. REID. I ask unanimous consent that the Senate now proceed to the consideration of the conference report to accompany H.R. 2112, an act making consolidated appropriations for the Departments of Agriculture, Commerce, Justice, Transportation, and Housing and Urban Development and related programs; that there be up to 90 minutes of debate, equally divided between the two leaders or their designees; that upon the use or yielding back of time, the Senate proceed to vote on the adoption of the conference report; further that the vote on adoption be subject to a 60 affirmative-vote threshold.

SOURCE: *Congressional Record*, November 17, 2011, S7673.

---

in Box 8.3. Conference managers seek a rule when they want to waive the 3-day layover requirement (either to meet deadlines or exploit favorable political circumstances) or to prevent points of order against the conference report for procedural violations. Conference reports are seldom rejected. As a congressional attorney explained:

> [The] chief reason conference reports pass is the basic rule that such reports must be adopted or rejected as a whole. . . . Thus, the question for Members is not how they feel about any particular provision, but how they feel about the bill as a whole, and they can always justify a vote for a conference report on the ground that they accepted the distasteful parts only to save the good ones.[71]

Outright rejection of a conference report kills the bill and may require a repetition of the entire legislative process. This becomes particularly significant in the weeks immediately before the final adjournment of a Congress, when members face the choice of accepting the bill as is; recommitting it to a conference committee, in all probability jeopardizing final approval; or killing the bill, knowing no time is left to move a revised bill through Congress.

Once both houses approve the conference report, the papers are delivered to the house that originated the measure. A copy of the bill as finally agreed to by Congress is prepared by an enrolling clerk. The **enrolled bill** is signed by the Speaker and presiding officer of the Senate, or by other authorized officers, and sent to the president. In a first-time-ever enrollment ceremony, Speaker Hastert and Senate President Pro Tempore Strom Thurmond, R-S.C., electronically signed a Year 2000 (Y2K) liability bill and sent it via

---

BOX 8.3 Calling Up a Conference Report by
Special Rule

PROVIDING FOR CONSIDERATION OF CONFERENCE REPORT
ON H.R. 2112, CONSOLIDATED AND FURTHER CONTINUING
APPROPRIATIONS ACT, 2012

Ms. Foxx. Mr. Speaker, by direction of the Committee on Rules, I call up
House Resolution 467 and ask for its immediate consideration.

The Clerk read the resolution, as follows:

H.RES. 467

Resolved, that upon adoption of this resolution it shall be in order to consider the conference report to accompany the bill (H.R. 2112) making appropriations for Agriculture, Rural Development, Food and Drug Administration,
and Related Agencies programs for the fiscal year ending September 30, 2012,
and for other purposes. All points of order against the conference report and
against its consideration are waived. The conference report shall be considered
as read. The previous question shall be considered as ordered on the conference report to its adoption without intervening motion except: (1) 1 hour of
debate; and (2) one motion to recommit if applicable.

THE SPEAKER pro tempore. The gentlewoman from North Carolina is recognized for 1 hour.

Ms. Foxx. Mr. Speaker, for the purpose of debate only, I yield the customary 30 minutes to the gentlewoman from New York (Ms. Slaughter), pending
which I yield such time as I may consume.

SOURCE: *Congressional Record*, November 17, 2011, H7733.

---

e-mail to the president. "For the first time in history Congress is sending
an electronically signed bill to the president," declared the Senate majority
leader.[72] Congress also transmitted a signed paper version of the measure to
the White House. "Bill signing" ceremonies are sometimes organized by the
Speaker and Senate majority leader, separately or together if both are of the
same party, to focus public attention on the measure or to showcase partisan
colleagues facing tough reelection fights.[73]

Although most enrolled bills are sent quickly to the White House, sometimes there are delays of a few days or weeks in getting them there. A measure's length and complexity might slow its processing by the enrolling
clerks, or the delay might be intentional. For example, to eliminate a bill

as a campaign issue and to free the president from electoral pressures, its transmittal can be timed by party leaders so the chief executive has until after Election Day to decide whether to sign or **veto** (or **pocket veto**, if Congress has adjourned) the measure.[74]

Presidential Approval or Veto

Under the Constitution (Article I, Section 7), the president has qualified veto power. The president's options are four. First, the president can sign measures into law. Once an enrolled bill is sent to the White House, the president has 10 days, excluding Sundays, to sign or veto the bill. President Obama created a small controversy when, for apparently the first time ever, he authorized a staff aide to use an autopen to sign a bill into law. The president was in France when the autopen was used. Customarily, a White House aide would hop on a plane and bring the enrolled bill to the president for an in-person signature. In this case, there was no time to fly an aide to that country before an antiterrorism law expired.[75] On two other occasions when President Obama was not in Washington, he has authorized staff to affix his signature to bills with the autopen. He is "the only president ever to use the mechanical device to sign legislation."[76]

Second, the president can disapprove of legislative acts, subject to the ability of Congress during its 2-year life to override the vetoes by a two-thirds vote, a quorum being present, of each house. The large vote required to override a veto means that the threat of a veto can be used strategically by presidents to achieve their lawmaking goals. Third, if no action is taken within the 10-day period and Congress is in session, the bill automatically becomes law without the president's signature. Fourth, presidents may also use the "pocket veto." Unlike a regular veto, Congress has no opportunity to override a pocket veto.

With respect to the pocket veto, recall from the Constitution that presidents have 10 days (excluding Sundays) to decide whether to sign or veto legislation, "unless the Congress by their Adjournment prevents its Return, in which case it shall not be a Law." At issue is the question of when a congressional adjournment prevents a return. There is no definitive Supreme Court ruling on this matter. Periodically, controversies erupt between Congress and the White House when presidents try to pocket veto measures when Congress adjourns for several days or weeks during intra- or intersession breaks. A key reason for the controversy: Each chamber authorizes the clerk of the House or the secretary of the Senate, as the case may be, to receive veto messages from the president when either chamber is not in session, obviating, in Congress's judgment, presidential use of the pocket veto.[77] (Both legislative chambers acknowledge the president's power to pocket veto measures when Congress adjourns at the conclusion of the second session.)

On some occasions, recent presidents have simultaneously invoked in their *return veto* message on a bill their constitutional power also to *pocket veto* that measure. Scholars and congressional parliamentarians sometimes call this the "protective return" veto, or two vetoes for one bill.[78] From the House and Senate's perspective, a president who exercises both a pocket and return veto on legislation is admitting that Congress's recess or adjournment did not prevent its receipt of veto messages and ability to attempt an override. Conversely, presidents justify using both veto approaches (return and pocket) for several reasons: to assert their right to use the pocket veto on the measure, to avoid litigation, and to leave no doubt that a bill is vetoed.

Woodrow Wilson wrote that the president, in using the veto power, "acts not as the executive but as a third branch of the legislature."[79] The president can use the veto, or the threat of a veto, to advance legislative and political goals. Often, the threat of a veto is itself enough to persuade Congress to change its legislative course, because attracting the two-thirds vote required in each house to override presidential vetoes is difficult. Periodically, the administration will submit Statements of Administration Policy to Congress highlighting, for example, the president's problems with certain legislation. One senator vividly described the president's power when he told the Senate why a conference committee agreed to a specific compromise: "There is another fundamental reason we did it—that is because we faced the veto, that great, big monster of a veto."[80]

Presidents use their veto power because they consider a measure to be unconstitutional, believe it encroaches on the chief executive's powers and duties, or hold that it represents ill-advised policies. When President Richard Nixon vetoed the 1973 War Powers Resolution (which Congress subsequently enacted by overriding his veto), he cited all three factors as the basis of his action. Vetoing bills because they cost too much is another favorite rationale of presidents.

Chief executives may issue "signing statements" to accompany a piece of legislation they have signed into law. Signing statements, although not mentioned in the Constitution, have been used by presidents at least since the time of James Monroe's presidency (1817–1825). President George W. Bush, however, employed them more often than any other president to reassert and strengthen what is called the "unitary theory" of executive power. As interpreted by Bush, this theory allowed the president to override statutory provisions he claimed would impinge on his constitutional prerogatives as commander in chief. When Congress banned the torture of terrorists (P.L. 109-148), for example, the president held that the law trespassed on his powers as commander in chief.

Signing statements have aroused the concern of Congress because they seem to provide the president with an unofficial line-item veto, allowing him to decide which parts of bills to implement or ignore. On the other hand, other analysts believe that signing statements have little effect on the administration of laws.[81] President Obama vowed that he would use signing statements "only when it is appropriate to do so as a means of discharging my constitutional responsibilities."[82] When President Obama issued his first signing statement on March 11, 2009, he was quickly criticized by GOP lawmakers for endorsing Bush's view that some parts of laws are optional.[83] The president has continued to issue signing statements challenging statutory provisions that in his judgment infringe on his powers.[84] To minimize legislative–executive controversies over the chief executive's enforcement of laws, it was reported that President Obama decided to issue fewer signing statements. Instead, the president utilizes legal opinions (which are secret) from the Justice Department's Office of Legal Counsel to ignore statutory provisions that office says are unconstitutional.[85]

Presidents contemplate how vetoes can be employed to advance their electoral and policy agendas, especially when their party does not control Congress. As national elections approach, for example, presidents will use the veto against an opposition Congress to show how their policies differ from the other party's and thus highlight their fundamental beliefs to the electorate. Conversely, an opposition Congress will send measures to the White House that it expects the president to veto. This strategy could be called the politics of differentiation or contrast politics.

When the president vetoes a measure, the Constitution provides that "he shall return it with his Objections to that House in which it shall have originated" and that chamber shall "proceed to reconsider it." This means that some action must be taken, but not necessarily a veto override vote. Neither chamber is under any obligation to schedule an override attempt. Party leaders may realize they have no chance to override and may not even attempt it. Because of popular support for the president's action, or for other reasons, the political environment may not be conducive to a successful override. Thus, a motion may be made to refer the message to committee rather than risk a loss on override. If an override attempt fails in one chamber, the process ends and the bill dies. If it succeeds, the measure is sent to the other chamber, where a second successful override vote makes it law. The Constitution requires roll-call votes on override attempts.

Whether signed by the president, allowed to become law without the president's signature, or passed over a veto, the bill becomes a public law and is sent to the National Archives and Records Administration for deposit and publication in *Statutes at Large,* an annual volume that compiles all bills that have become law. (Figure 8.2 shows an example of a public law.)

126 STAT. 156   PUBLIC LAW 112–96—FEB. 22, 2012

Public Law 112–96
112th Congress

An Act

Feb. 22, 2012
[H.R. 3630]

To provide incentives for the creation of jobs, and for other purposes.

Middle Class Tax
Relief and Job
Creation Act
of 2012.
26 USC 1 note.

Be it enacted by the Senate and House of Representatives of the United States of America in Congress assembled,

SECTION 1. SHORT TITLE; TABLE OF CONTENTS.

(a) SHORT TITLE.—This Act may be cited as the "Middle Class Tax Relief and Job Creation Act of 2012".

(b) TABLE OF CONTENTS.—The table of contents for this Act is as follows:

FIGURE 8.2   Public Law

CASE STUDY

A Procedural Sketch: The Surface
Transportation Conference, 2012

BACKGROUND

Speaker Boehner's signature issue for 2012 was to be a 5-year, $260 billion transportation bill (H.R. 7). Dissension within his party over cost and policy issues prevented the measure from ever reaching the floor. Meanwhile, on March 14, the Senate approved by a large bipartisan margin (74–22) their version of the transportation funding extension: a 2-year, $109 billion measure (S. 1813). Both chambers and parties faced a June 30 deadline, when funding for transportation projects would end. The result: Many highway and mass-transit projects might lapse and numerous workers could lose their jobs at the prime construction season. In addition, failure to pass the legislation—"Moving Ahead for Progress in the 21st Century," or MAP-21—would mean a 10th short-term extension of transportation funding, underscore Congress's inability to govern effectively, and create potential electoral grief for various legislators in the upcoming November elections. (Not since 2005 had Congress enacted a multiyear transportation measure. That law expired in 2009. Since then, nine short-term extensions kept transportation programs in operation.)

HOUSE ACTION

On April 18, the House passed a 90-day extension of transportation funding by a 293-to-127 vote. The bill (H.R. 4348) included proposals to attract the votes of persuadable Republicans and Democrats, such as expediting construction of the so-called Keystone pipeline (carrying oil from Canada to the Gulf states) and blocking regulations affecting coal issued by the Environmental Protection Agency. The inclusion of these matters was also designed to broaden the "scope" of H.R. 4348 and make these issues "conferencable," thus strengthening the House's bargaining position given the Senate's comprehensive transportation bill. Transportation Chair John Mica, Fla., even stated that the provisions in H.R. 7, which died in committee, should be among the outstanding issues, or "matters in disagreement," before the conference. "You can do anything in conference," exclaimed Mica.[86] House and Senate rules restrict conferees to those matters in disagreement between the House and Senate bills. Conferees are not to consider new matters that neither chamber acted on when each passed their respective bills. Senate conferees successfully resisted Mica's contention but not without help, as noted below, from the party leaders of the House and Senate.

SENATE ACTION

On April 24, the Senate took up H.R. 4348, struck all the text after the enacting clause, which gives legal force to measures—"Be it enacted by the Senate and House of Representatives of the United States of America in Congress Assembled"—and substituted the language of S. 1813. Note that the Senate agreed to a bill carrying the House number—one chamber must act on the other's bill, essential to the convening of a conference. In this case, the Senate transformed S. 1813 into an amendment called a "complete substitute" or an "amendment in the nature of a substitute." The Senate then insisted on its amendment to H.R. 4348, requested a conference with the House, and authorized the presiding officer to name conferees. *(The next day, April 25, by unanimous consent, the House disagreed to the Senate amendment and agreed to a conference. By these actions—one chamber insisting on its amendment and the other disagreeing to it—the House and Senate formally entered the "stage of disagreement." These dual actions invariably trigger the convening of a conference committee.)*

SENATE CONFEREES

Size and ratio are among the factors that influence the selection of Senate conferees. Given the legislation's importance, Majority Leader Reid began discussions with GOP leader Mitch McConnell about those twin topics. Reid's concern was that Senator Max Baucus, D-Mont., would have to be a conferee.[87] Baucus chaired the Finance Committee (the panel responsible for finding the revenue to fund highway projects), and he also served as a senior member of the Environment and Public Works Committee. Baucus was a proponent of constructing the Keystone pipeline, but the Obama Administration and many Senate Democrats wanted to delay construction pending analyses of the pipeline's environmental impact in the affected states. As an unrelated energy issue and not part of S. 1813, Keystone could impede the two chambers' ability to reconcile their differences.

Reid achieved his desired two-seat party advantage of eight Democrats and six Republicans. Thus, if Baucus voted with all the Senate's GOP conferees on a motion to add the Keystone project to the conference report, it would produce a tie vote (7 to 7). Tie votes lose in the legislative process. Recall the informal "unit rule" that governs conference proceedings: Each chamber's conferees decide among themselves—by consensus or majority vote—either to approve or reject compromises that they propose or that are offered by the other house. (Formally, the presiding officer simply names the conferees; he or she has no real authority to select conferees. On major legislation, the majority- and minority-party leaders are pivotal in choosing conferees, but they also heed the suggestions of the relevant committee chairs or ranking minority members, as the case might be.)

HOUSE CONFEREES

Speaker Boehner named 33 conferees—20 Republicans and 13 Democrats—with most (21) chosen from the Transportation and Infrastructure Committee; 3 conferees each were appointed from the other four panels with some jurisdiction over the legislation. Significantly, the Speaker named eight freshman Republicans as conferees, in part to have them develop a stake in the compromise product and then convince their nonconferee GOP colleagues to vote for the conference report.[88]

MOTIONS TO INSTRUCT CONFEREES (HOUSE)

After the House agreed to the conference, but before the conferees were named, the ranking Democrat on Transportation offered a nonbinding motion to instruct the House's conferees to simply accept the Senate's amendment, which would clear the bill (H.R. 4348) for presidential consideration. The House voted to reject this advisory motion. Only one valid motion to instruct is in order at this juncture, and priority in offering the motion is accorded a minority party member. Subsequently, under the House's 20-calendar/10-legislative-day rule, if the conferees have failed to report within either time period, then any number of motions to instruct are in order on one legislative day's notice. Any legislator, regardless of party, may offer these motions. Nearly a dozen motions to instruct were proposed at this stage to pressure House conferees to take certain actions, such as ending tax-haven abuse and requiring the conferees to resolve their differences by a certain date. *(The Senate makes infrequent use of instruction motions, even though they can be made at almost any time during the conference committee's existence. The Senate did not instruct its transportation conferees.)*

CONFERENCE NEGOTIATIONS

The transportation conference convened publicly on May 8 with Senator Barbara Boxer, D-Calif., the head of the Environment Committee, as the overall chair of the conference. (It was Senator Boxer's turn to serve as overall conference chair, because Mica had headed the previous conference of the two jurisdictionally parallel panels.) Members expressed optimism at the May 8 meeting that they could resolve their differences by the June 30 deadline. The two Senate leaders of the conference, Boxer and her ranking member on the Environment Committee, Senator Jim Inhofe, R-Okla., initiated the bargaining process by presenting a comprehensive package for resolving their bicameral differences. House negotiators responded with a series of counteroffers.[89] Later, when the negotiations appeared to break down, the two Senators hand-delivered to Mica a transportation funding plan. "Their symbolic gesture was intended as a show of good faith in a Congress where trust has been in short supply."[90]

Despite scores of private discussions among the conferees and relevant legislative staff, as well as pressure from the president, outside groups, and nonconferee lawmakers, progress slowed in early June given the strong differences between the chambers over various issues. Each party and chamber blamed the other for the stalled negotiations.[91] Simply put, it was not in the political or policy interest of either chamber or party to compromise early. "Blinkmanship" through delay might enable each chamber or party to attain their preferred policy objectives and minimize criticism that either "caved" too quickly to the other side. Inhofe, one of the most conservative senators, was especially active as a mediator with House conservatives, urging them to back the transportation measure. He reminded them that conservatives traditionally favored expenditures for national security and infrastructure.

Finally, with only 11 days left before the June 30 deadline and conference progress stymied—in part because House conferees were insisting that certain provisions in H.R. 7 had to be included in the conference report—Speaker Boehner and Majority Leader Reid met with Boxer and Mica. Boehner and Reid gave the two their marching orders: Return to the bargaining table and work even harder to reach a compromise.[92] In the end, with both sides giving up issues—for example, Republicans dropped a provision expediting construction of the Keystone oil pipeline and Democrats accepted a loosening of environmental standards for new transportation projects—the conference report (H. Rept. 112-557) was filed on June 28. Needless to say, the members and relevant congressional staff worked long days, nights, and weekends to turn the accord into proper legal language and to write the joint explanatory statement that accompanies conference reports.

NEW MATTER ADDED TO THE CONFERENCE REPORT

Significantly, the transportation conference report contained two unrelated major provisions (student loans and flood insurance)—separate bills that had reached a legislative impasse in both chambers and were mired in political controversy. Like the transportation bill, the student loan issue faced a deadline of June 30, when the interest rates on college loans would double. Senators Reid and McConnell negotiated an accord on the student loan issue, which was acceptable to Speaker Boehner. The congressional leadership chose the transportation conference report as the vehicle to carry the 1-year freeze on student interest rates for an important reason: It had become a "must-pass" legislative train leaving the congressional station on time and heading to the White House. In addition, there were overlapping offsets (pension law changes) that could be used to help pay for both student loans and transportation projects. As Senator McConnell stated, "This [conference report] is fully paid for with a package of offsets mostly included in the Senate-passed highway bill."[93]

The other unrelated matter added during the transportation conference was a bill reported by the Senate Banking Committee extending the National Flood Insurance Program for 5 years. The bill's purpose was to require people who live near dams or levees to purchase flood insurance. This requirement aroused the ire of various senators on both sides of the aisle, and they blocked Senator Reid from acting on the bill. Like transportation and student loans, the flood insurance program also faced a deadline: the start of the 2012 Atlantic hurricane season, which runs from June 1 to November.[94] Thus, the flood insurance program was folded into transportation conference report to expedite its enactment into law.

HOUSE APPROVAL

The House acted first on the conference report. (Recall the custom directing the chamber that agrees to a conference to act first on the conference report.) With lawmakers anxious to depart the capital for July 4th celebrations back home, the House on Friday, June 29, took up the transportation conference report. A special rule (H. Res. 717) from the Rules Committee, which the House adopted, waived all points of order against the conference report, including the requirement that conference reports lay over for 3 session days so members have time to review the contents. When Republicans assumed control of the House, they promised to abide by the 3-day rule to give lawmakers an opportunity to learn what was in conference reports. Practical exigencies allowed the 3-day rule to be set aside. Similarly, the GOP promised not to bundle unlike bills into omnibus measures, as with the transportation conference report. As GOP Representative Virginia Foxx, N.C., stated, Republicans "prefer to have things broken up . . . and [vote] on them one by one."[95] Despite such misgivings, the conference report was agreed to by a vote of 373 to 52.

Opponents of the report were upset for both substantive and process reasons. As House Democratic conferee Edward Markey, Mass., who refused to sign the conference report and joint explanatory statement, explained about the process: "Conferees have been asked to sign an agreement we have had little or no time to review and the substance of the agreement was negotiated largely without input from most conferees."[96] Worth noting is that the special rule (H. Res. 717) allowed the House to take up a bill on Friday, June 29, via suspension procedure—normally in order only on Mondays, Tuesdays, and Wednesdays—that would temporarily extend transportation programs and student loan rates for 1 week. The purposes of this provision were to provide Congress more time, if needed, to enact the conference report and to avoid any lapse in highway construction or hike in student loan rates. The House employed suspension procedure to pass by voice vote a 1-week extension bill (H.R. 6064).[97]

SENATE APPROVAL

With House approval, the conference report was messaged to the Senate, where it was agreed to on June 29 by a vote of 74 to 19. Before the final vote was reached, the Senate waived three points of order against the conference report for violating Senate Rule XXVIII, involving "scope" and the availability of conference reports, as well as a provision of the 1974 Budget Act. To waive, or overcome, the three points of order required a vote of 60 senators in each case. Majority Leader Reid propounded a unanimous consent agreement that established the sequence for debating and voting on the three points of order. Moreover, the conference report would require 60 affirmative votes for passage.

The first point of order stated that the 596-page conference report violated Rule XXVIII's requirement that conference reports are to be publicly available for 48 hours prior to consideration on the floor. Majority Leader Reid moved to waive Rule XXVIII, which the Senate agreed to by a vote of 72 to 22. As a result, the point of order was rejected.

The second point of order involved the issue of "scope" under Rule XXVIII. Majority Leader Reid moved to waive all scope points of order. A senator then raised a specific scope point of order. It concerned a provision involving invasive species in the Great Lakes that was "slipped into the transportation conference report literally in the dark of night."[98] This provision was in neither the House's nor the Senate's transportation measure. Hence, this was a violation of Rule XXVIII's prohibition against "new matter" not addressed by either chamber being included in conference reports. Reid's motion to waive Rule XXVIII was adopted by a 66-to-28 vote, and the point of order fell.

The third point of order contended that the spending provided in the conference report exceeded the levels set in the concurrent budget resolution for fiscal year 2012. (These spending aggregates—budget authority and budget outlays—were set forth in the Budget Control Act of 2011.) Majority Leader Reid moved to waive all budget laws and concurrent budget resolutions that apply to the conference report. His motion was adopted by a 66-to-30 vote, and the point of order fell. The Senate then went on to enact the conference report by the required supermajority vote stipulated in the unanimous consent agreement. The 1-week extension measure (H.R. 6064) was also enacted by voice vote, clearing the bill for presidential consideration.

PRESIDENTIAL CONSIDERATION

On June 29, President Obama signed into law the 1-week extension measure. Thus, there was no stoppage of highway projects or increase in student loan rates. The extension measure also provided additional time for H.R. 4348—the 27-month, $109 billion surface transportation bill—to be put in proper form (enrolled) for presentation to the president. The cap on student interest rates was extended for 1 year and the flood insurance program until 2017. On July 6, President Obama signed H.R. 4348 into law (P.L. 112-141).

SUMMING UP

An array of actors, factors, and forces are ever present in enacting major bills into law. This was certainly the case with the surface transportation conference report. Among those that seem most significant to its enactment are these:

Deadlines

The enactment into law of the three disparate measures—surface transportation, student loan rates, and flood insurance—was influenced by deadlines. In fact, two sets of deadlines promoted passage of the conference report. The first was the June 30 expiration date for transportation programs and student loan rates, and the beginnings of the hurricane season in the Atlantic. Congressional failure to meet the deadlines would redound negatively on Congress and many of its lawmakers. The second deadline was the fast-approaching and traditional July 4 legislative break. Most lawmakers were anxious to depart Washington and head home or to other places. As one House member bluntly stated: "99.9 percent of us want to go home Friday [June 30]."[99] Both deadlines provided incentives for favorable action on surface transportation.

Leadership

An essential ingredient of leadership is followership. Democratic and Republican party and committee leaders excelled at putting together winning coalitions and devising procedures that carried the day for the conference report. And they did all this without earmarks. Bipartisanship within each chamber and between the two houses prevailed because most members wanted to avoid another extension and pass a longer-term transportation law that would benefit their communities and provide at least 27 months of funding certainty to the construction industry. That the top leader of each chamber stepped in forcefully to reenergize the stalled conference negotiations proved critical in moving the process forward to a successful bipartisan and bicameral outcome.

Politics

A variety of considerations is subsumed by this rubric. For example, on the campaign trail, President Obama was wooing student voters by criticizing Republicans for stalling legislation that would prevent a hike in student loan interest rates. To undermine the president's campaign against a "do-nothing," gridlocked Congress, it was imperative for Republicans, working with Democrats, to demonstrate their ability to pass legislation beneficial to the country. Failure to act would anger many voters, including college students, construction workers who could lose their jobs, and people who needed flood insurance. Needless to say, all three proposals enjoyed public popularity.

To conclude, Senator Boxer, the conference chair, said the lopsided vote for the conference report in both chambers "sends a tremendous signal to the people of America that we can work together."[100] Effective collaboration occurred because most lawmakers in both parties and chambers supported the hard work of deal-making required to reach compromises acceptable to the Republican House and Democratic Senate. "Finding consensus is never easy," wrote Senator Jay Rockefeller, D-W.Va., the chair of the Commerce Committee who was present at the signing of H.R. 4348, "but this was a major priority and making the country's roads, bridges, and highways safer and more efficient is good for all of us."[101] And good for most lawmakers is touting a major congressional accomplishment to voters in the November elections.

NOTES

1. Just as other ideas are implicit in the Constitution (e.g., separation of powers and checks and balances), so too is the requirement that absolutely identical bills must be enacted by the House and Senate (see the bicameral and present-ment clauses of the Constitution) before they are sent to the president.
2. Ada G. McCown, *The Congressional Conference Committee* (New York: Columbia University Press, 1927), 12. See also Lawrence Longley and Walter J. Oleszek, *Bicameral Politics: Conference Committees in Congress* (New Haven, Conn.: Yale University Press, 1989); Gilbert Steiner, *The Congressional Conference Committee, Seventieth to Eightieth Congresses* (Urbana: University of Illinois Press, 1951); and David J. Vogler, *The Third House: Conference Committees in the United States Congress* (Evanston, Ill.: Northwestern University Press, 1971).
3. *Congressional Record*, July 8, 1998, S7650.
4. Roy Swanstrom, *The United States Senate, 1787–1801*, 99th Congress, 1st sess., 1985, S. Doc. 99-19, 232.
5. *Congressional Record*, September 13, 1999, H8129.
6. Ibid., February 20, 1986, S1463.
7. Dave Boyer, "GOP Considers TV for Energy Hearings," *Washington Times*, April 26, 2002, A4.
8. *CQ Daily Monitor*, March 20, 2000, 3.
9. Gary Andres, "A Deal or No Deal," *Washington Times*, June 8, 2006, A19.
10. James V. Saturno, "The Origination Clause of the U.S. Constitution: Inter-pretation and Enforcement," *CRS Report RL31399*, March 15, 2011.
11. John Gramlich, "Reid Says House Is Holding Up Conference on Domestic Violence Legislation," *CQ Today*, May 22, 2012, 6. Also see John Gramlich, "Obstacle Emerges on Violence Bill,' *CQ Today*, May 18, 2012, 1. Worth not-ing is that "blue slips" have two procedural meanings. One, as noted, involves the origination clause of the Constitution. The other is a tradition unique to the Senate Judiciary Committee. Judiciary chairs commonly state that unless federal district and circuit court nominees receive the support of both of their

home-state senators via signatures on a blue slip, the Judiciary Committee will not conduct hearings on the judicial nominees. See Mitchell Sollenberger, "The Blue Slip: A Theory of Unified and Divided Government," *Congress & the Presidency*, May–August 2010, 125–156.

12. Russ Choma, "Senate Approves Additional Funds 'Cash for Clunkers,' Rejects Amendments," *Daily Report for Executives*, August 7, 2009, A-26.

13. Richard Cohen, *National Journal*, July 28, 2001, 2396.

14. Alan K. Ota, "Senate GOP Freshman Find Power in House Counterparts' Numbers," *CQ Today*, July 25, 2011, 1.

15. Senate Committee on Rules and Administration, *Congressional Handbook*, U.S. Senate ed. (Washington, DC: Government Printing Office, 1994), III–30.

16. *Congressional Record*, March 21, 1974, 7589. See also *Congressional Record*, April 10, 1974, 10569.

17. Steve Teske, "House, Senate Lawmakers Continue Work on SCHIP Compromise Reauthorization Bill," *Daily Report for Executives*, September 19, 2007, A-45.

18. *Congressional Record*, December 28, 2008, E2665.

19. Steven T. Dennis, "Pelosi, Hoyer Promise 72 Hours to Review Health Bill," *Roll Call*, January 14, 2010, online edition.

20. For a detailed analysis of the procedural complexities associated with the amendment exchange procedure, see Elizabeth Rybicki, *Amendments Between the Houses: Procedural Options and Effects* (CRS Report R41003), January 13, 2012.

21. Richard S. Beth, Valerie Heitshusen, Bill Heniff Jr., and Elizabeth Rybicki, *Leadership Tools for Managing the U.S. Senate* (paper delivered at the 2009 annual meeting of the American Political Science Association, Toronto, Canada, September 3–6, 2009), 12.

22. Paul Kane and Lori Montgomery, "GOP Senators Seek to Block Defense Bill to Delay Health-Care Vote," *Washington Post*, December 18, 2009, A3.

23. See *Congressional Record*, December 16, 2009, S13295–S13296, on filling the tree and the motion to refer by Senator Reid; December 18, 2009, S13407, for the successful cloture vote; and December 19, 2009, S13476, for Senate passage of the defense bill.

24. John Stanton, "GOP Blocks Appointment as Senate Adjourns," *Roll Call*, December 24, 2009, online edition.

25. *Congressional Record*, December 20, 1982, S15757.

26. Richard F. Fenno Jr., *The Power of the Purse* (Boston: Little, Brown, 1966), 610.

27. Lindsey Layton, "Californians Shape Up as Force on Environmental Policy," *Washington Post*, December 29, 2008, A3.

28. John Ferejohn, "Who Wins in Conference Committee?" *Journal of Politics* (November 1975): 1033–1046; and Walter J. Oleszek, "House–Senate Relationships: Comity and Conflict," *The Annals* (January 1974): 80–81.

29. Elizabeth Drew, *Senator* (New York: Simon and Schuster, 1979), 174.

30. *Congressional Record*, May 23, 2001, S5527.

31. Janet Hook and Peter Wallsten, "Border Battle Now a GOP Turf War," *Los Angeles Times*, June 22, 2006, online edition.

32. *Enactment of a Law*, 97th Congress, 2d sess., 1992, S. Doc. 97-20, 24.

33. Carl Hulse and Robert Pear, "Feeling Left Out on Major Bills, Democrats Turn to Stalling Others," *New York Times*, May 3, 2004, A18.

34. Ceci Connolly, "Legislation Goes Overboard as Legislators Eye the Exits," *Congressional Quarterly Weekly Report*, October 1, 1994, 2755.
35. *Congressional Record*, May 16, 2000, S3991.
36. Ibid., July 18, 1985, H5937.
37. *Washington Times*, February 14, 1995, A11.
38. Mary Agnes Carey, "Hastert's Choice of Conferees Diminishes Prospects for Survival of House's Managed Care Bill," *CQ Weekly*, November 6, 1999, 2657.
39. *Congressional Record*, March 2, 2006, S1600.
40. Ibid., March 3, 2006, S1755.
41. Alan K. Ota, "With DeLay Setting a Partisan Tone, House Stands Firm on Child Credit," *CQ Weekly*, June 21, 2003, 1531.
42. John Cochran, "Management by Objective: How Frist Deals in 51–49 Senate," *CQ Weekly*, August 30, 2003, 2063.
43. Jonathan Allen and John Cochran, "The Might of the Right," *CQ Weekly*, November 8, 2003, 2762.
44. *Congressional Record*, July 29, 1981, S8711.
45. Ibid., August 3, 1989, H5003.
46. For an example of a majority-party member offering an unusual instruction motion, see *Congressional Record*, November 8, 2001, H7945.
47. *Congressional Record*, June 23, 1983, H4435.
48. *CQ Daily Monitor*, August 8, 1994, 3.
49. In 2003, for example, Democrats offered numerous motions to instruct, urging House conferees to provide a child tax credit to families earning between $10,000 and $26,000. A goal of Democrats was to make Republicans appear insensitive to the needs of low-income working families.
50. Robert Pear, "Negotiators Stall on Patients' Rights Bill," *New York Times*, May 26, 2000, A15.
51. Jackie Koszczuk, "After Half a Century, He's Still Got a To-Do List," *CQ Weekly*, February 20, 2006, 475.
52. Samuel Goldreich, "Domenici, Tauzin Say They Will Write Energy Bill," *CQ Today*, September 12, 2003, 6.
53. Emily Pierce, "Tax Conference Getting 'Parental Supervision,'" *Roll Call*, May 22, 2003, 26.
54. *New York Times*, July 23, 1981, A19. See also Michael J. Malbin, *Unelected Representatives: Congressional Staff and the Future of Representative Government* (New York: Basic Books, 1980), Chap. 5.
55. Ted Siff and Alan Weil, *Ruling Congress* (New York: Grossman, 1975), 184.
56. Julie Rovner, "Senators Form 'Working Group' to Watch Medicare Negotiations," *CongressDailyAM*, August 1, 2003, 7.
57. Joseph Anselmo, "GOP Leaders Take a Short Time-Out in Final Push on Omnibus Energy Bill," *CQ Today*, October 2, 2003, 5.
58. Laurie Kellman, "Senators Lament Cutting Anti-Terror Bill Features," *Washington Times*, April 17, 1996, A6.
59. *Congressional Record*, August 1, 1984, S9605.
60. *CQ's Congressional Insight*, October 19, 1990, 1.
61. Quoted in Charles L. Clapp, *The Congressman* (Washington, D.C.: Brookings, 1962), 249.
62. For a rare point of order against a conference report for violating scope, see *Congressional Record*, November 14, 2002, H8824.

63. House Rule XXII, which deals with House–Senate relations, also stipulates that it is not in order to consider a conference report that proposes to amend the Internal Revenue Code unless a tax complexity analysis has been prepared either by the Joint Committee on Taxation or the Committee on Ways and Means.

64. *Congressional Record,* November 7, 2007, S14043.

65. Ibid., September 30, 2009, S9965.

66. Floyd M. Riddick and Alan S. Frumin, *Senate Procedure: Precedents and Practices* (Washington, DC: Government Printing Office, 1992), 463. Today, the Senate usually employs a "reasonably related" standard to assess whether unrelated matter is included in conference reports.

67. Martin Gold, Michael Hugo, Hyde Murray, Peter Robinson, and A. L. "Pete" Singleton, *The Book on Congress* (Washington, DC: Big Eagle, 1992), 343.

68. Martin Vaughan and Susan Davis, "With Extra Time and Bush's Help, CAFTA Squeaks Through," *CongressDailyPM,* July 28, 2005, 2.

69. *Congressional Record,* December 22, 2005, H13181.

70. Ibid., January 4, 2007, H27.

71. Charles Tiefer, *Congressional Practice and Procedure* (New York: Greenwood Press, 1989), 818.

72. Matthew Rarey, "Congress Breaks into Cyberspace With Electronically Signed Bill," *Washington Times,* July 16, 1999, A3.

73. Erin Billings and John Stanton, "Leaders Boost Profiles of Senate's Endangered," *Roll Call,* March 2, 2006, 22.

74. David R. Sands, "Veto by Obama Raises Questions," *Washington Times,* January 12, 2010, A4.

75. Nancy Benac, "Obama Takes Faux Presidential Signature Into a Different Realm," *USA Today,* June 27, 2011, 4A.

76. Dave Boyer, "Republicans Question Obama's Use of Autopen to Sign 'Cliff' Bill,'" *Washington Times,* January 4, 2013, A3.

77. See, for example, John H. Cushman Jr., "Congress Lets President Delay His Tax Bill Veto," *New York Times,* October 23, 1992, A14.

78. See Robert J. Spitzer, "Growing Executive Power: The Strange Case of the 'Protective Return' Pocket Veto," *Presidential Studies Quarterly,* September 2012, 637–655.

79. Woodrow Wilson, *Congressional Government* (Boston: Houghton Mifflin, 1885), 52. Wilson wrote that the "president is no greater than his prerogative of veto makes him; he is, in other words, powerful rather as a branch of the legislature than as the titular head of the Executive" (p. 260).

80. *Congressional Record,* December 20, 1982, S15678.

81. Dan Friedman, "On the Other Hand," *National Journal,* March 28, 2009, 54. See also Philip J. Cooper, "George W. Bush, Edgar Allen Poe, and the Use and Abuse of Presidential Signing Statements," *Presidential Studies Quarterly,* September 2005, 515–532.

82. See David Nather, "New President, Old Precedent," *CQ Weekly,* July 27, 2009, 1760–1762.

83. Charlie Savage, "Obama Takes a New Route to Opposing Parts of Laws," *New York Times,* January 9, 2010, A9.

84. Charlie Savage, "Provisions in Budget Bill Are Challenged by Obama," *New York Times,* December 24, 2011, A13.

85. Michael D. Shear, "Obama Pledges to Limit Use of Signing Statements," *Washington Post,* March 10, 2009, A4.
86. Kathryn Wolfe and Burgess Everett, "Transportation Conferees Begin Talks," *Roll Call,* May 8, 2012, 17.
87. Meredith Shiner, "Baucus Could Be Key GOP Ally on Pipeline," *Roll Call,* April 25, 2012, 3.
88. Ibid., "GOP Freshmen Key to Highway Bill," *Roll Call,* May 7, 2012, 3.
89. Christine Grimaldi and Nancy Ognanovich, "House Republican Conferees Prepare Counteroffer to Senate Reauthorization Draft," *Daily Report for Executives,* June 7, 2012, A-37.
90. Ashley Halsey III, "The Personal Touch on Transportation," *The Washington Post,* June 6, 2012, A17.
91. Keith Laing and Pete Kasperowicz, "Highway Talks Break Down, Accusations Fly," *The Hill,* June 14, 2012, 1. See also Russell Berman, Alexander Bolton, and Keith Laing, "Reid, GOP Brawl Over Highway Bill," *The Hill,* June 6, 2012, 1.
92. During the first week of June, Speaker Boehner stated that if the conferees could not reach an accord, he would have the House vote on a 6-month transportation funding extension, leaving the matter to be reconsidered after the November elections. Senator Boxer criticized the Speaker's proposal, but it was Representative Mica's view that "the speaker's intent was to put as much pressure on the conferees as possible to try to conclude their work." Christine Grimaldi, Anthony Adragna, and Jonathan Nicholson, "Boehner Floats Transportation Extension; House GOP Conferees Make Counteroffer," *Daily Report for Executives,* June 8, 2012, A-23.
93. *Congressional Record,* June 29, 2012, S4735.
94. Jeff Baker, "Congress Passes Flood Insurance Measure Reauthorizing Program for Five Years," *Daily Report for Executives,* July 2, 2012, EE-13.
95. Lauren Smith and Jennifer Scholtes, "Despite Grumbling, Flood Insurance Likely to Pass," *CQ Today,* June 28, 2012, 7. Over in the Senate, Conference Chair Barbara Boxer agreed with Representative Foxx. Senator Boxer said, "I don't like the fact that we cast one vote and there are three subjects. It is very difficult for the people back home to understand it." *Congressional Record,* June 29, 2012, S4743.
96. *Congressional Record,* June 28, 2012, E1177.
97. The special rule (H. Res. 717) also stated that, if needed, the House could consider on June 29 a concurrent resolution correcting the enrollment of H.R. 4348. Enrollment means preparing an accurate copy of the bill, usually on parchment paper, for presentation to the president. The enrolling process can be lengthy and laborious, depending on the complexity of the final form of the legislation.
98. *Congressional Record,* June 29, 2012, S4741.
99. Kathryn A. Wolfe and Burgess Everett, "Transportation Bill Inching Forward to Passage," *Politico,* June 29, 2012, 3.
100. *Congressional Record,* June 29, 2012, S4760.
101. Heather Caygle, "Obama Signs Surface Transportation Reauthorization Measure Through FY2014," *Daily Report for Executives,* July 9, 2012, A-23.

CHAPTER 9

Legislative Oversight

A FUNDAMENTAL objective of legislative oversight is to hold executive officials accountable for the implementation of delegated authority. As one senator expressed it,

> I believe that oversight is one of the Congress's most important constitutional responsibilities. We must do more than write laws and decide policies. It is also our responsibility to perform the oversight necessary to insure that the administration enforces those laws as Congress intended.[1]

Another senator underscored this view: "We've delegated so much authority to the executive branch of government, and we ought to devote more time to oversight then we do."[2]

Consider the huge expansion of executive influence in the modern era. If the founding fathers returned to observe their handiwork, they would likely be shocked by such developments as the multiplicity of presidential roles, the creation of a "presidential branch" of government (the Office of Management and Budget [OMB], the National Security Council, and the like), and the establishment of so many federal agencies and departments, such as the Department of Homeland Security. Importantly, oversight enables Congress to challenge unwarranted assertions of executive power, to raise and ask the tough fiscal and policy questions of public officials, and to help administrative leaders fix (or avoid) mistakes.

Congressional oversight is the continuing review by the House and Senate, especially through their committee structures, of how effectively, efficiently, and frugally the executive branch is carrying out congressional mandates. It implies some form of "supervision," "watchfulness," or "review" of executive actions and activities. Only by investigating how a statute is being administered can Congress discover deficiencies in the original statute and make necessary adjustments and refinements. After all, laws passed by Congress are often general guidelines, and sometimes their wording is deliberately vague or convoluted. Under authority granted by Congress, administration of statutes commonly requires executive agencies to draft federal regulations and agency officials to undertake day-to-day program management.

Congress's "watchdog" role is crucial for other reasons. Oversight shines the spotlight of public attention on many significant issues, allowing the American people to make informed judgments about executive performance, policy success or failure, and the conduct of officeholders who serve in the federal government. "The informing function of Congress," wrote

Woodrow Wilson in his classic 1885 study of the legislative branch, "should be preferred even to its legislative function." He added:

> Unless Congress have and use every means of acquainting itself with the acts and dispositions of the administrative agents of the government, the country must be helpless to learn how it is being served; and unless Congress both scrutinize these things and sift them by every form of discussion, the country must remain in embarrassing, crippling ignorance of the very affairs which it is most important it should understand and direct.[3]

Another fundamental goal of oversight is to protect Congress's policy-making role and its place in our constitutional separation-of-powers system as the "first branch" of government. The huge growth of the executive establishment has produced a policymaking rival to Congress. Administrators do more than simply "faithfully execute" our laws according to the intent (which may be vague) of Congress. Federal agencies are filled with knowledgeable career and noncareer experts who, among other things, write rules and regulations that have the force of law; formulate policy initiatives for the White House and Congress; interpret statutes in ways that may expand their discretionary authority or, conversely, undercut legislative intent; and shape policy development by Congress, in part by "selling" their ideas to lawmakers and committees via hearings, agency reports, and other means.

OVERSIGHT: AN OVERVIEW

Congress's oversight roles are both to take stock of national governmental responsibilities and to ensure, as the Constitution states, that "the laws are faithfully executed" by the president and federal administrators. Oversight has been part of the principal functions of the legislative branch since the nation's beginning. Congress's power of the purse, its authority to pass laws that create programs and agencies, its power of impeachment and confirmation, and its right to investigate executive-branch activities are among the explicit and implicit oversight functions rooted in the Constitution. The framers, according to historian Arthur M. Schlesinger Jr., believed the review function did not require specific mention in the Constitution. "It was not considered necessary to make an explicit grant of such authority," wrote Schlesinger. "The power to make laws implied the power to see whether they were faithfully executed."[4]

Congress formalized its legislative oversight function in the Legislative Reorganization Act of 1946. That act required congressional committees to exercise "continuous watchfulness" of the agencies under their jurisdictions and implicitly divided oversight functions into three areas:

1. Authorizing committees (such as Agriculture, Armed Services, and Commerce) conduct "legislative oversight." They are required to review federal programs and agencies under their jurisdictions and,

if necessary, to propose legislation or use other means to remedy deficiencies they uncovered.

2. "Fiscal oversight" was assigned to the Appropriations Committees of each chamber, which were to scrutinize agency spending and hold agencies accountable for their fiscal decisions.

3. Wide-ranging "investigative oversight" over the executive branch was assigned to the House Oversight and Government Reform Committee and the Senate Homeland Security and Governmental Affairs Committee. Their job is to probe for inefficiency, waste, and corruption in the federal government. To some degree, all committees perform each type of oversight.

Each of the three overlapping types of oversight—legislative, fiscal, and investigative—aims to fulfill the basic goals or purposes of oversight, such as clarifying statutory intent; evaluating program administration and performance; eliminating waste, fraud, abuse, and red tape; reviewing whether programs have outlived their usefulness; ensuring that programs and agencies are administered in a cost-effective and economical manner; and correcting executive abuses of authority.

Congress has also enacted many other laws that strengthen its oversight capacities. These laws establish mechanisms, procedures, or entities within the executive branch that provide Congress with oversight-related information and assessments of administrative activities. They include statutes that address, for example, paperwork reduction, whistleblower protection, the preparation of regular financial statements by individual departments and agencies, and the purchase of the most cost-effective information technology. Among additional noteworthy statutes are the following.

The Government Performance and Results Act of 1993 (GPRA) aims to promote more cost-effective federal spending by requiring agencies to set strategic goals (e.g., a statement of their basic missions and the resources required to achieve those objectives) and to prepare annual performance plans and annual performance reports, which are submitted to Congress and the president. A fundamental purpose of the GPRA is to hold agencies accountable for setting goals and measuring their performance. The law also aims to assist Congress in determining agency budgets by identifying which programs are effective and which are ineffective by providing credible information on agency performance or nonperformance. The GPRA might over time also help reduce unnecessary duplication and overlap among federal agencies that implement similar policy areas. As a House majority leader noted as he held up a pizza box

If this were a cheese pizza, it would be inspected by the [Food and Drug Administration]. If it were a pepperoni pizza, it would be inspected by the [U.S. Department of Agriculture]. . . . We definitely have a great deal of duplication here.[5]

Eighteen years later, on January 4, 2011, the GPRA Modernization Act was signed into law (P.L. 111-352). Among its basic purposes are to establish new goal-setting and performance measures for policy areas that cross-cut agency jurisdictions; promote wider opportunities for Congress and nonfederal stakeholders "to influence how agencies and OMB set goals and assess performance"; and increase the availability of agency performance reports over the Internet.[6] The new and old GPRA laws aim, in short, to strengthen Congress's and the president's capacity to assess agency and program performance and to ensure that taxpayer dollars are spent wisely. (In this era of spending austerity, Congress is considering a number of possible laws to oversee federal spending, such as the bipartisan Digital Accountability and Transparency Act. This act proposes the creation of an oversight commission "to monitor all government spending, including federal awards, grants, contracts, loans, and other assistance.")[7]

The Congressional Review Act of 1996 (CRA) enables Congress to review and disapprove agency rules, and provides expedited procedures in the Senate, but not the House, for the consideration of joint resolutions of disapproval. Under the CRA, all final agency rules must be submitted to the House and Senate before they can go into effect. The House and Senate then have 60 session days following the submission of the rules to act on a joint resolution of disapproval. If the House and Senate do not act on a disapproval resolution, or if either body defeats the measure, the rule will go into effect. Conversely, if both chambers enact a joint resolution of disapproval but it is vetoed by the president, the rule will become effective subject to Congress's ability to override the veto.

As for expedited procedures for the Senate, the CRA provides that they may be used for disapproval resolutions "at any time within 60 days of Senate session after the rule in question has been published in the *Federal Register* and received by both houses of Congress."[8] Then, if the committee to which a disapproval resolution has been referred fails to report the measure within 20 calendar days, any 30 senators can file a petition to discharge the resolution from the committee. It will then be placed on the legislative calendar. Any senator (usually the majority leader) may then offer a nondebatable motion to proceed to the disapproval resolution. If this motion is adopted, the disapproval resolution itself is subject to 10 hours of debate with no amendments. When debate ends, the CRA states that "the Senate automatically proceeds to vote on the resolution."[9] In short, there is no opportunity to filibuster disapproval resolutions. (The House usually considers disapproval resolutions per a special rule from the Rules Committee.)

The law has been little used by Congress to block agency rules. For example, since the law went into effect, only one rule has been rejected (an ergonomics rule in 2001), despite federal agencies finalizing "over 3,500 regulations per year in each of the last three years."[10] Various structural and interpretive ambiguities, such as "whether a disapproval resolution may be directed at part of a rule," account for its limited use.[11] Members also acknowledge that the law contains a fatal flaw: The president can veto the joint resolution of disapproval—"which is likely if the underlying rule is developed during his administration."[12] Congress is unlikely to override the veto given the two-thirds vote required of each chamber. Still, the law is available to either chamber to express its views about agency rulemaking. Congressional Republicans in the 112th Congress (2011–2013) introduced more disapproval resolutions "than at any time in the history of the Congressional Review Act."[13]

Congress, too, can employ its spending power to stipulate that no appropriated funds shall be used by federal entities to develop, enforce, or implement unwanted rules or regulations. Today, appropriations measures are replete with policy ("limitation") riders limiting or cutting off funds to agencies charged, for example, with implementing two of President Barack Obama's signature legislative achievements: the Affordable Care Act and Wall Street reform. Outside groups can also bring suit in federal court to block what they consider to be illegally promulgated rules.

Passage of the landmark Congressional Budget and Impoundment Control Act of 1974 (see Chapter 2) strengthened Congress's review capabilities by directing the Government Accountability Office (GAO)—a legislative support agency—to assist House and Senate committees in program evaluation and in the development of "methods for assessing and reporting actual program performance."

The Federal Funding Accountability and Transparency Act, informally called the "Google your government" law, requires the OMB "to provide a user-friendly, searchable database" of nearly $1 trillion in federal grants and contracts.[14] The potential inherent in the law is that it could enable any interested citizen or watchdog group to monitor federal spending, thereby providing greater transparency and accountability to the government's funding decisions. Many "citizen auditors" would no doubt share their evaluation of federal expenditures with congressional lawmakers and committees. This development might be dubbed "the democratization of oversight" or "the public as watchdog."

Recent presidents have taken steps to employ technology to enhance government transparency, provide easier access to information, and promote more citizen interaction with federal officials and agencies. In this Internet age, the federal government has an estimated 24,000 Internet sites, with many departments and agencies hosting "blogs, Facebook pages, YouTube channels, Twitter feeds and even ambitious virtual worlds on Second Life."[15] For example, to give the public easier access to government information, President Obama directed "all federal agencies to make at least two government services available on the iPhone and other mobile devices."[16] To encourage interactive oversight between citizens and federal policymakers, the Obama Administration launched in September 2011 a "We the People" petition site. If 25,000 citizens (increased to 100,000 citizens in January 2013) sign a petition urging a change in federal policy, the White House will respond (meetings, statements, online postings, etc.) to the issue within 30 days. A White House official said the threshold was raised "to ensure that we're able to continue to give the most popular ideas the time they deserve."[17] The petition site, however, soon became a handy "lobbying tool for interest groups in Washington."[18]

When Republicans won control of the 112th House, they revived an online program they used when they were in the minority—called "You Cut." People can vote online at Majority Leader Eric Cantor's, Va., website and "select one of the three government programs to cut. The proposal with the most votes will be introduced as a bill, with the public able to track its progress on the website."[19] Although "You Cut" bills are unlikely to pass the Democratic Senate, they underscore the GOP's commitment to rein in government spending.

Formalizing Oversight

The House and Senate have always had authority to investigate programs and agencies of the executive branch. The first congressional investigation in American history, in 1792, delved into the conduct of the government in the wars against the Indians. One of the broadest investigations was an 1861 inquiry into the conduct of the Civil War. Other notable probes have included investigations into the Crédit Mobilier scandal in 1872 to 1873, the "Money Trust" in 1912, the Teapot Dome scandal in 1923, stock exchange operations in 1932 to 1934, and defense spending during World War II. In the mid-1980s, a House and Senate select committee jointly investigated the Iran-contra affair, which involved covert and deceptive operations by the National Security Council and others during the Reagan Administration. The hearings were televised nationally. More recently, House and Senate panels have conducted inquiries into a host of international issues (Iraq, Afghanistan, Libya, and Syria, for example) and national matters (the Wall Street meltdown, cybersecurity, tax reform, and health care, for instance).

The 1946 reorganization act stated Congress's intention to exercise its investigative authority primarily through standing committees rather than by means of specially created investigating committees. (In 1995, the House amended its rules to grant explicit authority to the Speaker to appoint "special ad hoc oversight committees for the purpose of reviewing specific matters within the jurisdiction of two or more standing committees.") The 1946 act provided for continuous review of programs instead of sporadic hearings whenever errors, malfeasance, or injustices surfaced. The continuous watchfulness precept of the act implied that Congress would henceforth participate actively in administrative decision making, in line with the observation that "administration of a statute is, properly speaking, an extension of the legislative process."[20]

During the 1970s, both houses amended their rules to grant additional oversight authority to the standing committees. The Legislative

Reorganization Act of 1970 rephrased in more explicit language the oversight duties of the committees and required most House and Senate panels to issue biennial reports on their oversight activities. The House Committee Reform Amendments of 1974 assigned "special oversight" responsibilities to several standing committees. The Senate adopted the same approach, called "comprehensive policy oversight," when it adopted the Committee System Reorganization Amendments of 1977. Both special oversight and comprehensive policy oversight are akin to the broad review authority granted the House Oversight and Government Reform Committee and the Senate Homeland Security and Governmental Affairs Committee.

Explained Senator Adlai E. Stevenson III, D-Ill. (1970–1981), floor manager during Senate debate on the 1977 change:

> Standing committees are directed and permitted to undertake investigations and make recommendations in broad policy areas—for example, nutrition, aging, environmental protection, or consumer affairs—even though they lack legislative jurisdiction over some aspects of the subject. Such oversight authority involves subjects that generally cut across the jurisdictions of several committees. Presently, no single committee has a comprehensive overview of these policy areas. [This rule change] corrects that. It assigns certain committees the right to undertake comprehensive reviews of broad policy issues.[21]

Selected Additional Rules Governing Oversight

Other notable changes were made in House and Senate rules regarding oversight. For example, the House directed its committees to create oversight subcommittees, undertake futures research and forecasting, and review the impact of tax expenditures (credits, incentives, and the like) on matters that fall within their respective jurisdictions.[22] The Senate required each standing committee to include regulatory impact statements in committee reports accompanying the legislation it sends to the floor. One of these statements, for example, might evaluate the amount of additional paperwork that would result from enactment of a proposed bill.

In 1995, the House adopted a new rule requiring all standing committees to prepare by February 15 of the first session of each Congress a comprehensive oversight plan. The objective was

> to ensure that committees make a more concerted, coordinated and conscientious effort to develop meaningful oversight plans at the beginning of each Congress and to follow through on their implementation, with a view to examining the full range of laws under their jurisdiction over a period of five Congresses.[23]

Four years later, in a move designed to encourage more monitoring of administrative performance, the House amended its rules to permit committees to have a sixth subcommittee (under House rules, most standing committees are limited to five subcommittees) if it is an oversight subcommittee. When the 109th Congress (2005–2007) began, the House adopted another rule "directing committees to review matters within their jurisdiction to ferret out duplicative government programs as part of their oversight planning at the beginning of each Congress."[24]

Soon after the 111th Congress (2009–2011) convened, the House amended its rules "to require each standing committee to hold at least three hearings per year on waste, fraud and abuse under each respective committee's jurisdiction." House committees are obligated to hold a hearing if "an agency's financial statements are not in order" and if a program under a committee's jurisdiction is "deemed by GAO to be at high risk for waste, fraud, and abuse."[25] The GOP-controlled 112th House continued the above rule changes but added a new provision to Rule X, Clause D, requiring committees during the development of their oversight plan "to include proposals to cut or eliminate mandatory and discretionary programs that are inefficient, duplicative, outdated, or more appropriately administered by State or local governments." The 113th House amended its rules to authorize committee chairs to request the GAO to conduct duplication analysis of any bill or joint resolution referred to that committee. Further, committee reports on those measures shall include a statement "indicating whether any provision of the measure establishes or reauthorizes a program of the Federal Government known to be duplicative of another Federal program."

Congress requires a large array of oversight devices because it faces an executive establishment of massive size and diffuse direction. As a scholar wrote: "We should not deceive ourselves into thinking that the Federal Government of the future will be a shrinking violet, retreating to the modest proportions it had in George Washington's or Grover Cleveland's time."[26] Many reasons account for the expansion in the size and reach of the national government. Domestic and international crises, such as wars and global economic meltdowns, fuel the increase of federal responsibilities. Complexity is another factor. New problems and issues constantly provoke calls for governmental action. Today, the federal government must address topics ranging from pandemics to currency exchange rates to global warming. A population of more than 300 million people creates its own set of national governmental issues (health care, law enforcement, transportation, and so on).

Many individuals, lawmakers, and presidents regularly call for "less government," contending that the size and reach of the national government saps individual initiative and threatens personal freedom. Yet numerous voters—even those philosophically opposed to big government—support a large number of the government's specific roles and may even welcome their selective expansion in ensuring clean air and water, a strong national defense, law enforcement, and safety from terrorist attacks. In his assessment of government, and the dualistic ideas about government held by many Americans, President Obama stated:

> Our predecessors understood that government could not, should not, solve every problem. They understood that there are instances when the gains in security from government action are not worth the added constraints on our freedom. But they also understood that the danger of too much government is matched by the perils of too little; that without the leavening hand of wise policy, markets can crash, monopolies can stifle competition, the vulnerable can be exploited.[27]

Whatever a person's views about the government's role or performance, its activities, responsibilities, and services affect every lawmaker's constituents. Thus, Congress has as one of its essential functions the monitoring and checking of the authority and resources it grants the federal bureaucracy. In carrying out its oversight responsibilities, Congress must be able to choose from a variety of techniques to hold agencies accountable so that if one technique proves ineffective, committees and members can employ others, singly or in combination.

TECHNIQUES OF OVERSIGHT

The objectives of oversight vary from committee to committee and member to member. The focus or emphasis might be political, programmatic, or both: promoting administrative efficiency and economy in government; protecting and supporting favored policies and programs; airing an administration's failures and wrongdoing or its achievements and successes; publicizing a particular member's or a committee's goals; reasserting congressional authority vis-à-vis the executive branch; assuaging the interests of pressure groups; generating favorable publicity for programs; or winning electoral support from voters or groups.

Needless to say, the press and media play a large and often controversial role (publicizing information that the government prefers to keep secret, for example) in investigating and reporting on governmental activities. Still, it is worth recalling a statement made by former Supreme Court Justice Potter Stewart:

> In the absence of governmental checks and balances present in other areas of national life, the only effective restraint upon executive policy and power in the area of national defense and international affairs may lie in an enlightened citizenry. . . . Without an informed and free press, there cannot be an enlightened people.[28]

A 14-month *USA Today* investigation enlightened Congress and the public about the "dangers posed by lead-contaminated soil around forgotten [lead smelter] factory sites [across the nation] that spewed lead particles into neighborhoods [and the surrounding soil] for decades before closing in the 1960s or 1970s."[29] Lawmakers moved quickly to urge the Environmental Protection Agency (EPA) to "take immediate action" to "ensure that people living near these sites, especially children, are safe."[30] Newspaper reports also brought to light the lavish and wasteful conferences for employees conducted by the General Services Administration (GSA), the federal agency responsible for supervising the government's real-estate holdings, overseeing federal contracting, and promoting cost-effective governmental operations. For example, a Las Vegas conference, which featured clowns, mind readers, and expensive parties, cost the taxpayers $823,000. A hearing conducted by the House Transportation and Infrastructure Committee saw Chair John Mica, R-Fla., rip into "GSA officials for spending taxpayers' money so lavishly while Americans themselves are struggling in tough economic times."[31] At a Washington-area award ceremony for GSA employees that cost $268,732, "the agency spent $20,578 on 4,000 drumsticks for a drum-playing exercise, $28,364 on 4,000 picture frames that included digital displays telling the time and temperature, and $7,697 on a reception that included a guitarist and violinist," not to mention $44 million in bonuses for selected employees.[32]

Hearings and Investigations

The traditional method of exercising congressional oversight is through committee hearings and investigations into executive branch operations. Legislators need to know how effectively federal programs are working and how well agency officials are responding to committee directives. And they want to know the scope and intensity of public support for government programs to assess the need for legislative changes.

For more than 200 years, Congress has conducted investigations of varying types with varying results. Along the way, there have been abuses and excesses, successes and accomplishments. Although no explicit provision in the Constitution authorizes Congress to conduct investigations, the Supreme Court has decided in several cases that the investigative function is essential to the legislative function. In *Watkins v. United States* (1957), for example, the Court declared that the "power of the Congress to conduct investigations is inherent in the legislative process. That power is broad. It encompasses inquiries concerning the administration of existing laws as well as proposed or possibly needed statutes."

The Supreme Court has also made clear that the investigative power is not unlimited, and Congress has no authority, for example, "to expose for the sake of exposure." Congress, too, has established procedures (e.g., the right of witnesses before investigative hearings to be accompanied by their own counsel) to ensure that individuals are treated fairly when they testify before committees. The rules of each chamber empower its committees to issue subpoenas that require witnesses to testify and to produce relevant documents. Individuals who refuse to comply with a subpoena issued in either chamber could be cited for contempt and be subject to criminal or civil penalties.[33] Typically, legislative–executive controversies surrounding the threat or issuance of subpoenas or contempt citations are resolved through private negotiations that produce agreements satisfactory to both branches. This was not the case in 2012 when Attorney General Eric Holder was held in contempt by the House of Representatives.

Holder Held in Contempt. The House Oversight and Government Reform Committee, chaired by Darrell Issa, R-Calif., voted along party lines to hold Attorney General Holder in contempt of Congress. The committee's charge was that Holder had not furnished relevant documents pertaining to "Operation Fast and Furious," an undercover gun-trafficking operation went awry that was conducted by the Phoenix division of the Bureau of Alcohol, Tobacco, Firearms and Explosives (a unit of the Justice Department). The program's goal was to allow guns to enter Mexico illegally, follow the gun smugglers, and then arrest the violent criminals associated with Mexico's drug cartels. The operation went astray when Bureau personnel lost track of the guns and a Border Patrol officer was killed in a shootout with drug dealers in possession of the "lost" weapons.

House and Senate committees pressed to learn the details of the flawed operation. Initially, a Justice Department official denied that any weapons were lost, but that contention was quickly proven false, which provoked legislative charges of a "cover up" by the Justice Department. Attorney General Holder refuted that charge and turned over to Chairman Issa's committee scores of documents relating to the murder of the agent and other relevant material. Despite subpoenas for additional Justice documents, the attorney general refused to produce the requested material for the committee. President Obama even asserted "executive privilege"—a presidential prerogative used to ensure candid communication between the chief executive and his top advisors—because the disclosure of the documents "would chill the candor of future internal deliberations." However, it is unclear whether the president's assertion "trumps Congress's right to subpoena internal communications within an agency."[34]

On June 28, 2012, for the first time ever, the House voted 255 to 67 to hold a sitting attorney general in contempt for not providing to a House committee certain documents pertaining to the gun-trafficking operation. Each party blasted the other for the contempt vote, which provoked a walkout from the chamber by many Democrats who refused to vote for "what they called an 'illegitimate' charade."[35] Republicans asserted that it was their constitutional duty to protect their oversight authority and to uncover all the details and documents associated with "Operation Fast and Furious." Democrats also called the contempt action politically motivated and designed to embarrass the president in an election year. In the view of the attorney general, "I've become a symbol of what [Republicans] don't like about the positions this Justice Department has taken [on issues such as immigration, voting rights, and gay marriage]." He added: "I am also a proxy for the president in an election year. You have to be exceedingly naïve to think that vote was about . . . documents."[36]

What happens next to the attorney general is unclear, except the near certainty of additional legal and political wrangling. Whether Holder will be compelled to turn over the documents wanted by the House is an open question. Under its inherent contempt power, the House could arrest and jail Holder until he turns over the documents. This approach, however, is viewed by many officials as unseemly, over-the-top, and virtually unenforceable. Another option for the House is to ask Department of Justice attorneys to prosecute the attorney general under criminal contempt statutes. It is unlikely that Justice lawyers would prosecute their boss. Moreover, this approach raises separation-of-powers issues, especially when the president asserts executive privilege and directs an executive official not to release documents to Congress. A third, and perhaps the most likely, approach is authorization provided in H. Res. 706 for the Committee on Oversight and Government Reform to hire counsel and "go into court to seek a declaratory judgment by the Federal court to enforce the subpoenas that have been presented by this committee to the Attorney General."[37] To be sure, the House has other options to pressure the attorney general to turn over the pertinent documents, such as cutting funds for the Justice Department, impeaching the attorney general, or passing a resolution censuring Attorney General Holder.[38]

The success or failure of investigating panels hinges on the skill of their committee leaders, the degree of bipartisan cooperation among members, and good preparatory work by competent staff. Surprise and luck are also factors. As Senator Daniel K. Inouye, D-Hawaii, the only veteran of both the Watergate and Iran-contra investigating committees, noted:

> I happened to be [at a hearing on Watergate] . . . and the question was asked by one of the Republican staffers [Fred Thompson, minority counsel and later a GOP senator from Tennessee] to one of the lesser witnesses [former Nixon White House aide Alexander P. Butterfield]. Thompson asked, "Mr. Butterfield, are you aware of any listening devices in the Oval Office of the President?" Butterfield responded, "I was aware of listening devices, yes sir."[39]

The rest, said Senator Inouye, was history.

Although excessive use of hearings and investigations can bog down governmental processes, judicious use of such tools helps maintain a more responsive bureaucracy while supplying Congress with information needed to formulate new legislation and to inform the public.[40] Committee members and committee staffs may conduct oversight hearings around the country (field hearings) to observe firsthand public programs in operation and to take testimony from citizens and local officials.

Legislative Veto

In 1932 Congress began to include provisions in statutes that, while delegating authority to the executive branch, reserved to Congress the right to approve or disapprove executive actions based on that authority within a specified time period. This procedure, known as the legislative veto and mentioned earlier with respect to the CRA, allows one or both chambers, by majority vote, to veto certain executive branch initiatives, decisions, and regulations. In a similar maneuver, Congress sometimes authorizes committees—the committee veto—to approve, or disapprove, executive actions (see Box 9.1).

The legislative veto was an attractive oversight technique because, even though Congress seldom exercised its veto prerogative to overturn agency decisions, committees and members felt that the practice kept federal administrators sensitive and responsive to congressional interests. It was employed in legislation dealing with both domestic and international issues. The legislative veto also served executive branch purposes by permitting agencies to make binding decisions without going through the lengthy lawmaking process.

On June 23, 1983, however, the Supreme Court declared in a historic decision, *Immigration and Naturalization Service v. Chadha,* that the legislative veto was unconstitutional. In a 7-to-2 vote, the Court majority said the device violated the separation of powers, the principle of bicameralism, and the presentation clause of the Constitution (legislation passed by both chambers must be presented to the president for a signature or veto). The decision, wrote Justice Byron R. White in a dissent, "strikes down in one fell swoop provisions in more laws enacted by Congress than the court has cumulatively invalidated in its entire history."

BOX 9.1   A Committee Veto

For the appropriation account "Transportation Administrative Service Center," no assessments may be levied against any program, budget activity, subactivity or project funded by this statute "unless notice of such assessments and the basis therefore are presented to the House and Senate Committees on Appropriations and are approved by such Committees." Department of Transportation and Related Agencies Appropriations Act 2001, 114 Stat. 1356A-2 (2000).

SOURCE: Cited in *Congressional Oversight Manual,* Congressional Research Service, January 3, 2007, 95.

Despite the *Chadha* ruling, Congress still employs legislative and committee vetoes. As scholar Louis Fisher pointed out:

In response to the Court's ruling, Congress repealed some legislative vetoes and replaced them with joint resolutions, which satisfy the [Supreme Court's] ruling because joint resolutions must pass both Houses and be presented to the President. However, Congress has also continued to enact legislative vetoes to handle certain situations. From June 23, 1983 to the end of the [110th Congress, hundreds of legislative vetoes of generally the committee-veto variety] have been enacted into law.[41]

Indeed, Congress and the executive branch have adapted to the post-*Chadha* era largely through informal accommodations and statutory adjustments. On one hand, executive agencies want discretion and flexibility in running their programs; on the other hand, Congress is generally unwilling to grant open-ended authority to executive entities. The legislative and committee vetoes remain important review devices because both branches recognize their value.

Authorizing Process as Oversight

Not only does Congress have the authority to create or abolish executive agencies and transfer functions between or among them, it also can enact "statutes authorizing the activities of the departments, prescribing their internal organization and regulating their procedures and work methods."[42] The authorization process is an important oversight tool. As a House member observed during debate on a bill to require annual congressional authorization of the Federal Communications Commission (FCC):

Our subcommittee hearings disclosed that the FCC needs direction, needs guidance, needs legislation, and needs leadership from us in helping to establish program priorities. Regular oversight through the reauthorization process, as all of us know in Congress, is necessary, and nothing brings everybody's attention to spending more forthrightly than when we go through the reauthorization process.[43]

Significant issues are often raised during the authorization process, especially in this spending austerity era, given rising deficits and debt. Lawmakers may ask such questions as: Can an agency be made smaller? If a program or agency did not exist, would it be created today? Should functions that overlap several agencies be merged or consolidated? What fundamental changes need to be made in how various agencies operate? If federal functions are to be eliminated or outsourced to the states, what functions and whose federal jobs should be cut? Are government agencies issuing unnecessary and burdensome rules and regulations? GOP-controlled House authorizing committees during the 112th Congress were especially aggressive in striving to curb or roll back federal regulations issued by the Obama Administration, taking up bills with names such as The Regulatory Freeze for Jobs Act (H.R. 4078), The Red Tape Reduction and Small Business Job Creation Act (H.R. 4078), and The SEC Regulatory Accountability Act (H.R. 2308).

The authorizing process, however, is often not exercised consistently as an oversight tool. Many programs and agencies fail to be reauthorized for years, yet they still continue to operate because appropriators provide funding for them. For example, Congress did not reauthorize the Department of Justice from 1980 until 2002. Similarly, the Department of State has not been subject to an authorization law since 2002. The lack of an authorization law for that department, noted the chair of the House Foreign Affairs Committee, "has eroded Congress's foreign policy leverage with the Department of State."[44] While lawmakers give many reasons for failing to reauthorize federal programs or entities (conflict between the chambers and branches or too little time, for example), the consequence is "increasingly poor congressional oversight over federal programs."[45] In the judgment of Senator John McCain, R-Ariz., "In the years that I have been here, I have seen a tremendous shift in the authority and responsibility from the authorizing committees to the appropriating committees."[46]

Appropriations Process as Oversight

Congress probably exercises its most effective oversight of agencies and programs through the appropriations process. By cutting off or reducing funds, Congress can abolish agencies or curtail programs. For example, dozens of federal programs were targeted for funding reductions or termination by Republicans in the 112th House.[47] Conversely, by increasing funds, Congress can build up neglected program areas or provide more resources for priority initiatives. In either case, Congress has formidable power to shape ongoing public policies. The power is exercised mainly by the House and Senate Appropriations Committees, particularly through their powerful subcommittees, whose broad budgetary recommendations are usually not changed significantly by the full committee or by the House and Senate. The House Appropriations Committee also has a separate survey and investigations (S&I) staff (made up mostly of former FBI, CIA, GAO, and other professionals) that often reviews spending by the defense and intelligence community.[48] Their reports are not made public. (Somewhat akin to the S&I unit is the Senate's Permanent Subcommittee on Investigations, whose small staff conducts a wide variety of confidential investigations—such as those into the financial crisis, money laundering, government waste—before the panel goes public with hearings and reports.)[49]

The Appropriations Committees define the precise purpose for which money may be spent, adjust funding levels, and often attach provisos prohibiting expenditures for certain purposes. The appropriations process as an oversight technique, notes congressional budget expert Allen Schick, is comparable to a Janus-like weapon: "The stick of spending reductions in case agencies cannot satisfactorily defend their budget requests and past performance, and the carrot of more money if agencies produce convincing success stories or the promise of future results."[50] The appropriations process is a potent tool for requiring federal officials to justify the continued existence of their programs and agencies and to comply with the appropriators' directives.

For example, the House Appropriations Subcommittee on Homeland Security stated in its report on the Department of Homeland Security appropriations bill that the "Coast Guard is directed to submit quarterly reports to the [Appropriations] Committee on its actions with respect to this plan [to properly maintain its vessels and aircraft]." Lack of compliance with this directive produced a different outcome the next year. The panel stated that it was

> extremely frustrated in the Coast Guard's apparent disregard for Congressional direction and has reduced funding for headquarters directorates by $5 million. . . . The Committee cannot adequately oversee Coast Guard programs when the agency fails to answer basic questions or fails to provide timely and complete information[51]

When the National Weather Service misdirected the expenditure of appropriated funds without notification to the House and Senate Appropriations Committees, the Weather Service's director resigned and the relevant appropriations subcommittees conducted weeks of investigation. The Senate chair and ranking member of the Commerce-Justice-Science Appropriations Subcommittee stressed that they will closely oversee the Weather Service's budget so that "a full accounting of these [unauthorized budget moves] are brought to light, and to restore Congress's confidence in the [Commerce] Department's budget process."[52] (The Weather Service is a unit of the Department of Commerce.)

Members also add amendments to appropriations measures, as noted earlier—or the bills may include spending limitations when reported from committee—that restrict or prohibit agencies from carrying out certain functions. For example, Senator Tom Harkin, D-Iowa, offered an amendment, approved by the Senate, that stated that none of the funds provided to the Department of Labor by an appropriations bill "shall be used to promulgate or implement any regulation" redefining worker eligibility for overtime pay.[53] "These amendments," wrote two senators, "are an important way for Congress to save taxpayers from wasted agency spending, and they enjoy a long-standing precedent because of their use by Republican and Democratic Congresses alike to rein in the excesses of Republican and Democratic administrations."[54]

Inspectors General

Congress has created statutory offices of inspectors general in more than 70 major federal agencies and departments. The inspectors general are located in every cabinet department and major agency, including the Central Intelligence Agency (CIA). Granted wide latitude and independence by the

Inspectors General Act of 1978, as amended in 1988 and again in 2008, these officials conduct investigations and audits of their agencies to improve efficiency, end waste and fraud, and discourage mismanagement. Inspectors general "are the government's first line of defense against fraud," noted Senator Charles Grassley, R-Iowa.[55]

Collectively, the inspector general offices employ about 12,000 auditors, investigators, and other personnel. Congress has also created special inspectors general to eliminate waste and fraud for reconstruction in Afghanistan and Iraq. For example, the special inspector general for Afghanistan stated that his mission is to "assess the progress of Afghan security forces during the drawdown" of U.S. troops, monitoring the Afghan government's ability "to take over basic programs that the United States is spending money to build," and to root out and expose corruption.[56] An inspector general report about that nation determined that a

> U.S. initiative to spend hundreds of millions of dollars on construction projects in Afghanistan, originally pitched as a vital tool in the military campaign against the Taliban, is running so far behind schedule that it will not yield benefits until most U.S. combat forces have departed the country.[57]

When many sectors of the banking, financial, and housing industry collapsed in 2008, Congress created a special inspector general to oversee the more than $700 billion bailout of the financial system. To monitor the $787 billion economic stimulus package (the American Recovery and Reinvestment Act), 23 inspectors general from different agencies worked on "accountability, doing the oversight, the audits, and any necessary investigations," explained Earl Devaney, who was in overall charge of coordinating and tracking how the stimulus money was being spent, uncovering fraud trends, and identifying the "best practices for detecting fraud."[58] One of those fraud-fighting techniques used by inspector general auditors is forensics. "Forensic auditing combines advanced computer investigative work—such as data mining and analysis, combining the content of computer hard drives, and conducting in-depth Web searches—with traditional auditing and accounting techniques to investigate fraud."[59]

The inspectors general strive to keep Congress fully and currently informed about federal activities, problems, and program performance through the issuance of semiannual and other reports. To be sure, they frequently testify before House and Senate committees. The inspector general of the Department of Health and Human Services said about the job, "I believe that a successful IG [inspector general] must . . . be willing to go beyond just the traditional after-the-fact investigations and audits. Instead, the IG should . . . not just detect, but also prevent fraud and abuse."[60] That department's inspector general also informed Congress that his office had recovered about $1.2 billion in unnecessary health expenditures during the first 6 months of fiscal year 2012.[61] There are occasions, too, when inspectors general feel the "wrath of government bosses or their supporters in

Congress after investigations cited agencies for poor performance, excessive spending, or wasted money."[62]

Lawmakers like the idea of having an independent office of inspector general located within an agency performing a watchdog role for Congress. For example, Senator Charles Grassley, R-Iowa, periodically takes the floor to discuss inspector general audits of the Department of Defense, examining their cost and effectiveness.[63] (The Pentagon has been unable for years to audit its books completely to determine where all the money it receives is obligated and spent.[64]) Recent available figures show that inspector general investigations and audits saved the government $43.8 billion during 2009–2010; produced 6,200 indictments and criminal charges; prosecuted successfully 5,900 criminal cases; and suspended or debarred 4,500 employees for misconduct.[65] The House, in the wake of internal bank and post office scandals, created its own Office of Inspector General in 1992; the position was filled the next year. One function of the House inspector general is to conduct audits of the chamber's financial activities. (The House periodically may contract with a major accounting firm to conduct a comprehensive auditing review of its spending practices.)

Nonstatutory and Informal Controls

Congress also is able to influence federal administrators using various informal means. Executive officials, conscious of Congress's power over the purse strings, are attuned to the nuances of congressional language in hearings, floor debate, committee reports, and conference reports. For example, in committee reports, the verbs *shall, expect, urge, recommend, desire,* and *feel* display in roughly descending order how obligatory a committee comment or viewpoint is intended to be.[66] If federal administrators believe congressional directives to be unwise, they are more likely to ask for informal consultation with members and committee staff than to seek new laws. In fact, executive officials are routinely in frequent contact with committee members and staff. Analyzing the House Appropriations Committee's relationship with the federal bureaucracy, one scholar wrote:

> [There] is a continuing and sometimes almost daily pattern of contacts between the Committee on Appropriations and the executive branch. When Congress is not in session, communication continues by telephone or even, on occasion, by visits to the homes of members of the committee. If the full story were ever known, the record probably would disclose a complex network of relationships between members of the Committee on Appropriations and its staff and officials, particularly budget officers, in the executive branch.[67]

Such informal contacts enable committees to exercise policy influence in areas in which statutory methods might be inappropriate or ineffective. Noteworthy is that top staff of the House and Senate Intelligence Committees travel monthly to CIA headquarters to closely monitor drone attacks against militants in places such as Pakistan and Yemen. As Senator

Diane Feinstein, D-Calif., the chair of the Senate intelligence panel, stated, committee staff have held monthly "in-depth oversight meetings to review strike records and question every aspect of the program including legality, effectiveness, precision, foreign policy implications, and the care taken to minimize noncombatant casualties."[68] Informal methods of program review are probably the most prevalent techniques of oversight.

Members sometimes urge their colleagues, administrative agencies, and the courts to exercise caution in interpreting committee reports, floor debate, and other nonstatutory matters as expressions of the intent of Congress. Abner J. Mikva, one of the relatively few public officials to have served in all three national branches of government (as a House member, federal judge, and President Bill Clinton's White House counsel), recounted a story about the pitfalls of interpreting a bill's legislative history:

> I remember when [Rep. Morris K.] Mo Udall (D-Ariz., 1961–1991) was managing the strip-mining bill, and there had been all sorts of problems getting it through. They'd put together a very delicate coalition of support. One problem was whether the states or the feds would run the program. One member got up and asked, "Isn't it a fact that under this bill the states will continue to exercise sovereignty over strip mining?" And Mo replied, "You're absolutely right." A little later someone else got up and asked, "Now is it clear that the Federal Government will have the final say on strip mining?" And Mo replied, "You're absolutely right." Later, in the cloakroom, I said, "Mo, they can't both be right." And Mo said, "You're absolutely right."[69]

Interpreting statutory intent is a hot issue at the Supreme Court because legal phraseology is often ambiguous. Justice Antonin Scalia advocates that judges, in clarifying statutory language, reject committee hearings, reports, or floor debate (congressional history), which can be conflicting and have not been voted on. Instead, they should focus on the exact legal language and the statutory text in which it is embedded (the plain-meaning principle). Justice Stephen G. Breyer, by contrast, recommends use of congressional history in statutory interpretation so judges can better understand the goals and objectives of the legislation signed into law.[70] "It is dangerous," says Breyer, "to rely exclusively upon the literal meaning of a statute's words."[71]

Government Accountability Office Audits and Reports

The Government Accountability Office (GAO), created by the Budget and Accounting Act of 1921, is known as Congress's watchdog. One of its primary functions is to conduct financial and management audits. For example, in one study, GAO "reported that 19 of 24 Federal agencies . . . could not fully explain how they had spent taxpayer money appropriated by Congress."[72] GAO also conducts reviews of executive agencies and programs at the request of committees and members of Congress to ensure that public funds are properly spent. GAO reported, for instance, that the "Navy keeps an average of $7.5 billion worth of spare parts and other goods it doesn't need every year because of poor planning and management." Commenting on the report he requested, Senator Bernie Sanders, I-Vt., exclaimed: "The idea we are spending many billions of dollars every year for parts that are not needed or not used by the Navy is absolutely unacceptable."[73]

In addition, GAO conducts field investigations of administrative activities and programs, prescribes accounting standards for the executive branch, prepares policy analyses, and provides legal opinions on government actions and activities. Two examples illustrate this work. At the start of each new Congress, GAO transmits various reports to top party and committee leaders of government operations at "high risk" due to their "greater vulnerabilities to fraud, waste, abuse, and mismanagement or the need for transformation to address economy, efficiency, or effectiveness challenges."[74] Another GAO report stated that after it had identified "81 areas where the government double-spends or could cut costs, President Obama and Congress have solved just four of them."[75] To be sure, the GAO and inspectors general coordinate audits to avoid duplication. A difference between the two organizations, opined an inspector general, is that the "GAO approach is more macro and global, and we're more focused on internal agency operations."[76]

The GAO, which has a staff of about 3,300, submits hundreds of reports to Congress annually on ways to root out waste and fraud in government programs and to promote program performance. GAO studies frequently lead to the introduction of legislation, congressional hearings, or cost-saving administrative changes. The head of the GAO, the comptroller general, is appointed for a single 15-year term by the president, subject to the advice and consent of the Senate. The GAO works only for Congress.

Reporting Requirements

Numerous laws require executive agencies to submit periodic reports to Congress and its committees. As one scholar explained:

> Reporting requirements are provisions in law requiring the executive branch to submit specified information to Congress or committees of Congress. Their basic purpose is to provide data and analysis Congress needs to oversee the implementation of legislation and foreign policy by the executive branch.[77]

Some reports are of minimal value because they are couched in broad language that reveals little about program implementation; others may be more specific. Some reports address large policy issues; others, the narrow interests of a small number of lawmakers. (One way to resolve problems in the legislative process, such as mobilizing support from lawmakers who are uncertain about the worth of a program or activity, is to ask an agency for a report.) Generally, however, the report requirement encourages self-evaluation by the executive branch and promotes agency accountability to Congress. For example, when Congress became exasperated with Pentagon delays in implementing a major reorganization of defense offices, it directed the secretary of the army "to report every 30 days to Congress on what he [was] doing to put the legislation into place."[78] Thus, reports can "drive a reluctant bureaucracy to comply with laws it would otherwise ignore."[79]

Periodically, Congress and the executive branch recommend the elimination of certain reports (currently there are about 5,000 reports submitted to Congress).[80] Sometimes the impulse to eliminate reports reflects legislative and executive concern about micromanagement of executive affairs by legislative committees. The ever-present tension, and even distrust, that suffuses legislative–executive relations explains to a large degree why Congress gets involved in managerial details and demands reports from federal entities. "We wrote an extraordinary amount of detail into the Clean Air Act," said one House member, "because we didn't trust the Environmental Protection Agency . . . with too much discretion."[81] The concern about reporting requirements involves weighing Congress's need for information to conduct evaluations of agencies and programs against the imposition of burdensome, costly, or irrelevant obligations on executive entities. That balance can be hard to achieve. For example, when the Pentagon placed a 10- to 15-page limit on reports to Congress, the House Armed Services chair, Buck McKeon, R-Calif., wrote to Defense Secretary Leon Panetta demanding that he rescind the page-limit policy. "We cannot do our job if the department does not provide adequate information," exclaimed Chairman McKeon.[82] (The Pentagon sends Congress more than 500 reports annually.)

Ad Hoc Groups and Outside Commissions

Numerous formal and informal groups and caucuses of Senate and House members focus on specific issues and programs and monitor executive branch activities. For example, the Congressional Automotive Caucus works with appropriate government agencies to resolve issues associated with the automobile industry. In the minority, Democrats or Republicans lack the ability to hold hearings, conduct investigations, or subpoena witnesses. As a result, the Democratic or GOP Policy Committees may conduct informal hearings or forums on issues that, in their estimation, receive little scrutiny by the opposition-controlled standing committees.[83]

Outside organizations also provide Congress with information on inadequacies in federal programs and other problems with the bureaucracy and exert pressure for more ambitious oversight. For example, private watchdog groups, such as Citizens Against Government Waste and the Project on Government Oversight regularly identify federal projects that, in their judgment, are a waste of taxpayers' dollars. Think tanks such as the Brookings Institution and the Heritage Foundation periodically study public policy issues and advise members of Congress and others on how well federal agencies and programs are working. More broadly, Congress receives much free advice from all kinds of groups on how to cut back the size of government and, alternatively, how to make federal programs and departments work more effectively. Groups also point out which federal activities might be candidates for expansion, elimination, or devolution to the states. Recall that advances in technology have encouraged bloggers and average citizens to get involved in monitoring governmental activities and spending decisions.

A recent trend is congressional creation of a number of quasi-legislative commissions to undertake oversight on its behalf. These entities are statutorily created, limited in duration and scope, and composed of "respected members seen as separated from [partisan] politics."[84] As one congressional journalist wrote, the "impulse to outsource oversight is becoming the new normal on Capitol Hill."[85] The national commission to investigate the September 11, 2001, terrorist attacks on the United States is a model example. The chair and vice chair of the 9/11 Commission—former New Jersey Governor Thomas Kean and former Rep. Lee Hamilton of Indiana, respectively—explained why Congress turns to outside commissions. "Congress cannot deal with the toughest questions facing the nation," they wrote.

> Because of divisiveness in the country, the dizzying twenty-four-hour news cycle, the constant need to raise funds and travel back and forth to a home district, the complexity of some bills, and the pressure on members to be partisan team players, it is harder for Congress to take the time to work through issues and build consensus. So many tough issues now get foisted off on commissions.[86]

To investigate two other "tough issues," Congress formed in 2006 a bipartisan Commission on Wartime Contracting in Iraq and Afghanistan to investigate federal contracting abuses in those countries, such as cost overruns, poor planning, and shoddy workmanship. Three years later, Congress established the Financial Crisis Inquiry Commission to investigate and make recommendations per "the causes, domestic and global, of the current financial and economic crisis."[87]

Senate Confirmation Process

High-ranking public officials are chosen by the president "by and with the Advice and Consent of the Senate," in accord with the Constitution. In general, the Senate gives presidents wide latitude in selecting cabinet members, but it closely scrutinizes judicial and diplomatic appointments as well as nominees to regulatory boards and commissions. Increasingly in recent years, Senate committees are probing the qualifications, independence, and policy predilections of presidential nominees, seeking information on everything from physical health to financial assets. As one commentator noted:

> These days, if you want to run for office [or] accept a position of public trust, everything is relevant. Your moral, medical, legal and financial background, even your college records, become the subject of public scrutiny. In the old days, the scrutiny was done in private, and certain transgressions could be considered irrelevant.[88]

Today, frustration with the confirmation process is running high. "The nomination system is a national disgrace," wrote one scholar of the presidential appointment process.[89] For example, a new development that has aroused concern is not only wider use of filibusters (or their threats) to block nominees but also their use to neuter an agency by not confirming its director. This precedent-breaking action occurred when President Obama named Richard Cordray to head a new Consumer Financial Protection Bureau, a bureaucratic entity strongly opposed by numerous Senate Republicans. Norman Ornstein, a noted analyst and scholar, called such Senate efforts to cripple agencies a new and disturbing trend. "If your view is that an agency shouldn't exist, and so you're going to use your one vote against a nominee, that's fine," said Ornstein. "But using the filibuster to raise the [confirmation] bar to 60 votes, not because they're awful people, but because you're trying to delegitimize an agency, that's very far over the line."[90] "Nonsense," responded GOP Senator Richard Shelby, Ala., who stated that both parties have stalemated confirmations to impede agency operations.[91] To be sure, senators of both parties are not reluctant to threaten to delay certain nominations through the use of "holds" or filibusters. These actions give lawmakers greater leverage to influence administration actions.

Nominees often complain, too, about lengthy delays that can turn the process into an ordeal and the rough treatment some of them receive from senators and outside groups. As one account noted, "Slow-walking nominations is a bipartisan sport."[92] However, as former Senator Robert C. Byrd, D-W.Va., pointed out, if the Senate "rushes through a nomination without adequate investigation, it is accused of 'consent without advice' or 'half rubber, half stamp.'"[93] Many senators, too, are concerned about the Obama Administration's designation of numerous policy "czars" who are not subject to Senate confirmation.[94]

Nomination hearings establish a public record of the policy views of nominees, on which appointed officials can be called to account at a later time. "We all ask questions at confirmation hearings, hoping to obtain answers that affect actions," observed Senator Carl Levin, D-Mich.[95] Committees may also extract pledges from nominees that they will testify at hearings when requested to do so, with the not-so-subtle threat that otherwise the appointee's name will not be sent to the full Senate for consideration. Important to note is that senators regularly consult with and provide advice to presidents during the prenomination phase.[96]

Program Evaluation

Program evaluation is an approach to oversight that uses social science and management methodology, such as surveys, cost-benefit analyses, efficiency studies, and evidence-based models, to assess the effectiveness of ongoing programs. It is a special type of oversight that has been specifically included in many agency appropriations bills since the late 1960s and in the 1974 Congressional Budget and Impoundment Control Act. The studies often are carried out by the GAO, think tanks, and by the executive agencies themselves.[97] President Obama even named the government's first chief performance officer to measure the effectiveness of government programs in meeting their objectives. "All programs—from Medicare to small-business loans—will be judged based on their progress in meeting certain quantifiable goals developed with input from agencies, Congress, management experts and the public."[98] An OMB director for President Obama stressed the importance of statistical and data analysis in empirically evaluating federal programs. "We are making huge investments [in health care and education systems] without doing enough to measure what works and what doesn't," he said.[99] He added: "Rigorous, independent program evaluations can be a key resource in determining whether government programs are achieving their intended outcomes as well as possible and at the lowest possible cost."[100]

Despite the multiplicity of methods to evaluate programs, members of Congress sometimes disagree about how to measure performance. Several factors frequently account for their divergent perspectives. For one thing, they may not agree on the objectives of certain programs. Public laws often are the products of conflicts and compromises, and when those compromises are translated into legislative language, ambiguity about program goals may be the result. Many policies have competing objectives or produce unintended results. In addition, no agreement may have been reached about criteria—quantitative or qualitative—for determining program success or failure. Finally, even if decision makers agree on objectives and criteria, they may interpret the assessments differently. Members and committees who support particular programs are unlikely to view with favor evaluations that recommend repeal or revision of those programs.

Casework

Each senator's and representative's office handles thousands of requests each year from constituents seeking help in dealing with executive agencies. The requests range from inquiries about lost Social Security checks or delayed pension payments to disaster relief assistance and complicated tax appeals to the Internal Revenue Service. "Constituents perceive casework in nonpolitical terms," wrote two scholars. "They expect their representatives to provide [this service]."[101] As a House member wrote:

> Last year, one of my constituents, a 63-year-old man who requires kidney dialysis, discovered that he would no longer be receiving Medicare because the Social Security Administration thought he was dead. Like residents of Southern Indiana who have problems dealing with the federal bureaucracy, this man contacted my district office and asked for help. Without difficulty, he convinced my staff that he was indeed alive, and we in turn convinced the Social Security Administration to resume sending him benefits.[102]

Most congressional offices employ specialists, called caseworkers, to process these types of petitions. Yet, depending on the importance or complexity of a case, the members themselves may contact federal officials, bring up the matter in committee, or discuss the case on the floor. Casework has the positive effect of bringing quirks in the administrative machinery to members' attention. And solutions to an individual constituent's problems can suggest legislative remedies on a broader scale.

Studies by Supporting Agencies

In addition to the GAO, Congress receives support from the Congressional Research Service and the Congressional Budget Office. Each prepares (or contracts for) reports or studies to assist committees and members in reviewing federal agency activities, expenditures, and performance. Their analyses can spark legislation to correct administrative shortcomings.

Resolutions of Inquiry

House members may introduce a privileged simple resolution, called a resolution of inquiry, which requests the president or the head of an executive department to furnish specific factual information and documentation to the House about the administration of a particular federal program. (A resolution of inquiry enjoys its privileged status only if it asks for facts and not opinions from either the president or a cabinet secretary. There is no exact Senate counterpart to these resolutions.) A House member explained some objectives of a resolution of inquiry: "It is a vehicle to provide information to Congress, to foster cooperation between the executive and legislative branches, and to encourage auditing of how taxpayers' dollars are spent."[103] House precedents state that the "effectiveness of such a resolution derives from comity between the branches of government rather than from any element of compulsion."[104] The House has no rule to enforce these resolutions other than to use its regular processes: committee hearings, lawmaking, funding, and the like.

House rules stipulate that if the resolution of inquiry is not reported by a committee within 14 legislative days of its introduction—which includes the 2 calendar days for the filing of minority or additional views by committee members—any lawmaker can offer a privileged motion to discharge the committee of the resolution. However, if a committee reports the resolution—either favorably, unfavorably, or without recommendation—by the 14-day deadline, the motion to discharge loses its privileged status and the House is under no obligation to take up the measure. A committee's failure to report means that any lawmaker could offer a nondebatable privileged motion to discharge the resolution from the panel. That motion could be tabled (or killed), however. A resolution brought to the floor, which rarely occurs, is debatable under the 1-hour rule. As congressional expert Christopher Davis notes, in more than 25 years, "only two resolutions of inquiry have received action on the House floor."[105]

In today's polarized House environment, resolutions of inquiry are a handy procedural tool for the minority party. Not only can these resolutions be framed to embarrass the administration—for example, directing the Treasury secretary to transmit to the House all information about the large bonuses paid to American International Group (AIG) executives using taxpayer-provided bailout dollars, compensation which made the public furious—they can consume committees' valuable time. Typically, committee chairs are certain to report these resolutions to prevent minority members from taking control of the floor agenda by offering the privileged discharge motion. Although history demonstrates that resolutions of inquiry can produce the requested information from the president or head of the executive department, they have evolved in the contemporary House to be a stratagem of the minority party. As Davis's study confirms, "Since the 108th Congress [2003–2005], only 1 in 65 resolutions of inquiry introduced was authored by a congressional majority party member."[106]

Oversight by Individual Members

Some members conduct their own personal reviews of agency activities and develop ways to publicize what they believe to be examples of governmental waste and inefficiency. Senator William Proxmire, D-Wis. (1957–1989), periodically bestowed a "Golden Fleece Award" on agencies that, in his estimation, were wastefully spending tax dollars.[107] Rep. Berkley W. Bedell, D-Iowa (1975–1987), utilized another technique: "One of the practices I have is to make unannounced visits to the executive branch of the Government. I simply select an agency at random, open a door, walk in, and start asking questions of the people who work in that office."[108] Senator Charles Grassley, R-Iowa, has also tried the personal approach. He "marched into the Department of Health and Human Services headquarters . . . asserting his congressional right to receive" the information he requested.[109]

A number of individual lawmakers in the House and Senate, whether in the majority or minority, are noted for their oversight effectiveness and diligence. Among the notables in the House are Republicans Fred Upton, Mich., and John Mica, Fla., and Democrats John Dingell, Mich., the longest serving House member ever, and Henry Waxman, Calif. For example, in the minority, Waxman employed a rarely used law, dubbed the "Seven Members Rule," which states that upon the request of seven members of the House Oversight and Government Reform Committee or five members of the Senate Homeland Security and Governmental Affairs Committee, "an executive agency . . . shall submit any information requested of it relating to any matter within the jurisdiction of the committee."[110]

In the Senate, Republicans Charles Grassley and Tom Coburn, Okla., are well known as formidable overseers of the executive branch. Senator Grassley has long emphasized the importance of oversight to his colleagues. "I have been conducting oversight of the executive branch since I first came to the Senate. I take oversight very seriously," he stated. "It is often an overlooked function for Members of Congress. It is not a glamorous function. It is a lot of hard work." As an "equal opportunity overseer," Senator Grassley investigates wrongdoing whether it is a Democratic or Republican administration.[111]

Senator Coburn targets waste and duplication of programs throughout the federal government, releases reports that highlight unnecessary spending, and places them on his Senate website. For example, Senator Coburn publicized a study titled "Wastebook: A Guide to Some of the Most Wasteful and Low Priority Government Spending of 2011." "Robot dragons, video games, Christmas trees, snow cone machines, and chocolate" are, in his judgment, examples of wasteful spending by the federal government.[112] Senator Coburn also has taken the lead in identifying and eliminating duplicative federal programs. He called on GAO to do a study of program overlap, and it found large duplication throughout the federal government. For example, there are more than 100 transportation programs, 82 teacher quality programs, 56 financial literacy programs, and 47 job-training programs. Senator Coburn believes that billions of dollars could be saved by consolidating many duplicative programs.[113] The chief federal performance office agrees. In a mid-January 2012 memorandum to the heads of executive departments and agencies and independent regulatory agencies, the official urged these administrative leaders to determine what the government "needs to stop doing. Duplicative programs make government less effective, waste taxpayer dollars, and make it harder for the American people to navigate government services."[114]

On occasion, individual members will conduct ad hoc field oversight hearings. These sessions usually permit constituents to testify about their problems with federal agencies. They usually garner favorable publicity for the legislator, too. Field hearings, underscored one account, are "excellent opportunities for constituent services and coverage by the hometown press."[115]

IMPEACHMENT

The ultimate check on the executive and judicial branch is the removal power, and it is vested exclusively in Congress. Article II, Section 4 of the Constitution states: "The President, Vice President, and all Civil Officers of the United States, shall be removed from office on Impeachment for, and Conviction of, Treason, Bribery, or other high Crimes and misdemeanors." The House has the authority to impeach an official by majority vote. (Impeachment, in effect, is the formal lodging of charges against an official.) House trial managers then prosecute the case before the Senate, where a two-thirds vote is required for conviction. In the history of the United States, the House has impeached 19 persons—two presidents, one Supreme Court justice, one senator, one cabinet officer, and 14 federal judges. Of those, the Senate convicted seven judges, who were removed from office.

The House impeached President Andrew Johnson in 1868, after Radical Republicans in the House charged that he had violated the Tenure of Office Act by dismissing the secretary of war. The Senate acquitted Johnson by a single vote. President Richard Nixon resigned in 1974, after the House

Judiciary Committee voted articles of impeachment; he faced probable impeachment and conviction. In December 1998, President Bill Clinton became the first elected president to be impeached by the House (Johnson was not elected; he became president when Abraham Lincoln was assassinated). The charges against Clinton were perjury and obstruction of justice. Two months later, the Senate voted acquittal on both of these articles of impeachment.[116]

OVERSIGHT TRENDS AND INCENTIVES

Legislators and scholars often complain that congressional oversight is irregular and shallow. Several scholars suggest that over time there has been greater legislative interest in the process.[117] As one specialist of congressional oversight explained:

> There are no authoritative, comprehensive statistics on the amount of oversight or even the number of specialized investigations throughout the history of Congress. This absence is, in part, because scholars have disagreed as to what constitutes oversight and, therefore, how it should be measured. Nonetheless, some statistics . . . are available. . . . These data tend to show that Congress has increased its oversight activity over history, particularly over the past three decades.[118]

Oversight attracts interest because a fundamental topic of public debate is the appropriate role of the national government, especially given the nation's large fiscal deficits and debt. As one senator put it: "The two most important questions policymakers must ask themselves are, 'What should government be doing?' and 'At what level of government should it be done?'" People may react negatively to big government in the abstract, but voters, as noted earlier, often support more rather than less government in many areas, especially safety and security in the aftermath of the September 11, 2001, terrorist attacks. Lawmakers, too, typically defend government programs supported by their constituents.

Among other factors that often contribute to heightened interest in oversight are the following:

- Public dissatisfaction with and concern about government waste, fraud, program performance, and escalating deficits ($1.4 trillion in 2012) and debt (in excess of $16 trillion in 2012 and rising);
- Congressional assertiveness and long-standing distrust of the executive branch in the wake of such cumulative events as the Vietnam War, Watergate, the Iran-contra affair, the decade-long war in Afghanistan, and the collapse of many banks and financial institutions that gave rise to the Great Recession;
- Influx of representatives and senators, many Tea Party endorsed, who are skeptical about the national government's ability to resolve many

public problems and want to shrink significantly "big government's" role in the polity;

- Proliferation of federal programs and regulations that touch the lives of practically every citizen, and citizens who, in turn, inform their elected officials about problems they are encountering with federal agencies
- Proliferation of interest groups and trade associations that pressure Congress to examine government actions that affect their special interests;
- Availability of staff resources, new technologies, and procedural tools, which permits the new breed of aggressive legislators to scrutinize federal activities; and
- Aggressive investigative reporting into executive activities by the print and broadcast media, including independent bloggers and "good government" groups, such as the Washington-based Project on Government Oversight.

Divided government (one party in control of the White House, the other in control of Congress, or at least one chamber), which is what the electorate got following the November 2010 and 2012 elections, provides another incentive for oversight. Opposition lawmakers, for example, monitor and supervise agency activities and, at the same time, are on the lookout for ways to bash the administration politically. As a scholar concluded:

> Policy divergence is most likely to occur under divided government, so the majority party in Congress will want to constrain the agencies under the president's control. In addition, members of the majority party may believe that they can benefit from using oversight to emphasize policy differences between their party and the president's party, and if in the case of such hearings and investigations they embarrass a president and his agency, this is not an insignificant [political] side benefit.[119]

By comparison, under unified government, President Obama's administration did not face the deluge of subpoenas during the 111th Congress (2009–2011) that occurred during the 112th Congress when the House was controlled by Republicans. For example, GOP-controlled House committees issued subpoenas to numerous executive officials, investigated scandals of wasteful government spending, criticized the president for delaying the nomination of inspectors general for several major agencies, scrutinized federal loan guarantees to a solar panel manufacturer (Solyndra) that went bankrupt, and held numerous hearings castigating the president's Affordable Care Act and the Wall Street reform law. Worth mentioning is that history demonstrates, as with President Jimmy Carter's administration, that unified government is no bar to tough investigative oversight.

Political incentives, to be sure, motivate members to oversee the bureaucracy. The opportunity to receive favorable publicity back home is a potential electoral bonus for lawmakers. Committee and subcommittee chairs "seek a high pay off—in attention from the press and other agencies—when selecting federal programs to be their oversight targets."[120] Oversight targets are especially plentiful when partisan ideological disagreements between or among the elective branches are strong, as in the case of the Tea Party–infused Republican 112th House and the Democratic administration. Lawmakers understand, too, that some investigations carry political risks if they have the potential to arouse constituency opposition back home.

LACK OF CONSENSUS ON OVERSIGHT

Despite the importance of Congress's oversight functions, many members and commentators still fault congressional efforts in this area. As a senator said:

> Congressional oversight is something that, unfortunately, we probably don't do as much as we should. That is what committee meetings are for. That is what audits are for. When you pass a law and say here is where we want to go, then you have to say: How are we getting there? We don't do that well.[121]

Several factors help account for this general perception, although those who are the targets of oversight—executive-branch officials and many others—no doubt prefer to be left alone. First, no clear consensus has emerged on how to measure oversight, quantitatively or qualitatively. As a result, members' anxiety about Congress's ability to review the massive federal establishment remains high. Quantitatively, no one knows how much oversight Congress is doing. Undercounting characterizes statistical analyses of oversight no matter what definition of that activity is employed. Part of the problem is that legislative review is a ubiquitous activity carried out by many entities: committees, members' offices, legislative support agencies, and committee and personal staff aides. Almost any committee hearing, for example, even ones ostensibly devoted to formulating new legislation, might pay considerable attention to reviewing past policy implementation. Qualitatively, little agreement exists among members on the criteria that can be used to evaluate effective oversight.

Second, some legislators favor oversight objectives that appear impossible to meet. They would like to see Congress conduct comprehensive reviews of the entire executive establishment. But then they find Congress's selective and unsystematic oversight approach generally unsatisfactory even when there is more of it. As some see it, oversight is too often a guerrilla foray rather than the continual watchfulness contemplated by the 1946 Legislative Reorganization Act. "It requires a blunder of major proportions, a calamity that is poorly addressed, before you get oversight," remarked a political scientist.[122] In general, Congress conducts dual types of oversight: "fire alarm" and "police patrol." The former occurs when outside events or public interest triggers agency reviews; it is episodic and reactive in character. The latter is proactive and involves deliberate House and

Senate committee decisions to oversee on a regular basis federal activities under their jurisdiction.[123]

Third, committees and individual members sometimes wonder if they have much impact or influence on the bureaucracy. Exclaimed Rep. Jim Wright, D-Tex. (1955–1989), who served as Speaker from 1987 to 1989:

> Fighting the red tape and the overregulation of bureaucratic rulemaking and guideline writing are among the most frustrating things any of us have had to do in Congress—it is almost like trying to fight a pillow. You can hit it—knock it over in the corner—and it just lies there and regroups. You feel sometimes as though you are trying to wrestle an octopus. No sooner do you get a hammerlock on one of his tentacles than the other seven are strangling you.[124]

Fourth, oversight may produce more questions than answers. Congress finds it easier "to highlight what's going wrong and to blame it on someone," declared a senator, "than to try to determine what to do about it."[125] And even with more oversight, agency problems can remain uncorrected absent sustained and determined follow-through by the relevant congressional committees.

Fifth, Congress seeks to shape executive actions to its own objectives, not simply to conduct or commission neutral evaluation studies of departmental activities. Oversight is part of the legislative–executive tug-of-war that characterizes the U.S. separation-of-powers system. According to a noted analyst:

> The key issue for Congress is not administrative performance but its ability to influence agency actions. Congress is interested in performance, but it expresses this interest by seeking dominion over agencies. The distribution of political power between the legislative and executive branches, not simply [or even mainly] the quality of programs, is at stake.[126]

Congress is sometimes frustrated by its inability to control and coordinate a fragmented and sophisticated bureaucracy. For example, occasionally Congress confronts the issue of whom to hold accountable for program performance when a contractor workforce is carrying out the bulk of a department's activities under the supervision of federal employees. More broadly, thousands of nonfederal employees—defense contractors, state and local officials, or university administrators—are increasingly carrying out activities once performed by civil servants. As a result, it is harder for Congress to hold accountable those who administer policies or deliver services.

Another development that has the potential to weaken congressional oversight is lockbox government. Federal officials are looking for ways to avoid the constraints of the congressional appropriations process by encouraging the passage of laws that give them a guaranteed funding stream for a specific activity. For example, federal oil and gas royalties flow into the Land and Conservation Fund to be spent on congressionally designated environmental programs. A consequence of removing agencies and programs from the regular appropriations process is that it robs "legislators of an opportunity to hold agency officials accountable for policy decisions. If functions are spun off to private organizations, oversight could be weakened further."[127]

Despite Congress's general interest in oversight, other considerations limit its effective performance. For one thing, legislators still have too little time to devote to their myriad tasks, including oversight. Huge investments of time, energy, and staff assistance are required to ferret out administrative inadequacies. The term *lawmaker* suggests where most House and Senate members prefer to spend much of their time. As former Speaker Newt Gingrich, R-Ga., pointed out:

> This is the city [Washington, D.C.] which spends almost all of its energy trying to make the right decisions and almost none of its energy focusing on how to improve implementing the right decisions. And without implementation, the best ideas in the world simply don't occur.[128]

Some members are reluctant to support massive investigations that may reveal only that a program is working fairly well—a determination that does not attract much constituent attention or media coverage. "Effective oversight is, of necessity, time-consuming and tedious," said a senator.

> To do it right, you have to hear an endless stream of witnesses, review numerous records, and at the end of it you may find an agency was doing everything right. It is much more fun to create a new program.[129]

(Creating new federal initiatives, however, can be difficult during periods of escalating deficits and debt, and when "pay-fors" have to be found for program creation.)

Many members, however, accept that much of their effort in this area is unglamorous. Moreover, the review process is sometimes inhibited by the alliances that develop among committees, agencies, and clientele groups. Examples of these subgovernments or "iron triangles," as the alliances are called, are the axis of the House and Senate Veterans Affairs Committees, the Department of Veterans Affairs, and the veterans groups, and the combination of the congressional Agriculture Committees, the Department of Agriculture, and the various farm groups. Each component of such an alliance is usually supportive of the other. In such cases, committees find it harder to review agency programs critically absent countervailing views and forces.

Some policy areas are also harder for Congress to oversee. Intelligence and national security issues are prime examples. Congress must conduct most of its intelligence oversight in secret without the monitoring aid of outside interest groups plentiful in other policy domains, and the lawmakers who serve on the intelligence committees are subject to an array of restrictions that inhibit the disclosure of sensitive material even to their colleagues, let alone to the media or others. Intelligence is also a highly complex and technically substantive area. There is defense intelligence, tactical intelligence, strategic intelligence, and so on, that require years of study and analysis. Moreover, members of each chamber's intelligence panels are subject to tenure limits, to reduce the chances that lawmakers will be co-opted by the intelligence community.[130]

In short, Congress will decide how it can best pursue its oversight responsibility. Much will depend on the political climate of the times, the willingness of lawmakers to watch and analyze executive-branch activities, the partisan composition and policy priorities of the legislative branch, and Congress's relationship with the executive branch. This relationship may range from cooperative to confrontational, but fundamental to Congress's job is that it ensures executive policies work effectively and reflect the values of the American people, anticipate long-range trends, and meet the continuing challenges of a changed world.

NOTES

1. *Congressional Record,* June 21, 1983, S8822.
2. Geoff Earle, "Dems Did Oversight Better, Says Grassley," *The Hill,* May 13, 2004, 2.
3. Woodrow Wilson, *Congressional Government* (Boston: Houghton Mifflin, 1885), 303.
4. Arthur M. Schlesinger Jr. and Roger Burns, eds., *Congress Investigates: A Documented History, 1792–1974,* vol. 1 (New York: Chelsea House, 1975), xix.
5. Jennifer Kabbany, "Armey Targets Waste in Federal Agencies," *Washington Times,* February 12, 1999, A6.
6. For a detailed analysis of the GPRA Modernization Act, see Clinton T. Brass, *Changes to the Government Performance and Results Act (GPRA): Overview of the New Framework of Products and Processes* (CRS Report R42379), February 29, 2012. The quoted material is from page 1 of this report.
7. Cheryl Bolen, "Commission to Oversee Spending Passes Overwhelmingly in House," *Daily Report for Executives,* April 26, 2012, A-13.
8. James E. McCarthy and Larry Parker, *EPA Regulation of Greenhouse Gases: Congressional Responses and Options* (CRS Report R41212), June 8, 2010, 9.
9. Ibid. The CRA also provides that "once the motion to proceed is adopted, the [disapproval] resolution becomes 'the unfinished business of the Senate until disposed of,' and a non-debatable motion may be offered to limit the time for debate further" (p. 10).
10. Jonathan Adler, "Would the REINS Act Rein in Federal Regulation?" *Regulation* (Summer 2011): 24. REINS is an acronym for "Regulations of the Executive in Need of Scrutiny." There were important political changes that produced successful repeal of the ergonomics rule. The rule was developed by the Clinton Administration. With the 2000 election of George W. Bush as president, and both chambers controlled by Republicans, the 2001 disapproval resolution for the Clinton-era ergonomics rule was not vetoed by President Bush after it passed the Congress.
11. Morton Rosenberg, "Whatever Happened to Congressional Review of Agency Rulemaking? A Brief Overview, Assessment, and Proposal for Reform," *Administrative Law Review* (Fall 1999): 1060.

12. Curtis W. Copeland, *The Federal Rulemaking Process: An Overview* (CRS Report RL32240), August 28, 2008, 15.
13. Gregory Korte, "'Legislative Veto' Little-Used Tool," *USA Today*, September 19, 2011, 7A.
14. Bill Myers, "'Google Your Government' Database Bill Signed Into Law," *Washington Examiner*, September 29, 2006, 17.
15. Mark Stencel, "Information Underload," *CQ Weekly*, February 16, 2009, 342.
16. Paul Barbagallo, "Obama Requires Federal Agencies to Offer Services on Mobile Devices," *Daily Report for Executives*, May 24, 2012, A-1.
17. Andrew Khouri, "White House Ups the Ante for Petition Website: 100,000 Signatures," *Los Angeles Times*, January 16, 2013, online edition.
18. Kevin Bogardus, "'We the People' Petition Site Now the Newest Tool in K Street Repertoire," *The Hill*, April 20, 2012, 10. See also Joseph Marks, "The Truth Behind Transparency," *Government Executive*, June 2012, 21–29.
19. Sean Lengell, "GOP Revives 'You Cut' Program," *Washington Times*, May 12, 2011, A3.
20. David B. Truman, *The Governmental Process* (New York: Knopf, 1953), 439. The continuous watchfulness provision was retitled legislative "review" in the Legislative Reorganization Act of 1970.
21. *Congressional Record*, February 1, 1977, S2897.
22. Michael J. Malbin, *Unelected Representatives* (New York: Basic Books, 1979). See Chapter 6 for an analysis of a House oversight subcommittee in action.
23. *Congressional Record*, January 4, 1995, H35.
24. Ibid., January 4, 2005, H13.
25. Ibid., January 14, 2009, H268.
26. *Workshop on Congressional Oversight and Investigations*, 96th Congress, 1st sess., 1979, H. Doc. 96-217, 198.
27. Quoted in Tom Shoop, "Defensive Activism," *Government Executive*, October 2009, 6.
28. Quoted in Daniel Schorr, "The Government's Current War With the Free Press," *Christian Science Monitor*, July 7, 2006, 9.
29. Alison Young, "Senate Digs Into 'Ghost Factory' Risk," *USA Today*, July 13, 2012, 3A.
30. Ibid., "Senators Seek Lead Tests at Old Sites," *USA Today*, May 10, 2012, 1A.
31. Susan Ferrechio, "Lawmakers Blast GSA for Its Bonuses, Junkets," *Examiner*, August 2, 2012, 11.
32. Andy Medici, "New GSA Scandal Prompts IG Probe," *Federal Times*, July 23, 2012, 1. The $44 million cited is from the Ferrechio article in Footnote 30. See also Jim McElhatton, "GSA Scandal Grows as Dozens of Events Face Probe for Waste," *Washington Times*, August 2, 2012, A1.
33. Todd B. Tatleman, "Congress's Contempt Power: Three Mechanisms for Enforcing Subpoenas," *Government Information Quarterly* 25 (2008): 592–624. See also Morton Rosenberg, *When Congress Comes Calling, a Primer on the Principles, Practices, and Pragmatics of Legislative Inquiry* (Washington, DC: Constitution Project, 2009).
34. Charlie Savage, "Republicans and White House Escalate Fight on Gun Inquiry," *New York Times*, June 21, 2012, A3. See also Louis Fisher, "An Overbroad Executive Privilege Claim," *National Law Journal* 34 (July 30, 2012): 34.
35. Jonathan Strong, "In Historic Vote, AG Holder Held in Contempt," *Roll Call*, June 29, 2012, 1.

36. Sari Horwitz, "Holder Says He's a Proxy for Obama," *Washington Post*, July 3, 2012, A2. See also Richard Serrano, "GOP Investigators Fault Five ATF Officials in Gun-Tracking Fiasco," *Los Angeles Times*, July 30, 2012, online edition.

37. *Congressional Record*, June 28, 2012, H4418.

38. See Josh Chafetz, "Should Boehner Arrest Holder?" *Washington Post*, June 22, 2012, A15.

39. *Washington Post*, March 17, 1994, A15.

40. Congressional requests for executive agency information may be blocked by executive privilege. See Raoul Berger, *Executive Privilege: A Constitutional Myth* (Cambridge, Mass.: Harvard University Press, 1974); Bernard Schwartz, "Executive Privilege and Congressional Investigatory Power," *California Law Review* (March 1959): 350; "Symposium: United States v. Nixon," *UCLA Law Review* (October 1974): 140; and *U.S. v. Nixon*, 418 U.S. 683 (1974).

41. Information supplied by Louis Fisher, noted specialist on the separation of powers, Law Library, Library of Congress. See Louis Fisher, "The Legislative Veto Invalidation: It Survives," *Law and Contemporary Problems* (Autumn 1993): 273–292.

42. Joseph P. Harris, *Congressional Control of Administration* (Washington, DC: Brookings, 1964), 284.

43. Quoted in Louis Fisher, "Annual Authorizations: Durable Roadblocks to Biennial Budgeting," *Public Budgeting and Finance* (Spring 1983): 38.

44. *Congressional Record*, July 17, 2012, H4883.

45. David Baumann, "Government on Autopilot," *National Journal*, March 13, 1999, 689.

46. *Congressional Record*, September 29, 2009, S9903. Senator McCain made this comment in the context of a statement about the corrupting effects of earmarks in appropriations bills.

47. Sean Reilly, "Dozens of Federal Programs to Be Eliminated," *Federal Times*, January 23, 2012, 5.

48. In October 2006, Appropriations Chair Jerry Lewis, R-Calif., dismissed most of the S&I staff. See Steven T. Dennis, "House Appropriations Dismisses 60 Investigators," *CQ Today*, October 19, 2006, online version. In 2007, David Obey, Wis., then Democratic chair of the Appropriations Committee, reconstituted the S&I team. GOP Chair Hal Rogers, Ky., considers the recommendations of the S&I staff when making funding decisions. See John Stanton, "'Doing More With Less' on Oversight," *Roll Call*, October 27, 2011, 1.

49. See John Aloysius Farrell, "The Raptor," *National Journal*, February 11, 2012, 24–28.

50. *Workshop on Congressional Oversight and Investigations*, 199.

51. "Department of Homeland Security Appropriations Bill, 2005," *House Report 108–541*, June 15, 2004, 60, and "Department of Homeland Security Appropriations Bill, 2006," *House Report 10-979*, May 13, 2005, 58.

52. *CQ's Budget Tracker*, June 20, 2012, 4. See also Robert Barnes, "Weather Service Director Retires," *Washington Post*, May 29, 2012; Lisa Rein and Jason Samenow, "Weather Service Rebuffed on Funds," *Washington Post*, May 30, 2012, A13; and Kerry Young and Niels Lesnewski, "After Weather Service's Unauthorized Moves, Senators Object to NOAA Request," *CQ Today*, May 30, 2012, 6.

53. *Congressional Record*, September 5, 2003, S11136; Helen Dewar, "Senate Blocks Overtime Revamp," *Washington Post*, September 11, 2003, A1.
54. Slade Gorton and Larry Craig, "Congress's Call to Accounting," *Washington Post*, July 27, 1998, A23.
55. Senator Chuck Grassley, "The Federal Government Needs an IG in Chief," *Politico,* July 22, 2009, 30.
56. Kevin Baron, "New Afghanistan IG Promises More Investigations," *National Journal Daily*, July 18, 2012, 14.
57. Rajiv Chandrasekaran, "Report Questions Afghan Strategy," *Washington Post*, July 30, 2012, A1.
58. Edward Pound, "Q&A with Earl Devaney," *National Journal,* March 14, 2009.
59. Elise Castelli, "A New Tactic in the Fight on Fraud," *Federal Times,* January 12, 2009, 1.
60. *The Inspectors General Act: 20 Years Later*, hearings before the Senate Committee on Governmental Affairs, 105th Congress, 2d sess., September 9, 1998, S. Hrg. 105737, 4. See also K. Daniel Glover, "In the Belly of the Beast," *National Journal*, November 1, 2003, 3350–3352.
61. Janet Swann, "OIG Announces an Expected $1.2 Billion in Recoveries for First Half of FY 2012," *Daily Report for Executives*, May 30, 2012, A-1.
62. Larry Margasak, "Gov't Watchdogs Under Attack From Bosses," *Los Angeles Times*, December 27, 2006, online edition.
63. *Congressional Record*, March 14, 2012, S1672–S1673.
64. Megan Scully, "Senators Seek Advance on Pentagon Audit," *CQ Today*, November 28, 2011, 1, and Scully, "The Pentagon Premium," *National Journal*, July 16, 2011, 16–22.
65. Charles Clark, "Into the Limelight," *Government Executive*, March 2011, 24.
66. Michael Kirst, *Government Without Passing Laws* (Chapel Hill: University of North Carolina Press, 1969), 37. See also William Rhode, *Committee Clearance of Administrative Decisions* (East Lansing: Michigan State University Press, 1959).
67. Holbert N. Carroll, *The House of Representatives and Foreign Affairs*, rev. ed. (Boston: Little, Brown, 1966), 172. A good example of nonstatutory controls involves the reprogramming of funds within executive accounts. Reprogramming refers to the expenditure of funds for purposes not originally intended when Congress approved the department's budget. Agencies secure approval for reprogramming from the appropriate House and Senate committees.
68. Ken Dilanian, "Congress Zooms in on Drone Killings," *Los Angeles Times*, June 25, 2012, online edition.
69. *New York Times*, May 12, 1983, B8. See also *New York Times*, October 22, 1982, A16.
70. See, for example, Robert A. Katzmann, "Justice Breyer: A Rival for Scalia on the Hill's Intent," *Roll Call*, May 30, 1994, 5, 15. See also Cornell Clayton, "Separate Branches Separate Politics: Judicial Enforcement of Congressional Intent," *Political Science Quarterly* (Winter 1994–1995): 843–872; *Interbranch Relations, Hearings Before the Joint Committee on the Organization of Congress*, 103d Congress, 1st sess., June 29, 1993.
71. Jonathan Kaplan, "High Court to Congress: Say What You Mean," *The Hill*, February 5, 2003, 21.
72. *Congressional Record*, June 27, 2006, H4675.

73. Matt Kelley, "GAO Details Billions in Navy Excess," *USA Today*, December 17, 2008, 7A.
74. Government Accountability Office, Report to Congressional Committees, *High-Risk Series: An Update* (GAO-11-278), February 2011.
75. Stephen Dinan, "GAO: Follow-Up Weak on Cost-Cutting Report," *Washington Times*, February 29, 2012, A1.
76. Clark, "Into the Limelight," 22.
77. Ellen C. Collier, "Foreign Policy by Reporting Requirement," *Washington Quarterly* (Winter 1988): 75.
78. *New York Times*, December 31, 1987, A20.
79. Guy Gugliotta, "Reporting on a Practice That's Ripe for Reform," *Washington Post*, February 11, 1997, A19.
80. See *Reports to Be Made to Congress,* House Document 111-4, 111th Congress, 1st sess., January 6, 2009.
81. Phillip Davis, "After Losing Pollution Battle, White House Seizes Victory," *Congressional Quarterly Weekly Report*, May 23, 1992, 1440. See also Pamela Fessler, "Complaints Are Stacking Up as Hill Piles on Reports," *Congressional Quarterly Weekly Report*, September 7, 1991, 2562–2566.
82. Austin Wright, "DOD Skimps on Reports to Congress, McKeon Charges," *Politico*, July 12, 2012, 16. See also Al Kamen, "In War on Paper, Pentagon's Pique Speaks Volumes," *Washington Post*, July 12, 2012, A15. Some units of the Pentagon established a 10-page limit on reports to Congress.
83. John Stanton, "Democrats Put Money on New Oversight Plan," *Roll Call*, January 25, 2006, 19.
84. Steven R. Ross, Raphael A. Prober, and Gabriel K. Gillett, "The Rise and Permanence of Quasi-Legislative Independent Commissions," *Journal of Law and Politics*, Spring 2012, 418, 457. The three authors are attorneys who specialize in congressional investigations. Ross also served as general counsel of the U.S. House of Representatives from 1983 to 1993.
85. Gail Russell Chaddock, "Congress's New Cops," *Christian Science Monitor,* May 10, 2009, 19.
86. Thomas H. Kean and Lee H. Hamilton, *Without Precedent: The Inside Story of the 9/11 Commission*, 2006, 318.
87. An overview of the work of these two commissions, as well as of the 9/11 panel, is discussed in Ross, Prober, and Gillett, "The Rise and Permanence of Quasi-Legislative Independent Commissions," 436–444.
88. George Archibald, "Panel Ties Funding to Ridge Testimony," *Washington Times*, March 22, 2002, A1.
89. G. Calvin McKenzie, "Hung Out to Dry." *Washington Post*, April 1, 2001, B5.
90. Gregory Korte, "Senate Politics Shut Down Some Agencies," *USA Today*, December 28, 2011, 7A.
91. Ibid. In this article, Donald Ritchie, the official Senate historian, said that research conducted by his office did not find "any precedent for making an agency powerless by not confirming anyone to run it."
92. Ruth Marcus, "Advise and Stall," *Washington Post,* October 7, 2009, A25. Also see Nelson W. Cunningham, "Holds, Delays on Cabinet Picks Hurting American Businesses," *The Hill,* October 7, 2009, 32.
93. *Congressional Record*, July 29, 1987, S21504.

94. Ralph Lindeman, "Sen. Feingold Signals Interest in Legislation to Curb Use of Policy Czars in White House," *Daily Report for Executives,* October 7, 2009, A-26; Joe Markman, "Panel Finds No Fault With Obama System of Policy 'Czars,'" *Los Angeles Times,* October 7, 2009, online edition; and Kara Rowland, "Sen. Feingold Criticizes Obama's Use of 'Czars,'" *Washington Times,* October 7, 2009, A10.

95. *New York Times,* April 14, 1983, B10.

96. See, for example, Mitchel A. Sollenberger, *The President Shall Nominate: How Congress Trumps Executive Power* (Lawrence: University of Kansas Press, 2008).

97. See, for example, George C. Edwards III, *Implementing Public Policy* (Washington, DC: CQ Press, 1980); Robert T. Nakamura and Frank Smallwood, *The Politics of Policy Implementation* (New York: St. Martin's Press, 1980); and *Program Evaluation: Improving the Flow of Information to the Congress* (General Accounting Office Report, GAO/PEMD-95-1), January 1995, 84.

98. Elise Castelli, "How Does Your Program Measure Up?" *Federal Times,* May 18, 2009, 1.

99. Carrie Dann, "Orszag: More Must Be Done to Evaluate Federal Programs," *CongressDailyPM,* May 7, 2009, 2.

100. Ralph Lindeman, "OMB Announces Initiative to Improve Evaluations of Programs in Budget Process," *Daily Report for Executives,* October 8, 2009, A-1.

101. John R. Johannes and John C. McAdams, "Entrepreneurs or Agent: Congressmen and the Distribution of Casework, 1977–1978," *Western Political Quarterly* (September 1987): 549.

102. Lee H. Hamilton, "Constituent Service and Representation," *New Bureaucrat* (Summer 1992): 12.

103. *Congressional Record,* July 14, 1988, E2397.

104. Richard S. Beth, *Resolutions of Inquiry in the House of Representatives: A Brief Description* (Congressional Research Service Report 87-365), April 22, 1987, 2.

105. Christopher M. Davis, *Resolutions of Inquiry: An Analysis of Their Use in the House, 1947–2009* (CRS Report, R40879), October 29, 2009, 8.

106. Ibid., 9.

107. See *Christian Science Monitor,* August 5, 1982, 1.

108. *Congressional Record,* June 8, 1983, H3737.

109. Marc Kaufman, "Senator's HHS Trip for Antibiotic Data Yields Only Ire," *Washington Post,* June 15, 2006, A10.

110. Ben Pershing, "Waxman Invokes Arcane Rule in Suit," *Roll Call,* March 25, 2002, 3.

111. *Congressional Record,* November 1, 2011, S6990.

112. Humberto Sanchez, "Coburn Report Targets Robot Dragons, Video Game History," *Roll Call,* December 20, 2011, online edition.

113. *Congressional Record,* November 28, 2011, S7891–S7892. Also see Senator Tom Coburn, "Congress Can Save Billions by Stopping Duplication," *Examiner,* March 5, 2012, 25.

114. Jeffrey D. Zients, "Memorandum for Heads of Executive Departments and Agencies, and Independent Regulatory Agencies" (M-12-07), January 13, 2012, 1.

115. Dana Milbank, "Bringing the Mountain, or at Least the Hill," *Washington Post,* April 21, 2009, A2.
116. Peter Baker, *The Breach: Inside the Impeachment and Trial of William Jefferson Clinton* (New York: Scribner, 2000).
117. See, especially, Joel D. Aberbach, *Keeping a Watchful Eye: The Politics of Congressional Oversight* (Washington, DC: Brookings Institution Press, 1990).
118. *History of the United States House of Representatives, 1789–1994,* H. Doc. 103-324 (Washington, DC: Government Printing Office, 1994), 262. Frederick Kaiser, specialist, Congressional Research Service, Library of Congress, wrote this study's chapter on oversight.
119. Charles R. Shipan, "Congress and the Bureaucracy," in *The Legislative Branch,* ed. Paul Quirk and Sarah Binder (New York: Oxford University Press, 2005), 437.
120. Richard Cohen, "King of Oversight," *Government Executive,* September 1988, 17.
121. *Congressional Record,* June 12, 2000, S4945.
122. Robin Toner, "For Republicans, a Swelling Tide of Trouble," *New York Times,* September 29, 2005, A21.
123. Matthew D. McCubbins and Thomas Schwartz, "Congressional Oversight Overlooked: Police Patrols Versus Fire Alarms," *American Journal of Political Science* (February 1984): 165–179.
124. *Workshop on Congressional Oversight and Investigations,* 5.
125. Ibid., 144.
126. Allen Schick, "Politics Through Law: Congressional Limitations on Executive Discretion," in *Both Ends of the Avenue,* ed. Anthony King (Washington, DC: American Enterprise Institute for Public Policy Research, 1983), 166.
127. Alasdair Roberts, "Lockbox Government," *Government Executive,* May 2000, 28.
128. Tichakorn Hill, "Gingrich: Government's Problem is 'Gotcha' Culture," *Federal Times,* July 18, 2005, 12.
129. *Congress Speaks: A Survey of the 100th Congress* (Washington, DC: Center for Responsive Politics, 1988), 163.
130. See Mark Lowenthal, *Intelligence: From Secrets to Policy,* 2d ed. (Washington, DC: CQ Press, 2003), and Frank Smist, *Congress Oversees the United States Intelligence Community, 1947–1994,* 2d ed. (Knoxville: University of Tennessee Press, 1994).

CHAPTER 10

A Dynamic Process

ANYONE WHO views lawmaking in Congress as a precise, neat process of drafting, debating, and approving legislation overlooks the dynamic forces at work on Capitol Hill. It is not a static institution, in part because of the constant influx of new members who bring fresh views, ideas, and perspectives to the lawmaking process. Thus, "the reality of passing legislation on Capitol Hill," observed Senator Richard Durbin, D-Ill., "deals a lot with people. If you don't understand the people and the power they have, you're not likely to succeed."[1]

For better or worse, the interests, pressures, perceptions, and prejudices of members of Congress change quickly, a result in part of the election cycle but also of other conditions and influences. The demands made by the presidency and the courts, international events, lobbying groups, and media disclosures are some of the ever-present forces that affect lawmaking. Congress is an institution in which procedures reflect and, in turn, perpetuate the messiness, openness, pragmatism, compromise, and deliberateness so characteristic of much of American policymaking. As a House chair said: "Legislation is like a chess game more than anything else. It is a seemingly endless series of moves, until ultimately somebody prevails through exhaustion, or brilliance, or because of overwhelming public sentiment for their side."[2] Senator Orrin Hatch, R-Utah, provided this explanation of why certain ideas become law and others do not.

> Bills become law generally for one of three reasons. First, a member makes the bill a top priority and is willing to expend the time and effort to build sufficient support to guarantee its passage. Second, a large group of constituents in multiple jurisdictions make passing a bill more politically attractive than doing nothing. Third, Congress is forced to respond to an event so tragic or compelling that the event itself overwhelms all possible criticism.[3]

At various stages of the legislative process, a winning coalition must be formed to carry a policy recommendation up the next rung of the legislative ladder; otherwise, its progress is jeopardized. Along the way, that coalition changes as the forces that mold it also change. Meanwhile, while some coalitions are forming to advance legislation, others may be forming to tear it down. There are also occasions in today's polarized Congress when the two parties vote for or against consequential legislation as solid blocs, a pattern common to parliamentary systems. If opponents fail in one session of Congress, they always can come back in the next to try again. In the judgment of Senator Alan K. Simpson, R-Wyo. (1979–1997), "In politics there are no right answers, only a continuing flow of compromises between groups resulting in a changing, cloudy, and ambiguous series of public decisions where appetite and ambition compete openly with knowledge and wisdom."[4]

OBSERVATIONS ABOUT LAWMAKING

Despite its built-in—and frequently beneficial—inefficiencies, Congress's lawmaking role is firmly grounded in the Constitution. But the preeminent place envisioned for Congress by the drafters of the Constitution has been modified by the growth in executive power that characterized the 20th century and, so far, the 21st century as well. What has emerged to a large degree, especially with respect to national and domestic security, is what could be called the "presidential branch" of government.

Whether the elective branches are united or divided in terms of party control, the basic point is that with assertive presidents, "Congress must constantly stand guard for increased encroachment by the President on the basic powers of the House and Senate because of the danger that these powers can be absorbed or redistributed to the advantage of the chief executive."[5] Instead of standing guard, Congress at times simply goes along with accretions of power to the president. Still, the constitutional separation of powers has preserved for Congress an independent role that distinguishes it from legislative bodies in most other democracies.

The mechanics of legislating influence the policymaking process. Procedural details and nuances have a crucial policy impact, and understanding why certain policies are adopted and others are not is impossible without an appreciation of the rules, precedents, and practices governing the process. Substance, in short, can be shaped through procedure. The Senate's tradition of lengthy debate is "a wonderful tool to . . . expose legislation to more careful consideration," said a Senate Democratic leader. "You hold many of these pieces of legislation up to the light of day and share the concerns you have with the American public, and that exposure is extremely powerful."[6] However, the deliberative character of the Senate has been in some decline, given such developments as wider use of procedural devices such as "filling the amendment tree," the demands on senators' time (campaigning, fundraising, meeting with constituents, etc.) that keep them away from the chamber, and the circumvention of the committee process. As Senator Carl Levin, D-Mich., observed: "The unique thing about the Senate is we're supposed to debate—frequently and at length. And we're supposed to be deliberative. It's been allowed, I believe, to decline in that regard."[7]

Congress's informal procedures and practices are often as important as its formal rules. For example, neither chamber needed rules changes to permit lawmaking through megabills that are hundreds or thousands of pages in length. These bills emerged from a variety of governing challenges (issue complexity, fiscal deficits, jurisdictional overlap, and the like) that compound the difficulties of lawmaking—and augment the authority of party leaders—and from legislative–executive conflicts. As a legislative scholar noted: "Leaders gain power with omnibus bills and, because they assemble omnibus bills, are afforded the opportunity to advance party agenda items." He added that omnibus legislating "also helps Congress by veto-proofing items the president opposes. Legislation that is headed to a veto stands a better chance in an omnibus bill alongside main items the president supports."[8] Rank-and-file lawmakers sometimes lament the use of megabills, even though they may vote for them, because they usually have little time to learn the content of these massive bills even with legislative rules changes mandating such things as a 3-day availability requirement for measures before they are taken up in the House or the requirement in the Senate for conference reports to be available on the Internet 48-hours prior to their consideration on the floor. Needless to say, members' demand for sufficient time to read bills and reports sometimes runs counter to party leaders' recognition that "legislative timing [of floor action] plays a big role in whether a bill will pass because support can be fleeting."[9] (Speaker John Boehner wanted to avoid the use of omnibus bills carrying unrelated provisions, but political realities required their use on some occasions. See the appendix to Chapter 8.)

Moreover, no rules changes mandated that legislators must play both the inside game (maneuvering behind the scenes at multiple lawmaking stages to pick up support for legislation) and the outside game (generating public support) to push controversial measures through the House and Senate. "Being a good legislator means you have to do both," remarked a House leader. "If you are going to pass important legislation, you have to both deal with Members and put together coalitions in the country."[10]

The rules of the game are as important in illuminating the outcomes of the legislative process as they are in comprehending who wins at any competition—the presidential nominating system, for example. The electoral strategy of a presidential candidate in the general campaign cannot be fully appreciated without understanding the electoral college or the techniques of raising campaign funds. Similarly, one cannot comprehend the behavior of members of Congress as participants in policy formation without knowledge of the formal and informal rules and procedures under which they operate.

Congressional rules and practices shape policy outcomes. For example, according to Senate Rule XXII, an extraordinary majority of the Senate is required to invoke cloture. Therefore, in the Senate a well-organized minority of 41 lawmakers can block passage of legislation desired by a majority—such as in contemporary Senates, as well as in the 1950s and 1960s when civil rights legislation was repeatedly delayed by the opponents' use of the filibuster. Final policy outcomes also are influenced by special rules from the House Rules Committee, which may limit or prevent amendments from being offered on the floor by minority party members.

The rules themselves may change in response to events, policy goals, or other conditions and circumstances. Some rules are modified or ignored, while new ones come out of struggles over a particular problem. The mixed results and unanticipated consequences that attend some procedural revisions can even disgruntle members who originally supported rules changes. For example, simplifying the complexities of the budget process, which today can require members to vote over and over on the same issue as they consider authorization, appropriation, budget, or tax measures, is no easy task when 535 lawmakers want a say in how and what fiscal decisions are to be made.

An ostensibly procedural decision also can be used to mask a policy objective. When members vote to table (kill) an amendment, procedurally it appears as if they are merely postponing consideration of it. But such a procedure may sidetrack the proposal permanently while allowing members to say they did not take a position on the amendment. (Today, "spin doctors" often devise campaign attack ads that transform procedural votes into members' actual policy preference.)

Important, too, are the differences in the way the two chambers operate. Each chamber functions under rules and procedures that reflect its basic constitutional design. A close examination of the differences as well as the similarities between the two bodies is indispensable to an accurate understanding of how Congress functions. Unlike those of the House, said Senator Robert C. Byrd, D-W.Va., the rules in the Senate favor the minority:

> They were meant to favor the minority to prevent the majority from running over the minority. That is why there is a Senate. That is why this Senate ought to remain a Senate and not become a second House of Representatives.[11]

The most significant and enduring feature of the rules is that they usually require bills to pass through a labyrinth of decision points before they can become law. Generally, passing legislation is more difficult than defeating it. To move their bills through the multiple decision points, each a potential roadblock, members of Congress must engage in a constant cycle of coalition building, using various bargaining techniques. The shifting coalitions typically combine, dissolve, and recombine in response to the widely varying issues and needs of members. Unlike in the past, when a few barons dominated legislative policymaking, today's Congress operates in an environment in which scores of members have some—and often significant—bargaining power.

Coalition building is possible primarily for two reasons. First, members of Congress, who represent diverse constituencies, are not equally concerned about every item on the legislative agenda. Second, members pursue many objectives other than the enactment of legislation. They may seek reelection, election to higher office, appointment to prestigious committees, or personal conveniences such as additional staff or office space. These conditions create numerous opportunities for coalition building through three major types of bargaining—logrolling, compromise, and the distribution of legislative and nonlegislative favors (primarily by the congressional leadership). For example, to win the 60 Democratic votes in the 111th Congress to pass President Barack Obama's health care law, and with Republicans in solid opposition, Senate Majority Leader Harry Reid, D-Nev., had to make policy concessions to several on-the-fence party colleagues to win their support. The press gave names to these concessions, names such as the "Louisiana Purchase" and the "Cornhusker Kickback." Republicans criticized these deals as "buying" the votes of the Democratic senators.

Another factor determining whether a series of majority coalitions can be built is the extent to which members are in general agreement that a law is required or inevitable on a particular subject. Members may have widely divergent views on the solution to the problem, but they usually will work toward compromising their differences when dealing with must-pass legislation. However, in today's hyperpartisan era, it is often difficult to reach compromises, even on must-pass bills, when many lawmakers insist that their policy preferences are right for the nation. As a House minority-party member said about why her party regularly votes against the majority's legislation: "It is really because we have a very different philosophy about what makes this country successful."[12] Speaker Boehner once bluntly said of compromise: "I reject the word."[13]

Although the U.S. Constitution is a bundle of compromises, many of today's lawmakers and voters view the legislative "give-and-take" process as a sellout of one's principles and a sign of political weakness. A key issue for lawmakers is determining when, or if, to seek common ground and political accommodation with those who do not share their views, especially if they have staked out firm positions and promised constituents that they would never vote contrary to those positions. Members who break their public pledges may face unwanted consequences, such as challengers in primary elections. As a House member explained:

> Compromise is not easy, especially in today's contentious atmosphere. Certainly it's not as easy as telling true believers what they want to hear, and it requires special courage in a changed political environment in which prominent media figures attack anyone who deviates from their view of what is right, in which every issue is seen as a tactical battlefield for the next campaign, and in which the political parties each depend on voters who scorn the very notion of compromise.[14]

Time influences the entire congressional process. "I'd like to get something done before we leave," said the Senate banking chair about the need to revamp the nation's financial regulatory structure. "I don't want to wait too long to miss the sense of urgency to get something done."[15] Recall from Chapter 2 how deadlines, such as raising the debt ceiling or preventing a government shutdown, can provoke the strategy of brinksmanship between the parties, branches, and chambers. As the 2-year cycle of a Congress runs its course, every procedural device that can be employed has a policy consequence—either delaying or speeding up the processing of legislation.

Frequently, as the countdown to final adjournment occurs, the bargaining process shifts into high gear. Bills that have been deadlocked for months may be moved along swiftly as logrolling and compromises save bills in which members have a vested interest. Deadlines and threatened or actual procedural and policy crises frequently activate the lawmaking process.

> [The] sharpness of the ideological, political, and partisan divisions [in contemporary Congresses] means that most controversial areas come down to end games; every major player is willing to wait, believing that he, she, or they will have maximum leverage at the end of the tunnel.[16]

Stalled legislation dies if not enacted before Congress's final adjournment.

During the past several decades, Congress has undergone significant transformations. Some of the changes resulted from the 1995 GOP takeover of Congress after Republicans had been the House minority for 40 years; other changes have been under way for some time or have recently assumed greater significance. Together, they have influenced the character of Congress's procedural and policy politics. Among these developments are the following.

Centralization of Authority in the Speakership

Recent Speakers of the House, such as Jim Wright, D-Tex. (1987–1989), and Thomas S. Foley, D-Wash. (1989–1995), had an impressive array of formal and informal powers that strengthened their hand in the lawmaking process. Neither, however, compares with authority exercised by Speaker Newt Gingrich, R-Ga. (1995–1999), in the House and in the larger political system. Strongly supported by party colleagues, especially junior Republicans, Gingrich took command of the House in the mid-1990s as few leaders before him had. Not only did he set the nation's agenda when he assumed the Speakership, functioning as the House's chief executive officer and relying on Majority Leader Dick Armey of Texas to be the chief operating officer on the House floor, but he also bypassed the custom of seniority to handpick loyalists to chair committees crucial to the success of the Republican agenda. As one congressional journalist noted about Gingrich's first 100 days in office,

> The notion of a House that's balkanized into legislative fiefdoms . . . has become antiquated. Instead, the House is driven by a Speaker who wields extraordinary power and by rank-and-file Members who are intent on proving to a skeptical public that they can change how Washington works.[17]

In an unprecedented event and path-breaking expansion of the bully pulpit role long associated with presidents, Speaker Gingrich requested—and received for free—prime-viewing television time to address the nation after House action on the GOP's governing agenda, called the "Contract with America."[18] But congressional history demonstrates that centralized authority is not a permanent condition in either chamber; instead, the forces of centralization versus decentralization are constantly in play, and they regularly adjust and reconfigure in response to new conditions and circumstances. And so later, as intraparty dissent with his leadership increased at the end of the 105th Congress (1997–1999), Gingrich left the House, in large measure because he had lost the support of many GOP colleagues. A skillful insurgency leader, Gingrich had difficulty adjusting to the formidable job of governing the House.

His successor, J. Dennis Hastert, R-Ill. (1999–2007), operated somewhat differently than Gingrich had in his leadership post. Not only did Hastert prefer a lower public profile than that favored by Gingrich, but he also stressed more consultation with the Republican rank and file. Hastert consolidated power in a trio of top GOP leaders—himself (as Speaker), the majority leader (Tom DeLay, Tex.), and the majority whip (Roy Blunt, Mo., now a senator). The three were able to move "top agenda items while wielding a historically small margin of control in a remarkably polarized House."[19] Hastert still exercised significant top-down command of the House and his party. Like Gingrich, Hastert was not reluctant to bypass standing committees, utilize task forces, select party loyalists as conferees, impose sanctions against uncooperative chairs or partisan colleagues, instruct committee chairs to deal with certain bills, restrict the role of minority-party members, or construct majorities exclusively from within GOP ranks. "The job of the Speaker," he said in articulating his governing philosophy, "is *not* to expedite legislation that runs counter to the wishes of the majority of his majority."[20] In fact, Hastert advised Speaker Boehner that if he had to rely too frequently on Democratic votes to pass legislation, "you're not in power anymore."[21]

Speaker Nancy Pelosi's, D-Calif. (2007–2011), leadership style emulated, and some say exceeded, that of Gingrich and Hastert—a top-down, centralized approach—rather than following the consultative model of earlier Democratic Speakers, such as Thomas "Tip" O'Neill, Mass. (1977–1987). As Pelosi's counterpart in the Senate, Majority Leader Reid, said about her: "She runs the House with an iron hand."[22] In the view of Henry Waxman, D-Calif., then chair of the House Energy and Commerce Committee and a close ally of the Speaker: "She's much more involved in the details and whipping the votes and trying to get the best substance than any Democratic Speaker I've ever seen."[23] (Waxman served with four other Democratic Speakers, beginning with Carl Albert, Okla., 1971–1977.) Speaker Pelosi, in brief, was a hands-on Speaker who was not reluctant to assert her authority in shaping controversial legislation and mobilizing the votes to win their passage in the House.

GOP Speaker Boehner (2011–), as a former committee chair himself—Education and the Workforce and a principal author of the No Child Left Behind legislation—did devolve authority to his committee chairs, empowering them to recommend legislation for House consideration. Boehner served with the three previous Speakers and disliked their "top-down" command style of running the House. He worked to avoid the bypassing of committee consideration on major bills and having a select few in the Speaker's office write bills in secret. He also ensured that appropriations bills were brought to the floor under open rules, unlike the practice of the three previous Speakers. However, Speaker Boehner has had a much harder time holding his party together on major votes, losing several key issues on the House floor. With 87 freshman Republicans—many of whom are Tea Party endorsed and all of whom are committed to reducing the government's size and role, cutting taxes, and favoring deep reductions in federal spending for social programs—Speaker Boehner often could not deliver the votes from his party after negotiating with the president or Senate Leader Reid. Fundamental to leadership is followership, and Speaker Boehner lacked sufficient GOP followers. In the view of House Democrat Jim McGovern, Mass., the Speaker "has to constantly please [the Tea Party conservatives], and they cannot be pleased enough." Or as conservative Republican Jim Jordan of Ohio explained: "As I tell folks, the speaker has to deal with Obama and Harry Reid and crazy conservatives like me."[24]

Noteworthy is that Senate party leaders, particularly the majority leader, have accrued more authority. A few examples make the point. Bear in mind that the minority leader and individual members have an array of parliamentary prerogatives to foil the best-laid plans of the majority leader. First, the majority leader is pivotal in determining the Senate's agenda: what to bring up, when to bring measures or matters to the floor, and what not to call up. With campaigning by legislating commonplace today, the majority leader can structure floor decision making in a manner to attract votes in the November elections and thus facilitate his party's continued control of the chamber. For example, with weak economic growth and unemployment stuck at about 8%, it is not surprising that in the lead-up to the November 2012 elections, Senator Reid brought to the floor numerous bills that emphasized job creation.

Second, the majority leader has the important prerogative of first recognition. By "filling the amendment tree" (see Chapter 6), the majority leader can function as a one-person "gatekeeper" or "House Rules Committee," deciding whether other senators can call up their amendments. Third, the majority leader is often the lead negotiator in crafting unanimous consent agreements that promote Senate passage of controversial legislation.

The heightened partisanship in the House and Senate motivates leaders in both chambers—majority and minority—to encourage, and often get, party loyalty on various key votes. "Procedure is always a party vote," emphasized a former House GOP leader.[25] These votes, as mentioned earlier, are sometimes used as campaign ammunition. Constituents "will decide whether they cast the right votes" on procedural issues, exclaimed a minority House Democrat. "I don't think most voters think, 'Well, it's a procedural issue, it didn't really matter.'"[26] Majority members reply that the electorate can distinguish between votes on substance versus procedural votes for campaign purposes.

Perhaps the most compelling argument majority party leaders can make to their partisans is that if they are to maintain control, they must stick together and do whatever it takes politically and procedurally to retain their majority status. Similarly, minority leaders urge their members to follow the leadership's playbook because it will lead to majority control. "Without unity, we really can't make ourselves heard," noted a Senate minority leader. "When you have multi-voices, you have no voice."[27] Senate GOP leader Mitch McConnell made it abundantly clear to his party colleagues that they must stay united and oppose President Obama's policies if they are to reclaim control of the Senate. "Republicans need to stick together as a team," exclaimed Senator McConnell. Or as a GOP senator summarized McConnell's strategy: "If Obama was for it, we had to be against it."[28]

Party Branding and Messaging

Both congressional parties in each chamber regularly employ a mix of political marketing strategies to win outside support for their fundamental procedural and policy priorities. They have theme teams, message groups, and "war rooms," and hold numerous party meetings to develop, coordinate, and transmit a clear, coherent, and unified message ("talking points") to the public. Today, there are as many, or more, staff aides skilled in public relations as there are policy specialists. The parties also hire consultants to assist them in devising effective communication or "message" strategies and in using words as political weapons. For example, congressional Republicans substitute the words "death tax" for the inheritance tax and "socialized medicine" or "Obamacare" for President Obama's landmark law (the Patient Protection and Affordable Care Act) that overhauled the health care system. Recognizing that Republicans had won the messaging strategy in characterizing the health law as "Obamacare," the president began to use the word himself but in a positive way: "Yes, I care about the health of people." Democrats understand that persuasive messaging strategies are important factors in accomplishing their legislative goals. As Pelosi, the Democratic House leader, once said: "We can do all we can with our inside maneuvering, but without the outside mobilization we'll never achieve what is possible."[29]

Key objectives of such efforts are to frame the national debate in a way that activates public support—particularly from each party's electoral base—behind GOP or Democratic congressional objectives and that rebuts attacks by opponents. Both congressional parties employ field hearings, interactive websites, rallies, focus groups, online petitions, blogs, podcasts, cable TV, polls and surveys, town meetings, Spanish-language websites, news conferences, Twitter, Facebook, talk radio appearances, newspaper articles, media events, bus tours, and more—all with the primary objective of winning public support for their causes and candidates.

Making major policy innovations today usually requires combining various external campaigning techniques with internal procedural coordination (e.g., who should offer amendments, when, and where). For example, in late 2010, after Democratic discontent with messaging on the health care issue and the loss of seats in the November election, Senate Majority Leader Reid created the Democratic Policy and Communications Center and named Senator Charles Schumer of New York to head it. The center's goals are to create greater message coherence and to "coordinate message and legislative strategy, provide Members with the tools that they need to communicate with voters and put Republicans on the defensive in their home states."[30] An objective of these efforts is to build extra political pressure to pass priority legislation.

Another aspect of the inside–outside game is the notion of "branding"— a marketing technique designed to shape the collective public reputation of a party. It has at least two key dimensions. One is to hold or to win power by trying to keep the other party on the defensive by portraying it negatively—for example, "tax-and-spend" Democrats or Republicans belonging to the "Party of No." Branding also is used positively to strengthen public regard for one or the other party. As two scholars point out, branding demands "that lawmakers market their partisan and programmatic wares to concerned constituencies and a politically interested public" and, in the process, "popularize their parties' trademarks" (e.g., Democrats as defenders of well-liked entitlement programs, such as Social Security and Medicare, and Republicans as champions of limited government and tax cuts).[31]

In brief, the distinction between campaigning and governing is blurred or sometimes obliterated in the House or Senate. Parties in both chambers regularly use the floor to spotlight their priorities, to activate outside supporters, and to win public support for their agendas. As a senator said: "The Senate has become a campaign platform." Or as a representative exclaimed about use of the House to send political messages rather than solve public problems:

> What drives me nuts about this place is that, when I came here [in 1969], it used to be that you had at least a year after you were elected where you could get the people's business done before the next election intruded. Now, the way politics has been nationalized, the election intrudes virtually every day, and it becomes more intense at an earlier time.[32]

Congress and the Information Age

Congress is wired to a high-tech world that enables members, party leaders, and constituents to communicate politically and quickly to shape the legislative process. Technology has had and will continue to have a major impact on Congress, including on the campaign trail (e.g., Internet fundraising or the microtargeting of electoral messages). Three points illustrate the case. First, Congress's agenda has been transformed because of developments in technology, telecommunications, and other aspects of the information age. Issues of electronic commerce, Internet security, privacy, nanotechnology, net neutrality, copyright, secrecy, and other related matters increasingly occupy the attention of lawmakers.

Second, electronic advocacy has added a plebiscitary quality to congressional policymaking. Today, many citizens and interest groups make their preferences known almost instantaneously to lawmakers via e-mail or various social-networking sites. Bloggers, for example, successfully influenced policymaking in the Senate when they helped overcome opposition to an earmark reform amendment and to a bill allowing citizens to use the Internet to monitor federal spending.[33] In another example of virtual lawmaking, Senator Durbin held a series of online discussions with policy experts, politically engaged citizens, and others, enlisting their assistance in drafting a bill "to ensure the widest affordable high-speed Internet access."[34]

Lawmakers also reach out to constituents to encourage interactive exchanges via their office or committee websites. This approach gives lawmakers the potential to communicate with many more constituents, including those who cannot attend members' town-hall meetings in the district for various reasons (lack of transportation, e.g.). Some members prefer holding virtual rather than face-to-face meetings with constituents to avoid being castigated or harangued by angry voters.[35] Members also post blogs on their websites and use Twitter to communicate in "real time" with their constituents (Twitter Town Halls, e.g.).[36]

A study found that "about 85 percent of Members have Twitter accounts."[37] Another study determined that congressional social media managers found "Facebook to be the most effective tool to both understand constituents' views and to communicate the views of their members."[38] In a first-ever House activity, Rep. Mike Honda, D-Calif., enlisted the support of his constituents in designing his website. "It is my hope that this process can empower the public to collaborate with Members of Congress," Honda said. "No longer will individuals simply petition their representatives— instead they should be our most valued advisors."[39] An issue for Congress is how to maintain an effective balance between representative government (where policy usually proceeds slowly) and electronic democracy (where fast action is often the objective).

Third, the strategy for moving legislation, as noted earlier, is as much technological—television, radio, the Internet, blogs, and so on—as it is political or procedural. Lawmakers understand the importance of technology in framing issues, molding public opinion, wooing colleagues, and generating grassroots support to advance policy initiatives on Capitol Hill. Lawmakers have hired "new media" staff aides to design their websites, educate members on innovative technologies and communications techniques (posting blogs, Tweeting, ensuring their presence on various social-networking sites, and so on) and integrate the new technology with fundraising and coalition building.[40] For example, House Majority Whip Kevin McCarthy, R-Calif., encouraged his GOP colleagues to use the "social networking site Twitter to interact with constituents and explain their votes" on various issues.[41] Technology, too, is one of many factors that influence how legislators make decisions. "We're in the Information Age and we're making decisions in so many different areas that it's a huge help," said Rep. Kevin Brady, R-Tex. "From a policy standpoint, [computer technology is] very productive for me and it's a very productive way to learn."[42]

Ad Hoc Lawmaking

Today, ad hoc lawmaking is a growth industry on Capitol Hill. At least two different tracks are available for the consideration of legislation. On the first track are measures that follow traditional textbook lawmaking (the so-called "regular order")—introduction of a bill, referral to committee, hearings and markup, floor deliberation and conference action, and presidential consideration. What the regular order is can prompt disagreement. For example, some lawmakers accept the "first-track" definition. Others suggest that the regular order occurs when legislative policymaking simply evolves without party leadership direction and supervision. Still others view the regular order in chamber-specific terms. In the House, the regular order could mean that all regular appropriations bills should be brought to the floor with open rules; further, they should all be enacted into law by the start of the fiscal year. In the Senate, the regular order would always grant senators the opportunity to offer and debate a reasonable number of nonrelevant amendments to legislation.

On the second track are the priority measures of each party, which may provoke legislative gridlock, as well as run-of-the-mill measures that get caught up in partisan battles and may become hostages to larger concerns. In these cases, ad hoc lawmaking is often the name of the game, including heightened use of deadlines and brinksmanship as action-forcing devices. To be sure, the regular process is bypassed when congressional leaders and the White House negotiate legislative compromises in secret. Members find new uses for old rules, employ innovative devices, or bypass traditional procedures and processes altogether to achieve their political and policy objectives. In a hard-to-govern era because of factors such as rancorous partisanship, the complexity of many issues, and the mounting fiscal deficit and debt, new and unexpected procedural twists to lawmaking are to be expected.

The politics of procedure is different today than in earlier periods. Then, procedural issues were basically an insider's game, driven largely by various tactical considerations (logrolls or compromises, e.g.) associated with forging winning coalitions. Today, the process of building coalitions on major party and institutional priorities is inseparable from larger, outside political forces (including the power of interest groups, the intensity of 24/7 media coverage, instantaneous communications, and so on) that influence how Congress operates. The result is a lawmaking process that is more free-flowing, open, and less predictable than in the past.

Resurgence of Sharp Partisanship

Parties have always been important in Congress. Among other things, they organize the House and Senate and advocate substantive agendas. Partisanship is important and useful because it identifies the principles and ideals that orient each party. Former House Majority Leader DeLay (2003–September 2005) strongly defended a zero-sum (one side wins and the other loses) form of partisanship in his farewell speech to the House. He stated: "For all its faults, it is partisanship based on core principles that clarifies our debates, that prevents one party from straying too far from the mainstream, and that constantly refreshes our politics with new ideas and new leaders."[43]

Another House Republican offered a different perspective.

> I never cease to be amazed at how day after day . . . we put on our adversarial robes and we pick up our adversarial clubs and then we go about our business. But, unfortunately, the adversarial process often leads us to be more concerned with scoring political points than we are with winning solutions.[44]

In a particularly blunt assessment of partisan rancor in the House, Jim Cooper, D-Tenn., declared: "This is not a collegial body anymore. It is more like gang behavior. Members walk into the chamber full of hatred. They believe the worst lies about the other side."[45] The factors that fomented such partisan rancor are many, such as the changing composition of the two parties, with liberals in the Democratic party and conservatives in the Republican party and little or no philosophical overlap between them; the two parties' intense policy disagreements; partisan media outlets that amplify and promote interparty conflict; and the proliferation of interest groups affiliated with one party or the other that demand ideological "purity" from lawmakers if they are to receive campaign assistance.

A result of the hyperpartisanship is that today's Congress sometimes acts as a quasi-parliamentary body, with lawmakers from one party crafting legislation only among themselves and voting as a unified bloc against the other, whose members are equally united in opposition. The intensity and extent of partisan conflict in the contemporary Congress raises questions about the body's ability to engage in meaningful bipartisan deliberation and mutual accommodation. Scholars assert that Congress is "broken" and "dysfunctional."[46] Others agree that Congress needs repair in various areas (the nominations process, budgeting, and so on) but note that it is never nonfunctional. In many ways, they suggest, Congress is functioning as the Founding Fathers intended. Senate Majority Leader Reid, who frequently laments and is frustrated by the stalemates, partisan battles, and party conflicts that often suffuse the lawmaking and nominating processes, stated:

> Congress is not broken. Congress works the way it should. Does that mean it is always a very pleasant, happy place? Do I wish it weren't as difficult as it has been in the last few months? I wish it was much better than that. That is where we are.
>
> Through all the years and conflicts we have had, we have been able to come together and reach reasonable conclusions. The great experiment that started in 1787 has been very successful. . . . I am not proud of the conflict we have had these last many months, but I am satisfied we have been able to come together to find a solution.[47]

Acrimony and nastiness between the parties is certainly nothing new. "Congress has always been a partisan place," said John Dingell, D-Mich., the longest serving House member ever, "but never has the atmosphere been as negative and divisive as it is today."[48] Various scholars and commentators have highlighted the reasons for this development. To reemphasize, they include changes in the constituency bases of the two parties. Democrats have generally become more liberal, and Republicans have become far more conservative, placing each party's priority agenda squarely at odds with the other's. Added to this mix is the ongoing and intense struggle between Democrats and Republicans to win the electoral battle for long-term control of the House and Senate.[49] With partisan command of the House and Senate shifting more frequently in recent years—recall the three "wave" elections of 2006, 2008, and 2010—the minority party often views actions that stymie majority policy achievements as an effective route back to majority control. It is much easier electorally for the minority to run against a "do-nothing" than a "do-something" Congress.

Although bitter partisanship in the 1990s and 2000s is more evident in the "majority-rule" House than in the Senate, it is surfacing more frequently in that latter chamber, even with its reputation for comity and greater reciprocity among its smaller membership. "When I came to the Senate in 1959," said the late Senator Byrd, the longest serving lawmaker ever in the House and Senate combined, "there was partisanship. [GOP Minority Leader] Everett Dirksen was a partisan. [Democratic Majority Leader] Mike Mansfield was a partisan. But they were not bitter partisans. We didn't have the negativism, the bitter partisanship that we have seen rule the Senate . . . and it is getting worse."[50] In the judgment of congressional scholar Ross Baker: "It's gotten so bad now that [at times] Republicans don't want to be seen publicly in the presence of Democrats or have a Democrat profess friendship for them or vice versa."[51] Numerous lawmakers who voluntarily depart the House or Senate often give as one of their reasons the partisan rancor that makes legislative service unpleasant and legislative accomplishments hard to achieve.

The breakdown of civility and trust in an environment of partisan polarization compounds the difficulties faced by each chamber in producing legislation. Members of opposite parties who disagree with each other are not just viewed as rivals but, as noted earlier, as political enemies. In the judgment of former Senate Majority Leader Tom Daschle, D-S.D. (2001–2002): "Because we can't bond, we can't trust. Because we can't trust, we can't cooperate. Because we can't cooperate, we become dysfunctional."[52] Moreover, when procedural rules are used solely for dilatory or message purposes, it becomes that much harder for lawmakers to work together in a collegial manner.

The Return of Deficits

In 2001, the Congressional Budget Office (CBO) projected a surplus of $5.6 trillion over 10 years. Today, CBO projects a 10-year deficit of $10 trillion, stemming largely from tax cuts, entitlement expenditures, the war against terrorists, homeland security requirements, and the severe economic recession, which reduces tax revenues and increases spending for unemployment compensation and other federal safety-net programs. In 2008, the deficit was $459 billion, a 1-year record. Four years later, the deficit was more than $1 trillion. How much is a trillion dollars? President Ronald Reagan explained it this way: "If you had a stack of thousand-dollar bills in your hand only 4 inches high, you'd be a millionaire. A trillion dollars would be a stack of thousand-dollar bills 67 miles high."[53]

Escalating annual deficits, combined with a national debt in 2013 exceeding $17 trillion, raise important questions for which there are no easy answers. Many economists argue that the nation cannot continue indefinitely on a course of ever-increasing deficit and debt, especially given the retirement of the "baby boom" generation, some 80 million people born between 1946 and 1964, with 10,000 retiring every week. How will Congress be able to pay for the retirement (Social Security) and health care needs (Medicare and Medicaid) of this expanding demographic group of aging retirees while also funding competing priorities, such as education, transportation, or defense? The country faces a critically important issue. As expressed by Federal Reserve Chair Ben Bernanke, "The fundamental decision that the Congress, the administration and the American people must confront is how large a share of the nation's economic resources to devote to federal government programs."[54] In fact, this fundamental issue is largely what the November 2012 elections were about: the role and reach of the federal government. In the view of a freshman House Republican, Mo Brooks of Arkansas (who was reelected), the elections represented a fierce political battle over the future direction of the country.

> November [2012] is the fight for our country. And we have people who are basically socialist, bigger government, higher tax fans who have one viewpoint. And you have people who believe in smaller government, individual liberty, lower taxes, free enterprise versus socialism. That's the battle. What you're seeing in the Senate and House is messaging to help the public better understand what the options are.[55]

Elections have consequences, as the saying goes, and President Obama handily won reelection to a second term. Congressional Democrats won eight additional seats in the still-GOP-controlled House and increased by two seats their margin of control in the Senate. During his inaugural speech on January 21, 2013, President Obama outlined an ambitious agenda that emphasized a substantial role for government in areas such as immigration, gun control, and climate change. He also highlighted the importance of federal programs such as Social Security, Medicare, and Medicaid. These programs, he said, "do not sap our initiative. They do not make us a nation of takers. They free us to take the risks that made this country great." The president also became the first president in an inaugural speech to urge an end to discrimination against gays. GOP Senate leader McConnell (and no doubt Representative Brooks) called the president's speech "disappointing" and declared that it was a return to the era of liberalism.[56] The extent to which President Obama can win the support of Congress and the country for his objectives remains unclear at this juncture.

The Continuity of Congress

After the September 11, 2001, attacks, Congress faced an issue that it rarely had to confront in the past: its own survival in the event of a catastrophic attack on the legislative branch that kills or incapacitates most lawmakers. Scores of complex issues are raised by a calamity that could prevent the House or Senate from functioning. Only a few will be mentioned to highlight the complicated issues that surround preserving representative government in the event of a catastrophe.

A major issue that confronts the House more than the Senate is how to quickly replace House members when a large number are killed or incapacitated in a terrorist attack. Under the 17th Amendment to the Constitution, most state legislatures have authorized their governors to fill Senate vacancies, which typically occurs quickly.[57] (A few states, such as Alaska and Connecticut, have laws that disallow gubernatorial appointments. The seat is left vacant until a special election is held.) The House is another story, however. Constitutionally, the only method to fill House vacancies is special elections, which generally occur 90 to 120 days after a legislator's death, retirement, or resignation. The Constitution makes no provision for repopulating the House if scores of lawmakers are killed or disabled, a situation that calls into question the institution's ability to function when there are numerous vacancies and many areas of the country lack representation. In such an event, the president might declare martial law and "act unilaterally without the check of Congress."[58]

In 2005, the president signed a law (P.L. 109-55) that called on the states with vacant House seats to hold expedited (within 49 days) special elections in the event of extraordinary circumstances. Many lawmakers oppose this idea and argue that the Constitution should be amended to authorize the appointment of temporary House members in the event of a calamity that causes mass vacancies (25% or more of the House membership is dead or incapacitated, e.g.). To date, Congress has shown little interest in amending the Constitution to permit the interim emergency appointment of House members in the event of a catastrophe that kills or incapacitates scores of members.

Another concern is the establishment of a quorum in the House. Under the Constitution, "a majority of each [chamber] shall constitute a quorum to do Business." However, under precedents stated in the House rulebook, this has been interpreted to mean "that after the House is once organized the quorum consists of a majority of those Members chosen, sworn, and living whose membership has not been terminated by resignation or action of the House." Thus, if only five House members were chosen, sworn, and alive after a tragic event, a vote of 3 to 2 would be sufficient to make crucial policy and political decisions, such as the selection of a new Speaker, even from the minority party. The question, then, is whether decisions made by a handful of lawmakers would be viewed as legitimate by the country.[59]

A related issue is if catastrophic circumstances left scores of lawmakers incapacitated and unable to carry out their legislative duties. How would the House or Senate function if a request for a quorum call or a recorded vote revealed fewer than 218 representatives or 51 senators in attendance? To deal with this issue, the House adopted a "provisional quorum" rule on the opening day of the 109th Congress, which remains in effect today. It states that after a series of quorum calls (totaling 72 hours) reveal the House's inability to establish a quorum, the number of lawmakers who are present will then constitute a provisional quorum for the House to conduct business.[60] The constitutionality of the provisional quorum rule remains an open question.

And so the dynamic interplay between policymaking and the rules continues. Precedents and practices are revised or abandoned and new ones established, often with great difficulty, in response to changing needs and pressures. "We always learn in this organization, even though we may think the rules are fixed and firm," stated a senator, "how the fertility of the minds of the Members manages to find ways to expand those rules."[61] Or as Senator Byrd pointed out, the "Senate doesn't operate under the rules it operated under when I came here and that existed up until a few years ago."[62]

Congress's dynamism is ensured by the regular infusion of new members, changing events and conditions, and the fluctuating expectations of citizens. If Congress reduces or increases its lawmaking activity, it usually is not by accident but as a reaction to the members' perceptions of what their constituents and the country want. For its part, the nation expects Congress to use its considerable powers and policymaking procedures to help resolve, or at least allay, the pressing issues facing the country. This expectation is sometimes hard to achieve, in part because mistrust between the legislative parties—provoked by their sharp ideological differences—makes problem solving on major issues difficult to accomplish. Still, Congress's constitutional role is to address the tough domestic and global issues that face the nation. Its "job is to understand them thoroughly, weigh the benefits and interests of an astounding variety of Americans, and consider carefully how to move forward" to enact constructive legislation.[63]

NOTES

1. Iian Gaff and Mary Lynn Jones, "Lessons About Congress Not Taught in School," *The Hill*, August 7, 2002, 13.
2. *Washington Post*, June 26, 1983, A14.
3. Orrin Hatch, *Square Peg: Confessions of a Citizen Senator* (New York: Basic Books, 2002), 70.
4. *Congressional Record*, May 20, 1987, S6798.
5. Robert V. Remini, *The House: The History of the House of Representatives* (Washington, DC: Smithsonian Books, 2006), 467.
6. *New York Times*, April 9, 1995, 18.
7. Jeremy W. Peters, "Bipartisan Filibuster Deal Is Taking Shape in Senate," *New York Times*, January 24, 2013, A16.
8. Glen S. Kurtz, "Omnibus Legislating: An Institutional Reaction to the Rise of New Issues," in *Policy Dynamics*, ed. Frank Baumgartner and Bryan Jones (Chicago: University of Chicago Press, 2002), 212, 225.
9. Susan Ferrechio, "Congressional Leaders Right Against Posting Bills Online," *Examiner*, October 6, 2009, 14.
10. Richard Cohen, "Taking Advantage of Tax Reform Means Different Strokes for Different Folks," *National Journal*, June 22, 1985, 1459.
11. *Congressional Record*, February 23, 1988, S1124.
12. Carl Hulse, "Legislative Hurdles in an Era of Conflict, Not Compromise," *New York Times*, June 20, 2010, A18.
13. Quoted in Deborah Tannen, "Democracy Needs the Art of the Compromise," *Politico*, June 16, 2011, 28.
14. Lee H. Hamilton, "We Need to Embrace Compromise, Not Insult It," *Center on Congress at Indiana University*, May 16, 2011, 2. See also Amy Gutmann and Dennis Thompson, *The Spirit of Compromise* (Princeton, NJ: Princeton University Press, 2012).
15. Bill Swindell and Dan Friedman, "Dodd: No Obstacles With Shelby on Overhaul," *CongressDailyPM*, October 8, 2009, 4.
16. Norman Ornstein, "Let the End Games Begin," *Roll Call*, September 12, 1994, A23.
17. Richard Cohen, "The Transformers," *National Journal*, March 4, 1995, 528–529.
18. *New York Times*, April 8, 1995, 1.
19. Ben Pershing, "Smith Spars With Leaders," *Roll Call*, March 26, 2003, 13.
20. Quoted in *The Cannon Centenary Conference: The Changing Nature of the Speakership*, House Document No. 108-204 (Washington, DC: Government Printing Office, 2004), 62. Emphasis on *not* is added.
21. Karen Robillard, "Dennis Hastert Warns Boehner on His 'Rule,'" *Politico*, January 3, 2013, online edition.
22. *Congressional Record*, December 5, 2007, S14752.

23. Edward Epstein, "Struggle in the Best of Scenarios," *CQ Weekly*, January 4, 2010, 17.
24. John Aloysius Farrell, "Boehner's Last Chance," *National Journal*, May 12, 2012. The McGovern quote is on page 21, and Jordan's is on page 19.
25. David Rogers and Jeannie Cummings, "Democrats Aim to Stir Public as Impeachment Nears," *Wall Street Journal*, December 14, 1998, A20.
26. Kathleen Hunter, "Republicans Face Pressure to Vote in Lock Step," *Roll Call*, February 17, 2011, 18.
27. Eliza Newlin Carney, "Running Interference," *National Journal*, November 22, 1997, 2362.
28. Michael Grunwald, "The Party of No," *Time*, September 3, 2012, 44.
29. John Nichols, "Is This the New Face of the Democratic Party?" *The Nation*, August 6–13, 2001, 13.
30. David M. Drucker and Steven T. Dennis, "Friction Strains Senate War Room," *Roll Call*, June 14, 2011, 3.
31. Gary Lee Malecha and Daniel J. Reagan, *The Public Congress: Congressional Deliberation in a New Media Age* (New York: Routledge, 2012), 69–70.
32. Bob Benenson and Jonathan Allen, "It's Looking Like Blue Skies All Over Again," *CQ Weekly*, November 26, 2007, 3541.
33. Robert Bluey, "How Bloggers Took on Harry Reid and Won on Earmark Reform," *Examiner*, January 18, 2007, 18.
34. Joelle Tessler, "Virtual Lawmaking," *CQ Weekly*, August 6, 2007, 2341.
35. Billy House, "Hide and Speak: Taking the Place of Town Halls?" *National Journal Daily*, April 27, 2012, 1. See also Emily Cahn, "More Members Are Using Social Media to Interact With Their Constituents," *Roll Call*, January 4, 2013, 7, and Jacob R. Strauss, Matthew Eric Glassman, Colleen J. Shogan, and Susan Navarro Smelcer, "Communicating in 140 Characters or Less: Congressional Adoption of Twitter in the 111th Congress," *PS, Political Science and Politics* (January 2013): 60–66.
36. Andie Coller, "Lawmakers All a-Twitter," *Politico*, February 3, 2009, 27. See also Jessica Estepa, "Royce's Blog," *Roll Call*, July 12, 2011, 20; Rebecca Neal, "Tweeting on the Hill," *Federal Times*, October 5, 2009, 2; and James Oliphant, "Tweet, Follow or Get Out of the Way," *Los Angeles Times*, March 3, 2009, online edition.
37. Kate Tummarello, "Call Me . . . Hold On, It's Taken?" *Roll Call*, September 14, 2011, 17.
38. Ethan Klapper, "Like This: Hill Offices Prefer Facebook for Social Media," *National Journal Daily*, July 26, 2011, 22.
39. Emily Yehle, "Campus Notebook," *Roll Call*, October 8, 2008, 3.
40. Winter Casey, "Hill Tunes in to New Media," *National Journal*, March 7, 2009, 50.
41. Kara Rowland, "As GOP Deputy Whip, Kevin McCarthy Is on Political Fast Track," *Washington Times*, March 10, 2009, B3. See also Rachael Bade, "Amash Explains Votes on Facebook," *Roll Call*, May 11, 2011, 23, and Rep. John Boehner (R-Ohio), "New-Media Tools Boost Transparency, Help to Hold Congress Accountable," *The Hill*, October 15, 2009, 30.
42. George Archibald, "Technology Lets Lawmakers Remain Connected," *Washington Times*, September 12, 1999, C-10. See also James A. Thurber and Colton Campbell, ed., *Congress and the Internet* (Upper Saddle River, NJ: Prentice Hall, 2003).

43. *Congressional Record,* June 8, 2006, H3549.
44. Ibid., June 26, 2009, H7674.
45. Quoted in Joe Nocera, "The Last Moderate," *New York Times,* September 6, 2011, A25.
46. See, for example, Thomas E. Mann and Norman J. Ornstein's two books: *The Broken Branch* (New York: Oxford University Press, 2006) and *It's Even Worse Than It Looks* (New York: Basic Books, 2012).
47. *Congressional Record,* August 1, 2011, S5156.
48. Rep. John Dingell, "Dingell's Own Half Century," *Roll Call,* June 16, 2005, 23.
49. See, for example, Ronald Brownstein, *The Second Civil War: How Extreme Partisanship Has Paralyzed Washington and Polarized America* (New York: Penguin Press, 2007), and Sean M. Theriault, *Party Polarization in Congress* (New York: Cambridge University Press, 2008).
50. *Los Angeles Times,* January 30, 1995, A12.
51. David M. Herszenhorn, "In Health Vote, a New Vitriol," *New York Times,* December 24, 2009, A14.
52. David Rogers, "The Lost Senate," *Politico,* October 9, 2009, 14.
53. John Maggs, "The Trillion-Dollar Deficit," *National Journal,* November 1, 2008, 34.
54. Quoted in Michael Barone, "Big Government Becomes the Battle-Line Issue," *Examiner,* August 12, 2009, 12.
55. Jake Sherman, "For Congress, a Slow Week With Medals, Gridlock," *Politico,* April 19, 2012, 3.
56. Peter Schroeder, "McConnell: Obama's Speech Is Proof 'Era of Liberalism is Back,'" *The Hill,* January 23, 2013, 3.
57. In 2009, the Senate Judiciary Subcommittee on the Constitution recommended an amendment to the U.S. Constitution that would prevent governors from appointing senators, requiring the states to hold special elections to fill Senate vacancies. The stimulus for this proposal was the gubernatorial appointment of four senators to the 111th Congress. They were Michael Bennet of Colorado, Roland Burris of Illinois, Kirsten Gillibrand of New York, and Ted Kaufman of Delaware. All four replaced sitting senators who joined the Obama Administration. The author of the constitutional amendment, Senator Russell Feingold, D-Wis., who was defeated for reelection to the 112th Congress, said: "When over 12 percent of our citizens are represented by someone in the Senate who they did not elect, I think that's a problem for our system of democracy." See Kathleen Hunter, "Coburn to Vote for Senatorial Appointment Amendment in Committee," *CQ Today,* July 30, 2009, 14. The late senator Edward Kennedy, D-Mass., recommended instead that governors make interim appointments to fill Senate vacancies until a special election can be held. In addition, the person named to fill the Senate vacancy on a temporary basis would pledge not to run for the seat. See Norman Ornstein, "Edward Kennedy's Gift to the Senate—and the Country," *Roll Call,* September 23, 2009, 6, 36.
58. John C. Fortier, *Testimony Before the House Judiciary Subcommittee on the Constitution, Civil Rights, and Civil Liberties on "Continuity of Congress in the Wake of a Catastrophic Attack,"* July 23, 2009, 4. See also www.continuity ofgovernment.org. Mr. Fortier is a research fellow at the American Enterprise Institute, Washington, DC.

59. For a good treatment of these types of issues, see *Preserving Our Institutions: The Continuity of Congress, The First Report of the Continuity of Government Commission*, May 2003. The commission is a joint project of the American Enterprise Institute and the Brookings Institution.

60. John Bryan Williams, "How to Survive a Terrorist Attack: The Constitution's Majority Quorum Requirement and the Continuity of Congress," *William and Mary Law Review* 48 (2006): 1025–1090.

61. *Congressional Record*, February 26, 1988, S1521.

62. Ibid., July 26, 2000, S7614.

63. Lee H. Hamilton, "Why Isn't Congress More Efficient?" *Center for Congress at Indiana University*, October 1, 2007, 2.

Glossary of Selected Congressional Terms

act: The term for legislation once it has passed both houses of Congress and has been signed by the president or has been passed over the president's veto, thus becoming law. Also used in parliamentary terminology for a bill that has been passed by one house and engrossed. (See *engrossed bill, law*.)

adjournment to a day certain: Adjournment under a motion or resolution that fixes the next time of meeting. Under the Constitution, neither house can adjourn for more than 3 days without the concurrence of the other. A session of Congress is not ended by adjournment to a day certain.

adjournment *sine die*: Adjournment without definitely fixing a day for reconvening; literally "adjournment without a day." Usually connotes the final adjournment of a session of Congress. A session can continue until noon, January 3, of the following year, when, under the Twentieth Amendment to the Constitution, it automatically terminates. Both houses must agree to a concurrent resolution for either house to adjourn for more than 3 days.

amendment in the nature of a substitute: An amendment that seeks to replace the entire text of a bill. Passage of this type of amendment strikes out everything after the enacting clause and inserts a new version of the bill. A *substitute amendment* proposes to replace the entire text of a pending amendment.

amendments: Proposals of members of Congress to alter the language, provisions, or stipulations in bills or in other amendments. An amendment is usually printed, debated, and voted on in the same manner as a bill.

appeal: A member's challenge of a ruling or decision made by the presiding officer of the chamber. In the Senate, the senator appeals to members of the chamber to override the decision. If carried by a majority, sometimes a supermajority vote, the appeal nullifies the chair's ruling. In the House, the decision of the Speaker traditionally has been final; rarely are appeals to reverse the Speaker's stand successful. To appeal a ruling is considered an attack on the Speaker.

appropriations bills: Bills that give legal authority to spend or obligate money from the Treasury. The Constitution disallows money to be drawn from the Treasury "but in Consequence of Appropriations made by Law."

An appropriations bill usually provides the monies approved by authorization bills but not necessarily the full amount permissible under the authorization measures. By congressional custom, an appropriations bill originates in the House, and it is not supposed to be considered by the full House or Senate until the related authorization measure is enacted. Appropriations bills are either general or one of two specialized types. (See *continuing resolutions, supplemental appropriations bills*.) There is also "emergency" spending legislation, a designation determined by Congress and the president. This type of extra spending is exempt from rules and procedures that apply to regular appropriations bills or direct spending measures.

authorization bill: Basic, substantive legislation that establishes or continues the legal operation of a federal program or agency, either indefinitely or for a specific period of time, or which sanctions a particular type of obligation or expenditure. An authorization normally is a prerequisite for an appropriation or other kind of budget authority. Under the rules of both the House and Senate, the appropriation for a program or agency may not be considered until its authorization has been considered. (These rules may be waived or not be observed.) An authorization also may limit the amount of budget authority to be provided or may authorize the appropriation of "such sums as may be necessary."

bill: Most legislative proposals before Congress are in the form of bills and are designated by "H.R." in the House of Representatives or "S." in the Senate, according to the chamber in which they originate, and by a number, assigned in the order in which they are introduced during the 2-year period of a congressional term. Public bills deal with general questions and become public laws if approved by Congress and signed by the president. Private bills deal with individual matters such as claims against the government, immigration and naturalization cases, and land titles, and they become private laws if approved and signed by the president. (See also *concurrent resolution, joint resolution, resolution*.)

bills introduced: In both the House and the Senate, any number of members may join in introducing a single bill or resolution. The first member listed is the sponsor of the bill, and all members' names following the sponsor's name are the bill's cosponsors. Many bills are committee bills and are introduced under the name of the chair of the committee or subcommittee. All appropriations bills fall into this category. A committee frequently holds hearings on related bills and may agree to one of them or to an entirely new bill. When introduced, a bill is referred to the committee or committees that have jurisdiction over the subject of the bill. Under the standing rules of the House and Senate, bills are referred by the Speaker in the House and by the presiding officer in the Senate. In practice, the House and Senate parliamentarians act for these officials and refer the vast majority of bills. (See also *clean bill, report*.)

budget authority: Authority to enter into obligations that will result in immediate or future outlays involving federal funds. The basic forms of budget authority are appropriations, contract authority, and borrowing authority. Budget authority may be classified by (1) the period of availability (1 year, multiple years, or without a time limitation), (2) the timing of congressional action (current or permanent), or (3) the manner of determining the amount available (definite or indefinite).

budget outlays: Money spent in a given fiscal year, as opposed to money appropriated for that year. One year's budget authority can result in outlays over several years, and the outlays in any given year result from a mix of budget authority from that year and prior years. Budget authority is similar to putting money into a checking account. Outlays occur when checks are written and cashed.

Calendar Wednesday: On Wednesdays in the House, only committee chairs or authorized committee members may invoke Calendar Wednesday procedure (House Rule XV). A committee chair, for example, gives notice to the House on Tuesday that he or she will seek recognition to call up a bill on Calendar Wednesday. Under this procedure, any bill from either the House Calendar or the Union Calendar, except bills that are privileged, may be called up. General debate is limited to 2 hours. Bills called up from the Union Calendar are considered in the Committee of the Whole. Calendar Wednesday procedure is rarely used.

calendars: Agendas or lists of business awaiting possible action by each chamber. The House uses four legislative calendars. (See *Discharge Calendar*, *House Calendar*, *Private Calendar*, and *Union Calendar*.)

In the Senate, all legislative matters reported from committee go on one calendar. They are listed in the order in which committees report them, or the Senate places them on the calendar, but they may be called up out of order by the majority leader, either by obtaining unanimous consent of the Senate or by a motion to call up a bill. The Senate uses one nonlegislative calendar; it is devoted to treaties and nominations. (See *Executive Calendar*.)

clean bill: Frequently, after a committee has finished a major revision of a bill, one of the committee members, usually the chair, will assemble the changes and what is left of the original bill into a new measure and introduce it as a clean bill. The revised measure, which is given a new number, is then referred back to the committee, which reports it to the floor for consideration. This procedure often is a timesaver, because committee-recommended changes in a clean bill do not have to be considered and voted on by the chamber. Reporting a clean House bill also protects committee amendments that might be subject to points of order on germaneness.

cloture: The formal procedure by which a filibuster can be ended in the Senate. A motion for cloture can apply to any measure before the Senate, including a proposal to change the chamber's rules. The signatures of

16 senators are needed for introduction of a cloture motion, and to end a filibuster the cloture motion must be approved by three fifths of the entire Senate membership (60 if there are no vacancies). However, to end a filibuster against a proposal to amend the standing rules of the Senate, a two-thirds vote of senators present and voting is required. The cloture request is put to a roll-call vote 1 hour after the Senate meets on the second day after introduction of the motion. If approved, the bill or amendment in question comes to a final vote after 30 hours of consideration (including debate time and the time it takes to conduct roll calls, quorum calls, and other procedural motions). (See *filibuster*.)

Committee of the Whole: The working title of what is formally the Committee of the Whole House on the state of the Union. Its membership is composed of all House members sitting as a committee. Any 100 members who are present on the floor of the chamber constitute a quorum of the committee. Usually, any legislation must have passed through the regular legislative committee or the Appropriations Committee and must have been placed on the calendar before it can be heard by the Committee of the Whole. Technically, the Committee of the Whole considers only bills directly or indirectly appropriating money, authorizing appropriations, or involving taxes or charges on the public. Because the Committee of the Whole need number only 100 representatives, a quorum is more readily attained, and legislative business is expedited. Before 1971, members' positions were not individually recorded on votes taken in the Committee of the Whole.

When the full House resolves itself into the Committee of the Whole, it supplants the Speaker with a chair. It then debates a measure and possibly proposes amendments, with votes on amendments as needed. When the committee completes its work on a measure, it dissolves itself by rising. The Speaker returns, and the chair of the Committee of the Whole reports to the House that the committee's work has been completed. At this time, members might demand a roll-call vote on any first-degree amendment adopted in the Committee of the Whole.

committees: Entities of the House or Senate that prepare legislation for action by the parent chamber or conduct investigations as directed by the parent chamber. Most standing committees are divided into subcommittees, which study legislation, hold hearings, and report bills, with or without amendments, to the full committee. Only the full committee, not a subcommittee, can report legislation to the House or Senate.

concurrent resolution: A concurrent resolution, designated "H. Con. Res." or "S. Con. Res.," must be adopted by both houses, but it is not sent to the president for a signature and therefore does not have the force of law. A concurrent resolution, for example, is used to fix the time for adjournment of a Congress. It also is used as a vehicle for expressing the sense of Congress on various foreign policy and domestic issues, and it serves as a vehicle for coordinated decisions on the federal budget under the 1974

Congressional Budget and Impoundment Control Act. (See also *bill, joint resolution, resolution.*)

conference: A meeting between representatives of the House and the Senate to reconcile differences when the chambers pass dissimilar versions of the same bill. Members of the conference committee are appointed formally by the Speaker and the presiding officer of the Senate and are called managers, or conferees, for their respective chambers.

A majority of the managers for each house must reach agreement on the provisions of the bill (usually a compromise between the versions of the two chambers) before it can be considered by either chamber in the form of a conference report. When the conference report goes to the floor, it cannot be amended, and, if it is not approved by both chambers, the bill may go back to conference or a new conference may be convened. Informal practices largely govern bargaining in conference committees.

Bills that are passed by both houses with only minor differences need not be sent to conference. Either chamber may concur in the other's amendments, completing action on the legislation. Sometimes leaders of the committees of jurisdiction work out an informal compromise instead of having a formal conference.

continuing resolutions: Joint resolutions drafted by Congress that continue appropriations for specific ongoing activities of a government department or departments when a fiscal year begins and Congress has not yet enacted all the regular appropriations bills for that year. The continuing resolution usually specifies a maximum rate at which the agency may incur obligations. This usually is based on the rate for the previous year, the president's budget request, or an appropriations bill for that year passed by either or both houses of Congress but not cleared.

CUTGO ("cut-as-you-go"): A formal rule adopted by the 112th House that replaced the "pay-as-you-go" rule, or PAYGO. PAYGO stated that tax cuts or hikes in entitlement spending needed to be offset by tax increases or entitlement cuts. CUTGO stipulates that spending for entitlement programs must be paid for only by spending cuts to existing programs, not by tax increases.

Discharge Calendar: The House calendar to which motions to discharge committees are referred when they have the required number of signatures (218) and are awaiting floor action

discharge a committee: Occasionally, attempts are made to relieve a committee from jurisdiction over a measure before it. This is attempted more often in the House than in the Senate, and the procedure seldom is successful. The Senate often discharges a committee by the unanimous consent of the chamber's membership. (See *unanimous consent.*)

In the House, if a committee does not report a bill within 30 legislative days after the measure is referred to it, any member may file a discharge motion. Once offered, the motion is treated as a petition needing the signatures of 218 members (a majority of the House). After the required signatures have been obtained, there is a delay of 7 days. Thereafter, on the second and fourth Mondays of each month, except during the last 6 days of a session, any member who has signed the petition must be recognized, if he or she so desires, to move that the committee be discharged. Debate on the motion to discharge is limited to 20 minutes, and if the motion is carried, consideration of the bill becomes a matter of high privilege.

If a resolution to consider a bill is held up in the Rules Committee for more than 7 legislative days, any member may enter a motion to discharge the committee. The motion is handled like any other discharge petition in the House. (For Senate procedure, see *discharge resolution.*)

discharge petition: (See *discharge a committee.*)

discharge resolutions: In the Senate, special motions that any senator may introduce to relieve a committee from consideration of a bill before it. The resolution can be called up for Senate approval or disapproval in the same manner as any other Senate business. This type of resolution is rarely used. (For House procedure, see *discharge a committee.*)

division vote: (See *standing vote.*)

earmark: A congressional earmark, as defined in House rules, means a provision or report language included primarily at the request of a member, delegate, resident commissioner, or senator, providing, authorizing, or recommending a specific amount of discretionary budget authority, credit authority, or other spending authority for a contract, loan, loan guarantee, grant, loan authority, or other expenditure with or to an entity, or targeted to a specific state, locality, or congressional district, other than through a statutory or administrative formula-driven or competitive award process. (See also *limited tax benefit* and *limited tariff benefit*)

enacting clause: Key phrase in bills beginning "Be it enacted by the Senate and House of Representatives. . . ." A successful motion to strike it from legislation kills the measure.

engrossed bill: The final copy of a bill as passed by one chamber, with the text as amended by floor action and certified by the clerk of the House or the secretary of the Senate.

enrolled bill: The final copy of a bill that has been passed in identical form by both chambers. It is certified by an officer of the house of origin (clerk of the House or secretary of the Senate) and then sent on for the signatures of the House Speaker, the Senate president pro tempore, and the president of the United States. An enrolled bill is printed on parchment.

Executive Calendar: This is a nonlegislative calendar in the Senate on which treaties and nominations are listed after being reported from committee.

filibuster: A time-delaying tactic associated with the Senate and used by a minority in an effort to prevent a vote on a bill or amendment that probably would pass if voted on directly. The most common method is to take advantage of the Senate's rules permitting unlimited debate, but other forms of parliamentary maneuvering may be used. The stricter rules used by the House make filibusters more difficult, but delaying tactics are employed occasionally through various procedural devices allowed by House rules, such as motions to adjourn. (See *cloture*.)

5-minute rule: A debate-limiting rule of the House that is invoked when the House sits as the Committee of the Whole. Under the rule, a member offering an amendment is allowed to speak 5 minutes in favor, and an opponent of the amendment is allowed to speak 5 minutes in opposition. Debate is then closed. In practice, amendments regularly are debated more than 10 minutes, with members gaining the floor by offering pro forma amendments or obtaining unanimous consent to speak longer than 5 minutes. (See *strike out the last word*.)

germane: Pertaining to the subject matter of the legislation at hand. House amendments must be germane to the bill being considered. The Senate requires that amendments be germane when they are proposed to general appropriations bills, bills being considered once cloture has been adopted, or, frequently, when proceeding under a unanimous consent agreement placing a time limit on consideration of a bill. The 1974 Budget Act also requires that amendments to concurrent budget resolutions be germane. In the House, floor debate must be germane, and the first 3 hours of debate each day in the Senate must be germane to the pending business.

House Calendar: A listing for action by the House of public bills that do not directly or indirectly appropriate money or raise revenue

joint resolution: A joint resolution, designated "H.J. Res." or "S.J. Res.," requires the approval of both houses and the signature of the president, just as a bill does, and has the force of law if approved. No practical difference exists between a bill and a joint resolution.

A joint resolution generally is used to deal with a limited matter, such as a single appropriation. Joint resolutions also are used to propose amendments to the Constitution. They must pass both chambers in identical form but do not require a presidential signature; they become a part of the Constitution when three fourths of the states have ratified them.

law: An act of Congress that has been signed by the president or passed over the president's veto by Congress. Public bills, when signed, become public laws and are cited by the letters P.L. and a hyphenated number (P.L. 113-1). The three digits before the hyphen correspond to the Congress, and the one or more digits after the hyphen refer to the numerical sequence in which the bills were signed by the president during that Congress. Private bills, when signed, become private laws.

legislative days: The day extending from the time either house meets after an adjournment until the time it next adjourns. Because the House normally adjourns from day to day, legislative days and calendar days usually coincide. But in the Senate, a legislative day may, and frequently does, extend over several calendar days. (See *recess*.)

limited tariff benefit: A provision modifying the Harmonized Tariff Schedule of the United States in a manner that benefits 10 or fewer entities

limited tax benefit: Any revenue-losing provision that provides a federal tax deduction, credit, exclusion, or preference to 10 or fewer beneficiaries under the Internal Revenue Code of 1986

marking up bills: Going through the contents of pieces of legislation in committee or subcommittee, considering their provisions in large and small portions, acting on amendments to provisions and proposed revisions to the language, inserting new sections and phraseology, and so on. If a bill is extensively amended, the committee's version may be introduced as a separate bill, with a new number, before being considered by the full House or Senate. (See *clean bill.*)

motion: In the House or Senate chamber, a request by a member to institute any one of a wide array of parliamentary actions. A member moves for a certain procedure, the consideration of a measure or amendment, and so on. The precedence of motions, and whether they are debatable, is set forth in the House and Senate manuals.

1-minute speeches: Addresses by House members usually at the beginning of a legislative day. The speeches may cover any subject but are limited to 1 minute's duration.

override a veto: If the president disapproves a bill and sends it back to Congress with his objections, Congress may try to override his veto and enact the bill into law. Neither house is required to attempt to override a veto. The override of a veto requires a recorded vote with a two-thirds majority in each chamber. The question put to each house is: "Shall the bill pass, the objections of the president to the contrary notwithstanding?" (See also *pocket veto, veto.*)

pairs: Voluntary arrangements between two lawmakers, usually on opposite sides of an issue. If passage of the measure requires a two-thirds majority vote, a pair would require two members favoring the action to one opposed to it. The names of lawmakers pairing on a given vote are printed in the *Congressional Record.*

pocket veto: The act of the president in withholding approval of a bill after Congress has adjourned. When Congress is in session, a bill becomes law without the president's signature if the president does not act on it within 10 days, excluding Sundays, of receiving it. But if Congress adjourns *sine die* within that 10-day period, the bill will die even if the president does not formally veto it. (See also *veto.*)

point of order: An objection raised by a member that the chamber is departing from rules governing its conduct of business. The objector cites the rule violated, and the chair sustains the objection if correctly made. The correct order is restored by the chair suspending proceedings of the chamber, until the House or Senate conforms to the prescribed order of business.

president of the Senate: Under the Constitution, the vice president of the United States is president of the Senate and presides on various occasions. In the vice president's absence, the president pro tempore, or a majority party senator designated by the president pro tempore, presides over the chamber.

president pro tempore: The chief officer of the Senate in the absence of the vice president; literally, but loosely, "president for a time." The president pro tempore, a constitutionally recognized position, is elected by the full membership of the Senate. The recent practice has been to choose the senator of the majority party with the longest period of continuous service.

previous question: A motion for the previous question, when carried, has the effect of cutting off all debate, preventing the offering of further amendments, and forcing a vote on the pending matter. In the House, the previous question is not permitted in the Committee of the Whole. The motion for the previous question is a debate-limiting device and is not in order in the Senate.

Private Calendar: In the House, private bills dealing with individual matters such as claims against the government, immigration, and land titles are put on this calendar. The Private Calendar must be called on the first Tuesday of each month; the Speaker may call it on the third Tuesday of each month as well.

privilege: Privilege relates to the rights of members of Congress and to the relative priority of the motions and actions they may make in their respective chambers. The two are distinct. Privileged motions deal with legislative business. Questions of privilege concern members themselves.

privileged motion: The order in which bills, motions, and other legislative measures are considered by Congress is governed by strict priorities. A motion to table, for example, is more privileged than a motion to recommit. Thus, a motion to recommit can be superseded by a motion to table, and a vote would be forced on the latter motion only. A motion to adjourn, however, takes precedence over a tabling motion and is therefore considered of the highest privilege. (See also *questions of privilege*.)

pro forma amendments: Ostensible amendments in the House that a member offers not to make any changes in a bill or amendment but only to receive debate time. (See *strike the last word*.)

questions of privilege: These are matters affecting members of Congress individually or collectively. Matters affecting the rights, safety, dignity, and integrity of proceedings of the House or Senate as a whole are questions of privilege in both chambers.

Questions involving individual members are called questions of personal privilege. A member rising to ask a question of personal privilege is given precedence over almost all other proceedings. An annotation in the House rules points out that the privilege is derived chiefly from the Constitution, which gives a member a conditional immunity from arrest and an unconditional freedom to speak in the House. (See also *privileged questions*.)

quorum: The number of members whose presence is necessary for the transaction of business. In the Senate and House, it is a majority of the membership: 51 in the Senate and 218 in the House. A quorum is 100 in the

Committee of the Whole. If the absence of a quorum is disclosed in either chamber, the Constitution authorizes a smaller number "to compel the Attendance of absent Members, in such Manner . . . as each House may provide."

reading of a bill: Traditional parliamentary procedure requires bills to be read three times before they are passed. This custom is of little modern significance. Normally, a bill is considered to have its first reading when it is introduced and printed, by title, in the *Congressional Record*. In the House, its second reading comes when floor consideration begins. The second reading in the Senate is supposed to occur on the legislative day after the measure is introduced but before it is referred to committee. The third reading (again, by title) takes place when floor action has been completed on amendments.

recess: Distinguished from adjournment in that a recess does not end a legislative day and therefore does not interrupt unfinished business. The rules in each house set forth certain matters to be taken up and disposed of at the beginning of each legislative day. The House usually adjourns from day to day. The Senate often recesses, thus meeting on the same legislative day for several calendar days or even weeks at a time.

recognition: The Speaker of the House has an unchallengeable right of recognition. The presiding officer of the Senate must recognize the first person that he or she sees who is seeking recognition, with priority always granted to the majority leader.

recommit: A motion, made on the floor after a bill has been debated, to return it to the committee that reported it. If approved, recommittal usually is a death blow to the bill. In the House, a motion to recommit can be made only by a member opposed to the bill, and in recognizing a member to make the motion, the Speaker gives preference to members of the minority party over majority party members.

A motion to recommit may include instructions to the committee to report the bill again with specific amendments or by a certain date. Or the instructions may direct that a particular study be made, with no definite deadline for further action. If the recommittal motion includes instructions to "report the bill back forthwith" and the motion is adopted, floor action on the bill continues; the committee does not actually reconsider the bill.

reconsider a vote: A motion to reconsider the vote by which an action was taken has, until it is disposed of, the effect of putting the action in abeyance. In the Senate, the motion can be made only by a member who voted on the prevailing side of the original question or by a member who did not vote at all. In the House, it can be made only by a member on the prevailing side.

A common practice in the Senate after close votes on an issue is a motion to reconsider, followed by a motion to table the motion to reconsider. On this motion to table, senators usually vote as they voted on the original question, which allows the motion to table to prevail, assuming there are no switches. The matter then is finally closed and further motions to reconsider are not entertained. In the House, as a routine precaution, a motion to reconsider usually is made every time a measure is passed. Such a motion almost always is tabled immediately, thus eliminating the possibility of future reconsideration, except by unanimous consent. Motions to reconsider must be entered in the Senate within the next 2 days of session after the original vote has been taken. In the House, they must be entered either on the same day or on the next succeeding day the House is in session.

recorded votes: Votes on which each member's stand is individually made known. In the Senate, this is accomplished through a roll call of the entire membership, to which each senator on the floor must answer "yea," "nay," or if he or she does not wish to vote, "present." Since January 1973, the House has used an electronic voting system for recorded votes, including yea-and-nay votes formerly taken by roll calls. A recorded vote is commonly obtained on questions in the House via a request for the constitutional yeas and nays (one fifth of those present), on the demand of one fifth (44 members) of a quorum, or one fourth (25 members) of a quorum in the Committee of the Whole. (See *yeas and nays*.)

report: Both a verb and a noun as a congressional term. A committee that has been examining a bill referred to it by the parent chamber reports, or votes out, its findings and recommendations to the chamber when it completes consideration. This process is called reporting a bill.

A report is the document setting forth the committee's explanation of its action. Senate and House reports are numbered separately and are designated "S. Rept." or "H. Rept." When a committee report is not unanimous, the dissenting committee members may file a statement of their views, called minority views and referred to as a minority report. Members in disagreement with some provisions of a bill may file additional or supplementary views. Sometimes, a bill is reported without a committee recommendation. Adverse reports occasionally are submitted by legislative committees. When a committee is opposed to a bill, it usually fails to report the measure at all.

resolution: A simple resolution, designated "H. Res." or "S. Res.," deals with matters entirely within the prerogatives of one house or the other. It requires neither passage by the other chamber nor approval by the president, and it does not have the force of law. Many resolutions deal with the rules or procedures of one house. They also are used to express the sentiments of a single house, such as condolences to the family of a deceased member, or to comment on foreign policy or executive business. A simple resolution is the vehicle for a rule from the House Rules Committee. (See also *concurrent resolution, joint resolution, rules*.)

riders: Amendments, usually not germane, that their sponsors hope to get through more easily by including them in other, often "must-pass," legislation. Riders become law if the bills embodying them are enacted. Amendments providing legislative directives in appropriations bills are examples of riders, though technically legislation is banned from appropriations bills. The House, unlike the Senate, has a strict germaneness rule. Thus, riders often are Senate devices to get legislation enacted quickly or to bypass lengthy House consideration and, possibly, opposition.

rules: The term has two specific congressional meanings. A rule may be a standing order governing the conduct of House or Senate business and listed among the permanent rules of either chamber. The rules deal with matters such as the duties of officers, the order of business, admission to the floor, parliamentary procedures on handling amendments and voting, and jurisdictions of committees.

In the House, a rule also may be a resolution reported by the Rules Committee to govern the handling of a particular bill on the floor. The committee may report a rule, also called a special order, in the form of a simple resolution. If the resolution is adopted by the House, the temporary rule becomes as valid as any standing rule and lapses only after action has been completed on the measure to which it pertains. A rule sets the time limit on general debate. It also may waive points of order against provisions of the bill in question, such as nongermane language, or against certain amendments intended to be proposed to the bill from the floor. It may even forbid all amendments or all amendments except those proposed by the legislative committee that handled the bill. In this instance, it is known as a closed or gag rule as opposed to an open rule, which puts no limitation on floor amendments, thereby leaving the bill completely open to alteration by the adoption of germane amendments.

Speaker: The presiding officer of the House of Representatives and the overall leader of the majority party in the chamber. The Speaker is selected by the caucus of the majority party's members and is formally elected by the full House at the beginning of each new Congress.

standing committees: (See *committees.*)

standing vote: A nonrecorded vote used in both the House and the Senate. (A standing vote also is called a *division vote.*) Members in favor of a proposal stand and are counted by the presiding officer. Then members opposed stand and are counted. There is no record of how individual members voted.

strike the last word (or requisite number of words): A motion whereby a House member is entitled to speak for 5 minutes on an amendment then being debated by the chamber. A member gains recognition from the chair by moving to strike out the last word of the amendment or section of the bill under consideration. The motion is pro forma, requires no vote, and does not change the amendment being debated.

substitute amendment: A discrete amendment that replaces the entire text of a pending amendment. Passage of a substitute amendment effectively kills the original amendment by supplanting it. The substitute also may be amended. (See also *amendment in the nature of a substitute*.)

supplemental appropriations bills: Legislation appropriating funds after the regular annual appropriations bill for a federal department or agency has been enacted. A supplemental appropriation provides additional budget authority beyond original estimates for programs or activities, including new programs authorized after the enactment of the regular appropriations act. (See also *appropriations bills*.)

suspension of the rules: Often a time-saving procedure for passing bills in the House. The wording of the motion, which may be made by any member recognized by the Speaker, is: "I move to suspend the rules and pass the bill. . . ." A favorable vote by two thirds of those present is required for passage. Debate is limited to 40 minutes, and no amendments from the floor are permitted. If a two-thirds favorable vote is not attained, the bill may be considered later under regular procedures. The suspension procedure is in order every Monday, Tuesday, and Wednesday and is intended to be reserved for noncontroversial bills.

table: A motion to lay on the table is not debatable in either house, and usually it is used to achieve final, adverse disposition of a matter. Tabling motions on amendments are effective debate-ending devices in the Senate.

unanimous consent: Proceedings of the House or Senate and action on legislation often take place upon the unanimous consent of the chamber, whether or not a rule of the chamber is being violated. Unanimous consent is employed to expedite floor action, especially in the Senate, and frequently is used for both substantive and routine matters. For example, senators may request the unanimous consent of the Senate to have specified members of their staff present on the floor during debate on an amendment.

unanimous consent agreements: A device used in the Senate to expedite legislation. Much of the Senate's legislative business, dealing with both minor and controversial issues, is conducted through unanimous consent or unanimous consent agreements. On major legislation, such agreements often are printed and transmitted to all senators in advance of floor debate. Once agreed to, they are binding on all members unless the Senate, by unanimous consent, agrees to modify them. An agreement may list the order in which various bills are to be considered, specify the length of time bills and amendments are to be debated and when they are to be voted on, and, frequently, require that all amendments introduced be relevant to the bill under consideration. In this regard, unanimous consent agreements are the Senate's version of rules issued by the House Rules Committee for bills pending in the House. (See *rules*.)

Union Calendar: Bills that directly or indirectly appropriate money or raise revenue are placed on this calendar of the House according to the date they are reported from committee.

veto: Disapproval by the president of a bill or joint resolution (other than one proposing an amendment to the Constitution). When Congress is in session, the president must veto a bill within 10 days—excluding Sundays—of receiving it; otherwise, the bill becomes law without the president's signature. When the president vetoes a bill, it must be returned to the house of origin with a message stating the president's objections. (See also *override a veto*, *pocket veto*.)

voice vote: In either the House or Senate, members answer "aye" or "no" in chorus, and the presiding officer decides the result. The term also is used loosely to indicate action by unanimous consent or without objection.

yeas and nays: The Constitution requires that yea-and-nay votes be taken and recorded when requested by one fifth of the members present. In the House, the Speaker determines whether one fifth of the members present requested a vote. In the Senate, practice requires only 11 members (one fifth of 51). The Constitution requires the yeas and nays on a veto override attempt. (See *recorded vote*.)

Selected Bibliography

Chapter 1. Congress and Lawmaking

Arnold, R. Douglas. *The Logic of Congressional Action*. New Haven, Conn.: Yale University Press, 1990.

Bacon, Donald C., Roger H. Davidson, and Morton Keller, eds. *The Encyclopedia of the United States Congress*, 4 vols. New York: Simon and Schuster, 1995.

Binder, Sarah A. *Minority Rights, Majority Rule: Partisanship and the Development of Congress*. New York: Cambridge University Press, 1997.

Dodd, Lawrence C., and Bruce I. Oppenheimer, eds. *Congress Reconsidered*, 9th ed. Washington, DC: CQ Press, 2009.

Gross, Bertram M. *The Legislative Struggle*. New York: McGraw-Hill, 1953.

Lee, Frances E., and Bruce I. Oppenheimer. *Sizing Up the Senate: The Unequal Consequences of Equal Representation*. Chicago: University of Chicago Press, 1999.

Luce, Robert. *Legislative Procedures*. Boston: Houghton Mifflin, 1922.

———. *Legislative Assemblies*. Boston: Houghton Mifflin, 1924.

———. *Legislative Principles*. Boston: Houghton Mifflin, 1930.

———. *Legislative Problems*. Boston: Houghton Mifflin, 1935.

Panagopoulos, Costas, and Joshua Schank. *All Roads Lead to Congress: The $300 Billion Fight Over Highway Funding*. Washington, DC: CQ Press, 2008.

Quirk, Paul J., and Sarah A. Binder, eds. *The Legislative Branch*. New York: Oxford University Press, 2005.

Schneider, Judy, and Michael L. Koempel. *Congressional Deskbook*, 5th ed. Alexandria, Va.: TheCapitol.Net, 2007.

Silbey, Joel H., ed. *Encyclopedia of the American Legislative System*, 3 vols. New York: Charles Scribner's Sons, 1994.

Smith, Steve S., Jason M. Roberts, and Ryan J. Vander Wielen. *The American Congress Reader*. New York: Cambridge University Press, 2009.

Tiefer, Charles. *Congressional Practice and Procedure: A Reference, Research, and Legislative Guide*. New York: Greenwood Press, 1989.

Chapter 2. The Congressional Budget Process

Fenno, Richard F., Jr. *The Power of the Purse*. Boston: Little, Brown, 1966.

Joyce, Philip. *The Congressional Budget Office*. Washington, DC: Georgetown University Press, 2011.

LeLoup, Lance T. *Parties, Rules and the Evolution of Congressional Budgeting*. Columbus: Ohio State University Press, 2005.

Meyers, Roy T. *Strategic Budgeting*. Ann Arbor: University of Michigan Press, 1996.

Munson, Richard. *The Cardinals of Capitol Hill*. New York: Grove Press, 1993.

Palazzolo, Daniel J. *Done Deal? The Politics of the 1997 Budget Agreement*. Chatham, NJ: Chatham House, 1999.

Rubin, Irene S. *Balancing the Federal Budget.* New York: Chatham House, 2003.

Schick, Allen. *Congress and Money.* Washington, DC: Urban Institute Press, 1980.

———. *The Capacity to Budget.* Washington, DC: Urban Institute Press, 1990.

———. *The Federal Budget: Politics, Policy, Process,* 3rd ed. Washington, DC: Brookings Institution Press, 2007.

Strahan, Randall. *New Ways and Means: Reform and Change in a Congressional Committee.* Chapel Hill: University of North Carolina Press, 1990.

Wildavsky, Aaron. *The Politics of the Budgetary Process,* 4th ed. Boston: Little, Brown, 1984.

Wilmerding, Lucius. *The Spending Power.* New Haven, Conn.: Yale University Press, 1943.

Chapter 3. Preliminary Legislative Action

Cooper, Joseph. *The Origins of the Standing Committees and the Development of the Modern House.* Rice University Monograph in Political Science, vol. 56, no. 3, Summer 1970.

Davidson, Roger H., and Walter J. Oleszek. *Congress Against Itself.* Bloomington: Indiana University Press, 1977.

Deering, Christopher J., and Steven S. Smith. *Committees in Congress,* 3rd ed. Washington, DC: CQ Press, 1997.

Evans, C. Lawrence. *Leadership in Committee.* Ann Arbor: University of Michigan Press, 1991.

Fenno, Richard F., Jr. *Congressmen in Committees.* Boston: Little, Brown, 1973.

Frisch, Scott, and Sean Q. Kelly. *Committee Assignment Politics in the U.S. House of Representatives.* Norman: University of Oklahoma Press, 2006.

King, David C. *Turf Wars: How Congressional Committees Claim Jurisdiction.* Chicago: University of Chicago Press, 1997.

Krehbiel, Keith. *Information and Legislative Organization.* Ann Arbor: University of Michigan Press, 1991.

Maltzman, Forrest. *Competing Principals: Committees, Parties, and the Organization of Congress.* Ann Arbor: University of Michigan Press, 1997.

Wilson, Woodrow. *Congressional Government.* Boston: Houghton Mifflin, 1885.

Chapter 4. Scheduling Legislation in the House

Cooper, Joseph, and David W. Brady. "Institutional Context and Leadership Style: The House From Cannon to Rayburn." *American Political Science Review* (June 1981): 411–425.

Cox, Gary W., and Matthew D. McCubbins. *Legislative Leviathan: Party Government in the House.* Berkeley: University of California Press, 1993.

———. *Setting the Agenda: Responsible Party Government in the House of Representatives.* New York: Cambridge University Press, 2005.

Green, Matthew. *The Speaker of the House: A Study of Leadership.* New Haven, Conn.: Yale University Press, 2010.

Hardeman, D. B., and Donald C. Bacon. *Rayburn.* Austin: Texas Monthly Press, 1987.

A History of the Committee on Rules. Committee Print, 97th Congress, 2d sess. Washington, DC: Government Printing Office, 1983.

Peters, Ronald M., Jr. *The American Speakership,* 2d ed. Baltimore, Md.: Johns Hopkins University Press, 1997.

Rae, Nicol, and Colton C. Campbell. *New Majority or Old Minority? The Impact of Republicans on Congress.* Lanham, Md.: Rowan and Littlefield, 1999.

Rohde, David. *Parties and Leaders in the Postreform House.* Chicago: University of Chicago Press, 1991.

Chapter 5. House Floor Procedure

Alexander, DeAlva Stanwood. *History and Procedure of the House of Representatives.* Boston: Houghton Mifflin, 1916.

Bach, Stanley, and Steven S. Smith. *Managing Uncertainty in the House of Representatives: Adaptation and Innovation in Special Rules.* Washington, DC: Brookings Institution Press, 1988.

Damon, Richard E. *The Standing Rules of the U.S. House of Representatives.* Doctoral dissertation, Columbia University, 1971.

Froman, Lewis A. *The Congressional Process: Strategies, Rules, and Procedures.* Boston: Little, Brown, 1967.

Harlow, Ralph V. *The History of Legislative Methods in the Period Before 1825.* New Haven, CT: Yale University Press, 1917.

MacNeil, Neil. *Forge of Democracy: The House of Representatives.* New York: David McKay, 1963.

Peters, Ronald M., Jr. and Cindy Simon Rosenthal. *Speaker Nancy Pelosi and the New American Politics.* New York: Oxford University Press, 2010.

Polsby, Nelson W. "The Institutionalization of the House of Representatives." *American Political Science Review* (March 1968): 144–168.

Sinclair, Barbara. *Legislators, Leaders, and Lawmaking: The U.S. House of Representatives in the Postreform Era.* Baltimore: Johns Hopkins University Press, 1995.

Smith, Steven S. *Call to Order: Floor Politics in the House and Senate.* Washington, DC: Brookings Institution Press, 1989.

Chapter 6. Scheduling Legislation in the Senate

Clark, Joseph S. *The Senate Establishment.* New York: Hill and Wang, 1963.

Den Hartog, Chris, and Nathan Monroe. *Agenda Setting in the U.S. Senate: Costly Consideration and Majority Party Advantage.* New York: Cambridge University Press, 2011.

Ehrenhalt, Alan. "Special Report: The Individualist Senate." *Congressional Quarterly Weekly Report,* September 4, 1982, 2175–2182.

Fenno, Richard F., Jr. *Learning to Legislate: The Senate Education of Arlen Specter.* Washington, DC: CQ Press, 1991.

Harris, Fred R. *Deadlock or Decision: The U.S. Senate and the Rise of National Politics.* New York: Oxford University Press, 1993.

Hibbing, John R., ed. *The Changing World of the U.S. Senate.* Berkeley, CA: IGS Press, 1990.

Rudman, Warren. *Combat: Twelve Years in the U.S. Senate.* New York: Random House, 1996.

Chapter 7. Senate Floor Procedure

Arenberg, Richard A., and Robert B. Dove. *Defending the Filibuster: The Soul of the Senate*. Bloomington: Indiana University Press, 2012.

Binder, Sarah A., and Steven S. Smith. *Politics or Principle? Filibustering in the United States Senate*. Washington, DC: Brookings Institution Press, 1997.

Burdette, Franklin L. *Filibustering in the Senate*. Princeton, NJ: Princeton University Press, 1940.

Campbell, Colton, and Nicol C. Rae, eds. *The Contentious Senate*. Lanham, MD: Rowman and Littlefield, 2001.

Caro, Robert A. *Master of the Senate*. New York: Alfred A. Knopf, 2002.

Evans, Rowland, and Robert Novak. *Lyndon B. Johnson: The Exercise of Power*. New York: New American Library, 1966.

Gold, Martin B. *Senate Procedure and Practice*. Lanham, MD: Rowman and Littlefield, 2004.

Harris, Joseph P. *The Advice and Consent of the Senate*. Berkeley: University of California Press, 1953.

Koger, Gregory. *Filibustering: A Political History of Obstructionism in the House and Senate*. Chicago: University of Chicago Press, 2010.

Loomis, Burdett, ed. *Esteemed Colleagues: Civility and Deliberation in the U.S. Senate*. Washington, DC: Brookings Institution Press, 2000.

Matthews, Donald. *U.S. Senators and Their World*. Chapel Hill: University of North Carolina Press, 1960.

Mucciaroni, Gary, and Paul Quirk. *Deliberative Choices: Debating Public Policy in Congress*. Chicago: University of Chicago Press, 2006.

Shuman, Howard E. "Senate Rules and the Civil Rights Bill: A Case Study." *American Political Science Review* (December 1957): 955–975.

Sinclair, Barbara. *The Transformation of the U.S. Senate*. Baltimore, MD: Johns Hopkins University Press, 1989.

Taylor, Andrew J. *The Floor in Congressional Life*. Ann Arbor: University of Michigan Press, 2012.

Wawro, Gregory J., and Eric Schickler. *Filibuster: Obstruction and Lawmaking in the U.S. Senate*. Princeton, NJ: Princeton University Press, 2006.

Chapter 8. Resolving House–Senate Differences

Fenno, Richard F., Jr. *The United States Senate: A Bicameral Perspective*. Washington, DC: American Enterprise Institute for Public Policy Research, 1982.

Longley, Lawrence D., and Walter J. Oleszek. *Bicameral Politics: Conference Committees in Congress*. New Haven, CT: Yale University Press, 1989.

McCown, Ada C. *The Congressional Conference Committee*. New York: Columbia University Press, 1927.

Pressman, Jeffrey L. *House vs. Senate: Conflict in the Appropriations Process*. New Haven, CT: Yale University Press, 1966.

Steiner, Gilbert. *The Congressional Conference Committee, Seventieth to Eightieth Congresses*. Urbana: University of Illinois Press, 1951.

Vogler, David J. *The Third House: Conference Committees in the U.S. Congress*. Evanston, IL: Northwestern University Press, 1971.

Chapter 9. Legislative Oversight

Aberbach, Joel D. *Keeping a Watchful Eye: The Politics of Congressional Oversight.* Washington, DC: Brookings Institution Press, 1990.

Bond, Jon R., and Richard Fleisher, eds. *Polarized Politics: Congress and the President in a Partisan Era.* Washington, DC: CQ Press, 2000.

Fisher, Louis. *Constitutional Conflicts Between Congress and the President,* 4th ed., revised. Lawrence: University of Kansas Press, 1997.

Foreman, Christopher H. *Signals From the Hill: Congressional Oversight and the Challenge of Social Regulation.* New Haven, CT: Yale University Press, 1988.

Gilmour, Robert S., and Alexis A. Halley, eds. *Who Makes Public Policy: The Struggle for Control Between Congress and the Executive.* Chatham, NJ: Chatham House, 1994.

Harris, Joseph P. *Congressional Control of Administration.* Washington, DC: Brookings Institution Press, 1964.

Light, Paul C. *Monitoring Government: Inspectors General and the Search for Accountability.* Washington, DC: Brookings Institution Press, 1993.

Ogul, Morris S. *Congress Oversees the Bureaucracy.* Pittsburgh, PA: University of Pittsburgh Press, 1976.

West, William F. *Controlling the Bureaucracy.* Armonk, NY: M. E. Sharp, 1995.

Chapter 10. A Dynamic Process

Bailey, Stephen K. *Congress Makes a Law.* New York: Columbia University Press, 1950.

Binder, Sarah A. *Stalemate: Causes and Consequences of Legislative Gridlock.* Washington, DC: Brookings Institution Press, 2003.

———. *Minority Rights, Majority Rule: Partisanship and the Development of Congress.* New York: Oxford University Press, 1997.

Brady, David W., and Matthew D. McCubbins, eds. *Party, Process, and Political Change in Congress: New Perspectives on the History of Congress.* Stanford, CA: Stanford University Press, 2002.

Casey, Chris. *The Hill on the Net: Congress Enters the Information Age.* Chestnut Hill, MA: Academic Press, 1996.

Davidson, Roger H., ed. *The Postreform Congress.* New York: St. Martin's Press, 1992.

Evans, C. Lawrence, and Walter J. Oleszek. *Congress Under Fire: Reform Politics and the Republican Majority.* Boston: Houghton Mifflin, 1997.

Hibbing, John R., and Elizabeth Thiess-Morse. *Congress as Public Enemy.* New York: Cambridge University Press, 1995.

Jones, Charles O. "A Way of Life and Law." *American Political Science Review* (March 1995): 1–9.

Krehbiel, Keith. *Pivotal Politics: A Theory of Lawmaking.* Chicago: University of Chicago Press, 1998.

Lee, Frances E. *Beyond Ideology: Politics, Principles, and Partisanship in the U.S. Senate.* Chicago: University of Chicago Press, 2009.

Mann, Thomas E., and Norman J. Ornstein. *The Broken Branch.* New York: Oxford University Press, 2005.

Polsby, Nelson W. *How Congress Evolves: Social Bases of Institutional Change.* New York: Oxford University Press, 2004.

Redman, Eric. *The Dance of Legislation.* New York: Simon and Schuster, 1973.

Remini, Robert V. *The House: The History of the House of Representatives.* New York: HarperCollins, 2006.

Schickler, Eric. *Disjointed Pluralism: Institutional Innovation and the Development of the U.S. Congress.* Princeton, NJ: Princeton University Press, 2001.

Sinclair, Barbara. *Party Wars: Polarization and the Politics of National Policy Making.* Norman: University of Oklahoma Press, 2006.

———. *Unorthodox Lawmaking,* 3d ed. Washington, DC: CQ Press, 2007.

Sundquist, James L. *The Decline and Resurgence of Congress.* Washington, DC: Brookings Institution Press, 1981.

Theriault, Sean. *Party Polarization in Congress.* New York: Cambridge University Press, 2008.

Thurber, James A., and Colton C. Campbell, eds. *Congress and the Internet.* Upper Saddle River, NJ: Prentice Hall, 2003.

Wirls, Daniel, and Stephen Wirls. *The Invention of the United States Senate.* Baltimore, MD: Johns Hopkins University Press, 2004.

Wolfensberger, Donald R. *Congress and the People: Deliberative Democracy on Trial.* Washington, DC: Woodrow Wilson Center Press, 2000.

Zelizer, Julian E., ed. *The American Congress.* Boston: Houghton Mifflin, 2004.

Internet Sources

Architect of the Capitol (www.aoc.gov)

Clerk of the House (www.clerk.house.gov)

CNN (www.cnn.com)

Congressional Budget Office (www.cbo.gov)

CQ Weekly (www.cq.com)

C-SPAN (www.c-span.org)

Government Accountability Office (www.gao.gov)

Government Printing Office (www.gpo.gov)

The Hill (www.thehill.com)

House of Representatives (www.house.gov)

Library of Congress (www.loc.gov/index.html)

National Journal (www.nationaljournal.com)

Roll Call (www.rollcall.com)

Senate (www.senate.gov)

Washington Post (www.washingtonpost.com)

White House (www.whitehouse.gov)

Index

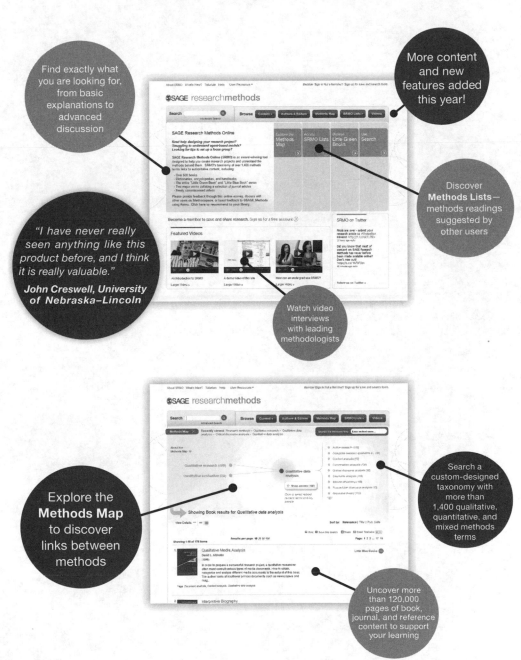